GENERAL COMPETITIVE ANALYSIS

ADVANCED TEXTBOOKS IN ECONOMICS

VOLUME 12

NORTH-HOLLAND
AMSTERDAM · NEW YORK · OXFORD · TOKYO

GENERAL COMPETITIVE ANALYSIS

KENNETH J. ARROW
Stanford University, CA, USA

FRANK H. HAHN
University of Cambridge, England

NORTH-HOLLAND
AMSTERDAM · NEW YORK · OXFORD · TOKYO

ELSEVIER SCIENCE PUBLISHERS B.V.
Sara Burgerhartstraat 25
P.O. Box 211, 1000 AE Amsterdam, The Netherlands

Distributors for the United States and Canada:

ELSEVIER SCIENCE PUBLISHING COMPANY INC.
655, Avenue of the Americas
New York, N.Y. 10010, U.S.A.

First edition: 1971
Second printing: 1980
Third printing: 1983
Fourth printing: 1986
Fifth printing: 1988
Sixth printing: 1991

Transferred to digital printing 2007

ISBN: 0 444 85497 5

PREFACE

Tradition is a matter of much wider significance. It cannot be inherited, and if you want it you must obtain it by great labour.
—T.S. Eliot, *Tradition and the Individual Talent*

Much of this book is concerned with the analysis of an idealized, decentralized economy. In particular, it is supposed, in the main, that there is perfect competition and that the choices of economic agents can be deduced from certain axioms of rationality. Only recently has a fairly complete and rigorous examination of this long-developing construction become possible.

It is our intent to give a systematic exposition of the subject. In the course of doing so, it became clear that a considerable amount of unexplored intellectual territory could be traversed without sacrificing the basically expository aims of the work; indeed, in many cases, the filling-in of gaps gives a more systematic feel to the whole. Also, in most cases, we have offered new proofs of the known results in competitive equilibrium theory.

Acknowledgments of priority are to be found in the **Notes** at the end of each chapter; we have not tried to give detailed histories there, only the first significant statement of each result. Theorems in the text not cited in the **Notes** are either so well known at this stage that reference would be pedantic or are, to the best of our knowledge, original with the authors.

The book is strictly a joint effort, and both authors are responsible for all errors. In the actual writing, one author had the initial responsibility for each chapter, which was then subject to repeated criticism and emendation by the other; in several cases, the tâtonnement went through several more steps. Doubtless, this process would have gone still further if the authors had not learned by bitter experience that the time in which recontract takes place is in fact coincident with real time. Arrow wrote the initial drafts of Chapters 1 and 3–8 and Mathematical Appendices B and C, Hahn those of Chapters 9–14 and Mathematical

Appendix A. Both authors wrote sections of Chapter 2.

Note should be made that certain topics that some readers might expect to find here are not covered; they were omitted to hold the physical and intellectual compass of the book within reasonable bounds and to preserve some semblance of unity of approach. (1) We have omitted all discussion of markets with a continuum of traders, a study of great potential importance in our judgment introduced in recent years by Aumann and pursued by Debreu, Hildenbrand, Vind, and the younger Belgian and Israeli schools. This work requires the use of measure theory, which would have been a formidable addition to the advanced mathematical prerequisites we already demand of our readers. In Chapters 7 and 8, however, we have attempted to go as far as we can in this direction without the use of measure theory. (2) Since our emphasis is on the general equilibrium of the economy, we have not covered in detail specific theorems on the theories of the firm and the household; only such results as are needed for general equilibrium analysis are discussed. This means also that we have been satisfied to base the theory of the household on the assumption of a preference ordering and have not examined the growing literature that bases this theory on some form of revealed preference assumption. (3) We have refrained also from a development of welfare economics, except for some theorems that also play a role in the descriptive theory of general equilibrium. It is expected that other volumes in this series of texts on mathematical economics and econometrics will deal with the theories of the firm and the household and with welfare economics. (4) The extension of general equilibrium theory to the case of uncertainty is given only the most cursory treatment in Chapter 5. On the one hand, the economics of uncertainty is a large topic that cannot be given adequate treatment here; on the other hand, the general equilibrium theory is still in an early stage of development.

It is natural and proper to ask whether this enquiry into an economy, apparently so abstracted from the world, is worthwhile. We may answer in the usual way by drawing attention to the enormously complex nature of the material that economists study and the accordingly urgent need for simplification and so abstraction. This, however, leaves open the question of why the particular simplifications here used should be the appropriate ones.

Our answer is somewhat different. There is by now a long and fairly imposing line of economists from Adam Smith to the present who have sought to show that a decentralized economy motivated by self-interest and guided by price signals would be compatible with a coherent disposition of economic resources that could be regarded, in a well-defined sense, as superior to a large class of possible alternative dispositions. Moreover, the price signals would operate in a way to establish this degree of coherence. It is important to understand how surprising this claim must be to anyone not exposed to this tradition. The immediate "common sense" answer to the question "What will an economy motivated by individual greed and controlled by a very large number of different agents look like?" is probably: There will be chaos. That quite a different answer has long been claimed true and has indeed permeated the economic thinking of a large number of people who are in no way economists is itself sufficient grounds for investigating it seriously. The proposition having been put forward and very seriously entertained, it is important to know not only whether it *is* true, but also whether it *could be* true. A good deal of what follows is concerned with this last question, which seems to us to have considerable claims on the attention of economists.

If confirmation of the proposition we have been discussing has been found in a particular formalization of the economy, it then becomes interesting to see how robust this result is. Will it survive a change in assumption from a perfectly competitive to an imperfectly competitive economy? Will it be overturned by external economics, by apparent irrationalities such as "judging quality by price" or by lack of sufficient "future markets" and the special role that might be taken by the medium of exchange? Some answers to these questions have been suggested in what follows. Other questions, of course, remain. But the point is this: It is not sufficient to assert that, while it is possible to invent a world in which the claims made on behalf of the "invisible hand" are true, these claims fail in the actual world. It must be shown just how the features of the world regarded as essential in any description of it also make it impossible to substantiate the claims. In attempting to answer the question "Could it be true?", we learn a good deal about why it might not be true.

Our view, therefore, is that an intellectually challenging theory of decentralized economics exists, has and is being taken seriously, and so deserves the most careful logical scrutiny.

We have paid some attention here also to the possibility of using the idealized constructions in comparing different economies. On the whole, our conclusion is that the postulates are too weak to allow one to make much headway. This can be taken as evidence of the deficiency of the theory. It can also be taken to show its strength, however, for it suggests that sufficient degrees of freedom have been left for empirical information to make a difference to prediction; it is not a totally a priori construction.

Note on Conventions of Notations and Cross References

All vectors are in boldface; components of a vector have the same symbol as the vector, but in italic and are distinguished from one another by subscripts. For example, if $\mathbf{x}$ is a vector, x_i is its ith component. Where the context makes it clear, no special notation is employed to distinguish row from column vectors. For example, in the inner product $\mathbf{xy}$, it is taken for granted that here $\mathbf{x}$ is a row vector and $\mathbf{y}$ a column vector.

The notation for vector inequalities is as follows: $\mathbf{x} \geq \mathbf{y}$ means $x_i \geq y_i$, all i; $\mathbf{x} > \mathbf{y}$ means $x_i \geq y_i$, all i, $x_i > y_i$ for at least one i; and $\mathbf{x} \gg \mathbf{y}$ means $x_i > y_i$ for all i.

A set is usually indicated by a capital italic letter. A vector sum of sets of vectors is indicated by an ordinary summation sign, $\sum$. A cartesian product of sets of vectors is indicated by $\times$; for both, running indices indicate the range of summation. Thus, if, for each index f, Y_f is a set of possible production vectors, then their vector sum, the social production possibility set, is indicated by $\sum_f Y_f$, while their cartesian product, which is the set of possible production allocations, is denoted by $\times_f Y_f$. A set defined as a cartesian product of an indexed family of sets with an italic letter is designated with the corresponding capital script letter, thus, $\mathscr{Y} = \times_f Y_f$, and any element of it with the corresponding small script letter, thus, y is a typical member of $\mathscr{Y}$.

If a set is defined by some property of its members, it is written with curly brackets in which the typical element of the set is written first, succeeded, after a vertical line, by the property in question. For example, $A = \{\mathbf{x} \mid \mathbf{x} > \mathbf{0}\}$ is the set of all vectors $\mathbf{x}$ with the property that all its elements are non-negative and at least one is positive.

A pair of curly brackets enclosing a single vector denotes the set consisting of that vector alone, for example, $\{\mathbf{x}^0\}$. If A and B are sets, $A \sim B$ denotes the set-theoretic difference of A and B, that is, the set of all elements of A that are not also in B.

Matrices usually are denoted with capital italic letters or are represented by parentheses surrounding the typical element. For example, (x_{ij}) is the matrix X with typical element x_{ij}. Transposition is denoted by a prime.

Detailed notation will be found in each chapter.

In any chapter or appendix, assumptions, lemmas, theorems, definitions, and displayed expressions are numbered consecutively. Assumptions, theorems, and definitions are referred to by their respective initial letters capitalized; for example, A.3.1 is the first assumption in Chapter 3, T.3.1 the first theorem, and Lemma 3.1 the first lemma. A corollary is given the number of its main theorem. If there is more than one corollary to a given theorem, a prime is placed after the number of the second; for example, Corollary 2 is the corollary to, say, T.3.2 and Corollary 2′ is its second corollary.

Acknowledgments

The work reported on in this book has been developed in the last 20 years, and our indebtedness to a few of our contemporaries is very great. The influence of the splendid work of Debreu and his brilliant expository volume, *Theory of Values,* will be obvious everywhere in what follows. We have attempted to answer some questions he did not pose and our methods of proof are in a number of instances quite different, but the theory in its present form would not have existed without him. Our debt to McKenzie and to Hurwicz is also sufficiently great to call for special attention here. All of us in turn are indebted to the seminal work of Wald, who gave the first rigorous treatment of general equilibrium analysis in the literature, and to Koopmans' activity analysis of production, which shaped the basic nature of the models we are dealing with.

James Mirrlees read much of the manuscript, and we have benefited from a number of his suggestions, but most especially the treatment of utility functions in Chapter 4, Section 2, is due to him.

We are greatly indebted to the United States Office of Naval Research, which has supported the preparation of this book under contracts successively with Stanford University and Harvard University. At various stages, we enjoyed the stimulating environments and facilities of the Center for Advanced Study in the Behavorial Sciences and of Churchill College.

We are grateful also to Dan Christiansen and Masahiro Okuna for their careful preparation of the indexes.

Finally, we are glad to acknowledge the indispensable aid of Laura Staggers at Stanford University, Dorothy Brothers at the Center for

Advanced Study in the Behavioral Sciences and Sheila V. Conroy at Harvard University, who contributed not only their great abilities as typists, but also unlimited patience in incorporating our innumerable revisions, persistence in deciphering our incomprehensible handwriting, and sympathy on the numerous occasions when it was needed.

Kenneth J. Arrow
F. H. Hahn

August 1971

CONTENTS

Chapter One

HISTORICAL INTRODUCTION

This is the use of memory
For liberation . . .

History may be servitude,
History may be freedom. . . .
—T. S. Eliot, *Little Gidding*

1. The Classical Economists

There are two basic, incompletely separable, aspects of the notion of general equilibrium as it has been used in economics: the simple notion of determinateness, that the relations describing the economic system must be sufficiently complete to determine the values of its variables, and the more specific notion that each relation represents a balance of forces. The last usually, though not always, is taken to mean that a violation of any one relation sets in motion forces tending to restore it (it has been shown (see Section 12.6) that this hypothesis does not imply the stability of the entire system). In a sense, almost any attempt to give a theory of the whole economic system implies the acceptance of the first part of the equilibrium notion; and Adam Smith's "invisible hand" is a poetic expression of the most fundamental of economic balance relations, the equalization of rates of return, as enforced by the tendency of factors to move from low to high returns.

The notion of equilibrium ("equal weight," referring to the condition for balancing a lever pivoted at its center) was familiar to mechanics long before the publication of *The Wealth of Nations* in 1776, and with it the notion that the effects of a force may annihilate it (e.g., water finding its own level), but there is no obvious evidence that Smith drew his ideas from any analogy with mechanics. Whatever the source of the concept, the notion that a social system moved by independent actions in pursuit of different values is consistent with a final coherent state of balance, and one in which the outcomes may be quite different from those intended by the agents, is surely the most important intellectual contribution that economic thought has made to the general understanding of social processes.

Smith also perceived the most important implication of general equilibrium theory, the ability of a competitive system to achieve an allocation of resources that is efficient in some sense. Nothing resembling a rigorous argument for, or even a careful statement of the efficiency proposition can be found in Smith, however.

Thus it can be maintained that Smith was a creator of general equilibrium theory, though the coherence and consistency of his work may be questioned. *A fortiori*, later systematic expositors of the classical system, such as Ricardo, Mill, and Marx, whose work filled in some of Smith's logical gaps, can all be regarded as early expositors of general equilibrium theory. In some ways, Marx came closer in form to modern theory in his scheme of simple reproduction (*Capital*, Vol. II), studied in combination with his development of relative price theory (Vols. I and III), than any other classical economist, though he confuses everything by his attempt to maintain simultaneously a pure labor theory of value and an equalization of rates of return on capital.[1]

There is, however, a very important sense in which none of the classical economists had a true general equilibrium theory: None gave an explicit role to demand conditions. No doubt the more systematic thinkers among them, most particularly J. S. Mill, gave verbal homage to the role of demand and the influence of prices on it, but there was no genuine integration of demand with the essentially supply-oriented nature of classical theory. The neglect of demand was facilitated by the special simplifying assumptions made about supply. A general equilibrium theory is a theory about both the quantities and the prices of all commodities. The classical authors found, however, that prices appeared to be determined by a system of relations, derived from the equal-rate-of-profit condition, into which quantities did not enter. This is clear enough with fixed production coefficients and a single primary factor, labor, as in Smith's famous exchange of deer and beavers; and it was the great accomplishment of Malthus and Ricardo to show that land could be brought into the system. If, finally, Malthusian assumptions about population implied that the supply price of labor was fixed in terms of goods, then even the rate of return on capital could be determined (though the presence of capital as a productive factor and recipient of rewards was clearly an embarrassment to the classical authors, as

[1] For some modern reconstructions of classical theories as general equilibrium models, see Samuelson [1957, 1959].

it remains to some extent today); indeed, with the Malthusian assumption, the model again had a single primary factor, land.

Thus, in a certain definite sense, the classical economists had no true theory of resource allocation, since the influence of prices on quantities was not studied and the reciprocal influence denied.[1] But the classical theory could survive neither the logical problem of explaining relative wages of heterogeneous types of labor nor the empirical problem of accounting for wages that were rising steadily above the subsistence level. It is in this context that the neoclassical theories emerged about 1870, with all primary resources in the role that land alone had had before.

(In all fairness to the classical writers, it should be remarked that the theory of foreign trade in the form given to it by Mill was a genuine general equilibrium theory. Of course, the assumptions made, particularly factor immobility, were very restrictive.)

2. The Contributions of Walras

The full recognition of the general equilibrium concept can be attributed unmistakably to Walras [1874, 1877], though many elements of the neoclassical system had been worked out independently by W. Stanley Jevons and by Carl Menger.[2] The economic system is made up of households and firms. Each household owns a set of resources, commodities useful in production or consumption, including different kinds of labor. For any given set of prices, then, a household has an income from the sale of its resources and, with this income, it can choose among all alternative bundles of consumer goods whose cost, at the given prices, does not exceed the household's income. Thus, the demand by households for any consumer good is a function of the prices of both consumer goods and resources. The firms were assumed (at least in the earlier

[1] The classical failure to see clearly the allocational nature of the economic problem has been most forcefully argued by F. H. Knight [1935].

[2] Schumpeter and others have called attention to Isnard [1781] as a creator of general equilibrium theory. According to the account given by Theocharis [1961, 1966–70], Isnard's model for the pure exchange case amounts to assuming that no individual holds more than one asset and that all demand functions are of unit elasticity in income and in own price. Under these conditions, relative prices are shown to be the solution of a system of simultaneous linear equations. Production is also introduced, with the usual fixed-coefficient assumptions. The spirit of the model is very much closer to the later neoclassical writers than to the contemporary classicists.

versions) to be operating under fixed coefficients. Then the demand for consumer goods determined the demand for resources, and the combined assumptions of fixed coefficients and zero profits for a competitive system implied relations between the prices of consumer goods and resources. An *equilibrium* set of prices, then, was a set such that supply and demand were equated on each market; under the assumption of fixed coefficients of production, or more generally, of constant returns to scale, this amounted to equating supply and demand on the resource markets, with prices constrained to satisfy the zero-profit condition for firms. Subsequent work of Walras, J. B. Clark, Wicksteed, and others generalized the assumptions about production to include alternative methods, as expressed in a production function. The marginal productivity considerations helped to determine the prices of resources.

That there exists an equilibrium set of prices was argued from the equality of the number of prices to be determined with the number of equations expressing the equality of supply and demand on all markets. Both are equal to the number of commodities, say n. In this counting, Walras recognized that there are two offsetting complications. (a) Only relative prices affect the behavior of households and firms, hence the system of equations have only $n - 1$ variables, a point that Walras expressed by selecting one commodity to serve as *numeraire*, with the prices of all commodities being measured relative to its price. (b) The budgetary balance of each household between income and the value of consumption and the zero-profit condition for firms together imply what has come to be known as Walras' law: The market value of supply equals that of demand for any set of prices, not merely the equilibrium set; hence, the supply-demand relations are not independent. If supply equals demand on $n - 1$ markets, then the equality must hold on the nth.

Walras went further and discussed the stability of equilibrium, essentially for the first time (that is, apart from some brief discussions by Mill in the context of foreign trade) in his famous but rather clumsy theory of *tâtonnements* (literally "gropings" or "tentative proceedings"). Suppose, as Walras did, a set of prices arbitrarily given; then supply may exceed demand on some markets and fall below on others (unless the initial set is in fact the equilibrium set, there must be at least one case of each, by Walras' law). Suppose the markets are considered in some definite order. On the first market, adjust the price so that supply and demand are equal, given all other prices; this will normally require raising the price if demand initially exceeded supply, decreasing it in the opposite case. The change in the first price will change supply and demand on all other markets. Repeat the process with the second and subsequent markets. At the end of one round the last market will be in equilibrium, but none of the others need be because the adjustments on subsequent markets will destroy the equilibrium achieved on any one. However, Walras argued, the supply and demand functions for any given commodity will be more affected by the changes in its own price than by changes in other prices; hence, after one round the markets should be more nearly in equilibrium than they were to begin with, and with successive rounds the supply and demand on each market will tend to equality.

It seems clear that Walras did not literally suppose that markets come into equilibrium in some definite order. Rather, the story is a convenient way of showing how the market system in fact could solve the system of equilibrium relations. The dynamic system, more properly expressed, asserted that the price on any market rises when demand exceeds supply and falls in the opposite case; the price changes on the different markets were to be thought of as occurring simultaneously.

Finally, Walras had a still higher aim for general equilibrium analysis: to study what is now called *comparative statics*, in other words, the laws by which the equilibrium prices and quantities vary with the underlying data (resources, production conditions, or utility functions). But little was actually done in this direction.

3. Edgeworth and Pareto: Group Rationality and Allocation

From Adam Smith's invisible hand on, the classical economists held that competitive equilibrium yielded what was in some none-too-well-defined sense an optimal allocation of resources. Edgeworth [1881] and Pareto [1909, p. 534] clarified considerably the relation between competitive equilibria and optimal allocations by starting from the latter.

Edgeworth considered a pair of individuals, with initial resources of two commodities, who were trying to arrange a trade between them. He did not assume that they were operating under the rules of the competitive game, but rather that they could make any trades they wished. He assumed that (a) they would not make a trade if there was another that would be more beneficial for both and (b) neither would make a trade that would make him worse off than in the absence of trade. He showed that there was a whole set of allocations, which he called the *contract curve*, satisfying these conditions, of which the competitive equilibrium was one. He went on to suppose that, instead of two individuals, there were two types of individuals, all individuals of the same type having the same utility function and the same endowment of initial resources. He generalized the previous assumptions about the conditions for satisfactory trade; no multilateral trade among the participants would be completed if there was some subset of them that could make another trade among themselves, using only their own resources, that would benefit them more than the initially proposed trade. This condition generalizes both (a) and (b) above. He then came to the remarkable conclusion that as the number of individuals of each type became large, the range of possible trades shrank toward the competitive equilibrium. Thus, a general bargaining process turns out to have a close relation to general competitive equilibrium.

Pareto's special contribution is a suitable definition of optimal resource allocation, essentially the satisfaction of condition (a) of Edgeworth's contract curve. He recognized, but did not rigorously show that an optimum in his sense could always be achieved as a competitive equilibrium starting from some suitable initial allocation of endowments.

4. Partial Equilibrium Analysis

Cournot [1838] and later Jenkin [1870] and the neoclassical economists employed extensively the partial equilibrium analysis of a single market. The demand and supply of a single commodity are conceived of as functions of the price of that commodity alone; the equilibrium price is that for which demand and supply are equal. This form of analysis must be viewed either as a pedagogical device to take advantage of the ease of graphical representation of one-variable relations or as a first approximation to general equilibrium analysis in which repercussions through other markets are neglected.

Partial equilibrium analysis is to be regarded as a special case of general equilibrium analysis. The existence of one market presupposes that there must be at least one commodity beyond that traded on that market, for a price must be stated as the rate at which an individual gives up something for the commodity in question. If there was really only one commodity in the world, there would be no exchange and no market.

Suppose for the moment that there are only two commodities, say 1 and 2. Because of homogeneity, demand and supply are determined by the ratio of the price of commodity 1 to that of commodity 2, that is, the price of commodity 1 with commodity 2 as numeraire. From Walras' law, equilibrium on market 1 ensures equilibrium on market 2. Partial equilibrium analysis of market 1 is, in the case of two commodities, fully equivalent to general equilibrium analysis.

Analysis of a two-commodity world may have considerable didactic usefulness as a way of studying general equilibrium through a special case admitting of simple diagrammatic representation, but it may be asked if partial equilibrium analysis has any empirical interest for a world of many commodities. An answer is provided by the following theorem, due independently to Hicks [1939] and Leontief [1936]: If the relative prices of some set of commodities remain constant, then for all analytical purposes the set can be regarded as a single composite commodity, the price of which can be regarded as proportional to the price of any member of the set and the quantity of which is then defined so that expenditure (price times quantity) on the composite commodity is equal to the sum of the expenditures on the individual commodities in the set. In symbols, if the prices $p_1, \ldots, p_m$ of a set of commodities $1, \ldots, m$ satisfy the conditions $p_i = \rho \bar{p}_i$ ($\bar{p}_i$ a constant for each i while ρ may vary), then we can take ρ to be the price of the composite commodity, and

$$\sum_{i=1}^{m} \bar{p}_i q_i$$

to be the quantity, where q_i is the quantity of the ith good.

The Hicks–Leontief aggregation theorem can be used to justify partial equilibrium analysis. Suppose that a change in the price of commodity 1 leaves the relative prices of all others unchanged. Then insofar as we are considering only disturbances to equilibrium from causes peculiar to the market for commodity 1, the remaining commodities can be regarded as a single composite commodity, and partial equilibrium analysis is valid.

The assumption of strict constancy of relative prices of the other commodities will not usually be valid, of course, but it may hold approximately in many cases of practical interest. It is sufficient for the purpose that the changes in the relative prices of other commodities induced by a change in the price of the commodity being studied do not in turn induce a significant shift in supply or demand conditions on the market for that commodity.

5. Developments During and After the 1930's: Existence and Uniqueness

The next truly major advances did not come until the 1930's. There were two distinct streams of thought, one beginning in German-language literature and dealing primarily with the existence and uniqueness of equilibrium, the other, primarily in English, dealing with stability and comparative statics. The former started with a thorough examination of Cassel's simplification [1924] of Walras' system, an interesting case of work that had no significance in itself, but whose study turned out to be extraordinarily fruitful. Cassel assumed two kinds of goods: commodities that enter into the demand functions of consumers and factors that are used to produce commodities (intermediate goods were not considered). Each commodity is produced from factors with constant input-output coefficients. Factor supplies are supposed totally inelastic. Let a_{ij} be the amount of factor i used in the production of one unit of commodity j, x_j the total output of commodity j, v_i the total initial supply of factor i, p_j the price of commodity j, and r_i the price of factor i. Then the condition that demand equal supply for all factors reads

$$\sum_j a_{ij}x_j = v_i \qquad \text{for all } i, \tag{1}$$

while the condition that each commodity be produced with zero profits reads

$$\sum_i a_{ij}r_i = p_j \qquad \text{for all } j. \tag{2}$$

The system is completed by the equations relating the demand for commodities to their prices and to total income from the sale of factors. In total there are as many equations as unknowns. But three virtually simultaneous papers by Zeuthen [1932], Neisser [1932], and von Stackelberg [1933] showed in different ways that the problem of existence of meaningful equilibrium is deeper than equality of equations and unknowns. Neisser noted that even with perfectly plausible values of the input-output coefficients, a_{ij}, the prices or quantities that satisfy (1) and (2) might well be negative. Von Stackelberg noted that (1) constitutes a complete system of equations in the outputs x_j, since the factor supplies, v_i, are data, but nothing had been assumed about the numbers of distinct factors or distinct commodities. If, in particular, the number of commodities was less than that of factors, equation (1), in general, would have no solution.

Zeuthen reconsidered the meaning of equation (1). He noted that economists, at least since Carl Menger, had recognized that some factors (e.g., air) are so abundant that there would be no price charged for them. These would not enter into the list of factors in Cassel's system. But, Zeuthen argued, the division of factors into free and scarce should not be taken as given *a priori*. Hence, all that can be said is that the use of a factor should not exceed its supply, but if it falls short, then the factor is free. In symbols, (1) is replaced by

$$\sum_j a_{ij}x_j \leq v_i; \qquad \text{if the strict inequality holds, then } r_i = 0. \quad (1')$$

To a later generation of economists to whom linear programming and its generalizations are familiar, the meaning of this step needs no elaboration; equalities are replaced by inequalities and the vital notion of the complementary slackness of quantities and prices introduced.

Independently of Zeuthen, Schlesinger, a Viennese banker and amateur economist, came to the same conclusion. He went much further, however, and intuitively grasped the crucial point that replacement of equalities by inequalities also resolves the problems raised by Neisser and von Stackelberg. Schlesinger [1933–34] realized the mathematical complexity of a rigorous treatment and, at his request, Oskar Morgenstern put him in touch with a young mathematician, Abraham Wald. The result of their collaboration was the first rigorous analysis of general competitive equilibrium. In a series of papers [1933–34, 1934–35] (see Wald [1936, 1951] for a summary), Wald demonstrated the existence of competitive equilibrium in a series of alternative models, including the Cassel model and a model of pure exchange. Competitive equilibrium was defined in the Zeuthen sense, and the essential role of that definition in the justification of existence is made clear in the mathematics.

Wald's papers were of forbidding mathematical depth, not only in the use of sophisticated tools, but also in the complexity of the argument. As they gradually came to be known among mathematical economists, they probably served as much to inhibit further research by their difficulty as to stimulate it.

Help finally came from development of a related line of research, John von Neumann's theory of games (first basic paper published in 1928; see von Neumann and Morgenstern [1944]). This historical relation between game theory and economic equilibrium has paradoxical elements. Game theory has developed several very general notions of equilibrium, which, in principle, should either replace the notion of competitive equilibrium or include it as a special case. Indeed, one such equilibrium notion, that of the *core*, is identical with Edgeworth's contract curve; it was introduced by Gillies [1953] and applied to specifically market situations by Shubik [1959] and, in a manner much closer to standard economic thought, by Scarf [1962] (see Chapter 8). The principal stimulation of game theory to equilibrium theory has been through the use of mathematical tools developed in the former and used in the latter with entirely different interpretations. Von Neumann himself made the first such application in his celebrated paper on balanced economic growth [1937, 1945]. In this model, there were no demand functions, only production. The markets in each period had to be in equilibrium in the Zeuthen sense, but beyond this was equilibrium in a second sense, which may be termed *stationary equilibrium*. The equilibrium configuration had to be the same from period to period. To prove the existence of equilibrium, von Neumann demonstrated that a certain ratio of bilinear forms had a saddle point, a generalization of the theorem that showed the existence of equilibrium in two-person zero-sum games. In game theory, however, the variables of the problem were probabilities (of choosing alternative strategies), while in the application to equilibrium theory one set of variables was prices and the other the levels at which productive activities were carried on.

Von Neumann deduced his saddle-point theorem from a generalization of Brouwer's fixed-point theorem, a famous proposition in topology. A simplified version of von Neumann's theorem was presented a few years later by the mathematician Shizuo Kakutani, and Kakutani's theorem has been the basic tool in virtually all subsequent work. (Statements and proofs of Brouwer's and Kakutani's theorems are found in Mathematical Appendix C.) With these foundations, plus the influence of the rapid development of linear programming on both the mathematical (again closely related to saddle-point theorems) and economic[1] sides, it was perceived independently by a number of scholars that existence theorems of greater simplicity and generality than Wald's were now possible. The first papers were those of McKenzie [1954] and Arrow and Debreu [1954]. Subsequent developments were due to Hukukane Nikaidô [1956] and Hirofumi Uzawa, Debreu, and McKenzie [1959, 1961]. The most complete systematic account of the existence conditions is in Debreu [1959]; the most general version is also in Debreu [1962].

6. Developments During and After the 1930's: Stability and Comparative Statics

Independently of this development of the existence conditions for equilibrium, the Anglo-American literature contained an intensive study of the comparative statics and stability of general competitive equilibrium. Historically, it was closely related to analyses of the second-order conditions for maximization of profits by firms and of utility by consumers; the most important contributors were John R. Hicks, Harold Hotelling, Paul Samuelson, and R. G. D. Allen. In particular, Hicks [1939] introduced the argument that the stability of equilibrium carried with it some implications for the shapes of the supply and demand functions in the neighborhood of equilibrium; hence, the effects of small shifts in any one behavior relation may be predicted, at least as to sign. Hicks' definition of stability has been replaced in subsequent work by Samuelson's [1941, 1942]; however, Hicks showed that (locally) stability in his sense was equivalent to a condition that has played a considerable role in subsequent research. Let z_i be the excess demand (demand less supply) for the ith commodity; it is in general a function of $p_1, \ldots, p_n$, the prices of all n commodities. Then Hicks' definition of stability was equivalent to the condition that the principal minors of the matrix whose elements were $\partial z_i/\partial p_j$ had determinants that were positive or negative according as the number of rows or columns included was even or odd.

[1] See Koopmans [1951a] for a collection of the work of George B. Dantzig, Albert W. Tucker, Harold W. Kuhn, Tjalling C. Koopmans and others, and John F. Nash, Jr. [1950].

Hicks also sought to derive comparative-statistics conclusions about the response of prices to changes in demand functions. Presently accepted theorems derive the same conclusions, from somewhat different premises, however (see Chapter 10).

Samuelson formulated the presently accepted definition of stability. It must be based, he argued, on an explicit dynamic model concerning the behavior of prices when the system is out of equilibrium. He formalized the implicit assumption of Walras and most of his successors: The price of each commodity increases at a rate proportional to excess demand for that commodity. This assumption defines a system of differential equations; if every path satisfying the system and starting sufficiently close to equilibrium converges to it, then the system is stable. Samuelson was able to demonstrate that Hicks' definition is neither necessary nor sufficient for his and that the economic system is stable if the income effects on consumption are sufficiently small. He proposed a general *correspondence principle* that all meaningful theorems in comparative statics derive either from the second-order conditions on maximization of profits by firms or of utility by consumers or from the assumption that the observed equilibrium was stable. In fact, very few useful propositions are derivable from this principle.

The current trend in comparative statics and stability dates from the work of Mosak [1944] and Metzler [1945]. The emphasis has tended to be a little different from Samuelson's correspondence principle; rather, the tendency has been to formulate hypotheses about the excess-demand functions that imply both stability and certain results in comparative statics.

7. The Structure of Price Determination and the Uniqueness of Equilibrium

A development of the period since 1948 has been a more detailed analysis of the relations between prices of factors and prices of produced goods. It is typically assumed in these analyses that (a) each commodity is either an original factor or a produced good, but never both, and (b) there is no joint production; that is, each production process has exactly one output, though it may have several inputs.

The case in which it is assumed, in addition, that production takes place under conditions of fixed coefficients leads to relatively simple analysis. The condition of zero profit for all processes leads to a system of linear equations. In the simple case in which all inputs are original factors, prices of commodities that are produced in any positive amount are related to factor prices by equations (2) (Section 1.5). Note that if there is only one primary commodity, then the relative prices of all commodities are determined by the technological coefficients. On the other hand, if the number of factors does not exceed the number of commodities produced and if the matrix (a_{ij}) has a rank equal to the number of factors (equals number of rows), then the factor prices are uniquely determined by the commodity prices.

These obvious conclusions turn out to generalize very considerably. The first extensions were to the case in which there are intermediate commodities, that is, produced goods used as inputs into the production of goods (Leontief [1941]). Consider again only commodities produced in some positive amount so that the zero-profit condition holds for each production process. Now let a_{ij} be the amount of produced good i used in the production of one unit of commodity j and let b_{kj} be the amount of original factor k used in the production of one unit of commodity j. As before, let p_j be the price of produced commodity j and let v_k be the price of original factor k. Then the zero-profit conditions are written:

$$p_j = \sum_i p_i a_{ij} + \sum_k v_k b_{kj}$$

or, in matrix and vector notation,

$$\mathbf{p} = \mathbf{p}A + \mathbf{v}B, \tag{3}$$

where $\mathbf{p}$ and $\mathbf{v}$ are the vectors with components p_j and v_k, respectively, and A and B are the matrices with elements a_{ij}, b_{kj}, respectively. Then (3) can be written

$$\mathbf{p}(I - A) = \mathbf{v}B, \tag{4}$$

and, if $I - A$ is non-singular,

$$\mathbf{p} = \mathbf{v}B(I - A)^{-1}. \tag{5}$$

Hence, commodity prices are determined by factor prices; in particular, if there is only one original factor, it remains true that relative prices of produced goods are completely determined by the technical coefficients, independent of demand. Also, if the rank of the matrix B equals the number of factors (rows), then it can be seen from (4) that factor prices are uniquely determined by the prices of commodities.

It should be remarked that the commodity prices determined by (4) are necessarily non-negative if factor prices are, and if a natural condition on A is satisfied. Specifically, it follows from the definitions of A and B and the assumption that there is no joint production that the elements of A and B are non-negative. Now assume that the system is productive in the sense that it is possible to produce a positive amount of every produced good if we ignore limitations due to factor scarcities; in symbols, there exists a non-negative vector $\mathbf{x}$ such that $A\mathbf{x} \ll \mathbf{x}$ (i.e., every component of $A\mathbf{x}$ is less than the corresponding component of $\mathbf{x}$). Then it follows from a well-known mathematical theory of Perron and Frobenius that the matrix $I - A$ is non-singular and that the elements of $(I - A)$ are non-negative. For $\mathbf{v}$ non-negative, $\mathbf{v}B$ is non-negative, and hence $\mathbf{p} = \mathbf{v}B(I - A)^{-1}$ is non-negative. (For an exposition, see Karlin [1959, Vol. I, pp. 245–246 and 256–258]; for the mathematical theory, see Karlin [1959, Vol. I, 246–256] or Mathematical Appendix A.)

Work since 1948 has demonstrated that these relations between commodity and factor prices generalize to the case involving alternative methods of production (but the hypothesis of no joint production is maintained). Samuelson [1951] and Georgescu-Roegen [1951] showed that with one primary factor it is still true that relative prices of produced goods are determined by the technology, independent of demand conditions. This is, in a certain sense, a surprising resuscitation of the classical theory in which prices are determined by supply conditions alone. Since competitive production always minimizes costs, it follows that the technique actually chosen for the production for any commodity is also independent of demand conditions, though it will depend, in general, on technological conditions in other industries. For more extended discussion, see Section 2.11.

The conditions for the determination of factor prices by commodity prices were studied by Samuelson [1948, 1953–54]; the problem arose in the context of foreign trade, which is assumed to equalize commodity prices across countries. In fact, the question of the conditions under which commodity prices determine factor prices is a special case of the conditions for the uniqueness of general equilibrium prices, specifically the case in which demand for commodities is perfectly elastic.

In general, there is no need that equilibrium be unique, and examples of non-uniqueness have been known since Marshall. Wald [1936] initiated the study of sufficient conditions for the uniqueness of competitive equilibrium. Both of his alternative sufficient conditions have since become major themes of the literature: The weak axiom of revealed preference holds for the market-demand functions or all commodities are gross substitutes (for the definition, see D.9.5).

An error in Samuelson's conditions for factor price determination was corrected by Gale and Nikaidô [1965], who supplied the mathematical basis for a fairly general uniqueness theorem, which generalizes, in particular, Wald's condition of gross substitutability (see Sections 9.2–9.3).

Note

The material of this chapter is drawn from Arrow [1968].

Chapter Two

MARKET EQUILIBRIUM: A FIRST APPROACH

To be or not to be, that is the question.
—W. Shakespeare, *Hamlet*

1. The Problem

We shall be considering a number of constructions representing economies in which agents take the terms at which they may transact as independently given. This, of course, is a feature of a perfectly competitive economy. A consequence of this is that part of the environment relevant to the decisions of economic agents consists of the prices of various goods that they take as given. Our main concern will be the description of situations in which the desired actions of economic agents are all mutually compatible and can all be carried out simultaneously, and for which we can prove that for the various economies discussed, there exists a set of prices that will cause agents to make mutually compatible decisions.

In carrying out this program we have imposed a number of restrictions on the matters covered and the degree of generality aimed at. Many of these restrictions are removed in the following chapters. Our first omission will be the rigorous discussion of the choices of economic agents; this will be found in Chapters 3 and 4. Our basic, and often implied, hypothesis is that agents have a complete ordering of points in the space of their possible choices and that, of the choices they can actually make in a given market situation, none is taken if there exists one that is preferred. These ideas are sufficiently familiar to justify invoking them informally before establishing them thoroughly. Our second omission, to be put formally presently, is that we shall be exclusively concerned with situations in which, for each set of prices, there is only one "best" choice for each agent. This will allow us to deal with demand and supply functions rather than with "correspondences" (i.e., situations in which the demand for a good, say at a given set of prices, must be represented by a set rather than by a number). The omission is rectified in Chapters 3–5 and further discussed below.

We start our discussion with a consideration of a very abstract kind of economy and then proceed to analyze a number of more restricted situations.

2. Goods and Prices

A good may be defined by its physical characteristics, its location in space, and the date of its delivery. Goods differing in any of these characteristics will be regarded as different. Services are regarded as goods. We shall suppose here that the number of different goods is finite.

We shall write p_i as the price of the ith good and we define $\mathbf{p}$ as the n-dimensional *row* vector with components p_i $(i = 1, \ldots, n)$. All prices are expressed in fictional unit of account—say "bancors" —and all prices are viewed from the present. Thus if "i" is a given good to be delivered at some location "A" in "T" periods from now, then p_i is the price that must be paid now for delivery of that good at that place at that time. This supposes the existence of all possible futures markets, a highly unrealistic assumption with which we shall dispense at a later stage.

3. The Excess-Demand Functions

Demand and supply decisions are taken by two kinds of agents: *households* and *firms*. The two are distinguished by the property that firms do, and households do not, take production decisions. This distinction is convenient.

Let x_{hi} be the decision of household h with respect to good i. Then, if $x_{hi} < 0$, we shall say that i is a service supplied by household h; when x_{hi} is non-negative, then i will be a good demanded by h, where this concept includes zero demand. We let $\mathbf{x}_h$ represent the n-dimensional *column* vector with components x_{hi}. Summation over households is indicated by omitting the subscript h. Thus, we have

$$x_i = \sum_h x_{hi} \qquad \mathbf{x} = \sum_h \mathbf{x}_h.$$

We write y_{fi} as the decision of firm f with respect to good i. We regard $y_{fi} < 0$ as denoting that i is an input demanded by f, while y_{fi} non-negative means that i is supplied by f where this concept includes zero supply. Also, $\mathbf{y}_f$ is the n-dimensional column vector with components y_{fi}. Summation over firms is indicated by omitting the subscript f. Thus, we have

$$y_i = \sum_f y_{fi} \qquad \mathbf{y} = \sum_f \mathbf{y}_f.$$

If there are any quantities of goods available in the economy before there is any production or market exchange, then we shall take it that these goods are owned by households. We write $\bar{x}_{hi}$ as the amount of good i owned by household h, and note that for good sense this must be a non-negative quantity. As before, $\bar{\mathbf{x}}_h$ is the n-dimensional column vector with components $\bar{x}_{hi}$ and summation over households is indicated by omitting the subscript h.

Market equilibrium is concerned with the compatibility of the decisions of the different firms and households, and therefore we are interested in the difference between the demand for a good and its total supply. The latter is the sum of the production of the good and the quantities of it available before production. Thus, the total supply of good i is $y_i + \bar{x}_i$. We define the excess demand for good i (written z_i) by

$$z_i = x_i - y_i - \bar{x}_i \qquad i = 1, \ldots, n.$$

We write $\mathbf{z}$ for the n-dimensional column vector with components z_i and refer to it as the *excess-demand vector*. Taking $\bar{\mathbf{x}}$ and $\bar{\mathbf{x}}_h$ as given, we regard $\mathbf{z}$ as a function of $\mathbf{p}$. We shall sometimes refer to $z_i < 0$ as an *excess supply* of good i. We put this formally:

ASSUMPTION 1 (F). To any $\mathbf{p}$ there corresponds a unique number $z_i(\mathbf{p})$ called the *excess-demand function* for i and so a unique vector of excess-demand functions $\mathbf{z}(\mathbf{p})$. We have $z_i(\mathbf{p}) = x_i(\mathbf{p}) - y_i(\mathbf{p}) - \bar{\mathbf{x}}_i$ and call $x_i(\mathbf{p})$ the *demand function* and $y_i(\mathbf{p})$ the *supply function.*[1]

It is quite important to understand why this assumption is indeed restrictive, and we consider a simple example by way of illustration for which F will not hold. Suppose that, given $\mathbf{p}$, there is a unique household response $x_i(\mathbf{p})$. Suppose further that good i is produced by firm f, which produces no other kind of good, while no other firm produces i. Let the firm choose $\mathbf{y}_f$, among all the choices of $\mathbf{y}_f$ open to it, so as to maximize $\mathbf{p}\mathbf{y}_f$, its profits. Assume that $\mathbf{p}$ is such that this maximization is possible and is achieved for $\mathbf{p}\mathbf{y}_f = 0$,

[1] Of course $\mathbf{y}(\mathbf{p})$ is a vector and contains negative components so that this use of the notion "supply function" is not that of the textbook.

but that the firm produces under constant returns to scale. Then evidently for $k > 0$, $k\mathbf{y}_f$ will also maximize profits and so $\mathbf{p}$ does not determine the total supply of good i uniquely and F does not hold. Other examples are possible, none of which relies on unrealistic postulates. It is clear, therefore, that we shall have to regard F as an assumption that, at some stage, we must do without.

There is one other important point that requires emphasis. The number $z_i(\mathbf{p})$ will later be derived from a proper theory of the actions of economic agents, households, and firms. It tells us what the excess demand for i will be if all attempted to carry out their preferred actions at $\mathbf{p}$. The excess-demand function is thus an *ex ante* concept; it is hypothetical in the sense that the actual purchases and sales may differ from those that the theory of the decisions of agents tells us would be the purchases and sales regarded as proper by the agents at $\mathbf{p}$.[1] Indeed, at $z_i(\mathbf{p})$ positive, for instance, it clearly would not be possible for all the agents to complete the transactions with respect to i that they regard as desirable at $\mathbf{p}$.

4. The Main Assumptions

In this section we introduce the main assumptions to be used in this chapter. Many of these will be deduced as propositions from more basic postulates later in this book (Sections 3.4 and 4.5).

The first assumption asserts that the actions of agents depend on the rates at which goods exchange one against another and not at all on the rate at which goods exchange against the (fictional) unit of account, in this case, bancors. This assumption should not be misunderstood. If one of the goods acts as a medium of exchange, for instance, then it too will have a price in terms of unit of account, and it is not asserted that the rate at which goods exchange against this particular good, the medium of exchange, is of no consequence to the decisions of economic agents. We write this assumption formally:

ASSUMPTION 2 (H). $\mathbf{z}(\mathbf{p}) = \mathbf{z}(k\mathbf{p})$ for all $\mathbf{p} > \mathbf{0}$ and $k > 0$; the excess-demand functions are *homogeneous of degree zero in* $\mathbf{p}$.

A consequence of H is that we may fix the level of $\mathbf{p}$ arbitrarily without restricting our analysis in any way. For our purposes, this

[1] See Sections 13.6 and 14.4 for detailed discussions.

is most conveniently done by considering only those prices that belong to the n-dimensional simplex S_n, which is defined by

$$S_n = \left\{\mathbf{p} \,\middle|\, \sum_i^n p_i = 1, \quad \mathbf{p} > \mathbf{0}\right\}.$$

It may be objected that this procedure is rather drastic because it precludes from consideration situations in which all prices are zero and also situations in which some price is negative.

First we note that if we wished to examine an economy from which the "economic problem" of scarcity is absent, we could do so by supposing everyone to own some quantities of a good, the price of which we set equal to unity so that all the other goods have a zero price. This we can do while restricting all $\mathbf{p}$ to be in S_n. The proper representation of such an economy could not be achieved by setting $\mathbf{p} = \mathbf{0}$.

There is also a technical reason for excluding $\mathbf{p} = \mathbf{0}$ from consideration. Suppose H holds for $k \geq 0$ and not just for $k > 0$. Now consider two price vectors, $\mathbf{p}$ and $\mathbf{p}'$, with $\mathbf{z}(\mathbf{p}) \neq \mathbf{z}(\mathbf{p}')$. Then by H, $\mathbf{z}(k\mathbf{p}) = \mathbf{z}(\mathbf{p})$ and $\mathbf{z}(k\mathbf{p}') = \mathbf{z}(\mathbf{p}')$ for $k > 0$. Evidently, if we allow k to approach zero, the two vectors of the excess-demand functions must approach different limits, from which we conclude that $\mathbf{z}(\mathbf{p})$ is not continuous at $\mathbf{p} = \mathbf{0}$. But we certainly would find it very inconvenient to have to do without the continuity of the excess-demand function at any point of the price domain we consider, and in this instance nothing of economic interest would be gained.

The reason for excluding negative prices is less cogent and also less necessary for the subsequent analysis, though we shall maintain it for simplicity. If a good has a negative price, then the individual selling that good has to give up units of some other good or goods with positive price as well. If he also has the option of disposing of the good without giving up any other good with a positive price, it is reasonable to suppose that he will prefer this option. Thus the exclusion of negative prices from consideration is justified if we suppose that there always exists the option of *free disposal*, for then no one would be willing to transact at a negative price and so a negative price could not arise. In this chapter and elsewhere in the book, free disposal is postulated.

The second assumption derives from the fact that, stealing apart, no agent can plan a greater expenditure on goods and services than the receipts he plans to obtain from the sale of goods and services.

By our definition of goods (Section 2.2), this "accounting restraint" includes borrowing and lending. The individual borrows by selling goods now for future delivery and he lends by buying goods now for future delivery.

The difference between the total value of all purchases planned by households and firms and the total value of sales planned by them is evidently $\mathbf{pz}$. We shall now give reasons for taking this number to be non-positive. Suppose that all firms aim to maximize their profits and that they all have the choice of not engaging in any productive activity. Clearly, since $\mathbf{py}$ is the profits of all firms taken together, we may take it that $\mathbf{py}$ is always non-negative. Next suppose that every household h receives a given fraction, $d_h \geq 0$, of the total profits of firms and that

$$\sum_h d_h = 1.$$

Then h may choose any $\mathbf{x}_h$ that satisfies

$$\mathbf{px}_h - \mathbf{p\bar{x}}_h - d_h\mathbf{py} \leq 0. \tag{1}$$

If we can suppose further that a household always prefers $\mathbf{x}_h$ to $\mathbf{x}'_h$ if $\mathbf{x}_h > \mathbf{x}'_h$ and that it will never choose an action if a preferred one is available, then the reader can verify that $\mathbf{x}_h$ will always be such as to make the expression in (1) equal to zero. Summing (1) over h then gives $\mathbf{pz} = 0$.

These are the underlying rationalizations of the assumption that we now put formally.

ASSUMPTION 3 (W). For all $\mathbf{p} \in S_n$, $\mathbf{pz(p)} = 0$ (Walras' law). In what follows we shall need another, rather technical assumption.

ASSUMPTION 4 (C). The vector excess-demand function, $\mathbf{z(p)}$, is continuous over its domain of definition, S_n.

Assumption C implies that $\mathbf{z(p)}$ is bounded everywhere, since S_n is a compact set, which here means that it is closed and bounded. In particular, this means that the demand for a free good is bounded; every individual becomes satiated with respect to any particular good. Unfortunately this assumption comes close to being inconsistent with the reasoning underlying W, which requires that at any point the household is unsatiated with respect to at least one good. A weaker continuity assumption that permits unlimited demand for free goods will be introduced in Section 2.8.

It may help the reader to have an example of the violation of C. Suppose again that good i is produced only by firm f, which produces no other goods. Given the prices of all goods other than i, assume the average cost curve of f to be U shaped.[1] Let p_i^* be the lowest price at which the firm can cover average costs. Then by the usual assumptions, the firm's output will be zero for all $p_i < p_i^*$, while we stipulate that there is a positive output at p_i^*. It can be left to the reader to verify that C will be violated. Since this example is not fanciful, we must conclude that C indeed may be a serious restriction on our analysis. Although this assumption can be somewhat relaxed after F is abandoned, we cannot do without something very close to it in many of the results to be given both in this chapter and in this book. However, we hope to draw some conclusions for the working of an economic system in certain of the cases in which C is violated.

5. Equilibrium

Economic agents may be taken to reach their decisions in the light of what they want and what they can get. If tastes and technology are given, and if the goods owned by individuals and households are also given, then the variables influencing their decisions are the prices prevailing in the various markets. If at some set of admissible prices (i.e., for us some $\mathbf{p}$ in S_n) all these decisions can be carried out simultaneously, then we may say that these decisions are compatible and that the prices are equilibrium prices. There are really two sets of ideas involved in this notion of equilibrium. On the one hand, in such a situation every agent can achieve what he wishes to achieve. On the other hand, if tastes, technology, and the ownership of goods remain given, there will be no mechanism to bring about a change in $\mathbf{p}$. Under the conditions postulated, it is argued that a change in prices is a signal, the consequence of incompatibility in the decisions of agents. This is a familiar notion, the "law of demand and supply," which is discussed more extensively in Chapters 11, 12, and 13.

[1] Since we have taken $\mathbf{p} \in S_n$, the curve must be thought of as constructed as follows: Take any $\mathbf{p} \in S_n$, and suppose that at this $\mathbf{p}$ there is at least one point on i's average cost curve equal to p_i. Now, say, raise p_i to p_i' and multiply all other prices by $k < 1$ so that the new $\mathbf{p}' \in S_n$. Again find a point on the average cost curve at $\mathbf{p}'$ that is equal to p_i'. Proceed in this way to trace the whole curve.

Before we formalize this idea we must take note of a special point. The decision to supply a good in a perfectly competitive economy is not a decision to supply so-and-so much to such-and-such agents, but simply to exchange so-and-so much of the good for other goods. If the price ruling for a good is zero and agents plan to supply some of it, then by the assumption of free disposal (see discussion of H in Section 2.4), we may simply say that agents decide to dispose of a certain amount of the good. Clearly this decision can be carried out by our assumption, whatever the demand of other agents for that good may be. If this demand were greater than the amount offered, however, then the decisions of the demanding agents could not be carried to fruition. From this we conclude that while we would never be willing to regard a situation with positive excess demand in some market as an equilibrium, an excess supply in a market where the price is zero is quite consistent with our notion of an equilibrium. All this seems agreeable to common sense and it remains to put it more formally.

DEFINITION 1 (E). $\mathbf{p}^*$ in S_n is called an *equilibrium* if $\mathbf{z}(\mathbf{p}^*) \leq \mathbf{0}$, where $\mathbf{z}(\mathbf{p})$ is derived from the "preferred" actions of agents.

That this formal definition indeed corresponds to our discussion of the equilibrium concept can be seen with the aid of the following theorem.

THEOREM 1. If W and $\mathbf{z}(\mathbf{p}^*) \leq \mathbf{0}$, then $z_i(\mathbf{p}^*) < 0$ implies that $p_i^* = 0$.

Proof. Since $\mathbf{p}^*$ is in S_n, it follows from the assumptions of T.2.1 that every element in the sum $\mathbf{p}^* z(\mathbf{p}^*)$ is non-positive. Then, if, contrary to what is asserted, $p_i^* > 0$, it must be that $\mathbf{p}^* z(\mathbf{p}^*) < 0$, which contradicts W. Since no price can be negative, this completes the proof.

In several respects D.2.1 is incomplete because it does not specify the conditions that must hold for each agent if his decision is to be the "best" open to him at $\mathbf{p}^*$. This, however, must be postponed until Chapters 3 and 4. Here we must be satisfied with our rather informal treatment.

It should also be noted that there is no reason to suppose that there is only one equilibrium price vector. The question of the "uniqueness" of an equilibrium will be fully explored in Chapter 9.

Here we simply introduce a piece of notation: We write E for the set of equilibrium price vectors,

$$E = \{\mathbf{p} \mid \mathbf{z}(\mathbf{p}) \leq \mathbf{0}; \quad \mathbf{p} \in S_n\}.$$

6. The Existence of Equilibrium—the Case of Two Goods

This section is to serve as an introduction to the proof that in general, given our assumptions, the set E is not empty. It is hoped that it will facilitate a proper appreciation of the roles of the various assumptions in the proof. In what follows we take all $\mathbf{p}$ to be in S_n.

Consider, in a two-good economy, the two price vectors

$$\mathbf{p}' = (0,1) \quad \text{and} \quad \mathbf{p}'' = (1,0).$$

We suppose that neither $\mathbf{p}'$ nor $\mathbf{p}''$ is in E, else there is nothing to prove. But then it must be that $z_1(\mathbf{p}') > 0$ and $z_2(\mathbf{p}'') > 0$. Consider the first of these. By W we have $0z_1(\mathbf{p}') + 1z_2(\mathbf{p}') = 0$. If, contrary to our assertion, we had $z_1(\mathbf{p}') \leq 0$, then the first term would certainly be zero and so also $z_2(\mathbf{p}') = 0$, which contradicts the supposition that $\mathbf{p}'$ is not in E. The same argument establishes the inequality for $z_2(\mathbf{p}'')$.

Now let

$$\mathbf{p}(m) = m\mathbf{p}' + (1 - m)\mathbf{p}'' \qquad \text{with } 1 \geq m \geq 0.$$

By W, one of the numbers $z_1(\mathbf{p}(m))$ and $z_2(\mathbf{p}(m))$ is positive and the other negative when $m \neq 0,1$, unless $\mathbf{p}(m) \in E$. Suppose then, without loss of generality, that $z_1(\mathbf{p}(m^0)) < 0$ for some $m^0 \neq 0,1$. Now let m increase from m^0 to 1. We already know that $z_1(\mathbf{p}(0))$ is positive, and therefore, as m approaches zero, somewhere $z_1(\mathbf{p}(m))$ must change sign. But, by C, it cannot change sign without becoming zero. Suppose this happens at m^*. Then $\mathbf{p}(m^*)$ is in E, for, by W, it must be that $z_2(\mathbf{p}(m^*)) = 0$.

We note the important role of C in this demonstration. Without it we could not exclude the possibility of a change in the sign of z_1, as m approaches zero, without its ever becoming equal to zero. Of course we also relied heavily on W, but this assumption does not appear to be very restrictive. As was indicated in the discussion of C, however, the latter will certainly exclude a number of perfectly possible situations from consideration. Later in the book, an investigation of some of these possibilities should help us to form some judgment as to the likelihood that the coherence of decisions implied by equilibrium is attainable by actual economies. In this, however, due care will have to be taken not to confuse the statement "an equilibrium cannot be shown to exist" with the statement "no equilibrium is possible."

In Figure 2-1 we illustrate the proposition just established for a two-good economy. In the diagram the horizontal axis is of unit length.

7. The Existence of an Equilibrium: Many Goods

When we turn to the economy with many goods, it is clear that the simple procedure of Section 2.6 will not serve, although the lessons we have learned will continue to be of interest, as we shall see. Indeed, the best introduction to the general case is probably achieved by staying with the two-good case a little longer.

Take any arbitrary point **p** on the horizontal axis of Figure 2-1 so that **p** is in S_n. At the point chosen in the figure, $z_1(\mathbf{p})$ is positive and $z_2(\mathbf{p})$ is negative. Let us adopt the following rules:

(1) Raise the price of the good in positive excess demand.
(2) Lower or at least do not raise the price of the good in excess supply, but never lower the price below zero.

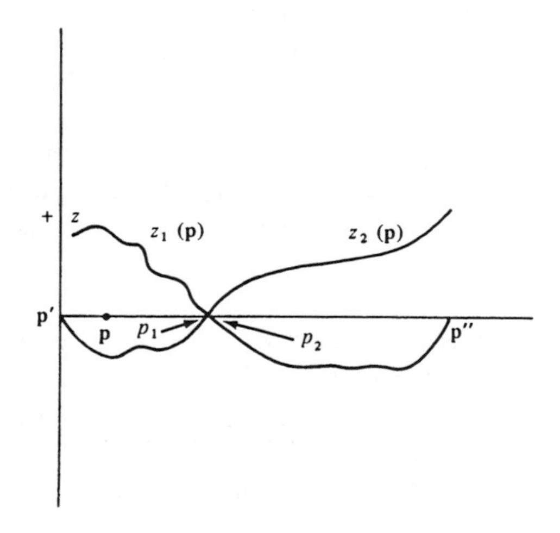

Figure 2-1

(3) Do not change the price of a good in zero excess demand.
(4) Multiply the resulting price vector by a scalar, leaving relative prices unchanged, so that the new price vector you obtain is in S_n.

If we are successful in carrying out these rules we can say: Given any **p** in S_n, we have a routine for finding another point in S_n. Another way of putting this is to say that our procedure gives us a *mapping* of S_n into itself. We note that if **p** is an equilibrium, then the mapping will give us **p** again. The converse will also be true: If the mapping takes us from **p** back to **p**, then equilibrium exists. The question then is: Does at least one such point exist? In our two-good example the answer is clearly "yes." Suppose that neither $\mathbf{p}'$ nor $\mathbf{p}''$ is the point we seek. We know that at $\mathbf{p}'$ the rules tell us to raise the price of good 1 and at $\mathbf{p}''$ they tell us to raise the price of good 2. By W, though, we can never be asked to raise the prices of both goods at any **p**. Hence, at $\mathbf{p}(m)$ with $1 \neq m \neq 0$, the rules instruct us to lower the price of some good, say the first. But then by C at some $\mathbf{p}(m^*)$, the rules tell us not to change the price of the first good (because $z_1(\mathbf{p}(m^*)) = 0$), and then by W it follows also that we must not change the price of the second good. Hence, $\mathbf{p}(m^*)$ is a point of the kind we seek.

All this is really a repetition of the argument of the previous section in slightly different terms. When we come to the case of many goods, our method will have to be somewhat different. As much as possible, we shall use the economics of our problem to construct a procedure that satisfies the rules we have given. We can use C to establish that the rules give a continuous mapping. Then we will appeal to a mathematical theorem that assures us that there will be at least one point in S_n that the mapping returns to itself. We then will appeal again to our economics to show that this point is the equilibrium we seek.

Step 1: Construction of mapping. We first seek a continuous function with the following three properties:

$$M_i(\mathbf{p}) > 0 \quad \text{if and only if } z_i(\mathbf{p}) > 0, \tag{2a}$$

$$M_i(\mathbf{p}) = 0 \quad \text{if } z_i(\mathbf{p}) = 0, \tag{2b}$$

$$p_i + M_i(\mathbf{p}) \geq 0. \tag{2c}$$

It is intended that $M_i(\mathbf{p})$ represent an adjustment to an existing price so that a price vector $\mathbf{p}$ is transformed into a new price vector with components $p_i + M_i(\mathbf{p})$.

Functions satisfying (2) exist; for one example, let $M_i(\mathbf{p}) = \max(-p_i, k_i z_i(\mathbf{p}))$, where $k_i > 0$. Since $M_i(\mathbf{p})$ is a continuous transformation of p_i and z_i, it is certainly continuous by C.

To verify (2a), first suppose $z_i(\mathbf{p}) > 0$. Since $p_i \geq 0$, $k_i z_i(\mathbf{p}) > -p_i$, so that $M_i(\mathbf{p}) = k_i z_i(\mathbf{p}) > 0$. Conversely, if $z_i(\mathbf{p}) \leq 0$, then either $M_i(\mathbf{p}) = k_i z_i(\mathbf{p}) \leq 0$ or $M_i(\mathbf{p}) = -p_i \leq 0$. It is easy to verify that (2b) and (2c) hold.

An even simpler, though less intuitive, example of a function satisfying (2) is $M_i(\mathbf{p}) = \max(0, k_i z_i(\mathbf{p}))$, $k_i > 0$.

For functions satisfying (2), we easily deduce

$$M_i(\mathbf{p}) z_i(\mathbf{p}) \geq 0 \qquad \text{all } i. \tag{3}$$

It will be seen that if we interpret $p_i + M_i(\mathbf{p})$ as the ith component of the new price vector that the mapping produces, given $\mathbf{p}$, the procedure for finding these new prices satisfies rules discussed earlier. However, while all $p_i + M_i(\mathbf{p})$ are certainly non-negative, there is nothing to ensure that they will add up to one. In other words, if we write $\mathbf{p} + \mathbf{M}(\mathbf{p})$ as the row vector of the new prices (components $p_i + M_i(\mathbf{p})$), then there is no reason to suppose that $\mathbf{p} + M(\mathbf{p})$ is in S_n when $\mathbf{p}$ is in S_n. Since we seek a mapping of S_n into itself, we must modify the mapping.

An obvious way of doing this is as follows: Let $\mathbf{e}$ be the n-dimensional column vector with all components unity. Then $[\mathbf{p} + M(\mathbf{p})]\mathbf{e}$ is certainly non-negative. If we are certain that this number is strictly positive, then we may take the mapping given by

$$\mathbf{T}(\mathbf{p}) = \frac{\mathbf{p} + \mathbf{M}(\mathbf{p})}{[\mathbf{p} + \mathbf{M}(\mathbf{p})]\mathbf{e}}. \tag{4}$$

The reader can now verify that (4) obeys all of the four rules we have laid down, in particular, that the vector $\mathbf{T}(\mathbf{p})$ is in S_n.

We now show that (4) is indeed a possible mapping by proving that for all $\mathbf{p} \in S_n$, $[\mathbf{p} + \mathbf{M}(\mathbf{p})]\mathbf{e} > 0$. If not, then for some $\mathbf{p} \in S_n$, $\mathbf{p} + \mathbf{M}(\mathbf{p}) = \mathbf{0}$ by 2(c). But then

$$0 = [\mathbf{p} + \mathbf{M}(\mathbf{p})]\mathbf{z}(\mathbf{p}) = \mathbf{p}\mathbf{z}(\mathbf{p}) + \mathbf{M}(\mathbf{p})\mathbf{z}(\mathbf{p}) = \mathbf{M}(\mathbf{p})\mathbf{z}(\mathbf{p})$$

by W. But then by (3), $M_i(\mathbf{p}) z_i(\mathbf{p}) = 0$, all i. Since $\mathbf{p} \in S_n$, it must be that $p_i > 0$, some i, so for that i, $M_i(\mathbf{p}) = -p_i < 0$. This, however, must mean $z_i(\mathbf{p}) = 0$, which in turn by (2b) implies that $M_i(\mathbf{p}) = 0$, a contradiction. Hence, $[\mathbf{p} + \mathbf{M}(\mathbf{p})]\mathbf{e} > 0$ for all $\mathbf{p} \in S_n$.

Step 2: The mathematical result. We first define some of the notions of our introductory remarks more formally.

DEFINITION 2. (a) If $\mathbf{T}(\mathbf{p})$ is a mapping that takes points in S_n into points in S_n, then the mapping is said to map S_n into itself.

(b) If for some $\mathbf{p}^*$ we have $\mathbf{p}^* = \mathbf{T}(\mathbf{p}^*)$, then $\mathbf{p}^*$ is called a *fixed point* of $\mathbf{T}(\mathbf{p})$.

The theorem we use in this chapter is called Brouwer's fixed-point theorem, and it is stated as follows: Every continuous mapping of a compact convex set into itself has a fixed point. The proof of this result will be found in T.C.1; convexity is defined in D.B.7. Here we need confirm only that the set S_n that we are interested in satisfies the requirements of the theorem.

Certainly if $\mathbf{p}$ and $\mathbf{p}'$ are in S_n, then for any m with $1 \geq m \geq 0$, the vector $\mathbf{p}(m) = m\mathbf{p} + (1 - m)\mathbf{p}'$ is in S_n, since $\mathbf{p}(m)$ is non-negative and $\mathbf{p}(m)\mathbf{e} = 1$. Hence, S_n is convex. Since S_n is clearly bounded and since the limit point of any sequence of price vectors in S_n is itself in S_n, S_n is compact.

Step 3: The fixed point of T(p) is an equilibrium. At the fixed point, we have $\mathbf{p}^* = \mathbf{T}(\mathbf{p}^*)$, that is,

$$\{[\mathbf{p}^* + \mathbf{M}(\mathbf{p}^*)]\mathbf{e}\}\mathbf{p}^* = \mathbf{p}^* + \mathbf{M}(\mathbf{p}^*)$$

or

$$\mathbf{M}(\mathbf{p}^*) = \lambda \mathbf{p}^*, \tag{5}$$

where $\lambda = [\mathbf{p}^* + \mathbf{M}(\mathbf{p}^*)]\mathbf{e} - 1$. Take the inner product of (5) on both sides with $\mathbf{z}(\mathbf{p}^*)$, and use W to find

$$\mathbf{M}(\mathbf{p}^*)\mathbf{z}(\mathbf{p}^*) = \lambda \mathbf{p}^*\mathbf{z}(\mathbf{p}^*) = 0.$$

As before, $M_i(\mathbf{p}^*)z_i(\mathbf{p}^*) = 0$, all i, by (3). Hence, $z_i(\mathbf{p}^*) > 0$ would imply $M_i(\mathbf{p}^*) = 0$, which contradicts (2a). Hence, $z_i(\mathbf{p}^*) \leq 0$, all i. By D.2.1, $\mathbf{p}^*$ is an equilibrium.

We summarize the result of this section formally:

THEOREM 2. If F, H, W, and C, then an equilibrium for a competitive economy with a finite number of goods exists.

We have thus been able to establish that for the economy here described there exists a set of "signals"—market prices—that will lead agents to make decisions that are mutually compatible. This is by no means a trivial result, and we repeat that careful reflection on the roles of the various assumptions in establishing it is very desirable because there are certainly economies that interest us in which coherence in decentralized decisions may not be possible, or at least for which it cannot be proved possible. Thus important issues in the judgment of decentralized systems are at stake.

8. Equilibrium under a Weakened Continuity Condition

As noted in Section 2.4, C implies in its present form that the demand for free goods is bounded. We shall want to weaken this restriction for several reasons: It is not unreasonable that demand for at least some goods might approach infinity as the price approaches zero; as already noted, the non-satiation hypothesis that underlies Walras' law is at least partly inconsistent with satiation in any single good; the assumption that all goods are gross substitutes, an assumption frequently made in the literature on stability and uniqueness and repeatedly used by us in later chapters of this book, implies that demands may approach infinity as prices go to zero.

We must be careful, however, in stating the weakened continuity assumption. A simple possibility might be to admit that an excess demand function $z_i(\mathbf{p})$ can take on the value $+\infty$ in addition to finite values and to define continuity in an obvious extension of the usual definition (i.e., if $z_i(\mathbf{p})$ approaches infinity along one converging sequence of price vectors, it must do so on every sequence converging to the same limit). This assumption indeed implies the existence of equilibrium, but it cannot be derived from a utility-maximization theory of household behavior. Consider the following example. There are three goods, and the household has a utility function

$$U(\mathbf{x}) = x_1^{1/2} + x_2^{1/2} + x_3^{1/2},$$

which is in no way pathological. Let the initial endowment be one unit of commodity 3, and suppose that $p_3 = 1$, while p_1 and p_2 are both varying and approaching 0. The usual calculations for demand functions show that

$$x_1(\mathbf{p}) = \frac{1}{p_1 + (p_1^2/p_2) + p_1^2}.$$

From the paths along which p_1 and p_2 both approach zero, it is possible to choose one for which p_1^2/p_2 approaches any given non-negative real number or indeed $+\infty$. Then $x_1(\mathbf{p})$ can be made to approach any given non-negative real number, or $+\infty$. Thus no definition can be given to $x_1(0,0,1)$ that is consistent with continuity in any sense. We must therefore regard $\mathbf{x}(\mathbf{p})$ as undefined at the point (0,0,1).

However, it can be seen that $x_1(\mathbf{p}) + x_2(\mathbf{p}) + x_3(\mathbf{p})$ approaches $+\infty$. We can calculate that

$$x_3(\mathbf{p}) = \frac{1}{(1/p_1) + (1/p_2) + 1}$$

and therefore certainly approaches zero as p_1 and p_2 approach 0 in any direction. Since $p_3 = 1$, $p_3x_3(\mathbf{p}) \to 0$. From the budget constraint,

$$p_1x_1(\mathbf{p}) + p_2x_2(\mathbf{p}) \to 1.$$

We can calculate also that

$$(p_1 - p_2)x_1(\mathbf{p}) - 1 = -\frac{(1 + u^2v)}{(u + u^2v)},$$

where $u = p_1/p_2$, $v = 1 + p_2$. For p_2 small, v can be regarded as constrained to a right-hand neighborhood of 1. Since the right-hand side is negative as u varies over positive values and v over its range and since it approaches $-\infty$ as u approaches 0 and -1 as u approaches $+\infty$, it is clearly negative and bounded away from 0. However,

$$p_2[x_1(\mathbf{p}) + x_2(\mathbf{p})] = [p_1x_1(\mathbf{p}) + p_2x_2(\mathbf{p}) - 1] - [(p_1 - p_2)x_1(\mathbf{p}) - 1];$$

since the first term on the right-hand side approaches 0 and the second is negative and bounded away from 0, it follows that $p_2[x_1(\mathbf{p}) + x_2(\mathbf{p})]$ is positive and bounded away from 0. Since $p_2 \to 0$, it must be that $x_1(\mathbf{p}) + x_2(\mathbf{p}) \to +\infty$, and, since $x_3(\mathbf{p})$ approaches 0, $x_1(\mathbf{p}) + x_2(\mathbf{p}) + x_3(\mathbf{p})$ approaches $+\infty$.

It will be shown later (T.4.8) that this result is a general implication of utility maximization. At present, we simply assume that the sum of excess demands approaches infinity whenever excess demand is undefined.

Before restating the continuity assumption formally, we introduce another.

Assumption 5 (B). There exists a positive finite number R such that for all $\mathbf{p}$ in S_n, $z_i(\mathbf{p}) > -R$, all i; $\mathbf{z}(\mathbf{p})$ is *bounded from below*.

B can be justified by supposing that the amount that can be produced of any one good at any one time not infinitely removed from the present is finite, that the quantities of goods initially owned by households also can properly be taken as finite, and that it is not fanciful to suppose that the quantity of any one service a household is capable of supplying at a moment of time is also not infinite. Assumption B is superfluous if C is postulated, but not if it is relaxed as below.

Assumption 6 (C′). The excess-demand function, $\mathbf{z}(\mathbf{p})$, is defined for all $\mathbf{p} \gg \mathbf{0}$ and possibly for other $\mathbf{p}$ and is continuous wherever defined. If $\mathbf{z}(\mathbf{p})$ is not defined for $\mathbf{p} = \mathbf{p}^0$, then

$$\lim_{p \to \mathbf{p}^0} \sum_i z_i(\mathbf{p}) = +\infty.$$

In view of C′, we can define, by convention,

$$\sum_i z_i(\mathbf{p})$$

to take on the value $+\infty$ for all $\mathbf{p}$ for which $\mathbf{z}(\mathbf{p})$ is not defined.

We now show that the previous equilibrium proof can be modified so as to be valid if C is replaced by B and C′.

We take $\mathbf{M}(\mathbf{p})$ to have the properties (2), but now require only that it be continuous wherever $\mathbf{z}(\mathbf{p})$ is defined and therefore continuous. The previous examples show that this is possible. Then (3) is still valid, as is the conclusion that $[\mathbf{p} + \mathbf{M}(\mathbf{p})]\mathbf{e} > 0$.

For convenience of notation, let,

$$Z(\mathbf{p}) = \sum_i z_i(\mathbf{p}).$$

Now introduce a continuous function, $\alpha(Z)$, defined for all real numbers Z such that $0 \leq \alpha(Z) \leq 1$, all Z, $\alpha(Z) = 0$ for $Z \leq 0$, $\alpha(Z) = 1$ for $Z \geq Z_1$, where $Z_1 > 0$. Then define $\alpha(\mathbf{p}) = \alpha[Z(\mathbf{p})]$ and

$$N(p) = \begin{cases} [1 - \alpha(\mathbf{p})]\mathbf{M}(\mathbf{p}) + \alpha(\mathbf{p})\mathbf{e}' & \text{if } \mathbf{z}(\mathbf{p}) \text{ is defined,} \\ \mathbf{e}' & \text{if } \mathbf{z}(\mathbf{p}) \text{ is undefined.} \end{cases} \tag{6}$$

Here $\mathbf{e}'$ is the row vector whose components are all 1. $\mathbf{N}(\mathbf{p})$ is so chosen that it coincides with $\mathbf{M}(\mathbf{p})$ if $Z(\mathbf{p}) \leq 0$ (a region in which we know any possible equilibrium must lie) and becomes a strictly positive vector if $\mathbf{z}(\mathbf{p})$ is undefined or indeed if $Z(\mathbf{p}) \geq Z_1$ and therefore, by C′, in any neighborhood of a point where $\mathbf{z}(\mathbf{p})$ is undefined.

Obviously, $\mathbf{N}(\mathbf{p})$ is continuous wherever $\mathbf{z}(\mathbf{p})$ is defined. Suppose $\mathbf{z}(\mathbf{p})$ is undefined for $\mathbf{p} = \mathbf{p}^0$. By C′, we can find a neighborhood of $\mathbf{p}^0$ such that $Z(\mathbf{p}) \geq Z_1$ for all $\mathbf{p}$ in the neighborhood for which $\mathbf{z}(\mathbf{p})$ is defined. Then $N(\mathbf{p}) = \mathbf{e}'$ for all such $\mathbf{p}$; it also equals $\mathbf{e}'$ for all $\mathbf{p}$ for which $\mathbf{z}(\mathbf{p})$ is not defined and in particular $\mathbf{p} = \mathbf{p}^0$, so that $\mathbf{N}(\mathbf{p})$ is constant at $\mathbf{e}'$ throughout the neighborhood and is certainly continuous.

Since $0 \leq \alpha(\mathbf{p}) \leq 1$, it follows from (6) that, where $\mathbf{z}(\mathbf{p})$ is defined, $M_i(\mathbf{p}) \leq 1$ implies $N_i(\mathbf{p}) \geq M_i(\mathbf{p})$ and, therefore, $p_i + N_i(\mathbf{p}) \geq p_i + M_i(\mathbf{p}) \geq 0$, while $M_i(\mathbf{p}) > 0$ implies $N_i(\mathbf{p}) > 0$ and, therefore, $p_i + N_i(\mathbf{p}) > p_i \geq 0$. Hence, certainly $p_i + N_i(\mathbf{p}) \geq 0$, all i. Also, if $M_i(\mathbf{p}) > 0$, some i, then $\mathbf{p} + \mathbf{N}(\mathbf{p}) > \mathbf{0}$, so that $[\mathbf{p} + N(\mathbf{p})]\mathbf{e} > 0$, while if $M_i(\mathbf{p}) \leq 0$, all i, then $\mathbf{p} + N(\mathbf{p}) \geq \mathbf{p} + \mathbf{M}(\mathbf{p})$, $[\mathbf{p} + \mathbf{N}(\mathbf{p})]\mathbf{e} \geq [\mathbf{p} + \mathbf{M}(\mathbf{p})]\mathbf{e} > 0$. Thus, if $\mathbf{z}(\mathbf{p})$ is defined, $[\mathbf{p} + \mathbf{N}(\mathbf{p})]\mathbf{e} > 0$; if $\mathbf{z}(\mathbf{p})$ is not defined, then $[\mathbf{p} + \mathbf{N}(\mathbf{p})]\mathbf{e} = (\mathbf{p} + \mathbf{e}')\mathbf{e}$ is certainly greater than 0.

It follows that the mapping

$$T(\mathbf{p}) = \frac{\mathbf{p} + N(\mathbf{p})}{[\mathbf{p} + \mathbf{N}(\mathbf{p})]\mathbf{e}}$$

is a continuous transformation of the fundamental price simplex, S_n, into itself and, therefore, has a fixed point, $\mathbf{p}^*$. In the equation $T(\mathbf{p}^*) = \mathbf{p}^*$, if we substitute the definition of $T(\mathbf{p})$ and solve for $\mathbf{N}(\mathbf{p}^*)$, we find

$$\mathbf{N}(\mathbf{p}^*) = \lambda \mathbf{p}^*,$$

where $\lambda = [\mathbf{p}^* + \mathbf{N}(\mathbf{p}^*)]\mathbf{e} - 1$. If $\mathbf{z}(\mathbf{p}^*)$ were undefined, then $N(\mathbf{p}^*) = \mathbf{e}'$, from which it follows that $\mathbf{p}^* \gg \mathbf{0}$, a contradiction since $\mathbf{z}(\mathbf{p}^*)$ would then be defined. Multiply both sides of the above equation by $\mathbf{z}(\mathbf{p}^*)$; from (W), $\mathbf{N}(\mathbf{p}^*)\mathbf{z}(\mathbf{p}^*) = 0$, or from (6),

$$[1 - \alpha(\mathbf{p}^*)]\mathbf{M}(\mathbf{p}^*)\mathbf{z}(\mathbf{p}^*) + \alpha(\mathbf{p}^*)Z(\mathbf{p}^*) = 0.$$

Note that, by definition, $Z(\mathbf{p}) = \mathbf{e}'\mathbf{z}(\mathbf{p})$. But from (3), $[1 - \alpha(\mathbf{p}^*)] \times \mathbf{M}(\mathbf{p}^*)\mathbf{z}(\mathbf{p}^*) \geq 0$, so that $\alpha(\mathbf{p}^*)Z(\mathbf{p}^*) \leq 0$. Since $\alpha(\mathbf{p}^*) > 0$ would imply $Z(\mathbf{p}^*) > 0$ by construction, we must have $\alpha(\mathbf{p}^*) = 0$. Hence, $\mathbf{M}(\mathbf{p}^*)\mathbf{z}(\mathbf{p}^*) = 0$, which implies that $\mathbf{p}^*$ is an equilibrium price vector as before.

THEOREM 3. If F, H, N, B, and C′, then an equilibrium for a competitive economy with a finite number of goods exists.

9. Restricted Futures Markets

The economy we have been considering is an abstract one in many respects, but perhaps the most serious departure from what we expect the world to be "really like" is the supposition that there are enough futures markets to produce "coherence" not only in the markets for current goods, but also in the markets for future goods. This hypothesis "telescopes" the future into the present, and although this occurs at least partially in certain markets, we know that it does not take place either universally or over the distant future. There are explanations for this, which have a good deal to do with the uncertainty agents have regarding the future state of the environment that is relevant to their present decisions. We do not now propose to formally introduce uncertainty into the story and will instead take a route following the signposts that are already available to us.

The first point is this: It is quite possible that when the economy we have been considering is in equilibrium, there are some markets in which there are no transactions of any kind. For instance, in partial equilibrium analysis, where we take the prices of all goods other than the one we are considering as given, the situation is represented by a supply curve that everywhere lies above the demand curve; both curves intersect the vertical axis. An obvious question is "To what extent is a market in which no transactions take place a market at all?" This is not our main concern. Instead, suppose that the market for the delivery of shoes next week is of this type. Clearly it is not implied that no one contemplates either acquiring shoes next week or selling them next week. Instead, it may be, for instance, that those hoping to get shoes next week on the whole expect there to be a cost-saving innovation in their manufacture, while those who hope to sell them expect no such thing. Evidently, although markets are formally in equilibrium, the system has failed to produce intertemporal coherence since agents have made plans on differing views of the terms on which shoes will exchange against other things, both of which cannot be correct. It is preferable, therefore, to say that no futures market in shoes exists if, when we stipulate such a market, every equilibrium of the system so constructed is found to be one in which no transactions take place in that market.

The second point is connected with the first. If the number of transactions in a market is small (in the limit zero), it is hard to continue the assumption that the agents in this market take the price as given. The point is obvious and, insofar as futures markets tend to be "narrow" for the reasons of the previous paragraph and also because the proper definition of a good for future delivery may have to be peculiarly fine to allow for intervening technological change, the manner in which we have incorporated futures markets into the system is likely to be pretty misleading in many instances. We might do less violence to the facts to stipulate instead that such markets do not exist.

The last point we can make here without a detailed discussion of uncertainty is that our foregoing analysis has postulated that there is only a finite number of markets. Since there is no reason to suppose that "time must have a stop," we have implicitly limited the number of futures markets that exist, and so also the extent in time to which we can say that coherence of decisions is possible. The reason for this limitation on our analysis is at least partly the desire to avoid the analytical and conceptual difficulties of infinite-dimensional spaces at this stage. As economists, we recognize, however, that the limitation also makes good sense if for no other reason than the facts of birth and death. To suppose that I now contract for the delivery of a pair of shoes to my grandson, whom I expect to be born twenty years from now, is itself somewhat fanciful. To suppose further that I have correctly foreseen the situation in which my grandson will find himself and that in these circumstances he will value the shoes in a way correctly known by me now is certainly dubious. Even if we allow contingent futures contracts such as, "For a price to be paid now, deliver a pair of shoes to my grandson if he exists and is twenty years old in forty years' time, and if not, deliver nothing," we would certainly expect such markets to be pretty narrow and to become narrower as the future recedes; quite apart from anything else, it is not clear how far the benevolence of an individual of a given generation extends to future generations.

For these reasons and others having to do with uncertainty, it is desirable to have an analysis of a competitive system in which universal futures markets are not postulated. To this we now turn.

10. Temporary or Short-Period Equilibrium

The absence of futures markets does not mean that an individual cannot engage in the intertemporal transfer of goods. If storage is possible, I can plan today to exchange apples for oranges tomorrow by storing apples for one day. Naturally, this decision will be influenced by current prices, storage and transaction costs, and the prices expected to prevail in the future. Here we shall take it that each agent regards his price expectations as certain, or at any rate that he is unwilling to pay anything to insure his future transactions (i.e., to make certain that the transaction can be carried out at the terms expected). This leads to the following difficulty: Should there be no difference between the transaction and storage costs of different goods, then the reader can verify that an agent would be indifferent about which good to store, and this would lead to difficulties with assumption F. All this is due to the artificial exclusion of the forces of uncertainty. In addition, we must not forget durable goods, that is, those goods not annihilated by a current act of consumption.

To overcome all these difficulties with one hand tied behind our backs, we shall arbitrarily postulate (a) that all storing is done by households who may rent such durable production goods as they have to producers and (b) that all households have preferences over the goods stored such that at any set of current and expected prices they store one and only one combination of goods. The second assumption is not as terrible as it seems, since it "mimics" in its consequences the forces of uncertainty that are excluded here. The first assumption is pretty harmless at the moment.

So far we have made it possible, through storage, for agents to plan to exchange present for future goods in the absence of futures markets. But the reverse operation cannot be carried out if there are no futures markets at all. By assumption, there is no way I can obtain more of a good now by promising to deliver a quantity of some good at a future date. In order not to exclude this possibility, we shall assume that there exists a futures market in at least one physical good (e.g., the medium of exchange) for all relevant future dates.

It is now advisable to put all this in more formal language before we consider the difference the new set of postulated circumstances will make to the conclusions of earlier sections.

It will be convenient to regard the services a given durable productive good renders as distinct from that good itself. If there are, say, m durable productive goods, there will be m additional goods, the services rendered by the durables. All these goods have the same date.

Let there be N current goods as defined above, and in addition, let there be one physical good at a fixed location at T intervals into the future, for which contracts for future delivery and sale can be made now. There are then $N + T$ goods altogether. The vector $\mathbf{p}$ is now the $N + T$-dimensional row vector of their current prices. In addition, agents have expectations as to the prices at future dates for the N physical goods currently being traded. We here ignore the invention of new goods, regard "location" as inessential, and suppose that no good deteriorates through use or storage. Suppose that agents are concerned only with the future over T periods. Then we write $\mathbf{q}_h$ as the NT-dimensional vector of prices expected by household h, and if there are H households, we write $\mathbf{q}$ as the HNT-dimensional vector of expected prices.

The price relevant to the current plans of household h is $(\mathbf{p}, \mathbf{q}_h)$. As before, we suppose that the household owns a stock of goods represented by the vector $\bar{\mathbf{x}}_h$. Also as before, we shall write x_{hi} as the amount of the good i demanded by h either for storage or consumption. Recall here that goods are still distinguished not only by their physical characteristics, but also by date. We write $\mathbf{x}_h$ as the demand vector of household h and regard a negative component as a plan to supply a service, which category now includes the offer of the services of a piece of productive equipment. Summation over households is again shown by the omission of the subscript h. Lastly, we write $\mathbf{x}^*$ as the vector consisting of the first $N + T$ components of $\mathbf{x}$ and $\bar{\mathbf{x}}^*$ as the vector consisting of the first $N + T$ components of $\bar{\mathbf{x}}$. These components represent the N current goods and the T futures of the single physical good assumed to have a futures market.

We now introduce

ASSUMPTION 7. Firms cannot stock goods of any kind, they cannot enter into "futures" contracts, and the production process of each firm can be completed in the current period.

This assumption is highly unrealistic, of course, because it puts all intertemporal transactions in the household sector. But although it excludes a number of matters of great economic interest, for example, investment plans by firms, it is relatively harmless for the rather formal problem of this section.[1] At the moment, we note that A.2.7 allows us to suppose that firms do not form any price expectations.

We write $\mathbf{y}_f$ as the production choice of firm f and, for convenience take it to have $N + T$ components, of which the last T are certainly zero. A negative component again denotes an input, which category now includes the services of productive equipment hired from households. As usual, the omission of the subscript f indicates summation over f.

We define $\mathbf{z}$ by

$$\mathbf{z} = \mathbf{x} - \bar{\mathbf{x}} - \mathbf{y}$$

so that $\mathbf{z}$ is the vector of excess demands in the N current markets for current goods and the T current markets for the future delivery of the only physical good with a futures market. Evidently we may take $\mathbf{z}$ to depend on $(\mathbf{p},\mathbf{q})$. We now introduce

Assumption 8. (a) $\mathbf{z}$ satisfies assumption F: $\mathbf{z} = \mathbf{z}(\mathbf{p},\mathbf{q})$ is a vector-valued function.

(b) $\mathbf{z}$ satisfies assumption W: $\mathbf{pz} = 0$ for all $(\mathbf{p}; \mathbf{q})$ considered.

(c) $\mathbf{z}$ satisfies assumption H: $\mathbf{z}(\mathbf{p},\mathbf{q}) = z(k\mathbf{p},k\mathbf{q})$.

(d) $\mathbf{z}$ satisfies assumption C over S_{N+T} for fixed $\mathbf{q}$.

These suppositions are neither more nor less restrictive than they were in our earlier discussion, and we do not explain or justify them further here.

Since $\mathbf{z}$ is the vector of excess demands for current goods and the single physical good with futures markets, we cannot deduce from knowledge of $\mathbf{z}$ what the market situations for goods in subsequent time periods will be. Accordingly, we are justified in the nomenclature of the following definition:

Definition 3. $(\mathbf{p}^*,\mathbf{q})$ is a *temporary equilibrium* if $\mathbf{z}(\mathbf{p}^*,\mathbf{q}) \leq \mathbf{0}$.

Once again this definition is justified as in our earlier discussion. It is important to remember, however, that the "coherence of decisions" we talked about there now refers to the markets represented in $\mathbf{z}$ only.

[1] This and other assumptions will be removed in the detailed treatment in Chapter 6.

The question of interest now is whether a temporary equilibrium exists. We prove that indeed it does.

The existence of a competitive equilibrium for fixed $\mathbf{q}$ is assured by the following argument: Normalizing $\mathbf{p}$ so that $\mathbf{p} \in S_{N+T}$ also implies by H that the expectation vector $\mathbf{q}$ has been normalized. For fixed $\mathbf{q}$ we may write $\mathbf{z} = \mathbf{z}(\mathbf{p},\mathbf{q}) = \hat{\mathbf{z}}(\mathbf{p})$. The vector-valued function $\hat{\mathbf{z}}(\mathbf{p})$ has all the properties of $\mathbf{z}(\mathbf{p})$ in our previous discussion of "existence" except H. But H was never invoked in the proof of T.2.2. Hence, we may use the same proof to establish the existence of a temporary equilibrium.

We have shown that, whatever the expectations of agents of future prices might be and however much these expectations may differ among agents, there exists a set of prices in the current markets such that all the actions agents plan to undertake in these markets can indeed be carried out. This seems to be a comforting result to have, but it is not unimportant to bear in mind that the conclusion is limited by the assumptions on which it is based and, in particular, that the proof of the existence of equilibrium prices does not constitute a claim that these prices in fact will be established.

To understand the limitations imposed by A.2.8, consider the following example. When we consider a system, we take its past as given, and in particular, we take the stock of durable productive equipment inherited from the past as given. Suppose that the production opportunities open to the economy (the *production set* for the economy) are such that with the inherited equipment (or rather with the maximum services the equipment can yield in the current period), there is an upper bound on the quantity of certain labor services that can be "usefully" employed. By "usefully" we mean that the employment of some more of that labor service makes possible a change in the vector of outputs of the economy. Next, suppose that the plans of households have the following property: If the *i*th good is the service supplied by households we have just discussed, then for all $\mathbf{p}$ in S_{N+T} for which $p_i \geq p_i'$ the amount of the service supplied exceeds some fixed positive number, while for $p_i < p_i'$ none of it will be supplied. Of course, this violates A.2.8.(d) as the supply function of the service is not now continuous over the relevant domain. It is now possible, in light of our other suppositions in this example, that for all $\mathbf{p}$ in S_{N+T} for which $p_i \geq p_i$, the demand of firms for this household service is less than the amount offered by households, say, because they always offer more than the upper bound of the amount that can be usefully employed. Thus, no equilibrium may exist. If we consider that the physiological needs of people make it impossible for them to offer labor services without positive consumption and if we also take note of the specificity of much productive equipment to particular uses, it is clear that the example is not farfetched. Of course, the same difficulty could have arisen in the world with a complete set of futures markets. In that case, however, households would have had the additional option of selling their services forward and firms may have been willing to buy them in conjunction with the future services of durable equipment, so that the realism of the postulated conditions of the example would have been less compelling.

So far it has been supposed that, given the normalization of **p**, the prices expected by agents may be taken as given. It is more reasonable, though, to take expected prices as influenced, at least to some extent, by current prices. Our main result, however, will not be affected if we stipulate:

ASSUMPTION 9. For each household h the expected price vector $\mathbf{q}_h$ is a continuous function $\mathbf{q}_h(\mathbf{p})$ of $\mathbf{p}$ in

$$S_{N+T} = \left\{\mathbf{p} \mid \mathbf{p} > \mathbf{0};\ \sum_i p_i = 1\right\}.$$

Given this assumption, we may again eliminate $\mathbf{q}$ from $\mathbf{z}(\mathbf{p},\mathbf{q})$ and write the vector of excess-demand functions as $\hat{\mathbf{z}}(\mathbf{p})$. In conjunction with A.2.8(d), we may take it that $\hat{\mathbf{z}}(\mathbf{p})$ is continuous over S_{N+T}. We may then use the same mapping as in Section 2.7 to map S_{N+T} into itself and proceed as we did there to establish the existence of an equilibrium.

THEOREM 4. Under assumptions A.2.7, A.2.8, and A.2.9, a temporary equilibrium exists.

It behooves us to draw attention to the restrictiveness of A.2.9. It is true that in a number of studies it has appeared that agents forecast prices they think will rule in the future by extrapolating from past and present prices. Moreover, such extrapolation procedures would satisfy the assumption under discussion. Yet we must recall that for the purposes of an existence proof, the postulated continuity must be over the whole of S_{N+T}, and it is harder to claim that this is the case from the emprical evidence. In particular, it may be argued that there are certain $\mathbf{p}$ in S_{N+T} so different from any prices that ruled before our investigation started that agents will consider their routinized method of expectation formation inadequate should such $\mathbf{p}$ occur. If this is so (and no doubt instances in economic history come to mind in which it certainly appears to have been so), then A.2.9 is unlikely to be satisfied. In any event, this is an area of economics in which our ignorance is so great that it would be very unwise to regard our assumption as more than tentative and, of course, convenient for our purposes.

11. Short-Period Equilibrium: A Special Case

The short-period model we have been considering, although restricted by certain assumptions, is of a pretty general sort and could be made more general still without too much difficulty (e.g., we could easily do without the assumption that firms make no intertemporal decisions). We have seen that there is a well-defined meaning for the equilibrium of such an economy, and we have seen what we must postulate in order to establish that such equilibrium exists. In this section we will examine the short-period equilibrium of a somewhat different economy. It is an economy we shall wish to discuss further elsewhere in this book. For brevity, we shall refer to it as the *Leontief* (L) *economy* because it is closely connected with the work of that economist. It is described by the following set of assumptions:

ASSUMPTION 10. (a) If $\mathbf{y}_f$ is a possible choice for firm f, then so is $k\mathbf{y}_f$ with $k > 0$. *Constant returns to scale* (CR).

(b) Every possible $\mathbf{y}_f$ for firm f has only one non-negative component, namely y_{ff}. *No joint production.*

(c) There are no durable production goods.

In view of CR, we may, for all $y_{ff} > 0$, define

$$\mathbf{y}'_f = \frac{\mathbf{y}_f}{y_{ff}}$$

and be certain that if $\mathbf{y}_f$ is a possible choice for f, then so is $\mathbf{y}'_f$.

We now suppose that the Nth component of y'_f represents the input of a labor service and postulate:

ASSUMPTION 11. No household can supply a labor service other than that represented by the label N. We call this the assumption of *one non-produced input.* All household demand functions satisfy H.

We shall wish to restrict the possible production choices further by

ASSUMPTION 12. (a) $y'_{fN} < 0$ for all $\mathbf{y}_f \neq 0$ that f can choose. *No output without labor input.*

(b) For each f, there exists a vector $\mathbf{y}_f$ such that

$$\sum_{j \neq N} y_{fj} > 0.$$

The system is *productive.* (Note that this condition need hold only for a suitable choice of units.)

Finally, let us now take $\mathbf{p}$ to be an N-dimensional price vector, S_N to be the *N-dimensional* price simplex, and define C_f by

$$C_f = p_f - \mathbf{p}\mathbf{y}'_f.$$

Evidently C_f is the unit production cost at $\mathbf{p}$ when $\mathbf{y}'_f$ is chosen. We postulate

ASSUMPTION 13. (a) For every $\mathbf{p}$ in S_N there is a choice of $\mathbf{y}'_f(\mathbf{p})$ such that $C^*_f(\mathbf{p}) = p_f - \mathbf{p}\mathbf{y}'_f(\mathbf{p}) \leq \mathbf{p}_f - \mathbf{p}\mathbf{y}'_f$, all possible $\mathbf{y}'_f$.

(b) $C^*_f(\mathbf{p})$ is continuous over S_N.

(c) Necessary conditions for the equilibrium of economic agents in the L-economy at $\mathbf{p}^*$ are

$$\text{(i)} \quad p^*_f \leq C^*_f(\mathbf{p}^*) \qquad \text{all } f,$$

$$\text{(ii)} \quad p^*_f y_{ff}(\mathbf{p}^*) = C^*_f(\mathbf{p}^*) y_{ff}(p^*) \qquad \text{all } f.$$

No production at negative profit and zero equilibrium profits.

This, with one exception to be introduced later, completes the specification of the L-economy. We shall postpone a proper discussion of the various assumptions until we have established certain properties of this economy. Here, however, we may note that CR implies a situation we took as an example of the violation of F. It is clear, therefore, that we cannot hope to discuss the L-economy exclusively in terms of excess-demand functions. It is at this stage that A.2.13(c) proves useful. This assumption is based on the Walrasian view that production as such involves no costs, psychic or otherwise, other than the amount that has to be paid to inputs required for production.[1] Hence, if at some $\mathbf{p}$ a firm is found to make a profit, there is

[1] A.2.13(a) and (b) can be deduced from the production conditions (see Section 3.4, especially T.3.7).

an inducement for some agents in the economy not presently engaged in production to become so engaged. The profit here referred to is the maximum profit. By the same token, if profits are zero, then the scale of production is a matter of indifference to the firm CR.

Our first task is to show that there exist prices satisfying A.2.13(c). Our procedure once again will be to find a mapping of S_N into itself and to show that the fixed point of this mapping is the price vector we seek.

Consider the following mapping:

$$T_f(\mathbf{p}) = \min\left[1; \frac{(1 - kp_N)}{V(\mathbf{p})}\right] C_f^*(\mathbf{p}), \quad f = 1, \ldots, N-1; 1 > k > 0 \tag{7a}$$

$$T_N(\mathbf{p}) = \max[1 - V(\mathbf{p}); kp_N] \tag{7b}$$

where

$$V(\mathbf{p}) = \sum_{f \neq N} C_f^*(\mathbf{p}). \tag{7c}$$

We shall first verify that (7) does indeed take points of S_N into points in S_N.

(a) By the definition of $C_f^*(\mathbf{p})$ and the assumption of no joint production, we have $C_f^*(\mathbf{p}) \geq 0$, all $\mathbf{p}$ and all f. Hence, certainly $T_f(\mathbf{p}) \geq 0$, all f, $T_N(\mathbf{p}) \geq 0$, all $\mathbf{p}$. We note that the assumption of "no output without labor input" implies that $V(\mathbf{p})$ can be only zero when $p_N = 0$.

(b) Suppose that $1 - V(\mathbf{p}) < kp_N$. Then by (7), $T_f(\mathbf{p}) = (1 - kp_N)C_f^*(\mathbf{p})/V(\mathbf{p}), f = 1, \ldots, N-1$, and $T_N(\mathbf{p}) = kp_N$. Adding gives

$$\sum_f T_f(\mathbf{p}) = 1.$$

(c) If $1 - V(\mathbf{p}) \geq kp_N$, then by (7), $T_f(\mathbf{p}) = C_f^*(\mathbf{p}), f = 1, \ldots, N-1$, and $T_N(\mathbf{p}) = 1 - V(\mathbf{p})$. Adding gives

$$\sum_f T_f(\mathbf{p}) = 1.$$

Since, by A.2.13(b), the functions $C_f^*(\mathbf{p})$ are continuous over S_N, the mapping in (7) is also continuous and thus has a fixed point $\mathbf{p}^*$. We now show that $\mathbf{p}^*$ satisfies the zero-profit condition. In doing this we shall first assume that $p_N^* > 0$ and then prove that this is indeed the case.

Since then $0 < p_N^* = T_N(\mathbf{p}^*)$ and $k < 1$, it must be that $p_N^* = 1 - V(\mathbf{p}^*)$ or else $p_N^* = kp_N^*$. So we have

$$1 - V(\mathbf{p}^*) > kp_N^*,$$

from which it then follows that

$$p_f^* = T_f(\mathbf{p}^*) = C_f^*(\mathbf{p}^*) \qquad f = 1, \ldots, N-1,$$

so that the fixed point certainly satisfies A.2.13(c). It remains only to show that indeed $p_N^* > 0$.

Since $\mathbf{p}^*$ is in S_N, the supposition that $p_N^* = 0$ would imply that

$$p_m^* = \max_f p_f^* > 0 \qquad m < N. \tag{8}$$

Also from (7), $p_N^* = 0$ implies that

$$1 - V(\mathbf{p}^*) \leq 0. \tag{9}$$

Let $\mathbf{y}_m$ be the vector described in A.2.12(b), with $f = m$, $\mathbf{y}_m' = \mathbf{y}_m / y_{mm}$; note that

$$\sum_{j \neq N} y_{mj}' > 0.$$

From A.2.13(a), $C_m^*(\mathbf{p}^*) \leq p_m^* - \mathbf{p}^*\mathbf{y}_m'$, so that

$$p_m^* - C_m^*(\mathbf{p}^*) \geq \mathbf{p}^* y_m' = \sum_{j \neq N} p_j^* y_{mj}' \geq p_m^* \sum_{j \neq N} y_{mj}' > 0,$$

where use has been made of the facts that $p_N^* = 0$, $p_j^* \leq p_m^*$, and $y_{mj}' \leq 0$ for $j \neq m$. From (7) and (9).

$$p_f^* = \frac{1}{V(\mathbf{p}^*)} C_f^*(\mathbf{p}^*) \leq C_f^*(\mathbf{p}^*) \qquad f = 1, \ldots, N-1.$$

Since not both these inequalities can hold, we conclude that indeed $p_N^* > 0$.

We now note that by A.2.12(a) and A.2.13(a), $p_N^* > 0$ implies $C_f(\mathbf{p}^*) > 0$, all f, and so it follows that $p_f^* > 0$, all f. Moreover, we have shown that there exists $\mathbf{p}^*$ in S_N, which satisfies A.13(c). We summarize:

THEOREM 5. If A.2.10–A.2.13 inclusive, then there exists a strictly positive $\mathbf{p}^*$ in S_N such that $p_f^* = C_f^*(\mathbf{p})$, $f = 1, \ldots, N-1$, and $p_N^* = 1 - V(\mathbf{p}^*)$.

This result is pleasant, but it is not yet sufficient to establish the existence of an equilibrium for the L-economy; it remains to show that all markets can be cleared at $\mathbf{p}^*$. (Recall that $\mathbf{p}^* \gg \mathbf{0}$, so that excess supplies are inconsistent with equilibrium.) To do so, we unfortunately require another assumption:

ASSUMPTION 14. Let $\mathbf{x}'(\mathbf{p}^*)$ be the $N-1$-dimensional vector of household demand at $\mathbf{p}^*$ for all goods other than the Nth.[1] Then if $\bar{\mathbf{x}}'$ is the $N-1$-dimensional vector of the goods owned by households, $\mathbf{x}'(\mathbf{p}^*) - \bar{\mathbf{x}}' > \mathbf{0}$.

We note that for $\bar{\mathbf{x}}' = \mathbf{0}$, this assumption will always hold provided households supply some of the labor service. However, with $\bar{\mathbf{x}}' \neq \mathbf{0}$, the assumption is evidently quite restrictive; we will comment on this again.

Now if all markets for non-labor services are cleared, we require that

$$\sum_f y'_{fj}(\mathbf{p}^*) y_{ff}(\mathbf{p}^*) = x'_j(\mathbf{p}^*) - \bar{\mathbf{x}}'_j \qquad j = 1, \ldots, N-1.$$

On writing $\mathbf{h}(\mathbf{p}^*)$ for the $N-1$-dimensional vector with components $y_{ff}(\mathbf{p}^*)$ and $H(\mathbf{p}^*)$ for the $(N-1) \times (N-1)$ matrix with typical element $y'_{fj}(\mathbf{p}^*)$, we have to solve

$$H(\mathbf{p}^*)\mathbf{h}(\mathbf{p}^*) = x'(\mathbf{p}^*) - \bar{\mathbf{x}}' \tag{10}$$

for $\mathbf{h}(\mathbf{p}^*) > 0$. From A.2.10(b), $H(\mathbf{p}^*)$ is a matrix with non-positive off-diagonal elements and positive diagonal elements. Also,

$$\sum_{j \neq N} p_j^* y'_{fj}(\mathbf{p}^*) = -p_N^* y'_{fN}(\mathbf{p}^*) > 0$$

by T.2.5 and A.2.12(a). Hence (see Appendix A, Remark 2), $H(\mathbf{p}^*)$ has a non-negative inverse. This, together with A.2.14, then leads to $\mathbf{h}(\mathbf{p}^*) > \mathbf{0}$.

We are now left only with the market for labor services. By the definition of $\mathbf{p}^*$, we have, writing $\tilde{p}^*$ for the $N-1$ vector of prices excluding p_N^*,

$$\tilde{p}^* H(\mathbf{p}^*)\mathbf{h}(\mathbf{p}^*) = -p_N^* \sum_f y'_{fN}(\mathbf{p}^*) y_{ff}(\mathbf{p}^*),$$

which is the value of the total demand for labor by firms. By W we have also

$$\tilde{\mathbf{p}}^*(\mathbf{x}'(\mathbf{p}^*) - \bar{\mathbf{x}}') = -p_N^* x_N(\mathbf{p}^*),$$

[1] We take the expected price vector $\mathbf{q}$ to be a continuous function of $\mathbf{p}$ and have eliminated it from the excess-demand function.

which is the value of the labor services supplied by households. Hence, multiplication of both sides of (10) by $\tilde{\mathbf{p}}^*$, since we know that $p_N^* > 0$, shows that the labor market is also in equilibrium at $\mathbf{p}^*$. We summarize:

THEOREM 6. If A.2.10–A.2.14 then a strictly positive equilibrium for the L-economy exists.

Let us discuss some of the features of this economy and, in particular, examine the role of the various assumptions we have made.

We note that if an equilibrium exists, we are able to determine $\mathbf{p}^*$ without reference to the forces of demand at all. This is one of the most striking properties of the L-economy. Moreover, we have, by T.2.5,

$$\tilde{p}^* H(\mathbf{p}^*) = -p_N^* y_N'(\mathbf{p}^*), \tag{11}$$

where $y_N'(\mathbf{p}^*)$ is the $N - 1$ vector with components $y_{fN}'(\mathbf{p}^*)$. Therefore,

$$\tilde{p}^* = -p_N^* y_N'(\mathbf{p}^*)[H(\mathbf{p}^*)]^{-1}.$$

As the example in the footnote[1] makes clear, this means that we may express the equilibrium price of every produced commodity as made up of the direct and indirect labor costs of producing one unit of that commodity.

[1] Consider the case in which $H(\mathbf{p}^*)$ is 2×2 and so y_N' is 2-dimensional. Omitting the argument $\mathbf{p}^*$, we may write

$$H(\mathbf{p}^*) = \begin{bmatrix} 0 & y_{fF}' \\ y_{Ff}' & 0 \end{bmatrix} + I = \text{say, } -A + I,$$

where I is the diagonal unit matrix. Evidently, A is non-negative, and by the postulate A.2.12(b), we have

$$[H(\mathbf{p}^*)]^{-1} = I + A + A^2 + \cdots.$$

So

$$\tilde{\mathbf{p}}^* = p_N^* \mathbf{y}_N'(I + A + A^2 + \cdots),$$

from which, for instance, p_F^* is given by

$$p_F^* = [y_{FN}' + y_{fF}' y_{fN}' + y_{fF}' y_{Ff}' y_{FN}' + \cdots] p_N^*.$$

The first term in the bracket measures the direct labor input required per unit of output of firm F, the second term measures the labor input required to produce the output of firm f required to produce one unit of output of firm F, and so on.

Since **p*** is determined without reference to demand conditions, it follows also that we now do not need any elaborate assumptions to ensure that all demand functions are continuous over S_N. Indeed, the theory of household behavior can be left in a most rudimentary state. All we need is H and W, the most innocuous of the assumptions. For all these reasons, the L-economy has proved attractive to many economists. But the number of assumptions we have made suggests that this simplicity is achieved at certain costs.

The role of constant returns to scale in achieving our results is clear. If we did not make the assumption, we could not determine the prices that do not exceed unit costs without reference to the scale of production, and so to the forces of demand. If certain durable goods (their services) were used in production and the quantity of these goods available arbitrarily specified, then once again prices could not be determined independently of demand conditions. As the services of durable goods used currently are not produced currently, the price of these services cannot be determined from the conditions of production, but must be found from the conditions of market equilibrium, which, in turn, involve the forces of demand. Moreover, we cannot determine the prices of goods currently produced until we know the prices of the services of durables. If we do not take the amount of durables as arbitrarily given, and make some further assumptions, these consequences can be avoided. Exactly the same reasoning explains why we found it necessary to postulate that there is only one kind of labor service. When we consider the variety of such services in practice, it is clear that not too much reliance should be placed on the L-model.

The assumption of "no output without labor input" is somewhat stronger than is strictly required. Its consequence is, of course, to ensure that all equilibrium prices are strictly positive. Had we postulated instead that for some particular good only, we could get no output without labor input, you can verify that all our arguments and conclusions would continue to hold, except the proposition that **p*** is strictly positive. Had we dropped the assumption altogether, we would have had an equilibrium situation in which all produced goods might have a zero price—an uninteresting case. In any case, this particular assumption is not particularly unpalatable.

The use we have made of the supposition that the system is productive is evident. It enabled us to ensure a semi-positive solution for (10).

The assumption that the system is productive is one we probably should want to impose on models other than the L-economy, and it seems quite agreeable to casual experience. Matters are rather different when it comes to the postulate that households are net demanders of some produced goods and net suppliers of none (A.2.14). Without this assumption, there might be transactions in a good that can be, but is not, produced. Indeed, the equilibrium market price of that good, that is, the situation in which the excess demand for that good is non-positive, might then be below the minimum unit cost of producing it. Evidently the forces of demand will be involved in the determination of prices. The assumption has no immediate appeal unless it is argued that we may take households not to hold any quantities of the producible goods. Without this postulate, then not only might we lose the special features of the L-economy, but we will also have to proceed along different lines to prove the existence of an equilibrium, in order to deal with excess demands not satisfying F (see Chapter 5).

There remains A.2.13. In part (a) of this assumption we ensured the existence of a unique cost-minimizing choice $\mathbf{y}_f'$ for all $\mathbf{p}$. This allowed us without further argument to treat the market clearing problem as we did in (10). The same point is involved here as in assumption F and is not at all important in a general treatment. Part (b) is explained on the same grounds as those invoked in the discussion of C. Both assumptions can be deduced as consequences of somewhat more fundamental restrictions on the set of possible production choices of firms. This is done in Chapter 3, where the realism of this procedure is also considered.

After all this, we may judge that the L-economy is an interesting construction, if for no other reason than that it helps us to understand earlier theories, such as the labor theory of value, but it seems somewhat unlikely that a pure "cost of production theory" of prices is capable of reflecting adequately the complexities of the real world. There are several directions, however, in which the analysis can be extended. We note only one of these here.

Suppose that inputs precede output by "one period"; production takes time. We are interested in situations in which the price expected by everyone for the period $t + 1$ is the same as that at t. However, the price that would actually be paid at t for a good to be delivered at $t + 1$ differs from the current price for current delivery by an arbitrarily given "discount factor." This is a familiar and elementary idea; we do not propose to discuss here the determination of the equilibrium discount factor.

We continue to postulate A.2.10–A.2.12, as well as A.2.13(a) and (b). In particular, note that there are still no durable inputs. A.2.13(c) is modified as follows:

ASSUMPTION 13. (c*) A necessary condition of equilibrium is,

$$\text{(i)}\quad p_f^* \leq RC_f^*(\mathbf{p}^*) \qquad \text{all } f,$$
$$\text{(ii)}\quad p_f^* y_{ff}^* = RC_f^*(\mathbf{p}^*) y_{ff}^* \qquad \text{all } f,$$

where R is a scalar, $R \geq 1$ (R^{-1} is the discount factor).

The question is whether for given R, there exists $\mathbf{p}^*$ satisfying A.2.13(c*). Now let

$$C_f^{**}(\mathbf{p}) = RC_f^*(\mathbf{p}),$$
$$f \neq N,$$
$$V^*(\mathbf{p}) = \sum_{f \neq N} C_f^{**}(\mathbf{p}),$$

and let $T^*(\mathbf{p})$ be the mapping in (7) with the new definitions. It is easy to check that if we just assume $p_N^* > 0$ the mapping does indeed have a fixed point satisfying A.2.13(c*). However, A.2.13(b) does not now ensure that

$$p_m^* - C^{**}(\mathbf{p}^*) \geq \mathbf{p}^* \mathbf{y}_m',$$

so our earlier line of proof that $p_N^* > 0$ may fail. Indeed, it is clear that the assumption that the system is productive cannot ensure the above inequality for arbitrarily large R. On the other hand, the argument is clearly safe for $R = 1$. We conclude:

The time-using economy has an equilibrium satisfying A.13(c*) for any given R not exceeding some $\bar{R} > 1$.

The market-clearing equations are now also changed since current inputs must be provided by the outputs of past production decisions. This is not pursued here.

12. Stock and Flow Equilibrium

If we consider again the short-period equilibrium of the economy of Section 2.10, we see that since, at $\mathbf{p}^*$, all agents are capable of carrying out the transactions they wish to carry out, it will also be true that, after these transactions, they will find themselves holding goods (if any) in just the quantities they had planned. This simply means that if people can carry out the desired change in their stocks —transact so much and so much of the particular good over the given time interval—then they will also find that they hold as much of the good as desired. In general, however, prices will differ not only from one period to the next, but also from what they had been expected to be. The prices here are those that establish temporary equilibrium at each moment in time. This means that the quantities of various goods that agents wish to hold will differ at different moments of time.

It is evidently both useful and legitimate to distinguish between an economy in which there is the full complement of futures markets, or that behaves as though there were such a full complement, and one that is not so fortunate. The equilibrium of the former economy might be called a "full" or "long-run" equilibrium, while the latter may be analyzed by means of a sequence of short-run equilibria. In the literature we find a further distinction, as is evident in the title of this section. If we think of the quantity of a good offered for sale, we must specify, for good sense, the period over which this is so, and similarly for the quantity demanded. Hence, both quantities have a time dimension: so-and-so much per unit of time. When we think of the amount of a good an agent wishes to store, we think of the amount he wishes to have at a moment of time, and no time dimension is involved. The former are called "flow" variables and the latter "stock" variables. If we change the units in which we measure time, then the flow variables are affected, but the stock variables are not. In the literature, then, a distinction is drawn between a situation in which all flow markets are cleared, a *flow equilibrium*, and a situation in which all agents find they have the stocks they desire, a *stock equilibrium*.

In the light of what has already been said, this distinction can have force only if we regard as a flow equilibrium a situation in which not all agents are carrying out the transactions they regard as most satisfactory at the ruling prices, although all flow markets are cleared. This goes counter to the definition of an equilibrium that we have employed throughout this chapter. Consider a typical example. It may be that at a given set of prices currently ruling and given expected prices, flow markets are cleared because some agents are prepared to satisfy what would otherwise be an excess flow demand by holding less of a good than they would like ("unintended" dishoarding), while others hold more of a good than they would like and so prevent what otherwise would be a flow excess supply (unintended hoarding). Evidently, in this view we may have flow equilibrium and stock disequilibrium. But the notion of an equilibrium has clearly been widened to include situations in which agents themselves are not in equilibrium in the sense that they do not carry out the transactions most satisfactory to themselves at the ruling prices.

It is not at all clear that the nomenclature of the literature is a good one, simply because it is not helpful to have the same name to describe quite different situations. In any case, in this volume the distinction between stock and flow equilibrium will become relevant only in the analysis of what, in our definition, are disequilibrium situations.

Connected with the distinction we have been discussing is the device of "period analysis." This can be helpful in overcoming some of the conceptual problems raised by continuous time, but it can also be misleading. For instance, Swedish authors at one time found it helpful to define the length of the period by the time interval over which prices could be taken as fixed. Starting with given prices at the beginning of the period, a flow equilibrium over the period, then, would involve stock disequilibrium at the end of the period unless the economy was in full equilibrium. They then traced the economy from period to period by using certain rules for changing prices. In an economy with many agents, however, it seems unnatural to suppose that they all not only adjust their preferred action at discrete intervals, but they do so at the same moment. If that is not so, then such adjustments will be taking place more or less continuously. To this must be added the fact that period analysis leads to a formulation in terms of "difference equations," which are capable of producing motions for the system that are not possible if the formulation is in terms of differential equations, so that what started as an aid to visualization may finish by being pretty misleading. In any event, it is noticeable that the discussion of this paragraph quite naturally ran in terms of what, from the agents' point of view, are plainly disequilibrium processes and confirms the view that these matters are best treated when we come to consider such processes.

Notes

Existence theorems of the general nature of T.2.2 were first proved by Wald [1933–34, 1934–35]; for systematic expositions of several interrelated results, see Wald [1936, 1951]. Wald assumed demand functions arising from the household sector together with Cassel's system of fixed coefficient relations for production (see Section 1.5). If factors are identified with final goods so that the production of final good i requires one unit of factor i and nothing else, then Wald's result is the same as T.2.2, though his assumptions were considerably stronger; see Wald [1951, pp. 372–373].

McKenzie [1954] established an existence theorem that is more general than Wald's with regard to production assumptions; however, if specialized to the case of exchange, it is identical to Wald's.

Both Wald and McKenzie assumed that the demand for a free good was infinite, more precisely that $z_i(\mathbf{p}^\nu) \to +\infty$ for any sequence $\{\mathbf{p}^\nu\}$ for which $\mathbf{p}^\nu \to \mathbf{p}^0$, where $p_i^0 = 0$. As the discussion in Section 2.8 shows, this assumption is not compatible, in general, with utility maximization.

Equilibrium in a model of no joint production, as discussed in Section 2.11, was discussed extensively by Leontief [1941] for the special case in which there are fixed coefficients for the production of each commodity. The crucial role of the productivity assumption, A.2.12(b) in our notation, was first stressed by Hawkins and Simon [1949]. The generalization of these results to the case of variable coefficients is due independently to Georgescu-Roegen [1951] and Samuelson [1951].

Chapter Three

PRODUCTION DECISIONS AND THE BOUNDEDNESS OF THE ECONOMY

Specializing is necessary to efficiency, which is a form of altruism, and however narrow the specialist becomes, we ought to pardon him if he does good work.

—B. Russell, *The Autobiography of Bertrand Russell**

1. General Principles and Illustrative Examples

The three basic elements of the theory of production under competitive conditions are its organization through separate firms, the delimitation of the production possibilities of each firm, and the choice among these possibilities by the principle of profit maximization at given prices. In this section, we will discuss these points informally and comment on some revisions and extensions of the simple concepts of supply and demand functions made necessary by a careful analysis. By illustrations, we will show especially the possible importance of multi-valued supply and demand relations.

First, we will consider the description of a firm's production possibilities. In general, a firm will use many inputs to produce several outputs; there is no need to confine attention to the single-product firm. Any possible state of production of the firm, then, is a statement that outputs of certain commodities in certain amounts can be achieved by inputs of other commodities in other given amounts. We will agree as a convention that positive quantities will represent outputs and negative quantities inputs. Any such specification of possible relations between inputs and outputs will be termed an *activity*; the set of all activities available to the firm will be called its *production possibility set.*

The word "possible" in the preceding paragraph refers to technological knowledge, not to availability of resources; to say that an activity is possible means only that if the firm possessed the specified

* Little, Brown and Co., Boston, 1957, p. 246.

inputs, the corresponding outputs could be produced. Thus, the production possibility set is a description of the state of the firm's knowledge about the possibilities of transforming commodities.

For simplicity in following the discussion in this and the following two chapters, it will be convenient to assume that production and all other economic activity is timeless; inputs and outputs are contemporaneous, and no consideration is given to the future in anyone's decisions. It should be made clear, however, that time can be introduced into the system by a mere reinterpretation of the symbols, so that the model of general competitive equilibrium has a broad application.

The distinction between pure technological possibility and feasibility, that is, possibility plus the availability of resources, cannot always be maintained strictly. We will find it convenient to consider some commodities as being private to a firm or group of firms (e.g., managerial ability or, in the case of foreign trade, domestic factor supplies). Then the following two descriptions of reality are equivalent:

(1) including the private commodities with all others among the components of the activity vectors and adding to the system a statement prohibiting the flow of these commodities out of the firm or group of firms;
(2) deleting the private commodities from the activity vectors and considering among the set of possible vectors in the remaining components only those vectors whose demands for the private commodities can be satisfied with the available supplies.

Given a set of prices for all commodities, it is possible to calculate for each activity its *profit*, the excess of the values of its outputs over the value of its inputs; for some activities, of course, profit may be negative. The assumptions of perfect competition imply that, at any set of prices regarded as given to it, each firm chooses an activity that yields it at least as much profit as any other possible.

Some of the possible complexities in a general and rigorous theory of production decisions can best be brought out through examples. We start with perhaps the simplest possible assumption about possible activities: There is one output that is proportional to the quantity of the one input.

In accordance with our notational principles, we take the input y_1 to be negative and the output y_2 to be positive; then we have assumed that the activities are those of the form

$$y_1 = -ay_2 \qquad y_2 \geq 0, \tag{1}$$

where a is some positive constant. If p_1 and p_2 are the prices of input and output, respectively, then the profit is

$$p_1y_1 + p_2y_2 = (p_2 - ap_1)y_2,$$

as seen by substituting from (1). Now the firm's profit-maximizing decision can easily be calculated. If $p_2 < ap_1$, then profits are negative if $y_2 > 0$ and 0 if $y_2 = 0$; thus, the profit-maximizing decision is to set $y_2 = 0$ (and, from (1), also set $y_1 = 0$), in other words, not to engage in production at all. If $p_2 = ap_1$, a more curious situation arises; profits are 0 no matter what level is chosen for y_2. Hence, any value of y_2 can be regarded as profit-maximizing, provided that the appropriate value of y_1 is chosen at the same time. Equivalently, we can say that any vector satisfying (1) is profit maximizing. Finally, if $p_2 > ap_1$, an increase in y_2 always increases profits. Strictly speaking, there is no profit-maximizing activity, since for any pair (y_1,y_2) satisfying (1), there is another that yields higher profits. In ordinary terms, the supply and demand functions must be regarded as undefined in this case.

We note that the classification of cases depended only on the *price ratio*, p_2/p_1. The case just studied is represented graphically in Figure 3-1. In Figure 3-1a, the line OA (assumed indefinitely

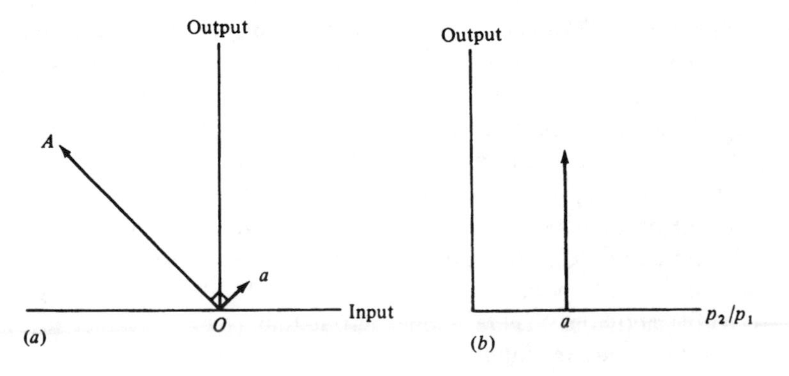

Figure 3-1

prolonged) is the set of possible activities. For price vectors with slope less than a, that is, making an obtuse angle with OA, profits can always be increased by a small decrease in scale; hence only the origin can be optimal. A price vector with slope a is perpendicular to OA everywhere; hence no change in scale will change profits, so that every point of OA is profit maximizing. Finally, a price vector with a slope greater than a, making an acute angle with OA at any point, yields additional profits for any increase in scale and so can define no profit-maximizing activity. In Figure 3-1b, the supply curve for the product implied by Figure 3-1a is presented. The quantity supplied depends, of course, only on the price ratio; it is zero for price ratios less than a, it can be any value whatever indifferently at a, and it is undefined above a.

This trivial case has been examined in such detail to bring out three points, stated in increasing order of importance: For some price vectors, the firm may find it most profitable to engage in the activity of doing nothing; for some price vectors, there is no profit-maximizing activity; for some price vectors, there is a whole set of activities, each of which is profit maximizing, in the sense that there is no other activity that yields a higher profit. Thus, for a general theory, we must relax the assumptions of the last chapter, according to which supply and demand are both defined and single valued for each price vector.

Some further examples will be useful. Suppose there are two types of activity, of which one is more efficient in the simple sense of more output per unit of input, but can be carried out to a limited scale, beyond which a less efficient type of activity must be used. (The more efficient activity may require some input private to the firm and limited in quantity.) The case is represented in Figure 3-2.

Clearly, for a price vector with slope less than a, the maximum profit again is zero, obtainable only at the origin. When the slope equals a, all activities on the line OA yield equal (zero) profit, while the price vector makes an obtuse angle with all points representing activities at higher scales, which therefore cannot be optimal, so that the profit-maximizing activities are those on OA. If the slope lies between a and b, the profit must be increasing with scale up to A and decreasing thereafter; hence the profit-maximizing point is uniquely A as the output-input price ratio increases from a to b; supply of the output and demand for the input are completely price-

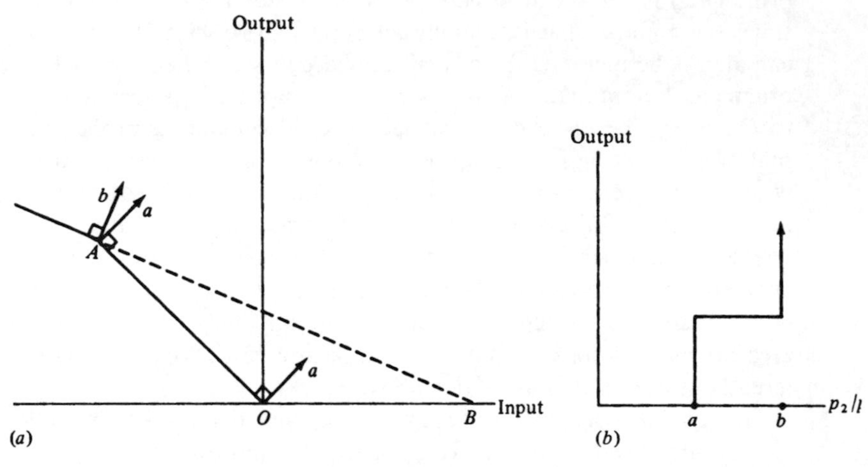

Figure 3-2

inelastic in this interval. When the price ratio is *b*, all points from *A* on are equally profitable, since the price vector is perpendicular to all of them. The amount of profit (divided by the price of the input) is represented by the intersection *B* of the perpendicular to the price vector at any given activity level with the input axis; therefore, the profit is positive as soon as the price ratio rises above *a*. For price ratios above *b*, the profit-maximizing activity is undefined again, since any increase in scale is profitable.

This is the first example of diminishing returns to scale. The new feature is the possibility of positive profits, which can be obtained whenever the price ratio exceeds *a*.

In Figures 3-3a and 3-3b, we exhibit continuously diminishing returns to scale. In this case, any given price vector with slope between *a* and *b* does define a unique profit-maximizing activity, since the price vector can be perpendicular to only one point. Profits are necessarily positive for price ratios greater than *a*, since the intercept of the perpendicular to the price vector (which is also the tangent to the production possibility curve) clearly cuts the input axis to the right of the origin, as at *B*. As the price ratio approaches *b*, the optimum scale approaches infinity; for price ratios at or above *b*, the profit-maximizing activity is undefined.[1]

[1] Note that the level of maximum profits at any given price vector may approach either a finite or an infinite limit as the price ratio approaches *b*.

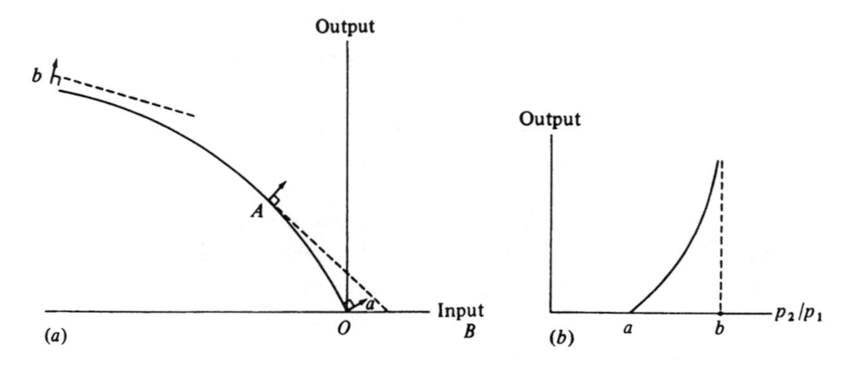

Figure 3-3

For a final example of considerable general interest, we show in Figures 3-4a and 3-4b a case of increasing returns followed by diminishing returns. Consider first any price vector with slope less than a. It may make an obtuse angle with all possible vectors, so that none are optimal. Alternatively, it may be the perpendicular to some possible activity, such as B; but then the profit, measured by C, is negative, so that B is inferior to the origin. The output-input price ratio a is the smallest value that is perpendicular to the curve of possible production vectors at a point A that yields a zero profit at the ratio a. Hence, for that ratio, A and O both represent profit-maximizing activities; for higher values of a, the supply curve

---

Consider, for examples, the following possible input-output relations (recall that $y_1 \leq 0$):

$$y_2 = 1 - y_1 - e^{y_1} \tag{a}$$

$$y_2 = -y_1 + (-y_1)^{1/2}. \tag{b}$$

With p_1 fixed at 1, the optimum scale of production in both cases approaches infinity ($y_1 \to -\infty, y_2 \to +\infty$) as p_2 approaches 1, but the profits at the optimum level approach 1 for (a) and $+\infty$ for (b). Note also that when p_2 rises beyond 1, we can achieve infinite profit even in case (a), in the sense that a profit as large as prescribed can be obtained by a sufficiently large scale of operations.

follows as in Figure 3-3. We note again that the profit-maximizing activity is multi-valued at the price ratio a.

Another way of looking at this case is illuminating. Imagine the original production possibility curve modified by replacing the curved section OA by the straight line OA. The case is now exactly like that of Figure 3-2. The supply curves are also the same, except that at the price ratio a the profit-maximizing set of activities contains just two points in Figure 3-4, while in Figure 3-2 it contains the same two points plus all those lying between them. Thus the modified production possibility curve, obtained by straightening out the hollows, yields a supply curve that is a smoothed version of the original. This smoothing process will be important in discussing the extent to which the existence of general equilibrium is affected by the presence of increasing returns (see Chapter 7).

Finally, we mention briefly the aggregation of the profit-maximizing decisions of individual firms. First, consider for each firm a single chosen activity vector. Because of the convention about signs—positive for outputs and negative for inputs—the net output of any commodity by the productive sector can be obtained by simple addition of the outputs of the individual firms; the amount produced by one firm and used by another for further production simply cancels out. The net aggregate "output" will turn out to be negative for some commodities; these are net inputs needed from the household sector, such as labor services.

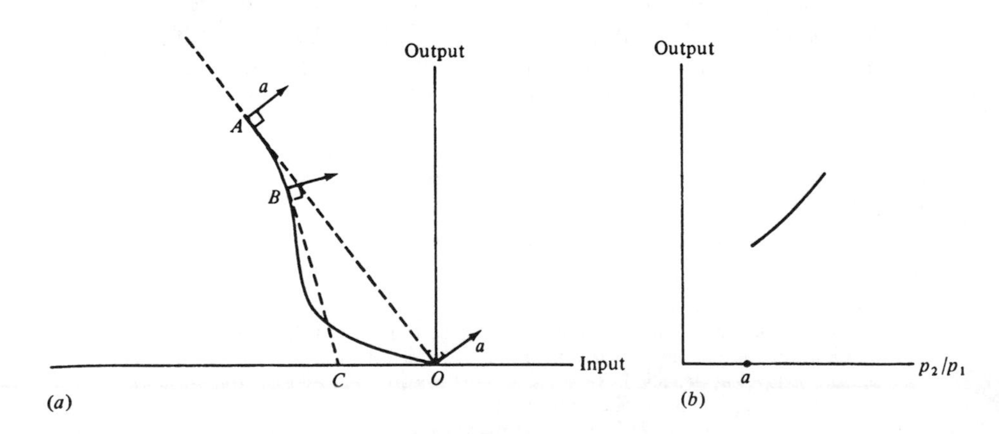

Figure 3-4

If at a given set of prices one or more of the firms has more than one set of profit-maximizing activities, then correspondingly the aggregate supply or demand must be multi-valued; any aggregate activity vector that can be formed by choosing a profit-maximizing vector for each firm and adding them up is an aggregate supply vector for that set of prices.

Finally, we note that if at a given set of prices the profit-maximizing vector is undefined for some firm, the aggregate supply vector must also be regarded as undefined.

2. Production Possibility Sets of Individual Firms

DEFINITION 1. The *production possibility* set for firm f, denoted by Y_f, is the set of activity vectors possible to the firm.

The components of an activity vector include all commodities; positive components refer to output, negative ones to inputs, and zeros to commodities neither purchased nor sold by the firm. An element of Y_f will usually be denoted by $\mathbf{y}_f$.

First we introduce two trivial assumptions about production possibilities. The first states that it is always possible for the firm to engage in no activity.

ASSUMPTION 1. $\mathbf{0} \in Y_f$.

The second is more of a convention than an assumption.

ASSUMPTION 2. Y_f is closed.

That is, if there are technologically possible activities arbitrarily close to a given activity, then we include the given activity among the possible ones. Clearly, little would be lost by sacrificing this assumption; for example, instead of there being a profit-maximizing activity for some set of prices, there would be a sequence of possible activities approaching a given vector such that the profit derived from any given activity is less than that derived from any member of the sequence beginning sufficiently far out.

A more serious restriction to be imposed on the production possibility sets of individual firms is that they are convex sets. The property of convexity can be derived from two, more elementary hypotheses: divisibility and additivity. Production is said to be *divisible* if, whenever y is an activity, λy is an activity for $0 \leq \lambda \leq 1$.

Production is said to be *additive* if, whenever $\mathbf{y}^1$ and $\mathbf{y}^2$ are activities, $\mathbf{y}^1 + \mathbf{y}^2$ is an activity. In this notation, production exhibits *constant returns to scale* if, whenever $\mathbf{y}$ is an activity, $\lambda\mathbf{y}$ is an activity for all $\lambda \geq 0$. The mathematical equivalent to the economic property of constant returns to scale is that of being a *cone*: a set of vectors that contains $\lambda\mathbf{x}$ for all $\lambda \geq 0$ if it contains $\mathbf{x}$.

LEMMA 1. If production is divisible and additive, then the production possibility set is convex and exhibits constant returns to scale, that is, it is a convex cone.

Proof. If $\mathbf{y}^1$ and $\mathbf{y}^2$ are activities, then, by divisibility, $\lambda\mathbf{y}^1$ and $(1 - \lambda)\mathbf{y}^2$ are activities, for $0 \leq \lambda \leq 1$, and $\lambda\mathbf{y}^1 + (1 - \lambda)\mathbf{y}^2$ is an activity, by additivity, demonstrating convexity.

Let $\mathbf{y}$ be an activity, $\lambda \geq 0$. Let n be the largest integer not exceeding λ, $v = \lambda - n$. Then $0 \leq v < 1$, and $v\mathbf{y}$ is an activity by divisibility. Let $\mathbf{y}^i = \mathbf{y}$ $(i = 1, \ldots, n)$, $\mathbf{y}^{n+1} = v\mathbf{y}$. Then $\mathbf{y}^i$ is an activity $(i = 1, \ldots, n + 1)$, and

$$\sum_{i=1}^{n+1} \mathbf{y}^i = \lambda\mathbf{y}.$$

From additivity it follows by induction that $\lambda\mathbf{y}$ is an activity.

The realism of the two hypotheses may be discussed briefly. First, consider divisibility, to which the more serious objections can be raised. In principle, we must distinguish between divisibility of commodities and divisibility of activities. There are many commodities (water, butter) that come in clearly divisible form and some (sugar, sand) for which the indivisible units are so small that the assumption of divisibility is clearly an excellent approximation. On the other hand, there are many commodities, particularly instruments of production (shovels, stamping mills) that come in indivisible units. Certainly, if commodities are indivisible, activities involving them cannot be divisible. If it is possible to use one shovel, it does not follow that there is any process in which half a shovel can be used. A more sophisticated example is that of storage containers. The usefulness of a storage container is proportional to the surface area (that is, if the thickness of the walls is constant; it may have to increase somewhat with volume to resist the pressure of the contents). Therefore, the input is proportional to the two-thirds power of the output. This case can be regarded formally as one of indivisibility; given the geometric shape of the container, containers of different size should be regarded as different commodities, each of which comes only in integer amounts. (This case is possibly of wide economic importance. To a very considerable extent, the manufacturing of commodities in continuous-process industries, such as chemicals, is the handling of materials in a sequence of containers. It has been observed empirically that the cost of a chemical plant of fixed type rises less than proportionately to the capacity and indeed roughly as the 0.6 power.)

Even if the divisibility of commodities is accepted, at least as an approximation, that of divisibility of production activities does not follow as a logical truth. Rather it is an empirical generalization that, for the great majority of ordinary production processes, a uniform reduction in scale preserves feasibility.

The assumption of additivity, on the other hand, can always be defended and indeed made essentially tautologous. The usual criticism of additivity is that if all inputs are doubled, it still may not be possible to double outputs because of limiting conditions such as inability to manage larger organizations. This means merely that some relevant input has been omitted. If all relevant inputs are listed, there is no reason why two activities cannot both be carried on if their inputs are available.

Some care must be taken, however, in the interpretation of the additivity assumption in the context of economic equilibrium. As already remarked, not all inputs are, in fact, marketed. For the moment, let $\mathbf{y}$ be a possible production vector in which all commodities, marketed or not, are included as components, and let Y be the set of possible production vectors (for a particular firm). If divisibility and additivity are assumed, then Y is a convex cone. Suppose that some of the components are marketed, while others are private to the firm. For any vector $\mathbf{y}$, let $\mathbf{y}^M$ and $\mathbf{y}^P$ be the vectors formed by considering only the marketed and private components, respectively. For the firm, assume that the private components are given: $\mathbf{y}^P = \bar{\mathbf{y}}^P$. From the viewpoint of the study of markets, only the vector $\mathbf{y}^M$ is relevant; that is, we are interested in the set of vectors $Y^M = \{\mathbf{y}^M \mid (\mathbf{y}^M, \bar{\mathbf{y}}^P) \in Y\}$. It is trivial to observe that the convexity of Y implies the convexity of Y^M, but Y^M need not exhibit constant returns to scale.

From this point on, suppose that the components of $\mathbf{y}$ are all marketed. Then the discussion justifies the tentative assumption:

ASSUMPTION 3. Y_f is convex.

According to the previous argument, non-convexity arises only because of indivisibility of commodities. Clearly, its economic significance is relatively less when the number of units is large. Thus, the difference between one stamping mill and none is important, but if the relevant choice is between 100 and 101 shovels, the assumption of divisibility is unlikely to be seriously misleading. The effects of non-convexity on the existence of equilibrium will be reconsidered along these lines in Chapter 7.

3. Production Possibility Set of the Entire Economy

The entire production side of the economy is assumed composed of a finite number of (potential or actual) firms. The total production of the economy is the sum of the productions of the individual firms. Note that if a commodity is an input to one firm and an output from another, the net output for society is the difference between the two. If $\mathbf{y}_f$ is the production vector for firm f, then

$$\mathbf{y} = \sum_f \mathbf{y}_f$$

is the production vector for society.

Let Y be the social production possibility set. Then, formally,

DEFINITION 2. $Y = \left\{\mathbf{y} = \sum_f y_f \mid y_f \in Y_f, \ \text{all} f\right\} = \sum_f Y_f.$

A production vector may be regarded as *possible for a set of firms* if it is the sum of vectors, each possible for a different firm of the set. Then, from D.3.2 and A.3.1, it is easy to see that any production vector possible for a set of firms is possible for society as a whole (i.e., for the set of all firms). Let $f_1, \ldots, f_K$ be distinct firms, and suppose

$$\mathbf{y}_{f_k} \in Y_{f_k} \qquad (k = 1, \ldots, K).$$

Set $\mathbf{y}_f = \mathbf{0}$ if f is distinct from any of the firms f_k; by A.3.1, $\mathbf{y}_f \in Y_f$, all f. By D.3.2,

$$\sum_k \mathbf{y}_{f_k} = \sum_f \mathbf{y}_f \in Y.$$

LEMMA 2. For any set of distinct firms, $f_1, \ldots, f_k$, $\sum_k Y_{f_k} \subset Y$.

Remark. The firms must be assumed distinct, because we are, in effect, assuming additivity across firms, but not necessarily across processes within a firm. It is the assumption of possible limitational factors to the firm that gives it its individuality.

We will also refer to the set of possible *production allocations* that define the production vector for each firm. This is the Cartesian product of the production possibility sets for the individual firms.

DEFINITION 3. $\mathcal{Y} = \bigtimes_f Y_f = \{\mathbf{y}_1, \ldots, \mathbf{y}_F \mid \mathbf{y}_f \in \mathbf{Y}_f, \quad \text{all } f\}$

where F is the number of firms. Note that

$$\sum_f \mathbf{y}_f$$

is a linear mapping of the set of possible production allocations into commodity space.

THEOREM 1. $\mathbf{0} \in \mathcal{Y}$; $\mathcal{Y}$ is closed and convex.

This theorem follows trivially from A.3.1–A.3.3.

Corollary 1. $\mathbf{0} \in Y$; Y is convex.

Proof. From T.3.1, since Y is the image of $\mathcal{Y}$ under the linear mapping

$$\sum_f \mathbf{y}_f,$$

it does not follow from A.3.1–A.3.3 alone that Y is closed; this property requires A.3.4 below.

If Y_f is unbounded, then at certain $\mathbf{p}$ it may be that the firm would like to produce on an infinitely large scale. This possibility, as such, does not make it impossible to conduct an analysis of market equilibrium with positive prices; although the firm is taken to suppose that it can sell and buy whatever quantities it likes at the going prices, the economy, in fact, may be incapable of producing outputs and using inputs in unlimited amounts. Indeed, if we are interested in a world of scarcity, we ought to exclude the possibility. We will examine a fairly weak assumption that ensures this.

ASSUMPTION 4. If $y \in \mathcal{Y}$ and $\sum_f \mathbf{y}_f \geq \mathbf{0}$, then $y = \mathbf{0}$.

A.3.4 defines the problem of scarcity when

$$\sum_f \mathbf{y}_f > \mathbf{0};$$

it states that society cannot produce something for nothing by any organization of its entire production apparatus. It is important to observe that this basic property of a social production possibility set cannot be deduced from the corresponding properties of the firm production possibility sets. If, in A.3.4, we let $\mathbf{y}_f = \mathbf{0}$ for all firms but one, then we can deduce the corresponding statement for a firm; that is, it cannot be that $\mathbf{y}_f > \mathbf{0}$ for any possible $\mathbf{y}_f \in Y_f$. But the converse is not true; from this last statement, A.3.4 cannot be deduced. For example, if firm A produces 2 units of commodity 2 from 1 unit of commodity 1 and firm B produces 2 units of commodity 1 from 1 unit of commodity 2, then neither firm has outputs without inputs, but together they can have a net output of 1 unit of each commodity with no net inputs.

When

$$\sum_f \mathbf{y}_f = \mathbf{0},$$

A.3.4 says further that no non-trivial, socially possible production process can be completely undone by another. For the validity of this irreversibility postulate, it suffices that there exists at least one non-produced input that is needed, directly or indirectly, for all production; labor provides an obvious example. Alternatively, if production takes time and differently dated commodities are distinguished, then reversal of a process would require that some outputs precede the corresponding inputs.

Assumption A.3.4 implies that the economy must have an initial endowment of resources in order to produce anything. Let the initial endowment be denoted by $\bar{\mathbf{x}}$.

DEFINITION 4. The social production possibility vector $\mathbf{y}$ is *feasible* if it is possible and

$$\mathbf{y} + \bar{\mathbf{x}} \geq \mathbf{0}.$$

The set of feasible production possibility vectors is denoted by

$$\hat{Y} = Y \cap \{\mathbf{y} \mid \mathbf{y} + \bar{\mathbf{x}} \geq \mathbf{0}\}.$$

DEFINITION 5. The production allocation $\mathscr{y}$ is *feasible* if $\mathbf{y}_f$ is possible for each f (i.e., if $\mathscr{y} \in \mathscr{Y}$) and if

$$\sum_f \mathbf{y}_f + \bar{\mathbf{x}} \geq 0.$$

The set of feasible production allocations is denoted by

$$\hat{\mathscr{Y}} = \mathscr{Y} \cap \left\{ \mathscr{y} \,\middle|\, \sum_f \mathbf{y}_f + \bar{\mathbf{x}} \geq \mathbf{0} \right\}.$$

A feasible vector or allocation is one that society is capable of carrying out, given the existing resources.

For later reference, it is important to add one more assumption, namely that the resources and technology of society together permit the supply of a positive amount of all goods.

ASSUMPTION 5. For some $\bar{\mathbf{y}} \in Y$, $\bar{\mathbf{x}} + \bar{\mathbf{y}} \gg \mathbf{0}$.

Note that if $\mathbf{y}$ is the social production possibility vector, $\mathbf{y} + \bar{\mathbf{x}}$ is the net supply, which must be non-negative for feasibility. To insist on the possibility of strict positivity means something like the following: Divide the commodities into produced and non-produced. The non-produced commodities all must be available initially in positive amounts (a commodity that is neither produced nor available initially can surely be disregarded). If the divisibility of production is assumed, assumption A.3.5 is equivalent to the surely innocuous proposition that if non-produced goods were available in unlimited quantities, it would be feasible to produce a positive amount of any given produced good. Let P be the set of produced goods, N the set of non-produced goods, and for each $i \in P$, let $\mathbf{y}^i$ be a vector with a positive output of commodity i that would be feasible if there were no restrictions on the availability of non-produced inputs. That is,

$$y_i^i > 0 \qquad y_j^i \geq 0 \qquad \text{for } j \in P.$$

Let n be the number of produced goods,

$$\bar{\bar{\mathbf{y}}} = \sum_{i \in P} \frac{1}{n} \mathbf{y}^i;$$

$\bar{\bar{\mathbf{y}}}$ is a convex combination of vectors in Y, so $\bar{\bar{\mathbf{y}}} \in Y$. Also,

$$\bar{\bar{\mathbf{y}}}_i > 0 \qquad \text{all } i \in P,$$

by construction. For $i \in N$, $\bar{x}_i > 0$; then choose α, $0 < \alpha \leq 1$, so that

$$\bar{x}_i + \alpha \bar{\bar{\mathbf{y}}}_i > 0 \qquad \text{all } i \in N.$$

Since $\bar{x}_i \geq 0$, $i \in P$,

$$\bar{x}_i + \alpha \bar{\bar{\mathbf{y}}}_i > 0 \qquad \text{all } i \in P.$$

Let $\bar{\mathbf{y}} = \alpha\bar{\bar{\mathbf{y}}}$. Since Y is divisible, $\bar{\mathbf{y}} \in Y$, and by construction, $\bar{\mathbf{x}} + \bar{\mathbf{y}} \gg 0$, as assumed in A.3.5.

Now it is essential to demonstrate that the set of feasible production allocations is bounded. For any real number ξ, let

$$\xi^+ = \max(\xi,0) \qquad \xi^- = \max(-\xi,0),$$

so that

$$\xi = \xi^+ - \xi^- \qquad \xi^+ \geq 0 \qquad \xi^- \geq 0.$$

For a vector, $\mathbf{x}$, define upper and lower bounds,

$$U(\mathbf{x}) = \sum_i x_i^+ \qquad L(\mathbf{x}) = \sum_i x_i^-.$$

Obviously, a set of vectors, S, is bounded if and only if $U(\mathbf{x})$ and $L(\mathbf{x})$ are both bounded from above as x varies over S.

THEOREM 2. If A.3.1–A.3.4 hold, then the set of feasible production allocations, $\hat{\mathscr{Y}}$, is compact and convex.

Proof. For any $\mathscr{y} \in \mathscr{Y} = \times_f Y_f$, let $\mathbf{y} = \sum_f \mathbf{y}_f$. Then

$$\sum_f (y_{fi}^+ - y_{fi}^-) = \sum_f y_{fi} = y_i \geq -y_i^-,$$

or

$$\sum_f y_{fi}^+ + y_i^- \geq \sum_f y_{fi}^-.$$

Sum over i. Then

$$U(\mathscr{y}) + L\left(\sum_f \mathbf{y}_f\right) \geq L(\mathscr{y}). \tag{2}$$

For $\mathscr{y} \in \hat{\mathscr{Y}}$, $\mathscr{y}$ is feasible; that is,

$$\sum_f \mathbf{y}_f \geq -\bar{\mathbf{x}},$$

so that

$$L\left(\sum_f \mathbf{y}_f\right) \leq U(\bar{\mathbf{x}}) \qquad \text{for } \mathscr{y} \in \hat{\mathscr{Y}}. \tag{3}$$

L and U may be thought of as indices of inputs and outputs, respectively; then

$$L\left(\sum_f \mathbf{y}_f\right)$$

is an index of *net* inputs to society, while $L(\mathscr{y})$ and $U(\mathscr{y})$ are indices of inputs and outputs, respectively, totalled over firms without cancelling inputs of one firm against outputs of another.

Let us expand $\hat{\mathscr{Y}}$ to include all allocations for which the inputs satisfy (3); that is, define

$$\mathscr{Y}^* = \mathscr{Y} \cap \left\{\mathscr{y} \mid L\left(\sum_f \mathbf{y}_f\right) \leq U(\bar{\mathbf{x}})\right\}. \tag{4}$$

To prove $\hat{\mathscr{Y}}$ bounded, it certainly suffices to show that the larger set, $\mathscr{Y}^*$, is bounded. Also, $\mathscr{Y}$ is closed by T.3.1, the set

$$\left\{\mathscr{y} \mid L\left(\sum_f \mathbf{y}_f\right) \leq U(\bar{\mathbf{x}})\right\}$$

is closed since it is defined by the continuous function

$$L\left(\sum_f \mathbf{y}_f\right)$$

and the intersection of closed sets is closed, so that $\mathscr{Y}^*$ is closed.

From (2) and the definition of $\mathscr{Y}^*$, (4),

$$U(\mathscr{y}) + U(\bar{\mathbf{x}}) \geq L(\mathscr{y}) \qquad \text{for } \mathscr{y} \in \mathscr{Y}^*; \tag{5}$$

hence, to prove the boundedness of $\mathscr{Y}^*$, it suffices to show that $U(\mathscr{y})$ is bounded there, for then the boundedness of $L(\mathscr{y})$ follows by (5).

If $U(\mathscr{y}) \leq 1$, all $\mathscr{y} \in \mathscr{Y}^*$, then there is nothing to prove. Suppose that $U(\mathscr{y}) > 1$, some $\mathscr{y} \in \mathscr{Y}^*$. For any such $\mathscr{y}$, let $\alpha = 1/U(\mathscr{y}) < 1$. By divisibility, $\alpha \mathbf{y}_f \in Y_f$, all f, so that $\alpha\mathscr{y} \in \mathscr{Y}$. Also,

$$L\left(\sum_f \alpha y_f\right) = \alpha L\left(\sum_f \mathbf{y}_f\right) \leq \alpha U(\bar{\mathbf{x}}) \leq U(\bar{\mathbf{x}}),$$

so that $\alpha\mathscr{y} \in \mathscr{Y}^*$. Also, $U(\alpha\mathscr{y}) = \alpha U(\mathscr{y}) = 1$, by definition of α. Let

$$\mathscr{Y}^{**} = \mathscr{Y}^* \cap \{\mathscr{y} \mid U(\mathscr{y}) = 1\}.$$

It has just been shown that

$$\text{if} \quad U(\mathscr{y}) > 1 \quad \text{and} \quad \alpha = \frac{1}{U(\mathscr{y})}, \quad \text{then} \quad \alpha\mathscr{y} \in \mathscr{Y}^{**}.$$

To prove the boundedness of $\mathscr{Y}^*$, note that it is sufficient to show that

$$L\left(\sum_f \mathbf{y}_f\right) \text{ bounded away from zero on } \mathscr{Y}^{**}. \tag{6}$$

Suppose (6) true. Then for any $\mathscr{y}$ for which $U(\mathscr{y}) > 1$,

$$L\left(\sum_f \alpha \mathbf{y}_f\right) = \alpha L\left(\sum_f \mathbf{y}_f\right) \geq c > 0,$$

so that

$$U(\mathscr{y}) = \frac{1}{\alpha} \leq \frac{L\left(\sum_f \mathbf{y}_f\right)}{c} \leq \frac{U(\bar{\mathbf{x}})}{c};$$

thus, for $\mathscr{y} \in \mathscr{Y}^*$, either $U(\mathscr{y}) \leq 1$ or $U(\mathscr{y}) \leq U(\bar{\mathbf{x}})/c$, so that $U(\mathscr{y})$ is certainly bounded on $\mathscr{Y}^*$, and $\mathscr{Y}^*$ is bounded.

It remains to demonstrate (6). The set, $\mathscr{Y}^{**}$, is clearly closed; since $U(\mathscr{y})$ is bounded on it by definition, (5) implies that $\mathscr{Y}^{**}$ is bounded and therefore compact. Recall that a continuous function actually assumes a minimum value as the argument varies over a compact set; that is, if $f(\mathbf{x})$ is continuous for $\mathbf{x} \in S$, where S is compact, then, for some $\bar{\mathbf{x}} \in S$, $f(\mathbf{x}) \geq f(\bar{\mathbf{x}})$, all $\mathbf{x} \in S$. It follows that if $f(\mathbf{x}) > 0$, for $\mathbf{x} \in S$, then $f(\mathbf{x}) \geq c > 0$, all $\mathbf{x} \in S$, where $c = f(\bar{\mathbf{x}})$. Since

$$L\left(\sum_f \mathbf{y}_f\right)$$

is a continuous function of $\mathscr{Y}$ on $\mathscr{Y}^{**}$, it suffices that

$$L\left(\sum_f \mathbf{y}_f\right) > 0 \qquad \text{on } \mathscr{Y}^{**}$$

in order that (6) hold.

Since $U(\mathbf{0}) = 0 \neq 1$, then $\mathscr{y} \neq 0$ for $\mathscr{y} \in \mathscr{Y}^{**}$. By A.3.4,

$$\sum_f \mathbf{y}_f$$

has at least one negative component, so that

$$L\left(\sum_f \mathbf{y}_f\right) > 0 \qquad \text{for } \mathscr{y} \in \mathscr{Y}^{**},$$

as required.

Thus, $\hat{\mathscr{Y}}$ has been proved bounded. By definition, it is the intersection of closed convex sets and therefore is closed and convex. A closed bounded set is compact, so that T.3.2 has been demonstrated.

Corollary 2. Y is closed.

Proof. That $\bar{\mathbf{x}}$ was actually the endowment vector did not enter the proof of T.3.2; what was shown was that the set

$$\mathscr{Y} \cap \left\{ y \,\middle|\, \sum_f \mathbf{y}_f + \tilde{\mathbf{x}} \geq \mathbf{0} \right\} \tag{7}$$

is compact for any vector $\tilde{\mathbf{x}}$. Let $\mathbf{y}^0$ be a limit point of Y. Then there is a sequence, $\{\mathbf{y}^\nu\}$, $\mathbf{y}^\nu \in Y$, $\mathbf{y}^\nu \to \mathbf{y}^0$. By D.3.2, there is, for each ν, a production allocation y^ν such that

$$\sum_f \mathbf{y}_f^\nu = \mathbf{y}^\nu.$$

Since $\mathbf{y}^\nu \to \mathbf{y}^0$, we can certainly find a vector $\tilde{\mathbf{x}}$, with $-\tilde{\mathbf{x}} \ll \mathbf{y}^0$, such that

$$\sum_f \mathbf{y}_f^\nu + \tilde{\mathbf{x}} \geq \mathbf{0} \qquad \text{all } \nu.$$

Then y^ν belongs to the compact set (7) for all ν. Therefore there exists a subsequence converging to some y^0 belonging to $\mathscr{Y}$; hence,

$$\mathbf{y}^\nu = \sum_f \mathbf{y}_f^\nu \quad \text{converges to} \quad \sum_f \mathbf{y}_f^0$$

along the subsequence. But $\mathbf{y}^\nu \to \mathbf{y}^0$; hence

$$\mathbf{y}^0 = \sum_f \mathbf{y}_f^0 \in Y.$$

4. Costs, Profits, and Supply

In this section, we will show how some of the assumptions of Chapter 2 can be derived as propositions in the theory of production and establish a few results that will be used later in the book. A complete study of profit and supply functions is not intended.

Suppose first that, in addition to A.3.1–A.3.3, we postulate that Y_f is bounded above. Clearly this is not an assumption we should wish to retain indefinitely—it excludes, for instance, the case of constant returns to scale. When it is made, however, then for given $\mathbf{p} \in S_n$, the function $\mathbf{p}\mathbf{y}_f$ always attains a maximum on Y_f. Accordingly, we introduce

DEFINITION 6.

$$\pi_f(\mathbf{p}) = \max_{\mathbf{y}_f \in Y_f} \mathbf{p}\mathbf{y}_f,$$

where $\pi_f(\mathbf{p})$ is the *profit function* of firm f.

By A.3.1 we have $\pi_f(\mathbf{p}) \geq 0$, all $\mathbf{p} \in S_n$. We may also define

DEFINITION 7. $Y_f(\mathbf{p}) = \{\mathbf{y}_f \mid \mathbf{p}\mathbf{y}_f = \pi_f(\mathbf{p}), \quad \mathbf{y}_f \in Y_f\}$ where $Y_f(\mathbf{p})$ is the *supply correspondence* of firm *f*.

Of course, some components of members of $Y_f(\mathbf{p})$ will be negative. These denote demands.

We now prove.

THEOREM 3. If Y_f is bounded, then (a) $\pi_f(\mathbf{p})$ is a continuous convex function over S_n; (b) $Y_f(\mathbf{p})$ is a convex set for each $\mathbf{p}$.

Proof. (a) Let $\mathbf{p}, \mathbf{p}' \in S_n$, $\mathbf{p}(\alpha) = \alpha\mathbf{p}' + (1 - \alpha)\mathbf{p}$, $0 \leq \alpha \leq 1$, and let $\mathbf{y}_f \in Y_f(\mathbf{p})$, $\mathbf{y}'_f \in Y_f(\mathbf{p}')$, $\mathbf{y}^\alpha_f \in Y_f[\mathbf{p}(\alpha)]$. Then by D.3.6 and D.3.7,

$$\mathbf{p}\mathbf{y}^\alpha_f \leq \mathbf{p}\mathbf{y}_f \qquad \mathbf{p}'\mathbf{y}^\alpha_f \leq \mathbf{p}'\mathbf{y}'_f.$$

Hence, multiplying the first inequality by $(1 - \alpha)$, the second by α, and adding yield

$$\pi_f[\mathbf{p}(\alpha)] \leq (1 - \alpha)\pi_f(\mathbf{p}) + \alpha\pi_f(\mathbf{p}'),$$

so that $\pi_f(\mathbf{p})$ is convex.

To demonstrate continuity, let $\{\mathbf{p}^\nu\}$ be a sequence of price vectors converging to $\mathbf{p}^0$. For each ν, let $\mathbf{y}^\nu_f \in Y_f(\mathbf{p}^\nu)$. Then, for any $\mathbf{y}_f \in Y_f$, $\mathbf{p}^\nu\mathbf{y}^\nu_f \geq \mathbf{p}^\nu\mathbf{y}_f$ for all ν. Since Y_f is compact, the sequence, $\{\mathbf{y}^\nu_f\}$, is bounded. Let $\mathbf{y}^0_f$ be any limit point; then $\mathbf{p}^0\mathbf{y}^0_f \geq \mathbf{p}^0\mathbf{y}_f$ for any $\mathbf{y}_f \in Y_f$, so that by D.3.6 and D.3.7, $\mathbf{y}^0_f \in Y_f(\mathbf{p}^0)$ and $\pi_f(\mathbf{p}^0) = \mathbf{p}^0\mathbf{y}^0_f$. Since $\mathbf{y}^0_f$ was any limit point of the bounded sequence $\{\mathbf{y}^\nu_f\}$ and since $\pi_f(\mathbf{p}^\nu) = \mathbf{p}^\nu\mathbf{y}^\nu_f$, it has been shown that $\pi_f(\mathbf{p}^\nu) \rightarrow \pi_f(\mathbf{p}^0)$, and therefore, $\pi_f(\mathbf{p})$ is a continuous function.

(b) Let $\mathbf{y}_f, \mathbf{y}'_f \in Y_f(\mathbf{p})$. Then for $0 \leq \alpha \leq 1$, let $\mathbf{y}_f(\alpha) = \alpha\mathbf{y}_f + (1 - \alpha)\mathbf{y}'_f$.

$$\mathbf{p}\mathbf{y}_f(\alpha) = \alpha\mathbf{p}\mathbf{y}_f + (1 - \alpha)\mathbf{p}\mathbf{y}'_f = \alpha\pi_f(\mathbf{p}) + (1 - \alpha)\pi_f(\mathbf{p}) = \pi_f(\mathbf{p}).$$

But $\mathbf{y}_f(\alpha) \in Y_f$ by A.3.3 and so belongs to $Y_f(\mathbf{p})$ by D.3.4.

If one is willing to assume Y_f to be *strictly* convex, the results can be strengthened. (A set is strictly convex if every *proper* convex combination of two points of the set belongs to the interior of the set relative to the smallest linear space containing it. If the set has full dimensionality then the relative interior is the interior in the usual sense. A proper convex combination of $\mathbf{x}^1$ and $\mathbf{x}^2$ is a point $\mathbf{x} = \alpha\mathbf{x}^1 + (1 - \alpha)\mathbf{x}^2$, for some α, $0 < \alpha < 1$.) We also assume that Y_f *admits free disposal*, in other words, that $\mathbf{y}_f \in Y_f$ and $\mathbf{y}'_f \leq \mathbf{y}_f$ imply that $\mathbf{y}'_f \in Y_f$. A set that admits free disposal necessarily has full dimensionality.

THEOREM 4. Let Y_f be bounded and strictly convex and admit free disposal. Then (a) $\pi_f(\mathbf{p})$ is a strictly convex function, and (b) $Y_f(\mathbf{p})$ has only one element for each $\mathbf{p}$ and can be written as a function, $\mathbf{y}_f(\mathbf{p})$.

Proof. Suppose that $\mathbf{y}_f$ and $\mathbf{y}'_f$ both belong to $Y_f(\mathbf{p})$. Then, in the previous notation and by the remarks just made, $\mathbf{y}_f(\alpha)$ belongs to the interior of Y_f if $0 < \alpha < 1$. Then there exists $\mathbf{y}''_f \gg \mathbf{y}_f(\alpha)$, $\mathbf{y}''_f \in Y_f$. But then, since $\mathbf{p} > 0$, $\mathbf{p}\mathbf{y}''_f > \mathbf{p}\mathbf{y}_f(\alpha) = \pi_f(\mathbf{p})$ by T.3.3(b), a contradiction to D.3.6 and D.3.7. It also follows that, for $0 < \alpha < 1$, the inequalities used in proving T.3.3(a) are all strict, so that $\pi_f(\mathbf{p})$ must be strictly convex.

This theorem shows that the discussion in the previous chapter, in particular assumption A.2.1, was based on the implicit supposition of diminishing returns to scale. We can also easily prove the other assumptions made there. Of course, A.2.2, homogeneity of degree zero, follows immediately from the nature of the maximization process as far as the production side goes. Walras' law (A.2.3) cannot be discussed without considering the consumption sector, but continuity (A.2.4) can now be demonstrated.

THEOREM 5. Let Y_f be bounded and strictly convex and admit free disposal. Then $\mathbf{y}_f(\mathbf{p})$ is continuous over S_n.

Proof. Let $\mathbf{p}^\nu \to \mathbf{p}^0 \in S_n$, and $\mathbf{y}_f^\nu = \mathbf{y}(\mathbf{p}^\nu)$. Since Y_f is compact, $\mathbf{y}_f^\nu \to \mathbf{y}_f^0 \in Y_f$ along some subsequence. By definition of the supply function, $\mathbf{p}^\nu[\mathbf{y}_f^\nu - \mathbf{y}_f(p^0)] \geq 0$, all ν, so that, taking limits along the selected subsequence, $\mathbf{p}^0[\mathbf{y}_f^0 - \mathbf{y}_f(\mathbf{p}^0)] \geq 0$. However, from the uniqueness of the profit-maximizing commodity vector for each $\mathbf{p}$, asserted in T.3.4(b), $\mathbf{y}_f^0 = \mathbf{y}_f(\mathbf{p}^0)$. Since this holds for any limit point, $\mathbf{y}_f^0$, T.3.5 has been established.

Let us now return to the profit function. Since $\pi_f(\mathbf{p}) = \mathbf{p}\mathbf{y}_f(\mathbf{p})$, it is certainly continuous. We will show that π_f is, in fact, differentiable and that $\partial\pi_f/\partial p_i = y_{fi}(\mathbf{p})$. This means that, to a linear approximation, the effect on profits of changing a price is the same whether inputs and outputs are adjusted optimally or left unchanged.

By definition of profits and profit maximization, we have, for any change $\mathbf{h}$ in the price vector,

$$\pi_f(\mathbf{p}+\mathbf{h}) = (\mathbf{p}+\mathbf{h})\mathbf{y}_f(\mathbf{p}+\mathbf{h}) \geq (\mathbf{p}+\mathbf{h})\mathbf{y}_f(\mathbf{p}) = \mathbf{p}\mathbf{y}_f(\mathbf{p}) + \mathbf{h}\mathbf{y}_f(\mathbf{p})$$
$$= \pi_f(\mathbf{p}) + \mathbf{h}\mathbf{y}_f(\mathbf{p}),$$

$$\pi_f(\mathbf{p}) = \mathbf{p}\mathbf{y}_f(\mathbf{p}) \geq \mathbf{p}\mathbf{y}_f(\mathbf{p}+\mathbf{h}) = (\mathbf{p}+\mathbf{h})\mathbf{y}_f(\mathbf{p}+\mathbf{h}) - \mathbf{h}\mathbf{y}_f(\mathbf{p}+\mathbf{h})$$
$$= \pi_f(\mathbf{p}+\mathbf{h}) - \mathbf{h}\mathbf{y}_f(\mathbf{p}+\mathbf{h}).$$

Hence,

$$\frac{\mathbf{h}[\mathbf{y}_f(\mathbf{p}+\mathbf{h}) - \mathbf{y}_f(\mathbf{p})]}{|\mathbf{h}|} \geq \frac{\pi_f(\mathbf{p}+\mathbf{h}) - \pi_f(\mathbf{p}) - \mathbf{h}\mathbf{y}_f(\mathbf{p})}{|\mathbf{h}|} \geq 0.$$

From T.3.4, $\mathbf{y}_f(\mathbf{p}+\mathbf{h}) - \mathbf{y}_f(\mathbf{p})$ approaches 0 as $\mathbf{h}$ approaches 0; since $\mathbf{h}/|\mathbf{h}|$ is certainly bounded, the left-hand member of the above inequality approaches 0, and therefore,

$$\lim_{\mathbf{h}\to 0} \frac{\pi_f(\mathbf{p}+\mathbf{h}) - \pi_f(\mathbf{p}) - \mathbf{h}y_f(\mathbf{p})}{|\mathbf{h}|} = 0;$$

by definition, $\pi_f(\mathbf{p})$ is differentiable for any $\mathbf{p} \in S_n$, while, by letting $\mathbf{h} = t\mathbf{e}^i$, where $\mathbf{e}^i$ is the ith unit row vector, $(0, \ldots, 0,1,0, \ldots, 0)$, with 1 in the ith place, we see that $\partial\pi_f/\partial p_i = y_{fi}$.

THEOREM 6. If Y_f is bounded and strictly convex and admits free disposal, then the profit function $\pi_f(\mathbf{p})$ is everywhere differentiable and $\partial\pi_f/\partial p_i = y_{fi}(\mathbf{p})$.

If it is assumed, in addition, that the profit function is *twice* differentiable, certain very familiar propositions of production theory emerge. By T.3.6,

$$\frac{\partial^2\pi_f}{\partial p_i \partial p_j} = \frac{\partial y_{fi}}{\partial p_j}.$$

But if π_f is twice continuously differentiable, then the matrix $(\partial^2\pi_f/\partial p_i\partial p_j)$ is symmetric; since π_f is convex, it is also positive semi-definite.

Corollary 6. If Y_f is bounded and strictly convex and admits free disposal and if the profit function, $\pi_f(\mathbf{p})$, is twice differentiable, then (a) $\partial y_{fi}/\partial p_j = \partial y_{fj}/\partial p_i$ for all i and j; (b) the matrix $(\partial y_{fi}/\partial p_j)$ is positive semi-definite; and in particular, (c) $\partial y_{fi}/\partial p_i \geq 0$.

Lastly, let us consider the special case discussed in Section 2.11 under the title, the L-economy. Here Y_f is a convex cone and not strictly convex. Instead we consider the normalized cone,

$$Y'_f = \left\{ \mathbf{y}'_f \mid \mathbf{y}'_f = \frac{1}{y_{ff}} \mathbf{y}_f, \quad \mathbf{y}_f \in Y_f, y_{ff} > 0 \right\};$$

recall the "no joint production" assumption, A.2.10(b). With the further assumption that positive output requires some input, it is easy to show that Y'_f is bounded. We can now define:

DEFINITION 8. The *unit profit function* for a firm having only a single output and constant returns to scale is defined as

$$\pi'_f(p) = \sup_{Y'_f \in Y_f} \mathbf{p}\mathbf{y}'_f.$$

The minimum unit cost function of Section 2.11, $C^*_f(\mathbf{p})$, then is defined by

$$C^*_f(\mathbf{p}) = p_f - \pi'_f(\mathbf{p}).$$

It follows at once from T.3.3 that

THEOREM 7. $C^*_f(\mathbf{p})$ is a continuous concave function over S_n.

Thus the use of the fixed point in establishing the existence of equilibrium in an L-economy (see A.2.13(b)) is justified.

Finally, we note a very simple, but much-used, implication of profit maximization.

THEOREM 8. If $\mathbf{y}^k_f \in Y_f(\mathbf{p}^k)$, $k = 1,2$, then $(\mathbf{p}^1 - \mathbf{p}^2)(\mathbf{y}^1_f - \mathbf{y}^2_f) \geq 0$.

In particular, under the hypotheses of T.3.5,

$$(\mathbf{p}^1 - \mathbf{p}^2)[\mathbf{y}_f(\mathbf{p}^1) - \mathbf{y}_f(\mathbf{p}^2)] \geq 0.$$

Proof. Profit maximization implies that $\mathbf{y}^1_f$ is at least as profitable as $\mathbf{y}^2_f$ at prices $\mathbf{p}^1$ and vice versa.

$$\mathbf{p}^1\mathbf{y}^1_f \geq \mathbf{p}^1\mathbf{y}^2_f \qquad \mathbf{p}^2\mathbf{y}^2_f \geq \mathbf{p}^2\mathbf{y}^1_f.$$

If these inequalities are added and the terms regrouped, the theorem is established.

Notes

The general outlines of production theory in this chapter are common to the neoclassical tradition and need no special reference. The analysis of production into activities, which underlies the entire chapter and which constitutes a synthesis of the earlier "fixed-coefficient" and "production function" viewpoints, seems to have first appeared in the classic paper of von Neumann [1937, 1945] on economic growth. A systematic development of production theory from the activity analysis viewpoint first appeared in Koopmans [1951b]; the crucial importance of assumptions of the type of A.3.4 in establishing the boundedness of the set of feasible production allocations first appeared there.

Section 2. For more extended discussion of the possibilities for and meaning of divisibility in production, see the interchange between Chamberlin [1948, 1949] and Hahn [1949] and also Menger [1954].

Section 3. It has been shown by Debreu [1962] that, in fact, irreversibility is not necessary to the existence theorems to be established in Chapter 5, but the proofs appear to become more complicated. In view of the high acceptability of the irreversibility assumption, we have not felt it worthwhile to seek the added generality.

Section 4. Most of the development of this section is parallel to the corresponding theorems in consumer demand theory due primarily to Slutzky [1915]. More specifically, the application to the theory of the firm and particularly Corollary 6 appears in Hotelling [1932]. The method of proof follows that of McKenzie [1956–57] for the consumer demand case; see also Karlin [1959, Vol. I, pp. 265–273].

Chapter Four

CONSUMER DECISIONS AND EFFICIENT ALLOCATIONS

A levelling rancorous rational sort of mind
That never looked out of the eye of a saint
Or out of a drunkard's eye.
—W. B. Yeats, *Seven Sages*

1. Consumer Choice

It is assumed that there are a finite number of households, indexed by h; $\mathbf{x}_h$ will represent the consumption vector of household h. Each household is also assumed to hold an initial endowment, $\bar{\mathbf{x}}_h$, of goods; for convenience in exposition, we assume that it sells this endowment at the going prices and uses the income to purchase consumption goods. Thus, all consumption can be regarded as non-negative.

The preferences of the households extend, among other commodities, to choices between labor and leisure and among different kinds of labor. Similarly, among the endowments of the household, the most important in practice are the capacities to perform different types of labor. To represent labor services, some slightly artificial conventions are needed.

Let L be the set of labor services. For a labor service $i \in L$, let x_{hi}, the endowment, be understood to mean the maximum amount of that service that household h is capable of supplying under any circumstances. Thus, if i is a skill not possessed by h, $\bar{x}_{hi} = 0$. If i is an arduous occupation, it may be physically impossible to supply it at a very high rate; then $\bar{x}_{hi}$ will be small. We define the individual's "demand" for labor service i, x_{hi}, as the extent to which his supply of that service falls short of the maximum he is capable of supplying; the amount of labor of type i supplied is then $\bar{x}_{hi} - x_{hi}$. Thus, if the individual is capable of teaching for 12 hours a day and also capable of driving a bus for 12 hours a day and if, in fact, he teaches for eight hours a day and does not drive a bus at all, then his demand for "teaching leisure" is four hours and that for "bus-driving leisure" 12 hours. The conventions used imply the constraints

$$0 \leq x_{hi} \qquad (i \in L).$$

If $x_{hi} < \bar{x}_{hi}$ $(i \in L)$, then the individual is supplying labor of type i in the amount $\bar{x}_{hi} - x_{hi}$. If $x_{hi} > \bar{x}_{hi}$, then the individual is a net demander of labor of type i in the amount $x_{hi} - \bar{x}_{hi}$; the second case might arise, for example, for domestic or repair services. In the notation introduced in Chapter 3, the net supply of labor of type i by household h is $(x_{hi} - \bar{x}_{hi})^-$, the net demand is $(x_{hi} - \bar{x}_{hi})^+$.

The amount of all types of labor that can be supplied is constrained not merely by capabilities, but also by the scarcity of time itself. We have not specified in what units labor is measured, so let τ_{hi} be the amount of time that labor activity i requires per unit. (Ordinarily, we measure labor by time, so that $\tau_{hi} = 1$, but it might be measured in terms of tasks performed, for example.) There is some limit T on the amount of time in the period under analysis (e.g., 24 hours in a day), so that the total labor supplied cannot exceed T;

$$\sum_{i \in L} \tau_{hi}(x_{hi} - \bar{x}_{hi})^- \leq T.$$

It is also true that at least some types of consumption of goods (other than types of leisure) require time. Let τ_{hi} be the amount of time required to consume a unit of good i $(i \notin L)$; let τ'_{hi} be the amount of time required to consume the services of a unit of labor of type i. Then the time constraint becomes

$$\sum_{i \in L} \tau_{hi}(x_{hi} - \bar{x}_{hi})^- + \sum_{i \in L} \tau'_{hi}(x_{hi} - \bar{x}_{hi})^+ + \sum_{i \notin L} \tau_{hi}x_{hi} \leq T.$$

Later on, the general equilibrium model will be reinterpreted to apply to many time periods simultaneously. The individuals are assumed to make their labor and consumption choices simultaneously for the future as well as for the present. Then there is a time constraint for each period.

For subsequent purposes this detailed description of the consumption possibility set will be used only as informal justification for certain axioms. The set has been characterized as the set of non-negative vectors that, in addition, satisfy certain inequalities. It is easy to verify that the set of vectors $\mathbf{x}_h$, which satisfy these inequalities, is convex.

ASSUMPTION 1. The consumption possibility set X_h for individual h is closed and convex; $\mathbf{x}_h \geq 0$ for $\mathbf{x}_h \in X_h$.

Note that the time constraints are satisfied with strict inequality if $x_{hi} = \bar{x}_{hi}$ $(i \in L)$, $x_{hi} = 0$ $(i \notin L)$. Then we can choose α, $0 < \alpha < 1$, so that the time constraints are satisfied by the vector $\bar{\bar{\mathbf{x}}}_h$ defined by $\bar{\bar{x}}_{hi} = \alpha \bar{x}_{hi}$ $(i \in L)$, $\bar{\bar{x}}_{hi} = 0$ $(i \notin L)$. Then certainly

$$\begin{aligned} \bar{\bar{x}}_{hi} &\leq \bar{x}_{hi} && \text{all } i, \\ \bar{\bar{x}}_{hi} &< \bar{x}_{hi} && \text{if } \bar{x}_{hi} > 0. \end{aligned}$$

This argument justifies the assumption,

ASSUMPTION 2. There exists a possible consumption vector $\bar{\bar{\mathbf{x}}}_h \in X_h$, such that

$$\begin{aligned} \bar{\bar{x}}_{hi} &\leq \bar{x}_{hi} && \text{all } i, \\ \bar{\bar{x}}_{hi} &< \bar{x}_{hi} && \text{if } \bar{x}_{hi} > 0, \end{aligned}$$

where $\bar{\mathbf{x}}_h$ is the initial endowment for household h.

The income of a household is assumed to derive from two sources: the sale of the initial endowment and the share held by the household in the profits of firms. It is assumed that household h owns a fraction, d_{hf}, of firm f and shares to that extent in the profits. Of course, d_{hf} must be non-negative, though it may be zero, and for each firm the total amount of profits is allocated to different households.

ASSUMPTION 3. For each household h the total income M_h at any set of prices $\mathbf{p}$ and any given set of production decisions $\mathbf{y}_f$ is given by

$$M_h = \mathbf{p}\bar{\mathbf{x}}_h + \sum_f d_{hf}(\mathbf{p}\mathbf{y}_f) \qquad \text{where } d_{hf} \geq 0, \sum_h d_{hf} = 1.$$

As stated, A.4.3 implies that each firm is a partnership, since the household shares in losses as well as profits. However, since $0 \in Y_f$, a profit-maximizing firm will always choose $\mathbf{y}_f$ so that $\mathbf{p}\mathbf{y}_f \geq \mathbf{p}\mathbf{0} = 0$; therefore, at an equilibrium in which firms maximize profits, it could have been assumed equally well that the firms are incorporated, with limited liability for stockholders.

The aim of the household is to choose the most preferred point among the commodity vectors available to it at a given set of prices and a given income. Its preferences are, as usual, assumed to be defined by an ordering of all commodity vectors in its consumption possibility set. The following assumptions will be made:

ASSUMPTION 4. For each h, there is a relation, $\succsim_h$ (interpreted "preferred or indifferent"), for pairs of elements in the consumption possibility set, X_h, with the following properties:

(a) Transitivity:

$$\mathbf{x}_h^1 \succsim_h \mathbf{x}_h^2 \quad \text{and} \quad \mathbf{x}_h^2 \succsim_h \mathbf{x}_h^3 \quad \text{imply} \quad \mathbf{x}_h^1 \succsim_h \mathbf{x}_h^3;$$

(b) Connexity:

$$\text{For all } \mathbf{x}_h^1 \text{ and } \mathbf{x}_h^2 \text{ in } X_h, \text{ either } \mathbf{x}_h^1 \succsim_h \mathbf{x}_h^2 \text{ or } \mathbf{x}_h^2 \succsim_h \mathbf{x}_h^1;$$

(c) Continuity:

$$\text{For any given } \mathbf{x}_h^0, \text{ the sets } \{\mathbf{x}_h \mid \mathbf{x}_h \succsim_h \mathbf{x}_h^0\}$$
$$\text{and } \{\mathbf{x}_h \mid \mathbf{x}_h^0 \succsim_h \mathbf{x}_h\} \text{ are closed;}$$

(d) Semi-strict convexity:

$$\text{If } \mathbf{x}_h^1 \succ_h \mathbf{x}_h^2 \text{ and } 0 \leq \alpha < 1, \text{ then } (1 - \alpha)\mathbf{x}_h^1 + \alpha\mathbf{x}_h^2 \succ_h \mathbf{x}_h^2;$$

(e) Non-satiation:

$$\text{There is no } \mathbf{x}_h^0 \text{ such that } \mathbf{x}_h^0 \succsim_h \mathbf{x}_h \text{ for all } \mathbf{x}_h \in X_h.$$

The notation $\succ_h$ used in (d) is defined by

$$\mathbf{x}_h^1 \succ_h \mathbf{x}_h^2 \quad \text{means} \quad \mathbf{x}_h^1 \succsim_h \mathbf{x}_h^2 \quad \text{and not} \quad \mathbf{x}_h^2 \succsim_h \mathbf{x}_h^1;$$

that is, $\mathbf{x}_h^1 \succ \mathbf{x}_h^2$ means that $\mathbf{x}_h^1$ is preferred to $\mathbf{x}_h^2$. In view of Connexity (b),

$$\mathbf{x}_h^1 \succ_h \mathbf{x}_h^2 \quad \text{if and only if not} \quad \mathbf{x}_h^2 \succsim_h \mathbf{x}_h^1.$$

The assumptions of A.4.4 are fairly standard. Parts (a) and (b) state simply that the individual is capable of ranking alternative commodity vectors in order of preference. Part (c) and the term "continuity" attached to it, may be slightly less familiar. The preference ordering is assumed to be continuous in the sense that a strict preference between two vectors is not altered if either is altered by sufficiently small amounts; in symbols, if $\mathbf{x}_h^1 \succ_h \mathbf{x}_h^2$, then there are neighborhoods, N_1 and N_2, of $\mathbf{x}_h^1$ and $\mathbf{x}_h^2$, respectively, such that $\mathbf{x}_h \succ_h \mathbf{x}_h^2$ for all $\mathbf{x}_h \in N_1$ and $\mathbf{x}_h^1 \succ_h \mathbf{x}_h$ for all $\mathbf{x}_h \in N_2$.

This statement is equivalent to A.4.4(c). Suppose, for example, there was no such neighborhood, N_1. Then in every neighborhood of $\mathbf{x}_h^1$ there would exist $\mathbf{x}_h$ such that $\mathbf{x}_h^2 \succsim_h \mathbf{x}_h$, that is, a member of the set $\{\mathbf{x}_h \mid \mathbf{x}_h^2 \succsim_h \mathbf{x}_h\}$. Since (c) asserts that this set is closed, it must contain $\mathbf{x}_h^1$ by definition of a closed set; that is, $\mathbf{x}_h^2 \succcurlyeq_h \mathbf{x}_h^1$, contrary to the assumption $\mathbf{x}_h^1 \succ_h \mathbf{x}_h^2$.

The assumption (d) of convexity is, as always, something of a stumbling block; it will be seen in Chapter 7 that it can be relaxed. The semi-strictness condition is designed to avoid local satiation, as shown by the following lemma.

LEMMA 1. (a) Local non-satiation: For every $\mathbf{x}_h^1 \in X_h$ there exists $\mathbf{x}_h^2 \in X_h$ arbitrarily close to $\mathbf{x}_h^1$ for which $\mathbf{x}_h^2 \succ_h \mathbf{x}_h^1$.

(b) Convexity: For any $\mathbf{x}_h^0$, the set $\{\mathbf{x}_h \mid \mathbf{x}_h \succcurlyeq_h \mathbf{x}_h^0\}$ is convex.

Proof. (a) By A.4.4(e), there exists $\mathbf{x}_h^3 \succ \mathbf{x}_h^1$. By (d), $\mathbf{x}_h^2 = (1 - \alpha)\mathbf{x}_h^3 + \alpha\mathbf{x}_h^1 \succ_h \mathbf{x}_h^1$ for $0 \le \alpha < 1$. For α arbitrarily close to 1, $\mathbf{x}_h^2$ can be made arbitrarily close to $\mathbf{x}_h^1$.

(b) Let $\mathbf{x}_h^1$ and $\mathbf{x}_h^2 \in \{\mathbf{x}_h \mid \mathbf{x}_h \succcurlyeq_h \mathbf{x}_h^0\}$, and let $\mathbf{x}_h = (1 - \alpha)\mathbf{x}_h^1 + \alpha\mathbf{x}_h^2$, $0 \le \alpha \le 1$. We seek to prove that $\mathbf{x}_h \succcurlyeq \mathbf{x}_h^0$ for all α. This is trivial if $\alpha = 0$ or 1, so assume $0 < \alpha < 1$. From A.4.4(b), assume without loss of generality that $\mathbf{x}_h^1 \succcurlyeq_h \mathbf{x}_h^2$. Choose $\mathbf{x}_h^*$ so that $\mathbf{x}_h^* \succ_h \mathbf{x}_h^1$, $\mathbf{x}_h^*$ arbitrarily close to $\mathbf{x}_h^1$. Then $\mathbf{x}_h^* \succ_h \mathbf{x}_h^2$ by transitivity and A.4.4(b). Let $\mathbf{x}_h^{**} = (1 - \alpha)\mathbf{x}_h^* + \alpha\mathbf{x}_h^2$. By A.4.4(d), $\mathbf{x}_h^{**} \succ_h \mathbf{x}_h^2$, and by transitivity, $\mathbf{x}_h^{**} \succ_h \mathbf{x}_h^0$, and, in particular, $\mathbf{x}_h^{**} \in \{\mathbf{x}_h \mid \mathbf{x}_h \succcurlyeq_h \mathbf{x}_h^0\}$. Since $\mathbf{x}_h^*$ is arbitrarily close to $\mathbf{x}_h^1$, $\mathbf{x}_h^{**}$ can be chosen arbitrarily close to $\mathbf{x}_h$. Hence, $\mathbf{x}_h$ is a limit point of the set $\{\mathbf{x}_h \mid \mathbf{x}_h \succcurlyeq_h \mathbf{x}_h^0\}$; by continuity (A.4.4(c)) $\mathbf{x}_h$ belongs to this set.

Analogous to the choice of production vectors in the profit-maximizing firm, there is a choice of preferred consumption vectors by the household. We will speak of a *preferred* vector for a given set $S \subset X_h$ as a vector $\hat{\mathbf{x}}_h$ such that $\hat{\mathbf{x}}_h \in S$ and $\hat{\mathbf{x}}_h \succcurlyeq_h \mathbf{x}_h$ for all $\mathbf{x}_h \in S$. The demand functions or their generalizations are the preferred vectors $\mathbf{x}_h \in X_h$ for the set satisfying the budget constraint,

$$\mathbf{p}\mathbf{x}_h \le M_h.$$

As in the case of the firm, no preferred vector need exist; suppose the price of a commodity is zero and the household is never satiated with regard to that commodity. Further, it is also possible that there is not a unique preferred point; there may be a set of commodity vectors satisfying the budget constraint, indifferent to each other and preferred to all other bundles in X_h satisfying the budget constraint. This possibility requires that the indifference surfaces have flat sections, as, for example, when two commodities are perfect substitutes or when one commodity does not enter into consumption at all.

Remark. If $\mathbf{p} > 0$, as we shall assume, and $\mathbf{p}\mathbf{y}_f \geq 0$, all f, then the possible consumption vector, $\bar{\mathbf{x}}_h$, whose existence was guaranteed by A.4.2, obviously satisfies the budget constraint. Thus, in any competitive equilibrium, we can assume that the individual will achieve a satisfaction (in terms of the ordering about to be introduced) at least as high as that achievable from $\bar{\mathbf{x}}_h$.

To ensure the existence of equilibrium, the demand for commodities should vary continuously with the prices, in some appropriate sense of continuity. The hypotheses made do not ensure this result. Suppose there are two goods in the economy, and an individual has an initial stock of good 1, but none of good 2 and no share of any firm. Hold the price of good 2 constant, and let p_1 approach 0. The budget constraint requires that

$$p_1 x_{h1} \leq p_1 x_{h1} + p_2 x_{h2} \leq p_1 \bar{x}_{h1},$$

so that for $p_1 > 0$, $x_{h1} \leq \bar{x}_{h1}$. On the other hand, when $p_1 = 0$, the set of commodity vectors compatible with the budget constraint is the set of all pairs, $(x_{h1},0)$, and the chosen value of x_{h1} may be considerably larger than $\bar{x}_{h1}$. This discontinuity will necessarily occur in some part of the price space, except in the unrealistic case in which the household has a positive initial holding of all goods.

On the other hand, there is another optimization problem that is very similar to choice of the preferred point under a budget constraint, but for which the chosen point varies, in an appropriate sense, continuously with prices. This is the problem of choosing $\mathbf{x}_h$ to minimize the cost of achieving a given level of satisfaction, or formally, minimizing $\mathbf{p}\mathbf{x}_h$ subject to the constraint that $\mathbf{x}_h \succcurlyeq_h \mathbf{x}_h^0$ for some prescribed $\mathbf{x}_h^0$. The chosen bundle is usually known in economic literature as the *compensated* demand function, since real income (level of satisfaction) is held constant, we imagine, by accompanying each change of price vector with a change of nominal income so that the commodity vector indifferent to the original one can be achieved.

The uncompensated and compensated demand functions are closely related.

LEMMA 2. If $\mathbf{x}_h^*$ is a preferred vector subject to a budget constraint, $\mathbf{p}\mathbf{x}_h \le M_h$, $\mathbf{x}_h \in X_h$, then $\mathbf{x}_h^*$ minimizes $\mathbf{p}\mathbf{x}_h$ subject to the constraint $\mathbf{x}_h \succcurlyeq_h \mathbf{x}_h^*$.

Proof. Suppose the conclusion is false. Then there exists $\mathbf{x}_h^1 \succcurlyeq_h \mathbf{x}_h^*$, for which $\mathbf{p}\mathbf{x}_h^1 < \mathbf{p}\mathbf{x}_h^*$. By local non-satiation (Lemma 4.1(a)), there exists $\mathbf{x}_h^2$ arbitrarily close to $\mathbf{x}_h^1$, for which $\mathbf{x}_h^2 \succ_h \mathbf{x}_h^1$ and, therefore, $\mathbf{x}_h^2 \succ_h \mathbf{x}_h^*$. By choosing $\mathbf{x}_h^2$ close enough to $\mathbf{x}_h^1$ we can guarantee $\mathbf{p}\mathbf{x}_h^2 \le \mathbf{p}\mathbf{x}_h^* \le M_h$, which contradicts the hypothesis that $\mathbf{x}_h^*$ is preferred in the budget constraint.

The converse of Lemma 4.2 is valid only if expenditures are above the minimum possible.

LEMMA 3. If $\mathbf{x}_h^*$ minimizes $\mathbf{p}\mathbf{x}_h$ subject to the constraint $\mathbf{x}_h \succcurlyeq_h \mathbf{x}_h^0$ and if $\mathbf{p}\mathbf{x}_h^* > \mathbf{p}\mathbf{x}_h^1$ for some $\mathbf{x}_h^1 \in X_h$, then $\mathbf{x}_h^*$ is preferred in the budget constraint, $\mathbf{p}\mathbf{x}_h \le \mathbf{p}\mathbf{x}_h^*$.

Proof. Consider any $\mathbf{x}_h' \in X_h$ for which $\mathbf{p}\mathbf{x}_h' \le \mathbf{p}\mathbf{x}_h^*$. Let

$$\mathbf{x}_h(\alpha) = (1 - \alpha)\mathbf{x}_h' + \alpha\mathbf{x}_h^1;$$

then

$$\mathbf{p}\mathbf{x}_h(\alpha) = (1 - \alpha)\mathbf{p}\mathbf{x}_h' + \alpha\mathbf{p}\mathbf{x}_h^1 < \mathbf{p}\mathbf{x}_h^* \qquad \text{for } 0 < \alpha \le 1.$$

If $\mathbf{x}_h(\alpha) \succcurlyeq_h \mathbf{x}_h^0$, then by hypothesis, $\mathbf{p}\mathbf{x}_h^* \le \mathbf{p}\mathbf{x}_h(\alpha)$. Hence, $\mathbf{x}_h^0 \succ_h \mathbf{x}_h(\alpha)$ and, therefore, $\mathbf{x}_h(\alpha) \in \{\mathbf{x}_h \mid \mathbf{x}_h^0 \succcurlyeq_h \mathbf{x}_h\}$. Since this last set is closed, it contains $\lim_{\alpha \to 0} \mathbf{x}_h(\alpha) = \mathbf{x}_h'$. Since $\mathbf{x}_h^* \succcurlyeq_h \mathbf{x}_h^0$, $\mathbf{x}_h^* \succcurlyeq_h \mathbf{x}_h'$ for any $\mathbf{x}_h'$ for which $\mathbf{p}\mathbf{x}_h' \le \mathbf{p}\mathbf{x}_h^*$.

In fact, the failure of the compensated demand functions to agree with the uncompensated functions on the boundary of the price domain is useful, for it can be shown that the compensated demand functions are continuous in an appropriate sense. Since these functions may be multi-valued, as we have seen, we need a broader concept of continuity. A multi-valued function will be called a *correspondence*; we define the correspondence $\Phi(\mathbf{x})$ to be *upper semi-continuous* if for any sequences $\{\mathbf{x}^\nu\}$, $\{\mathbf{y}^\nu\}$, the conditions $\mathbf{x}^\nu \to \mathbf{x}$, $\mathbf{y}^\nu \to \mathbf{y}$, $\mathbf{y}^\nu \in \phi(\mathbf{x}^\nu)$, imply that $\mathbf{y} \in \Phi(\mathbf{x})$.

Also, defining the *compensated demand correspondence*, $X_h(\mathbf{p},\mathbf{x}_h^0) = \{\mathbf{x}_h' \mid \mathbf{x}_h' \text{ minimizes } \mathbf{p}\mathbf{x}_h \text{ subject to } \mathbf{x}_h \in X_h, \mathbf{x}_h \succcurlyeq_h \mathbf{x}_h^0\}$.

LEMMA 4. $X_h(\mathbf{p},\mathbf{x}_h^0)$ is upper semi-continuous in $\mathbf{p}$ for fixed $\mathbf{x}_h^0$.

Proof. Let $\{\mathbf{p}^\nu\}$ be a sequence with $\mathbf{p}^\nu \to \mathbf{p}$; suppose $\mathbf{x}_h^\nu \in X_h(\mathbf{p}^\nu,\mathbf{x}_h^0)$ and $\mathbf{x}_h^\nu \to \mathbf{x}_h$. Then $\mathbf{x}_h^\nu \succcurlyeq_h \mathbf{x}_h^0$, all ν, and by continuity of preferences, $\mathbf{x}_h \succsim_h \mathbf{x}_h^0$. Take any $\mathbf{x}'_h$ such that $\mathbf{x}'_h \succsim_h \mathbf{x}_h^0$. Then, by definition of $X_h(\mathbf{p}^\nu,\mathbf{x}_h^0)$, $\mathbf{p}^\nu\mathbf{x}_h^\nu \leq \mathbf{p}^\nu\mathbf{x}'_h$. In the limit, $\mathbf{p}\mathbf{x}_h \leq \mathbf{p}\mathbf{x}'_h$.

Q.E.D.

We will not in fact make use of Lemma 4.4 as it stands, but it motivates the strategy for proving the existence of competitive equilibrium used in Chapter 5. It is easier to establish the existence of an equilibrium in a compensated sense because the compensated demand correspondences are continuous; then it has to be shown (with the aid of an additional assumption) that the compensated equilibrium assigns each individual an expenditure above the minimal possible, so that the individual is in fact achieving a preferred point under the budget constraint.

2. Utility Functions

It turns out that the assumption A.4.4 made on the preference relation suffices to permit a continuous numerical representation.

DEFINITION 1. A real-valued function, U_h, defined on X_h, is a *utility function* if it has the property that $\mathbf{x}_h^1 \succsim_h \mathbf{x}_h^2$ if and only if $U_h(\mathbf{x}_h^1) \geq U_h(\mathbf{x}_h^2)$.

The numerical representation, although it can be dispensed with, is extremely useful in simplifying the proofs.

Since we are dealing with a single household in this section, we will omit the subscript h in all uses in order to lighten the notational burden. Also, for the purpose of establishing the existence of a continuous utility function, we will not need the full force of A.4.4, only assumptions (a), (b), and (c) (transitivity, connexity, and continuity).

The two assumptions that play the most important roles in demonstrating the existence of a numerical representation are the continuity of the ordering (A.4.4(c)) and the convexity of X (actually, the latter could be replaced by the much weaker assumption that any two points in X could be connected by a continuous path entirely contained in X; for a convex set, the line segment joining two given points is such a path).

First, a utility function is constructed for a subset of X. Specifically, an arbitrary element, $\mathbf{x}^0 \in X$, is chosen, and a continuous utility function is constructed for the subset of X for which $\mathbf{x} \succsim \mathbf{x}^0$. The method is simple: For any $\mathbf{x}$ satisfying this condition, the utility of $\mathbf{x}$, $U(\mathbf{x})$, is taken to be the distance from $\mathbf{x}^0$ to the set of points preferred or indifferent to $\mathbf{x}$. (By the distance from a point to a set is meant the *smallest* distance from the given point to any point of the set.)

Then let

$$C(\mathbf{x}) = \{\mathbf{x}' \mid \mathbf{x}' \succcurlyeq \mathbf{x}\}$$

be the upper contour set through $\mathbf{x}$. By A.4.4(c), this set is closed. Let $\rho(\mathbf{x}) = |\mathbf{x} - \mathbf{x}^0|$, the distance from $\mathbf{x}^0$ to $\mathbf{x}$. Since $\rho(\mathbf{x}')$ is a continuous function bounded from below (it is non-negative) and $C(\mathbf{x})$ is closed, $\rho(\mathbf{x}')$ has a minimum as $\mathbf{x}'$ varies over $C(\mathbf{x})$. We define

$$U(\mathbf{x}) = \min_{\mathbf{x}' \in C(\mathbf{x})} \rho(\mathbf{x}), \tag{1}$$

and we will show that $U(\mathbf{x})$ is indeed a continuous utility function. The minimum in (1) is taken on at one or more points of $C(\mathbf{x})$; let

$$M(\mathbf{x}) = C(\mathbf{x}) \cap \{\mathbf{x}' \mid \rho(\mathbf{x}') = U(\mathbf{x})\}. \tag{2}$$

Since $M(\mathbf{x}) \subset C(\mathbf{x})$, clearly $\mathbf{x}' \succcurlyeq \mathbf{x}$ for all $\mathbf{x}' \in M(\mathbf{x})$. In fact, it must be that $\mathbf{x}' \sim \mathbf{x}$. Suppose that $\mathbf{x}' \in M(\mathbf{x})$, $\mathbf{x}' \succ \mathbf{x}$. There is, by Continuity, a neighborhood of $\mathbf{x}'$ such that $\mathbf{x}'' \succcurlyeq \mathbf{x}$ for all $\mathbf{x}''$ in the neighborhood. Choose $\alpha > 0$, but sufficiently small so that $(1 - \alpha)\mathbf{x}' + \alpha\mathbf{x}^0 \succcurlyeq \mathbf{x}$; in particular, choose $\alpha < 1$. But

$$\begin{aligned}\rho[(1 - \alpha)\mathbf{x}' + \alpha\mathbf{x}^0] &= |(1 - \alpha)\mathbf{x}' + \alpha\mathbf{x}^0 - \mathbf{x}^0| \\ &= (1 - \alpha)|\mathbf{x}' - \mathbf{x}^0| = (1 - \alpha)\rho(\mathbf{x}') = (1 - \alpha)U(\mathbf{x}).\end{aligned}$$

By definition (1), $U(\mathbf{x}) \leq \rho[(1 - \alpha)\mathbf{x}' + \alpha\mathbf{x}^0]$, so that $(1 - \alpha)U(\mathbf{x}) \geq U(\mathbf{x})$ or $U(\mathbf{x}) \leq 0$. Since $U(\mathbf{x})$ has been defined to be non-negative, $U(\mathbf{x}) = 0$. Therefore $\rho(\mathbf{x}') = 0$, or $\mathbf{x}' = \mathbf{x}^0$. Since we are considering only $\mathbf{x} \succcurlyeq \mathbf{x}^0$, however, the assumption $\mathbf{x}' \succ \mathbf{x}$ has been contradicted.

$$\text{If} \quad \mathbf{x}' \in M(\mathbf{x}), \quad \text{then} \quad \mathbf{x}' \sim \mathbf{x}. \tag{3}$$

To show that $U(\mathbf{x})$ is a utility function, it suffices by D.4.1 and Connexity, A.4.4(b), to show that $\mathbf{x}^1 \succcurlyeq \mathbf{x}^2$ implies $U(\mathbf{x}^1) \geq U(\mathbf{x}^2)$ and that $\mathbf{x}^1 \succ \mathbf{x}^2$ implies $U(\mathbf{x}^1) > U(\mathbf{x}^2)$. The first follows immediately from the definition of $U(\mathbf{x})$, (1), and Transitivity (A.4.4(a)); Transitivity implies that $C(\mathbf{x}^1) \subset C(\mathbf{x}^2)$, the minimization in (1) occurs over a subset, and hence the minimum achieved cannot be any lower. Now suppose that $\mathbf{x}^1 \succ \mathbf{x}^2$. Then $M(\mathbf{x}^1) \subset C(\mathbf{x}^1) \subset$

$C(\mathbf{x}^2)$. If $U(\mathbf{x}^1) = U(\mathbf{x}^2)$, then $M(\mathbf{x}^1) \subset M(\mathbf{x}^2)$, by (2). If $\mathbf{x}' \in M(\mathbf{x}^1)$, then by (3), $\mathbf{x}' \sim \mathbf{x}^1$ and also $\mathbf{x}' \sim \mathbf{x}^2$, so that $\mathbf{x}^1 \sim \mathbf{x}^2$, a contradiction. Since we know that $U(\mathbf{x}^1) \geqq U(\mathbf{x}^2)$ and have just shown that $U(\mathbf{x}^1) \neq U(\mathbf{x}^2)$, it must be that $U(\mathbf{x}^1) > U(\mathbf{x}^2)$. Therefore $U(\mathbf{x})$ is a utility function for those $\mathbf{x} \in X$ for which $\mathbf{x} \succcurlyeq \mathbf{x}^0$.

To demonstrate that $U(\mathbf{x})$ is a continuous function, it suffices to show that for every real number u, the two sets $\{\mathbf{x} \mid U(\mathbf{x}) \geq u\}$ and $\{\mathbf{x} \mid U(\mathbf{x}) \leq u\}$ are closed. Consider the first set. Let $\{\mathbf{x}^\nu\}$ be a sequence such that $U(\mathbf{x}^\nu) \geq u$, all ν, $\mathbf{x}^\nu \to \mathbf{x}$. Let $\mathbf{x}'$ be any element of $M(\mathbf{x})$; by Lemma 4.1(a), we can choose $\mathbf{x}'' \succ \mathbf{x}'$ and arbitrarily close. Certainly, $U(\mathbf{x}'') \leq \rho(\mathbf{x}'')$, by (1). On the other hand, since $\mathbf{x}'' \succcurlyeq \mathbf{x}'$ and $\mathbf{x}' \sim \mathbf{x}$, by (3), $\mathbf{x}'' \succ \mathbf{x}$. By Continuity, $\mathbf{x}'' \succcurlyeq \mathbf{x}^\nu$ for all ν sufficiently large, $U(\mathbf{x}'') \geq U(\mathbf{x}^\nu) \geq u$, so that $\rho(\mathbf{x}'') \geq u$. But $\mathbf{x}''$ can be chosen as close as desired to $\mathbf{x}'$; since $\rho(\mathbf{x})$ is continuous, we can assert that $u \leq \rho(\mathbf{x}') = U(\mathbf{x})$, so that the set $\{\mathbf{x} \mid U(\mathbf{x}) \geq u\}$ has been shown to be closed.

Now let $\{\mathbf{x}^\nu\}$ be any sequence such that $U(\mathbf{x}^\nu) \leq u$, all ν, $\mathbf{x}^\nu \to \mathbf{x}$. For each ν, choose $\mathbf{x}'^\nu \in M(\mathbf{x}^\nu)$. Since $\rho(\mathbf{x}'^\nu) = U(\mathbf{x}^\nu)$, we have that $\rho(\mathbf{x}'^\nu) \leq u$, all ν. Thus, the sequence $\{\mathbf{x}'^\nu\}$ is bounded and therefore has a limit point $\mathbf{x}'$, for which $\rho(\mathbf{x}') \leq u$. Since $\mathbf{x}'^\nu \sim \mathbf{x}^\nu$, by (3) and $\mathbf{x}^\nu \to \mathbf{x}$, it follows, by restricting attention to the subsequence of $\{\mathbf{x}'^\nu\}$ that converges to $\mathbf{x}'$, that $\mathbf{x}' \sim \mathbf{x}$, where use is made of the Continuity of preferences. Then by definition of $U(\mathbf{x})$ and the fact that it is a utility function,

$$U(\mathbf{x}) = U(\mathbf{x}') \leq \rho(\mathbf{x}') \leq u,$$

so that the set $\{\mathbf{x} \mid U(\mathbf{x}) \leq u\}$ is indeed closed, and therefore, $U(\mathbf{x})$ is a continuous utility function over the set $\{\mathbf{x} \mid \mathbf{x} \succcurlyeq \mathbf{x}^0\}$.

It remains to extend $U(\mathbf{x})$ in some appropriate way to the entire consumption possibility set, X. If there is a least preferred point, that is, a point $\mathbf{x}^0$ such that $\mathbf{x} \succcurlyeq \mathbf{x}^0$ for all $\mathbf{x} \in X$, then simply choose $\mathbf{x}^0$ in the previous construction. Otherwise, for every $\mathbf{x} \in X$, there exists $\mathbf{x}' \in X$ such that $\mathbf{x} \succ \mathbf{x}'$, and we consider this case. It will be shown next that

Any compact non-null subset of X contains
a least preferred point.

To see this, consider first any finite subset X'' of X. Then by Transitivity, there certainly exists a least preferred point $\mathbf{x}''$ of X''.

Now let X' be any compact subset of X and X'' any finite subset of X'. By Transitivity, we see that

$$X' \cap \{\mathbf{x}' \mid \mathbf{x}'' \succcurlyeq \mathbf{x}'\} \subset X' \cap \{\mathbf{x}' \mid \mathbf{x} \succcurlyeq \mathbf{x}'\} \qquad \text{for all } \mathbf{x} \in X'',$$

or equivalently,

$$X' \cap \{\mathbf{x}' \mid \mathbf{x}'' \succcurlyeq \mathbf{x}'\} = \bigcap_{\mathbf{x} \in X''} [X' \cap \{\mathbf{x}' \mid \mathbf{x} \succcurlyeq \mathbf{x}'\}];$$

that is, the set of consumption vectors $\mathbf{x}'$ in X' not superior to $\mathbf{x}''$ is the intersection of the sets of consumption vectors not superior to the various members of X''. Since $\mathbf{x}''$ belongs to the left-hand set, we see that the intersection on the right is non-null. The sets

$$X' \cap \{\mathbf{x}' \mid \mathbf{x} \succcurlyeq \mathbf{x}'\}$$

are compact sets. If we consider the entire family of such sets as $\mathbf{x}$ varies over X', it has been shown that the intersection of any finite subfamily is non-null. By a well-known theorem of analysis, it follows that the intersection of all such sets is non-null, so that there exists $\mathbf{x}^*$ such that,

$$\mathbf{x}^* \in X' \cap \{\mathbf{x}' \mid \mathbf{x} \succcurlyeq \mathbf{x}'\} \qquad \text{for all } \mathbf{x} \text{ in } X',$$

and therefore $\mathbf{x} \succcurlyeq \mathbf{x}^*$ for all $\mathbf{x} \in X'$, $\mathbf{x}^* \in X'$.

In particular, for any fixed positive integer μ, the set $X \cap \{\mathbf{x} \mid |\mathbf{x}| \leq \mu\}$ is compact; it is non-null for all μ sufficiently large. By (4), it has a least preferred point, $\mathbf{x}^{0\mu}$. Further, since

$$X \cap \{\mathbf{x} \mid |x| \leq \mu\} \subset X \cap \{\mathbf{x} \mid |\mathbf{x}| \leq \mu + 1\},$$

it must be true that $\mathbf{x}^{0\mu} \succcurlyeq \mathbf{x}^{0,\mu+1}$ for all μ.

Since we are now assuming that X has no least preferred point, it is true that for every μ there exists an $\mathbf{x} \in X$ such that $\mathbf{x}^{0\mu} \succ \mathbf{x}$. By construction, it must be that $|\mathbf{x}| > \mu$. For any $\mu' \geq |\mathbf{x}|$, $\mathbf{x}^{0\mu'} \preccurlyeq \mathbf{x}$, by construction. Now define $\mu(\nu)$ recursively as follows:

$$\mu(1) = \min\{\mu \mid X \cap \{\mathbf{x} \mid |\mathbf{x}| \leq \mu\} \quad \text{is non-null}\},$$
$$\mu(\nu + 1) = \min\{\mu \mid \mathbf{x}^{0\mu(\nu)} \succ \mathbf{x}^{0\mu}\}.$$

By the previous discussion, $\mu(\nu + 1) \geq \mu(\nu) + 1$, so that $\mu(\nu) \geq \nu$, and in particular $\mu(\nu) \to +\infty$. Define

$$\mathbf{x}^{\nu} = \mathbf{x}^{0\mu(\nu)};$$

then $\mathbf{x}^\nu \succ \mathbf{x}^{\nu+1}$. Further, for any $\mathbf{x} \in X$, $\mathbf{x} \succcurlyeq \mathbf{x}^{0\mu}$ for $\mu \geq |\mathbf{x}|$; therefore, for any $\mathbf{x} \in X$, $\mathbf{x} \succcurlyeq \mathbf{x}^\nu$ for all ν sufficiently large.

The sequence $\{\mathbf{x}^\nu\}$ has two basic properties: It is strictly decreasing in preference, $\mathbf{x}^\nu \succ \mathbf{x}^{\nu+1}$ for all ν, and every $\mathbf{x} \in X$ is preferred or indifferent to $\mathbf{x}^\nu$ for all ν sufficiently large.

We can take in turn each $\mathbf{x}^\nu$ as the $\mathbf{x}^0$ of our earlier construction and find a continuous utility function for the set $\{\mathbf{x} \mid \mathbf{x} \succcurlyeq \mathbf{x}^\nu\}$. Let $U(\mathbf{x};\mathbf{x}^\nu)$ be this utility function. As is well known and obvious, if U is a utility function and $F(u)$ is a strictly increasing function on the real numbers, then $F[U(\mathbf{x})]$ is also a utility function in the sense of D.4.1. If F is continuous, then so is $F[U(\mathbf{x})]$. In particular, if $F(u) = a + bu$, $b > 0$, then $a + bU(\mathbf{x})$ is a continuous utility function. Further, by suitable choice of a and b, this utility function can be made to assume prescribed values at two given points.

We will choose arbitrarily the utility values for the points $\mathbf{x}^\nu$. Then, for each ν, a utility function will be chosen, by the procedure just given, to assume the prescribed values at $\mathbf{x}^{\nu-1}$ and $\mathbf{x}^\nu$; if $\nu = 1$, only the value at $\mathbf{x}^1$ is prescribed. Finally, the utility function is defined for any given $\mathbf{x}$ as the value of the utility function associated with $\mathbf{x}^\nu$ for the smallest ν for which $\mathbf{x} \succcurlyeq \mathbf{x}^\nu$.

Formally, let $\{u^\nu\}$ be a strictly decreasing sequence of real numbers. For each ν, define $U_\nu(\mathbf{x}) = a_\nu + b_\nu U(\mathbf{x};\mathbf{x}^\nu)$ for $\mathbf{x} \succcurlyeq \mathbf{x}^\nu$ by choosing a_ν, b_ν so that $U_\nu(\mathbf{x}^{\nu-1}) = u_{\nu-1}$, $U_\nu(\mathbf{x}^\nu) = u_\nu$. (For $\nu = 1$, we require only that $U_1(\mathbf{x}^1) = u_1$.) Then for each $\mathbf{x}$, there is precisely one ν such that $\mathbf{x}^{\nu-1} \succ \mathbf{x} \succcurlyeq \mathbf{x}^\nu$, or else $\mathbf{x} \succcurlyeq \mathbf{x}^1$. Let $U(\mathbf{x}) = U_\nu(\mathbf{x})$.

The function $U(\mathbf{x})$ is then defined for all x. It remains to show, first, that $U(\mathbf{x})$ is a utility function, and second, that it is continuous. It is obvious that if $\mathbf{x}^a \sim \mathbf{x}^b$, then $U(\mathbf{x}^a) = U(\mathbf{x}^b)$. Suppose $\mathbf{x}^a \succ \mathbf{x}^b$. There are three possibilities: (a) $\mathbf{x}^a \succ \mathbf{x}^b \succcurlyeq \mathbf{x}^1$; (b) $\mathbf{x}^{\nu-1} \succ \mathbf{x}^a \succ \mathbf{x}^b \succcurlyeq \mathbf{x}^\nu$ for some ν; (c) $\mathbf{x}^a \succcurlyeq \mathbf{x}^\nu \succ \mathbf{x}^b$ for some ν. If (a) holds, then $U(\mathbf{x}^a) = U_1(\mathbf{x}^a)$, $U(\mathbf{x}^b) = U_1(\mathbf{x}^b)$; since U_1 is a utility function, $U(\mathbf{x}^a) > U(\mathbf{x}^b)$. If (b) holds, then similarly, $U(\mathbf{x}^a) = U_\nu(\mathbf{x}^a)$, $U(\mathbf{x}^b) = U_\nu(\mathbf{x}^b)$, and again $U(\mathbf{x}^a) > U(\mathbf{x}^b)$. If (c) holds, let ν' be the smallest ν such that $\mathbf{x}^a \succcurlyeq \mathbf{x}^\nu$, and ν'' the largest ν such that $\mathbf{x}^\nu \succ \mathbf{x}^b$; clearly, $\nu' \geq \nu''$, so that $u_{\nu'} \geq u_{\nu''}$. Then $U(\mathbf{x}^a) = U_{\nu'}(\mathbf{x}^a) \geq U_{\nu'}(\mathbf{x}^{\nu'}) = u_{\nu'}$, and $U(\mathbf{x}^b) = U_{\nu''+1}(\mathbf{x}^b) < U_{\nu''+1}(\mathbf{x}^{\nu''}) = u_{\nu''} \leq u_{\nu'} \leq U(\mathbf{x}^a)$. Hence, $U(\mathbf{x})$ is a utility function.

It remains to prove continuity. If $\mathbf{x} \succ \mathbf{x}^1$ or $\mathbf{x}^{\nu-1} \succ \mathbf{x} \succcurlyeq \mathbf{x}^\nu$ for some ν, then the same relation holds for $\mathbf{x}'$ sufficiently close to $\mathbf{x}$, by

Continuity, so that $U(\mathbf{x}') = U_1(\mathbf{x}')$ or $U_\nu(\mathbf{x}')$ in a neighborhood of $\mathbf{x}$; since the functions $U_\nu(\mathbf{x})$ are continuous at $\mathbf{x}$, so is $U(\mathbf{x})$.

Now suppose $\mathbf{x} \sim \mathbf{x}^\nu$ for some ν. Let $\{\mathbf{x}^\rho\}$ be a sequence such that $\mathbf{x}^\rho \to \mathbf{x}$. If $\mathbf{x}^\rho \succcurlyeq \mathbf{x}$, all ρ, then $\mathbf{x}^{\nu-1} \succ \mathbf{x}^\rho$ for ρ sufficiently large, if $\nu > 1$. Hence, $U(\mathbf{x}^\rho) = U_\nu(\mathbf{x}^\rho)$ for ρ large; by continuity of $U_\nu(\mathbf{x})$, $U_\nu(\mathbf{x}^\rho) \to U_\nu(\mathbf{x}) = U(\mathbf{x})$. Similarly, if $\mathbf{x} \succ \mathbf{x}^\rho$ for all ρ, $\mathbf{x}^\rho \succcurlyeq \mathbf{x}^{\nu+1}$ for ρ sufficiently large, $U(\mathbf{x}^\rho) = U_{\nu+1}(\mathbf{x}^\rho)$ for ρ large, and $U(\mathbf{x}^\rho) \to U_{\nu+1}(\mathbf{x}) = U_{\nu+1}(\mathbf{x}^\nu) = u_\nu = U(\mathbf{x})$. Finally, if the sequence $\{\mathbf{x}^\rho\}$ contains some members inferior to $\mathbf{x}$ and others not inferior, we can divide it into two sequences, for each of which $U(\mathbf{x}^\rho)$ converges to $U(\mathbf{x})$.

THEOREM 1. Every preference ordering satisfying A.4.4(a)–(c) and defined over a convex set can be represented by a continuous utility function.

To state the implications of A.4.4(d) for the utility function, introduce the definition

DEFINITION 2. A function $f(\mathbf{x})$ is said to be semi-strictly quasi-concave if

$$f(\mathbf{x}^1) \geq f(\mathbf{x}^2) \quad \text{implies} \quad f[\alpha\mathbf{x}^1 + (1-\alpha)\mathbf{x}^2] \geq f(x^2), \qquad 0 \leq \alpha \leq 1$$

and

$$f(\mathbf{x}^1) > f(\mathbf{x}^2) \quad \text{implies} \quad f[\alpha\mathbf{x}^1 + (1-\alpha)\mathbf{x}^2] > f(\mathbf{x}^2), \qquad 0 < \alpha \leq 1.$$

As noted earlier, if $U(\mathbf{x})$ is a continuous utility function, then for any $b > 0$, $a + bU(\mathbf{x})$ is also a continuous utility function. This freedom of choice will be used here to set a zero utility level. With $b = 1$, we can always ensure that $U(\bar{\bar{\mathbf{x}}}) = 0$, where $\bar{\bar{\mathbf{x}}}$ is the possible consumption vector named in A.4.2.

Then, with the aid of Lemma 4.1, we state

Corollary 1. Under A.4.1 and A.4.4, for every household h there is a continuous semi-strictly quasi-concave utility function, $U_h(\mathbf{x}_h)$, defined on X_h, such that for every $\mathbf{x}_h$, there exists $\mathbf{x}'_h$ arbitrarily close, for which $U_h(\mathbf{x}'_h) > U_h(\mathbf{x}_h)$, and such that $U_h(\bar{\bar{\mathbf{x}}}_h) = 0$ for a commodity vector, $\bar{\bar{\mathbf{x}}}_h \in X_h$, such that $\bar{\bar{\mathbf{x}}}_{hi} \leq \bar{x}_{hi}$, all i, $\bar{\bar{x}}_{hi} < \bar{x}_{hi}$ if $\bar{x}_{hi} > 0$.

The aim of the consumer, then, is to maximize $U_h(\mathbf{x}_h)$ subject to $\mathbf{x}_h \in X_h$, $\mathbf{px} \leq M_h$, where M_h is defined in A.4.3.

3. Individual- and Market-Excess Demands

In the discussion of equilibrium, we are primarily interested in excess demands on the market, that is, vectors $\mathbf{z}$ of the form

$$\mathbf{z} = \sum_h \mathbf{x}_h - \mathbf{y} - \bar{\mathbf{x}}, \qquad \mathbf{x}_h \in X_h, \mathbf{y} \in Y.$$

Here, because of our conventions as to signs,

$$\sum_h \mathbf{x}_h$$

is the aggregate vector of demands by households, $\mathbf{y}$ the aggregate vector of goods supplied by firms, and $\bar{\mathbf{x}}$ the aggregate vector of supplies initially available before production. The excess-demand vector is a function of the decisions of all units of the economy, households and firms:

$$\mathbf{z} = \sum_h \mathbf{x}_h - \sum_f \mathbf{y}_f - \bar{\mathbf{x}} \qquad \mathbf{x}_h \in X_h, \mathbf{y}_f \in Y_f.$$

In D.3.3 we introduced the notion of a production allocation, which is a large vector composed of vectors, each of which is a possible production vector for one firm. As noted, it is an element of the Cartesian product of the production possibility sets of the different firms, $\times_f Y_f$. Analogously, we introduce

DEFINITION 3. A *consumption allocation* is any element, x, of

$$\mathscr{X} = \times_h X_h,$$

and an *allocation*, $w = (x,y)$, is a consumption allocation and a production allocation, that is, an element of the set

$$\mathscr{W} = \mathscr{X} \times \mathscr{Y}.$$

DEFINITION 4. The *excess demand* is a linear function over the set of allocations,

$$\mathbf{z}(w) = \sum_h \mathbf{x}_h - \sum_f \mathbf{y}_f - \bar{\mathbf{x}},$$

where

$$w = (x,y) \in \mathscr{W}.$$

To say that an allocation is feasible is simply to say that the corresponding excess-demand vector is non-positive in each component, for then for each commodity aggregate supply, both from production and from initial endowment, exceeds or equals aggregate requirements of consumers.

DEFINITION 5. An allocation, ω, is *feasible* if $\mathbf{z}(\omega) \leq 0$. The set of feasible allocations will be denoted by

$$\hat{\mathscr{W}} = \mathscr{W} \cap \{\omega \mid \mathbf{z}(\omega) \leq 0\}.$$

THEOREM 2. The set of feasible allocations, $\hat{\mathscr{W}}$, is compact and convex.

Proof. From D.4.3., A.4.1., and A.3.3, $\mathscr{W}$ is a Cartesian product of convex sets and, therefore, convex. Since $\mathbf{z}(\omega)$ is a linear function, by D.4.4, the set $\{\omega \mid \mathbf{z}(\omega) \leq 0\}$ is convex. By D.4.5, $\hat{\mathscr{W}}$ is the intersection of convex sets and, therefore, convex.

Let $\hat{\mathscr{Y}}'$ be the projection of $\hat{\mathscr{W}}$ on $\mathscr{Y}$, that is,

$$\hat{\mathscr{Y}}' = \mathscr{Y} \cap \{y \mid \mathbf{z}(x,y) \leq 0 \quad \text{for some } x \in \mathscr{X}\},$$

and similarly let $\hat{\mathscr{X}}$ be the projection of $\hat{\mathscr{W}}$ on $\mathscr{X}$,

$$\hat{\mathscr{X}} = \mathscr{X} \cap \{x \mid \mathbf{z}(x,y) \leq 0 \quad \text{for some } y \in \mathscr{Y}\}.$$

If $y \in \hat{\mathscr{Y}}'$, then

$$\sum_f \mathbf{y}_f + \bar{\mathbf{x}} \geq \sum_h \mathbf{x}_h \geq 0,$$

for some $x \in \mathscr{X}$, so that, by D.3.5, $\hat{\mathscr{Y}}' \subset \hat{\mathscr{Y}}$, where $\hat{\mathscr{Y}}$ is the set of feasible production allocations. Then $\hat{\mathscr{Y}}$ is bounded, as shown in T.3.2., and therefore, so is $\hat{\mathscr{Y}}'$.

If $x \in \hat{\mathscr{X}}$, then $x \geq 0$ and

$$\sum_h \mathbf{x}_h \leq \bar{\mathbf{x}} + \sum_f \mathbf{y}_f \qquad \text{for some } y \in \mathscr{Y}.$$

But then y must belong to $\hat{\mathscr{Y}}'$, by definition, and therefore, is bounded above. If $x \geq 0$,

$$\sum_h \mathbf{x}_h \text{ bounded above} \qquad \text{for } x \in \hat{\mathscr{X}},$$

then $\hat{\mathscr{X}}$ must be bounded. If the projections of $\hat{\mathscr{W}}$ on both $\mathscr{X}$ and $\mathscr{Y}$ are bounded, however, then $\hat{\mathscr{W}}$ itself must be bounded. Since it is obviously closed, it must be compact.

4. Feasible and Efficient Utility Allocations

We will be interested in the possibility that a given household achieves a certain utility level, and more generally, in the utility levels achieved by all households.

DEFINITION 6. The set of *u_h-possible consumption vectors* for household h is

$$X_h(u_h) = \{\mathbf{x}_h \mid U_h(\mathbf{x}_h) \geq u_h\}.$$

By a utility allocation, $\mathbf{u}$, we will mean a vector whose hth component, u_h, is a possible utility for household h.

DEFINITION 7. The set of *$\mathbf{u}$-possible consumption allocations* is

$$\mathscr{X}(\mathbf{u}) = \mathop{\times}_{h} X_h(u_h),$$

that is, the Cartesian product of the sets of u_h-possible consumption vectors for the different households h.

DEFINITION 8. The set of *$\mathbf{u}$-possible allocations* is

$$\mathscr{W}(\mathbf{u}) = \mathscr{X}(\mathbf{u}) \times \mathscr{Y};$$

that is, a $\mathbf{u}$-possible allocation is a $\mathbf{u}$-possible consumption allocation and a possible production allocation.

We will be interested in the excess demands corresponding to the u-possible allocations.

DEFINITION 9. The set of *$\mathbf{u}$-possible excess demands* is the image of $\mathscr{W}(\mathbf{u})$ under the linear mapping $\mathbf{z}(\omega)$, that is,

$$Z(\mathbf{u}) = \{\mathbf{z} \mid \mathbf{z} = \mathbf{z}(\omega) \quad \text{for some } \omega \in \mathscr{W}(\mathbf{u})\}.$$

Analogous to the notion of feasibility is that of *$\mathbf{u}$-feasibility*, the ability of the economy to achieve a utility allocation $\mathbf{u}$ within the limits of its resources.

DEFINITION 10. The set of *$\mathbf{u}$-feasible allocations* is the set of $\mathbf{u}$-possible allocations that also are feasible;

$$\hat{\mathscr{W}}(\mathbf{u}) = \mathscr{W}(\mathbf{u}) \cap \{\omega \mid \mathbf{z}(\omega) \leq \mathbf{0}\}.$$

DEFINITION 11. A *$\mathbf{u}$-feasible excess demand* is the excess demand corresponding to a $\mathbf{u}$-feasible allocation; that is, $\hat{Z}(\mathbf{u})$ is the image of $\hat{\mathscr{W}}(\mathbf{u})$ under the linear mapping $\mathbf{z}(\omega)$.

THEOREM 3. For each **u**, the set of **u**-feasible allocations $\hat{\mathscr{W}}(\mathbf{u})$ is compact and convex.

T.4.3 is proved exactly the same way as T.4.2, with X_n everywhere replaced by $X_h(u_h)$.

Corollary 3. For each **u**, $\hat{Z}(\mathbf{u})$ is compact and convex.

Proof. From T.4.3, since $\hat{Z}(\mathbf{u})$ is the image of $\hat{\mathscr{W}}(\mathbf{u})$ under a linear and therefore continuous mapping.

Among the feasible utility allocations, we wish to characterize those that are efficient in the appropriate sense, that of Pareto.

DEFINITION 12. A utility allocation $\mathbf{u}^1$ is *dominated* by $\mathbf{u}^2$ if $\mathbf{u}^2$ is feasible and $\mathbf{u}^2 \gg \mathbf{u}^1$. A utility allocation, **u**, is *Pareto efficient* if it is feasible and not dominated by any other feasible utility allocation.

We use the term "Pareto efficient" instead of the more common "Pareto optimal" because the latter term conveys more commendation than the concept should bear, since a Pareto-efficient allocation might assign extremely low utilities to some (indeed, possibly to all but one) households and thus not be optimal in any sense in which distributional ethics are involved. This definition differs somewhat from the conventional one, in which the statement $\mathbf{u}^2$ dominates $\mathbf{u}^1$ is interpreted to mean $\mathbf{u}^2 > \mathbf{u}^1$; that is, everyone is at least as well off and one person is better off. In our definition, the concept of efficiency is somewhat wider than usual; an allocation is efficient if there is no way of making everyone better off. The present definition leads to simpler results and avoids some special, odd cases.

The general plan of the analysis is to note that if **z** is an excess-demand vector for which $\mathbf{z} \ll \mathbf{0}$, it would appear to correspond to a dominated allocation, since everyone can be given more of every commodity; hence, if **u** is efficient, $Z(\mathbf{u})$ is disjoint from the set $\{\mathbf{z} \mid \mathbf{z} \ll \mathbf{0}\}$. The two sets are convex and the second has an interior; hence, we can find a separating hyperplane, which can be shown to imply a price system such that the utility allocation **u** is realized when each firm is maximizing profits and each household is minimizing the cost of achieving its prescribed utility level.

LEMMA 5. If $\mathbf{z} \in Z(\mathbf{u})$, there exist $\mathbf{z}', \mathbf{u}'$, with $\mathbf{z}' \in Z(\mathbf{u}')$, $\mathbf{z}'$ arbitrarily close to **z** and $\mathbf{u}' \gg \mathbf{u}$.

Proof. Let

$$\mathbf{z} = \sum_h \mathbf{x}_h - \sum_f \mathbf{y}_f - \bar{\mathbf{x}}, \qquad \text{where } \mathbf{x}_h \in X_h(u_h), \mathbf{y}_f \in Y_f.$$

By Corollary 1, $\mathbf{x}'_h$ can be chosen arbitrarily close to $\mathbf{x}_h$ with $U_h(\mathbf{x}'_h) > U_h(\mathbf{x}_h) = u_h$. Let

$$\mathbf{z}' = \sum_h \mathbf{x}'_h - \sum_f \mathbf{y}_f - \bar{\mathbf{x}}.$$

Then by D.4.9, $\mathbf{z}' \in Z(\mathbf{u}')$, where $u'_h = U_h(\mathbf{x}'_h)$.

LEMMA 6. If $\mathbf{u}$ is Pareto efficient, then $Z(\mathbf{u})$ is disjoint from $\{\mathbf{z} \mid \mathbf{z} \ll \mathbf{0}\}$.

Proof. Suppose $\mathbf{z} \in Z(\mathbf{u})$, $\mathbf{z} \ll \mathbf{0}$. By Lemma 4.5 we can find $\mathbf{z}' \ll \mathbf{0}$ for which $\mathbf{z}' \in Z(\mathbf{u}')$, $\mathbf{u}' \gg \mathbf{u}$. But then $\hat{Z}(\mathbf{u}')$ is non-null so that $\mathbf{u}'$ is feasible and dominates $\mathbf{u}$, contrary to the definition D.4.12 of Pareto efficiency.

We now use the well-known separation theorem for convex sets (see T.B.6).

LEMMA 7. If A and B are disjoint convex sets in a finite-dimensional space and at least one has an interior, then there exists a vector $\mathbf{p} \neq 0$ and a scalar c such that

$$\mathbf{p}\mathbf{x} \geq c \qquad \text{for all } \mathbf{x} \in A,$$
$$\mathbf{p}\mathbf{x} \leq c \qquad \text{for all } \mathbf{x} \in B.$$

LEMMA 8. If A is a convex set disjoint from the set $\{\mathbf{x} \mid \mathbf{x} \ll 0\}$, then there exists a vector $\mathbf{p} > 0$ for which $\mathbf{p}\mathbf{x} \geq 0$ for all $\mathbf{x} \in A$.

Proof. Choose $\mathbf{p}$ as in Lemma 7, with $B = \{\mathbf{x} \mid \mathbf{x} \ll \mathbf{0}\}$; note that B has an interior. Let $\mathbf{x}^0 \ll \mathbf{0}$, $\mathbf{e}^i$ be the vector with 1 in the ith component and 0 elsewhere, and $\lambda > 0$. Then

$$\mathbf{x}^0 - \lambda\mathbf{e}^i \ll \mathbf{0} \qquad \text{all } \lambda > 0,$$

so that

$$c \geq \mathbf{p}(\mathbf{x}^0 - \lambda\mathbf{e}^i) = \mathbf{p}\mathbf{x}^0 - \lambda p_i \qquad \text{all } \lambda > 0.$$

Divide through by λ and let λ approach infinity; then $p_i \geq 0$. Thus, $\mathbf{p} \geq \mathbf{0}$; since $\mathbf{p} \neq 0$, $\mathbf{p} > 0$.

Also, let $\mathbf{e}$ be the vector all of whose components are 1. Then $-\epsilon\mathbf{e} \ll \mathbf{0}$, all $\epsilon > 0$. Then $c \geq -\epsilon\mathbf{p}\mathbf{e}$; let ϵ approach 0, then $c \geq 0$.

Hence, from $\mathbf{px} \geq c$, all $\mathbf{x} \in A$, it can be concluded that $\mathbf{px} \geq 0$, all $\mathbf{x} \in A$.

We now combine the disjunction assured by Lemma 4.6 with the separation theorem, Lemma 4.8.

THEOREM 4. If $\mathbf{u}^0$ is Pareto efficient, there exists a vector $\mathbf{p}$ with the following properties:

(a) $\mathbf{p} > \mathbf{0}$;
(b) $\mathbf{pz} \geq 0$, all $\mathbf{z} \in Z(\mathbf{u}^0)$;
(c) $\mathbf{pz} = 0$, all $\mathbf{z} \in \hat{Z}(\mathbf{u}^0)$;
(d) if $(\mathscr{x}^0, \mathscr{y}^0) \in \hat{\mathscr{W}}(\mathbf{u}^0)$, so that the conditions $U_h(\mathbf{x}_h^0) \geq u_h^0$, $\mathbf{y}_f^0 \in Y_f$, and

$$\sum_h \mathbf{x}_h^0 \leq \sum_f \mathbf{y}_f^0 + \sum_h \bar{\mathbf{x}}_h,$$

are satisfied, then
(i) $\mathbf{px}_h$ is minimized over $X_h(u_h^0)$ at $\mathbf{x}_h^0$;
(ii) $\mathbf{py}_f$ is maximized over Y_f at $\mathbf{y}_f^0$;
(iii) the social budget constraint,

$$\sum_h \mathbf{px}_h^0 = \sum_h \left[\mathbf{p}\bar{\mathbf{x}}_h + \sum_f d_{hf}(\mathbf{py}_f^0)\right],$$

is satisfied.

Proof. Conclusions (a) and (b) are simple consequences of Lemmas 4.6 and 4.8; in other words, Pareto efficiency implies that $Z(\mathbf{u}^0)$ is disjoint from the set of strictly negative vectors, while Lemma 4.8 assures the existence of a vector, $\mathbf{p} > \mathbf{0}$, for which (b) is true. If $\mathbf{z} \in \hat{Z}(\mathbf{u}^0)$, then $\mathbf{z} \leq \mathbf{0}$ so that, from (a) $\mathbf{pz} \leq 0$; then (c) follows from (b). Note that, since $\mathbf{u}^0$ is feasible, $\hat{Z}(\mathbf{u}^0)$ is non-null.

Statements (b) and (c) can be rephrased as follows: The minimum value of $\mathbf{pz}$ for $\mathbf{z} \in Z(\mathbf{u}^0)$ is 0 and is attained at any $\mathbf{z}^0$ in $\hat{Z}(\mathbf{u}^0)$, that is, any $\mathbf{z}^0 \in Z(\mathbf{u}^0)$ for which $\mathbf{z}^0 \leq \mathbf{0}$.

The hypothesis of (d) is precisely that $\mathbf{z}^0 \leq \mathbf{0}$, where

$$\mathbf{z}^0 = \sum_h \mathbf{x}_h^0 - \sum_f \mathbf{y}_f^0 - \sum_h \bar{\mathbf{x}}_h.$$

For any $\mathbf{z}$ in $Z(\mathbf{u}^0)$, we can, by definition, choose $\mathbf{x}_h \in X_h(u_h^0)$, $\mathbf{y}_f \in Y_f$, so that

$$\mathbf{z} = \sum_h \mathbf{x}_h - \sum_f \mathbf{y}_f - \sum_h \bar{\mathbf{x}}_h.$$

Then $\mathbf{pz} \geq \mathbf{pz}^0$, or

$$\mathbf{p}\Big(\sum_h \mathbf{x}_h - \sum_f \mathbf{y}_f - \sum_h \bar{\mathbf{x}}_h\Big) \geq \mathbf{p}\Big(\sum_h \mathbf{x}_h^0 - \sum_f \mathbf{y}_f^0 - \sum_h \bar{\mathbf{x}}_h\Big)$$
$$\text{for all } \mathbf{x}_h \in X_h(u_h^0),\ \mathbf{y}_f \in Y_f.$$

Add $\mathbf{p}(\sum_h \bar{\mathbf{x}}_h)$ to both sides and rewrite slightly:

$$\sum_h \mathbf{px}_h - \sum_f \mathbf{py}_f \geq \sum_h \mathbf{px}_h^0 - \sum_f \mathbf{py}_h^0,$$
$$\text{all } \mathbf{x}_h \in X_h(u_h^0),\ \mathbf{y}_f \in Y_f.$$

The variables on the left-hand side are independent so that the inequality must hold term-by-term. In more detail, let $\mathbf{y}_f = \mathbf{y}_f^0$, all f, $\mathbf{x}_h = \mathbf{x}_h^0$ for $h \neq h'$. Then if we cancel all terms in $\mathbf{px}_h^0(h \neq h')$ and in $\mathbf{py}_f^0$ from both sides, we have

$$\mathbf{px}_{h'} \geq \mathbf{px}_{h'}^0 \qquad \text{for all } \mathbf{x}_{h'} \in X_{h'}(u_{h'}^0),$$

which is (i). Statement (ii) follows similarly; statement (iii) is simply a restatement of (c).

T.4.4 is the basic efficiency theorem of welfare economics. Any Pareto-efficient allocation can be realized as a sort of competitive equilibrium. If an omniscient state wishes to realize a given Pareto-efficient allocation, it computes a price vector, $\mathbf{p}$, satisfying hypotheses of the theorem. Then it chooses for each individual an initial endowment, $\bar{\mathbf{x}}_h$, and ownership shares, d_{hf}, in the different firms, so that

$$\mathbf{px}_h^0 = \mathbf{p}\bar{\mathbf{x}}_h + \sum_f d_{hf}(\mathbf{py}_f^0) \qquad \text{each } h$$

and, of course,

$$\sum_h \bar{\mathbf{x}}_h = \bar{\mathbf{x}} \qquad d_{hf} \geq 0 \qquad \sum_h d_{hf} = 1.$$

These equations certainly can be solved because of (d-iii). For example, let each individual h have the proportion

$$\frac{\mathbf{px}_h^0}{\sum_h \mathbf{px}_h^0}$$

of every initially available good and every firm.

Then, indeed, at the given prices, each firm will maximize its profits at the desired production vector and each household will minimize the cost of achieving the given utility level at the desired consumption vector, at the same time spending exactly the value of endowment in goods and shares. Thus, in a certain sense, any desired efficient allocation can be achieved by redistribution of initial assets, followed by the achievement of an equilibrium. However, there are several important qualifications that should be kept in mind.

The most obvious and perhaps most important qualification is that the assumptions made so far have to be satisfied. The most important of these are the convexity of production possibility sets and orderings (the first is much more significant, as the discussion in Chapter 7 will show). Also implicit so far has been the absence of externalities; preferences and production possibilities are not affected by the behavior of other economic agents. This problem will be considered again in Section 6.2.

The informational requirements as stated are far beyond the possible. Methods of successive approximations are needed, but this, in turn, implies an ability to measure utility levels already achieved.

The equilibrium, as defined, is not precisely the competitive equilibrium in the usual sense. As already noted in Section 4.1, it is rather a compensated equilibrium. The relations between these concepts are discussed in detail in Section 5.1.

Some of the initial endowments reflect labor skills; it is hard to imagine that, in fact, they can be redistributed from one individual to another. The redistribution must take the form of abstract purchasing power.

For any given distribution of initial assets, the resulting equilibrium might not be unique (see Chapter 9) or stable (see Chapters 11–13). Therefore, if the state merely allocates endowments, it cannot always be sure that the market will achieve the desired Pareto-optimal allocation. Of course, if the state also announces the price vector, then competitive forces will maintain that vector.

A more extended analysis of the welfare implications of T.4.4 is beyond the scope of this book, which is concerned with the properties of competitive equilibria; T.4.4 has been proved here as a step in demonstrating the existence of equilibrium.

It has not been implied that the price vector $\mathbf{p}$ that will support a given Pareto-efficient utility allocation is unique. The essential properties are (a) and (b) of T.4.4; any price satisfying those conditions automatically satisfies (c) and (d). It is obvious that if $\mathbf{p}$ satisfies (a) and (b), then so does $\lambda\mathbf{p}$ for any $\lambda > 0$. This is the usual homogeneity property of prices. Then, without loss of essential generality, we can restrict ourselves to price vectors $\mathbf{p}$ for which $\mathbf{pe} = 1$, where, it will be recalled, $\mathbf{e} = (1, \ldots, 1)$.

Even among these normalized price vectors there may be more than one satisfying (a) and (b). Let

DEFINITION 13. $U = \{\mathbf{u} \mid \mathbf{u}$ Pareto efficient$\}$ = *Pareto frontier.*

DEFINITION 14. $P(\mathbf{u}) = \{\mathbf{p} \mid \mathbf{p} > 0,\ \ \mathbf{pe} = 1, \mathbf{pz} \geq 0\ \text{ for all } \mathbf{z} \in Z(\mathbf{u})\}$.

T.4.4 asserts that $P(\mathbf{u})$ is non-null for $\mathbf{u} \in U$. We will consider $P(\mathbf{u})$ as a correspondence from U to $S_n = \{\mathbf{p} \mid \mathbf{p} > 0,\ \ \mathbf{pe} = 1\}$, the *price set*, the unit simplex for n-dimensional vectors, where n is the number of commodities.

We conclude this section with some lemmas on domination of utility allocations to be used in the next chapter.

In A.4.2 and Corollary 1, we introduced a possible consumption vector, $\bar{\bar{\mathbf{x}}}_h$, for each individual, which was used to define his zero utility level.

LEMMA 9. The utility allocation, $\mathbf{0}$, is dominated.

Proof. By A.3.5 there is a vector $\bar{\mathbf{y}}$ in the social production possibility set for which

$$\bar{\mathbf{x}} + \bar{\mathbf{y}} \gg \mathbf{0}. \tag{6}$$

For any commodity i, either $\bar{x}_i > 0$ or $\bar{x}_i = 0$. In the first case, $\bar{x}_{hi} \geq 0$, all h, $\bar{x}_{hi} > 0$, some h. By A.4.2, then, $\bar{x}_{hi} \geq \bar{\bar{x}}_{hi}$, all h, $\bar{x}_{hi} > \bar{\bar{x}}_{hi}$, some h, so that

$$\bar{x}_i > \bar{\bar{x}}_i = \sum_h \bar{\bar{\mathbf{x}}}_{hi},$$

and therefore

$$\bar{x}_i + \alpha\bar{y}_i > \bar{\bar{x}}_i \qquad \text{for } \alpha > 0 \text{ and sufficiently small.}$$

(Recall that some components of $\bar{\mathbf{y}}$ are negative.) If $\bar{x}_i = 0$, then $\bar{\bar{x}}_i = 0$, and from (6), $\bar{y}_i > 0$ so that

$$\bar{x}_i + \alpha\bar{y}_i > \bar{\bar{x}}_i.$$

Thus,

$$\bar{\bar{\mathbf{z}}} = \bar{\mathbf{x}} - \alpha\bar{\mathbf{y}} - \bar{\mathbf{x}} \ll 0,$$
$$\bar{\bar{\mathbf{x}}} = \sum_h \bar{\bar{\mathbf{x}}}_h \quad \bar{\bar{\mathbf{x}}}_h \in X_h(0) \qquad \text{all } h,$$

so that, by Lemma 4.6, $\mathbf{0}$ is a dominated utility allocation.

We will confine our attention to non-negative utility allocations. Then the Pareto-efficient utility allocations will be semi-positive. We note

LEMMA 10. If $\mathbf{u}$ and $\mathbf{u}'$ are feasible non-negative utility allocations, $\mathbf{u} \leq \mathbf{u}'$, and $u_h < u_h'$ for any h for which $u_h' > 0$, then $\mathbf{u}$ is dominated.

Proof. Let $\omega \in \hat{\mathscr{W}}(\mathbf{u})$, $\omega' \in \hat{\mathscr{W}}(\mathbf{u}')$. Since, by Lemma 4.9, $\mathbf{0}$ is dominated, there is an allocation $\omega^a \in \hat{\mathscr{W}}(\mathbf{u}^a)$, with $\mathbf{u}^a \gg \mathbf{0}$. Now consider the allocation $\omega^b = (1 - \alpha)\omega' + \alpha\omega^a$, $0 < \alpha \leq 1$; it is certainly feasible. We will show that by suitable choice of α we have $\mathbf{u}^b \gg \mathbf{u}$, where $u_h^b = U_h(\mathbf{x}_h^b)$. First, consider any h for which $u_h' = 0$; then $u_h = 0$. Either $\mathbf{x}_h^a \succ_h \mathbf{x}_h'$ or $\mathbf{x}_h' \succcurlyeq_h \mathbf{x}_h^a$. In the first case, by semi-strict convexity of preferences, A.4.4(d), $\mathbf{x}_h^b \succ_h \mathbf{x}_h'$, so that $u_h^b > U_h(\mathbf{x}_h') \geq u_h' = 0 = u_h$. In the second case, by Lemma 4.1(b), $u_h^b \geq U_h(\mathbf{x}_h^a) \geq u_h^a > 0 = u_h$. Now consider the households for which $u_h' > 0$; then $u_h' > u_h$. Then $u_h^b \geq u_h' > u_h$ for $\alpha = 0$; by continuity $u_h^b > u_h$ for $\alpha > 0$ and sufficiently small. Hence, $\mathbf{u}$ is dominated.

Remark. It is noted, for later reference, that the proof of Lemma 4.10 depends only on the validity of Lemma 4.9 and on the semi-strict convexity of preferences.

5. Some Continuity Theorems

Some of the sets introduced in the preceding sections are functions of utility levels. For the existence of equilibrium we will need to show that these set-valued functions or correspondences are continuous in appropriate senses. In addition to the concept of upper semi-continuity, already used in Section 4.1, we will need that of *lower semi-continuity*.

$\Phi(\mathbf{x})$ is lower semi-continuous if $\mathbf{x}^\nu \to \mathbf{x}^0$, $\mathbf{y}^0 \in \Phi(\mathbf{x}^0)$ implies that there exists a sequence $\{\mathbf{y}^\nu\}$ for which $\mathbf{y}^\nu \in \Phi(\mathbf{x}^\nu)$, $\mathbf{y}^\nu \to \mathbf{y}^0$. A correspondence $\Phi(x)$ is said to be *continuous* if it is both upper and lower semi-continuous.

LEMMA 11. The correspondence $X_h(u_h)$ defined in D.4.6, is convex for each given u_h and is continuous in u_h.

Proof. Convexity has already been noted. Suppose $u_h^\nu \to u_h^0$, $\mathbf{x}_h^\nu \in X_h(u_h^\nu)$, $\mathbf{x}_h^\nu \to \mathbf{x}_h^0$. By definition, $U_h(\mathbf{x}_h^\nu) \geq u_h^\nu$. Since U_h is continuous, $U_h(\mathbf{x}_h^0) \geq \mathbf{x}_h^0$, so that $\mathbf{x}_h^0 \in X_h(u_h^0)$ and $X_h(u_h)$ is upper semi-continuous.

Now suppose that $u_h^\nu \to u_h^0$ and $\mathbf{x}_h^0 \in X_h(u_h^0)$. Choose $\mathbf{x}_h^1$ so that $U_h(\mathbf{x}_h^1) > U_h(\mathbf{x}_h^0) \geq u_h^0$. Then, for each ν, precisely one of the three following possibilities holds:

$$\begin{aligned}
&\text{(a)} \quad u_h^\nu \geq U_h(\mathbf{x}_h^1);\\
&\text{(b)} \quad U_h(\mathbf{x}_h^1) > u_h^\nu \geq U_h(\mathbf{x}_h^0);\\
&\text{(c)} \quad U_h(\mathbf{x}_h^0) > u_h^\nu.
\end{aligned}$$

Since $u_h^\nu \to u_h^0$, (a) can hold only for finitely many ν by the definition of $\mathbf{x}^1$; for those ν, choose $\mathbf{x}_h^\nu$ to be any element of $X_h(u_h^\nu)$. If (c) holds, let $\mathbf{x}_h^\nu = \mathbf{x}_h^0$. On this subsequence (if infinite), $\mathbf{x}_h^\nu \to \mathbf{x}_h^0$ trivially, and $\mathbf{x}_h^\nu \in X_h(u_h^\nu)$.

Now suppose (b) holds. Let $\mathbf{x}_h(\alpha) = (1 - \alpha)\mathbf{x}_h^0 + \alpha\mathbf{x}_h^1$, $0 \leq \alpha \leq 1$. By continuity there exists α^ν, $0 \leq \alpha^\nu < 1$, for which $U_h[\mathbf{x}_h(\alpha^\nu)] = u_h^\nu$. Let $\mathbf{x}_h^\nu = \mathbf{x}_h(\alpha^\nu)$. Certainly, $\mathbf{x}_h^\nu \in X_h(u_h^\nu)$. It remains to show that if (b) holds for infinitely many ν, then $\mathbf{x}_h^\nu \to \mathbf{x}_h^0$ along that subsequence.

The sequence $\{\alpha^\nu\}$ is bounded and, therefore, has a limit point; let α^* be any such, and let $\mathbf{x}_h^* = \mathbf{x}_h(\alpha^*)$. Then $U_h(\mathbf{x}_h^*) = u_h^0$, since by assumption, $u_h^\nu \to u_h^0$. But since U_h is semi-strictly quasi-concave, $U_h[\mathbf{x}_h(\alpha)] > U_h(\mathbf{x}_h^0) \geq u_h^0$ for any $\alpha > 0$. Hence, $\alpha^* = 0$, and this must be the only limit point of the sequence $\{\alpha^\nu\}$. Therefore, $\mathbf{x}_h^\nu \to \mathbf{x}_h^* = \mathbf{x}_h^0$.

THEOREM 5. The correspondence $\mathscr{W}(u)$ defined in D.4.8 is convex for each $\mathbf{u}$ and continuous in $\mathbf{u}$.

Proof. Convexity has already been noted. For upper semi-continuity, suppose $\mathbf{u}^\nu \to \mathbf{u}^0$, $w^\nu \to w^0$, $w^\nu \in \mathscr{W}(\mathbf{u}^\nu)$. Write

$$w^\nu = (x^\nu, y^\nu) \qquad \text{where } x^\nu \in \mathscr{X}(\mathbf{u}^\nu),\ y^\nu \in \mathscr{Y},$$
$$w^0 = (x^0, y^0).$$

Then $\mathbf{x}_h^\nu \to \mathbf{x}_h^0$, and by Lemma 4.11, $\mathbf{x}_h^0 \in X_h(u_h^0)$, each h, or $x^0 \in \mathscr{X}(\mathbf{u}^0)$. Since $\mathscr{Y}$ is a closed set, and $y^\nu \in \mathscr{Y}$, all ν, $y^0 \in \mathscr{Y}$; by the definition of $\mathbf{u}$-possible allocations, $\mathscr{W}(\mathbf{u})$, in D.4.8 $w^0 \in \mathscr{W}(\mathbf{u}^0)$.

To prove lower semi-continuity, let $\mathbf{u}^\nu \to \mathbf{u}^0$, $\omega^0 \in \mathscr{W}(\mathbf{u}^0)$. By definition, $\omega^0 = (x^0, y^0)$, $\mathbf{x}_h^0 \in X_h(\mathbf{u}_h^0)$, $y^0 \in \mathscr{Y}$. Since the correspondence $X_h(u_h)$ is lower semi-continuous, we can find a sequence, $\{\mathbf{x}_h^\nu\}$, for each h, such that,

$$\mathbf{x}_h^\nu \in X_h(u_h^\nu) \qquad \mathbf{x}_h^\nu \to \mathbf{x}_h^0.$$

If we let $\omega^\nu = (x^\nu, y^0)$, then $\omega^\nu \in \mathscr{W}(u^\nu)$, $\omega^\nu \to \omega^0$, so that lower semi-continuity holds.

Corollary 5. The set of $\mathbf{u}$-feasible allocations, $\hat{\mathscr{W}}(\mathbf{u})$, is upper semi-continuous in $\mathbf{u}$.

Proof. From D.4.10, $\hat{\mathscr{W}}(\mathbf{u})$ is the intersection of two sets, one of which is upper semi-continuous in $\mathbf{u}$ by T.4.5 and the other of which is independent of $\mathbf{u}$.

Corollary 5′. The set of u-possible excess demands, $Z(\mathbf{u})$, is lower semi-continuous in $\mathbf{u}$.

Proof. Let $\mathbf{u}^\nu \to \mathbf{u}^0$, $\mathbf{z}^0 \in Z(\mathbf{u}^0)$. By D.4.9, $\mathbf{z}^0 = \mathbf{z}(\omega^0)$ for some $\omega^0 \in \mathscr{W}(\mathbf{u}^0)$. From T.4.5, then, there exists a sequence $\{\omega^\nu\}$ with $\omega^\nu \to \omega^0$, $\omega^\nu \in \mathscr{W}(\mathbf{u}^\nu)$. Let $\mathbf{z}^\nu = \mathbf{z}(\omega^\nu)$; then $\mathbf{z}^\nu \to \mathbf{z}^0$, $\mathbf{z}^\nu \in Z(\mathbf{u}^\nu)$, by D.4.9.

THEOREM 6. The set $P(\mathbf{u})$, as defined in D.4.14, is upper semi-continuous in $\mathbf{u}$, compact and convex for each $\mathbf{u}$, and is non-null for $\mathbf{u} \in U$.

Proof. Convexity and compactness follow trivially from the definition of $P(\mathbf{u})$. The non-nullity of the set for $\mathbf{u} \in U$ is the content of T.4.4. To see upper semi-continuity, suppose there are sequences $\mathbf{u}^\nu \to \mathbf{u}^0$, $\mathbf{p}^\nu \to \mathbf{p}^0$, $\mathbf{p}^\nu \in P(\mathbf{u}^\nu)$. Since $\mathbf{p}^\nu > 0$, $\mathbf{p}^\nu\mathbf{e} = 1$, it follows that $\mathbf{p}^0 \geq 0$, $\mathbf{p}^0\mathbf{e} = 1$, and therefore, $\mathbf{p}^0 > 0$. Take any $\mathbf{z}^0 \in Z(\mathbf{u}^0)$; by Corollary 5′, we can choose a sequence $\{\mathbf{z}^\nu\}$, where $\mathbf{z}^\nu \to \mathbf{z}^0$, $\mathbf{z}^\nu \in Z(\mathbf{u}^\nu)$, all ν. Since $\mathbf{p}^\nu \in P(\mathbf{u}^\nu)$, it follows by definition that $\mathbf{p}^\nu\mathbf{z}^\nu \geq 0$, and hence, by taking limits, $\mathbf{p}^0\mathbf{z}^0 \geq 0$. But then $\mathbf{p}^0$ satisfies the definition of $P(\mathbf{u}^0)$.

6. The Single-Valued Case

Analogously to Section 3.4, we will present some assumptions that ensure that the excess-demand correspondences of the household become single-valued functions, and we will then discuss some of their well-known properties.

As in Section 3.4, we assume that the set of commodities can be partitioned into two parts, for one of which the household is assumed to have no utility; that is, we can write the vector, $\mathbf{x}_h$, as $(\mathbf{x}_h^a,\mathbf{x}_h^b)$, where $U_h(\mathbf{x}_h) = U_h(\mathbf{x}_h^a,\mathbf{x}_h^b)$ is, in fact, independent of $\mathbf{x}_h^b$. Analogously to the assumption that Y_f is strictly convex with respect to those commodities that appear in it at all, we strengthen our assumptions on preferences to strict convexity; that is, if $\mathbf{x}_h^1 \succcurlyeq \mathbf{x}_h^2$ and $0 < \alpha < 1$, then $\alpha\mathbf{x}_h^1 + (1 - \alpha)\mathbf{x}_h^2 \succ \mathbf{x}_h^2$ provided $\mathbf{x}_h^1$ and $\mathbf{x}_h^2$ differ in some of the *a*-components. The demand for the *b*-commodities is 0 for all price levels; it is permissible, for simplicity, to assume that all commodities are *a*-commodities. (Some complication may arise from the fact that some commodities in the household's endowment are *b*-commodities, not desired for its own consumption; but we will carry income, M_h, as a separate variable when needed.)

For any given $\mathbf{p} \gg \mathbf{0}$, the set of commodity vectors in X_h that satisfy the budget constraint, $\mathbf{p}\mathbf{x}_h \leq M_h$, is a compact set, so there exists at least one $\mathbf{x}_h^0$, maximizing $U_h(\mathbf{x}_h)$ in this set. If $\mathbf{x}_h^1$ also maximized $U_h(\mathbf{x}_h^0)$ in this set, then $U_h(\mathbf{x}_h) = U_h(\mathbf{x}_h^1)$. Let $\mathbf{x}_h^2$ be a proper convex combination of the two; then it satisfies the budget constraint, but by strict quasi-concavity of the utility function, it has a higher utility than either, which contradicts the choice of $\mathbf{x}_h^0$.

THEOREM 7. If $U_h(\mathbf{x}_h)$ is strictly quasi-concave, then for every $\mathbf{p}$ there is, at most, one $\mathbf{x}_h^0$ that maximizes $U_h(\mathbf{x}_h)$ subject to $\mathbf{p}\mathbf{x}_h \leq M_h$, $\mathbf{x}_h \in X_h$. If $\mathbf{p} \gg \mathbf{0}$, there is one such $\mathbf{x}_h^0$.

In view of T.4.7, it is legitimate to define

DEFINITION 15. The *uncompensated demand function* $\mathbf{x}_h(\mathbf{p},M_h)$ is the unique $\mathbf{x}_h^0$ that maximizes $U_h(\mathbf{x}_h)$ subject to $\mathbf{p}\mathbf{x}_h \leq M_h$, $\mathbf{x}_h \in X_h$.

In general equilibrium theory, M_h is, in turn, a function of p, as defined by A.4.3.

DEFINITION 16. The *demand function* $\mathbf{x}_h(\mathbf{p}) = x_h[\mathbf{p},M_h(\mathbf{p})]$, where $M_h(\mathbf{p})$ is defined by A.4.3.

Then T.4.7 implies that the uncompensated demand function and the demand function are both well defined on a domain that includes all strictly positive price vectors. A particular consequence is the well-known weak assumption of revealed preference. If $\mathbf{x}_h^2$ is a vector satisfying the budget constraint $\mathbf{p}^1\mathbf{x}_h^2 \leq M_h^1$, but $\mathbf{x}_h^2 \neq \mathbf{x}_h(\mathbf{p}^1,M_h^1)$, then $U_h[\mathbf{x}_h(\mathbf{p}^1,M_h^1)] > U_h(\mathbf{x}_h^2)$. If in particular, $\mathbf{x}_h^2 =$

$\mathbf{x}_h(\mathbf{p}^2, M_h^2)$, it must maximize utility subject to the budget constraint, $\mathbf{p}^2\mathbf{x} \leq M_h^2$; therefore it must be that $\mathbf{x}_h(\mathbf{p}^1, M_h^1)$ does not satisfy that budget constraint.

Corollary 7 (Revealed Preference). If $\mathbf{p}^1\mathbf{x}_h(\mathbf{p}^2, M_h^2) \leq M_h^1$ and $\mathbf{x}_h(\mathbf{p}^1, M_h^1) \neq \mathbf{x}_h(\mathbf{p}^2, M_h^2)$, then $\mathbf{p}^2\mathbf{x}_h(\mathbf{p}^1, M_h^1) > M_h^2$.

From T.4.7, if $\mathbf{x}_h(\mathbf{p})$ is not defined for some $\mathbf{p}$, then there is no utility-maximizing $\mathbf{x}_h$ under the budget constraint. The lack of definition comes from the fact that the household is not satiated in some free goods so its demand is, in some appropriate sense, infinite.

The example given at the beginning of Section 2.8 shows, however, that some care must be taken in defining the sense in which demands may be infinite at zero price; even if the household is not satiated in any commodity, demands need not approach infinity as prices approach a limit in which some components are zero. On the other hand, in the same example it was shown that the sum of the demands for all commodities does approach infinity as any set of prices approaches 0. This is a general result, which will now be demonstrated, so that assumption A.2.6 can be justified by being derived from utility-maximizing considerations.

DEFINITION 17. We define

$$\sum_i x_{hi}(\mathbf{p})$$

in the natural way at any $\mathbf{p}$ for which $\mathbf{x}_h(\mathbf{p})$ is defined and as equal to $+\infty$ otherwise.

We will show that the function

$$\sum_i x_{hi}(\mathbf{p}),$$

so defined, is continuous. Continuity for an extended-real-valued function that can take on the value $+\infty$ has the usual meaning at any point where the function is finite, while for any sequence $\{\mathbf{p}^\nu\}$ approaching $\mathbf{p}^0$, where

$$\sum_i x_{hi}(\mathbf{p}^0) = +\infty,$$

we require that

$$\lim_{\nu \to \infty} \sum_i x_{hi}(\mathbf{p}^\nu) = +\infty,$$

on the subsequence (if infinite) for which

$$\sum_i x_{hi}(\mathbf{p}^\nu) < +\infty.$$

As the discussion in Section 4.1 (preceding Lemma 4.2) suggests, we are unlikely to achieve continuity in any sense if income is at the minimum possible. It will follow from Lemma 5.1 that M_h is above the minimum possible if and only if $M_h > 0$. We will therefore assume $M_h > 0$ for all possible prices—a strong assumption, because it means, in effect, that $\bar{\mathbf{x}}_h \gg \mathbf{0}$, unless the household owns shares in a firm that makes positive profits at any set of prices.

THEOREM 8. If the utility function $U_h(\mathbf{x}_h)$ is strictly quasi-concave and $M_h > 0$ for all $\mathbf{p}$, then $\mathbf{x}_h(\mathbf{p})$ is continuous in its domain of definition, which includes all $\mathbf{p} \gg 0$, and

$$\sum_i x_{hi}(\mathbf{p}),$$

as extended by D.4.17, is continuous everywhere on the unit simplex, S_n.

Proof. In this proof, we will drop the subscript h. Suppose $\mathbf{x}(\mathbf{p})$ is defined, but not continuous, at some price vector $\mathbf{p}$. Then there is a sequence $\{\mathbf{p}^\nu\}$, $\mathbf{p}^\nu \to \mathbf{p}$, and a positive number ϵ such that

$$|\mathbf{x}(\mathbf{p}^\nu) - \mathbf{x}(\mathbf{p})| \geq \epsilon > 0 \qquad \text{all } \nu.$$

Let

$$\beta_\nu = \frac{\epsilon}{|\mathbf{x}(\mathbf{p}^\nu) - \mathbf{x}(\mathbf{p})|},$$

$$\mathbf{x}'^\nu = \beta_\nu \mathbf{x}(\mathbf{p}^\nu) + (1 - \beta_\nu)\mathbf{x}(\mathbf{p}).$$

Since $0 < \beta_\nu \leq 1$, $\mathbf{x}'^\nu$ is a convex combination of two members of X and hence belongs to X. By quasi-concavity,

$$\text{if} \quad U[\mathbf{x}(\mathbf{p})] > U(\mathbf{x}'^\nu), \quad \text{then} \quad U(\mathbf{x}'^\nu) \geq U[\mathbf{x}(\mathbf{p}^\nu)]. \tag{7}$$

Since $|\mathbf{x}'^\nu - \mathbf{x}(\mathbf{p})| = \epsilon$, we can choose a subsequence for which $\mathbf{x}'^\nu \to \mathbf{x}'$, where $|\mathbf{x}' - \mathbf{x}(\mathbf{p})| = \epsilon$. Then $\mathbf{x}' \in X$, since X is closed.

Since $\mathbf{p}^\nu\mathbf{x}(\mathbf{p}^\nu) \leq M(\mathbf{p}^\nu)$,

$$\mathbf{p}^\nu\mathbf{x}'^\nu \leq \beta_\nu M(\mathbf{p}^\nu) + (1 - \beta_\nu)\mathbf{p}^\nu\mathbf{x}(\mathbf{p}) = \mathbf{p}^\nu\mathbf{x}(\mathbf{p}) + \beta_\nu[M(\mathbf{p}^\nu) - \mathbf{p}^\nu\mathbf{x}(\mathbf{p})].$$

As ν approaches infinity, $\mathbf{p}^\nu\mathbf{x}(\mathbf{p}) \to M(\mathbf{p})$, $M(\mathbf{p}^\nu) \to M(\mathbf{p})$, and β_ν remains bounded.

$$\mathbf{px}' \leq M(\mathbf{p}).$$

Since $\mathbf{x}' \neq \mathbf{x}(\mathbf{p})$, it follows by definition that $U(\mathbf{x}') < U[\mathbf{x}(\mathbf{p})]$; therefore

$$U(\mathbf{x}'^\nu) < U[\mathbf{x}(\mathbf{p})]$$

for ν sufficiently large; from (7), then, $U[\mathbf{x}(\mathbf{p}^\nu)] \leq U(\mathbf{x}'^\nu)$. Also, by continuity, we can choose $\lambda > 0$ so that $U(\mathbf{x}') < U[\lambda\bar{\bar{\mathbf{x}}} + (1 - \lambda)\mathbf{x}(\mathbf{p})]$, so that

$$U(\mathbf{x}'^\nu) \leq U[\lambda\bar{\bar{\mathbf{x}}} + (1 - \lambda)\mathbf{x}(\mathbf{p})] \qquad \nu \text{ large,}$$

and therefore

$$U[\mathbf{x}(\mathbf{p}^\nu)] \leq U[\lambda\bar{\bar{\mathbf{x}}} + (1 - \lambda)\mathbf{x}(\mathbf{p})],$$

which implies that

$$\mathbf{p}^\nu[\lambda\bar{\bar{\mathbf{x}}} + (1 - \lambda)\mathbf{x}(\mathbf{p})] \geq M(\mathbf{p}^\nu).$$

Let ν approach infinity.

$$\lambda\mathbf{p}\bar{\bar{\mathbf{x}}} + (1 - \lambda)M(\mathbf{p}) \geq M(\mathbf{p}),$$

or $\mathbf{p}\bar{\bar{\mathbf{x}}} \geq M(\mathbf{p})$. But as will be seen in Lemma 5.1, this is impossible if $M(\mathbf{p}) > 0$.

It remains to show that if $\mathbf{x}$ is not defined at $\mathbf{p}$, then for every sequence $\{\mathbf{p}^\nu\}$, $\mathbf{p}^\nu \to \mathbf{p}$, $\sum_i x_i(\mathbf{p}^\nu) \to \infty$. If not, then there is a sequence $\{\mathbf{p}^\nu\}$ converging to $\mathbf{p}$ for which $\{\mathbf{x}(\mathbf{p}^\nu)\}$ is bounded. Let $\mathbf{x}'$ be a limit point of the sequence. Since $\mathbf{p}^\nu\mathbf{x}(\mathbf{p}^\nu) \leq M(\mathbf{p}^\nu)$, $\mathbf{px}' \leq M(\mathbf{p})$. We show, in fact, that $\mathbf{x}'$ maximizes $U(\mathbf{x})$ subject to $\mathbf{px} \leq M(\mathbf{p})$; then $\mathbf{x}(\mathbf{p})$ would be defined equal to $\mathbf{x}'$, a contradiction. Consider any $\mathbf{x}''$ for which $U(\mathbf{x}'') > U(\mathbf{x}')$. Then, for some $\lambda > 0$,

$$U[\lambda\bar{\bar{\mathbf{x}}} + (1 - \lambda)\mathbf{x}''] > U(\mathbf{x}'),$$

and therefore

$$U[\lambda\bar{\bar{\mathbf{x}}} + (1 - \lambda)\mathbf{x}''] > U[\mathbf{x}(\mathbf{p}^\nu)],$$

for ν sufficiently large along the appropriate subsequence. By definition of $\mathbf{x}(\mathbf{p}^\nu)$, this implies that

$$\mathbf{p}^\nu[\lambda\bar{\bar{\mathbf{x}}} + (1 - \lambda)\mathbf{x}''] > M(\mathbf{p}^\nu).$$

Let ν approach infinity along the appropriate subsequence.

$$\mathbf{p}[\lambda\bar{\bar{\mathbf{x}}} + (1 - \lambda)\mathbf{x}''] \geq M(\mathbf{p}).$$

Since $M(\mathbf{p}) > 0$, $M(\mathbf{p}) > \mathbf{p}\bar{\bar{\mathbf{x}}}$, by Lemma 5.1. Hence,

$$\lambda M(\mathbf{p}) + (1 - \lambda)\mathbf{px}'' > M(\mathbf{p}),$$

or $\mathbf{px}'' > M(\mathbf{p})$. That is, any $\mathbf{x}''$ preferred to $\mathbf{x}'$ must be unavailable at income $M(\mathbf{p})$ and prices $\mathbf{p}$, or equivalently, $\mathbf{x}'$ maximizes $U(\mathbf{x})$ to $\mathbf{px} \leq M(\mathbf{p})$.

Now let us examine some well-known properties of compensated demand for those price vectors $\mathbf{p}$ for which $M_h > 0$. Define the function

$$C_h(\mathbf{p},u_h) = \inf\{\mathbf{px}_h \mid U_h(\mathbf{x}_h) \geq u_h, \quad \mathbf{x}_h \in X_h\},$$

and interpret it as the lowest cost for household h of attaining a prescribed utility level u_h, given the market prices $\mathbf{p}$. The compensated demand correspondence $\mathbf{x}_h(\mathbf{p}, u_h)$ is then defined by

$$\mathbf{x}_h(\mathbf{p},u_h) = \{\mathbf{x}_h \mid \mathbf{px}_h = C_h(\mathbf{p},u_h), \quad \mathbf{x}_h \in X_h\}.$$

If $U_h(\mathbf{x}_h)$ is strictly quasi-concave, $\mathbf{x}_h(\mathbf{p},u_h)$ has only one member for each $\mathbf{p}$ for which $C_h(\mathbf{p},u_h) > 0$ and, therefore, is a function. For by Lemma 4.3 and T.4.7, $\mathbf{x}_h(\mathbf{p},u_h)$ is the unique element that maximizes $U_h(\mathbf{x}_h)$ subject to the budget constraint, $\mathbf{px}_h \leq C_h(\mathbf{p},u_h)$, that is,

$$\mathbf{x}_h(\mathbf{p},u_h) = \mathbf{x}_h(\mathbf{p},M_h) \qquad \text{when } M_h = C_h(\mathbf{p},u_h). \tag{8}$$

The following theorem is proved in exactly the same way as T.3.4 and T.3.6, and we do not repeat the proof here.

THEOREM 9. Let $U_h(\mathbf{x}_h)$ be strictly quasi-concave. Then for all $\mathbf{p}$ for which $C_h(\mathbf{p},u_h) = \inf\{\mathbf{px}_h \mid U_h(\mathbf{x}_h) \geq u_h, \quad \mathbf{x}_h \in X_h\} > 0$,

(a) $\mathbf{x}_h(\mathbf{p},u_h)$ is a function,
(b) $C_h(\mathbf{p},u_h)$ is a strictly concave differentiable function of $\mathbf{p}$ over S_n for fixed u_h, where

$$\frac{\partial C_h}{\partial p_j} = x_{hj}(\mathbf{p},u_h).$$

If C_h is twice differentiable, then, by (b) of the theorem, the Jacobian with elements $\partial^2 C_h/\partial p_i \partial p_j$ is negative semi-definite and symmetric. Thus,

$$\frac{\partial^2 C_h}{\partial p_i \partial p_j} = \frac{\partial x_{hi}(\mathbf{p},u_h)}{\partial p_j} = \frac{\partial x_{hj}(\mathbf{p},u_h)}{\partial p_i}, \tag{9}$$

and the elements of the Jacobian are the substitution terms of traditional theory.

Now differentiate (8) with respect to p_j.

$$\frac{\partial \mathbf{x}_h(\mathbf{p},u_h)}{\partial p_j} = \frac{\partial \mathbf{x}_h(\mathbf{p},M_h)}{\partial p_j} + \left[\frac{\partial \mathbf{x}_h(\mathbf{p},M_h)}{\partial M_h}\right]\left(\frac{\partial C_h}{\partial p_j}\right);$$

substitution for $\partial C_h/\partial p_j$ from T.4.9(b) yields

$$\frac{\partial \mathbf{x}_h(\mathbf{p},u_h)}{\partial p_j} = \frac{\partial \mathbf{x}_h(\mathbf{p},M_h)}{\partial p_j} + \frac{\partial \mathbf{x}_h(\mathbf{p},M_h)}{\partial M_h} x_{hj};$$

the last term is the well-known income effect. Holding all other prices and money income constant, the effect of a change in one price, which is the first term on the right-hand side, can be expressed as the difference between a substitution effect and an income effect. From (9) and T.4.9, we deduce

THEOREM 10. Let $U_h(\mathbf{x}_h)$ be strictly quasi-concave. Then for all $\mathbf{p}$ for which $M_h > 0$,

(a) $$\frac{\partial x_{hi}(\mathbf{p},M_h)}{\partial p_j} + \left[\frac{\partial x_{hi}(\mathbf{p},M_h)}{\partial M_h}\right] x_{hj}(\mathbf{p},M_h) = \frac{\partial x_{hj}(\mathbf{p},M_h)}{\partial p_i} + \left[\frac{\partial x_{hj}(\mathbf{p},M_h)}{\partial M_h}\right] x_{hi}(\mathbf{p},M_h);$$

(b) the matrix with typical element,

$$\frac{\partial x_{hi}(\mathbf{p},M_h)}{\partial p_j} + \frac{\partial x_{hi}(\mathbf{p},M_h)}{\partial M_h} x_{hj},$$

is negative semi-definite; in particular,

$$\frac{\partial x_{hi}(\mathbf{p},M_h)}{\partial p_i} + \frac{\partial x_{hi}(\mathbf{p},M_h)}{\partial M_h} x_{hi} \leq 0.$$

Notes

Section 1. For the most part, the assumptions of this section are standard in the economic theory of the household. The treatment of different kinds of labor as displacements of different kinds of leisure and the consequent time constraint on types of leisure was introduced by Arrow and Debreu [1954, pp. 268–269]. The time constraints on consumption in general have been stressed by Becker [1965].

Section 2. Since the introduction of indifference surfaces by Pareto and Irving Fisher, it has been taken for granted that they could be represented by a utility function. Wold seems to have been the first to see the need of specifying assumptions under which the representation by a continuous utility function exists [1943–44, sections 31, 37]. Wold assumed that X_h is the entire non-negative orthant and that preference is strictly monotonic in each commodity. In that case, it is easy to verify that each possible consumption vector is indifferent to precisely one vector of the form $\mu\mathbf{e}$, and μ can be used as the utility function. A very considerable generalization, based on a mathematical paper by Eilenberg [1941], was achieved with deeper methods by Debreu [1954]; he assumed only the continuity of preferences and the connectedness of X_h (a property weaker than convexity). The construction of the utility function involves selection of a denumerable subset of X_h everywhere dense in it, defining a utility function by placing it inductively into one-to-one correspondence with the rational numbers on the unit interval, and extending this utility function to the entire consumption possibility set by a limiting process. The proof is straightforward, but lengthy; the result is valid in infinite-dimensional spaces with suitable properties. Further extensions are due to Rader [1963], who gives a simple construction, and to Debreu [1964]; the proof of one of the lemmas in the last paper has been notably simplified by Bowen [1968].

A more elementary approach in the spirit of Wold's can also be supplied for general convex X_h and continuous preferences. Choose any strictly positive price vector $\mathbf{p}^0$ and define $U_h(\mathbf{x})$ to be the cheapest way of buying a commodity vector not inferior to $\mathbf{x}$. Then if $\tilde{\mathbf{x}}$ minimizes $\mathbf{p}^0\mathbf{x}$ over X_h, it is very easy to verify that $U_h(\mathbf{x})$ is a continuous utility function over the subset of X_h for which $\mathbf{x}_h \succcurlyeq \tilde{\mathbf{x}}$. However, this utility function cannot be extended to the entire set X_h without additional assumptions; one set that suffices is to assume that X_h is polyhedral and preferences are convex.

The approach used here was suggested to the authors by James Mirrlees, to whom we are grateful.

Section 4. The basic theorem of welfare economics, T.4.4, has a well-known long history. The use of convex set theory to provide a rigorous statement is due independently to Arrow [1951] and Debreu [1951].

Section 6. Most of the material in this section is too familiar for reference; see also the Notes to Section 3.4. T.4.8 is new; the proof here is James Mirrlees' simplification of our original proof.

Chapter Five
THE EXISTENCE OF COMPETITIVE EQUILIBRIUM

At length I saw these lovers full were come
Into their torture of equilibrium.
—John Crowe Ransom,
The Equilibrists

1. Compensated and Competitive Equilibrium: Definitions and Interrelations

An (uncompensated) competitive equilibrium has the meaning usual in the economic literature: a set of prices and production and consumption allocations such that each firm maximizes profits at the given prices, each household maximizes utility at the given prices and with the income implied by those prices and its initial holdings of assets and profit shares, and aggregate consumption is feasible in not exceeding the sum of aggregate production and initial endowments. Formally,

DEFINITION 1. A price vector, $\mathbf{p}^*$, a consumption allocation, $\mathscr{x}^*$, and a production allocation, $\mathscr{y}^*$, constitute a *competitive equilibrium* if

(a) $\mathbf{p}^* > 0$;
(b) $\sum_h \mathbf{x}_h^* \leq \sum_f \mathbf{y}_f^* + \sum_h \bar{\mathbf{x}}_h$;
(c) $\mathbf{y}_f^*$ maximizes $\mathbf{p}^*\mathbf{y}_f$ subject to $\mathbf{y}_f \in Y_f$;
(d) $\mathbf{x}_h^*$ maximizes $U_h(\mathbf{x}_h)$ subject to $\mathbf{p}^*\mathbf{x}_h \leq M_h^* = \mathbf{p}^*\bar{\mathbf{x}}_f + \sum_f d_{hf}(\mathbf{p}^*\mathbf{y}_f^*)$.

As already suggested in Section 4.1, it is convenient as an intermediate step in deriving sufficient conditions for the existence of a competitive equilibrium to find sufficient conditions for the existence of another type of equilibrium, which we call a compensated equilibrium. This differs from the competitive equilibrium in the assumptions about consumer behavior; households are assumed to minimize the cost of achieving a given utility level, and it is then postulated separately that their income is sufficient to cover these minimum costs.

DEFINITION 2. A price vector, $\mathbf{p}^*$, a utility allocation, $\mathbf{u}^*$, a consumption allocation, $\mathscr{x}^*$, and a production allocation, $\mathscr{y}^*$, constitute a *compensated equilibrium* if

(a) $\mathbf{p}^* > 0$;
(b) $\sum_h \mathbf{x}_h^* \leq \sum_f \mathbf{y}_f^* + \sum_h \bar{\mathbf{x}}_h$;
(c) $\mathbf{y}_f^*$ maximizes $\mathbf{p}^*\mathbf{y}_f$ subject to $\mathbf{y}_f \in Y_f$;
(d) $\mathbf{x}_h^*$ minimizes $\mathbf{p}^*\mathbf{x}_h$ subject to $U_h(\mathbf{x}_h) \geq u_h^*$;
(e) $\mathbf{p}^*\mathbf{x}_h^* = M_h^*$.

As is already evident from Lemmas 4.2 and 4.3, there is a close relation between the two kinds of equilibria. In one direction the relation is very simple.

THEOREM 1. If $(\mathbf{p}^*, \mathscr{x}^*, \mathscr{y}^*)$ is a competitive equilibrium and $u_h^* = U_h(\mathbf{x}_h^*)$ for each h, then $(\mathbf{p}^*, \mathbf{u}^*, \mathscr{x}^*, \mathscr{y}^*)$ is a compensated equilibrium.

Proof. D.5.2(a)–(c) are identical with D.5.1(a)–(c). Lemma 4.2 asserts that a consumption vector that maximizes utility subject to a budget constraint also minimizes the cost of achieving that utility level, so that D.5:1(d) implies D.5.2(d). Finally, suppose that D.5.2(e) does not hold. From D.5.1(d), $\mathbf{p}^*\mathbf{x}_h^* < M_h^*$. But then, by Corollary 4.1, we can choose $\mathbf{x}_h'$ arbitrarily close to $\mathbf{x}_h^*$ such that $U_h(\mathbf{x}_h') > U_h(\mathbf{x}_h^*)$. In particular, $\mathbf{x}_h'$ can be chosen so that $\mathbf{p}^*\mathbf{x}_h' \leq M_h^*$, which is a contradiction to the assumption that $\mathbf{x}_h^*$ is utility maximizing under the budget constraint.

Corresponding to Lemma 4.3, a partial converse of T.5.1 is valid. First, we note

LEMMA 1. If $\mathbf{p} > 0$ and $\mathbf{p}\mathbf{y}_f \geq 0$, all f, then

(a) $M_h \geq 0$, all h;
(b) for any h, $M_h > 0$ if and only if $M_h > \mathbf{p}\bar{\bar{\mathbf{x}}}_h$.

Proof. By definition,

$$M_h = \mathbf{p}\bar{\mathbf{x}}_h + \sum_f d_{hf}(\mathbf{p}\mathbf{y}_f),$$
$$M_h - \mathbf{p}\bar{\bar{\mathbf{x}}}_h = \mathbf{p}(\bar{\mathbf{x}}_h - \bar{\bar{\mathbf{x}}}_h) + \sum_f d_{hf}(\mathbf{p}\mathbf{y}_f).$$

From the hypotheses, obviously, $M_h \geq 0$, all h. But from A.4.2, it is assumed that $\bar{\mathbf{x}} - \bar{\bar{\mathbf{x}}}_h \geq 0$ and that $\bar{\mathbf{x}}_h$ has exactly the same positive components (and the same zero components) as $\bar{\mathbf{x}}_h - \bar{\bar{\mathbf{x}}}_h$. Since $\mathbf{p} > 0$, $\mathbf{p}\bar{\mathbf{x}}_h > 0$ if and only if there is at least one component i for which both $p_i > 0$ and $\bar{x}_{hi} > 0$; similarly, $\mathbf{p}(\bar{\mathbf{x}}_h - \bar{\bar{\mathbf{x}}}_h) > 0$ if and only if there is at least one component i for which $p_i > 0$ and $\bar{x}_{hi} - \bar{\bar{x}}_{hi} > 0$. Hence,

$$\mathbf{p}\bar{\mathbf{x}}_h > 0 \quad \text{if and only if} \quad \mathbf{p}(\bar{\mathbf{x}}_h - \bar{\bar{\mathbf{x}}}_h) > 0.$$

Also, obviously,

$$M_h > 0 \quad \text{if and only if either} \quad \mathbf{p}\bar{\mathbf{x}}_h > 0 \quad \text{or} \quad \sum_f d_{hf}(\mathbf{p}\mathbf{y}_f) > 0;$$

$$M_h - \mathbf{p}\bar{\bar{\mathbf{x}}}_h > 0 \quad \text{if and only if either} \quad \mathbf{p}(\bar{\mathbf{x}}_h - \bar{\bar{\mathbf{x}}}_h) > 0 \quad \text{or} \quad \sum_f d_{hf}(\mathbf{p}\mathbf{y}_f) > 0.$$

These statements taken together imply the lemma.

In particular, Lemma 5.1 implies that if $M_h > 0$, then there is some $\mathbf{x}'_h$ $(= \bar{\bar{\mathbf{x}}}_h)$ in X_h for which $\mathbf{p}\mathbf{x}'_h < M_h$.

THEOREM 2. If $(\mathbf{p}^*, \mathbf{u}^*, \mathscr{x}^*, \mathscr{y}^*)$ is a compensated equilibrium and $M_h^* > 0$, all h, then $(\mathbf{p}^*, \mathscr{x}^*, \mathscr{y}^*)$ is a competitive equilibrium.

Proof. D.5.2(a)–(c) are identical with D.5.1(a)–(c). If $M_h^* > 0$, then, by D.5.2(e), $\mathbf{p}^*\mathbf{x}_h^* = M_h^* > \mathbf{p}^*\mathbf{x}'_h$ for some $\mathbf{x}'_h$ in $\mathbf{X}_h$, as just remarked. By Lemma 4.3, it follows from D.5.2(d) that $\mathbf{x}_h^*$ maximizes $U_h(\mathbf{x}_h)$ subject to the budget constraint, $\mathbf{p}^*\mathbf{x}_h \leq M_h^*$.

It is not necessarily true that at a compensated equilibrium every household has positive income. The absence of positive income implies that there cannot exist a possible consumption vector that costs less than total income (since all possible consumption vectors are non-negative); in view of Lemma 4.3, this raises the possibility that utility-maximizing and cost-minimizing behavior do not coincide. In particular, from the discussion preceding Lemma 4.2, there is a possibility that the uncompensated demand functions are discontinuous.

It can be shown, however, that at least one household has positive income.

LEMMA 2. If $(\mathbf{p}^*, \mathbf{u}^*, \mathscr{x}^*, \mathscr{y}^*)$ is a compensated equilibrium, then $M_h^* > 0$, for some h.

Proof. It suffices to prove

$$\sum_h M_h^* > 0.$$

By definition, however,

$$\sum_h M_h^* = \sum_h \left[\mathbf{p}^*\bar{\mathbf{x}}_h + \sum_f d_{hf}(\mathbf{p}^*\mathbf{y}_f^*)\right] = \sum_h \mathbf{p}^*\bar{\mathbf{x}}_h + \sum_h \sum_f d_{hf}(\mathbf{p}^*\mathbf{y}_f^*)$$
$$= \sum_h \mathbf{p}^*\bar{\mathbf{x}}_h + \sum_f \left(\sum_h d_{hf}\right)\left(\mathbf{p}^*\mathbf{y}_f^*\right) = \sum_h \mathbf{p}^*\bar{\mathbf{x}}_h + \sum_f \mathbf{p}^*\mathbf{y}_f^*,$$

since

$$\sum_h d_{hf} = 1 \qquad \text{for all } f.$$

We have assumed (A.3.5) that the economy is capable of supplying a positive amount of each good; that is, there exists a socially possible production vector, $\bar{\mathbf{y}}$, such that, $\bar{\mathbf{x}} + \bar{\mathbf{y}} \gg 0$. Since $\mathbf{p}^* > \mathbf{0}$,

$$\mathbf{p}^*\bar{\mathbf{x}} + \mathbf{p}^*\bar{\mathbf{y}} = \mathbf{p}^*(\bar{\mathbf{x}} + \bar{\mathbf{y}}) > 0.$$

Since $\mathbf{y}_f^*$ is profit maximizing over Y_f, each f,

$$\mathbf{y}^* = \sum_f \mathbf{y}_f^* \quad \text{is profit maximizing over} \quad Y = \sum_f Y_f,$$

so that

$$\sum_f \mathbf{p}^*\mathbf{y}_f^* = \mathbf{p}^*\mathbf{y}^* \geq \mathbf{p}^*\bar{\mathbf{y}},$$

and therefore,

$$\sum_h M_h^* = \mathbf{p}^*\bar{\mathbf{x}} + \sum_f \mathbf{p}^*\mathbf{y}_f^* > 0.$$

For our purposes, Lemma 5.2 will be useful later in establishing a condition under which a compensated equilibrium is also a competitive equilibrium. It is worthwhile, however, to note here that a sufficiency theorem for Pareto efficiency can be established at this stage, although this theorem is not directly relevant to our main aim of proving the existence of equilibrium.

THEOREM 3. If $(\mathbf{p}^*,\mathbf{u}^*,\mathscr{x}^*,\mathscr{y}^*)$ is a compensated equilibrium, then $\mathbf{u}^*$ is a Pareto-efficient utility allocation.

Proof. Suppose not. Then there would exist an allocation $(\mathscr{x}^1,\mathscr{y}^1)$, which is feasible,

$$\sum_h \mathbf{x}_h^1 \leq \sum_h \bar{\mathbf{x}}_h + \sum_f \mathbf{y}_f^1, \tag{1}$$

such that $U_h(\mathbf{x}_h^1) > u_h^*$, all h. Since $\mathbf{x}_h^*$ minimizes the cost of achieving the utility level u_h^*,

$$\mathbf{p}^*\mathbf{x}_h^* \leq \mathbf{p}^*\mathbf{x}_h^1 \qquad \text{all } h,$$

or, in view of D.5.2(e), the balanced budget condition,

$$M_h^* \leq \mathbf{p}^*\mathbf{x}_h^1 \qquad \text{all } h.$$

By Lemma 5.2, there is at least one h for which $M_h^* > 0$. By Lemma 5.1, $\mathbf{p}^*\mathbf{x}_h^* = M_h^* > \mathbf{p}^*\bar{\mathbf{x}}_h$ for that h, and therefore, $\mathbf{x}_h^*$ is also utility maximizing subject to the budget constraint $\mathbf{p}^*\mathbf{x}_h \leq M_h^*$, by Lemma 4.3. Since $U_h(\mathbf{x}_h^1) > U_h(\mathbf{x}_h^*) = u_h^*$ in this case, it must be that

$$M_h^* < \mathbf{p}^*\mathbf{x}_h^1 \qquad \text{some } h,$$

so that

$$\sum_h \mathbf{p}^*\mathbf{x}_h^1 > \sum_h M_h^* = \sum_h \mathbf{p}^*\bar{\mathbf{x}}_h + \sum_f \mathbf{p}^*\mathbf{y}_f^*. \tag{2}$$

On the other hand, from (1), since $\mathbf{p}^* > 0$,

$$\sum_h \mathbf{p}^*\mathbf{x}_h^1 \leq \sum_h \mathbf{p}^*\bar{\mathbf{x}}_h + \sum_f \mathbf{p}^*\mathbf{y}_f^1.$$

Finally, since $\mathbf{y}_f^*$ is profit maximizing, $\mathbf{p}^*\mathbf{y}_f^1 \leq \mathbf{p}^*\mathbf{y}_f^*$, all f, so

$$\sum_h \mathbf{p}^*\mathbf{x}_h^1 \leq \sum_h \mathbf{p}^*\bar{\mathbf{x}}_h + \sum_f \mathbf{p}^*\mathbf{y}_f^*,$$

in contradiction to (2).

It may be worthwhile noting at this point that the theorems and lemmas of this section depend on only a few of the assumptions made in Chapters 3 and 4; in particular, they do not depend on the convexity assumptions.

2. Mapping the Pareto Frontier into a Simplex

The main tool in proving the existence of equilibrium is Kakutani's fixed-point theorem (see T.C.4). This theorem states that an upper semi-continuous correspondence that maps points in a compact convex set into convex subsets of that set has a fixed point; that is, there is one point that belongs to the subset associated with it by the correspondence. As we will see in the next section, there is a very natural mapping whose fixed point can be seen to be a compensated equilibrium; but the domain from which the mapping takes place is, in part, the Pareto frontier (more precisely, the domain is the Cartesian product of several sets, one of which is the set of non-negative, Pareto-efficient utility allocations). However, the Pareto frontier certainly need not be itself a convex set. Indeed, since the utility functions are defined only up to monotone transformations, convexity, which is a cardinal property, can have no real significance.

Nevertheless, the non-negative Pareto frontier can be shown to be essentially identical to a convex set, in fact to a simplex, from the topological point of view. It is sufficient to show that there is a simplex, whose dimensionality is one less than the number of households, which can be mapped in one-to-one, continuous fashion into the non-negative Pareto frontier.

We will first note that the non-negative Pareto frontier can be mapped continuously into a unit simplex and then show that the inverse of this mapping is defined and unique for all elements of the simplex.

Let U' be the non-negative Pareto frontier, that is, the set

$$U' = U \cap \{\mathbf{u} \mid \mathbf{u} \geq \mathbf{0}\},$$

where U is the set of Pareto-efficient points (see D.4.13). By Lemma 4.9, $\mathbf{0}$ is not Pareto efficient, so every non-negative efficient allocation is semi-positive, and in particular,

$$\sum_h u_h > 0.$$

Then the mapping

$$\mathbf{v}(\mathbf{u}) = \frac{\mathbf{u}}{\left(\sum_h u_h\right)} \tag{3}$$

is well defined and continuous on U'. Further, we obviously have

$$\mathbf{v}(\mathbf{u}) \geq 0 \qquad \sum_h v_h(\mathbf{u}) = 1,$$

so that $\mathbf{v}(\mathbf{u})$ maps U' into a unit simplex, S_H, where H is the number of households.

Definition 3. The set of *relative utility vectors* is defined by

$$S_H = \left\{\mathbf{v} \mid \mathbf{v} \geq 0, \ \sum_h v_h = 1\right\}.$$

It is easy to see that if the inverse of $\mathbf{v}(\mathbf{u})$ is well defined, it must be continuous. To show that it is well defined is to say that the equation

$$\mathbf{v}(\mathbf{u}) = \mathbf{v}$$

has a unique solution, $\mathbf{u}$, for every $\mathbf{v} \in S_H$. If

$$\lambda = \sum_h u_h,$$

a positive scalar, then $\mathbf{v}(\mathbf{u}) = \mathbf{v}$ implies

$$\mathbf{u} = \lambda\mathbf{v} \qquad \text{for some } \lambda > 0, \mathbf{u} \in U'. \tag{4}$$

Conversely, if (4) holds, then clearly, from (3), $\mathbf{v}(\mathbf{u}) = \mathbf{v}$. Hence, it suffices to show that (4) holds for every $\mathbf{v} \in V$ for a unique λ.

The functions $U_h(\mathbf{x}_h)$ together define a mapping from the set of feasible consumption allocations to the set of feasible utility allocations. Since the set of feasible consumption allocations is compact, as implied by T.4.2, and the functions U_h are continuous, the set of feasible utility allocations is compact. For fixed $\mathbf{v}$, then, the set of scalars,

$$\{\lambda \mid \lambda\mathbf{v} \quad \text{a feasible utility allocation}\}, \tag{5}$$

is also compact. Since $\mathbf{0} = 0\mathbf{v}$ is certainly feasible for all $\mathbf{v}$ (let $x = \bar{\bar{x}}, y = 0$), the set (5) is non-null and hence has a maximum.

$$\bar{\lambda}(\mathbf{v}) = \max\{\lambda \mid \lambda\mathbf{v} \quad \text{a feasible utility allocation}\}.$$

We will show that $\lambda\mathbf{v}$ is efficient if and only if $\lambda = \bar{\lambda}(\mathbf{v})$; as previously remarked, this suffices for the existence of an inverse to $\mathbf{v}(\mathbf{u})$. If $\lambda > \bar{\lambda}(\mathbf{v})$, then, by definition, $\lambda\mathbf{v}$ is not feasible and, therefore, not efficient. Now suppose $\lambda = \bar{\lambda}(\mathbf{v})$. By definition, $\bar{\lambda}(\mathbf{v})\mathbf{v}$ is feasible. Suppose it were dominated; then, for some feasible $\mathbf{u}$, $\mathbf{u} \gg \bar{\lambda}(\mathbf{v})\mathbf{v}$ (see D.4.12). But then there exists $\lambda > \bar{\lambda}(\mathbf{v})$ for which $\mathbf{u} \geq \lambda\mathbf{v}$. Then $\lambda\mathbf{v}$ is feasible, contrary to the definition of $\bar{\lambda}(\mathbf{v})$. Hence, $\bar{\lambda}(\mathbf{v})\mathbf{v}$ is undominated and, therefore, efficient.

Since, as already remarked, $\mathbf{0} = 0\mathbf{v}$ is not efficient, it must be that

$$\bar{\lambda}(\mathbf{v}) > 0.$$

Suppose now $\lambda < \bar{\lambda}(\mathbf{v})$. Then trivially,

$$\lambda\mathbf{v} \leq \bar{\lambda}(\mathbf{v})\mathbf{v}, \quad \lambda v_h < \bar{\lambda}(\mathbf{v})v_h \quad \text{if} \quad \bar{\lambda}(\mathbf{v})v_h > 0.$$

By Lemma 4.13, then, $\lambda\mathbf{v}$ is dominated and, therefore, not efficient.

LEMMA 3. Let S_H be the simplex of relative utilities. Then there is a continuous function, $\mathbf{u}(\mathbf{v})$, mapping S_H into the non-negative Pareto frontier, such that $v_h = 0$ if and only if $u_h(\mathbf{v}) = 0$.

3. The Existence of Compensated Equilibrium

We are now ready to prove expeditiously the existence of a compensated equilibrium. We introduce two more pieces of notation,

$$s_h(\mathbf{p},\omega) = \mathbf{p}\left[\bar{\mathbf{x}}_h + \sum_f d_{hf}(\mathbf{p}\mathbf{y}_f) - \mathbf{x}_h\right] = M_h(\mathbf{p},\mathcal{Y}) - \mathbf{p}\mathbf{x}_h, \qquad (6)$$

the budgetary surplus for household h if prices are $\mathbf{p}$ and the allocation is ω, and

$$V(\mathbf{p},\omega) = S_H \cap \{\mathbf{v} \mid v_h = 0 \quad \text{if } s_h(\mathbf{p},\omega) < 0\}. \qquad (7)$$

We may think of (7) as an instruction to punish households that incur budgetary deficits by setting their relative utility, v_h, equal to 0, while imposing no conditions on other households. By Lemma 5.3, equating a relative utility to 0 is equivalent to equating the utility of that household to 0.

The idea of the mapping can be expressed simply. We start with a price vector, $\mathbf{p}$, a relative utility allocation, $\mathbf{v}$, and a feasible commodity allocation, ω. These need not be consistent with each other; we assume each arbitrarily chosen from its appropriate domain. The relative utility allocation determines uniquely a non-negative Pareto-efficient utility allocation, $\mathbf{u} = \mathbf{u}(\mathbf{v})$, by Lemma 5.3. Then there is a non-null set of price vectors, $P(\mathbf{u})$, that supports the allocation $\mathbf{u}$, by T.4.4 and D.4.14; by definition of efficiency and feasibility, there is a set of feasible allocations, $\hat{\mathscr{W}}(\mathbf{u})$, that permits the realization of the utility allocation $\mathbf{u}$, by D.4.10 and D.4.12; and the initial prices and allocation define budgetary surpluses and therewith a new set of relative utilities, by (6) and (7).

Since $\mathbf{u}$ is a function of $\mathbf{v}$, the sets of prices and of feasible allocations can be written $P[\mathbf{u}(\mathbf{v})]$ and $\hat{\mathscr{W}}[\mathbf{u}(\mathbf{v})]$, respectively.

The domain of the mapping, then, is the Cartesian product, $s_n \times S_H \times \hat{\mathscr{W}}$. s_n and S_H are simplexes and, therefore, compact convex sets; by T.4.2, $\hat{\mathscr{W}}$ is compact and convex. Hence, the domain is compact and convex.

The correspondence defined on $s_n \times V \times \hat{\mathscr{W}}$ is, formally,

$$P[\mathbf{u}(\mathbf{v})] \times V(\mathbf{p},\omega) \times \hat{\mathscr{W}}[\mathbf{u}(\mathbf{v})]. \qquad (8)$$

By the definitions already cited,

$$P[\mathbf{u}(\mathbf{v})] \subset P \qquad V(\mathbf{p},\omega) \subset S_H \qquad \hat{\mathscr{W}}[u(v)] \subset \hat{\mathscr{W}},$$

so that the correspondence does map the domain into subsets of itself. By T.4.6, $P(\mathbf{u})$ is compact and convex for fixed u and upper semi-continuous in $\mathbf{u}$; since $\mathbf{u}(\mathbf{v})$ is continuous in $\mathbf{v}$ and $\mathbf{u}$ is fixed for fixed $\mathbf{v}$, $P[\mathbf{u}(\mathbf{v})]$ is compact and convex for fixed $\mathbf{v}$, and upper semi-continuous in $\mathbf{v}$. From Theorem 4.5, Corollary 5, it follows similarly that $\hat{\mathscr{W}}[\mathbf{u}(\mathbf{v})]$ is compact and convex for fixed $\mathbf{v}$ and upper semi-continuous in v. From (7), for fixed $\mathbf{p}$ and ω, $V(\mathbf{p},\omega)$ is the intersection of a compact convex set, S_H, with a closed convex set and, therefore, is compact and convex. We wish to prove that it, too, is upper semi-continuous in its variables.

Let $\mathbf{p}^\nu \to \mathbf{p}^0$, $\omega^\nu \to \omega^0$, $\mathbf{v}^\nu \to \mathbf{v}^0$, $\mathbf{v}^\nu \in V(\mathbf{p}^\nu,\omega^\nu)$. Consider any h for which

$$s_h(\mathbf{p}^0,\omega^0) < 0. \tag{9}$$

Since s_h is a continuous function of $\mathbf{p}$ and ω, it must be that for ν sufficiently large $s_h(\mathbf{p}^\nu,\omega^\nu) < 0$. Then, by definition (7), $v_h^\nu = 0$ for all such ν. Trivially, $v_h^0 = 0$. But then we have shown that $v_h^0 = 0$ whenever (9) holds. Since $\mathbf{v}^\nu \in V$, all ν, it is certainly true that $v^0 \in V$; by (7), $v^0 \in V(p^0,\omega^0)$, as was to be proved.

Thus, all three components of the mapping (8) are compact and convex for fixed values of $\mathbf{p},\mathbf{v},\omega$ and, hence, so is the entire mapping. Also, all three components are upper semi-continuous functions of these variables and, hence, so is the entire mapping. By Kakutani's fixed-point theorem (see T.C.4), this mapping has a fixed point; that is, there is a point $(\mathbf{p}^*,\mathbf{v}^*,\omega^*) \in S_n \times S_H \times \hat{\mathscr{W}}$ such that

$$(\mathbf{p}^*,\mathbf{v}^*,\omega^*) \in P[\mathbf{u}(\mathbf{v}^*)] \times V(\mathbf{p}^*,\omega^*) \times \hat{\mathscr{W}}[\mathbf{u}(\mathbf{v}^*)]. \tag{10}$$

We show that this fixed point in fact satisfies all the conditions for a compensated equilibrium, as given in D.5.2. First, let

$$\mathbf{u}^* = \mathbf{u}(\mathbf{v}^*). \tag{11}$$

Then (10) can be written as the three statements,

$$\mathbf{p}^* \in P(\mathbf{u}^*), \tag{12}$$

$$\mathbf{v}^* \in V(\mathbf{p}^*,\omega^*), \tag{13}$$

$$\omega^* \in \hat{\mathscr{W}}(\mathbf{u}^*). \tag{14}$$

Recall the definitions of $P(\mathbf{u})$ (D.4.14) and $\hat{\mathscr{W}}(\mathbf{u})$ (D.4.10), and then use (12) and (14) in conjunction with the basic theorem on Pareto efficiency, T.4.4. From (12) and part (a) of T.4.4, D.5.2(a) holds. From the definition of $\hat{\mathscr{W}}(\mathbf{u})$, (14) implies D.5.2(b). From (14) and (12) together, part (d) of the theorem implies D.5.2(c) and (d) and also

$$\sum_h \mathbf{p}^*\mathbf{x}_h^* = \sum_h \left[\mathbf{p}^*\bar{\mathbf{x}}_h + \sum_f d_{hf}(\mathbf{p}^*\mathbf{y}_f^*)\right],$$

which, from (6), can be written

$$\sum_h s_h(\mathbf{p}^*,\omega^*) = 0. \tag{15}$$

We seek to show that D.5.2(e) holds; that is, $s_h(\mathbf{p}^*,\omega^*)=0$, all h. From (15), it suffices to show that $s_h(\mathbf{p}^*,\omega^*) \geq 0$, all h. Suppose, then, $s_h(\mathbf{p}^*,\omega^*) < 0$, some h. From (7) and (13), $v_h^* = 0$; by Lemma 5.3 and (11), $u_h^* = 0$. By construction, $\bar{\bar{\mathbf{x}}}_h \in X_h(0)$; since $\mathbf{x}_h^*$ minimizes $\mathbf{p}^*\mathbf{x}_h$ subject to $\mathbf{x}_h \in X_h(u_h^*) = X_h(0)$,

$$\mathbf{p}^*\mathbf{x}_h^* \leq \mathbf{p}^*\bar{\bar{\mathbf{x}}}_h \leq \mathbf{p}^*\bar{\mathbf{x}}_h \leq M_h^*.$$

The last two inequalities follow from the facts that $\bar{\bar{\mathbf{x}}}_h \leq \bar{\mathbf{x}}_h$ and $\mathbf{p}^*\mathbf{y}^* \geq \mathbf{p}^*\mathbf{0} = 0$, by profit maximization. Hence, the assumption $s_h(\mathbf{p}^*,\omega^*) < 0$ implies that $s_h(\mathbf{p}^*,\omega^*) \geq 0$, a contradiction.

THEOREM 4. Under the assumptions made, a compensated equilibrium exists.

4. The Existence of a Competitive Equilibrium

To complete the program of proving existence of competitive equilibrium, we have to use T.5.4 by giving a condition under which a compensated equilibrium is a competitive equilibrium. We already have such a condition in T.5.2, but by itself it is not very useful. Therefore, we need a sufficient condition that $M_h^* > 0$ for all h at a compensated equilibrium.

In terms of the example preceding Lemma 4.2, what is wanted is a condition to ensure that the price that the household receives for its sole asset does not approach zero. Intuitively, the condition required is that the asset in question be of value, directly or indirectly, to others, so that as the price declines there will eventually arise a demand that will equal supply at a positive price.

We will say that household h' is *resource related* to household h'' if some increase in those assets held by household h' in some positive amounts can be used in a reallocation of the entire economy so that no household is worse off and household h'' is strictly better off. Note that the only property of household h' that is relevant to the definition is a list of those commodities with which he is endowed in some positive amount; the only relevant property of household h'' is its utility function. Note too that the manner by which the additional endowments improve the lots of household h'' may be very indirect. Of course, they may enter directly into the utility function of h''; they may be factors of production used to produce commodities that increase the utility of h''; they may be neither of these, but rather, they may enable the production of commodities that increase the welfare of some other household, permitting the last to give up some other goods so that its utility level does not on balance fall below the initial level, while h'' is made better off by the goods given up.

DEFINITION 4. Household h' is said to be *resource related* to household h'' if, for every feasible allocation, $(\mathscr{x},\mathscr{y})$, there exists an allocation $(\mathscr{x}',\mathscr{y}')$ and a vector $\bar{\mathbf{x}}'$ such that $(\mathscr{x}',\mathscr{y}')$ would be feasible if the endowment were $\bar{\mathbf{x}}'$, that is,

$$\text{(a)} \quad \sum_h \mathbf{x}'_h \leq \sum_f \mathbf{y}'_f + \bar{\mathbf{x}}', \ \mathbf{x}'_h \in X_h, \ \mathbf{y}'_f \in Y_f;$$

everybody is at least as well off under $(\mathscr{x}',\mathscr{y}')$ as under $(\mathscr{x},\mathscr{y})$ and household h'' is better off,

$$\text{(b)} \quad U_h(\mathbf{x}'_h) \geq U_h(\mathbf{x}_h), \text{ all } h,$$
$$\text{(c)} \quad U_{h''}(\mathbf{x}'_{h''}) > U_{h''}(\mathbf{x}_{h''});$$

and $\bar{\mathbf{x}}'$ is an increase in endowment only for those commodities in the endowment of household h' in positive amounts,

$$\text{(d)} \quad \bar{\mathbf{x}}' \geq \bar{\mathbf{x}},$$
$$\text{(e)} \quad \bar{x}'_i > \bar{x}_i \text{ only if } \bar{x}_{h'i} > 0.$$

We use this definition to show that if, at a compensated equilibrium, some household has a positive income, then any household that is resource related to it has a positive income; in effect the first household has an effective demand for the endowment of the second and, therefore, makes its income positive.

LEMMA 4. Let M_h^* be the income of household h at some compensated equilibrium. If h' is resource related to h'' and $M_{h''}^* > 0$, then $M_{h'}^* > 0$.

Proof. Let the compensated equilibrium be $(\mathbf{p}^*,\mathbf{u}^*,\mathscr{x}^*,\mathscr{y}^*)$. By D.5.4, we can find a vector $\bar{\mathbf{x}}'$ and an allocation $(\mathscr{x}',\mathscr{y}')$ satisfying (a)–(e) with $(\mathscr{x},\mathscr{y})$ replaced by $(\mathscr{x}^*,\mathscr{y}^*)$. Since $\mathbf{x}_h^*$ minimizes $\mathbf{p}^*\mathbf{x}_h$ subject to $U_h(\mathbf{x}_h) \geq u_h^*$, it follows from (b) that

$$\mathbf{p}^*\mathbf{x}_h' \geq \mathbf{p}^*\mathbf{x}_h^* \qquad \text{all } h.$$

Since $M_{h''}^* > 0$, it follows, as in the proof of T.5.2, that $\mathbf{x}_{h''}^*$ maximizes $U_{h''}(\mathbf{x}_{h''})$ subject to $p^*\mathbf{x}_{h''} \leq p^*\mathbf{x}_{h''}^*$. From (c), then, it is impossible that $\mathbf{x}_{h''}'$ satisfies this budget constraint:

$$\mathbf{p}^*\mathbf{x}_{h''}' > \mathbf{p}^*\mathbf{x}_{h''}^*.$$

Thus,

$$\mathbf{p}^* \sum_h \mathbf{x}_h' > \mathbf{p}^* \sum_h \mathbf{x}_h^*.$$

By profit maximization, $\mathbf{p}^*\mathbf{y}_f^* \geq \mathbf{p}^*\mathbf{y}_f'$, all f, so that,

$$\mathbf{p}^* \sum_f \mathbf{y}_f' \leq \mathbf{p}^* \sum_f \mathbf{y}_f^*.$$

From D.5.2(e), summed over all h,

$$\mathbf{p}^* \sum_h \mathbf{x}_h^* = \sum_f \mathbf{p}^*\mathbf{y}_f^* + \mathbf{p}^*\bar{\mathbf{x}},$$

so that

$$\mathbf{p}^* \sum_h \mathbf{x}_h' - \mathbf{p}^* \sum_f \mathbf{y}_f' > \mathbf{p}^*\bar{\mathbf{x}}.$$

On the other hand, since $\mathbf{p}^* > \mathbf{0}$, it follows from D.5.4(a) that

$$\mathbf{p}^* \sum_h \mathbf{x}_h' - \mathbf{p}^* \sum_f \mathbf{y}_f' \leq \mathbf{p}^*\bar{\mathbf{x}}',$$

so that $\mathbf{p}^*(\bar{\mathbf{x}}' - \bar{\mathbf{x}}) > 0$. This is equivalent to saying that, for some i, both $p_i^* > 0$ and $\bar{x}_i' - \bar{x}_i > 0$. From D.5.4(e), this implies that, for some i, $p_i^* > 0$ and $\bar{x}_{h'i} > 0$, which implies that $\mathbf{p}^*\bar{\mathbf{x}}_{h'} > 0$, and therefore, $M_{h'}^* > 0$.

The condition that one household must be resource related to another is weak, in view of all the possible reallocations that are permitted. A still weaker relation is the following:

DEFINITION 5. Household h' is *indirectly resource related* to household h'' if there is a sequence of households, h_i, $(i = 0, \ldots, n)$, with $h_0 = h'$, $h_n = h''$, and h_i resource related to h_{i+1} $(i = 0, \ldots, n - 1)$.

An example will show that the relation "indirectly resource related" is, in fact, weaker (holds more often) than the relation "resource related." Consider a pure exchange economy with three households, 1, 2, and 3. Household h holds an initial stock of commodity h only; but the utility function of household 1 values only commodity 3, that of household 2 only commodity 1, and that of household 3 only commodity 2. Then it is easy to verify that household 1 is resource related to household 2 and household 2 to household 3, so that household 1 is indirectly resource related to household 3; but household 1 is not resource related to household 3, since, given an allocation in which households 1, 2, and 3 receive all of commodities 3, 1, and 2, respectively, an increase in the initial endowment of commodity 1 cannot be used to increase the utility of household 3.

Corollary 1. Let M_h^* be the income of household h at some compensated equilibrium. If h' is indirectly resource related to h'' and $M_{h''}^* > 0$, then $M_{h'}^* > 0$.

Proof. By definition, h_{n-1} is resource related to $h_n = h''$. Since $M_{h''}^* > 0$, $M_{h_{n-1}}^* > 0$, by Lemma 5.4. Then, repeating this argument, we must have $M_{h_{n-2}}^* > 0$, and so forth, so that finally $M_{h_0}^* = M_{h'}^* > 0$.

It is now simple to state and prove a theorem that ensures that at a compensated equilibrium $M_h^* > 0$, all h, and therefore, it is a competitive equilibrium by T.5.2.

THEOREM 5. If every household is indirectly resource related to every other and if all the other assumptions of Chapters 3 and 4 hold, then a competitive equilibrium exists.

Proof. Since all assumptions hold, there exists a compensated equilibrium, by T.5.4. By Lemma 5.2, $M_{h''}^* > 0$, some h''. By hypothesis, every household is indirectly resource related to household h'', so that by Corollary 1, $M_h^* > 0$, all h.

5. Equilibrium with Debt and Bankruptcy

If the proofs of T.5.4 and the lemmas and theorems leading to it are examined in detail, it will be seen that assumption A.4.2 (that the initial endowment more or less dominates an element, $\bar{\mathbf{x}}_h$, of the consumption possibility set) was used at only two points: in the proof of Lemma 4.9, that $\mathbf{0}$ is a dominated utility vector, and at the very end, to show the impossibility of a budgetary deficit at equilibrium; the mapping used ensures that a budgetary deficit ($s_h < 0$) implies zero utility, which can be achieved, however, without any deficit since the zero utility level can always be achieved without any trade at all. In ordinary language, assumption A.4.2 serves to avoid the possibility of bankruptcy.

Therefore, if we replace A.4.2 by the assumption that $\mathbf{0}$ is dominated, it turns out that an existence theorem for equilibrium with bankruptcy has been proved. We still have that (15) holds, so that budgetary surpluses total to zero, but it is no longer true that $s_h(\mathbf{p}^*, w^*) = 0$ for all h. Instead, for some households, $s_h < 0$ at equilibrium; they are the bankrupts. The mapping, however, does insist that the utility of a bankrupt be zero. If we drop A.4.2, we can redefine the zero utility level arbitrarily. We can now interpret it as the minimum level that society insists on providing for every household, even for those that cannot achieve this level in the marketplace. Of course, the budgetary deficits of the bankrupts must be balanced by budgetary surpluses of others; these may be interpreted as the taxes needed to be paid to maintain the minimum guaranteed utility level.

With this new concept of equilibrium, it is also possible to introduce initial debts into the system. In addition to their commodity endowments and their ownership of shares in firms, households may be supposed to start with debts owed to others or with credits owed by others. Let the instruments of debt be termed *bonds*, and let b_h be the initial bond holdings of household h. A negative value represents a net debtor position. In a closed economy

$$\sum_h b_h = 0.$$

A bond is an obligation to pay that may be stated in terms of units of account or in terms of some one commodity or in terms of a bundle of commodities. To cover all these cases, we suppose simply that b_h is measured in units of account and is a continuous function of prices. (Thus, if b_h^1 is the bond holding stated as an obligation to pay in units of commodity 1, $b_h = p_1 b_h^1$.)

With debts, the income of the household is

$$M_h = \mathbf{p}\bar{\mathbf{x}}_h + \sum_f d_{hf}(\mathbf{p}\mathbf{y}_f) + b_h(\mathbf{p}).$$

Then in an economy with bonds we can define a compensated equilibrium concept in which bankruptcy is allowed.

DEFINITION 6. In an economy with initial holdings of bonds, a price vector $\mathbf{p}^*$, a non-negative utility allocation $\mathbf{u}^*$, a consumption allocation $\mathscr{x}^*$, a production allocation $\mathscr{y}^*$, and a redistribution vector $\mathbf{s}^*$ constitute a *compensated equilibrium with bankruptcy* if D.5.2(a)–(d) hold, and in addition,

$$\text{(e)}\quad \mathbf{p}^*\mathbf{x}_h^* = M_h^* - s_h^* = \mathbf{p}^*\bar{\mathbf{x}}_h + \sum_f d_{hf}(\mathbf{p}^*\mathbf{y}_f^*) + b_h(\mathbf{p}^*) - s_h^*,$$

$$\text{(f)}\quad \sum_h s_h^* = 0,$$

$$\text{(g)}\quad u_h^* = 0 \text{ for any household for which } s_h^* < 0.$$

It is now obvious that the following theorem holds.

THEOREM 7. If the assumptions of Chapters 3 and 4, other than A.4.2, hold, if a zero utility level is prescribed for each household in such a way that there exists a feasible allocation $(\mathscr{x},\mathscr{y})$ for which $U_h(\mathbf{x}_h) > 0$, all h, and if $b_h(\mathbf{p})$ is continuous for each h,

$$\sum_h b_h(\mathbf{p}) = 0 \qquad \text{for all } \mathbf{p},$$

then there exists a compensated equilibrium with bankruptcy.

Remark 1. The conditions under which this compensated equilibrium is a competitive equilibrium and, indeed, the exact definition of a competitive equilibrium with bankruptcy remain open questions.

Remark 2. In Section 4.4, it was noted that a Pareto-efficient allocation possibly could be realized as a competitive equilibrium after some reallocation of the initial endowment. It is clear that a reallocation in real terms is not necessary; a reallocation by creating debts and credits would always do. If ω^* is a Pareto-efficient allocation that is sustained by a price vector $\mathbf{p}^*$, then if we define

$$b_h = \mathbf{p}^*\mathbf{x}_h - \left[\mathbf{p}^*\bar{\mathbf{x}}_h + \sum_f d_{hf}(\mathbf{p}^*\mathbf{y}_f^*)\right],$$

and if we define $u_h^* = U_h(\mathbf{x}_h^*)$, then it is obvious that $(\mathbf{p}^*,\mathbf{u}^*,\omega^*,\mathbf{0})$ constitutes a compensated equilibrium in the sense of D.5.6, indeed one in which no bankruptcy occurs in fact. For further discussion of the implications of bankruptcy for the existence of equilibrium, see Section 14.3.

6. Equilibrium under Uncertainty

We note briefly that the general equilibrium model of Chapters 3–5 has more than one interpretation. It is well known, of course, that the commodities can be regarded as differentiated in time or in space or in both even when they are physically identical. Then the equilibrium found is one in time or space. In the case of a spatial economy there would be different markets and different prices in different localities; more specific theorems might be obtained by noting that there are special kinds of activities, such as transportation, that transform commodities in one place to commodities in another; if these activities have special properties, such as constant returns, special theorems can be stated concerning the relations between prices in different locations.

Similarly, if the equilibrium model is regarded as extended in time, there will be different markets for commodities at different times. A market for a commodity to be delivered at some future time is a *futures* market. In the pure model, all markets, current and futures, are operating in the present; once the transactions have been carried out, there will be no need, in principle, for any more markets, since all future transactions will have already been contracted for. Note that allowance is made in this intertemporal model for the fact that production takes time; in a possible production vector, the positive components may all refer to future commodities, while the inputs are current. Again special assumptions about the nature of production, such as its recursive character, and in particular, about the transfer of commodities from the present to the future, as through storage, lead to the special theorems that constitute capital theory.

Rather than enlarge on these well-known themes, we will briefly discuss another interpretation. Suppose that, in fact, there is uncertainty about endowments and production. This can be established by saying that endowments and production possibilities depend on the *state of the world*; that is, a state of the world is a description so complete that, if known to be true, it would completely define all endowments and production possibilities. If there are finitely many states of the world, then the endowment of household h can be described by the numbers $\bar{x}_{his}$, the amount of commodity i held by household h if state s occurs. Similarly, a possible production vector for a firm, f, may depend on the state of the world (e.g., the dependence of farm output on weather). Thus $\mathbf{y}_{fs}$ is a possible production vector for firm f if state s occurs. We can describe endowments and production possibilities then by vectors whose components vary according to both commodity and state of the world. The vector $\bar{\mathbf{x}}_h$ has the components $\bar{x}_{his}$, where both i and s vary. A possible production vector $\mathbf{y}_f$ then has also components y_{fis}. The extent that some components are independent of the state of the world will be reflected in the fact that for some i, y_{fis} will be the same for all s, as will typically be true if some inputs have to be committed before knowing the state of the world.

If endowments and production possibilities depend on the state of the world, then the feasibility of an allocation depends, of course, on the state of the world, and therefore commitments to consumption must vary similarly. Hence, a consumption vector, $\mathbf{x}_h$, must have dimensions conforming to those of $\bar{\mathbf{x}}_h$ and $\mathbf{y}_f$, that is, its components must be written, $\mathbf{x}_{his}$. For a given state of the world, feasibility is defined as before; hence, it follows easily that with the new interpretation of the production and consumption vectors, feasibility is also defined as before. Now it means feasibility for all states of nature, in the sense that the commitments have enough flexibility to be always satisfiable.

It should be noted that a preference ordering for consumption vectors in the new interpretation contains elements of judgment about the likelihoods of the different states of the world as well as elements of evaluation of tastes. A consumption vector in the present sense can be regarded as a sequence of consumption vectors in the narrower sense, one for each state of the world; let $\mathbf{x}_{hs}$ be the vector with components x_{his}, where i varies over commodities. For simplicity of discussion assume that there are only two possible states of the world, $s = 1,2$. Thus, in comparing $\mathbf{x}_h = (\mathbf{x}_{h1},\mathbf{x}_{h2})$ with $\mathbf{x}'_h = (\mathbf{x}'_{h1},\mathbf{x}'_{h2})$, a small preference for $\mathbf{x}_{h1}$ over $\mathbf{x}'_{h1}$ may outweigh a very large preference for $\mathbf{x}'_{h2}$ over $\mathbf{x}_{h2}$ if state 2 is believed to be very unlikely to occur. The decomposition of a utility function for consumption vectors into elements of belief and of pure taste (as under certainty) has been the subject of much research; the expected-utility hypothesis of Bernoulli [1938, 1954] has been the most favored. According to this hypothesis, the preference ordering over consumption vectors $\mathbf{x}_h = (\mathbf{x}_{h1}, \ldots, \mathbf{x}_{hs}, \ldots)$ can be represented by a utility function with the special form

$$\sum_s \pi_{hs} U_h(\mathbf{x}_{hs}),$$

where $\pi_{hs} \geq 0$, all s, $\pi_{hs} > 0$, some s. Without loss of generality, we may assume

$$\sum_s \pi_{hs} = 1.$$

Then π_{hs} may be thought of as the probability of s as believed by household h (sometimes called *subjective* or *personal probability*), U_h a function reflecting tastes, including tastes for taking or rejecting risks as well as for choices among commodities. The function U_h associated with a given preference ordering is unique up to a linear transformation. The Bernoulli hypothesis has been shown by various writers to be implied in turn by seemingly weaker and more plausible sets of hypotheses; see Ramsey [1926], de Finetti [1937], von Neumann and Morgenstern [1947, Appendix], and Savage [1954].

With the new interpretation, the entire formalism of this and the preceding two chapters remains valid. Each commodity now must be interpreted as a contingent claim with the double index $i.s$, a promise to supply one unit of commodity i if state s occurs and nothing otherwise. The assumptions have to be reinterpreted, a task that will not be undertaken in detail here. For the most part, the arguments for the plausibility of these assumptions remain unchanged, but the assumption of convexity of preferences has a new implication in the case of uncertainty.

Consider a simple example. Suppose that there are just two states of the world and the preference ordering is symmetric with respect to them, that is, that $\mathbf{x}_h \sim_h \mathbf{x}'_h$ if $\mathbf{x}_{h1} = \mathbf{x}'_{h2}$ and $\mathbf{x}_{h2} = \mathbf{x}'_{h1}$. This could arise because the household judged the two states to be equally possible (in the Bernoulli case, if $\pi_{h1} = \pi_{h2}$) and if tastes in the two states were the same. Then convexity implies that $\mathbf{x}''_h = \frac{1}{2}\mathbf{x}_h + \frac{1}{2}\mathbf{x}'_h \succcurlyeq_h \mathbf{x}_h$. But $\mathbf{x}''_{h1} = \mathbf{x}''_{h2} = \frac{1}{2}\mathbf{x}_{h1} + \frac{1}{2}\mathbf{x}_{h2}$; that is, the certainty of the average bundle is preferred to a bundle varying by chance. Thus, *convexity of preferences under uncertainty implies risk aversion*. This may well be a plausible assumption for the usual run of business decisions, but it should be understood that an additional hypothesis is implied. It will be shown in Chapter 7 that even without convexity of preferences at least an approximate equilibrium exists.

The equilibrium will then yield a set of prices p_{is}^*, the price paid in return for a promise to supply one unit of commodity i if state s occurs and nothing otherwise. The firm then will be maximizing

$$\sum_i \sum_s p_{is}^* y_{is};$$

this is linear in input-output decisions, so that, in equilibrium, the firm acts as if it were risk-neutral. All the risk-bearing activities of the economy are carried on by households in accordance with their tastes for risk bearing and their assessments of the likelihoods of different states of the world. In effect, the households, in addition to their economic functions of satisfying their consumption needs and supplying inputs, will also be writing and selling insurance policies.

The approach sketched so far implies that there is a final settlement after one period when all uncertainty is resolved. This can be generalized. Suppose, to illustrate, that some information will be available at time 1, and all uncertainties will be resolved at time 2. Thus, there may be uncertainties about the weather in both periods; the state of the world involves a description of the weather in both periods. At time 1, however, only the weather at that time is known. Then the state of the world might be described by a pair of integers (s_1,s_2), where s_1 is known at time 1 and s_2 at time 2. Commodities now bear two subscripts denoting uncertainty, thus, $x_{his_1s_2}$. However, commitments for transactions at time 1 must in fact be independent of s_2, though not of s_1. Contracts for time 2 will depend, in general, on both s_1 and s_2.

With this more general interpretation, it is again possible to reinterpret the model of this and the last two chapters to show the existence of equilibrium. There is a very important qualification to the possibility of this interpretation of equilibrium under uncertainty that must be specified. For simplicity, we return to the one-period model. The participants in a market for a commodity conditional upon a state of the world all must know which state has occurred. Obviously, an individual whose endowment is different in all states of the world will know which has occurred. On the other hand, even an individual whose endowment is independent of the state of the world may still want to make conditional contracts because the terms on which he can buy goods depend on endowments and production possibilities of others, which, in turn, do depend on the state of the world. If, in fact, he is unable to enter into such contracts because he will never know the true state, the model of equilibrium under uncertainty just sketched is untenable. An individual who knows that information will become available to part of the market, but not to him, will be unable to enter into conditional contracts. But since he knows that future prices, in fact, will depend on this information, he treats them from his viewpoint as random variables. Thus, he may be led to take certain prudent actions, such as investing in highly safe securities, possibly money, which will be available to meet the future uncertainties. The single market for all uncertainties, present and future, must be dissolved into a sequence of markets that come into equilibrium at successive time points as information becomes available to some members of the economy. Then decisions are made in earlier markets on the basis of current estimates of the likelihoods of alternative possible outcomes on future markets.

A particular case of failures of markets to exist because of inequalities in information structure is the so-called *moral hazard*, to use a term found in insurance literature. An insurance company may be unwilling to sell an unduly large amount of fire insurance to a household because it creates an incentive to carelessness. The matter may be put this way in the formal language we have been using: There are three possible states of the world—no fire hazard, mild fire hazard, which leads to fire only when the household is careless, and severe fire hazard, which leads to fire regardless of precautions. According to the analysis of this section, there is an equilibrium in which the two kinds of fire hazard are distinguished and different insurance policies, with different premiums, written for each. Thus, the household might be compensated for the occurrence of a mild fire hazard, whether or not fire actually breaks out; whether it does depends on the household's carelessness, for which it bears full financial responsibility.

In fact, of course, the insurance company can only observe whether or not a fire has occurred; it cannot distinguish between mild and severe fire hazards. Therefore, it will write a single policy against fire. Then, however, the incentive for the household to be careful will be removed. An equilibrium can be shown to exist, but it will certainly not have the Pareto-efficiency properties of the pure model of equilibrium under uncertainty as first sketched in this section.

Notes

The first theorem on existence of equilibrium in a fully developed model of production and consumer choice, in which supply and demand may be multi-valued correspondences, is due to Arrow and Debreu [1954]; they were influenced by the earlier work of Wald, as well as by Nash's fundamental result on the somewhat related problem of existence of equilibrium points in n-person games (see Section 1.5 and Notes to Chapter 2). An independent proof was that of Nikaidô [1956]. A systematic presentation with much improvement is the subject of Debreu [1959]. The most general existence theorems, more general than those proved here, can be found in Debreu [1962].

While proving the existence of equilibrium with single-valued excess-demand functions in Chapter 2, it was sufficient to use a mapping from the price simplex into itself. The basic reason why the domain of the mapping is more complex here is because of the multi-valuedness of the excess demands; in the case of Chapter 2, specifying quantities as well would have been superfluous since prices uniquely determine quantities. McKenzie [1959] in fact has shown that a price-to-price mapping can be used even in the general case; however, since he assumes constant returns to scale, there are no profits to distribute, and hence, the problem of determining the profits of individual firms does not arise. In any case, his ingenious proof involves some artificialities that are avoided here.

The mapping used in Section 5.3 is novel. Negishi [1960] used a mapping that, like this, involved welfare-economic considerations, but in a considerably different way.

The problem created by discontinuity of uncompensated demand functions when some prices are zero was recognized by Arrow and Debreu [1954, Sections 4 and 5]; they stated a condition that ensured that the endowments of any household are desired, directly or indirectly, by others, so that incomes cannot fall to zero. A general and very elegant formulation of such a condition is due to McKenzie [1959, 1961], based on an earlier suggestion of Gale [1957]. The definitions of resource relatedness and indirect resource relatedness used in Section 5.4 are variants of McKenzie's.

The proofs of existence of competitive equilibrium in Arrow and Debreu and in McKenzie are based on approximations by economies in which continuity is not a problem because, in effect, the households have endowments with positive quantities of all commodities. The present discussion is closer to that of Debreu [1962]; he first proved the existence of what he calls a quasi-equilibrium, a concept closely related to, but not identical with, that of a compensated equilibrium and then stated conditions under which a quasi-equilibrium is a competitive equilibrium.

The interpretation of equilibrium theory for the case of uncertainty sketched in Section 5.6 was first introduced by Arrow [1953, 1963–64] for a pure exchange economy. The extension to production and to multi-period models is due to Debreu [1959, Chapter 7]. The relation between convexity of preferences and risk aversion was noted by Arrow [1953, Section 4; 1963–64, Section 4]. The difficulties created for this equilibrium concept by the varying information structures of the economic agents were noted by Radner [1968]; the particular problems of moral hazard were emphasized by Arrow [1963, 961–962; 1965, 55–56; 1970, 142–143].

Chapter Six

GENERAL EQUILIBRIUM UNDER ALTERNATIVE ASSUMPTIONS

The expense
Is what one thought and more.
—Yvor Winters,
At the San Francisco Airport

The existence of general equilibrium has been proved in the last chapter under the assumptions set forth in Chapters 3 and 4—the usual assumptions of the perfectly competitive economy. In this chapter, we will show that the methods of analysis used so far can also demonstrate the existence of equilibrium in several cases in which some of these conditions are relaxed.

1. Prices Affecting Utilities

It has been frequently suggested in the literature that an individual's preferences among commodity vectors are influenced by the prices; typically, it is argued that if the price of a commodity goes up, the commodity will be more highly valued (in the sense that, for any given quantities, the marginal rate of substitution between that commodity and any other increases) either because it serves as a better public demonstration of the household's wealth [Veblen, 1899] or because price is used by the household as an index of quality [Scitovsky, 1944–45]. The empirical importance of the price effect has never been assessed (it would be difficult to measure even in principle), but a modification of our general model to include this possibility will be didactically useful. It will be shown that the methods of analysis used can easily be modified to establish the existence of equilibrium in this case. This may seem surprising, because our methods are closely related to the optimality properties of competitive equilibrium; when the utility function is no longer a given for the economic system, but instead, varies with some of its variables (in this case, price) the significance of Pareto efficiency becomes obscure, since an allocation that is dominated at one set of prices is not dominated at another. However, we can use a concept that might be termed *conditional Pareto efficiency*: For any fixed price vector, we take the utility functions corresponding to it and find the Pareto-efficient allocations corresponding to them. Thus, the set of prices associated with a given Pareto-efficient allocation, as defined in T.4.4 and D.4.14, now depend upon the price initially given as well as the utility allocation. Other parts of the mapping used in Section 5.3 are modified similarly; the fixed point still exists and at this point the price that determines the utility functions is, in fact, the prevailing price, so that the final equilibrium situation is consistent.

Formally, we modify assumption A.4.3 as follows:

ASSUMPTION 1. For each price vector $\mathbf{p} > 0$, there is a preference ordering, $\succcurlyeq_{h\mathbf{p}}$ for each household h that satisfies all the conditions of A.4.3 and, in addition, varies continuously with $\mathbf{p}$ in the sense that it is represented by a utility function, $U_h(\mathbf{x}_h,\mathbf{p})$, that is jointly continuous in its arguments.

As before, we can, with no loss of generality, assume that $U_h(\bar{\mathbf{x}}_h,\mathbf{p}) = 0$, all $\mathbf{p}$; for example, first, let $U_h'(\mathbf{x}_h,\mathbf{p})$ be any utility function satisfying the hypotheses of A.6.1 and then define

$$U_h(\mathbf{x}_h,\mathbf{p}) = U_h'(\mathbf{x}_h,\mathbf{p}) - U_h'(\bar{\mathbf{x}}_h,\mathbf{p}).$$

For fixed $\mathbf{p}$, say, the functions $U_h(\mathbf{x}_h,\mathbf{p})$ are a set of utility functions, one for each household, and we can define the conditionally Pareto-efficient allocations for these functions. The set of conditionally efficient utility allocations may be denoted by $U(\mathbf{p})$; it varies, of course, with $\mathbf{p}$. However, for any fixed $\mathbf{p}$, the argument of Section 5.2 still holds; the non-negative elements of $U(\mathbf{p})$ can be mapped one-to-one and continuously onto a unit simplex, S_H, through a function, $\mathbf{v}(\mathbf{u},\mathbf{p})$; for each $\mathbf{p}$, this function has an inverse, $\mathbf{u}(\mathbf{v},\mathbf{p})$, mapping S_H into $U(\mathbf{p})$, which, it is easy to verify, is jointly continuous in its arguments.

For any fixed $\mathbf{p}$ and fixed conditionally efficient utility allocation, $\mathbf{u} \in U(\mathbf{p})$, there exists a price vector, $\mathbf{p}'$, that supports that allocation in the sense of T.4.4. In general, $\mathbf{p}'$ need not equal $\mathbf{p}$; it will be a condition of equilibrium that the equality hold. The set of such $\mathbf{p}'$, normalized to lie on the unit simplex for prices, will be denoted by $P(\mathbf{u},\mathbf{p})$. There is also a set of feasible allocations, $\mathscr{W}(\mathbf{u},\mathbf{p})$, for each $\mathbf{u}$ in $U(\mathbf{p})$ that achieve (at least) the utility levels prescribed, where utilities are measured by the utility function appropriate to the given price vector, $\mathbf{p}$.

Let $X_h(u_h,\mathbf{p})$ be the set of consumptions vectors, $\mathbf{x}_h \in X_h$, that achieve utility level at least u_h conditional upon the price vector $\mathbf{p}$. Then, from A.6.1, it is easy to generalize Lemma 4.11 to say that $X_h(u_h,\mathbf{p})$ is continuous jointly in u_h and $\mathbf{p}$. The upper semi-continuity argument proceeds exactly as before with obvious substitutions. For the proof of lower semi-continuity, we start with sequences, u_h^ν approaching u_h^0 and $\mathbf{p}^\nu$ approaching $\mathbf{p}^0$, with $\mathbf{x}_h^0 \in X_h(u_h^0,\mathbf{p}^0)$. Choose $\mathbf{x}_h^1$ so that $U_h(\mathbf{x}_h^1,\mathbf{p}^0) > U_h(\mathbf{x}_h^0,\mathbf{p}^0)$. By A.6.1, $U_h(\mathbf{x}_h^1,\mathbf{p}^\nu) > U_h(\mathbf{x}_h^0,\mathbf{p}^\nu)$ for ν sufficiently large. Then, at least for ν large, we can divide the sequence into three subsequences according as (a) $u_h^\nu > U_h(\mathbf{x}_h^1,\mathbf{p}^\nu)$ (which can hold only for finitely many ν), (b) $U_h(\mathbf{x}_h^0,\mathbf{p}^\nu) \leq u_h^\mu \leq U_h(\mathbf{x}_h^1,\mathbf{p}^\nu)$, and (c) $U_h(\mathbf{x}_h^0,\mathbf{p}^\nu) > u_h^\nu$. Then we can choose $\mathbf{x}_h^\nu \in X_h(u_h^\nu,\mathbf{p}^\nu)$, each ν, as before, and prove that $\mathbf{x}_h^\nu \rightarrow \mathbf{x}_h^0$.

Once the generalization of Lemma 4.11 has been accomplished, it follows exactly as before that the corresponding generalizations of Corollary 4.5 and T.4.6 hold, that is, that $\hat{\mathscr{W}}(\mathbf{u},\mathbf{p})$ and $P(\mathbf{u},\mathbf{p})$ are upper semi-continuous in $(\mathbf{u},\mathbf{p})$. The two sets are, exactly as before, convex and compact for each $(\mathbf{u},\mathbf{p})$.

Define $V(\mathbf{p},\omega)$ exactly as in 5.(7). Then there exists a fixed point of the correspondence

$$P[\mathbf{u}(\mathbf{v},\mathbf{p}),\mathbf{p}] \times V(\mathbf{p},\omega) \times \hat{\mathscr{W}}[\mathbf{u}(\mathbf{v},\mathbf{p}),\mathbf{p}]$$

that takes $S_n \times S_H \times \hat{\mathscr{W}}$ into subsets of itself. This fixed point is a compensated equilibrium.

To pass from a compensated to a competitive equilibrium, we again use the concept of resource relatedness. The definitions must be rephrased to hold for the utility functions conditional on every $\mathbf{p}$.

DEFINITION 1. Household h' is *resource related* to household h'' *for given price vector* $\mathbf{p}$ if D.5.4 holds when $U_h(\mathbf{x}_h)$ is everywhere replaced by $U_h(\mathbf{x}_h,\mathbf{p})$.

DEFINITION 2. Household h' is *resource related* to household h'' if it is resource related for every $\mathbf{p} > \mathbf{0}$.

The definition of being indirectly resource related remains as in D.5.5, with the new definition of being resource related substituted.

THEOREM 1. If the assumptions of Chapters 3 and 4 hold, except that A.4.3 is replaced by A.6.1 so that utilities may vary continuously with prices, then there exists a competitive equilibrium.

2. Externalities

In fact, not all the effects of the economic behavior of others are mediated through the price system. In general, it is usually held that the utility of a household and the production possibility set of a firm is itself affected by the allocation of resources among other households and firms. Such effects are usually termed, "externalities." We do not attempt a complete analysis of this concept here, but simply assume that the utility function of household h has the form, $U_h(\mathbf{x}_h,\omega)$. It is understood in this notation that the effect of ω on U_h does not depend on its $\mathbf{x}_h$-component, whose effect is represented explicitly. Formally, if ω^1 and ω^2 are two allocations that differ only in their $\mathbf{x}_h$-component, then

$$U_h(\mathbf{x}_h,\omega^1) = U_h(\mathbf{x}_h,\omega^2) \qquad \text{for all } \mathbf{x}_h.$$

This understanding permits us to ascribe meaning to the symbols $U_h(\mathbf{x}_h,\omega)$ even when the $\mathbf{x}_h$-component of ω differs from x_h; the former simply doesn't matter.

It should be noted that there are two somewhat different possible interpretations of $U_h(\mathbf{x}_h,\omega)$: It represents the preference ordering for $\mathbf{x}_h \in X_h$ for given values of the consumption vectors of other households and of production possibility vectors for firms; and it might represent a preference ordering over the entire space of allocations; the household may be assumed to have preferences with regard to the actions of others for all the usual reasons of externality (e.g., pollution of air or water). The second interpretation implies the first, though not conversely; if $U_h(\mathbf{x}_h,\omega)$ represents a preference ordering over allocations, then for fixed ω (with the understanding given above), it represents a preference ordering over X_h alone. For the purposes of welfare analysis, it is the second interpretation that is needed, but for descriptive analysis and the proof of existence of equilibrium, it is the first that is needed and will be assumed here. With this interpretation, we can enforce without difficulty the convention that $U_h(\overline{\mathbf{x}}_h,\omega) = 0$ for all ω. (This utility function would not satisfy the second interpretation, in general, since there is no reason why the household would be indifferent among allocations when $\mathbf{x}_h = \overline{\mathbf{x}}_h$; but such a utility function can be derived, of course, from a utility function over all allocations by subtracting the utility of $(\overline{\mathbf{x}}_h,\omega)$, the result being still consistent with the first interpretation.)

On the production side, we have a parallel situation; the production possibility set, Y_f, of firm f is no longer a constant. It varies with the allocation, $Y_f(\omega)$; again, the effect of ω is assumed not to depend upon its $\mathbf{y}_f$-component.

In accordance with the atomistic connotations of the concept of competitive equilibrium, each household and firm is assumed to take externalities as parametrically given. Formally,

DEFINITION 3. The pair $(\mathbf{p}^*,\omega^*)$ constitute a *competitive equilibrium with externalities* if D.5.1 holds with $U_h(\mathbf{x}_h)$ replaced everywhere by $U_h(\mathbf{x}_h,\omega^*)$ and Y_f by $Y_f(\omega^*)$.

That is, at the equilibrium, each household is maximizing utility under a budget constraint given the activities of all other households and of all firms, and each firm is maximizing profits given the activities of all households and all other firms.

On the consumptions side, the assumptions made are strictly parallel to those of the last section:

ASSUMPTION 2. For each allocation, ω, there is a preference ordering $\succcurlyeq_{h\omega}$ for each household h that satisfies all the conditions of A.4.3 and, in addition, varies continuously with ω in the sense that it is represented by a utility function $U_h(\mathbf{x}_h,\omega)$ that is jointly continuous in its arguments.

This assumption replaces A.4.3. As before, A.4.1 and A.4.2 are maintained.

On the production side, somewhat more complicated modifications must be made. Note that at equilibrium the firm is maximizing profits at fixed prices; hence, we cannot drop the convexity assumption on $Y_f(\omega)$, at least not completely, for with increasing returns there need not exist any maximum. On the other hand, we do not want to exclude the possibility of increasing returns to the economy as a whole. Indeed, one important implication of the notion of externalities (more specifically, external economies) has been the viability of competitive equilibrium under social-increasing returns. What happens, of course, is that the increasing returns are caused by the influence of one firm on another's productivity, an influence that for one reason or another is not compensated for in the market.

We first assume that the assumptions previously held about the production possibility sets of individual firms continue to hold for any given allocation.

ASSUMPTION 3. Assumptions A.3.1–A.3.3 hold with Y_f replaced by $Y_f(\omega)$.

We also assume

ASSUMPTION 4. For each f, $Y_f(\omega)$ is a continuous correspondence in ω.

Recall that a correspondence is continuous if it is both lower and upper semi-continuous.

Corresponding to D.3.3, D.4.6–D.4.8, and D.4.10, we have:

DEFINITION 4. $X_h(u_h,\omega) = \{\mathbf{x}_h \mid U_h(\mathbf{x}_h,\omega) \geq u_h\}$.

DEFINITION 5. $\mathscr{X}(\mathbf{u},\omega) = \underset{h}{\times} X_h(u_h,\omega)$.

DEFINITION 6. $\mathscr{Y}(\omega) = \underset{f}{\times} Y_f(\omega)$.

DEFINITION 7. $\mathscr{W}(\mathbf{u},\omega) = \mathscr{X}(u,\omega) \times \mathscr{Y}(\omega)$.

DEFINITION 8. $\hat{\mathscr{W}}(\mathbf{u},\omega) = \mathscr{W}(\mathbf{u},\omega) \times \{\omega \mid \sum_n \mathbf{x}_h \leq \sum_f \mathbf{y}_f + \sum_h \bar{\mathbf{x}}_h\}$;

that is, $\hat{\mathscr{W}}(\mathbf{u},\omega)$ is the set of **u**-feasible allocations conditional on an allocation ω.

We need an assumption to ensure the compactness of the last set. To this end, we make an assumption parallel to A.3.4 (impossibility of producing something from nothing), but apply it to a somewhat wider set than that of the actually possible production allocations that are mutually consistent. Define

DEFINITION 9. $Y_f^{**} = \{\mathbf{y}_f \mid \mathbf{y}_f \in Y_f(\omega)$ for some $(\omega)\}$,
Y_f^* is the closed convex hull of Y_f^{**}.

(For the definition of a convex hull, see D.B.12.)

ASSUMPTION 5. If $\mathbf{y}_f \in \mathbf{Y}_f^*$, each f, and $\sum_f \mathbf{y}_f = 0$, then $\mathbf{y}_f = 0$.

In words, even if we ascribe to each firm all the production possibility vectors it could have for any possible actions of other firms and then take the convex hull of that set, it would not have been so expanded as to permit either production without inputs or reversibility.

From A.6.5 we have a conclusion like T.3.2:

$$\left(\underset{f}{\times} Y_f^*\right) \cap \left\{\sum_f \mathbf{y}_f + \bar{\mathbf{x}} \geq 0\right\} \text{ is compact.}$$

Since $Y_f(\omega) \subset Y_f^*$, all f, it follows from the definitions, plus the assumption that X_h is bounded from below that $\hat{\mathscr{W}}(\mathbf{u},\omega)$ is compact for all $\mathbf{u}$ and ω.

The convexity of this set follows immediately from the convexity of $X_h(u_h,\omega)$ and of $Y_f(\omega)$ for fixed $\mathbf{u}$ and ω.

Also, just as in the previous section, the continuity of $X_h(u_h,\omega)$ in its arguments follows easily from the assumptions and from this, the continuity of $\mathscr{W}(\mathbf{u},\omega)$ follows from A.6.4. Again as in Section 6.1, we have for each ω, a set of conditionally Pareto-efficient allocations, $U(\omega)$, and for each $\mathbf{u}$ in $U(\omega)$, a non-null set of price vectors, $P(\mathbf{u},\omega)$, that support that allocation. From the continuity of $\mathscr{W}(\mathbf{u},\omega)$, it follows, as in the proofs of Corollary 4.5 and T.4.6, that $\hat{\mathscr{W}}(\mathbf{u},\omega)$ and $P(\mathbf{u},\omega)$ are upper semi-continuous correspondences.

Finally, for each ω, we can find a one-one continuous function mapping $U(\omega)$ into the unit simplex, S_H; let $\mathbf{u}(\mathbf{v},\omega)$ map S_H into $U(\omega)$. Then, again as in Section 6.1, $\mathbf{u}(\mathbf{v},\omega)$ is jointly continuous in the two variables.

Then the correspondence

$$P[\mathbf{u}(\mathbf{v},\omega),\omega] \times V(\mathbf{p},\omega) \times \hat{\mathscr{W}}[\mathbf{u}(\mathbf{v},\omega),\omega]$$

has a fixed point, which can be seen to be a compensated equilibrium in the sense that each household is minimizing the cost of achieving a given utility measured at the equilibrium allocation and similarly each firm is maximizing profits among the production vectors possible at the equilibrium allocation. It follows also that the equilibrium allocation is consistent, in that if each firm produces and each household consumes according to it, then the production vectors for each firm in fact will be possible because the external effects are those assumed.

For the passage to a competitive equilibrium, use

DEFINITION 10. Household h' is *resource related* to household h'' if definitions D.6.1 and D.6.2 hold with $\mathbf{p}$ replaced by ω.

THEOREM 2. Competitive equilibrium exists in the presence of externalities if assumptions A.6.2–A.6.5, A.4.1 and A.4.2 hold and if every household is indirectly resource related to every other.

In the presence of externalities, the competitive equilibrium is conditionally Pareto efficient, that is, Pareto efficient according to the utility functions and production possibility sets corresponding to the equilibrium allocation. Of course, the equilibrium is not Pareto efficient in any broader sense; other allocations may indeed improve the utility of all, when the utility considered is a function of the entire allocation.

By the same token, there are private pressures toward making deals not compatible with the competitive equilibrium. In particular, there can be profit in the merger of two or more firms, a profit that is absent in the absence of externalities.

3. Temporary Equilibrium

In Sections 2.9 and 2.10 we noted the need for a model of general equilibrium for a world in which households and firms planned on the basis of an assumed future, but in which future markets did not exist or were severely limited in scope. We now return to this issue in the context of the more general and detailed model of Chapters 3 and 4.

We will now see that the components of the possible production and consumption vectors extend over several periods of time. For simplicity, we will confine ourselves to two periods, present and future. We assume that the only commodities traded in currently are commodities of the current period plus bonds; a unit bond is a promise to pay one unit of the currency of account in the next period. Let the subscript b refer to bonds. We use here the notation $\mathbf{x}$ to refer to the vector of commodities currently traded in by households; thus $\mathbf{x} = (\mathbf{x}^1, x_b)$, *not* $\mathbf{x} = (\mathbf{x}^1, \mathbf{x}^2)$. Similarly, for firms, $\mathbf{y} = (\mathbf{y}^1, y_b)$ where y_b is the supply of bonds issued by firms, and $\mathbf{p} = (\mathbf{p}^1, p_b)$.

The main task of this section is to show how, by suitable modifications of the methods and concepts of Chapters 3–5, the existence of an equilibrium on the current markets can be established. Before going into details, we will discuss the main difficulties and the strategy for overcoming them. The modifications to be made to the definition of and assumptions on the production sets are straightforward except for one particular. Consider one firm whose production plan for the future has consequences in current markets because it affects the current value of the firm and the amount it will borrow. Since there is no current market for the resources of the subsequent period, the availability of resources then cannot be used to argue that production plans are bounded. This creates obvious difficulties, which are partly academic since it could be argued that a firm is "realistic enough" not to plan indefinitely large production. It is preferable, however, to incorporate the argument from realism into our construction in a way more in the spirit of the perfectly competitive model. We do this by insisting that the price expectations of firms be "sensible." This is done later in A.6.7(b).

As already noted, plans for future production must have consequences in current markets. In fact, we shall assume that each firm offers in the current bond market a quantity of bonds equal to its expected profit in the future. This means that there is a "current" representation of the future plans, which, in turn, allows us to incorporate these in the framework of our earlier discussion. This is made precise in (1) and D.6.12.

When we come to consumers, a number of special problems arise. First, we must decide what we mean by the initial endowment of bonds held by a household. We simply take it to equal its anticipated receipts of the future period; that is, it represents the maximum the household believes it could repay. Note that the household's anticipated receipts may differ from what any other agent would expect them to be, given the household's plans—that is, we allow for differences in price expectations.

The differences in expectations also mean that different households will value any given firm differently. We assume that the actual current market value of any firm is equal to the highest value any agent places on it and suppose that the ownership of the firm will shift to the hands of that household or those households that value it most highly (D.6.16 and A.6.9). Therefore, we now treat d_{hf}, the share of household h in firm f, as a variable of the equilibrium. All this leads to modifications in the manner in which we must write the households' budget constraints [see (10) and (15)].

We must ensure also that our assumptions about consumption possibility sets, A.4.1 and A.4.2, hold when reinterpreted in terms of current markets. This is fairly straightforward (see A.6.8, (16), and D.6.17).

Lastly there is the following problem. We know that the household utility depends on its future plans, and in the existence proof of Section 6.2, the utilities of the households played an important part. Our procedure incorporating the expected future into arguments about the present is to use a "derived utility function" (D.6.18). This will be the maximum utility of the household, given its first-period allocation, under an appropriate budget constraint. It will be obvious that this derived function can be treated as a function of current plans only, as is desired.

Proceeding to detailed argument, let us first consider the behavior of the firm. We take the viewpoint that the firm is an entity that, on its own, has expectations of future prices and maximizes profits in accordance with them. At the end of this section we will comment on this assumption.

We retain the assumptions on the production possibility sets of the individual firms with appropriate changes of notation and add a hypothesis that embodies the possibility of abandoning a productive enterprise without loss.

DEFINITION 11. The set of *possible two-period production vectors* for firm f is Y_f^{12}. An element is denoted by $\mathbf{y}_f^{12} = (\mathbf{y}_f^1, \mathbf{y}_f^2)$, where $\mathbf{y}_f^1$ are the components of $\mathbf{y}_f^{12}$ referring to the first period and $\mathbf{y}_f^2$ are those referring to the second period. We also refer to $\mathbf{y}_f^1$ and $\mathbf{y}_f^2$ as *first-period* and *second-period* production vectors, respectively.

The set of *possible two-period production allocations* for the economy is $\mathcal{Y}^{12} = \underset{f}{\times} Y_f^{12}$

ASSUMPTION 6. A.3.1–A.3.3 hold with $\mathbf{y}_f$ replaced by $\mathbf{y}_f^{12}$ and Y_f by Y_f^{12}. If $(\mathbf{y}_f^1, \mathbf{y}_f^2) \in Y_f^{12}$, then there exists $\mathbf{y}_f^{2'} \geq 0$ such that $(\mathbf{y}_f^1, \mathbf{y}_f^{2'}) \in Y_f^{12}$.

The firm observes current prices, $\mathbf{p} = (\mathbf{p}^1, p_b)$, and is assumed to have subjectively certain expectations for prices in period 2, $\mathbf{p}_f^2$; since there are no future markets, different firms may have different expectations. A production plan, $(\mathbf{y}_f^1, \mathbf{y}_f^2)$, yields net revenue $\mathbf{p}^1\mathbf{y}_f^1$ in period 1 and is expected to yield net revenue $\mathbf{p}_f^2\mathbf{y}_f^2$ in period 2. If bonds sell in period 1 at p_b, then a revenue of $\mathbf{p}_f^2\mathbf{y}_f^2$ in period 2 is equivalent on perfect markets to a first-period income of $p_b(\mathbf{p}_f^2\mathbf{y}_f^2)$. Without loss of generality, we can assume that the firm actually sells bonds to the extent of its anticipated second-period income; if, in fact, it does not do so, we can imagine that it does and then distributes the difference to its stockholders. Under the assumptions being made here, the two actions are completely indifferent to everyone. Its offering of bonds is

$$y_{fb} = \mathbf{p}_f^2\mathbf{y}_f^2, \tag{1}$$

and its current receipts from a given production plan are

$$\mathbf{p}^1\mathbf{y}_f^1 + p_b(\mathbf{p}_f^2\mathbf{y}_f^2). \tag{2}$$

The firm chooses its production plan so as to maximize (2) among all production plans $\mathbf{y}_f^{12} \in Y_f^{12}$. Provisionally, we will assume that all price expectations are totally inelastic, that is, that $\mathbf{p}_f^2$ is a datum for the firm independent of current prices. Then (1) maps the elements of Y_f^{12} into a set Y_f of $(n + 1)$-dimensional vectors; in effect, with fixed expectations, the firm's future possibilities amount to its ability to produce bonds for today's market.

DEFINITION 12. The set of *possible current production vectors*, $\mathbf{Y}_f$, for firm f is the image of Y_f^{12} under the linear mapping (1),

$$Y_f = \{\mathbf{y}_f \mid \mathbf{y}_f = (\mathbf{y}_f^1, y_{fb}) \text{ such that } y_{fb} = \mathbf{p}_f^2 \mathbf{y}_f^2 \text{ for some } (\mathbf{y}_f^1, \mathbf{y}_f^2) \in Y_f^{12}\}.$$

The set of *possible current production allocations is* $\mathscr{Y} = \times_f Y_f$.

It is easy to verify from A.6.6 that

$$\text{A.3.1–A.3.3 hold under D.6.12.} \tag{3}$$

From D.6.12 and (2):

$$\text{The firm maximizes } \mathbf{p}\mathbf{y}_f. \tag{4}$$

Suppose $p_b > 0$ and the firm has chosen a production plan, $\mathbf{y}_f^{12}$, for which there will be negative receipts in the future, $\mathbf{p}_f^2 \mathbf{y}_f^2 < 0$. Then by the second half of A.6.6, it is possible to choose another plan with higher profits.

$$\text{If } p_b > 0, \text{ then } \mathbf{p}_f^2 \mathbf{y}_f^2 - y_{fb} \geq 0 \text{ at any profit-maximizing plan.} \tag{5}$$

We now make an assumption about the impossibility of production without inputs and about irreversibility that is somewhat stronger than that obtained simply by replacing $\mathbf{y}_f$ by $\mathbf{y}_f^{12}$ and Y_f by Y_f^{12} in A.4.4. The reason the stronger assumption is needed is that future resource limitations do not directly restrain production, since there are no future markets on which they appear. We still do have the constraints on first-period resources and, in addition, we will, in accordance with (5), restrict ourselves at certain stages in the argument to plans for which $\mathbf{p}_f^2 \mathbf{y}_f^2 \geq 0$, since only those will satisfy our equilibrium conditions.

ASSUMPTION 7. (a) If $\sum_f \mathbf{y}_f^1 \geq 0$, then $\mathbf{y}_f^1 = 0$, all f.

(b) The future returns to any production plan requiring no first-period inputs are bounded for any firm; that is, $\mathbf{p}_f^2 \mathbf{y}_f^2$ is bounded as

$\mathbf{y}_f^2$ varies over all two-period production vectors $(0,\mathbf{y}_f^2)$ in Y_f^{12} with no current inputs.

We will argue that this assumption is not unreasonable. First, it must be understood that any factor availabilities in period 1 as the result of earlier production (e.g., durable capital goods or maturing agricultural products) are to be included in the initial endowment of current flows, $\bar{\mathbf{x}}^1$. Hence, the absence of net inputs means the absence of capital, labor, and current raw materials; it is reasonable, then, to conclude that no production takes place in period 1, that is, $\mathbf{y}_f^1 = 0$, all f. As far as (b) is concerned, if it were not true, then a firm could expect indefinitely large profits in the next period even if it would shut down today. But then the firm would know that its price expectations are not consistent with any equilibrium, so it is reasonable to argue that it does not hold any such expectations. Thus (b) is really a weak requirement on the rationality of expectations.

To have a temporarily useful terminology, we define

DEFINITION 13. The set of *quasi-feasible two-period production allocations* is,

$$\tilde{\mathscr{Y}}^{12} = \mathscr{Y}^{12} \cap \left\{ y^{12} \,\middle|\, \sum_f \mathbf{y}_f^1 + \bar{\mathbf{x}}^1 \geq 0, \quad \mathbf{p}_f^2 \mathbf{y}_f^2 \geq 0 \text{ for all } f \right\}.$$

From A.6.7, the argument used in the proof of T.3.2 can be easily adapted to prove

$$\tilde{\mathscr{Y}}^{12} \text{ is compact and convex.} \tag{6}$$

In the theory of consumer behavior, we apply again the assumptions made earlier to the intertemporal consumption vectors.

DEFINITION 14. The set of *possible two-period consumption vectors* for household h is X_h^{12}, with elements $\mathbf{x}_h^{12} = (\mathbf{x}_h^1,\mathbf{x}_h^2)$, the components being referred to as the *first-period* and *second-period* possible consumption vectors, respectively;

The set of *possible two-period consumption allocations* for the economy is

$$\mathscr{X}^{12} = \mathop{\times}_h X_h^{12}.$$

ASSUMPTION 8. A.4.1–A.4.3 hold under D.6.14 with $\mathbf{x}_h$, $U_h(\mathbf{x}_h)$, $\bar{\mathbf{x}}_h$, $\bar{\bar{\mathbf{x}}}_h$, and X_h replaced by x_h^{12}, $U_{12}(\mathbf{x}_h^{12})$, $\bar{\mathbf{x}}_h^{12}$, $\bar{\bar{\mathbf{x}}}_h^{12}$, and X_h^{12}, respectively. We assume also that $U_h^{12}(\mathbf{x}_h^1,\mathbf{x}_h^2)$ is not satiated in $\mathbf{x}_h^2$ for any $\mathbf{x}_h^1$.

Like the firm, the household knows current prices, including that of bonds, and anticipates second-period prices, $\mathbf{p}_h^2$. It plans purchases and sales for both periods. In each period, there is a budget constraint. The two constraints are linked through the purchase of bonds, which constitutes an expense in period 1 and a source of purchasing power in period 2 (or vice versa, if the household is a net borrower in period 1). The household can be considered to have an initial endowment of bonds, $\bar{x}_{hb}$, which is precisely its anticipated volume of receipts in period 2 (but see Remark 2 at the end of this section). The net purchase of bonds in period 1 is denoted then by $x_{hb} - \bar{x}_{hb}$. Total expenditures for goods and bonds in period 1 are $\mathbf{p}^1\mathbf{x}_h^1 + p_b(x_{hb} - \bar{x}_{hb})$, while planned expenditures in period 2 are $\mathbf{p}_h^2\mathbf{x}_h^2$. The purchasing power available in period 1 is the sum of the sale of endowment, $\mathbf{p}^1\bar{\mathbf{x}}_h^1$, and receipts from firms in that period. The planned receipts in period 2 equal the planned sale of endowment, $\mathbf{p}_h^2\bar{\mathbf{x}}_h^2$, plus receipts from firms in period 2, and this sum equals $\bar{x}_{hb}$, as remarked. The purchasing power planned to be available in period 2 is the repayment to the household of its net purchase of bonds, $x_{hb} - \bar{x}_{hb}$, plus planned receipts and, therefore, is simply x_{hb}.

One feature in this model is not present in the static model or its intertemporal analog with all future markets. Since different households hold different expectations of future prices, they have different expectations of the profitability of any particular firm. Hence, a market for shares in firms will arise; the initial stockholders may value the firm less highly than some others, and therefore, the stock of the firm should change hands.

After the firm has chosen its production plans, $\mathbf{y}_f^{12}$, household h values the plan according to current prices and its expectations of future prices.

DEFINITION 15. The *capital value of firm f according to household h* is

$$K_{hf}(\mathbf{p},\mathbf{y}_f^{12}) = \mathbf{p}^1\mathbf{y}_f^1 + p_b(\mathbf{p}_h^2\mathbf{y}_f^2).$$

The value of the firm in the market is the highest value that any household gives to it.

DEFINITION 16. The *market capital value of firm f* is

$$K_f(\mathbf{p},\mathbf{y}_f^{12}) = \max_h K_{hf}(\mathbf{p},\mathbf{y}_f^{12}).$$

We will assume that, for each production plan for each firm, there is at least one household that values the plan at least as highly as the firm itself does; we might rationalize this by noting that the firm's manager is presumably himself the head of a household.

ASSUMPTION 9. The market capital value of a firm is at least equal to the maximum profits anticipated by the firm itself; in symbols,

$$K_f(\mathbf{p},\mathbf{y}_f^{12}) \geq \mathbf{p}\mathbf{y}_f \qquad \text{for all } \mathbf{p} \text{ and all } \mathbf{y}_f^{12} \in Y_f^{12}.$$

From D.6.15 and D.6.16

$$K_f = \max_h[\mathbf{p}^1\mathbf{y}_f^1 + p_b(\mathbf{p}_h^2\mathbf{y}_f^2)] = \mathbf{p}^1\mathbf{y}_f^1 + p_b \max_h(\mathbf{p}_h^2\mathbf{y}_f^2),$$

since $\mathbf{p}^1\mathbf{y}_f^1$ and p_b are independent of h. Let

$$K_f^2(\mathbf{y}_f^2) = \max_h(\mathbf{p}_h^2\mathbf{y}_f^2). \tag{7}$$

If we recall that $\mathbf{p}\mathbf{y}_f = \mathbf{p}^1\mathbf{y}_f^1 + p_b(\mathbf{p}_f^2\mathbf{y}_f^2)$ then A.6.9 implies

$$K_f - \mathbf{p}\mathbf{y}_f = p_b(K_f^2 - \mathbf{p}_f^2\mathbf{y}_f^2) \geq 0. \tag{8}$$

Let $\bar{d}_{hf}$ be the share of firm f held initially by household h; we assume that it sells its shares at the market price and buys others, but only in those firms that it values at least as highly as any other household. We assume the absence of short sales. Let d_{hf} be its share of firm f after the stock market has operated. Its net receipts from sale less purchase of stocks (possibly negative, of course) are given by

$$\sum_f (\bar{d}_{hf} - d_{hf})K_f.$$

Also,

$$d_{hf} = 0 \quad \text{unless} \quad K_{hf} = K_f. \tag{9}$$

It will be recalled that the current receipts of the firm are given by (2) or (4); it is assumed that they are all distributed among its new owners, so that household h receives

$$\sum_f d_{hf}(\mathbf{p}\mathbf{y}_f).$$

Hence, the budget constraint for period 1 reads

$$\mathbf{p}^1\mathbf{x}_h^1 + p_b(x_{hb} - \bar{x}_{hb}) \leq \mathbf{p}^1\bar{\mathbf{x}}^1 + \sum_f d_{hf}(\mathbf{p}\mathbf{y}_f) + \sum_f (\bar{d}_{hf} - d_{hf})K_f. \tag{10}$$

In period 2, the household is responsible for its share of the bonds issued by firm f, a total of $\mathbf{p}_f^2\mathbf{y}_f^2$. According to its expectations, however, the firm will receive $\mathbf{p}_h^2\mathbf{y}_f^2$. From (9), the household invests only in firms whose production plans it values at least as highly as anyone else, so that from (7), any firm for which $d_{hf} > 0$ will be expected by household h to have second-period receipts K_f^2. Hence, the anticipated total receipts from firms in period 2 by household h will be

$$\sum_f d_{hf}(K_f^2 - \mathbf{p}_f^2\mathbf{y}_f^2).$$

From earlier remarks, then,

$$\bar{x}_{hb} = \mathbf{p}_h^2\bar{\mathbf{x}}_h^2 + \sum_f d_{hf}(K_f^2 - \mathbf{p}_f^2\mathbf{y}_f^2) \qquad \bar{\mathbf{x}}_h = (\bar{\mathbf{x}}_h^1, \bar{x}_{hb}). \tag{11}$$

Then

$$\bar{x}_b = \sum_h \bar{x}_{hb} = \sum_h (\mathbf{p}_h^2\bar{\mathbf{x}}_h^2) + \sum_f (K_f^2 - \mathbf{p}_f^2\mathbf{y}_f^2). \tag{12}$$

Note that $\bar{x}_b$ is a function of the $\mathbf{y}_f^2$'s, or to use an obvious notation, of $\mathscr{y}^2$, the second-period production allocation. Note also that, from (8), the summation terms in (11) and (12) are non-negative.

Now we seek to define a "minimal" current consumption vector, $\bar{\bar{\mathbf{x}}}_h$, that will satisfy the analog in this temporary equilibrium model of A.4.2. For this purpose, let

$$\bar{\bar{x}}_{hb} = \mathbf{p}_h^2\bar{\bar{\mathbf{x}}}_h^2 \qquad \bar{\bar{\mathbf{x}}}_h = (\bar{\bar{\mathbf{x}}}_h^1, \bar{\bar{x}}_{hb}). \tag{13}$$

From A.6.8 and A.4.2, we have assumed that $\bar{\bar{\mathbf{x}}}_h^1 \leq \bar{\mathbf{x}}_h^1$, $\bar{\bar{\mathbf{x}}}_h^2 \leq \bar{\mathbf{x}}_h^2$. Multiply through in the second inequality by $\mathbf{p}_h^2 \geq 0$, and use (11) and the definitions of $\bar{\bar{x}}_{hb}$; then $\bar{\bar{x}}_{hb} \leq \mathbf{p}_h^2\bar{\mathbf{x}}_h^2 \leq \bar{x}_{hb}$, and so, from the definition of $\bar{\bar{\mathbf{x}}}_h$ in (13), we have that

$$\bar{\bar{\mathbf{x}}}_h \leq \bar{\mathbf{x}}_h.$$

The assumptions imply also that $\bar{x}_{hi} > 0$ implies $\bar{\bar{x}}_{hi} < \bar{x}_{hi}$ $(i = 1, \ldots, n)$, since $\bar{x}_{hi} = \bar{x}_{hi}^1$ and $\bar{\bar{x}}_{hi} = \bar{\bar{x}}_{hi}^1$ for such i. We need to show only that the same is true when $i = b$. Suppose $\bar{x}_{hb} > 0$. From (11), there are two possibilities, $\bar{x}_{hb} > \mathbf{p}_h^2\bar{\mathbf{x}}_h^2$, or $\bar{x}_{hb} = \mathbf{p}_h^2\bar{\mathbf{x}}_h^2$. In the first case, since $\bar{\bar{x}}_{hb} \leq \mathbf{p}_h^2\bar{\mathbf{x}}_h^2$, as already seen, we certainly have $\bar{x}_{hb} > \bar{\bar{x}}_{hb}$. In the second case, the non-negative vectors, $\mathbf{p}_h^2$ and $\bar{\mathbf{x}}_h^2$, must have at least one positive component in common. Yet, since, by A.6.8 and A.4.2, any positive component of $\bar{\mathbf{x}}_h^2$ must also be a positive component of $\bar{\mathbf{x}}_h^2 - \bar{\bar{\mathbf{x}}}_h^2$, it follows that

$$\mathbf{p}_h^2(\bar{\mathbf{x}}_h^2 - \bar{\bar{\mathbf{x}}}_h^2) > 0,$$

or from the definition of $\bar{\bar{x}}_{hb}$ and the assumption that $\bar{x}_{hb} = \mathbf{p}_h^2 \bar{\mathbf{x}}_h^2$, $\bar{x}_{hb} > \bar{\bar{x}}_{hb}$. We conclude that A.6.8 and A.4.2 ensure

$$\bar{\mathbf{x}}_h \geq \bar{\bar{\mathbf{x}}}_h; \quad \text{if} \quad \bar{x}_{hi} > 0, \quad \text{then} \quad \bar{x}_{hi} > \bar{\bar{x}}_{hi}. \tag{14}$$

As already remarked, the anticipated budget constraint for period 2 is simply

$$\mathbf{p}_h^2 \mathbf{x}_h^2 \leq x_{hb}, \tag{15}$$

so it is convenient to introduce the following definition:

DEFINITION 17. The set of *current consumption vectors* is

$$X_h = \{\mathbf{x}_h \mid x_{hb} \geq \mathbf{p}_h^2 \mathbf{x}_h^2 \quad \text{for some } \mathbf{x}_h^{12} \in X_h^{12}\}.$$

The set of *current consumption allocations* is

$$\mathscr{X} = \bigtimes_h X_h.$$

From (15) and A.6.8, $x_{hb} \geq 0$, and also $\bar{\bar{\mathbf{x}}}_h \in X_h$. From A.6.8, (14), and D.6.17, we can conclude

A.4.1 and A.4.2 hold with the interpretations of $\bar{\mathbf{x}}_h$, $\bar{\bar{\mathbf{x}}}_h$, and X_h in (11), (13), and D.6.17, respectively. (16)

The maximization of $U_h^{12}(\mathbf{x}_h^1, \mathbf{x}_h^2)$ subject to the budget constraints (10) and (15) can be thought of as occurring in two stages. For any given $\mathbf{x}_h = (\mathbf{x}_h^1, x_{hb})$, we can maximize with respect to $\mathbf{x}_h^2$ subject to (15); the maximum is now a function of $\mathbf{x}_h^1$ and of x_{hb}, that is, of $\mathbf{x}_h$, with respect to which it can be maximized subject to (10).

DEFINITION 18. *First-period derived utility* is

$$U_h(\mathbf{x}_h) = \max U_h^{12}(\mathbf{x}_h^1, \mathbf{x}_h^2) \quad \text{subject to} \quad \mathbf{p}_h^2 \mathbf{x}_h^2 \leq x_{hb}.$$

We must assume that the maximum in D.6.18 actually exists. The existence depends primarily on $\mathbf{p}_h^2$, the household's anticipations of future prices. It will be assumed that the household is sufficiently realistic for this purpose; this is not an unreasonable assumption since the household would know, from the fact that a maximum does not exist, that the prices could not be equilibrium prices.

ASSUMPTION 10. For given $\mathbf{x}_h^1$, the function $U_h^{12}(\mathbf{x}_h^1, \mathbf{x}_h^2)$ assumes a maximum subject to the constraint $\mathbf{p}_h^2 \mathbf{x}_h^2 \leq x_{hb}$ for any x_{hb} permitting possible second-period consumption, that is, for any $\mathbf{x}_h \in X_h$.

From A.6.8 and A.4.1, it is easy to see that U_h is continuous. It is also true that it is semi-strictly quasi-concave. Suppose that

$$U_h(\mathbf{x}_h^a) > U_h(\mathbf{x}_h^b) \qquad \mathbf{x}_h = \alpha\mathbf{x}_h^a + (1 - \alpha)\mathbf{x}_h^b \quad 0 < \alpha < 1.$$

Then define $\mathbf{x}_h^{a2}$ as the possible second-period consumption vector that maximizes $U_h^{12}(\mathbf{x}_h^1,\mathbf{x}_h^2)$ with respect to $\mathbf{x}_h^2$ subject to the constraint $\mathbf{p}_h^2\mathbf{x}_h^2 \leq x_{hb}^a$; define $\mathbf{x}_h^{b2}$ similarly. By definition of a maximizing value,

$$U_h(\mathbf{x}_h^a) = U_h^{12}(\mathbf{x}_h^{a1},\mathbf{x}_h^{a2}), \qquad U_h(\mathbf{x}_h^b) = U_h^{12}(\mathbf{x}_h^{b1},\mathbf{x}_h^{b2}).$$

Now define $\mathbf{x}_h^2 = \alpha\mathbf{x}_h^{a2} + (1 - \alpha)\mathbf{x}_h^{b2}$. By semi-strict quasi-concavity of U_h^{12},

$$U_h^{12}(\mathbf{x}_h^1,\mathbf{x}_h^2) > U_h^{12}(\mathbf{x}_h^{b1},\mathbf{x}_h^{b2}).$$

But clearly $\mathbf{p}_h^2\mathbf{x}_h^2 \leq x_{hb}$. By definition of a maximum,

$$U_h(\mathbf{x}_h) \geq U_h^{12}(\mathbf{x}_h^1,\mathbf{x}_h^2) > U_h^{12}(\mathbf{x}_h^{b1},\mathbf{x}_h^{b2}) = U_h(\mathbf{x}_h^b),$$

which establishes the semi-strict quasi-concavity of U_h.

It is also very easy to establish that U_h is locally non-satiated in $\mathbf{x}_h$. By a suitable choice of origin, we can ensure that $U_h(\bar{\mathbf{x}}_h) = 0$.

> $U_h(\mathbf{x}_h)$ is continuous, semi-strictly quasi-concave, and admits no local satiation; $U_h(\bar{\mathbf{x}}_h) = 0$, U_h is strictly increasing in x_{hb} for any $\mathbf{x}_h^1$. (17)

These are, except for the last, the properties of U_h used in proof of existence in Chapters 3–5. The last clause follows from D.6.18 and the last part of A.6.8.

The aim of the household, then, is to maximize U_h subject to (10), which can be written

$$\mathbf{p}\mathbf{x}_h \leq M_h(\mathbf{p},\mathscr{y}^{12}), \tag{18}$$

where

$$M_h = \mathbf{p}\bar{\mathbf{x}}_h + \sum_f d_{hf}(\mathbf{p}\mathbf{y}_f) + \sum_f (\bar{d}_{hf} - d_{hf})K_f(\mathbf{p},\mathbf{y}_f^1,\mathbf{y}_f^2). \tag{19}$$

Another way of writing (19) will be useful. First, rewrite it slightly; note that by our notation $\mathbf{p}\bar{\mathbf{x}}_h = \mathbf{p}^1\bar{\mathbf{x}}_h^1 + p_b\bar{x}_{hb}$, then substitute from (11).

$$\begin{aligned} M_h &= \mathbf{p}\bar{\mathbf{x}}_h + \sum_f \bar{d}_{hf}(\mathbf{p}\mathbf{y}_f) + \sum_f (\bar{d}_{hf} - d_{hf})(K_f - \mathbf{p}\mathbf{y}_f) \\ &= \mathbf{p}^1\bar{\mathbf{x}}_h^1 + \sum_f \bar{d}_{hf}(\mathbf{p}\mathbf{y}_f) + p_b\left[\mathbf{p}_h^2\bar{\mathbf{x}}_h^2 + \sum_f \bar{d}_{hf}(K_f^2 - \mathbf{p}_f^2\mathbf{y}_f^2)\right] \end{aligned} \tag{20}$$

Recall that $K_f - \mathbf{p}\mathbf{y}_f = p_b(K_f^2 - \mathbf{p}_f^2\mathbf{y}_f^2)$ by (8). One important implication of (20) is that the actual final share allocation does not affect the household budget constraints and, therefore, does not affect the equilibrium. The reason is that, since shares in firms are assumed to be sold to those who value them most highly at a price equal to that value, each potential buyer is, in fact, indifferent between making the purchase and investing in bonds, and none of his other behavior is affected by the choice.

For later reference we note that $M_h \geq 0$ and, further, $M_h > 0$ if and only if $M_h > \mathbf{p}\bar{\mathbf{x}}_h$ at any possible equilibrium, specifically at any point at which firms are making non-negative planned profits. Then $\mathbf{p}\mathbf{y}_f \geq 0$, while $p_b(K_f^2 - \mathbf{p}_f^2\mathbf{y}_f^2) \geq 0$, for all f, by (8). From (20),

$$M_h \geq \mathbf{p}^1\bar{\mathbf{x}}_h^1 + p_b\mathbf{p}_h^2\bar{\mathbf{x}}_h^2.$$

From A.6.8 and A.4.2, we have, by the reasoning of Lemma 5.1,

$$M_h > 0 \quad \text{if and only if} \quad M_h > \mathbf{p}^1\bar{\mathbf{x}}_h^1 + p_b\mathbf{p}_h^2\bar{\mathbf{x}}_h^2 = \mathbf{p}\bar{\mathbf{x}}_h. \quad (21)$$

The last step follows from (13).

We now have all the threads of the model in hand. Since equilibrium occurs only on current markets, the only relevant prices are those for current commodities and bonds. Basically, the model is very similar to that of static competitive equilibrium; the aim of the firm is to maximize $\mathbf{p}\mathbf{y}_f$ subject to $\mathbf{y}_f \in Y_f$, according to (4) and D.6.12, while the consumer aims to maximize a (first-period derived) utility function subject to a budget constraint (18). The feasibility conditions for the current markets have the same form as before; demand for first-period commodities and for bonds shall not exceed supply, including the initial endowment of bonds as defined. However, there are two complications: The budget constraint, using the definition of M_h in (20), is somewhat different than that of Chapter 4, and more especially, it contains variables, the $\mathbf{y}_f^2$'s, that are not in the standard system; by (12) one component of the social endowment vector, namely, $\bar{x}_b$, also depends on y^2.

We define several types of allocations; notice that in none of them do the second-period consumption allocations enter, since they are not relevant to equilibrium. We do need the household demand for bonds, however.

DEFINITION 19. The set of *two-period allocations*, $\mathscr{W}^{12}$, is

$$\mathscr{W}^{12} = \mathscr{X} \times \mathscr{Y}^{12}.$$

The set of *current allocations* is

$$\mathscr{W} = \mathscr{X} \times \mathscr{Y}.$$

The set of *feasible current allocations* is

$$\hat{\mathscr{W}}(y^2) = \mathscr{W} \cap \left\{(x,y) \middle| \sum_h \mathbf{x}_h \leq \sum_f \mathbf{y}_f + \bar{\mathbf{x}}(y^2)\right\}.$$

The set of *quasi-feasible two-period allocations* is

$$\tilde{\mathscr{W}}^{12} = \mathscr{W}^{12} \cap \left\{(x,y^{12}) \middle| \sum_h \mathbf{x}_h^1 \leq \sum_f \mathbf{y}_f^1 + \bar{\mathbf{x}}^1, \quad \mathbf{p}_f^2\mathbf{y}_f^2 \geq 0, \quad \text{all } f\right\}.$$

Since $\bar{\mathbf{x}}$ (more specifically, $\bar{x}_b$) depends on y^2, feasibility of current allocations depends on y^2, as the notation seeks to make clear.

Any two-period production allocation, y^{12}, such that $(x,{}^1y^{12}) \in \tilde{\mathscr{W}}^{12}$ for some x, certainly satisfies the conditions

$$\sum_f \mathbf{y}_f^1 + \bar{\mathbf{x}}^1 \geq 0, \quad \mathbf{p}^2\mathbf{y}_f^2 \geq 0 \qquad \text{all } f,$$

and so belongs to the bounded set $\tilde{\mathscr{Y}}^{12}$, by D.6.13 and (6). Then $\bar{x}_b$, as a function of y^2, is also bounded; hence, from the conditions on the components of $\mathbf{x}_h$, the entire set, $\tilde{\mathscr{W}}^{12}$, must be bounded. It is obviously closed and convex.

$$\tilde{\mathscr{W}}^{12} \text{ is compact and convex.}$$

As before, we can define **u**-possible and **u**-feasible current allocations; the definitions remain unchanged, but it should be remarked that the set of **u**-feasible current allocations now depends upon y^2.

Let us formally define competitive and compensated temporary equilibrium.

DEFINITION 20. Competitive and compensated temporary equilibrium are defined exactly as before (see D.5.1 and D.5.2) with the notation introduced in this section, except that the variables $\mathbf{y}_f^2$ must be consistent with intertemporal profit maximization and the budget equations now take the form

$$\mathbf{p}\mathbf{x}_h = M_h(\mathbf{p},y^{12})$$

where the function M_h is defined by (19) or (20).

To prove existence of compensated equilibrium, the previous mapping has to be modified only slightly. For any given y^2, there is a set of Pareto-efficient current utility allocations, $U(\mathscr{y}^2)$, that depends upon $\mathscr{y}^2$ because it determines the initial endowment of bonds. For fixed $\mathscr{y}^2$, there is a function, $\mathbf{u}(\mathbf{v},\mathscr{y}^2)$, that maps the unit simplex, S_H, into $U(\mathscr{y}^2)$; the function, $\mathbf{u}(\mathbf{v},\mathscr{y}^2)$ is continuous in its variables. The correspondence to be used maps the set

$$S_n \times S_H \times \tilde{\mathscr{W}}^{12},$$

into subsets of itself. Any element of $\mathscr{W}^{12}$ defines, in particular, a second-period production allocation, $\mathscr{y}^2$. For fixed $\mathscr{y}^2$, there are correspondences, $P(\mathbf{u},\mathscr{y}^2)$ and $\hat{\mathscr{W}}(\mathbf{u},\mathscr{y}^2)$, which are upper semi-continuous with respect to their arguments where $\mathbf{u}$ varies over the set $U(\mathscr{y}^2)$ and which define the sets of prices and feasible current allocations, respectively, which correspond to a given Pareto-efficient utility allocation. A current production allocation in $\hat{\mathscr{W}}(\mathbf{u},\mathscr{y}^2)$ is itself the image of a two-period production allocation under the mapping (1), $y_{fb} = \mathbf{p}_f^2\mathbf{y}_f^2$. Hence, define

$$\hat{\mathscr{W}}^{12}(\mathbf{u},\mathscr{y}^2) = \{(\mathscr{x},\mathscr{y}^{12'}) \mid (\mathscr{x},\mathscr{y}) \in \hat{\mathscr{W}}(\mathbf{u},\mathscr{y}^2) \text{ where } \mathscr{y}^1 = \mathscr{y}^{1'}, y_{fb} = \mathbf{p}_f^2\mathbf{y}_f^{2'}, \text{ for all } f\}.$$

The notation $\mathscr{y}^{12'}$ is designed to emphasize that $y_f^{2'}$ need not equal the original $\mathbf{y}_f^2$; the latter entered only through its effect on $\bar{x}_b$. It is easy to see that $\hat{\mathscr{W}}^{12}(\mathbf{u},\mathscr{y}^2)$, is closed and convex and is upper semi-continuous in its arguments. We show that

$$\hat{\mathscr{W}}^{12}(\mathbf{u},\mathscr{y}^2) \subset \tilde{\mathscr{W}}^{12}. \tag{22}$$

If $\mathbf{p} \in P(\mathbf{u},\mathscr{y}^2)$, it follows from the last clause of (17) that $p_b > 0$. Then profit maximization implies that $\mathbf{p}_f^2\mathbf{y}_f^2 \geq 0$, according to (5). Since feasibility already implies that

$$\sum_f \mathbf{y}_f^1 + \bar{\mathbf{x}}^1 \geq \sum_h \mathbf{x}_h^1,$$

(22) follows from D.6.19.

If we now define

$$s_h(p,\omega^{12}) = M_h(\mathbf{p},\mathscr{y}^{12}) - \mathbf{p}\mathbf{x}_h,$$

where $\omega^{12} = (\mathscr{x},\mathscr{y}^{12})$, we can define

$$V(\mathbf{p},\mathscr{y}^{12}) = S_H \cap \{\mathbf{v} \mid v_h = 0 \quad \text{if } s_h(\mathbf{p},\omega^{12}) < 0\}.$$

From (14) and (20),

$$M_h \geq \mathbf{p}\bar{\bar{\mathbf{x}}}_h,$$

always.

The correspondence

$$P[\mathbf{u}(\mathbf{v},\mathscr{y}^2),\mathscr{y}^2] \times V(\mathbf{p},\mathscr{w}^{12}) \times \tilde{\mathscr{W}}^{12}[\mathbf{u}(\mathbf{v},\mathscr{y}^2),\mathscr{y}^2]$$

then has a fixed point, which can be seen to be a compensated equilibrium by the arguments of Section 5.3.

We have assumed that all price expectations are totally inelastic; this assumption can easily be relaxed.

ASSUMPTION 11. For each household and firm, anticipated second-period prices are a continuous function of current prices; that is, $\mathbf{p}_h^2(\mathbf{p})$ and $\mathbf{p}_f^2(\mathbf{p})$ are continuous functions.

We now interpret those assumptions that referred to anticipated second-period prices, namely, A.6.7, A.6.9, and A.6.10, to hold for all values of $\mathbf{p}_h^2$ and $\mathbf{p}_f^2$ in the ranges of the anticipation functions, $\mathbf{p}_h^2(\mathbf{p})$ and $\mathbf{p}_f^2(\mathbf{p})$.

The various functions and correspondences now depend explicitly on $\mathbf{p}$, through $\mathbf{p}_f^2$ and $\mathbf{p}_h^2$; all the relevant continuity properties are easily seen to hold. Thus, U_h depends on $\mathbf{p}$ through $\mathbf{p}_h^2$, Y_f and $\mathbf{p}$ through $\mathbf{p}_f^2$.

Now redefine

$$\tilde{\mathscr{W}}^{12} = \mathscr{W}^{12} \cap \left\{(\mathscr{x},\mathscr{y}^{12}) \,\middle|\, \sum_f \mathbf{y}_f^1 + \bar{\mathbf{x}}^1 \geq \sum_h \mathbf{x}_h^1,\ \ \mathbf{p}_f^2(\mathbf{p})\mathbf{y}_f^2 \geq 0 \text{ for all } f, \text{ for some } \mathbf{p}\right\}.$$

Since $\mathbf{p}_f^2(\mathbf{p})$ is a continuous function over a compact set, the unit simplex, its range is compact. It is then easy to demonstrate from A.6.7 that $\tilde{\mathscr{W}}^{12}$ is compact. It is not necessarily convex, but its convex hull, denoted by con $\tilde{\mathscr{W}}^{12}$, is both compact and convex (see Lemma B.3).

Both U_h and Y_f depend upon $\mathbf{p}$; also, the initial current endowment of bonds, $\bar{x}_b$, as defined by (12) also depends continuously on $\mathbf{p}$ through its dependence on the anticipated prices, $\mathbf{p}_f^2$ and $\mathbf{p}_h^2$. Now we can consider the set of current utility allocations that are Pareto efficient conditional upon $\mathbf{p}$ as well as $\mathscr{y}^2$. Let $U(\mathscr{y}^2,\mathbf{p})$ be this set; then, as before, there is a continuous function, $\mathbf{u}(\mathbf{v},\mathscr{y}^2,\mathbf{p})$, that maps the unit simplex, S_H, into $U(\mathscr{y}^2,\mathbf{p})$. We then define the correspondences

$$P(\mathbf{u},\mathscr{y}^2,\mathbf{p}), \quad \tilde{\mathscr{W}}(\mathbf{u},\mathscr{y}^2,\mathbf{p}), \quad \text{and} \quad \tilde{\mathscr{W}}^{12}(\mathbf{u},\mathscr{y}^2,\mathbf{p})$$

in obvious analogy to the inelastic case. As in (22),

$$\hat{\mathscr{W}}^{12}(\mathbf{u},\mathscr{y}^2,\mathbf{p}) \subset \tilde{\mathscr{W}}^{12} \subset \text{con } \tilde{\mathscr{W}}^{12}.$$

Then the correspondence

$$P[\mathbf{u}(\mathbf{v},\mathscr{y}^2,\mathbf{p}),\mathscr{y}^2,\mathbf{p}] \times V(\mathbf{p},\mathscr{y}^{12}) \times \hat{\mathscr{W}}^{12}[\mathbf{u}(\mathbf{v},\mathscr{y}^2,\mathbf{p}),\mathscr{y}^2,\mathbf{p}]$$

maps the set $S_n \times S_H \times \text{con } \tilde{\mathscr{W}}^{12}$ into subsets of itself and possesses a fixed point that, again, is a compensated equilibrium.

Finally, to show that the compensated equilibrium is a competitive equilibrium, we need a suitable definition of *resource relatedness.*

DEFINITION 21. Household h' is *resource related* to household h'' for given $\bar{\mathbf{x}}_b$ and $\mathbf{p}$ if D.5.4 holds when $\mathbf{y}_f$ is computed as of a fixed $\mathbf{p}_f^2$ determined by $\mathbf{p}$, $\mathbf{U}_h$ is computed as of a fixed $\mathbf{p}_h^2$ determined by $\mathbf{p}$, and $\bar{\mathbf{x}}_b$ is taken as given, and when the impact of an alternative allocation on these parameters is ignored.

Household h' is *resource related* to household h'' if it is so resource related for any given $\bar{\mathbf{x}}_b$ and $\mathbf{p}$.

Household h' is *indirectly resource related* to household h'' if D.5.5 holds.

THEOREM 3. Competitive temporary equilibrium exists if A.6.6–A.6.11 hold and if every household is indirectly resource related to every other.

Remark 1. The theory of the firm used here is somewhere between two currently popular views. It is "managerial" in that only the expectations of managers enter into the firm's decisions; stockholders appear only as passive investors. In contradistinction to theories such as those of Marris [1964] and Williamson [1964], however, we do not ascribe to managers any motives other than profit maximization according to their expectations. A more general model would introduce a utility function for managers that depends in some more complicated way on the firm's production vector and current and anticipated profits; we have not investigated such a model here.

An alternative theory has the firm maximizing the current market value of its stock; that is, the firm chooses $\mathbf{y}_f^{12}$ to maximize K_f. This could be included in the present model by identifying $\mathbf{p}_f^2$ with $\mathbf{p}_h^2$ for that household for which K_{hf} is a maximum, where, for each h, K_{hf} has itself been defined by maximizing over Y_f^{12} at given $\mathbf{p}$ and $\mathbf{p}_h^2$. The only difficulty with this theory in the present framework is that as current prices change, different households value the firm most highly, and so $\mathbf{p}_f^2$ might change discontinuously as $\mathbf{p}$ changes. This could be avoided if we assumed there is, in fact, a continuum of households filling up a whole area in $\mathbf{p}_h^2$-space for any given $\mathbf{p}$; then $\mathbf{p}_f^2$ as defined would vary continuously with $\mathbf{p}$. Such a theory requires advanced methods for analysis.

Remark 2. The model here has assumed that there are no debts in the initial period, though, in general, there will be debts at the beginning of the next period. The discussion of Section 5.5 is applicable here; if expectations are falsified, then it can happen that no equilibrium in the next period will exist without bankruptcy, because the distribution of debt that is the result of the present period's choices and, therefore, the initial distribution for the next period is inappropriate.

Remark 3. Of course, we are neglecting uncertainty. This is a more serious problem than we might think, for in the presence of uncertainty it is unreasonable to assume that bonds of different firms and households are perfect substitutes. If we are not willing to assume that all individuals have the same probability distributions of prices, then it is reasonable to suppose that any firm or household has more information about matters that concern it most, and therefore, a household will have different subjective probability distributions for the bonds of different firms. Then, if a given firm is the only supplier of a commodity (its bonds) for which there are no perfect substitutes, the capital markets cannot be assumed perfect.

Remark 4. The restriction to two periods prevents us from examining speculation in the market for shares based on other households' expectations, a matter to which Keynes [1936, pp. 154–159] dramatically called attention. In a three-or-more-period model, a household may buy shares in a firm because it has expectations that in the second period others will have expectations that will make it profitable to sell the shares then.

4. Equilibrium under Monopolistic Competition

We now return to a static formulation, assuming this time that there are some firms in the economy that are capable of exercising monopolistic or monopsonistic power over certain markets. We assume, however, the absence of interaction among the monopolistic firms. Each firm takes the current prices of products not under its control as given and perceives a demand (or supply) function that may or may not be correct. The perception is made on the basis of observed prices and allocation. It is assumed that, at least at equilibrium, the demand functions are correct at the observed point, though not necessarily elsewhere; in other words, for the quantities actually produced, the firm correctly perceives the prices that will clear the markets. It is not necessarily assumed, however, that the monopolistic firms correctly perceive the elasticities of demand at the equilibrium point.

The production possibility sets for monopolistic firms need not be convex; indeed, the non-convexity (in particular, the increasing returns to scale) is presumably one reason for the existence of monopoly. However, it is assumed that the prices charged by monopolistic firms are continuous functions of other prices and other production and consumption decisions. If we assume, in the usual way, that monopolists are maximizing profits according to their perceived demand curves, then what we are saying is that the perceived marginal revenue curves fall more sharply than marginal cost curves.

Though we will weaken the convexity assumptions on the production possibility sets of the monopolists, we still need to make some hypotheses that will ensure that the set of feasible production allocations satisfies some reasonable conditions, specifically that it is bounded if resources are bounded and that it is a set that does not break up into several parts or have holes in its middle. The second provision can be expressed more precisely by requiring that the sets of those production possibility vectors for the monopolistic sector that are compatible with feasibility for the entire production sector can be expressed as the image of a compact convex set under a continuous mapping.

The assumptions on the competitive sector will remain those made before.

There are two kinds of firms, competitive and monopolistic. A *subscript* C will indicate a vector of *all* commodities that is possible for a competitive firm or for the competitive sector as a whole; similarly a subscript M denotes a commodity vector possible for a monopolistic firm or sector. Thus, Y_{Cf} is the production possibility set for competitive firm f, Y_{Mg} for monopolistic firm g. The production possibility set for the competitive sector as a whole is

$$Y_C = \sum_f Y_{Cf}$$

and similarly,

$$Y_M = \sum_g Y_{Mg}.$$

The elements of these sets are represented by $\mathbf{y}$ with the appropriate subscripts. A monopolized commodity, of course, will not be the output of any vector in Y_C, but it may be an input. Also, we use the term "monopolized" to include "monopsonized."

ASSUMPTION 12. A.3.1–A.3.3 hold for the sets Y_{Cf}.

ASSUMPTION 13. $0 \in Y_{Mg}$ and Y_{Mg} is closed, for each g.

We now need an assumption that extends A.3.4 (impossibility of getting something for nothing) to include the monopolistic firms; since the production possibility sets of the latter need not be convex, we will imagine the assumption to hold even if these sets are replaced by their convex hulls (see Section B.4). In other words, the increasing returns are sufficiently limited so that if we were to expand the production possibility sets so as to ensure convexity, we would not violate the laws of conservation. The extension is somewhat less drastic than A.6.5 above.

ASSUMPTION 14. If con Y_{Mg} is the convex hull of Y_{Mg} and

$$\sum_f \mathbf{y}_{Cf} + \sum_g \mathbf{y}_{Mg} \geq 0,$$

where $\mathbf{y}_{Cf} \in \mathbf{y}_{Cf}$ and $\mathbf{y}_{Mg} \in \text{con } Y_{Mg}$, then

$$\mathbf{y}_{Cf} = 0 \qquad \text{all } f,$$

and

$$\mathbf{y}_{Mg} = 0 \qquad \text{all } g.$$

From A.6.12–A.6.14, it follows by the same proof as that of T.3.2 that

$$(\mathscr{Y}_C \times \text{con } \mathscr{Y}_M) \cap \{(y_C, y_M) \mid \mathbf{y}_C + \mathbf{y}_M + \bar{\mathbf{x}} \geq \mathbf{0}\} \quad \text{is compact.} \quad (23)$$

Here we have used the obvious extensions of earlier notation,

$$\mathscr{Y}_C = \mathop{\times}_f Y_{Cf}, \quad \mathscr{Y}_M = \mathop{\times}_g Y_{Mg}, \quad \text{con}\, \mathscr{Y}_M = \mathop{\times}_g \text{con}\, Y_{Mg},$$

$$\mathbf{y}_C = \sum_f \mathbf{y}_{Cf}, \quad \mathbf{y}_M = \sum_g \mathbf{y}_{Mg}.$$

Also, we introduce the following definitions; the superscript v implies that the convex hull of $\mathscr{Y}_M$, con $\mathscr{Y}_M$, has been substituted for $\mathscr{Y}_M$ in the corresponding definition.

$$\mathscr{W} = \mathscr{X} \times \mathscr{Y}_C \times \mathscr{Y}_M,$$
$$\mathscr{W}^v = \mathscr{X} \times \mathscr{Y}_C \times \text{con}\, \mathscr{Y}_M,$$
$$\hat{\mathscr{W}} = \mathscr{W} \cap \{(x, y_C, y_M) \mid \mathbf{x} \le \mathbf{y}_C + \mathbf{y}_M + \bar{\mathbf{x}}\},$$
$$\hat{\mathscr{W}}^v = \mathscr{W}^v \cap \{(x, y_C, y_M) \mid \mathbf{x} \le \mathbf{y}_C + \mathbf{y}_M + \bar{\mathbf{x}}\},$$

$\hat{\mathscr{W}}^v_C$ is the projection of $\hat{\mathscr{W}}^v$ on $\mathscr{X} \times \mathscr{Y}_C$,

$\hat{\mathscr{Y}}_M$ is the projection of $\hat{\mathscr{W}}$ on $\mathscr{Y}_M$.

From (23), it follows immediately that $\hat{\mathscr{W}}$ and $\hat{\mathscr{W}}^v$ are compact (we are assuming, as will be explained shortly, that all elements of $\mathscr{X}$ are non-negative). Then,

$$\hat{\mathscr{W}}^v_C \text{ and } \hat{\mathscr{Y}}_M \text{ are compact.} \tag{24}$$

We now make a basic assumption on the structure of the monopolistic production possibility sets. It amounts to saying that the extent of increasing returns there is not too great relative to the resources that the competitive sector would be capable of supplying. In D.B.4, we introduce the definition that a point $\mathbf{x}^1$ is *visible* from another point $\mathbf{x}^2$ in a set C if the line segment joining the two points is entirely contained in C.

ASSUMPTION 15. There exist allocations $x^0 \in \mathscr{X}$ and $y^0_C \in \mathscr{Y}_C$ and a neighborhood in $\mathscr{Y}_M$ such that, for all y^1_m in that neighborhood, (x^0, y^0_C, y^1_m) is feasible and every point of Y_{Mg} is visible from $\mathbf{y}^1_{Mg}$.

In terms of D.B.6, we assume that $\mathscr{Y}_M$ is strictly star shaped. This assumption is admittedly not very transparent. However, first note that if Y_{Mg} is convex, then A.6.15 is automatically satisfied if $\mathbf{y}^0_{Mg}$ can be chosen to be a relative interior point of Y_{Mg} for which (x^0, y^0_C, y^0_M) is feasible, for by definition, a convex set is one in which every point is visible from any other. More generally, suppose that the competitive sector (including households) is capable of achieving a net supply of all competitive commodities (see A.3.5 and following discussion); let the corresponding allocation in the competitive sector be (x^1, y_C^1), so that the competitive components of

$$\sum_h \mathbf{x}_h^1 - \sum_f \mathbf{y}_{Cf}^1 - \bar{\mathbf{x}}$$

are all negative, while the monopolistic components are all 0. If the production possibility set for the monopolistic sector admits free disposal, this vector certainly belongs to that set, since we can certainly assume it contains **0**. Further, since competitive goods in the aggregate are productive in the monopolistic sector, we can increase all components, monopolistic and competitive alike, and still have a possible vector for the monopolistic sector; the corresponding allocation will be taken to be (x^0, y_C^0, y_M^0), and it is certainly feasible. From the construction, it is reasonable to hold that the same is true for all neighboring points. Now consider for each g any other point of Y_{Mg}, say $\mathbf{y}_{Mg}$. The vector $\mathbf{y}_{Mg}^0$ contains its share of an input of competitive goods; as the vector moves along the line segment to $\mathbf{y}_{Mg}$, it may be assumed that the failures of convexity due to indivisibilities are overcome by inputs of competitive goods. The point is illustrated by Figure 6.1, where the horizontal axis gives the input, derived from the competitive sector, while the vertical axis gives the output. Let

$$\mathbf{z}_C = \sum_h \mathbf{x}_h - \bar{\mathbf{x}} - \sum_f \mathbf{y}_{Cf}$$

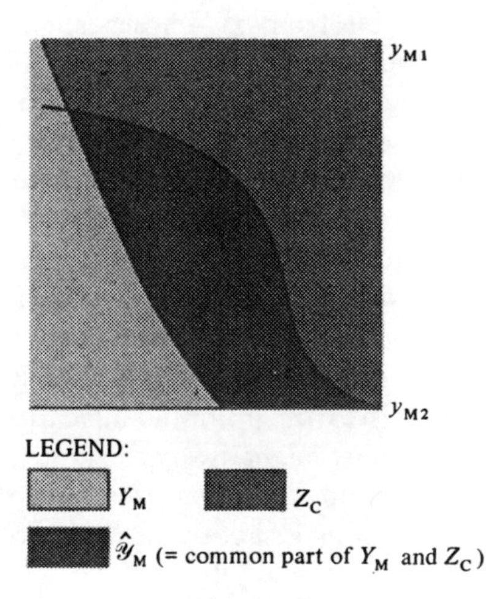

Figure 6-1

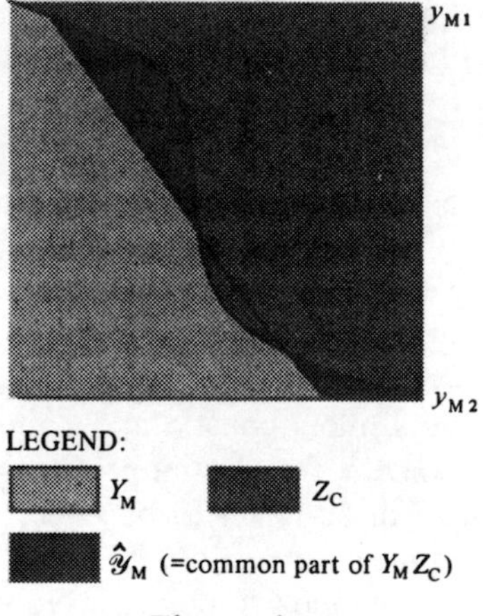

Figure 6-2

be any feasible excess-demand vector of the competitive sector, and let Z_C be the set of all such $\mathbf{z}_C$. In effect, $-\mathbf{z}_C$ is the vector of amounts made available to the monopolistic sector by the competitive sector; in general, $\mathbf{z}_C$ may have some positive components among the monopolized goods and these correspond to demands by the competitive sector on the monopolistic sector. In particular, in Figure 6-1, let $\mathbf{z}_C^1$ have a positive competitive component and a zero monopolistic component. Then any possible production for the monopolistic sector is visible from $\mathbf{z}_C^0$, chosen slightly larger than $\mathbf{z}_C^1$ in each component, and indeed, from any point in its neighborhood. On the other hand, if the competitive sector can produce only $\mathbf{z}_C^2$ with zero demand on the monopolistic sector, then there are points of Y_{Mg} not visible from $\mathbf{z}_C^2$ or any nearby point.

In Figure 6-2, we illustrate what the consequences might be of a failure of A.6.15. Suppose that the monopolistic commodity can be used by the competitive sector to increase its production. Then the set Z_C might take the indicated form. The darkest area is $\hat{\mathscr{Y}}_M$, which now consists of two disjoint areas. It is certainly conceivable that no equilibrium will exist; from an initial allocation corresponding to one area, the monopolist might always be motivated to choose a price that moves demand into the other area. At the very least, the weak assumptions we will make about the monopolist's behavior will not suffice to exclude this possibility.

Let y_M^1 belong to the neighborhood specified in A.6.15. Then, by definition, $y_M^1 \in \hat{\mathscr{Y}}_M$. Let y_M be any other element of $\hat{\mathscr{Y}}_M$ and y_M^2 a convex combination of the two. Since y_{Mg} is visible from y_{Mg}^1 in Y_{Mg}, y_M is visible from y_M^1. Because the feasibility condition is linear and the sets $\mathscr{X}$, $\mathscr{Y}_C$ are convex, it is immediate to verify that $y_M^2 \in \hat{\mathscr{Y}}_M$. Hence, every point of $\hat{\mathscr{Y}}_M$ is visible from every point in a neighborhood. We can now apply T.B.3 to assert

> There exists a continuous function with a unique inverse that maps $\hat{\mathscr{Y}}_M$ into a compact convex set A. (25)

We now turn to the behavior of the monopolist. At any given moment, the monopolists observe current prices and the current allocation and (individually) decide on their prices. We do not here necessarily derive their behavior from any hypothesis of profit—or utility—maximization, but we do assume that, whatever criterion they employ, their choices of prices and quantities will depend continuously on observations of the rest of the market. Under different alternative perceptions of demand conditions, the prices and quantities chosen will differ, but there will be a functional relation on which all the price-quantity choices will lie for given behavior of the rest of the economy. In equilibrium, the actual behavior of the monopolist will be jointly determined by the posited relation and the true demand relation derived from the behavior of the competitive sector.

We shall illustrate the assumptions in the conventional partial equilibrium analysis of monopoly. The monopolist believes that the demand curve is given by $p = d(y,\theta)$, where θ is a shift parameter. Let $R'(y,\theta)$ be the corresponding perceived marginal revenue curve for any θ and $C'(y)$ the monopolist's marginal cost curve. Then, for any given θ, output and price are determined as the solutions of the pair of equations $p = d(y,\theta)$, $C'(y) = R'(y,\theta)$. If we eliminate θ in these two relations, we have a single relation between p and y, say, $y = f(p)$. This relation might be termed the monopolist's supply curve. It is a relation between his price and his quantity that holds regardless of the demand curves he perceives. The actual equilibrium of the economy will be determined by this relation together with the true demand curve, say, $p = \bar{d}(y)$. The function $\bar{d}(y)$ need not coincide with the function $d(y,\theta)$, for any θ, if the monopolist's perceived family of demand curves does not include the true one. If p^*, y^* satisfy the two equations

$y^* = f(p^*)$ and $p^* = \bar{d}(y^*)$, then the monopolist will perceive the demand curve as that determined by the value of the shift parameter θ^* determined by the relation $p^* = d(y^*,\theta^*)$. He must perceive the correct actual demand, though not necessarily the true demand function.

Thus, we are assuming a stable relation between the price and quantity decisions of the monopolists, given the observations on prices and quantities in the rest of the economy. If we regard the monopolist's output as the dependent variable, we can think of it also as a function of all prices and quantities; this is not to imply that he takes his price as given, but rather that, given all other prices and all other quantities, his output decision is functionally related to his price decision. Given the monopolized outputs, the choice of competitive inputs to produce them is determined on a cost-minimizing basis. Hence, the total production decision of the monopoly is a function of all prices and quantities. Though we are not assuming profit maximization, it is necessary in a private-enterprise economy to insist on viability; no monopoly can be making a negative profit.

ASSUMPTION 16. For each monopolistic firm, g, the production vector is a continuous function, $\mathbf{y}_{Mg}(\mathbf{p},\omega)$, of prices and allocations such that $\mathbf{p}\mathbf{y}_{Mg}(\mathbf{p},\omega) \geq 0$ for all $\mathbf{p}$ and ω.

We now turn to the competitive sector, which determines the demand for monopolized goods. Some further notation is needed. For any fixed monopolistic production allocation, y_M, there is a range of feasible allocations for the competitive sectors, provided $y_M \in \mathscr{Y}_M$, namely, those allocations $\omega_C = (x,y_C)$ for which

$$\sum_h \mathbf{x}_h \leq \sum_f \mathbf{y}_{Cf} + \bar{\mathbf{x}} + \sum_g \mathbf{y}_{Mg} \qquad \mathbf{y}_{Cf} \in Y_{Cf},\ \mathbf{x}_h \in X_h.$$

The productive activity of the monopolistic sector can be treated as a modification of the initial endowment from the viewpoint of the competitive sector. The set of allocations ω_C satisfying these conditions will be denoted by $\mathscr{W}_C(y_M)$.

As in Section 4.4, especially D. 4.6–11, we shall be interested in feasible allocations in the competitive sector that yield each household at least a prescribed utility level. For any vector of utilities, $\mathbf{u}$, we define

$$\mathscr{W}_C(\mathbf{u},y_M) = \mathscr{W}_C(y_M) \cap \{(x,y_C) | U_h(\mathbf{x}_h) \geq u_h, \quad \text{all } h\}. \qquad (26)$$

We now repeat the assumptions on consumer behavior discussed in Chapter 4 with a rather technical strengthening of A.4.2.

ASSUMPTION 17. (a) Assumptions A.4.1, A.4.3, and A.4.4 hold.

(b) There exist possible consumption vectors $\bar{\bar{\mathbf{x}}}_h^k \in X_h$, $k = 1, 2$, not indifferent to each other, such that

$$\bar{\bar{\mathbf{x}}}_{hi}^k \leq \bar{\mathbf{x}}_{hi} \text{ (all } i) \quad \bar{\bar{\mathbf{x}}}_{hi}^k < \bar{\mathbf{x}}_{hi} \quad \text{if} \quad \bar{\mathbf{x}}_{hi} > 0 \qquad \text{for } k = 1, 2.$$

From (b), we can assume without loss of generality that

$$\bar{\bar{\mathbf{x}}}_h^2 \succ_h \bar{\bar{\mathbf{x}}}_h^1 \qquad \text{all } h.$$

The utility function, $U_h(\mathbf{x}_h)$, can be so chosen that $U_h(\bar{\bar{\mathbf{x}}}_h^1) = 0$, $U_h(\bar{\bar{\mathbf{x}}}_h^2) = 2$, all h. Then any household can clearly achieve a utility of more than 1 regardless of prices. Without loss of generality, then, we restrict ourselves, where appropriate, to allocations that achieve a utility of 1 at least for each individual. Define

$$\mathscr{W}(\mathbf{e}) = \mathscr{X}(\mathbf{e}) \times \mathscr{Y}_C \times \mathscr{Y}_M,$$

$$\hat{\mathscr{W}}(\mathbf{e}) = \mathscr{W}(\mathbf{e}) \cap \{(x, y_C, y_M) | \mathbf{x} \leq \mathbf{y}_C + \mathbf{y}_M + \bar{\mathbf{x}}\},$$

$$\hat{\mathscr{Y}}_M(\mathbf{e}) \text{ is the projection of } \hat{\mathscr{W}}(\mathbf{e}) \text{ on } \mathscr{Y}_M.$$

As before, $\mathbf{e}$ is the vector all of whose components are 1; in this case, its dimensionality is equal to H, the number of households.

The reasoning leading to (25) can be repeated with $\mathscr{Y}_M$ replaced by $\mathscr{Y}_M(\mathbf{e})$.

> There exists a continuous function, $\mathbf{a}(y_M)$, with a unique inverse, that maps $\mathscr{Y}_M(\mathbf{e})$ into a compact convex set A. (27)

For fixed $y_M \in \hat{\mathscr{Y}}_M(\mathbf{e})$, we can consider the range of feasible utility vectors in the competitive sector, that is, the set of vectors $\mathbf{u}$ for which $\hat{\mathscr{W}}(\mathbf{u}, y_M)$ is non-null. By definition of $\hat{\mathscr{Y}}_M(\mathbf{e})$, the vector $\mathbf{e}$ is always feasible, so there are always some non-negative utility vectors. We can consider then the range of non-negative Pareto-efficient utility allocations, $U(\mathscr{Y}_M)$. For each $\mathbf{u} \in U(\mathscr{Y}_M)$, the set of Pareto-efficient competitive allocations is $\hat{\mathscr{W}}_C(\mathbf{u}, y_M)$. By A.6.17, the reasoning leading to T.4.4, the basic theorem of welfare economics, is still valid here, so allocations in this set are all supported by a set of price vectors,

$$P_C(\mathbf{u}, y_M). \tag{28}$$

Since $\mathbf{e}$ is feasible, $\mathbf{0}$ is always dominated. Hence Lemma 4.13

remains valid (see the Remark to that lemma). Hence, the proof of Lemma 5.3 remains valid, so that, for fixed y_M, there is a function,

$$\mathbf{u}(\mathbf{v}, y_M),$$

mapping the unit simplex S_H into $U(y_M)$; the function, $\mathbf{u}(\mathbf{v}, y_M)$, can easily be seen to be continuous in both variables.

We now make an assumption that plays the same role as A.3.5, the ability of the economy to produce a positive amount of every good. This assumption was used to show that the aggregate income of the economy must be positive. Here, we simply make that assumption more directly.

ASSUMPTION 18. For any price vector $\mathbf{p}$, at least one of the following must hold:

(a) $\mathbf{p}\bar{\mathbf{x}} > 0$;
(b) for some f, $\mathbf{p}\mathbf{y}_{Cf} > 0$ for some $\mathbf{y}_{Cf} \in Y_{Cf}$;
(c) for any ω, $\mathbf{p}\mathbf{y}_{Mg}(\mathbf{p}, \omega) > 0$ for some g.

Suppose neither (a) nor (b) hold. Then all primary factors are free, and no competitive firm can make any profit. Then this assumption simply asserts that at least one monopolistic firm must be capable of making positive profits.

In defining equilibrium for monopolistic competition, we must provide for the distribution of monopolistic profits to households. The income of the household is now given by

$$M_h = \mathbf{p}\bar{\mathbf{x}}_h + \sum_f d^C_{hf}(\mathbf{p}\mathbf{y}_{Cf}) + \sum_g d^M_{hg}(\mathbf{p}\mathbf{y}_{Mg}), \tag{29}$$

where, of course,

$$d^C_{hf} \geq 0 \qquad d^M_{hg} \geq 0$$

$$\sum_h d^C_{hf} = 1 \qquad \sum_h d^M_{hg} = 1$$

so that

$$\sum_h M_h = \mathbf{p}\bar{\mathbf{x}} + \mathbf{p}\mathbf{y}_M + \mathbf{p}\mathbf{y}_C. \tag{30}$$

DEFINITION 22. A price vector, $\mathbf{p}^*$, and an allocation, $\omega^* = (x^*, y^*_C, y^*_M)$ constitute a *monopolistic competitive equilibrium* if

(a) $\mathbf{p}^* > 0$;
(b) $\sum_h \mathbf{x}^*_h \leq \sum_h \bar{\mathbf{x}}_h + \sum_f \mathbf{y}^*_{Cf} + \sum_g \mathbf{y}^*_{Mg}$;

(c) $\mathbf{y}^*_{Cf}$ maximizes $\mathbf{p}^*\mathbf{y}_{Cf}$ subject to $\mathbf{y}_{Cf} \in Y_{Cf}$;

(d) $\mathbf{x}^*_h$ maximizes $U_h(\mathbf{x}_h)$ subject to

$$\mathbf{p}^*\mathbf{x}_h \leq M^*_h = \mathbf{p}^*\bar{\mathbf{x}}_h + \sum_f d^C_{hf}(\mathbf{p}^*\mathbf{y}^*_{Cf}) + \sum_g d^M_{hg}(\mathbf{p}^*\mathbf{y}^*_{Mg});$$

(e) $\mathscr{y}^*_M = \mathscr{y}_M(\mathbf{p}^*,\omega^*)$.

The function

$$\mathscr{y}_M(\mathbf{p},\omega)$$

in part (e) of this definition is the allocation whose firm components are the functions

$$\mathbf{y}_{Mg}(\mathbf{p},\omega),$$

introduced in A.6.16.

Unlike the procedure of Chapter 5, we do not explicitly introduce a corresponding definition of compensated equilibrium. We shall still need an assumption of resource relatedness to prove the existence of monopolistic competitive equilibrium. We use definitions D.5.4–5 but relate them to the competitive sector only; monopolistic inputs and outputs are treated as alterations of the initial endowment.

ASSUMPTION 19. Every household is indirectly resource related to every other through the competitive sector alone for every initial endowment obtained by replacing $\bar{\mathbf{x}}$ by

$$\bar{\mathbf{x}} + \sum_g \mathbf{y}_{Mg} \quad \text{for some } \mathscr{y}_M \in \mathscr{y}_M(\mathbf{e}).$$

We now construct the mapping used to prove the existence of equilibrium. The basic principle of the mapping of Chapter 5 is retained, but modified to introduce both quantities used in the competitive sector and production decisions of monopolists. The monopolized commodities appear twice in the space in which the mapping takes place, but the mapping is so arranged that, at the fixed point, the two output variables corresponding to the same good are equal. The other variables in the mapping are, as before, prices and relative utilities. The prices in the image will be those that sustain an efficient allocation in the competitive sector for given monopolistic production decisions. For the image vector of relative utilities, the previous construction is modified in the obvious way. Simply define

$$s_h(\mathbf{p},\omega) = \mathbf{p}\mathbf{x}_h - M_h(\mathbf{p},\omega), \tag{31}$$

where $\omega = (x, y_C, y_M)$ and M_h is defined in (29),

$$V(\mathbf{p},\omega) = S_H \cap \{\mathbf{v} | v_h = 0 \quad \text{if} \quad s_h(\mathbf{p},\omega) < 0\}. \tag{32}$$

We also map the initial situation into the efficient allocation of commodities in the competitive sector, conditional on the outputs of the monopolistic sector. For the monopolistic sector, we would like the new value of the monopolistic production vector to be on the response function postulated in A.6.16. We also want this image to be in or correspond to a point in A, that is, equivalent to a production vector in $\hat{\mathscr{Y}}_M(\mathbf{e})$, the set that is indexed by A according to (27). The second property will be satisfied at equilibrium if there is one, but not in general for an arbitrary initial $\mathbf{p}$, ω. We therefore construct a mapping into A as follows. First, find $y_M(\mathbf{p},\omega)$, the monopolist's response according to A.6.16. Then map this point into $\hat{\mathscr{Y}}_M(\mathbf{e})$ in such a way that it is unchanged if it is already in this set. Then map the resulting point into A according to (27). To do this, choose y_M^0 to belong to the interior of the neighborhood specified in A.6.15. Clearly we can do this in such a way that

$$\mathbf{x}^0 \ll \mathbf{y}_C^0 + \mathbf{y}_M^0 + \bar{\mathbf{x}} \quad \text{for some} \quad x^0 \in \mathscr{X}(\mathbf{e}),\ \mathbf{y}_C^0 \in Y_C. \tag{33}$$

Let $p(y_M)$ be the gauge function for the set $\hat{\mathscr{Y}}_M(\mathbf{e})$ with center y_M^0 (see Section B.2, especially T.B.2). Then $y_M \in \hat{\mathscr{Y}}_M(\mathbf{e})$ if and only if $p(y_M) \leq 1$. Let $q(y_M) = \max[p(y_M), 1]$. Then $q(y_M) = 1$ for $y_M \in \hat{\mathscr{Y}}_M(\mathbf{e})$, $q(y_M) > 1$ for $y_M \in \mathscr{Y}_M(\mathbf{e})$. Define

$$y_M^1(\mathbf{p},\omega) = y_M^0 + \frac{y_M(\mathbf{p},\omega) - y_M^0}{q[y_M(\mathbf{p},\omega)]}, \tag{34}$$

$$\mathbf{a}^1(\mathbf{p},\omega) = \mathbf{a}[y_M^1(\mathbf{p},\omega)]. \tag{35}$$

In (34), we accept the monopolist's response if it permits a utility of at least 1 to each household (a utility that can be achieved without trade); if not, we move the response toward a given point until it satisfies this condition. In (35), we relabel this point to put it in a convex compact set.

We map the set

$$S_n \times S_H \times \mathscr{W}_C^v \times A$$

into the correspondence

$$P_C(\mathbf{u}, y_M) \times V(\mathbf{p},\omega) \times \mathscr{W}_C(\mathbf{u}, y_M) \times \{\mathbf{a}^1(\mathbf{p},\omega)\},$$

where

$$y_M \text{ satisfies the condition } \mathbf{a}(y_M) = \mathbf{a}, \text{ and } \mathbf{u} = \mathbf{u}(\mathbf{v}, y_M),$$

and $P_C(\mathbf{u},y_M)$ and $\mathscr{W}_C(\mathbf{u},y_M)$ are defined in (28) and (26), respectively. Then Kakutani's theorem guarantees the existence of a fixed point for this correspondence, $(\mathbf{p}^*,\mathbf{v}^*,w_C^*,\mathbf{a}^*)$. Let y_M^* be defined by

$$\mathbf{a}(y_M^*) = \mathbf{a}^*$$

and

$$\mathbf{u}^* = \mathbf{u}(\mathbf{v}^*,y_M^*).$$

Since

$$\mathbf{p}^* \in P_C(\mathbf{u}^*,y_M^*) \qquad w_C^* \in \mathscr{W}_C(\mathbf{u}^*,y_M^*), \tag{36}$$

it follows from T.4.4 that D.6.22 (a)–(c) hold, and also

$$\mathbf{x}_h^* \text{ minimizes } \mathbf{p}^*\mathbf{x}_h \text{ subject to } U_h(\mathbf{x}_h) \geq \mathbf{u}_h^*. \tag{37}$$

From (31) and (36), it follows, as in Section 5.3, that

$$\sum_h s_h(\mathbf{p}^*,w^*) = 0.$$

At the fixed point, $\mathbf{v}^* \in V(\mathbf{p}^*,w^*)$. Again as in Section 5.3, it follows that

$$s_h(\mathbf{p}^*,w^*) \geq 0 \qquad \text{all } h,$$

and therefore

$$s_h(\mathbf{p}^*,w^*) = 0 \qquad \text{all } h,$$

or equivalently,

$$\mathbf{p}^*\mathbf{x}_h^* = M_h^*. \tag{38}$$

We know that (37) and (38) imply that D.6.22(d) (utility maximization) holds if it can be demonstrated that $M_h^* > 0$ (see the proof of T.5.2). Because of A.6.19 (resource relatedness), it suffices to show that

$$\sum_h M_h^* > 0.$$

From (33), we know that

$$\mathbf{p}^*(\mathbf{y}_C^0 + \mathbf{y}_M^0 + \bar{\mathbf{x}}) > 0.$$

By profit maximization, $\mathbf{p}^*\mathbf{y}_C^* \geq \mathbf{p}^*\mathbf{y}_C^0$ and also $\mathbf{p}^*\mathbf{y}_C^* \geq 0$. Hence,

$$\mathbf{p}^*(\bar{\mathbf{x}} + \mathbf{y}_C^* + \mathbf{y}_M^0) > 0 \tag{39}$$

and

$$\mathbf{p}^*(\bar{\mathbf{x}} + \mathbf{y}_C^*) \geq 0.$$

From A.6.16,

$$\mathbf{p}^*\mathbf{y}_{Mg}(\mathbf{p}^*,\omega^*) \geq 0$$

and, therefore, summing over g,

$$\mathbf{p}^*\mathbf{y}_M(\mathbf{p}^*,\omega^*) \geq 0$$

so that

$$\mathbf{p}^*[\bar{\mathbf{x}} + \mathbf{y}_C^* + \mathbf{y}_M(\mathbf{p}^*,\omega^*)] \geq 0. \tag{40}$$

From (35), at the fixed point,

$$\mathbf{a}^1(\mathbf{p}^*,\omega^*) = \mathbf{a}^*,$$

or

$$y_M^1(\mathbf{p}^*,\omega^*) = y_M^*,$$

so from (34) and summing over g, we see that $\mathbf{y}_M^*$ is a convex combination of $\mathbf{y}_M^0$ and $\mathbf{y}_M(\mathbf{p}^*,\omega^*)$, with weights $1 - (1/q^*)$ and $(1/q^*)$, respectively, where

$$q^* = q[y_M(\mathbf{p}^*,\omega^*)].$$

Then, from (39) and (40),

$$\mathbf{p}^*(\bar{\mathbf{x}} + \mathbf{y}_C^* + \mathbf{y}_M^*) \geq 0, \tag{41}$$

and the strict inequality holds if $q^* > 1$. If, on the contrary, $q^* = 1$, then

$$\mathbf{y}_M^* = \mathbf{y}_M(\mathbf{p}^*,\omega^*),$$

and by A.6.16,

$$\mathbf{p}^*\mathbf{y}_M^* \geq 0.$$

Then equality can hold in (41) only if simultaneously

$$\mathbf{p}^*\bar{\mathbf{x}} = 0, \quad \mathbf{p}^*\mathbf{y}_C^* = 0, \quad \text{and} \quad \mathbf{p}^*\mathbf{y}_M^* = 0,$$

in contradiction to A.6.18. Therefore, the strict inequality holds in (41) in any case; by (30),

$$\sum_h M_h^* > 0$$

and, therefore, D.6.22(d) holds.

Since each household is maximizing utility and since each can achieve a utility of 2 without using the market, it must be that

$$u_h^* \geq 2 \qquad \text{all } h.$$

If y_M^* were changed to any y_M in its neighborhood, there would still exist competitive allocations feasible conditional on the monopolistic allocation y_M, which would achieve a utility strictly greater than 1 for each individual. Then y_M^* must belong to the interior of the set

$$\mathcal{Y}_M(\mathbf{e}).$$

By definition of the gauge function,

$$p(y_M^*) < 1.$$

By (34),

$$p(y_M^*) = \frac{p[y_M(\mathbf{p}^*,\omega^*)]}{q[(y_M\mathbf{p}^*,\omega^*)]} < 1.$$

From the definitions, this can happen only if $q^* = 1$, that is, if

$$y_M^* = y_M(\mathbf{p}^*,\omega^*),$$

which is D.6.22(e).

THEOREM 4. Under assumptions A.6.12–19, monopolistic competitive equilibrium exists.

Remark 1. No explicit mention has been made of product differentiation, a central theme of monopolistic competition theory, but note that the model admits the possibility that any monopolistic firm can produce a variety of goods. Suppose that all conceivable goods are included in the list of commodities; even what are usually regarded as varieties of the same good must be distinguished in this list if they are not perfect substitutes in both production and consumption. In general, a monopolist will find it profitable to produce a number of varieties. The definition of a monopoly implies that, for some reason or another, two different monopolists produce non-overlapping sets of goods, but of course the goods produced by one monopolist may be quite close substitutes for those produced by another. The usual idea in product differentiation—that a firm produces just one commodity—is not a convenient assumption for general equilibrium analysis, but it is equally certainly not a good description of the real world.

Remark 2. The notion of free entry, and with it the famous double-tangency solution of Chamberlin [1956, pp. 81–100] and Robinson [1933, pp. 93–94], has no role here either. The list of monopolists is assumed given, so that in effect there is a scarcity of the appropriate type of entrepreneurship, and there is no reason for profits to be wiped out. No doubt if there are several firms producing products that are close substitutes in consumption and have very similar production possibility sets otherwise, they should behave about the same way, and if there are enough of them, it may well be that each is making very little in the way of profit. But the question then is the one raised originally by Kaldor [1935]: Would not the elasticity of demand to the individual firm be essentially infinite, so that the situation is essentially one of perfect competition? This question has not been fully answered, since a more specific model defining close substitutes and their production possibilities has not yet been explicitly formulated.

Remark 3. An open and potentially important research area is the specification of conditions under which monopolistic behavior, as expressed in the function $y_M(\mathbf{p},\omega)$ is, in fact, continuous. The formulation is very general; it is certainly compatible with utility-maximizing behavior (e.g., preference for size or particular kind of expenditure or product) as well as profit-maximizing behavior. The assumption of continuity may be strong nevertheless; in effect, it denies the role of increasing returns as a barrier to entry. As demand shifts upward, the firm might pass from zero output (i.e., a purely potential existence) to a minimum positive output. A zero output must be interpreted as a price decision at a level corresponding to zero demand, but if the demand curve slopes downward, then entry at a positive level far removed from zero implies a discontinuous drop in price. The importance of this problem is not easy to assess. The situation can arise only if the (perceived) marginal revenue curve is, broadly speaking, flatter than the marginal cost curve (otherwise entry would be a continuous phenomenon) but the demand curve must also be relatively flat and therefore the price discontinuity may be mild even if the output discontinuity is large. Also, if there were only a single monopolist who correctly perceived the excess-demand correspondence of the competitive sector, he could choose his most preferred point, which would be then an equilibrium; the discontinuity of his behavior would be irrelevant. The problem may be important, however, if his perceptions are accurate only at equilibrium or if there are several monopolists; the discontinuity in the behavior of any one affects the perceived demand functions for the others, though, again, if the monopolists are relatively separated in markets and each is relatively small on the scale of the economy, then the discontinuities involved may be unimportant.

Remark 4. It must always be remembered that monopolistic competition models of the type discussed here ignore the mutual recognition of power among firms, the oligopoly problem.

Notes

Section 2. The analysis of this section was developed jointly with David Starrett. It is rather hard to make out from the usual literature whether it is assumed that competitive equilibrium is compatible with externalities. Chipman [1970] reviews some of the literature. In a particular case he shows how externalities that give rise to social-increasing returns, but private constant returns, are compatible with the existence of competitive equilibrium and even, under special circumstances, to Pareto efficiency. For a good general statement of the usual doctrine of equilibrium with externalities in production, see Bohm [1963, Chapter 2]. For a rigorous proof of the existence of equilibrium with externalities in consumption, see McKenzie [1955b].

Section 3. The analysis of temporary equilibrium was introduced by Hicks [1939, pp. 130–133]. A more recent methodological discussion can be found in Hicks [1965, Chapter VI]. The possibility of an existence theorem for temporary equilibrium was indicated by Saito [1961, pp. 233–236]. The results of this section have appeared in slightly different form in Arrow [1971].

Section 4. The model presented here is a formalization of Chamberlin's case of monopolistic competition with large numbers [1956, pp. 81–100; originally published in 1933]. As Triffin [1940] showed, the essential aspects of monopolistic competition appear as soon as we attempt to introduce some monopolies into a system of general competitive equilibrium. The only previous complete formal model is that of the brilliant paper of Negishi [1960–61], who proved an existence theorem for it, the only previous work of this type known to us. Negishi assumed that each monopolist produced only one commodity and maximized profits according to a perceived demand curve that was a function of all prices and the entire allocation, but, in particular, was linear in the price of the commodity. He saw the importance of insisting that at equilibrium the monopolist's perceived demand curve should at least pass through the observed price-quantity point. In his formulation, which was originally suggested by Bushaw and Clower

[1957, p. 181], the monopolist's price equaled the given one if, at the given allocation, supply and demand were equal for that commodity. Also, Negishi restricted attention to the case in which the monopolists have convex production possibility sets, a severe condition since the occurrence of monopoly is unlikely under those circumstances, as Negishi himself noted [p. 109, middle]. He raised the possibility of more general assumptions, similar to A.6.15.

A model intended to represent the ideas of this section has already been presented in Arrow [1971]. The results given there, however, while mathematically correct, suffer from considerable difficulties in interpretation. We are greatly indebted to Tatsuro Ichiishi, Keio University, and James Mirrlees, Oxford, for demonstrating to us the need for new thinking on these questions.

Chapter Seven

MARKETS WITH NON-CONVEX PREFERENCES AND PRODUCTION

A gulf profound as that Serbonian Bog
Betwixt Damiata and mount Casius old,
Where Armies whole have sunk.
—John Milton, *Paradise Lost*

1. Introduction

The assumptions of convexity of production (A.3.3) and of preferences (A.4.4(d)) have played an essential role in the proof of existence of competitive equilibrium. Convexity implies that responses of firms and households to changes in prices tend to be continuous; even when jumps occur (as under constant returns for a firm), every point in the whole interval between the two extremities of the jump is a permissible response so that there are no gaps in which an inequality between supply and demand can be fitted. This point can be seen for firms by contrasting Figures 3-1–3-3 with Figure 3-4 (see also the accompanying text). In Figure 7-1 we reproduce the production possibility set of Figure 3-4a and add the implied demand function for the input. Let commodity 1 be input and commodity 2 output. Then, for p_2/p_1 less than some critical price ratio, a, the firm will make negative profits at any positive output level and, therefore, will supply and demand zero. At $p_2/p_1 = a$, the firm will make a zero profit at precisely one non-zero activity, (y_1^a,y_2^a) and negative profits at all others. Thus, the profit-maximizing firm is indifferent between (0,0) and (y_1^a,y_2^a); the demand by the firm is two-valued, the values being 0 and $-y_1^a$. For $p_2/p_1 > a$, the demand will exceed $-y_1^a$.

Suppose the firm is the only one in the economy, the initial endowment of the economy (summed over all households) is $(\bar{x}_1,0)$, and commodity 1 does not enter anyone's utility function, so that the sole demand for the commodity arises from the firm's productive activity. Then if $0 < \bar{x}_1 < -y_1^a$, it is clear that no equilibrium price ratio exists. If $p_2/p_1 < a$, then supply of commodity 1 exceeds

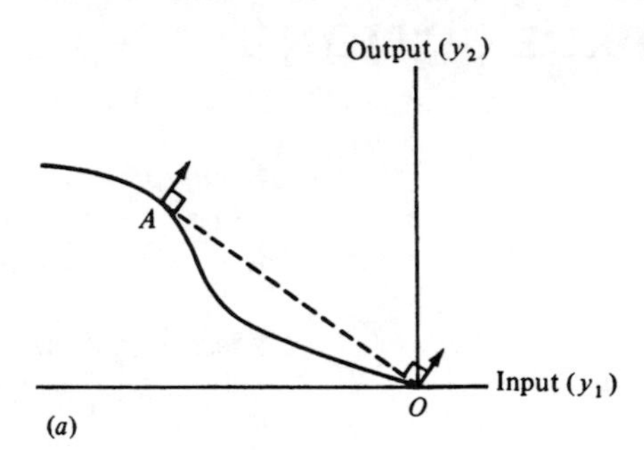

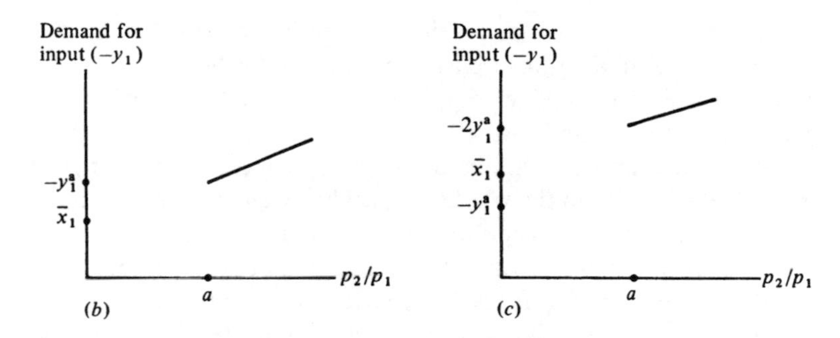

Figure 7-1

demand. If $p_2/p_1 > a$, then demand exceeds supply on that market. If $p_2/p_1 = a$, there is no behavior of the firm that simultaneously maximizes profits and absorbs exactly the available supply.

Suppose that Figure 7-1a were modified by adding to the production possibility set every production vector on or below the straight line segment OA. Then at the price ratio a all these points would yield a zero profit; the demand correspondence for the input would include the whole vertical segment from 0 to $-y_1^a$. Then the equilibrium input would be $\bar{x}_1$ and the equilibrium price ratio a. This comparison brings out more specifically the role of convexity in establishing the existence of equilibrium.

Since existence of equilibrium is not assured in the presence of non-convexity, it may be worthwhile to ask how close to equilibrium the economy can come, under the assumption that the firm is profit maximizing. Suppose first that $0 < \bar{x}_1 \leq -y_1^a/2$. Assume the price ratio is a. Then, if the firm purchases zero, there is an excess supply $\bar{x}_1$. If, on the contrary, the firm purchased $-y_1^a$—an equally profitable decision—demand would exceed supply by $-y_1^a - \bar{x}_1 \geq \bar{x}_1$. There is, then, a price ratio, a, and a profit-maximizing demand, 0, for which the absolute discrepancy between supply and demand does not exceed $-y_1^a/2$. If the price ratio were different from a, the discrepancy could not be smaller. Now, if we suppose that $-y_1^a/2 < \bar{x}_1 < -y_1^a$, the smallest discrepancy between supply and demand occurs at price ratio a and profit-maximizing demand $-y_1^a$; this time there is excess supply, but again the discrepancy does not exceed $-y_1^a/2$ in absolute value.

Now, to continue the example, suppose an economy with two identical firms, each with the production possibility set defined by Figure 7-1a. The aggregate demand for two firms is represented in Figure 7-1c. Then aggregate demand for commodity 1 is zero for $p_2/p_1 < a$, and it exceeds $-2y_1^a$ for $p_2/p_1 > a$. If $p_2/p_1 = a$, each firm will, as before, demand either zero or $-y_1^a$. Since neither, one, or both of the two firms may be demanding a positive amount of commodity 1, the aggregate demand at $p_2/p_1 = a$ is tri-valued, the three possible values being 0, $-y_1^a$, and $-2y_1^a$. Now, if $\bar{x}_1$ lies between 0 and $-2y_1^a$, it is clear that at the price ratio a we can arrange that the discrepancy between supply and demand not exceed $-y_1^a/2$ without violating the assumption that firms maximize profits; all that is needed is to choose that one of three possible magnitudes that is closest to $\bar{x}_1$.

This conclusion suggests the interesting implication that the possible discrepancies between supply and demand do not necessarily increase with the number of agents in the economy. Put another way, the ratio of the possible disequilibrium to the size of the economy decreases. The aim of this chapter is to give a general formulation of this result.

The possibility that, at the price ratio a, one firm may be operating while the other is not suggests another implication of non-convexity: At an equilibrium or approximate equilibrium it may be necessary that identical firms behave very differently.

The possibilities for validity or invalidity of the convexity hypothesis have been discussed in Section 3.2. It was argued there that non-convex production possibility sets could be expected to arise from indivisibilities in production processes.

It is similarly possible that the preference orderings of households do not satisfy the convexity condition A.4.4(d). Some pairs of commodities may be antagonistic in consumption. Whiskey and gin form a frequently cited pair of this kind. A more serious example is residential location. An individual may be indifferent between consuming seven days a week a day of living in California and consuming the same amount of living in Massachusetts, but he

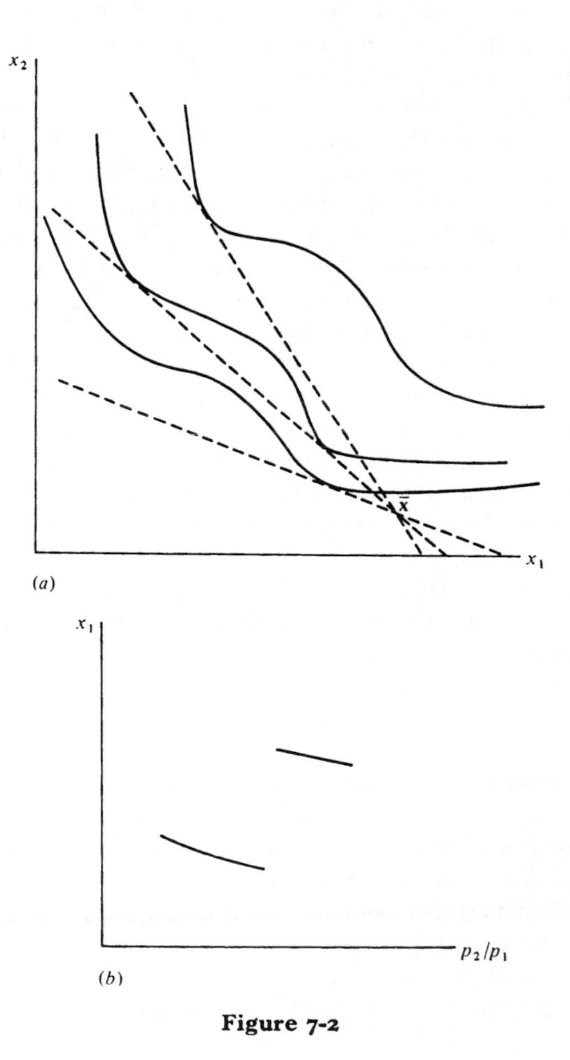

Figure 7-2

may well prefer either to splitting the week between the two. (On the other hand, a different choice may be made if the alternatives are London and Cambridge.) Evaluations of esthetic satisfaction of tastes, in general, are also unlikely to be convex. "There is no excellent Beauty that hath not some strangenesse in the proportion," says Bacon. "A man cannot tell whether Appelles or Albert Dürer were the more trifler; whereof the one would make a Personage by geometrical proportions; the other, by taking the best parts out of diverse Faces to make one excellent." Nor would a convex combination of *tripe à la mode de Caen* and *filet de sole Marguéry* be regarded highly by the gourmet (perhaps Chinese cuisine admits more convexity in preferences among its dishes than does the French). No doubt the root of any non-convexity in household preference orderings is some indivisibility; in any consumption activity, one input is the individual. For our purposes it suffices to recognize the possibility that preference orderings may exhibit non-convexities without seeking a deeper explanation.

Figure 7-2 illustrates the demands derived from non-convex preferences, analogous to those derived from non-convex production possibility sets in Figure 7-1. It is assumed that the household has an initial endowment vector, $\bar{\mathbf{x}}$. Then again the demand correspondence at some price ratio will be two valued, but it will have a gap.

2. The Method of Analysis and a Measure of Non-Convexity

In this chapter, we will state a general theorem on the degree to which an economy not satisfying the convexity assumptions in production and consumption nevertheless can possess approximately a competitive equilibrium; that is, we will show the existence of a price vector, a consumption vector for each household that minimizes the cost of achieving a given utility level and satisfies the budget constraint at those prices, and a production vector for each firm that maximizes profits at those prices, such that the social excess demand for all commodities is bounded in a manner determined by the degree of non-convexity of the preference orderings and the production possibility sets. Further, we can so determine this upper bound on the discrepancy that it does not increase with the size of the economy; hence, the discrepancy divided by some measure of the size of the economy (e.g., the number of economic agents) approaches zero. This result is stated with greater precision in T.7.1.

The method of analysis is the following. From the given economy, we construct a new one satisfying all the conditions of the existence theory of Chapters 3–5. Recall the definition of a convex hull. (See D.B.3, D.B.12, and T.B.7.) A vector $\mathbf{x}'$ is said to be the convex combination of the vectors in a finite set T if there exists a non-negative real-valued function, $\alpha(\mathbf{x})$, defined for $\mathbf{x} \in T$, such that,

$$\sum_{\mathbf{x} \in T} \alpha(\mathbf{x}) = 1 \qquad \sum_{x \in T} \alpha(\mathbf{x})\mathbf{x} = \mathbf{x}'.$$

We will say also that the set T spans x'. The *convex hull* of a set S is the set of all vectors, $\mathbf{x}'$, that are convex combinations of finite subsets of S. An alternative and equivalent definition is that the convex hull of S is the intersection of all convex sets of which S is a subset. It is clear that the convex hull of a convex set is the set itself; in general, the convex hull of S is the smallest convex set that contains S.

Starting with a given economy, then, we replace the production possibility set of each firm by its convex hull. Similarly, we replace the preference ordering of each household by an ordering that satisfies the convexity property; this is done by replacing each upper contour set, that is, $\{\mathbf{x}_h \mid \mathbf{x}_h \succcurlyeq_h \mathbf{x}_h^0\}$ for each possible $\mathbf{x}_h^0$, by its convex hull. We assume that the *convexified* economy so defined satisfies all the assumptions of Chapters 3–5. Then it has a competitive equilibrium, that is, a price vector, $\mathbf{p}^*$, and a feasible allocation, $\mathscr{w}^* = (\mathscr{x}^*, \mathscr{y}^*)$, where $\mathbf{x}_h^*$ is cost minimizing at some given level of the convexified utility and satisfies the budget constraint and $\mathbf{y}_f^*$ is profit maximizing in the convexified production possibility set. Each $\mathbf{x}_h^*$ is a convex combination of vectors that belong to the compensated demand correspondence for the original economy for some utility level and the given price vector, $\mathbf{p}^*$. It can be shown that we can choose, for each h, one among these vectors, say $\mathbf{x}_h^\dagger$, in such a way that

$$\left|\sum_h \mathbf{x}_h^* - \sum_h \mathbf{x}_h^\dagger\right|$$

is bounded by a magnitude that depends on the maximum degree of non-convexity of the preference orderings. Similarly, we can choose $\mathbf{y}_f^\dagger$, which is profit maximizing in the original production possibility set at $\mathbf{p}^*$, such that the discrepancy

$$\left|\sum_f \mathbf{y}_f^* - \sum_f \mathbf{y}_f^\dagger\right|$$

is bounded by a magnitude that depends on the maximum degree of non-convexity of the production possibility sets. The price vector, $\mathbf{p}^*$, and the allocation $\mathscr{W}^\dagger = (\mathscr{X}^\dagger, \mathscr{Y}^\dagger)$ together constitute an approximate equilibrium in the sense that the discrepancy between supply and demand is also bounded (with a modification for free goods). No matter how large the economy, the bound is determined by the maximum degree of non-convexity.

For a pure-exchange economy in the special case where X_h, the consumption possibility set, is the entire non-negative orthant, a considerably stronger conclusion can be derived; there is a feasible allocation $\mathscr{W}^{**}$ whose distance from the allocation $\mathscr{W}^\dagger$ is bounded similarly to the above. This implies that for each individual the distance between his bundle under the feasible allocation, $\mathbf{x}_h^{**}$, and his chosen bundle, $\mathbf{x}_h$, approaches zero as the number of participants in the economy grows.

We have referred vaguely to the "degree of non-convexity"; it is necessary to introduce a specific measure. First, we define the *radius* of a set S, rad(S), as the radius of the smallest ball (i.e., set of the form $\{\mathbf{x} \mid |\mathbf{x} - \mathbf{x}^0| \leq R\}$) containing S. We now define the *inner radius* $r(S)$ of a set as follows: for every $\mathbf{x} \in$ con S, there is, by definition, a finite subset $T \subset S$ that spans $\mathbf{x}$. For every such $\mathbf{x}$, find the infimum of rad(T) as T varies over all such spanning sets; then define $r(S)$ as the supremum over all $\mathbf{x}$ in con S of this infimum. Note that if $\mathbf{x} \in S$, it is, in particular, spanned by the one-element set $\{\mathbf{x}\}$ and therefore inf rad T over all spanning sets $T \subset S$ is 0. For a convex set, con $S = S$; hence, $r(S) = 0$ if and only if S is convex. Thus, $r(S)$ is a measure of non-convexity and will be used as such in this and the following chapter.

3. Approximation to Market Equilibrium

In accordance with the discussion in the previous section, we now assume that if each production possibility set is replaced by its convex hull, then all the assumptions of Chapter 3 are satisfied.

ASSUMPTION 1. A.3.1–A.3.4 hold when Y_f is replaced by con Y_f in each of them.

It is slightly less obvious how we replace a non-convex preference ordering by a convex one. The original preference ordering defines (and is defined by) the class of upper contour sets, that is, the class of all sets of the form $\{\mathbf{x}_h \mid \mathbf{x}_h \succsim_h \mathbf{x}_h^0\}$ as $\mathbf{x}_h^0$ varies over all elements in X_h. (Of course, many elements $\mathbf{x}_h^0$ may define the same upper contour set.) Of any two upper contour sets, one must always include the other; in particular, they may include each other, in which case they are identical. Now, if S_1 and S_2 are sets in the same vector space and $S_1 \subset S_2$, con $S_1 \subset$ con S_2. Hence, among the class of sets that are convex hulls of the upper contour sets, it must also be true of any pair of such sets that one includes the other. It is possible, therefore, to define a new ordering, which we may refer to as the *convexification* of the original, by the condition that $\mathbf{x}^1$ is preferred or indifferent to $\mathbf{x}^2$ (in the new ordering) if every convex hull of an upper contour set that contains $\mathbf{x}^2$ also contains $\mathbf{x}^1$ (see Figure 7-3). In symbols,

DEFINITION 1. $\mathbf{x}_h^1 \succsim_{hk} \mathbf{x}_h^2$ is defined to mean that for every $\mathbf{x}_h^0$ for which $\mathbf{x}_h^2 \in \text{con}\{\mathbf{x}_h \mid \mathbf{x}_h \succsim_h \mathbf{x}_h^0\}$, it is also true that $\mathbf{x}_h^1 \in \text{con}\{\mathbf{x}_h \mid \succsim_h \mathbf{x}_h^0\}$.

From the preceding remarks, the relation $\succsim_{hk}$ is certainly connected, while transitivity follows directly from D.7.1. Hence, $\succsim_{hk}$ is certainly an ordering. We now assume

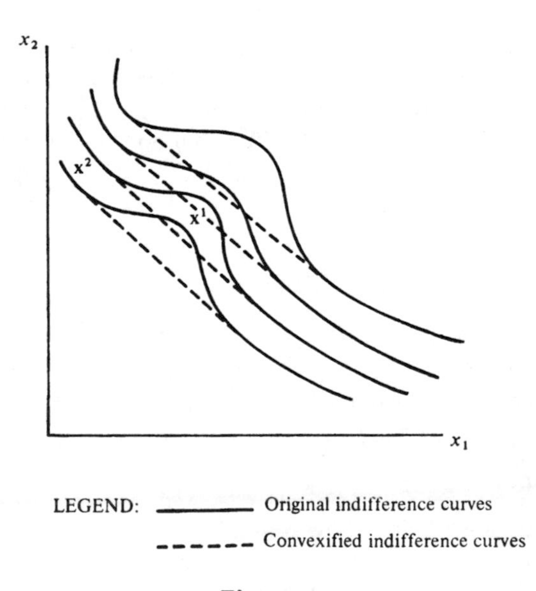

Figure 7-3

ASSUMPTION 2. A.4.1–A.4.4 hold when $\succsim_h$ is replaced by $\succsim_{hk}$.

No doubt, it is possible to specify assumptions on the original production possibility sets and preference orderings from which A.7.1–A.7.2 could be deduced, but we refrain here.

In view of the basic theorem, T.5.4, we can assert that, under these assumptions, there exists a compensated equilibrium for the convexified economy, in other words, that defined by replacing production possibility sets and upper contour sets by their convex hulls. That is, there exists a price vector $\mathbf{p}^*$ and an allocation $\mathscr{A}^* = (\mathscr{X}^*,\mathscr{Y}^*)$ such that $\mathbf{p}^* > \mathbf{0}$,

$$\mathbf{x}^* \leq \mathbf{y}^* + \bar{\mathbf{x}}, \tag{1}$$

$$\mathbf{y}_f^* \text{ maximizes } \mathbf{p}^*\mathbf{y}_f \text{ subject to } \mathbf{y}_f \in \text{con } Y_f, \tag{2}$$

$$\mathbf{x}_h^* \text{ minimizes } \mathbf{p}^*\mathbf{x}_h \text{ subject to } \mathbf{x}_h \succsim_{hk} \mathbf{x}_h^*, \tag{3}$$

$$\mathbf{p}^*\mathbf{x}_h^* = M_h^* = \mathbf{p}^*\bar{\mathbf{x}}_h + \sum_f d_{hf}(\mathbf{p}^*\mathbf{y}_f^*). \tag{4}$$

When convexity obtains, an equilibrium allocation achieves all of the following: feasibility, optimization for each individual at equilibrium prices (profit maximization for firms, cost minimization for given utility for households), and satisfaction of the household budget constraints. With non-convexity, of course, we cannot hope for so much. Instead, we will find a price vector and *two* allocations, one of which is feasible and the other optimal for each individual and satisfying household budget constraints at the given prices, such that in the aggregate the two allocations are close. Formally, we introduce the following definition.

DEFINITION 2. A *social-approximate* compensated equilibrium of modulus A is a price vector $\mathbf{p}^* > 0$ and two allocations, $\mathscr{A}^* = (\mathscr{X}^*,\mathscr{Y}^*)$ and $\mathscr{A}^\dagger = (\mathscr{X}^\dagger,\mathscr{Y}^\dagger)$, such that

(a) $\mathbf{x}^* \leq \mathbf{y}^* + \bar{\mathbf{x}}$,
(b) $p_i^* = 0$ if $x_i^* < y_i^* + \bar{x}_i$,
(c) $\mathbf{y}_f^\dagger$ maximizes $\mathbf{p}^*\mathbf{y}_f$ for $\mathbf{y}_f \in Y_f$,
(d) $\mathbf{x}_h^\dagger$ minimizes $\mathbf{p}^*\mathbf{x}_h$ subject to $\mathbf{x}_h \succsim_h \mathbf{x}_h^\dagger$,
(e) $\mathbf{p}^*\mathbf{x}_h^\dagger = M_h^\dagger = \mathbf{p}^*\bar{\mathbf{x}}_h + \sum_f d_{hf}(\mathbf{p}^*\mathbf{y}_f^\dagger) = M_h^* = \mathbf{p}^*\bar{\mathbf{x}}_h + \sum_f d_{hf}(\mathbf{p}^*\mathbf{y}_f^*)$,
(f) $|(\mathbf{x}^* - \mathbf{y}^*) - (\mathbf{x}^\dagger - \mathbf{y}^\dagger)| \leq A$.

Then the following theorem will be demonstrated.

THEOREM 1. Under A.7.1 and A.7.2, if L is such that $r(Y_f) \leq L$, all f, $r(\{\mathbf{x}_h \mid \mathbf{x}_h \succsim_h \mathbf{x}_h^\dagger\}) \leq L$, all h, then there exists a social-approximate compensated equilibrium of modulus $L\sqrt{n}$, where n is the number of commodities.

Proof. We take $\mathbf{p}^*$ and ω^* to be the equilibrium for the convexified economy, so that (1)–(4) are satisfied and, therefore, D.7.2 (a)–(b). Since $\mathbf{y}_f^* \in \text{con } Y_f$, $\mathbf{y}_f^*$ is the convex combination of at least one finite subset of Y_f. Among all such subsets, choose the one with the smallest radius; by the definition of inner radius and the assumption that $r(Y_f) \leq L$, we can find a set, $T_f \subset Y_f$, that spans $\mathbf{y}_f^*$ and for which $\text{rad}(T_f) \leq L$. By definition, there exists a non-negative-valued function, $\alpha(\mathbf{y}_f)$, defined for $\mathbf{y}_f \in T_f$, such that

$$\sum_{\mathbf{y}_f \in T_f} \alpha(\mathbf{y}_f)\mathbf{y}_f = \mathbf{y}_f^* \qquad \sum_{\mathbf{y}_f \in T_f} \alpha(\mathbf{y}_f) = 1.$$

Clearly, we can assume $\alpha(\mathbf{y}_f) > 0$ without loss of generality, for otherwise the corresponding $\mathbf{y}_f$ can be deleted from T_f without altering either of these relations. Then

$$\mathbf{p}^*\mathbf{y}_f^* = \sum_{Y_f \in T_f} \alpha(\mathbf{y}_f)\mathbf{p}^*\mathbf{y}_f;$$

but $\mathbf{y}_f \in Y_f \subset \text{con } Y_f$ for all $\mathbf{y}_f \in T_f$. By (2) (profit maximization), $\mathbf{p}^*\mathbf{y}_f^* \geq \mathbf{p}^*\mathbf{y}_f$ for all $\mathbf{y}_f \in T_f$. With $\alpha(\mathbf{y}_f) > 0$, all $\mathbf{y}_f \in T_f$, it is necessary that $\mathbf{p}^*\mathbf{y}_f = \mathbf{p}^*\mathbf{y}_f^*$ for all $\mathbf{y}_f \in T_f$, and therefore, certainly

$$\text{All } \mathbf{y}_f\text{'s in } T_f \text{ maximize } \mathbf{p}^*\mathbf{y}_f \text{ for } \mathbf{y}_f \in Y_f. \tag{5}$$

The set $\{\mathbf{x}_h \mid \mathbf{x}_h \succsim_{hk} \mathbf{x}_h^*\}$ is the convex hull of a set of the form $\{\mathbf{x}_h \mid \mathbf{x}_h \succsim_h \mathbf{x}_h^0\}$, for some x_h^0. By the same argument, then, we can find a finite subset S_h of this set, with $\text{rad}(S_h) \leq L$, such that S_h spans $\mathbf{x}_h^*$ and

$$\text{All } \mathbf{x}_h\text{'s in } S_h \text{ minimize } \mathbf{p}^*\mathbf{x}_h \text{ for } \mathbf{x}_h \succsim_h \mathbf{x}_h^0; \tag{6}$$

$$\mathbf{p}^*\mathbf{x}_h = \mathbf{p}^*\mathbf{x}_h^* \text{ for all } \mathbf{x}_h \text{ in } S_h. \tag{7}$$

From (6) it is clear also that we can choose $\mathbf{x}_h^0$ to be any element of S_h and that all elements of S_h are indifferent.

By the construction,

$$\begin{aligned}\mathbf{x}^* - \mathbf{y}^* &= \sum_h \mathbf{x}_h^* - \sum_f \mathbf{y}_f^* \in \sum_h \text{con } S_h + \sum_f \text{con}(-T_f)\\ &= \text{con}\Big[\sum_h S_h + \sum_f (-T_f)\Big].\end{aligned}$$

(For the last relation, see Lemma B.2.) Since rad S_h and rad$(-T_f)$ are all uniformly bounded by L, we can apply the Shapley–Folkman theorem (T.B.9) and assert the existence of

$$\mathbf{z}^\dagger \in \sum_h S_h + \sum_f (-T_f)$$

for which $|\mathbf{x}^* - \mathbf{y}^* - \mathbf{z}^\dagger| \leq L\sqrt{n}$; that is, we can find $\mathbf{x}_h \in S_h$ and $\mathbf{y}_f \in T_f$ such that

$$\mathbf{z}^\dagger = \sum_h \mathbf{x}_h - \sum_f \mathbf{y}_f.$$

Then, with the aid of (5)–(7), it is clear that D.7.2(c)–(f) hold, and T.7.1 is proved.

Remark. If the economy increases in size, say by increases in the numbers of firms and households of roughly similar types, then we may expect the upper bound, L, on the non-convexities to remain roughly constant; the theorem then assures us that the discrepancy between supply and demand (for non-free goods) will have the same upper bound in the aggregate and, therefore, will approach zero as a proportion to total supply or demand.

4. Approximation of Equilibrium for Individual Behavior

If we restrict ourselves to a pure exchange economy and assume that for each household the consumption possibility set, X_h, is the non-negative orthant, the approximate equilibrium has a much stronger property, namely, we can find an allocation with the same totals as $\mathscr{x}^*$ (therefore also feasible) that is close to the individual optimal allocation $\mathscr{x}^\dagger$. The closeness of two allocations is, of course, a much stronger property than the closeness of the market totals.

DEFINITION 3. *An individual-approximate* compensated equilibrium of modulus A is a price vector, $\mathbf{p}^* > 0$, and two allocations, $\omega^{**} = (\mathscr{x}^{**},\mathscr{y}^{**})$ and $\omega^\dagger = (\mathscr{x}^\dagger,\mathscr{y}^\dagger)$, such that

(a) $\mathbf{x}^{**} \leq \mathbf{y}^{**} + \bar{\mathbf{x}}$,
(b) $p_i^* = 0$ if $x_i^{**} < y_i^{**} + \bar{x}_i$,
(c) $\mathbf{y}_f^\dagger$ maximizes $\mathbf{p}^*\mathbf{y}_f$ for $\mathbf{y}_f \in Y_f$,
(d) $\mathbf{x}_h^\dagger$ minimizes $\mathbf{p}^*\mathbf{x}_h$ for $\mathbf{x}_h \succcurlyeq_h \mathbf{x}_h^\dagger$,
(e) $\mathbf{p}^*x_h^\dagger = M_h^\dagger = M_h^*$,
(f) $|\omega^{**} - \omega^\dagger| \leq A$.

Note that

$$|\omega^{**} - \omega| = \sqrt{\sum_h |\mathbf{x}_h^{**} - \mathbf{x}_h^\dagger|^2 + \sum_f |\mathbf{y}_f^{**} - \mathbf{y}_f^\dagger|^2}.$$

Hence, if m is the number of agents in the economy and A is a constant with respect to m, we can see by dividing both sides of (f) by m that the root-mean-square deviation between the bundles chosen by agents under the two allocations approaches zero.

THEOREM 2. In a pure-exchange economy where A.7.2 holds, X_h is the non-negative orthant for each h, and $r(\{\mathbf{x}_h \mid \mathbf{x}_h \succcurlyeq_h \mathbf{x}_h^\dagger\}) \leq L$ for all h, there exists an individual-approximate compensated equilibrium of modulus $L\sqrt{n}$.

Proof. We take $\mathbf{p}^*$ and $\omega^\dagger$ as in T.7.1. Take also ω^* as given in T.7.1, and we will find ω^{**} such that

$$\mathbf{x}^{**} = \mathbf{x}^*, \tag{8}$$

$$\mathbf{p}^*\mathbf{x}_h^{**} = \mathbf{p}^*\mathbf{x}_h^\dagger \quad \mathbf{x}_h^{**} \geq \mathbf{0} \qquad \text{all } h, \tag{9}$$

$$x_{hi}^\dagger - x_{hi}^{**} \text{ is not opposed in sign to } x_i^\dagger - x_i^* \text{ for all } h \text{ and } i. \tag{10}$$

If such ω^{**} can be found, it is clear from T.7.1 and (8) and (9) that D.7.3(a)–(e) are satisfied with $\mathbf{x}_h^{**} \in X_h$; it will be shown below that that T.7.1 and (10) imply D.7.3(f) with $A = L\sqrt{n}$.

We first show that (8)–(10) can be satisfied. Let

$$P = \{i \mid x_i^\dagger - x_i^* > 0\} \qquad N = \{i \mid x_i^\dagger - x_i^* \leq 0\}. \tag{11}$$

Conditions (8)–(10) then can be written

$$\sum_h x_{hi}^{**} = \sum_h x_{hi}^* \qquad (i \in P), \tag{12}$$

$$\sum_h x_{hi}^{**} = \sum_h x_{hi}^* \qquad (i \in N), \tag{13}$$

$$\sum_{i \in N} p_i^*(x_{hi}^{**} - x_{hi}^\dagger) = \sum_{i \in P} p_i^*(x_{hi}^\dagger - x_{hi}^{**}) = a_h, \qquad \text{say} \tag{14}$$

$$x_{hi}^{**} \geq 0 \qquad (i \in P), \tag{15}$$

$$x_{hi}^{**} \geq 0 \qquad (i \in N), \tag{16}$$

$$x_{hi}^\dagger - x_{hi}^{**} \geq 0 \qquad (i \in P), \tag{17}$$

$$x_{hi}^\dagger - x_{hi}^{**} \leq 0 \qquad (i \in N). \tag{18}$$

Since $\mathbf{x}_h^\dagger \in X_h$, $x_{hi}^\dagger \geq 0$; hence, $x_{hi}^{**} \geq 0$ for $i \in N$ if (18) holds. Therefore, condition (16) is redundant.

For $i \in P$, $x_i^\dagger > 0$ and $x_i^*/x_i^\dagger < 1$. Therefore, if we define

$$x_{hi}^{**} = \frac{x_i^*}{x_i^\dagger} x_{hi}^\dagger \qquad \text{for } i \in P,$$

(12), (15), and (17) will be satisfied. It remains to show that (13), (14), and (18) can be satisfied by choice of x_{hi}^{**} $(i \in N)$. From (17), $a_h \geq 0$. Let

$$a = \sum_h a_h \quad w_h = \frac{a_h}{a} \qquad \text{if } a > 0.$$

Let w_h be arbitrary non-negative with

$$\sum_h w_h = 1 \qquad \text{if } a = 0.$$

Define

$$x_{hi}^{**} = x_{hi}^\dagger + w_h(x_i^* - x_i^\dagger) \qquad \text{for } i \in N.$$

From the definition of N in (11), (18) certainly holds. Since

$$\sum_h w_h = 1,$$

(13) holds. Multiply by p_i^* and sum over $i \in N$:

$$\sum_{i \in N} p_i^*(x_{hi}^{**} - x_{hi}^\dagger) = w_h \sum_{i \in N} p_i^*(x_i^* - x_i^\dagger).$$

From T.7.1 and D.7.2(e), $\mathbf{p}^*\mathbf{x}_h^* = \mathbf{p}^*\mathbf{x}_h^\dagger$, and therefore,

$$\sum_{i \in N} p_i^*(x_i^* - x_i^\dagger) = \sum_h \sum_{i \in N} p_i^*(x_{hi}^* - x_{hi}^\dagger) = \sum_h \sum_{i \in P} p_i^*(x_{hi}^\dagger - x_{hi}^*)$$
$$= \sum_h a_h = a,$$

in view of (12), so that

$$\sum_{i \in N} p_i^*(x_{hi}^{**} - x_{hi}^\dagger) = w_h a = a_h;$$

that is, (14) holds. Hence, (8)–(10) have been shown to hold for a suitable allocation $\mathscr{x}^{**}$.

By T.7.1, $|\mathbf{x}^* - \mathbf{x}^\dagger| \leq L\sqrt{n}$, and then, by (8), $|\mathbf{x}^{**} - \mathbf{x}^\dagger| \leq L\sqrt{n}$.

But

$$|\mathbf{x}^{**} - \mathbf{x}^{\dagger}|^2 = \sum_i (x_i^{**} - x_i^{\dagger})^2,$$

and

$$(x_i^{**} - x_i^{\dagger})^2 = \left[\sum_h (x_{hi}^{**} - x_{hi}^{\dagger})\right]^2.$$

From (10), the sum in brackets consists of terms all of the same sign; hence,

$$(x_i^{**} - x_i^{\dagger})^2 \geq \sum_h (x_{hi}^{**} - x_{hi}^{\dagger})^2.$$

If we now sum over i, we see immediately that

$$|\mathscr{X}^{**} - \mathscr{X}^{\dagger}| \leq |\mathbf{x}^{**} - \mathbf{x}^{\dagger}| \leq L\sqrt{n},$$

as was to be shown.

Notes

Traditional economics texts frequently assumed the U-shaped cost curve in the context of a discussion of perfect competition; by implication, then, they were asserting something like the results of the present chapter. As the modern study of the theory of competitive equilibrium emphasized more strongly the importance of the convexity assumption, efforts began to relax it. Farrell [1959] noted first that non-convexities of individual economic units correspond to relatively small discontinuities in aggregate behavior. His paper gave rise to a considerable discussion, by Bator [1961] and especially by Rothenberg [1960], who showed graphically in great thoroughness how with large numbers of households the effect on aggregate demand is the same as if the concavities in the indifference curves were replaced by straight lines. A rigorous general treatment is due to Starr [1969], on whose work the present chapter is entirely based; he made use of some mathematical results developed by L. S. Shapley and J. H. Folkman, which have not yet been published by them, but which he reported in his paper.

An alternative, very bold approach has been taken by Aumann [1966]. To begin with, he assumes a continuum of households, each of infinitesimal endowment. Then, by use of some deep results in measure theory, he demonstrates the existence of competitive equilibrium without making any assumptions about convexity. This approach works because the discontinuity in the behavior of any individual has infinitesimal weight in the aggregate, but so far it has been confined to a pure-exchange economy.

Chapter Eight

THE CORE OF A MARKET ECONOMY

My bonds in thee are all determinate.
For how do I hold thee but by thy granting?
—William Shakespeare, *Sonnet 87*

1. Equilibrium in Bargaining

In the preceding chapters, and indeed in most of the remainder of the book, emphasis has been placed on the allocation of resources through a price system. All individuals (except monopolists and monopsonists) behave as though they can buy or sell unlimited quantities at prices taken as given by them. They do not take into account any resource limitation or tastes of the particular individual with whom they may be dealing.

An entirely different approach is to assume that allocations are arrived at through quantity bargaining. The bargains considered may be multilateral as well as bilateral. Thus any set of economic agents are permitted to allocate resources between themselves provided only that their initial endowments and productive capabilities are sufficient so that the allocation is feasible without using the resources of other individuals.

For simplicity, we first consider a pure exchange economy; production will be introduced in Section 8.5. We have to define some notions of equilibrium for bargains. These will take the form of specified conditions under which we would expect a bargain *not* to be maintained. One is the notion of dominance already introduced in defining Pareto efficiency (see D.4.12). Given a feasible allocation, $\mathscr{x}$, if there is another feasible allocation, $\mathscr{x}'$, such that every household is better off under $\mathscr{x}'$ than under $\mathscr{x}$, that is, $\mathbf{x}_h' \succ_h \mathbf{x}_h$, all h, then we expect that $\mathscr{x}$ cannot be the equilibrium of the bargaining process. Thus, we assume that equilibria in bargaining must be Pareto efficient. Again, an allocation is hardly an acceptable bargain if any individual is better off with his initial endowment than with the proposed allocation; thus, $\mathscr{x}$ is not a bargaining equilibrium if $\bar{\mathbf{x}}_h \succ_h \mathbf{x}_h$ for some h.

These two principles can be subsumed into a more general one: If any set of households can find an allocation x' that is feasible given only their endowments and such that each member of the set is better off under x' than under some given allocation x, it cannot be that x is a bargaining equilibrium. The two preceding principles are special cases in which the set of households in question consists of all households or one household, respectively. We now formalize these considerations by introducing the following definitions.

DEFINITION 1. A *coalition* is a set of households.

DEFINITION 2. An allocation, x, is *feasible for coalition S* if

$$\sum_{h \in S} \mathbf{x}_h \leq \sum_{h \in S} \bar{\mathbf{x}}_h.$$

Remark. Let V be the coalition composed of all households. Then an allocation that is feasible for V, according to D.8.2, is feasible in the usual sense (see D.4.5 for the special case in which there is no production).

DEFINITION 3. An allocation, x, is *blocked by coalition S* if there exists another allocation, x', that is feasible for coalition S such that $\mathbf{x}'_h \succ_h \mathbf{x}_h$ for all $h \in S$.

DEFINITION 4. The *core* of a (pure-exchange) economy is the set of all allocations that are feasible and not blocked by any coalition.

In particular, any allocation in the core is not blocked by the coalition of all households, and therefore, is Pareto efficient, nor is it blocked by a coalition consisting of any one household. These are properties possessed by the allocation corresponding to any competitive equilibrium, for any such is Pareto efficient and of course any household must be at least as well off at the competitive equilibrium as it would be without trade. This suggests what is, in fact, the case—that there is a close connection between allocations achievable as competitive equilibria and those achievable as a member of the core; but this connection holds only for economies in which competitive equilibria exist and cores are non-empty or at least where these conditions are approximately true. Further, and this is of great importance, the relation between competitive equilibria and unblocked allocations is especially close when any given economic agent is, in an appropriate sense, small relative to the entire market.

To clarify some of these remarks, consider first the thrice-familiar Edgeworth box case—pure exchange, two households, convex indifference maps (the usual restriction to two commodities is no simplification from the analytic viewpoint; it serves only to permit graphic representation). The core consists of all allocations that are Pareto efficient and that do not make either household worse off than if it were to consume only its endowment. If the endowments are sufficiently different in commodity proportions from each other, then, with suitable indifference maps, the potential gains from trade are large. The core contains the allocation that maximizes the utility of household 1 subject to the constraint that household 2's utility is at least what it receives from its endowment and, similarly, the corresponding allocation with the two households' roles reversed. For any utility level for household 1 between its endowment level and the above maximum, there will be an unblocked allocation that yields household 1 that utility level.

In particular, the competitive equilibrium (or equilibria, if not unique) is Pareto efficient and certainly neither household can be forced below its endowment utility level. Hence, the competitive equilibria are in the core. However, with two households, the core might be much larger than the set of competitive equilibria. Suppose now that a third household enters the economy. New possibilities of bargaining and, therefore, of blocking arise from the two-member coalitions. Thus, a proposed allocation is blocked not merely if any one household is driven below its endowment level, but also if any two members can jointly improve their lots by trades that do not involve the third. This suggests that in some sense the range of unblocked allocations becomes smaller when there are more households.

It turns out that there is a natural way of formalizing the idea that with large economies the core tends to be close to the competitive equilibria. Roughly speaking (see Section 8.3 for details), we consider a sequence of larger and larger economies and, for each one, an unblocked allocation. Then for each economy we can find a price system such that every coalition in every economy behaves approximately like a group of price-taking utility maximizers; that is, the difference between the quantities the coalition receives in the given unblocked allocation and the total demands of the same set of households at those prices if they maximize utility under competitive conditions is bounded uniformly in the size of the economy and of the coalition. Thus, for large coalitions, the approximation of the unblocked allocation to a competitive equilibrium is good relative to the magnitudes involved.

The implications of these conclusions are striking in many ways. They suggest that under appropriate hypotheses, especially convexity and the presence of all markets (absence of externalities), competitive equilibrium is very sturdy. There is no strong incentive for subgroups to try to coalesce and to achieve more than they could in the competitive equilibrium; for any such attempt would be unstable. This is contrary to the view sometimes expressed that competitive equilibrium has an inherent instability in that it would pay, for example, the owners of some one commodity to form a cartel and exploit their monopoly power. The theorems on the relation between competitive equilibria and the core suggest that any such attempt would be broken up by the formation of coalitions involving some buyers and some sellers of that commodity. The sellers ultimately can depend for sure only on what they can achieve by trade among themselves, and of course, this may be very little indeed.

In real life, no doubt, there are many qualifications to these conclusions. Perhaps the most important is the neglect of costs of forming coalitions. Actually, it is probably the fact that the costs of forming coalitions of different kinds of individuals are different rather than the mere existence of bargaining costs that is of critical importance. The competitive price system may be expected to prevail when all costs of bargaining are high relative to the costs of price-directed markets. If all costs of bargaining are low, then again the theory of the core may be the chief predictive device; the theorems of this chapter suggest that under appropriate conditions, the outcome will be very similar to that under perfect competition. On the other hand, if the costs of bargaining are not uniform for different coalitions, then indeed quite different results may prevail. Adam Smith suggested in a famous passage that producers of the same commodity find it easy to communicate with each other; in that case, the possibility of forming stable cartels to exploit consumers may be enhanced. No real theory of this type has yet been developed, however.

There is another qualification arising out of the possible rationality of seemingly irrational actions, a point that has emerged most especially in the discussions of strategy in the context of nuclear arms (see especially Schelling [1960]). If a coalition with monopoly power somehow makes it credible to all others that its demands will not be compromised no matter how much it suffers and that none of its members can be drawn off into side bargains, then it may indeed get its way. This is the value of burning one's bridges behind one. The difficulty with this type of argument is its asymmetry. If one coalition can threaten in this way, so can the coalition composed of all others; the result is mutual destruction, by no means an uncommon occurrence in international politics, but much rarer among those playing for economic advantage only. The asymmetry in expected behavior needed for the efficacy of threat strategies is plausible only when based either on differential bargaining costs (so that the counter-coalition cannot really form) or on extra-economic motives of loyalty to and identification with some group, such as nation, class, or race.

Then, if the economy is large, bargaining costs are low or at least uniform, and expectations of behavior are symmetric, the theorems on the core imply that departures from perfectly competitive behavior occur only when there are non-convexities or market failures of one kind or another.

2. Competitive Equilibria Are Unblocked

We already know that any competitive equilibrium is Pareto efficient (see T.5.3). By definition, any unblocked allocation is Pareto efficient. We now show, by using the same reasoning as before,

THEOREM 1. In a pure-exchange economy, if $(\mathbf{p}^*, \mathscr{x}^*)$ is a competitive equilibrium, then $\mathscr{x}^*$ belongs to the core.

Proof. Suppose $\mathscr{x}^*$ is blocked by coalition S (see D.8.1–D.8.4). Then there exists a coalition S and an allocation $\mathscr{x}'$ such that

$$\sum_{h \in S} \mathbf{x}'_h \leq \sum_{h \in S} \bar{\mathbf{x}}_h \tag{1}$$

and

$$\mathbf{x}'_h \succ_h \mathbf{x}^*_h \qquad \text{all } h \in S. \tag{2}$$

From the definition of competitive equilibrium (see D.5.1), $\mathbf{x}^*_h \succsim_h \mathbf{x}_h$ if $\mathbf{p}^*\mathbf{x}_h \leq \mathbf{p}^*\bar{\mathbf{x}}_h$ for all h; hence, from (2), $\mathbf{p}^*\mathbf{x}'_h > \mathbf{p}^*\bar{\mathbf{x}}_h$, all h in S, and therefore,

$$\sum_{h \in S} \mathbf{p}^*\mathbf{x}'_h > \sum_{h \in S} \mathbf{p}^*\bar{\mathbf{x}}_h.$$

Since $\mathbf{p}^* > 0$, however, it follows by multiplying both sides of (1) by $\mathbf{p}^*$ that

$$\sum_{h \in S} \mathbf{p}^*\mathbf{x}'_h \leq \sum_{h \in S} \mathbf{p}^*\bar{\mathbf{x}}_h,$$

a contradiction.

3. The Core Approximates the Competitive Equilibria

The near-converse to T.8.1 is much deeper and relies for proof on theorems due to Shapley and Folkman and to Starr on the extent to which the vector sum of a large number of sets is approximately a convex set (see Section B.4). We restate some concepts here.

First, the radius of any bounded set S, rad(S), is defined to be the radius of the smallest ball that contains S. Then, we define the *inner radius* of a set S as follows: Any point $\mathbf{x}$ in con S (the convex hull of S) is the convex combination of the members of at least one finite, and hence bounded, subset T of S. For any such $\mathbf{x}$, consider the infimum of rad(T) for subsets T of S that span $\mathbf{x}$, and then define the inner radius, $r(S)$, as the supremum over $\mathbf{x}$ in con S of these infima:

$$r(S) = \sup_{\mathbf{x} \in \text{con}\, S} \; \inf_{T \in S,\, T \text{ spans } \mathbf{x}} \text{rad}(T).$$

Note that if $\mathbf{x} \in S$, it is spanned by the one-element set consisting of itself, so that

$$\inf_{T \subset S,\, T \text{ spans } \mathbf{x}} \text{rad}(T) = 0.$$

Hence, if S is convex, so that $\mathbf{x} \in \text{con}\, S$ only if $\mathbf{x} \in S$, $r(S) = 0$, and conversely, $r(S) = 0$ only if S is convex. Therefore, $r(S)$ is a measure of the extent to which a set is non-convex.

We know that a vector sum of convex sets is convex. It is shown in T.B.10 that the vector sum of any number of sets that are of uniformly bounded non-convexity (as measured by the inner radius) uniformly approximates its convex hull. We restate the result here.

LEMMA 1. Let F be a family of sets in a given vector space of dimension n such that $r(S) \leq L$ for some L. For any finite subfamily $F' \subset F$, if

$$S' = \sum_{S \in F'} S,$$

then for every $\mathbf{x} \in \text{con } S'$, there exists $\mathbf{x}' \in S'$ such that $|\mathbf{x} - \mathbf{x}'| \leq L\sqrt{n}$.

Thus, no matter how many of the sets S are being added, the difference between the convex hull of the vector sum and the vector sum itself is uniformly bounded. In particular, the discrepancy between the vector *average* and its convex hull approaches zero where the vector average of a family of sets is obtained by dividing each element of the vector sum by the number of sets in the family.

We now state a very general relation between cores and competitive equilibria. In what follows, we shall understand by an *economy* any set of households, where a household is defined by a preference ordering and an endowment.

THEOREM 2. Consider a class of pairs $(E,\tilde{x})$, where E is an economy and $\tilde{x}$ is a member of the core of E (assumed non-empty). For each household h in any economy E, define

$$\tilde{X}_h = \{\mathbf{x}_h \mid \mathbf{x}_h \succcurlyeq_h \tilde{\mathbf{x}}_h\} \qquad X'_h = X_h \cup \{\bar{\mathbf{x}}_h\},$$

$$X''_h = \{\mathbf{x}''_h \mid \mathbf{x}''_h \geq \mathbf{x}'_h \quad \text{for some } \mathbf{x}'_h \text{ in } X'_h\}.$$

Assume that, for some L, $r(X''_h) \leq L$ for all h in all economies E in the class. Then there exists a constant M ($= 2L\sqrt{n}$, where n is the number of commodities) and, for each E, a vector $\mathbf{p}^* > \mathbf{0}$, $\mathbf{p}^*\mathbf{e} = 1$, such that for any economy E the following statements hold:

(a) $\sum_{h \in E} |\mathbf{p}^*(\tilde{\mathbf{x}}_h - \bar{\mathbf{x}}_h)| \leq M;$

(b) $\mathbf{p}^* \sum_{h \in E} \tilde{\mathbf{x}}_h - \sum_{h \in E} \min_{\mathbf{x}_h \succcurlyeq_h \tilde{\mathbf{x}}_h} \mathbf{p}^*\mathbf{x}_h \leq M.$

Before proceeding to the proof, let us first comment on the meaning of the hypotheses and the conclusions. The class of economies is quite arbitrary, but it may be thought of most usefully as a sequence of economies growing larger and larger in the sense of consisting of more and more households. The household characteristics of the different economies are statistically similar in the sense that the distribution of preference orderings and endowment vectors among them are not too remote from each other. Each economy in the class is assumed to have a non-empty core. This will certainly be true if each possesses a competitive equilibrium, by T.8.1. We do not exclude the possibility that households have non-convex indifference maps. However, it should be noted that as far as present theorems go, the existence of an element in the core is guaranteed only if preference orderings are convex; hence, it must be specially assumed that the core has at least one member.

The set $\tilde{X}_h$ is, for any given household, the upper contour set defined by the given allocation in the core. If there are any gains from trade at all, this set will not contain the original endowment point, $\bar{\mathbf{x}}_h$, so that X''_h will consist of an upper contour set (modified to allow for free disposal) plus all points to the northeast of $\bar{\mathbf{x}}_h$ (see Figure 8-1). In general, this set will not be convex even if the upper contour set is, so that $r(X''_h) > 0$. In Figure 8-1, the point in con X''_h whose spanning set has maximum radius is a point like $\mathbf{x}^1$, the spanning set for which consists of the points $\bar{\mathbf{x}}_h$ and $\mathbf{x}^2$, where $\mathbf{x}^2$ is on the indifference curve through $\tilde{\mathbf{x}}_h$. From Figure 8-1a it is clear that a necessary condition that $r(X''_h)$ be bounded uniformly for all households in all the economies considered is that we are considering economies and allocations that are sufficiently balanced that the gains from trade for any one household are bounded (so that the indifference curve through $\tilde{\mathbf{x}}_h$ is not too far away from $\bar{\mathbf{x}}_h$). Figure 8-1b illustrates a different possible case where $r(X''_h)$ is large, namely, where there is a sequence of households associated with successively

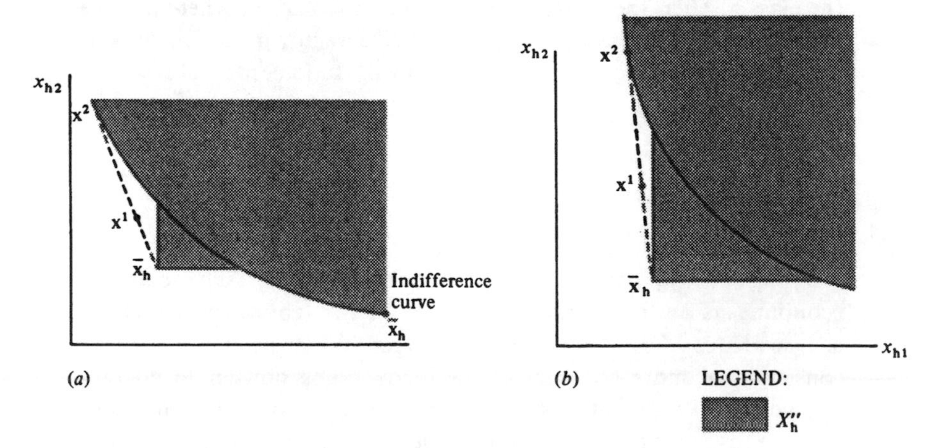

Figure 8-1

larger economies that are more and more nearly satiated with commodity 2 (relative to commodity 1) at levels only moderately greater than the initial endowment. Finally, though not illustrated, $r(X''_h)$ may become indefinitely large if the non-convexities in the indifference curve through $\bar{\mathbf{x}}_h$ become indefinitely large.

It thus appears that the assumption that $r(X''_h)$ is uniformly bounded means that gains from trade do not become unbalanced, that the households in the different economies have statistically similar preference orderings, and that the non-convexities in them are bounded.

The conclusions state that, for each pair consisting of an economy and an unblocked allocation for it, we can choose a price vector so that allocation approximately satisfies the conditions for a compensated equilibrium. Conclusion (a) asserts that the sum of the absolute deviations from the budget constraint for the entire economy is uniformly bounded over all economies. This conclusion has little force for small economies. But if both sides of (a) are divided by the number of members of the economy E, it is asserted that the *average* discrepancy from a budget constraint is bounded by a number that is inversely proportional to the size of the economy and therefore approaches zero for large economies. Conclusion (b) deals with the relation between the given unblocked allocation and the compensated demand. It asserts that the cost savings totalled over an entire economy in which each household achieves the utility associated with the given allocation in the cheapest possible way is also bounded uniformly; again, this implies that the unnecessary cost associated with the given allocation averaged over any large economy is very small.

Proof. For any economy E, let

$$X'' = \sum_{h \in E} X''_h.$$

Since X'' has been defined in terms of an allocation in the core of E, it follows that it must be disjoint from the set of strictly feasible social-demand vectors, that is, those for which

$$\mathbf{x} \ll \bar{\mathbf{x}} = \sum_{h \in E} \bar{\mathbf{x}}_h.$$

For suppose $\mathbf{x}'' \in X''$, $\mathbf{x}'' \ll \bar{\mathbf{x}}$. From the definitions of X_h'' and X'' there is a set S of the members of E such that

$$\mathbf{x}'' = \sum_{h \in S} \mathbf{x}_h'' + \sum_{h \in E \sim S} \bar{\mathbf{x}}_h', \qquad \text{where } \mathbf{x}_h'' \geq \mathbf{x}_h \text{ for some}$$

$$\mathbf{x}_h \in \tilde{X}_h, \bar{\mathbf{x}}_h' \geq \bar{\mathbf{x}}_h. \quad (3)$$

If S were the null set, $\mathbf{x}'' \geq \bar{\mathbf{x}}$, which is impossible if $\mathbf{x}'' \ll \bar{\mathbf{x}}$. This last condition can be written, from (3),

$$\sum_{h \in S} \mathbf{x}_h'' + \sum_{h \in E \sim S} \bar{\mathbf{x}}_h' \ll \sum_{h \in S} \bar{\mathbf{x}}_h + \sum_{h \in E \sim S} \bar{\mathbf{x}}_h,$$

and therefore,

$$\sum_{h \in S} \mathbf{x}_h + \sum_{h \in E \sim S} \bar{\mathbf{x}}_h \ll \sum_{h \in S} \bar{\mathbf{x}}_h + \sum_{h \in E \sim S} \bar{\mathbf{x}}_h,$$

or,

$$\sum_{h \in S} \mathbf{x}_h \ll \sum_{h \in S} \bar{\mathbf{x}}_h \qquad \mathbf{x}_h \in \tilde{X}_h \text{ for } h \in S.$$

Then, by Lemma 4.1(a), we can choose $\mathbf{x}_h' \succ_h \mathbf{x}_h$, $\mathbf{x}_h'$ arbitrarily close to $\mathbf{x}_h$ for each $h \in S$, so that

$$\sum_{h \in S} \mathbf{x}_h' \leq \sum_{h \in S} \bar{\mathbf{x}}_h,$$

and $\mathbf{x}_h' \succ_h \mathbf{x}_h \succcurlyeq_h \bar{\mathbf{x}}_h$, all $h \in S$. From D.8.2–D.8.3, the allocation $\tilde{x}$ is blocked by the allocation $\tilde{x}'$, contrary to assumption. Hence, we can assert

$$X'' \text{ is disjoint from } \{\mathbf{x} \mid \mathbf{x} \ll \bar{\mathbf{x}}\}. \quad (4)$$

Let $\mathbf{e}'$ be the column vector all of whose components are 1. We will consider all vectors of the form $\bar{\mathbf{x}} - \mu\mathbf{e}'$, $\mu \geq 0$, that belong to con X''. These points lie on a ray that starts from the social endowment point and proceeds in a strictly negative direction into the strictly feasible region as long as the points on the ray are convex combinations of the points in X'' (see Figure 8-2). Since

$$\bar{\mathbf{x}} = \sum_{h \in E} \bar{\mathbf{x}}_h$$

and $\bar{\mathbf{x}}_h \in X_h''$ by definition, $\bar{\mathbf{x}} \in X''$ and, therefore, certainly $\bar{\mathbf{x}} \in$ con X''. Hence, the endowment point, corresponding to $\mu = 0$, certainly belongs to the desired set. The set may or may not contain other points, for which $\mu > 0$. We wish to show that the set of such points is bounded uniformly for all economies considered.

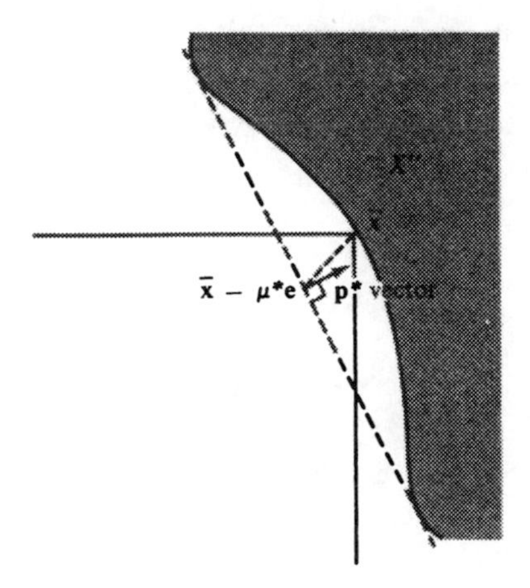

Figure 8-2

By Lemma 8.1, if $\bar{\mathbf{x}} - \mu\mathbf{e}' \in \text{con } X''$, we can find $\mathbf{x}'' \in X''$ such that

$$|\bar{\mathbf{x}} - \mu\mathbf{e}' - \mathbf{x}''| \leq M' = L\sqrt{n}.$$

But from (4), $\mathbf{x}'' - \bar{\mathbf{x}}$ must have at least one non-negative component.

$$|\bar{\mathbf{x}} - \mu\mathbf{e}' - \mathbf{x}''| = |\mu\mathbf{e}' + (\mathbf{x}'' - \bar{\mathbf{x}})| \geq \mu + \max_i(x_i'' - \bar{x}_i) \geq \mu,$$

so that

$$\bar{\mathbf{x}} - \mu\mathbf{e}' \in \text{con } X'' \quad \text{implies} \quad \mu \leq M'. \tag{5}$$

Since the set $\{\mu \mid \bar{\mathbf{x}} - \mu\mathbf{e}' \in \text{con } X''\}$ is bounded, it has a supremum, μ^*. Then the point $\bar{\mathbf{x}} - \mu^*\mathbf{e}'$ is necessarily a boundary point of con X''. Hence by a well-known theorem in convex set theory (see Corollary B.5), there is a supporting hyperplane to con X'' at that point, that is, a vector $\mathbf{p}^* \neq \mathbf{0}$ for which

$$\mathbf{p}^*\mathbf{x}'' \geq \mathbf{p}^*(\bar{\mathbf{x}} - \mu^*\mathbf{e}') \qquad \text{for all } \mathbf{x}'' \in \text{con } X''. \tag{6}$$

In particular, (6) holds for $\mathbf{x}'' \in X''$. But by construction, if $\mathbf{x}'' \in X''$, then so does $\mathbf{x}'' + \lambda\mathbf{u}$ for any $\lambda \geq 0$, $\mathbf{u} \geq \mathbf{0}$. If we replace $\mathbf{x}''$ by $\mathbf{x}'' + \lambda\mathbf{u}$ in (6), divide through by λ, and let λ approach infinity, we conclude that $\mathbf{p}^*\mathbf{u} \geq 0$ for all $\mathbf{u} \geq 0$, which implies that $\mathbf{p}^* \geq \mathbf{0}$; since $\mathbf{p}^* \neq \mathbf{0}$, $\mathbf{p}^* > \mathbf{0}$. From (6), we can assume without loss of generality that $\mathbf{p}^*\mathbf{e}' = 1$. Then we conclude from (6) that

$$\mathbf{p}^*\mathbf{x}'' \geq \mathbf{p}^*\bar{\mathbf{x}} - \mu^* \qquad \text{for all } \mathbf{x}'' \in \text{con } X'', \mathbf{p}^* > \mathbf{0}, \mathbf{p}^*\mathbf{e}' = 1. \tag{7}$$

For any coalition S, let in particular,

$$\mathbf{x}'' = \sum_{h \in S} \tilde{\mathbf{x}}_h + \sum_{h \in E \sim S} \bar{\mathbf{x}}_h;$$

since $\tilde{\mathbf{x}}_h \in X''_h$, $\bar{\mathbf{x}}_h \in X''_h$, $\mathbf{x}'' \in X'' \subset \text{con } X''$. Substitute in (7) and recall that

$$\bar{\mathbf{x}} = \sum_{h \in S} \bar{\mathbf{x}}_h + \sum_{h \in E \sim S} \bar{\mathbf{x}}_h;$$

then

$$\mathbf{p}^* \sum_{h \in S} (\bar{\mathbf{x}}_h - \tilde{\mathbf{x}}_h) \leq \mu^*. \tag{8}$$

Since (8) holds for any coalition S, it holds with S replaced by $E \sim S$.

$$\mathbf{p}^* \sum_{h \in E \sim S} (\bar{\mathbf{x}}_h - \tilde{\mathbf{x}}_h) \leq \mu^*. \tag{9}$$

Since the allocation $\tilde{x}$ is feasible,

$$\sum_h \tilde{\mathbf{x}}_h \leq \sum_h \bar{\mathbf{x}}_h;$$

since $\mathbf{p}^* > \mathbf{0}$,

$$\mathbf{p}^* \sum_h \tilde{\mathbf{x}}_h \leq \mathbf{p}^* \sum_h \bar{\mathbf{x}}_h,$$

or

$$\mathbf{p}^* \sum_{h \in S} (\tilde{\mathbf{x}}_h - \bar{\mathbf{x}}_h) + \mathbf{p}^* \sum_{h \in E \sim S} (\tilde{\mathbf{x}}_h - \bar{\mathbf{x}}_h) \leq 0.$$

Add this last result to (8).

$$\mathbf{p}^* \sum_{h \in E \sim S} (\tilde{\mathbf{x}}_h - \bar{\mathbf{x}}_h) \leq \mu^*. \tag{10}$$

In particular, let $S = \{h \mid \mathbf{p}^*\bar{\mathbf{x}}_h \geq \mathbf{p}^*\tilde{\mathbf{x}}_h\}$. Then

$\mathbf{p}^*(\bar{\mathbf{x}}_h - \tilde{\mathbf{x}}_h) = |\mathbf{p}^*(\tilde{\mathbf{x}}_h - \bar{\mathbf{x}}_h)|$ for $h \in S$, $\mathbf{p}^*(\tilde{\mathbf{x}}_h - \bar{\mathbf{x}}_h) = |\mathbf{p}^*(\tilde{\mathbf{x}}_h - \bar{\mathbf{x}}_h)|$

for $h \in E \sim S$. Then if we add (8) and (10) and use (5), conclusion (a) of the theorem follows.

Now let $\mathbf{x}_h^*$ minimize $\mathbf{p}^*\mathbf{x}_h$ subject to $\mathbf{x}_h \succcurlyeq_h \tilde{\mathbf{x}}_h$. Since $\mathbf{x}_h^* \in \tilde{X}_h \subset X''_h$,

$$\sum_h \mathbf{x}_h^* \in X'',$$

so that, from (7),

$$\mathbf{p}^* \sum_h \mathbf{x}_h^* \geq \mathbf{p}^*\bar{\mathbf{x}} - \mu^*,$$

or

$$\mathbf{p}^* \sum_h (\bar{\mathbf{x}}_h - \mathbf{x}_h^*) \leq \mu^*. \tag{11}$$

From the definition of S and (9),

$$\mathbf{p}^* \sum_h (\tilde{\mathbf{x}}_h - \bar{\mathbf{x}}_h) \leq \mathbf{p}^* \sum_{h \in E \sim S} (\tilde{\mathbf{x}}_h - \bar{\mathbf{x}}_h) \leq \mu^*. \tag{12}$$

Addition of (11) and (12) yields

$$\sum_h \mathbf{p}^*(\tilde{\mathbf{x}}_h - \mathbf{x}_h^*) \leq 2\mu^* \leq 2L\sqrt{n},$$

from (5), so that (b) of the theorem holds.

4. The Case of Finitely Many Types of Households

We now turn to a much studied special case of T.8.2, for which a stronger conclusion holds. Let us say that two households are of the same *type* if they have the same preference ordering and the same endowment vector. Suppose further we consider a sequence of economies with increasing numbers of households in which, however, there are only a fixed finite number of types of households in all the economies in the sequence. Suppose finally that the successive economies represent balanced expansions; specifically, assume that the numbers of households in the different types are equal for any one economy. Hence, the size of the economy is indicated by the number of households in any one type. The successive economies may be thought of as obtained by replication of one economy.

If it is assumed, in addition, that the preference orderings are convex, then it will be shown that, with a slightly different definition of blocking, any unblocked allocation must yield the same utility to any two individuals in the same type (since any two such individuals have the same indifference map, such an interpersonal comparison is meaningful). Thus an unblocked allocation, as far as utilities are concerned, can be characterized by the utility allocation to types; this has a fixed dimensionality as the size of the economy changes. It is obvious that the competitive equilibria for any economy of this class are simply replications of the competitive equilibria for the economy with one member per type, and each of these yields a utility allocation to types that is independent of the size of the economy. It turns out, remarkably, that the converse of this statement is true; if there is an unblocked allocation for each economy in the sequence that yields the same utility allocation to types for all the economies, then there is a price vector (the same for all economies) that, together with the given unblocked allocation, is a compensated equilibrium for the economy.

We assume, then, that there are m types of households; each type has, say, k members. We will index households with the double subscript ht, for the hth household of type t ($h = 1, \ldots, k$; $t = 1, \ldots, m$); the preference ordering, utility function, and endowment vector of household h,t will have the single subscript t.

It is convenient here to use a slightly different definition of blocking.

DEFINITION 5. An allocation, $\mathscr{x}$, is *weakly blocked* by coalition S if there exists another allocation, $\mathscr{x}'$, that is feasible for coalition S such that $\mathbf{x}'_h \succsim_h \mathbf{x}_h$ for all $h \in S$, $\mathbf{x}'_h \succ_h \mathbf{x}_h$ for at least one $h \in S$.

DEFINITION 6. An allocation is *strongly unblocked* if it is feasible and not weakly blocked by any coalition S.

THEOREM 3. Suppose there are m types of households, where all households of each type have the same endowment and the same preference ordering, and let there be k households of each type. Then

(a) The bundles yielded by any strongly unblocked allocation to two households of the same type must be indifferent in the preference ordering for that type.

(b) If the number of types and the endowments and preference orderings defining them remain constant, but k, the number of households in each type, varies, if, for each k, $\mathscr{x}^k$ is a strongly unblocked allocation such that $U_t(\mathbf{x}^k_{ht}) = u^k_t$ is the same for all k (it is independent of h by (a)), and if $r(X''_t)$ is finite when $k = 1$ for all t, then there is a price vector $\mathbf{p}^*$ such that $(\mathbf{p}^*, \mathbf{u}^k, \mathscr{x}^k)$ is a compensated equilibrium for all k, where $\mathbf{u}^k$ is the vector with mk components defined by $u^k_{ht} = u^k_t$.

Proof. (a) Let $\mathscr{x}$ be a feasible allocation, and suppose that for some t, say 1, there are two households, h' and h'', such that $U_1(\mathbf{x}_{h'1}) \neq U_1(\mathbf{x}_{h''1})$. Then for each t let the households be numbered so that household 1 has the least utility under the given allocation; that is,

$U_t(\mathbf{x}_{1t}) \leq U_t(\mathbf{x}_{ht})$, all h and t. Now define for each t the average bundle received by members of that type, namely,

$$\mathbf{x}_t^a = \sum_{h=1}^{k} \frac{\mathbf{x}_{ht}}{k}.$$

By semi-strict quasi-concavity, $U_t(\mathbf{x}_t^a) \geq U_t(\mathbf{x}_{1t})$, all t, while $U_1(\mathbf{x}_1^a) > U_1(\mathbf{x}_{11})$. Since $\mathscr{x}$ is feasible, it follows that

$$\sum_{t=1}^{m} \mathbf{x}_t^a = \frac{1}{k} \sum_{h=1}^{k} \sum_{t=1}^{m} \mathbf{x}_{ht} \leq \frac{1}{k} \sum_{h=1}^{k} \sum_{t=1}^{m} \bar{\mathbf{x}}_t = \sum_{t=1}^{m} \bar{\mathbf{x}}_t.$$

Consider the coalition that consists of all the households numbered 1 from all the types, that is, those with indices $1,t$ ($t = 1, \ldots, m$). Since household $1,t$ has endowment $\bar{\mathbf{x}}_t$, it follows that the allocation that gives every household in type t the commodity vector $\mathbf{x}_t^a$ is feasible for this coalition, and therefore, it has been shown that the allocation $\mathscr{x}$ is weakly blocked by this coalition. Then by D.8.5 and D.8.6, any allocation $\mathscr{x}$ with the property that $U_t(\mathbf{x}_{h't}) \neq U_t(\mathbf{x}_{h''t})$ for some t and some pair h',h'' is not strongly unblocked.

(b) By (a), then, if $\mathscr{x}$ is strongly unblocked, $\mathbf{x}_{h't} \sim_t \mathbf{x}_{h''t}$ for any t, h', h''. The sets

$$X_{ht} = \{\mathbf{x}_{ht} \mid \mathbf{x}_{ht} \succcurlyeq_t \bar{\mathbf{x}}_{ht}\}$$

are then the same for all h for any given t, and, therefore, the same must be true of the sets X''_{ht}, defined as in T.8.2, that is, $X''_{ht} = X''_{1t}$ for all h and t. Now note that

$$\text{con} \sum_{t=1}^{m} \sum_{h=1}^{k} X''_{ht} = k \text{ con} \sum_{t=1}^{m} X''_{1t}. \tag{13}$$

(Recall that for any set of vectors C, kC means the set obtained by multiplying each element of C by the scalar k.) To see the validity of (13), first note that for any convex set C, it is easy to establish that

$$\sum_{i=1}^{r} C = rC.$$

Second, as shown in Lemma B.2, the convex hull of a vector sum is the vector sum of the convex hulls. Thus, since $X''_{ht} = X''_{1t}$, all h,

$$\sum_{h=1}^{k} \text{con } X''_{ht} = \sum_{h=1}^{k} \text{con } X''_{1t} = k \text{ con } X''_{1t},$$

and therefore,

$$\text{con} \sum_{t=1}^{m} \sum_{h=1}^{k} X''_{ht} = \sum_{t=1}^{m} \sum_{h=1}^{k} \text{con } X''_{ht} = \sum_{t=1}^{m} k \text{ con } X''_{1t} = k \text{ con} \sum_{t=1}^{k} X''_{1t}.$$

Since $\tilde{x}$ is strongly unblocked, it certainly belongs to the core, and T.8.2 and its proof can be applied. Let

$$\mu^k = \sup\left\{\mu \,\middle|\, k \sum_{t=1}^{m} \bar{\mathbf{x}}_t - \mu \mathbf{e}' \in \text{con} \sum_{t=1}^{m} \sum_{h=1}^{k} X''_{ht}\right\}.$$

From (13), it is obvious that $\mu^k = k\mu^1$. From the hypothesis, the sets X_{ht} are independent of k, as well as of h; therefore, the same is true of X''_{ht}. Since there are then only finitely many distinct such sets and since $r(X''_{ht})$ is finite for each such, it follows that $r(X''_{ht})$ is bounded above uniformly over all households in all economies in the sequence formed by letting n increase indefinitely. Therefore, by (5), μ^k is bounded above uniformly in n. But if $\mu^k = k\mu^1 \geq 0$, this is possible only if $\mu^1 = 0$, and therefore $\mu^k = 0$, all k. We can take $M = 0$ in T.8.2. Then, $\mathbf{p}^*\tilde{\mathbf{x}}_h = \mathbf{p}^*\bar{\mathbf{x}}_h = \mathbf{p}^*\mathbf{x}_h^*$, that is, at the prices $\mathbf{p}^*$, $\tilde{\mathbf{x}}_h$ minimizes the cost of achieving its utility and, at the same time, that bundle satisfies the budget constraint. Hence, there is exactly a competitive equilibrium.

5. The Core of a Productive Economy

The preceding two theorems concern only the case of a pure exchange economy. Some care must be taken in the introduction of production into the theory of the core. Here we start without a concept of prices and *a fortiori* of profits. The model of Chapters 3–5, with production taking place in firms separate from households and profits then being distributed to the firms' owners, is inappropriate to the present discussion; it might be said that an adequate theory of bargaining should explain the formation of firms, not merely take them for granted.

As an alternative, it will be assumed that there is a production possibility set associated with each possible coalition. The simplest case is that in which this is the same, a convex cone Y, for each coalition. It will be seen later that, with a suitable redefinition of the commodity space, this condition is less restrictive than it might appear at first.

We can now generalize the definitions of feasibility.

DEFINITION 7. A consumption allocation, x, is *feasible* for a coalition, S, if, for some $\mathbf{y} \in Y$,

$$\sum_{h \in S} \mathbf{x}_h \leq \sum_{h \in S} \bar{\mathbf{x}}_h + \mathbf{y}.$$

The definitions of blocked allocations and of the core (D.8.3–D.8.4) remain unchanged, provided feasibility is understood in the sense of D.8.7.

An unblocked consumption allocation, $\tilde{x}$, then has associated with it a production vector, $\tilde{\mathbf{y}}$, which makes it feasible; the pair $(\tilde{x},\tilde{\mathbf{y}})$ will be referred to as an unblocked *allocation*. For any such allocation, we can define X''_h as in the statement of T.8.2. Now define

$$Z''_h = X''_h - Y \qquad Z'' = \sum_{h \in E} Z''_h.$$

Since Y is a cone,

$$\sum_{h \in S} Y = Y$$

for any coalition S. If we use D.8.7 and the definition of blocking, we can use the same reasoning as in the proof of T.8.2 to show the following extension of (4):

$$Z'' \text{ is disjoint from } \{\mathbf{x} \mid \mathbf{x} \ll \bar{\mathbf{x}}\}. \tag{14}$$

Assume that $r(Z''_h) \leq L$ for all h in all economies E for some L. We can then parallel the arguments of T.8.2. As there, the set $\{\mu \mid \bar{\mathbf{x}} - \mu\mathbf{e}'\} \in \operatorname{con} Z''$ has a supremum, μ^*, not exceeding $M = L\sqrt{n}$. Hence, we can find $\mathbf{p}^*$ so that

$$\mathbf{p}^*\mathbf{z}'' \geq \mathbf{p}^*\bar{\mathbf{x}} - \mu^* \qquad \text{for all } \mathbf{z}'' \in \operatorname{con} Z'', \mathbf{p}^* > \mathbf{0}, \mathbf{p}^*\mathbf{e}' = 1. \tag{15}$$

Since $Z'' = \sum_{h \in E} X'_h - \sum_{h \in E} Y = X'' - Y$, we have, from (15),

$$\mathbf{p}^*\mathbf{x}'' \geq \mathbf{p}^*\bar{\mathbf{x}} - \mu^* + \mathbf{p}^*\mathbf{y} \qquad \text{for all } \mathbf{x}'' \in X'', \mathbf{y} \in Y. \tag{16}$$

Clearly, then, $\mathbf{p}^*\mathbf{y}$ is bounded above for $\mathbf{y} \in Y$. Since Y is a cone, it must be that

$$\mathbf{p}^*\mathbf{y} \leq 0 \qquad \text{for all } \mathbf{y} \in Y. \tag{17}$$

If we set $\mathbf{y} = \mathbf{0}$ in (16), we have (7), so that (8) and (9) still hold. Since $(\tilde{x},\tilde{\mathbf{y}})$ is a feasible allocation,

$$\sum_h \tilde{\mathbf{x}}_h \leq \sum_h \bar{\mathbf{x}}_h + \tilde{\mathbf{y}},$$

and since $\mathbf{p}^* > 0$,

$$\mathbf{p}^* \sum_h \tilde{\mathbf{x}}_h \leq \mathbf{p}^* \sum_h \bar{\mathbf{x}}_h + \mathbf{p}^*\tilde{\mathbf{y}}. \tag{18}$$

In view of (7), however, (10) still holds, and therefore, T.8.2(a) can be deduced as before. From (18) and (8) (with $S = E$), we can also deduce

$$\mathbf{p}^*\tilde{\mathbf{y}} \geq -\mu^*. \tag{19}$$

Since (10) and (7) are still valid, it follows also that the argument leading to T.8.2(b) is still valid.

THEOREM 4. Consider a class of economies E such that the production possibility sets for all coalitions in a given economy are the same convex cone Y (which may depend on E). For each E, consider an allocation $(\tilde{x},\tilde{\mathbf{y}})$ in its core (assumed non-empty). For each household h in any economy E, define,

$$X_h = \{\mathbf{x}_h \mid \mathbf{x}_h \succcurlyeq_h \tilde{\mathbf{x}}_h\} \qquad X'_h = X_h \cup \{\bar{\mathbf{x}}_h\}$$
$$X''_h = \{\mathbf{x}''_h \mid \mathbf{x}''_h \geq \mathbf{x}'_h \text{ for some } \mathbf{x}'_h \in X'_h\} \qquad Z''_h = X''_h - Y.$$

Assume that, for some L, $r(Z''_h) \leq L$ for all h in all economies E in the class. Then there exists a constant M ($= 2L\sqrt{n}$, where n is the number of commodities) and, for each E, a vector $\mathbf{p}^* > 0$, such that for any economy E, the following statements hold:

(a) $\sum_{h \in E} |\mathbf{p}^*(\tilde{\mathbf{x}}_h - \mathbf{x}_h)| \leq M$;

(b) $\mathbf{p}^* \sum_{h \in E} \tilde{\mathbf{x}}_h - \sum_{h \in E} \min_{\mathbf{x}_h \succcurlyeq_h \tilde{\mathbf{x}}_h} \mathbf{p}^*\mathbf{x}_h \leq M$;

(c) $-M \leq \mathbf{p}^*\tilde{\mathbf{y}} \leq 0$; $\mathbf{p}^*\mathbf{y} \leq 0$, all y in Y.

Part (c) shows that the production decision may not be profit maximizing, but that the departure from profit maximization is bounded. Thus, for large economies, the difference between actual and maximum profits becomes small relative to any measure of the size of the economy.

We now argue that seemingly more general hypotheses about the production possibility sets available to coalitions lead essentially to the above assumption that every such production possibility set is the same convex cone (within a given economy). Essentially the argument is that any productive capacities that distinguish individuals as they enter into different coalitions can be treated as separate commodities. It will be assumed that households are of finitely many *productive types* (say, m in number); any two households of the same productive type are interchangeable in production.

DEFINITION 8. The *profile* of a coalition S, $\mathbf{k}(S)$, is an m vector such that $k_t(S)$ is the number of households of productive type t in S.

It will then be assumed that the production possibility set for a coalition S depends only on its profile and, therefore, can be represented as $Y[\mathbf{k}(S)]$. Thus, $Y(\mathbf{k})$ is a correspondence mapping vectors with non-negative integer components into production possibility sets. We assume first,

ASSUMPTION 1. For each non-negative integer vector $\mathbf{k}$, $Y(\mathbf{k})$ satisfies assumptions A.3.1–A.3.4.

Suppose two coalitions with the same profiles combine into one. In the absence of any kind of increasing returns to scale, the production possibility set may be presumed to undergo merely a scale expansion.

ASSUMPTION 2. For any non-negative integer N and any non-negative integer vector $\mathbf{k}$, $Y(N\mathbf{k}) = NY(\mathbf{k})$.

Although $Y(\mathbf{k})$ is defined in the first instance only for integer vectors, A.8.2 permits a natural extension to rational vectors. If $\mathbf{k}$ is rational, choose N so that $N\mathbf{k}$ is integer valued. Then $Y(N\mathbf{k})$ is well defined; we then *define* $Y(\mathbf{k})$ to mean $Y(N\mathbf{k})/N$, so that A.8.2 remains valid in the extended domain of definition. Note that this is a proper definition, for the set $Y(N\mathbf{k})/N$ is the same for any integer N for which $N\mathbf{k}$ is integer valued.

It is now reasonable to insist that the correspondence $Y(\mathbf{k})$ defined for rational vectors $\mathbf{k}$ has appropriate continuity properties. Specifically, it will be assumed that there exists a continuous correspondence, $Y(\mathbf{k})$, defined for all non-negative vectors $\mathbf{k}$, that coincides on the rationals with the just-described extension of $Y(\mathbf{k})$ from integer valued vectors $\mathbf{k}$. (Recall, from Section 4.5, that a correspondence is continuous if it is both lower and upper semi-continuous.)

ASSUMPTION 3. There exists a continuous correspondence $Y(\mathbf{k})$, defined for all $\mathbf{k} \geq \mathbf{0}$, such that for any non-negative rational $\mathbf{k}$ and positive integer N for which $N\mathbf{k}$ is integer valued, $Y(N\mathbf{k})/N = Y(\mathbf{k})$.

Suppose now that two disjoint coalitions, S_1 and S_2, combine into one. Presumably one possible way of organizing production would be to split again, produce in the component coalitions, and then total the resulting production vectors. In symbols then, $Y[\mathbf{k}(S_1)] + Y[\mathbf{k}(S_2)] \subset Y[\mathbf{k}(S_1 \cup S_2)]$. Since $\mathbf{k}(S_1 \cup S_2) = \mathbf{k}(S_1) + \mathbf{k}(S_2)$, we can write this assumption of *super additivity* as follows:

ASSUMPTION 4. $Y(\mathbf{k}^1) + Y(\mathbf{k}^2) \subset Y(\mathbf{k}^1 + \mathbf{k}^2)$ for any non-negative integer vectors $\mathbf{k}^1,\mathbf{k}^2$.

It is easy to verify, from the continuity of $Y(\mathbf{k})$, that the analogs of A.8.2 and A.8.4 hold for all non-negative $\mathbf{k}$, not merely those with integer values. Note first the following general lemma.

LEMMA 2. If $\Phi(\mathbf{x})$ is lower semi-continuous, $\psi(\mathbf{x})$ upper semi-continuous, and $\{\mathbf{x}^\nu\}$ a sequence converging to $\mathbf{x}$ such that $\Phi(\mathbf{x}^\nu) \subset \psi(\mathbf{x}^\nu)$, all ν, then $\Phi(\mathbf{x}) \subset \psi(\mathbf{x})$.

Proof. Let $\mathbf{y} \in \Phi(\mathbf{x})$. By definition of lower semi-continuity, there is a sequence $\{\mathbf{y}^\nu\}$, $\mathbf{y}^\nu \in \Phi(\mathbf{x}^\nu)$, all ν, $\mathbf{y}^\nu \rightarrow \mathbf{y}$. Then by hypothesis $\mathbf{y}^\nu \in \psi(\mathbf{x}^\nu)$, all ν, and by the upper semi-continuity of ψ, $\mathbf{y} \in \psi(\mathbf{x})$.

Corollary 2. If $\Phi(\mathbf{x})$ and $\psi(\mathbf{x})$ are continuous correspondences and $\{\mathbf{x}^\nu\}$ is a sequence converging to $\mathbf{x}$ such that $\Phi(\mathbf{x}^\nu) = \psi(\mathbf{x}^\nu)$, all ν, then $\Phi(\mathbf{x}) = \psi(\mathbf{x})$.

Now let λ be any non-negative real number, $\mathbf{k}$ any non-negative vector. Let $\{\lambda_\nu\}$ be a sequence of non-negative rational numbers converging to λ, $\{\mathbf{k}^\nu\}$ a sequence of non-negative rational vectors converging to $\mathbf{k}$, and for each ν, N_ν a positive integer such that $\lambda_\nu N_\nu$ and $\lambda_\nu N_\nu \mathbf{k}^\nu$ are both integer valued. Then, by A.8.2–A.8.3,

$$Y(\lambda_\nu N_\nu \mathbf{k}^\nu) = N_\nu Y(\lambda_\nu \mathbf{k}^\nu) = \lambda_\nu N_\nu Y(\mathbf{k}^\nu).$$

Divide the last equality by N_ν, and let ν approach infinity. From the continuity of Y and the Corollary to Lemma 8.2, $Y(\lambda\mathbf{k}) = \lambda Y(\mathbf{k})$.

For any non-negative vectors, $\mathbf{k}^1$ and $\mathbf{k}^2$, choose two sequences of non-negative rational vectors, $\{\mathbf{k}^{1\nu}\}$ and $\{\mathbf{k}^{2\nu}\}$, converging to $\mathbf{k}^1$ and $\mathbf{k}^2$, and then choose, for each ν, a positive integer N_ν so that $N_\nu \mathbf{k}^{1\nu}$ and $N_\nu \mathbf{k}^{2\nu}$ are both integer valued. From A.8.4,

$$Y(N_\nu \mathbf{k}^{1\nu}) + Y(N_\nu \mathbf{k}^{2\nu}) \subset Y[N_\nu(\mathbf{k}^{1\nu} + \mathbf{k}^{2\nu})] \qquad \text{all } \nu,$$

or from A.8.3,

$$N_\nu Y(\mathbf{k}^{1\nu}) + N_\nu Y(\mathbf{k}^{2\nu}) \subset N_\nu Y(\mathbf{k}^{1\nu} + \mathbf{k}^{2\nu}).$$

Divide through by N_ν and let ν approach infinity; then by Lemma 8.2, $Y(\mathbf{k}^1) + Y(\mathbf{k}^2) \subset Y(\mathbf{k}^1 + \mathbf{k}^2)$.

LEMMA 3. Under A.8.1–A.8.4, $Y(\lambda\mathbf{k}) = \lambda Y(\mathbf{k})$ for all $\lambda \geq 0$, $\mathbf{k} \geq \mathbf{0}$, and $Y(\mathbf{k}^1) + Y(\mathbf{k}^2) \subset Y(\mathbf{k}^1 + \mathbf{k}^2)$ for all $\mathbf{k}^1 \geq 0$, $\mathbf{k}^2 \geq 0$.

We must generalize again the definition of feasibility.

DEFINITION 9. An allocation $(\mathscr{x},\mathbf{y})$ is feasible for a coalition S if, for some $\mathbf{y} \in Y[\mathbf{k}(S)]$,

$$\sum_{h \in S} \mathbf{x}_h \leq \sum_{h \in S} \bar{\mathbf{x}}_h + \mathbf{y}.$$

The definitions of blocked allocations and of the core then remain unchanged in form.

THEOREM 5. Suppose that the production possibility sets of the coalitions in each economy E in a class satisfy A.8.1–A.8.4. For each E, consider an allocation $(\tilde{\mathscr{x}}, \tilde{\mathbf{y}})$ in its core (assumed non-empty). Define $Y = \{(\mathbf{y}, -\mathbf{k}) \mid \mathbf{y} \in Y(\mathbf{k})\}$. For each household h of productive type t in any economy E, define the following sets in $(n + m)$-space.

$$X_h = \{(\mathbf{x}_h, 0) \mid \mathbf{x}_h \succcurlyeq_h \tilde{\mathbf{x}}_h\}$$

$$X'_h = X_h \cup \{\bar{\mathbf{x}}_h, \mathbf{e}^{t(h)}\},$$

$$X''_h = \{\mathbf{x}''_h \mid \mathbf{x}''_h \geq \mathbf{x}'_h \quad \text{for some } \mathbf{x}'_h \in X'_h\},$$

$$Z''_h = X''_h - Y.$$

Assume that for some L, $r(Z''_h) \leq L$, for all h in all economies E in the class. Then there exists a constant $M = 2L\sqrt{n + m}$ and, for each E, an n vector $\mathbf{p}^* \geq \mathbf{0}$ and an m vector $\mathbf{w}^* \geq 0$, with $(\mathbf{p}^*, \mathbf{w}^*)\mathbf{e} = 1$, such that for any economy E, the following statements hold:

(a) $\sum_{h \in E} |\mathbf{p}^*(\tilde{\mathbf{x}}_h - \bar{\mathbf{x}}_h) - w^*_{t(h)}| \leq M;$

(b) $\mathbf{p}^* \sum_{h \in E} \tilde{\mathbf{x}}_h - \sum_{h \in E} \min_{\mathbf{x}_h \succcurlyeq_h \tilde{\mathbf{x}}_h} \mathbf{p}^*\mathbf{x}_h \leq M;$

(c) $\mathbf{w}^*\mathbf{k}(E) - M \leq \mathbf{p}^*\tilde{\mathbf{y}} \leq \mathbf{w}^*\mathbf{k}(E)$; $\mathbf{p}^*\mathbf{y} \leq \mathbf{w}^*\mathbf{k}(S)$, all $\mathbf{y} \in Y[\mathbf{k}(S)]$ and all $S \subset E$;

(d) for any economy E for which $k_t(E) > M$, all t, $\mathbf{p}^* > \mathbf{0}$.

The vector $\mathbf{e}^t$ is the unit m vector with 1 in the tth place and 0 elsewhere, and $t(h)$ is the productive type of household h. In the definition of Y, the sign of the profile k is reversed, since the productive types of the participants are to be regarded as inputs.

Proof. From Lemma 8.3, it follows immediately that Y is a convex cone. We can simply expand the commodity space by adding m new components as follows:

(a) The preference orderings of the households do not depend on the additional commodities.
(b) The endowment vector of a household of type t contains one unit of commodity $n + t$ and 0 of commodity $n + t'$ for any $t' \neq t$.
(c) The production possibility for every coalition is taken to be Y.

In view of (a), we can assume that in seeking for a blocking allocation we need only consider consumption vectors in which the quantities of the additional commodities are zero. Hence, the feasibility condition D.8.9 applied to the extended commodity space states (with $x_{hi} = 0$ for $i > n$)

$$\sum_{h \in S} \mathbf{x}_h \leq \sum_{h \in S} \bar{\mathbf{x}}_h + \mathbf{y} \qquad \mathbf{0} \leq \sum_{h \in S} \mathbf{e}^{t(h)} - \mathbf{k} \qquad (\mathbf{y}, -\mathbf{k}) \in Y,$$

where $t(h)$ is the productive type of household h. But obviously

$$\sum_{h \in S} \mathbf{e}^{t(h)} = \mathbf{k}(S),$$

so that, from the definition of Y, the last two conditions become $\mathbf{k} \leq \mathbf{k}(S)$, $\mathbf{y} \in Y(\mathbf{k})$, or since $Y(\mathbf{k})$ is certainly monotonic in $\mathbf{k}$, the single condition, $\mathbf{y} \in Y[\mathbf{k}(S)]$. Thus the feasibility condition in the extended space reduces to that already used. We can apply T.8.4 by straightforward reinterpretation of symbols. In particular, we let $(\mathbf{p}^*, \mathbf{w}^*)$ correspond to $\mathbf{p}^*$; then T.8.4(a)–(c) follow immediately. Further, if $\mathbf{p}^* = \mathbf{0}$, then $\mathbf{w}^*\mathbf{e}' = 1$, by the normalization used. If $k_t(E) > M$, all t, then $\mathbf{w}^*\mathbf{k}(E) > M$; but from the first inequality in (c), $\mathbf{w}^*\mathbf{k}(E) - M \leq 0$ if $\mathbf{p}^* = 0$, a contradiction. Hence, $\mathbf{p}^* > 0$ when $k_t(E) > M$, all t.

Remark. The quantities $\mathbf{w}_t^*$ are the distribution of pure profits. Under the assumptions made, two households of the same productive type receive the same dividends. Thus, these magnitudes might be thought of leading to the distribution parameters, d_{hf}, used in the model of Chapters 4 and 5. Then (a) asserts that the given unblocked allocation approximately satisfies the budget constraint for each coalition. The first part of (c) asserts that dividends in the aggregate are approximately equal to total profits; the second part asserts that no coalition can gain at the prevailing prices by engaging in separate production for the market. Statement (d) shows that for sufficiently large economies, at least, the price system is non-trivial.

If the productive types are identified with the types in Section 8.4, the following theorem is obvious.

THEOREM 6. Suppose there are m types of households, where all households of each type have the same endowment and the same preference ordering and are indistinguishable in production, so that the production possibility sets of the coalitions satisfy A.8.1–A.8.4. Suppose further that there are k households of each type, indexed as in the statement of T.8.3. Then

(a) The bundles yield by any strongly unblocked allocation to two households of the same type must be indifferent in the preference ordering for that type.

(b) If the numbers of types and the endowments, preference orderings, and coalition production possibility sets defining them remain constant, but k, the number of households in each type, varies, if, for each k, $(\tilde{\mathscr{x}}^k,\tilde{\mathbf{y}}^k)$ is a strongly unblocked allocation such that $U_t(\mathbf{x}^k_{ht}) = u^k_t$ is the same for all k (it is independent of h by (a)), and if $r(Z''_{1t})$ is finite when $k = 1$ for all t, then there is a price vector $\mathbf{p}^*$ and a dividend share d_t for each household of type t such that $(\mathbf{p}^*,\mathbf{u}^k,\mathscr{x}^k,\mathbf{y}^k)$ is a compensated equilibrium for all k, where $\mathbf{u}^k$ is the vector with mk components defined by $u^k_{ht} = u^k_t$, $\mathbf{y}^k$ maximizes $\mathbf{p}^*\mathbf{y}$ for $\mathbf{y}$ in the production possibility set for the coalition of all members of the economy with k members of each type, and the income, M^k_t, of any household of type t is

$$\mathbf{p}^*\bar{\mathbf{x}}_t + \sum_t d_t(\mathbf{p}^* y^k).$$

Notes

As discussed in Section 1.3, the concept of the core was introduced (though not with that terminology) by Edgeworth [1881, pp. 20–56], who gave a thorough analysis of the case of two individuals. He further suggested that with two types of households (in the sense of Section 8.4) the core would shrink to the competitive equilibria.

The concept of the core was introduced in the general theory of non-zero-sum games for which market economies are a special case. The first to apply it to market economies was Shubik [1959]. Shubik's work, like that of von Neumann and Morgenstern, Gillies, and Shapley, operated under the highly restrictive assumption of transferable utility.

The decisive step in giving a general treatment of Edgeworth's propositions while retaining his assumption of non-transferable utility is due to Scarf [1962], who proved T.8.3 (indeed, a more general form since he did not assume that the inner radii of certain sets must be finite). A greatly simplified presentation is due to Debreu and Scarf [1963], who also extended the results to the case of production, in which each coalition has access to the same production possibility set, which is a cone (this is a special case of T.8.6).

Aumann [1964] gave an alternative treatment of the core by assuming to begin with that the households form a continuum. Of course, his methods require sophisticated measure-theoretic arguments.

Scarf's theorem applies to a replicated economy, Aumann's to one that is a continuum. An alternative formulation of the problem is to consider a sequence of economies with successively greater numbers of participants and ask under what conditions the cores of these economies tend to approximate their equilibria. It is this approach that underlies the present analysis. The only (somewhat) similar approaches known to us are those of Nishino [1970, Theorem 8] and Hildenbrand [1970]. Nishino makes some strong assumptions about the utility functions and then asserts a theorem that, in a sequence of economies of increasing numbers of participants, there is a corresponding sequence of price vectors such that the maximum budgetary deficit of any household approaches zero. Hildenbrand's methods and theorems make strong use of measure theory, so only a rough version of his main result along these lines (his Corollary 1 to Theorem 2) will be stated: Given a sequence of finite economies converging (in an appropriate sense) to an economy with a continuum of households and, for each such economy, an unblocked allocation, if the sequence of allocations converges continuously to an allocation in the limit economy, then there is a price vector, $\mathbf{p}$, such that the sequence of allocations approaches the demand correspondences of the households uniformly. (The sequence of functions $\{f_\nu\}$ is said to converge continuously to a function, f, if $\mathbf{x}^\nu \to \mathbf{x}$ implies $f_\nu(\mathbf{x}^\nu) \to f(\mathbf{x})$.)

Chapter Nine

THE UNIQUENESS OF COMPETITIVE EQUILIBRIUM

Alone, alone, all, all alone,
Alone on a wide, wide sea.
—Samuel T. Coleridge,
The Ancient Mariner

1. The Problem

We return now to a world of excess demand functions discussed in Chapter 2. In particular, we assume F, H, W, B, and C′, that is, assumptions A.2.1–A.2.3, A.2.5, and A.2.6. The main question we will investigate is this: In what circumstances will it be true that the abstract economy discussed in the first part of Chapter 1 has only a single possible equilibrium $\mathbf{p}^*$ in S? The question is not only interesting in its own right, but requires an answer if one proposes to consider problems in comparative statics. Moreover, it will turn out that the analysis of the uniqueness of an equilibrium is very helpful in examining the dynamic behavior of general equilibrium systems.

Our procedure will be as follows. First, we shall show that if a purely mathematical condition is satisfied by the excess demand functions, then the equilibrium of the economy must be unique. We shall then take a good deal of time to discuss the possible economic cases that lead to the fulfillment of the mathematical condition, and we shall also note cases for which more direct or different approaches are possible.

2. The Main Assumptions

It will prove convenient in what follows to carry out the analysis in terms of excess supplies rather than excess demands. We write $s_i = -z_i$, all i. Of course, $s_i(\mathbf{p})$ is the excess supply function for good i. Also, if $\mathbf{p}^*$ is our equilibrium it must imply $s_i(\mathbf{p}^*) \geq 0$, all i. We postulate:

ASSUMPTION 1 (D). For all i and for all $\mathbf{p}$ in S_n, $s_i(\mathbf{p})$ is differentiable. The reader is reminded that this is a stronger assumption than C′.

The second assumption we shall need will be further discussed below when we have proved the basic result.

ASSUMPTION 2 (N). In every equilibrium of the system there is a good, give it the label n, for which

$$\sum_i s_i(\mathbf{p}) = -\infty$$

when $p_n = 0$. This good is called the *numeraire*.

Now, let us write $s_{ij}(p)$ as the partial derivative of s_i with respect to its jth argument at $\mathbf{p}$ and $J(\mathbf{p})$ as the $(n-1) \times (n-1)$ Jacobian matrix of these partials. (In $J(\mathbf{p})$, i and j run from 1 to $n-1$). We require the following definition.

DEFINITION 1 (GP). Let A be a square matrix and T a diagonal matrix of the same order as A, with -1 or $+1$ or both, along the main diagonal. Then if $\mathbf{v}$ is a column vector, A will be said to have the *Gale property* if for all T the problem $TAT\mathbf{v} \leq \mathbf{0}$, $\mathbf{v} \geq \mathbf{0}$, has only the solution $\mathbf{v} = \mathbf{0}$.

Remark. The Gale property (GP) can be given an alternative useful statement. Let $\mathbf{u}$ be any non-zero vector, $\mathbf{w} = A\mathbf{u}$. Choose the diagonal matrix T, with $t_{ii} = \pm 1$, so that $t_{ii}u_i > 0$ if $u_i \neq 0$, $t_{ii}w_i \leq 0$ if $u_i = 0$, and let $\mathbf{v} = T\mathbf{u} \geq \mathbf{0}$. Since $T = T^{-1}$, $\mathbf{u} = T\mathbf{v}$. Substitute in the definition of $\mathbf{w}$, and multiply both sides by T, so that $TAT\mathbf{v} = T\mathbf{w}$. Then GP is equivalent to the statement that $T\mathbf{w}$ has at least one positive component; that is, $t_{ii}w_i > 0$ for at least one i. By choice of T, it is impossible that $u_i = 0$, and it can be seen that u_i and w_i must be both positive or both negative. Thus GP is equivalent to the following statement: *For any non-zero* $\mathbf{u}$, *there is at least one non-zero component that has the same sign as the corresponding component of* $A\mathbf{u}$.

We now note,

LEMMA 1. If a matrix A has GP, then every principal minor must have GP.

Proof. Let

$$A = \begin{pmatrix} A_{11} & A_{12} \\ A_{21} & A_{22} \end{pmatrix},$$

and suppose A_{11} does not have GP. For some $\mathbf{v}^1$ and T_1, $T_1A_{11}T_1\mathbf{v}^1$

$\leq \mathbf{0}, \mathbf{v}^1 > \mathbf{0}$. Also, we can readily find T_2 such that $T_2 A_{21} T_1 \mathbf{v}^1 \leq \mathbf{0}$. Then let

$$T = \begin{pmatrix} T_1 & 0 \\ 0 & T_2 \end{pmatrix} \qquad \mathbf{v} = \begin{pmatrix} \mathbf{v}^1 \\ \mathbf{0} \end{pmatrix},$$

and find

$$TAT\mathbf{v} = \begin{pmatrix} T_1 A_{11} T_1 \mathbf{v}^1 \\ T_2 A_{21} T_1 \mathbf{v}^1 \end{pmatrix} \leq \mathbf{0},$$

which contradicts the assumption that A has GP.

The following definition was introduced by Hicks in his discussion of perfect stability.

DEFINITION 2. A matrix, A, is said to be *Hicksian* if all the principal minors have positive determinants.

LEMMA 2. A square matrix is Hicksian if and only if it has GP.

Proof. For a matrix of order one, both conditions are equivalent to the statement that the single element is positive. Suppose the lemma is true for matrices of order less than n, and let A be a matrix of order n.

First, suppose A has GP. It is certainly non-singular, for otherwise we could find $\mathbf{u}$ with $A\mathbf{u} = \mathbf{0}$, $\mathbf{u} \neq 0$, contrary to the Remark to D.9.1. Now choose u so that

$$A\mathbf{u} = \mathbf{e}(n),$$

where $\mathbf{e}(n)$ is the nth unit vector. From the Remark to D.9.1, it follows that $u_n > 0$. Let A_{nn} consist of the first $n - 1$ rows and columns of A. By Cramer's rule,

$$u_n = \frac{\det A_{nn}}{\det A}.$$

But by Lemma 9.1, A_{nn} has GP; by the induction hypothesis, A_{nn} is Hicksian and in particular $\det A_{nn} > 0$; hence $\det A > 0$. Since Lemma 9.1 and the induction hypothesis also ensure that the determinants of all principal minors of A other than A itself are positive, A must be Hicksian.

Now suppose that A is Hicksian, but does not have GP. Then for some $\mathbf{v} > \mathbf{0}$, $TAT\mathbf{v} \leq \mathbf{0}$. Since TAT is also Hicksian, we can replace it by A with no loss of generality.

If $\mathbf{v}$ has a zero component, partition its components into their positive and zero elements respectively, so that

$$\mathbf{v} = \begin{pmatrix} \mathbf{v}^1 \\ \mathbf{v}^2 \end{pmatrix} \qquad \mathbf{v}^1 \gg \mathbf{0},\ \mathbf{v}^2 = \mathbf{0}.$$

With the same partitioning of components write

$$A = \begin{pmatrix} A_{11} & A_{12} \\ A_{21} & A_{22} \end{pmatrix} \qquad \mathbf{w} = \begin{pmatrix} \mathbf{w}^1 \\ \mathbf{w}^2 \end{pmatrix}.$$

Then $A_{11}\mathbf{v}^1 = \mathbf{w}^1$, $\mathbf{v}^1 \gg \mathbf{0}$, $\mathbf{w}^1 \leq \mathbf{0}$. Yet if A is Hicksian, then, by D.9.2, so is every principal minor, and in particular, A_{11} is Hicksian and has GP by the induction hypothesis, a contradiction.

Now suppose $\mathbf{v}$ has no zero components, so that $\mathbf{v} \gg \mathbf{0}$. Let D be the diagonal matrix with $d_{ii} = -w_i/v_i \geq 0$, $A(t) = A + tD$. By induction on n, the order of the matrix, we show that $\det A(t) > 0$ for $t \geq 0$. The statement is trivial for $n = 1$; suppose it true for matrices of order $n - 1$. By expansion of a determinant on its ith row, we see that

$$\frac{\partial \det (A + D)}{\partial d_{ii}} = \det A_{ii},$$

where A_{ii} is the principal minor of A formed by deleting the ith row and column. Then,

$$\frac{d \det A(t)}{dt} = \sum_{i=1}^{n} d_{ii} \det A_{ii}(t).$$

By the induction hypothesis, $\det A_{ii}(t) > 0$, while $d_{ii} \geq 0$; hence $\det A(t)$ is a monotone increasing function of t. Since $\det A(0) = \det A > 0$ by hypothesis, $\det A(t) > 0$, all $t \geq 0$.

In particular, for $t = 1$, $A + D$ is non-singular. By construction, however, $D\mathbf{v} = -\mathbf{w}$, so that $(A + D)\mathbf{v} = \mathbf{0}$, $\mathbf{v} \gg \mathbf{0}$, a contradiction.

We now make the following assumption about the economic system.

ASSUMPTION 3. For all $\mathbf{p}$ in S_n, $J(\mathbf{p})$ has GP.

Later we give several sufficient conditions for A.9.3 to hold. However, it may be immediately observed from the Remark to D.9.1 that A.9.3 is equivalent to the following: For any small change in prices (relative to the numeraire), there is at least one commodity for which its price and its excess supply change in the same direction. Thus stated, the assumption A.9.3 seems comparatively innocuous. Yet it does rule out Giffen goods, at least if supply is fixed or highly inelastic, for if only one price changes GP requires that the excess supply of that good increase.

The fundamental result to be established can now be stated.

THEOREM 1. If D, N, and A.9.3, then there is only one $\mathbf{p}$ in S_n, call it $\mathbf{p}^*$, such that $s_i(\mathbf{p}^*) \geq 0$, all i. (H, W, B, and C′ are taken to hold.)

3. Proof of T.9.1

The proof will proceed by induction; that is we shall show first that the theorem is true for an economy with two goods ($n = 2$). Then we shall stipulate that it is true for an economy with $n - 1$ goods and show that it must also hold for an economy with n goods. In order to do this we shall make use of the fact that an n-goods economy in which the relative prices of two goods are fixed may be treated like an economy with $n - 1$ goods. We shall explore this idea first.

Consider an n-goods economy in which variables have been transformed as follows:

For all $\mathbf{p}$ in S with $p_n > 0$, let

$$q_i = p_i, \quad \mathfrak{s}_i = s_i, \quad (i < n - 1);$$
$$q_{n-1} = p_{n-1} + p_n;$$
$$\mathfrak{s}_{n-1} = as_{n-1} + (1 - a)s_n \qquad \text{where } a = \frac{p_{n-1}}{q_{n-1}}$$

and let $\mathfrak{s}$ be the $(n - 1)$ vector with components $\mathfrak{s}_i$, and $\mathbf{q}$ the $(n - 1)$ vector with components q_i.

The reader may verify the following properties of the construction:

(a) For all $\mathbf{p}$ in S_n, $\mathbf{q}$ is in S_{n-1};
(b) $\mathbf{q}\mathfrak{s}(\mathbf{q},a) = 0$ for all $\mathbf{q}$ in S_{n-1} (W holds);
(c) $\mathfrak{s}(\mathbf{q},a)$ satisfies H, C′, and B.

Hence by T.2.3 there exists, for fixed a, a vector $\mathbf{q}(a)$, such that $\mathfrak{s}(\mathbf{q}(a),a) \geq \mathbf{0}$ ($\mathbf{q}(a)$ is an equilibrium). Also, by N it must be that $q_{n-1}(a) > 0$.

It will now be convenient to have the nomenclature given below.

DEFINITION 3. The system $\mathfrak{s}$ with prices $\mathbf{q}$, given a, will be called the *reduced* economy $R(a)$.

We also define two vectors, **P** and **Q**, by

$$\mathbf{P} = \frac{\mathbf{p}}{p_n} \quad \text{and} \quad \mathbf{Q} = \frac{\mathbf{q}}{(1-a)q_{n-1}}.$$

By H, if $\mathbf{p}^*$ is an equilibrium for the n-goods economy, then so is $\mathbf{P}^*$, and if $\mathbf{q}(a)$ is an equilibrium for $R(a)$ then so is $\mathbf{Q}(a)$. Note that $Q_{n-1} = 1/(1-a)$, which is the value of q_{n-1} if we set $p_n = 1$.

Finally let $\mathbf{P}(a)$ be defined as follows:

$$P_i(a) = Q_i(a) \qquad \text{all } i < n-1$$

$$P_{n-1}(a) = \frac{a}{(1-a)}$$

$$P_n(a) = 1$$

Then for $i < n-1$, $s_i(\mathbf{q}(a),a) = s_i(\mathbf{P}(a))$. But $\mathbf{q}(a)$ is an equilibrium for $R(a)$ and so

$$\text{For } i < n-1,\ s_i(\mathbf{P}(a)) \geq 0, \text{ and } s_i(\mathbf{P}(a)) > 0 \text{ implies } P_i(a) = 0. \quad (1)$$

We shall also need the following:

LEMMA 3. If for all $0 \leq a \leq 1$, $R(a)$ has a unique equilibrium, $\mathbf{q}(a)$, then $\mathbf{q}(a)$ is continuous in a.

Proof. Consider a sequence $a^r \to a^0$, $0 \leq a^r \leq 1$. Let $\mathbf{q}^r = \mathbf{q}(a^r)$ be the equilibrium for a^r. Since the $\mathbf{q}$'s are bounded, there will be a convergent subsequence, say, $\mathbf{q}^{r_k} \to \mathbf{q}^0$. Since $\mathbf{s}(\mathbf{q}^r,a^r)$ is a vector of continuous functions,

$$\lim_{r\to\infty} \mathbf{s}(\mathbf{q}^r,a^r) = \mathbf{s}(\mathbf{q}^0,a^0).$$

But by construction, $\mathbf{s}(\mathbf{q}^r,a^r)) \geq 0$, all r, and so $\mathbf{s}(\mathbf{q}^0,a^0) \geq \mathbf{0}$. Then, by the uniqueness hypothesis, $\mathbf{q}^0 = \mathbf{q}(a^0)$. Evidently the same argument establishes the continuity of $\mathbf{Q}(a)$ for $a < 1$.

We may now proceed to the proof of T.9.1 by induction on the number of goods.

(a) T.9.1 is true for $n = 2$. For if $\mathbf{P}^* \neq \mathbf{P}^{**}$ are both equilibria, take $P_1^{**} > P_1^*$. But $J(\mathbf{p}) = s_{11}(\mathbf{P})$ has GP, so s_1 must be strictly increasing in P_1, that is, $s_1(\mathbf{P}^{**}) > s_1(\mathbf{P}^*) \geq 0$ and so $\mathbf{p}^{**}$ is not an equilibrium.

(b) Suppose the theorem true for $(n-1)$ goods, but false for n. Let $\mathbf{P}^* \neq \mathbf{P}^{**}$ be two equilibria in the n economy, and $\mathbf{Q}(a^*)$, $\mathbf{Q}(a^{**})$ the corresponding equilibria for $R(a^*)$ and $R(a^{**})$. (If $\mathbf{P}^*$ is an equilibrium for n, then for $a^* = P^*_{n-1}/Q^*_{n-1}$, $\mathbf{Q}(a^*)$ must be an equilibrium for $R(a^*)$ and similarly for $\mathbf{Q}(a^{**})$.) Since, by Lemma 9.1, $R(a)$, the Jacobian for which has GP, must have a unique equilibrium, we must have $a^* \neq a^{**}$. Take $a^* > a^{**}$.

(c) We first note that

$$\frac{ds_i(\mathbf{P}(a))}{da}\frac{dP_i(a)}{da} \leq 0 \qquad \text{all } i < n-1. \tag{2}$$

For if $ds_i(\mathbf{P}(a))/da > 0$, it follows from (1) that $s_i(\mathbf{P}(a')) > 0$ for $a' > a$ and sufficiently close, so that $P_i(a') = 0$, whence $dP_i(a)/da \leq 0$. By the same argument we have: $ds_i(\mathbf{P}(a))/da \leq 0$ implies $dP_i(a)/da \leq 0$.

Let T be the $(n-1) \times (n-1)$ diagonal matrix with $T_{ii} = +1$ or -1. We may evidently choose it so that

$$\frac{T_{ii}(dP_i(a))}{da} > 0 \quad \text{if} \quad \frac{dP_i(a)}{da} \neq 0, \tag{3}$$

$$T_{ii}\frac{ds_i(\mathbf{P}(a))}{da} \leq 0 \quad \text{if} \quad \frac{dP(a)}{da} = 0.$$

Note that since $P_{n-1}(a) = a/(1-a)$, $dP_{n-1}/da > 0$, we have

$$T_{n-1,n-1} > 0.$$

Let $\tilde{\mathbf{s}}(\mathbf{P}(a))$ be the vector of the first $(n-1)$ components of $\mathbf{s}(\mathbf{P}(a))$. By the chain rule,

$$\frac{d\tilde{\mathbf{s}}(\mathbf{P}(a))}{da} = J(\mathbf{P}(a))\frac{d\mathbf{P}(a)}{da}$$

so that

$$T\frac{d\tilde{\mathbf{s}}(\mathbf{P}(a))}{da} = TJ(\mathbf{P}(a))TT\frac{d\mathbf{P}(a)}{da}$$

or in obvious notation:

$$\mathbf{u} = TJ(\mathbf{P}(a))T\mathbf{v}. \tag{4}$$

From (3) and $dP_{n-1}/da > 0$ we have $\mathbf{v} > \mathbf{0}$. From (2) and (3) we know that the first $(n-2)$ components of $\mathbf{u}$ are non-positive.

Hence if $u_{n-1,n-1} \leq 0$, (4) would have a contradiction of GP. Hence $u_{n-1,n-1} > 0$ or

$$\frac{ds_{n-1}(\mathbf{P}(a))}{da} > 0.$$

But if both $\mathbf{P}^* = \mathbf{P}(a^*)$ and $\mathbf{P}^{**} = \mathbf{P}(a^{**})$ are equilibria then $s_{n-1}(P(a^{**})) \geq 0$ and so $s_{n-1}(P(a^*)) > 0$ since $a^{**} < a^*$. But then, by the definition of an equilibrium, $P^*_{n-1} = 0$ and so $a^* = 0$ and we cannot have $a^* > a^{**} \geq 0$. Hence $\mathbf{P}^*$ and $\mathbf{P}^{**}$ cannot both be equilibria.

4. A Weaker Assumption

The method of our proof suggests the following weakening of A.9.3:

ASSUMPTION 3′. $J(\mathbf{P})$ and all its principal submatrices have GP at all $\mathbf{P}$ in $E = \{\mathbf{P} \mid \mathbf{s}(\mathbf{P}) \geq \mathbf{0}\}$.

We show that this weaker version is sufficient to establish that E has only one member, proceeding in the same manner as in Section 9.3.

(a) Suppose that $n = 2$ and that $\mathbf{P}^*$ and $\mathbf{P}^{**}$ are in E. Also, $P_1^{**} > P_1^*$. Then, evidently, by A.9.3′ it must be that $s_1(\mathbf{P}^* + (\epsilon,0)) > 0$ and $S_1(\mathbf{P}^{**} - (\epsilon,0)) < 0$, for $\epsilon > 0$ and small enough. (Since $P_1^{**} > 0$, $s_1(\mathbf{P}^{**}) = 0$; since $P_1^* \geq 0$, $s_1(\mathbf{P}^*) \geq 0$.) But then by C′, since s_1 changes sign between the two price situations, there must be P_1^{***} with $P_1^{**} > P_1^{***} > P_1^*$, such that $\mathbf{P}^{***}$ is in E. Proceeding in this way we may find equilibrium values of P_1 arbitrarily close to P_1^*, but this clearly contradicts A.9.3′ for $J(\mathbf{P}^*)$. Hence there is only one equilibrium.

(b) We again suppose that A.9.3′ is sufficient, with the other conditions of T.9.1 to ensure uniqueness for an economy with $n - 1$ goods and proceed by induction in the same manner as in the previous section. In particular, we again use $R(a)$ and all the notation established there.

We know from the previous section that $ds_{n-1}(\mathbf{P}(a^*))/da > 0$, $ds_{n-1}(\mathbf{P}(a^{**}))/da > 0$. We take $a^* > a^{**}$. It follows that for $a' < a^*$ and close enough, $s_{n-1}(\mathbf{P}(a')) < 0$. By continuity, there exist a^{***} such that $a^* > a^{***} > a^{**}$, and $s_{n-1}(\mathbf{P}(a^{***})) = 0$. By construction, then, $\mathbf{P}(a^{***})$ is an equilibrium. Proceeding in this way, we must be able to find a arbitrarily close to a^{**} such that $\mathbf{P}(a)$ is an equilibrium. Clearly, then, A.9.3′ is contradicted. We have proved:

THEOREM 2. If D, N, and A.9.3′, then the competitive economy has a unique equilibrium.

Our main task now will be to examine a number of economic restrictions on the excess-demand functions that lead to the uniqueness of an equilibrium. We shall do this, roughly, in increasing order of generality (i.e., plausibility of the restrictions). In a number of cases, we shall be able to establish the required result without appeal to the two theorems we have just proved. In one case at least, we shall prove uniqueness and find that this could not be done by the use of the theorems. This underlines the important point that only *sufficient* conditions for a unique equilibrium to exist are available and that the ones we have utilized may well be a good deal stronger than others that may be found eventually. We shall also examine a number of examples.

5. A Partial Converse

It is clear that GP will not be a necessary condition for an economy to have a unique equilibrium. However, we now show that a rather stronger uniqueness postulate does indeed imply that the excess supply functions have GP at $\mathbf{p}^* \gg \mathbf{0}$.

The "reduced" economy that we constructed previously is only one of a large number of possible reduced economies. In particular, let N be any subset of the goods *not* including the numeraire and $\tilde{N}$ its complement in the set of goods. Let a superscript N or $\tilde{N}$ to a vector denote that it has all its components in N or $\tilde{N}$, respectively. Let $\boldsymbol{\beta}^N$ be non-negative and $h > 0$ a scalar, and write

$$\mathbf{p}^{\tilde{N}} = h\boldsymbol{\beta}^{\tilde{N}}.$$

Then we call $R(\boldsymbol{\beta}^N)$ the reduced economy having excess supply functions $(\mathbf{s}^N,\mathbf{s}^{\tilde{N}})$ and prices $(\mathbf{p}^N,h\boldsymbol{\beta}^{\tilde{N}})$. The idea is just as before except that now we construct reduced economies by arbitrarily fixing the relative prices of any subset of goods that includes the numeraire. We now prove

THEOREM 3. Suppose that for every possible N and $\boldsymbol{\beta}^{\tilde{N}}$, $R(\boldsymbol{\beta}^{\tilde{N}})$ has a unique equilibrium. Let the numeraire assumption N hold, and suppose the economy has a unique equilibrium at $\mathbf{p}^* \gg \mathbf{0}$. Then the Jacobian of excess supply functions has GP at $\mathbf{p}^*$ if all its principal minors are non-singular.

Remark. By analogy to Hicksian "perfect stability," we may call the first requirement of the theorem one of *perfect uniqueness.* Since, when N consists only of the numeraire, we have a reduced economy that is the actual economy, ordinary uniqueness is included in perfect uniqueness, but does not imply it. Hence the assumption of perfect uniqueness is certainly stronger.

Proof. (a) Let N contain the first $m + 1$ goods, and let N' be the first m of these. Also, let

$$\mathbf{p}^N = (\mathbf{p}^{N'}, p_{m+1}) \qquad p_{m+1} = \alpha k$$
$$\mathbf{p}^{\bar{N}} = (1 - \alpha)k\boldsymbol{\beta}^{\bar{N}} \qquad \boldsymbol{\beta}^{\bar{N}'} = (\boldsymbol{\beta}^{\bar{N}}, \alpha).$$

Choose $\boldsymbol{\beta}^{\bar{N}}$ so that the unique equilibrium of $R(\boldsymbol{\beta}^{\bar{N}})$, written as $(\mathbf{p}^{*N}, h^*)$ is also the equilibrium for the economy, that is, $\mathbf{p}^* = (\mathbf{p}^{*N}, h^*\boldsymbol{\beta}^{\bar{N}})$.

Let $(\mathbf{p}^{N'}(\alpha), \alpha k(\alpha), (1 - \alpha)k(\alpha))$ be the unique equilibrium of $R(\boldsymbol{\beta}^{\bar{N}'})$, that is, of $R(\boldsymbol{\beta}^{\bar{N}}, \alpha)$. For $\alpha < 1$, the assumption N ensures that $(1 - \alpha)k(\alpha) > 0$. Let

$$\mathbf{q}^{N'}(\alpha) = \frac{\mathbf{p}^{N'}(\alpha)}{(1 - \alpha)k(\alpha)}$$
$$\mathbf{q}^{N}(\alpha) = \left(\mathbf{q}^{N'}(\alpha), \frac{\alpha}{1 - \alpha}\right).$$

Then by H and perfect uniqueness there can be only one value of α, say α^*, such that

$$\frac{(\mathbf{p}^{*N}, h^*)}{(1 - \alpha^*)k(\alpha^*)} = \left(\mathbf{q}^{N'}(\alpha^*), \frac{\alpha^*}{1 - \alpha^*}, 1\right).$$

Also, $\alpha^* < 1$.

For $\alpha < \alpha^*$, consider the equilibrium of $R(\boldsymbol{\beta}^{\bar{N}}, \alpha)$. Let $s_i(\alpha) = s_i(\mathbf{q}^{N'}(\alpha), \alpha/(1 - \alpha), \boldsymbol{\beta}^{\bar{N}})$, $i = 1, \ldots, m$. For any α, $s_i(\alpha) = 0$, $(i = 1, \ldots, m)$ if we ignore free goods, as we may for these purposes. If $s_{m+1}(\alpha) = 0$, then the equilibrium for $R(\boldsymbol{\beta}^{\bar{N}}, \alpha)$ would also be an equilibrium for $R(\boldsymbol{\beta}^{\bar{N}'})$, which we know is unique; hence $s_{m+1}(\alpha) = 0$ if and only if $\alpha = \alpha^*$. Then $s_{m+1}(\alpha)$ has a constant sign for $\alpha < \alpha^*$; if that sign were positive, then $s_{m+1}(0) \geq 0$, and the equilibrium for $R(\boldsymbol{\beta}^{\bar{N}}, 0)$ would be a corner equilibrium for $R(\boldsymbol{\beta}^{\bar{N}'})$, contrary to uniqueness. Thus, $s_{m+1}(\alpha) < 0$ for $\alpha < \alpha^*$, or

$$d = \frac{s_{m+1}(\alpha) - s_{m+1}(\alpha^*)}{\alpha - \alpha^*} > 0.$$

Let $s_{ij} = \partial s_i/\partial p_j$; since $s_i(\alpha)$ is constant, that is, 0 for $i \leq m$,

$$\sum_{j=1}^{m+1} s_{ij} \frac{dq_j}{d\alpha} = 0,$$

when evaluated at the equilibrium of $R(\boldsymbol{\beta}^{\tilde{N}},\alpha)$ for any α. By the mean value theorem,

$$d = \sum_{j=1}^{m+1} s_{m+1,j} \frac{dq_j}{d\alpha},$$

where the derivatives are all evaluated at some α', $\alpha < \alpha' < \alpha^*$. Let S'_m be the matrix with elements s_{ij}, $i, j = 1, \ldots, m$, evaluated at α'. Then we can write

$$S'_{m+1} \frac{d\mathbf{q}^N}{d\alpha} = \begin{pmatrix} \mathbf{0} \\ d \end{pmatrix}.$$

Let S^*_m be the matrix with elements s_{ij}, $i, j = 1, \ldots, m$, evaluated at α^*. By hypothesis, S^*_m is non-singular, and therefore, for α' sufficiently close to α^*, S'_m is non-singular, all m. By Cramer's rule,

$$\frac{dq_{m+1}}{d\alpha} = \frac{d \det S'_m}{\det S'_{m+1}}.$$

Since $q_{m+1} = \alpha/(1 - \alpha)$, $dq_{m+1}/d\alpha > 0$. It has already been shown that $d > 0$; therefore $\det S'_m$ and $\det S'_{m+1}$ have the same sign. As α approaches α^*, α' approaches α^* and S'_m approaches S^*_m, each m. Since $\det S^*_m \neq 0$, it must be that $\det S^*_m$ and $\det S^*_{m+1}$ have the same non-zero sign. This holds for all m, so that $\det S^*_m$ has the same sign for all m.

To complete the proof it suffices to show that $\det S^*_1 = s_{11} > 0$, when s_{11} is evaluated at $\alpha = \alpha^*$ and $m = 0$ in the above argument. Then, as before, $s_1(\alpha) = s_1(\alpha p^*_1,h) < 0$ for $\alpha < \alpha^*$; if $s_{11} \neq 0$, it must be that $s_{11} > 0$.

It has now been shown that all the principal minors of $J(\mathbf{p}^*)$ have positive determinants; that is, $J(\mathbf{p}^*)$ is Hicksian by D.9.2 and, therefore, has GP by Lemma 9.2.

6. The Hicksian Economy

Consider an economy with only one household and let $\mathbf{p}^*$ be an equilibrium for that economy and $\mathbf{p}$ any other price vector. By W and the definition of an equilibrium, we have

$$\mathbf{ps(p^*)} \geq \mathbf{ps(p)}. \tag{5}$$

From the definition of s and the assumption of profit maximization,

$$\mathbf{p[x(p) - x(p^*)]} \geq \mathbf{p[y(p) - y(p^*)]}$$
$$\geq 0.$$

By the assumption that the weak axiom of revealed preference (WAR) holds for the household (see Corollary 4.6), it must be that

$$\mathbf{p^*}[x(\mathbf{p}) - x(p^*)] \geq 0,$$

whence again by the maximization of profits

$$\mathbf{p^*s(p^*)} \geq \mathbf{p^*s(p)}. \tag{6}$$

Since F (A.2.1) has been postulated, it must be that either $\mathbf{x(p)}$ costs strictly more at $\mathbf{p^*}$ than does $\mathbf{x(p^*)}$ or profits are strictly greater at $\mathbf{p^*}$ when $\mathbf{y(p^*)}$ is produced than when $\mathbf{y(p)}$ or both are produced. If not, there would be more than one supply or demand vector that satisfies agents at $\mathbf{p^*}$ and so not F. Hence the inequality in (6) is strict, and

$$\mathbf{p^*s(p)} < 0.$$

This is true for all $\mathbf{p} \neq \mathbf{p^*}$, and since $\mathbf{p^*}$ is non-negative, it follows that for all such $\mathbf{p}$ it is impossible that $\mathbf{s(p)} \geq \mathbf{0}$. Hence $\mathbf{p^*}$ is the unique equilibrium of this economy.

THEOREM 4. A one-household economy has a unique equilibrium.

Before we discuss the question of why this result is of some interest, it will be instructive to see whether it could be established by means of T.9.1 or T.9.2. For this purpose, consider the price vectors $\mathbf{P}$, where we have set $P_n = 1$. This supposes that N holds, a point to which we return. Also, we write $N(E)$ as the set of $\mathbf{P}$ for which $|\mathbf{P} - \mathbf{P^*}| \leq \epsilon$, where ϵ is positive and sufficiently small. Since $\mathbf{ps(p)} = 0$, we have, from (6), $(\mathbf{P} - \mathbf{P^*})\mathbf{s(P)} > 0$, so for $\mathbf{P}$ in E, up to terms of higher order,

$$(\mathbf{P} - \mathbf{P^*})\mathbf{s(P)} \approx (\mathbf{P} - \mathbf{P^*})\mathbf{s(P^*)} + (\mathbf{P} - \mathbf{P^*})J(\mathbf{P^*})(\mathbf{P} - \mathbf{P^*})' > 0. \tag{7}$$

Now, if $\mathbf{P^*}$ is strictly positive, the first term on the right-hand side of (6) is zero. Since (7) holds for all $\mathbf{P}$ in $N(E)$, it must be that $J(\mathbf{P^*})$

has GP. Suppose not; in other words, suppose there is a non-negative, non-zero vector, $\mathbf{v}$, and a diagonal matrix, T, with $t_{ii} = \pm 1$ such that $TJ(\mathbf{p}^*)T\mathbf{v} \leq \mathbf{0}$, whence $\mathbf{v}'TJ(\mathbf{p}^*)Tv \leq 0$. Clearly, there is some $\mathbf{P}$ in E such that for $k > 0$ and sufficiently small, we have $(\mathbf{P} - \mathbf{P}^*) = kT\mathbf{v}'$, and thus (7) is violated. Thus, if any equilibrium of the one-household economy must have strictly positive prices, A.9.3′ holds and we may use it to establish uniqueness. Also, of course, N causes no difficulty. If, however, $\mathbf{P}^*$ semi-positive is possible then we cannot establish that $J(\mathbf{P}^*)$ has GP and this method of proof fails us. Of course, if we postulate non-satiability of every good, an upper bound on stocks of goods and on the amount of any one good that can be produced, then we can exclude equilibria with some zero prices. Not only is that an assumption we do not need for T.9.4, but also the method of proof we employed to establish this theorem is considerably more direct than the alternative route via T.9.2 and does not require D. For this case, the work of the earlier sections was unnecessary.

It is now time that we inquired why this case should command our interest.

Intuition suggests that an economy in which all individuals are alike in some sense, will behave "as if" there were only one individual (with his space of possible choices suitably enlarged). If this is so, then the sense in which the households are alike is easy to deduce. Firstly, at any $\mathbf{p}$, the distribution of wealth between households must have no effect on the aggregate excess-demand (-supply) vector. Secondly, the redistribution effect of a price change must have no effect on the economy's excess-demand vector. Evidently, if the first requirement is met, then so is the second. Moreover, it is not hard to see that both requirements can be met only if starting from any arbitrary distribution of wealth among households and taking some wealth away from one of them and giving it to any other causes the loser to take decisions in the market that are opposite in sign and of the same absolute magnitude to the decisions taken by the gainers. Now we shall make this precise.

To do so it will be convenient to take the demand vector of a household as having no negative components. We do this by letting the household be endowed with maximum quantities of various kinds of leisure and by taking it to demand various kinds of leisure. The difference between the leisure of a kind demanded and the maximum there is is the supply of a service (Section 4.1). We shall not change notation to take account of this; however, $\mathbf{x}_h$ is now non-negative, and $\bar{\mathbf{x}}_h$ includes the leisure endowment. We also write $M_h = \mathbf{p}\bar{\mathbf{x}}_h + d_h\mathbf{p}\mathbf{y}$, the "wealth of h," and $\mathbf{x}_h = \mathbf{x}_h(\mathbf{p},M_h)$.

DEFINITION 4. The economy will be said to be *Hicksian* if

(a) for all $k > 0$ and all h, $\mathbf{x}_h(\mathbf{p},M_h) = (1/k)\mathbf{x}_h(\mathbf{p},kM_h)$, and
(b) if $\mathbf{x}'_h = \mathbf{x}_h/M_h = \mathbf{x}_h(\mathbf{p},1)$, $M_h > 0$, then $\mathbf{x}'_h$ is the same for all h (with $M_h > 0$).

The first part of this assumption postulates that all demands are linear and homogeneous in wealth (all households have linear Engel curves through the origin), while the second part requires the amount of anything demanded per unit wealth to be the same for all households (the Engel curves of households are parallel).

THEOREM 5. The Hicksian economy behaves as if there is only one household.

Proof. By D.9.4(a),

$$\sum_h \mathbf{x}'_h(\mathbf{p},1)M_h = \mathbf{x}(\mathbf{p}, M_1, \ldots, M_H),$$

the economy's demand. By D.9.4(b), if, say $M_h > 0$, this may be written as

$$\mathbf{x}'_H(\mathbf{p},1) \sum_h M_h,$$

and so $\mathbf{x}$ may be written as

$$\mathbf{x}\left(\mathbf{p}, \sum_h M_h\right),$$

that is, as depending only on total wealth and not on its distribution between households. Moreover, we may analyze the economy as if only household H exists.

We can show also that the Hicksian economy is the only one for which T.9.5 holds—the conditional of that theorem is both necessary and sufficient (Gorman [1953], Nataf [1953]). It is apparent that the restrictions involved are pretty stringent. It is hard to believe not only that all households are alike in this sense, but also that all Engel curves pass through the origin so that as an individual gets poorer and poorer he nonetheless continues to mix holidays, say, in the same ratio to bread, as he did when he was richer. Yet it ought to be recalled that all theorizing that makes use of community indifference curves must be based on the supposition that the economy is Hicksian and that there is a good deal of such theorizing. In any event, we have proved

Corollary 5. The Hicksian economy has a unique equilibrium.

We must now inquire, not unnaturally, whether we cannot find some more appealing economies with this property.

7. Gross Substitutes

We know from elementary theory of demand that, for a given household, the consequences of a given price change may be split into an "income" effect and a "substitution" effect (see T.4.10). If the jth price changes and the substitution term for the ith good is positive, then the two goods i and j are, in the literature, said to be substitutes. In this section we extend this notion to the whole excess-demand (-supply) function for i, that is to say we include income effects as well as supply effects in a classification of commodities.

DEFINITION 5 (GS). Two goods, i and j, $i \neq j$, are said to be *gross substitutes* at $\mathbf{p}$ when we have $s_{ij}(\mathbf{p}) < 0$ whenever $\mathbf{s}(\mathbf{p})$ is defined. (We may write equivalently: If $\mathbf{z}(\mathbf{p})$ is defined, then $z_{ij}(\mathbf{p}) > 0$.)

For the moment, we shall postpone a consideration of the realism of supposing all goods to be GS at some or at all $\mathbf{p}$ and proceed to establish a number of propositions about such an economy. In what follows we shall write $\mathbf{p}(i)$ as the vector $\mathbf{p}$ with zero in the ith place.

THEOREM 6. If all goods are GS at $\mathbf{p}$ and, for some i, $p_i = 0$, then $\mathbf{s}(\mathbf{p})$ is not defined at $\mathbf{p}$ and

$$\sum_j s_j(\mathbf{p}) = -\infty.$$

Proof. Suppose the theorem false so that, say, $\mathbf{p}(i) = \mathbf{p}$, $\mathbf{s}(\mathbf{p})$ defined. By H, for $k > 1$, $s_i[\mathbf{p}(i)] = s_i[k\mathbf{p}(i)]$, while for k close to 1, GS implies $s_i[\mathbf{p}(i)] < s_i[k\mathbf{p}(i)]$. This last inequality follows from the fact that at $k\mathbf{p}(i)$ all prices other than the ith are no lower than, and the ith is the same as, at $\mathbf{p}(i)$, and at least one price is higher.

Since we now have a contradiction, we conclude $\mathbf{s}(\mathbf{p})$ is not defined. But then, by C′ (A.2.6),

$$\sum_j s_j(\mathbf{p}) = -\infty.$$

Corollary 6. Let $\mathbf{p}^*$ be an equilibrium. Then, if all goods are GS at $\mathbf{p}^*$, it must be that $\mathbf{p}^* \gg \mathbf{0}$.

Corollary 6′. If, for all $\mathbf{p} \in S_n$, all goods are GS, then N holds.

THEOREM 7. If all goods are GS for every $\mathbf{p} \in E$ and if N holds, then E has only one member (equilibrium is unique).

Proof. Let $\mathbf{p}^* \in E$. Then we know that $\mathbf{p}^* \gg \mathbf{0}$. Since N holds, by T.9.6, we may use the normalized price vector $\mathbf{P}^*$, where $p_n^* = 1$. By H and GS,

$$\sum_{j \neq n} s_{ij}(\mathbf{P}^*)P_j^* = -s_{in}(\mathbf{P}^*) > 0 \qquad i = 1, \ldots, n-1. \tag{8}$$

Since $s_{ij}(\mathbf{P}) < 0$, $j \neq i$, $s_{ii}(\mathbf{P}^*) > 0$, it must be that $J(\mathbf{P}^*)$ has GP at $\mathbf{P}^*$. If not, there is some $\mathbf{v} > \mathbf{0}$ with $TJ(\mathbf{P}^*)T\mathbf{v} \leq \mathbf{0}$. Since $\mathbf{P}^* \gg \mathbf{0}$, we may define a vector $\mathbf{w}$, with components

$$w_i = \frac{v_i}{P_i^*},$$

and define $J(\mathbf{P}^*)$ as the matrix with elements $s_{ij}(\mathbf{P}^*)P_j^*$. Certainly, $TJ(\mathbf{P}^*)T\mathbf{w} \leq \mathbf{0}$, $\mathbf{w} > \mathbf{0}$. Then let

$$w_k = \max_j w_j.$$

Since $t_{kk}t_{jj} = +1$ or -1, for each j, it is easily verified that $t_{kk}^2 w_k \geq t_{kk}t_{jj}w_j$, all j. By use of GS, the kth component of $TJ(P^*)T\mathbf{w}$ satisfies the condition

$$\begin{aligned}\sum_{j \neq n} t_{kk}s_{kj}(\mathbf{P}^*)P_j^* t_{jj}w_j &= t_{kk}^2 s_{kk}(\mathbf{P}^*)P_k^* w_k + \sum_{\substack{j \neq n \\ j \neq k}} t_{kk}s_{kj}(\mathbf{P}^*)P_j^* t_{jj}w_j \\ &\geq s_{kk}(\mathbf{P}^*)P_k^* w_k + \sum_{\substack{j \neq n \\ j \neq k}} s_{kj}(\mathbf{P}^*)P_j^* w_k \\ &= \left(\sum_{j \neq n} s_{kj}(\mathbf{P}^*)P_j^*\right) w_k > 0,\end{aligned}$$

by (8), which contradicts $TJ(\mathbf{P}^*)T\mathbf{w} \leq \mathbf{0}$. Hence, $J(\mathbf{P}^*)$ does have GP, and T.9.2 proves the theorem.

Corollary 7. If all goods are GS for all $\mathbf{p} \in S_n$, then equilibrium is unique.

Of course, the proof of this corollary is trivial in the light of the theorem and Corollary 6′, but there are two available methods of establishing this result that make no appeal to T.9.2 and that it will be instructive to consider.

Suppose that $\mathbf{P}^*$ is an equilibrium and that $\mathbf{P} > \mathbf{0}$ is any different price vector. Let $v_i = P_i/P_i^*$, and suppose, say,

$$v_k = \max_j v_j = m.$$

Then, by H and the fact that $\mathbf{P}^*$ is an equilibrium, we have $0 = s_k(\mathbf{P}^*) = s_k(m\mathbf{P}^*)$. Now we can construct a sequence of price vectors, starting at $m\mathbf{P}^*$ and ending at $\mathbf{P}$, such that at each step of the sequence, the kth price remains unchanged while at least some other price is lowered and none is raised. By GS, then, s_k must increase with every step in the sequence and, in particular, $s_k(\mathbf{P}) > 0$. Since $\mathbf{P} \gg \mathbf{0}$, it follows that $\mathbf{P}$ cannot be an equilibrium. Since every equilibrium price vector must be strictly positive, the corollary follows at once. We note that in this elementary proof we have established, incidentally, a proposition concerning the excess supply of the good whose price rose in the greatest proportion between $\mathbf{P}^*$ and $\mathbf{P}$. This will be useful in another part of the book and, accordingly, we shall formally record it here.

THEOREM 8. Let $\mathbf{P} > \mathbf{0}$ and $\mathbf{P}' \gg \mathbf{0}$ be two unequal price vectors, v_i the ratio of the ith element of $\mathbf{P}$ to the ith element of $\mathbf{P}'$. Let $\max v_i = v_k$, $\min v_i = v_h$. Then, if for all $\mathbf{P}$, all goods are GS, $s_k(\mathbf{P}) > s_k(\mathbf{P}')$, $s_h(\mathbf{P}) < s_h(\mathbf{P})$.

The second inequality of this theorem is established in exactly the same manner as the first.

T.9.8 demonstrates in a striking way that GS certainly implies GP. Suppose there is a change in prices relative to a numeraire; if any have risen relative to the numeraire, the excess supply of the good with the largest price rise must have increased, while if any have fallen relative to the numeraire, the good whose price has fallen most must have had a decrease in excess supply. Thus, in any case, there is at least one commodity whose price has changed in the same direction as its excess supply, which is the essential property of GP, according to the Remark to D.9.1. When GS holds, we have much more specific information as to which excess supply must have risen or fallen.

The other alternative proof of Corollary 2 is not quite so simple, but it is worth having for its own sake and for its use in other parts of general equilibrium analysis. We shall prove the following, rather striking result.

THEOREM 9. If all goods are GS for all **p**, then if $\mathbf{p}^*$ is an equilibrium, $\mathbf{p}^*\mathbf{s}(\mathbf{p}) < 0$, for all $\mathbf{p} \neq \mathbf{p}^* \in S_n$.

It is clear that a proof of this theorem is also a proof of Corollary 2: Indeed, the conclusion to be proved is the same as the one we established for the economy with one household.

Proof. If we can establish that the expression $\mathbf{p}^*\mathbf{s}(\mathbf{p})$ is maximized uniquely at $\mathbf{p}^*$, then since by W, $\mathbf{p}^*\mathbf{s}(\mathbf{p}^*) = 0$ the theorem will have been proved.

Since **p** and $\mathbf{s}(\mathbf{p})$ are bounded above and C′, we know that a maximum for $\mathbf{p}^*\mathbf{s}(\mathbf{p})$ exists. Since, by T.9.6, $p_i = 0$ implies $\mathbf{s}(\mathbf{P})$ undefined and, therefore,

$$\sum_j s_i(\mathbf{p}) = -\infty,$$

the maximum must be an interior one, so that if it is attained at **p**,

$$\sum_j p_j^* s_{jk}(\mathbf{p}) = 0 \qquad k = 1, \ldots, n. \tag{9}$$

But by W and by virtue of $\mathbf{p}^* \gg 0$, we know that, for $\mathbf{p} = \mathbf{p}^*$,

$$\frac{\partial[\mathbf{ps}(\mathbf{p})]}{\partial p_k} = 0 = \sum_i p_i^* s_{ik}(\mathbf{p}^*),$$

since $s_k(\mathbf{p}^*) = 0$, so that (9) must hold at $\mathbf{p} = \mathbf{p}^*$. We show that it can hold for no other **p**.

If $\mathbf{p} \neq \mathbf{p}^*$ satisfies (9), let, say,

$$\frac{p_r}{p_r^*} = \max_j \frac{p_j}{p_j^*} = h.$$

By T.9.8, $s_r(\mathbf{p}) > 0$ since $s_r(\mathbf{p}^*) = 0$. By W,

$$\frac{\partial}{\partial p_r}(\mathbf{ps}(\mathbf{p})) = \sum_j p_j s_{jr}(\mathbf{p}) + s_r(\mathbf{p}) = 0$$

and so

$$\sum_j p_j s_{jr}(\mathbf{p}) < 0.$$

But then

$$0 = h \sum_j p_j^* s_{jr}(\mathbf{p}) = p_r s_{rr}(\mathbf{p}) + h \sum_{j \neq r} p_j^* s_{jr}(\mathbf{p}) < \sum_j p_j s_{jr}(\mathbf{p}) < 0,$$

which is impossible. Therefore, (9) is satisfied only at $\mathbf{p} = \mathbf{p}^*$. Since an interior maximum exists, the theorem is proved.

The result we have just established is a suitable point of departure for a consideration of the economics of the GS assumption in both its global (GS for all $\mathbf{p}$) and its local (GS for all $\mathbf{p} \in E$) forms.

The first point to emphasize is that the fact that WAR can be shown to hold in a comparison of any two price situations, of which one is an equilibrium, does not mean that this is true also for comparisons between any two arbitrarily chosen price situations. This is a fundamental difference between the Hicksian and the global GS case. In the former, non-intersecting community indifference surfaces exist; in the latter they generally do not. For instance, the reader may verify that if the utility functions of households are of the form

$$U_h = \prod_j x_{hj}^{\alpha_{hj}} \qquad \alpha_{hj} > 0, \text{ all } j \qquad \sum_j \alpha_{hj} = 1$$

then $\partial x_j / \partial p_i > 0$, all $j \neq i$, however much the constants α_{hj} may differ for different h. For instance, in a pure-exchange economy (an economy without production), this would certainly be enough to ensure global GS. It is true that in this example the Engel curves are linear, but they are not parallel for different households.

On the other hand, if we calculate the substitution terms for this example, we find that they are all positive for $i \neq j$, and this is a clue to a judgment as to the restrictiveness of the GS postulate. In general, elementary theory (see T.4.10) gives $\partial x_{hj} / \partial p_i$ by the expression below:

$$\frac{\partial x_{hj}}{\partial p_i} = \lambda_{ji}^h + (\bar{x}_{hi} - x_{hi}) r_j^h,$$

where λ_{ji}^h is the substitution term and r_j^h is household h's marginal propensity to buy good j. Omitting superscripts to denote summation over h gives

$$\frac{\partial x_j}{\partial p_i} = \lambda_{ji} + \sum_h (\bar{x}_{hi} - x_{hi}) r_j^h. \tag{10}$$

Now, if $\lambda_{ji} < 0$, the burden of ensuring (10) to be positive is thrown onto the income term. But this depends partly on the disparity in the marginal propensities r_j^h between households, and partly on the distribution of goods between households. For a given $\mathbf{p}$, there are many distributions of $\bar{\mathbf{x}}$ between households that leave $\mathbf{p}\bar{\mathbf{x}}_h$ the same for all h and so leave $\mathbf{x}_h$ unchanged. We can readily construct examples where (10) changes sign over such distributions. Nor is it clear what would be most helpful to postulate about the marginal propensities. If they are the same for all h and $\mathbf{p}$ is an equilibrium with $p_i > 0$, the income term evidently disappears altogether and GS will not hold. If the marginal propensities differ widely, then we will be able to find distributions of $\bar{\mathbf{x}}$ that lead (10) to change sign. If we then say that GS should only be postulated for a particular distribution, then the range of interesting application is rather restricted. To say that we also require $\lambda_{ji} > 0$, all $j \neq i$, would be very unrealistic because it is easy to think of examples of goods (petrol and motoring); for which we feel pretty sure that the assumption will be violated.

Another unpalatable implication of GS in the absence of production is that the elasticity of net demand for every good is less than -1. For if, say, a rise in the price of i raises the demand for every good other than i, then it must be that the total expenditure on good i diminishes. Lastly, there is the objection that the assumption forces us to conclude that demands go to infinity as the price of any good goes to zero.

When account is taken of production, the assumption of GS does not become any more convincing. Even if differentiability is assumed, there is no good reason to suppose that we may take $\partial y_j/\partial p_i < 0$ for $i \neq j$. Certainly, in the absence of joint production, a *ceteris paribus* rise, say, in p_i, will cause those producers who use i as an input to reduce (or not increase) their use of that input, so that we may argue that the net supply of good j of all producers, other than the ith, taken together, will not increase. However, the demand for good j by the producers of good i may increase sufficiently to cause an increase in the total net supply of good j. Indeed, there are no satisfactory assumptions, even in the absence of joint production, that imply all goods are gross substitutes in production alone. Thus, the main burden of the GS postulate falls on household demands.

To hypothesize, local GS only is weaker, largely because we require rather less of the income term in (10); at an equilibrium, since it is strictly positive, the sum of the terms multiplying r_j^h is zero. Certainly, then, if $\lambda_{ji} > 0, j \neq i$, and the covariance of r_j^h and $(\bar{x}_{hi} - x_{hi})$ is small, local GS seems reasonable. The smallness of the covariance in question could surely be defended also (Section 12.5), but once again we require $\lambda_{ji} > 0$ and that remains an unhappy postulate. Yet if production considerations are introduced again, we might feel less certain that local GS makes unreasonable demands on our credulity. Taking one thing with another, though, there seems plenty of reason for searching for more agreeable sufficient conditions for uniqueness than are provided by GS.

8. Weak Gross Substitutes

A slight weakening of GS is obtained by dropping the demand that, for all $j \neq i$, we have $s_{ij} < 0$ and replacing it with the requirement that all these terms are non-positive. As we shall see, even this slight relaxation of the conditions has considerable consequences for the uniqueness problem. We introduce the following nomenclature.

DEFINITION 6 (WGS). Two goods i and j, $i \neq j$, are said to be *weak gross substitutes* at $\mathbf{p}$ if $s_{ij}(\mathbf{p}) \leq 0$ when $\mathbf{s}(\mathbf{p})$ is defined.

In view of our preceding discussion, there is no need to emphasize that the increase in generality obtained by replacing GS by WGS is by no means great. On the principle of Occam's razor, however, we must certainly see whether this relaxation, however slight, still allows us to deduce some of the main results of the previous section.

If we are willing to add one more postulate to that of WGS, then indeed it will not be hard to show that all the theorems proved in the previous section will continue to hold for this new economy. We introduce this extra assumption in the following.

DEFINITION 7. The economy will be called *connected* at $\mathbf{p}$ if there is no set of goods I such that $s_{ij}(\mathbf{p}) = 0$ for all $i \in I, j \notin I$.

Suppose now that an economy has WGS and is connected at $\mathbf{p}^*$, an equilibrium. Then it can be left to the reader[1] to show that we can

[1] By connectedness, $s_{ij}(\mathbf{p}^*(i)) < 0$, some $j \neq i$, otherwise $s_{ij} = 0$ for $i \in I = \{i\}, j \notin I$. Suppose this is so only for $j = h$. Then, if $s_i(\mathbf{p}^*(i)) = s_i(\mathbf{k}(\mathbf{p}^*(i)))$, it must be that $p_h^* = 0$. Let $\mathbf{p}^*(i,h)$ be the vector with $p_i^* = p_h^* = 0$ and apply the same argument to $s_h(\mathbf{p}^*(i,h)) = s_h(k\mathbf{p}^*(i,h))$. Note that $s_{hj} < 0$, some $j \neq i,h$, for else we contradict connectedness. Proceeding in this way, we finish up with either $\mathbf{p}^* = \mathbf{0}$ or $s_j = -\infty$, some j.

use the same method of proof as in T.9.5 to establish that $\mathbf{p}^* \gg \mathbf{0}$. Next, consider $J(\mathbf{P}^*)$. By connectedness, it must be that $s_{in}(\mathbf{p}) \neq 0$, some i. Hence, all the right-hand sides in (8) are non-negative and at least one is positive. Proceeding as in the proof of T.9.7, we now have

$$\sum_{j \neq n} s_{kj}(\mathbf{P}^*)P_j^* w_j \geq w_k \left(\sum_{j \neq n} s_{kj}(\mathbf{P}^*)P_j^* \right) \geq 0.$$

If the first or second inequality is strict, there is nothing more to do, and we proceed as before. The first inequality fails to be strict only if, for all j for which $s_{kj}(\mathbf{P}^*) < 0$, we have $w_j = w_k$. Suppose, then, that $s_{kh}(\mathbf{P}^*) < 0$ and $w_h = w_k$. But then

$$\sum_{j \neq n} s_{hj}(\mathbf{P}^*)P_j^* w_j \geq w_h \left(\sum_{j \neq n} s_{hj}(\mathbf{P}^*)P_j^* \right) \geq 0.$$

Once again, if any inequality is strict, we have nothing more to do. Moreover, if the first inequality fails to be strict, then, by connectedness, there must be $j \neq k,h$ such that $s_{hj}(\mathbf{P}^*) < 0$ and $w_j = w_k$. Proceeding in this way, either all w's are equal—in which case, in view of $s_{in}(\mathbf{P}^*) < 0$, some i, the second inequality must be strict for some k—or the w's are not all equal and the first inequality must be strict for some k. Hence $J(\mathbf{P}^*)$ has GP. It then follows also that with WGS replacing GS in Corollary 6 and by adding the connectedness assumption, the conclusion of the corollary will continue to hold.

Next consider T.9.8 with WGS and connectedness instead of GS. Using the same notation as employed in the proof of that theorem, we note that $s_k(\mathbf{P})$ can only now fail to be positive, if for all j for which $s_{kj}(\mathbf{P}) < 0$, we have $v_k = v_j$. An argument exactly analogous to the one we have just used in discussing T.9.7 with the new assumptions shows that there must be some h such that $v_h = v_k$ and $s_h(\mathbf{P}) > 0$. Hence one of the goods whose price has risen by no smaller proportion from its equilibrium value than has that of any other good, must now be in excess supply. Since this is the result we need for the last crucial inequality employed in the proof of T.9.9, it follows that WGS and connectedness are sufficient to give $\mathbf{P}^*\mathbf{s}(\mathbf{P}) < 0$ all $\mathbf{P} \neq \mathbf{P}^*$.

It should be clear that the assumption that the economy is connected plays a considerable role in preserving all the results of GS for the case of WGS. Since a GS economy is certainly connected,

WGS and connectedness are weaker than GS, and this is some improvement. Now we must see how far we can go without connectedness.

THEOREM 10. Suppose for some $\mathbf{p}(i)$, $s_i(\mathbf{p}(i)) > 0$. Then $s_i(\mathbf{p}) > 0$ all $\mathbf{p} \in S$. (Recall that $\mathbf{p}(i)$ is the vector $\mathbf{p}$ with zero in the ith place.)

Proof. (a) By WGS and H, $s_{ii}(\mathbf{p}) \geq 0$, all $\mathbf{p} \in S$, and so

$$s_i(\mathbf{p}) \geq s_i(\mathbf{p}(i))$$

Therefore, we need to prove only that $s_i(\mathbf{p}(i)) > 0$, some $\mathbf{p}(i)$, implies $s_i(\mathbf{p}(i)) > 0$ all $\mathbf{p}(i) \in S$.

(b) If the theorem is false, there is, by C′, some $\mathbf{p}'(i)$ such that $s_i(\mathbf{p}'(i)) = 0$. Define $\mathbf{p}''(i)$ so that

$$p_j''(i) = \min[p_j(i), p_j'(i)].$$

Then, by WGS,

$$s_i(\mathbf{p}''(i)) \geq s_i(\mathbf{p}(i)) > 0. \tag{11}$$

Now let $\mathbf{p}(\alpha) = (1 - \alpha)\mathbf{p}''(i) + \alpha\mathbf{p}'(i)$, $0 \leq \alpha \leq 1$. By (11) and C′,

$$s_i(\mathbf{p}(\alpha)) > 0 \qquad \text{for } \alpha > 0 \text{ and sufficiently small.} \tag{12}$$

By construction, for $\alpha > 0$, $p_j(\alpha) > 0$ if and only if $p_j'(i) > 0$. For all such j, $s_{ij}(\mathbf{p}(\alpha)) = 0$. Otherwise, by WGS, $s_{ij}(\mathbf{p}(\alpha)) < 0$; then $s_i(\mathbf{p}(\alpha)) > s_i(k\mathbf{p}(\alpha))$, for $k > 1$ and sufficiently small, contradicting H. (Note that, by (12), $s_i(\mathbf{p}(\alpha)) = -\infty$ is impossible.) Then, for all j, either $s_{ij}(\mathbf{p}(\alpha)) = 0$ or $p_j(\alpha)$ is constant at 0, so that $s_i(\mathbf{p}(\alpha))$ is constant. Since $\mathbf{p}'(i) = \mathbf{p}(1)$,

$$s_i(\mathbf{p}(\alpha)) = s_i(\mathbf{p}'(i)) = 0 \qquad \text{all } \alpha > 0,$$

in contradiction to (12).

Corollary 10. Suppose that for some $\mathbf{p}'(i)$, $s_i[\mathbf{p}'(i)] = 0$. Then $s_i[\mathbf{p}(i)] = 0$ for all $\mathbf{p}(i)$.

Proof. If not, then there must be some $\mathbf{p}(i)$ such that $s_i[\mathbf{p}(i)] < 0$, for by T.9.10, there cannot be any $\mathbf{p}(i)$ such that $s_i[\mathbf{p}(i)] > 0$. Let

$$p_j''(i) = \min[p_j'(i), p_j(i)].$$

Then, by WGS, $s_i[\mathbf{p}''(i)] \geq 0$. By T.9.10, the inequality is not possible and so

$$0 = s_i[\mathbf{p}''(i)] > s_i[\mathbf{p}(i)].$$

Let $\mathbf{p}(\alpha) = (1 - \alpha)\mathbf{p}''(i) + \alpha\mathbf{p}(i)$. Then, for $\alpha > 0$ and small enough,

$$s_i[\mathbf{p}(\alpha)] > s_i[\mathbf{p}(i)],$$

and $p_j(\alpha) > 0$ if and only if $p_j(i) > 0$. Then, by the same argument as in T.9.10, we obtain $s_i[\mathbf{p}(1)] = s_i[\mathbf{p}(i)] > s_i[\mathbf{p}(i)]$, a contradiction.

The theorem and corollary we have just established must take the place of T.9.6 for the GS case. We see that we can no longer claim that $s_i(\mathbf{p}(i))$ is undefined, so we can no longer establish $\mathbf{p}^* \gg \mathbf{0}$. If a market reaches an equilibrium at a zero price, however, then it can never be in excess demand at any set of prices and this is a property of the situation that we shall exploit in the following:

THEOREM 11. Let $\mathbf{p}^* \in E$, the set of equilibrium price vectors. Then, if all goods are WGS at all $\mathbf{p}$, $\mathbf{p}^*\mathbf{s}(\mathbf{p}) < 0$, for all $\mathbf{p}$ not in E.

Before embarking on a proof of this theorem we should note that it is a good deal weaker than T.9.9; if true, it clearly does not enable us to deduce that E has a single member only. Nonetheless, we shall find that the result will be useful in characterizing the equilibrium set E. It will prove useful in later chapters as well.

Proof. (a) Let $R = \{i \mid p_i^* > 0\}$ and $R' = \{i \mid p_i^* = 0\}$. Let the subscript R to a vector denote that it has components in R and similarly for a subscript R'. Then, by WGS,

$$\mathbf{s}_R(\mathbf{p}_R,\mathbf{p}_{R'}) \leq \mathbf{s}_R(\mathbf{p}_R,\mathbf{0}).$$

Hence, if we can show that for all $(\mathbf{p}_R,\mathbf{0})$ not in E, $\mathbf{p}_R^*\mathbf{s}_R(\mathbf{p}_R,\mathbf{0}) < 0$, we shall have proved the theorem.

(b) If $i \in R$, $p_i = 0$, then

$$s_i(\mathbf{p}_R,\mathbf{0}) \leq 0.$$

Suppose not, that is, for some such i, $s_i(\mathbf{p}_R,\mathbf{0}) > 0$. Then, by T.9.9, $s_i(\mathbf{p}_R^*,\mathbf{0}) > 0$. But $p_i^* > 0$, and so we contradict $(\mathbf{p}_R^*,\mathbf{0}) \in E$.

(c) We propose to show that $\mathbf{p}^*\mathbf{s}(\mathbf{p})$ cannot reach a maximum at any $\mathbf{p}$ not in E. By the argument of (a), we note that the maximum must occur at some $(\mathbf{p}_R,\mathbf{0})$, where we may take $\mathbf{p}_R > \mathbf{0}$, and so a necessary condition for a maximum is

$$\sum_{j \in R} p_j^* s_{jk}(\mathbf{p}_R,\mathbf{0}) \geq 0, \qquad \text{all } k \in R. \tag{13}$$

Clearly (13) holds for $\mathbf{p}_R = \mathbf{p}_R^*$, and we must show that it cannot hold for any other $\mathbf{p}_R$.

Suppose (13) holds for $\mathbf{p}_R \neq \mathbf{p}_R^*$, and that the first r elements of $\mathbf{p}_R$ are zero. (Of course, r may be zero, i.e., no element of $\mathbf{p}_R$ is zero; the numbering is inessential.) Let $\mathbf{p}_R^*(r)$ be the vector $\mathbf{p}_R^*$ with its first r elements set equal to zero. Also let $k_i = p_i/p_i^*$ and number goods so that

$$k_{r+1} \geq k_{r+2} \geq \cdots \geq k_m,$$

where we take R as containing all $i \leq m$.

Then, by WGS, certainly

$$s_{r+1}(\mathbf{p}_R^*,\mathbf{0}) \leq s_{r+1}(\mathbf{p}_R^*(r),\mathbf{0})), \tag{14}$$

since in $\mathbf{p}_R^*(r)$ the prices of goods $i \leq r$ are lower than they are in $\mathbf{p}_R^*$ and no price is higher. By H,

$$s_{r+1}(\mathbf{p}_R^*(r),\mathbf{0}) = s_{r+1}(k_{r+1}\mathbf{p}_R^*(r),\mathbf{0}). \tag{15}$$

By the definition of k_{r+1}, it must be that $(r + 1)$th component of $k_{r+1}\mathbf{p}_R^*(r)$ is equal to p_{r+1}, while no component of $\mathbf{p}_R$ can exceed the corresponding component of $k_{r+1}\mathbf{p}_R^*(r)$. But by WGS,

$$s_{r+1}(k_{r+1}\mathbf{p}_R^*(r),\mathbf{0}) \leq s_{r+1}(\mathbf{p}_R,\mathbf{0}), \tag{16}$$

and so by (14), (15), and (16),

$$s_{r+1}(\mathbf{p}_R^*,\mathbf{0}) \leq s_{r+1}(\mathbf{p}_R,\mathbf{0}). \tag{17}$$

If in (17) the inequality is strict, we may argue as follows: Differentiating W with respect to p_{r+1} gives

$$\sum_{j \in R} p_j s_{j,r+1}(\mathbf{p}_R,\mathbf{0}) = -s_{r+1}(\mathbf{p}_R,\mathbf{0}). \tag{18}$$

From (17) and the fact that $(\mathbf{p}_R^*,\mathbf{0})$ is an equilibrium with $p_{r+1}^* > 0$, we deduce that the right-hand side of (18) is negative. Yet from the definition of k_{r+1} and WGS,

$$k_{r+1} \sum_{j \in R} p_j^* s_{j,r+1}(\mathbf{p}_R,\mathbf{0}) \leq \sum_{j \in R} p_j s_{j,r+1}(\mathbf{p}_R,\mathbf{0}),$$

and so in view of (18)

$$\sum_{j \in R} p_j^* s_{j,r+1}(\mathbf{p}_R,\mathbf{0}) < 0. \tag{19}$$

Since (19) contradicts (13), $\mathbf{p}^*\mathbf{s}(\mathbf{p})$ cannot attain a maximum at $(\mathbf{p}_R,\mathbf{0})$.

Suppose, then, the inequality in (17) is not strict. If $k_{r+2} = k_{r+1}$, it is easily checked that we can obtain (17) for s_{r+2}. If that inequality were strict, we would again get (19) for "$r + 2$" with the same conclusion. So consider $k_{r+2} < k_{r+1}$. Then every component $k_{r+1}p_i^*$ of $k_{r+1}\mathbf{p}_R^*(r)$, with $i > r + 1$, exceeds p_i. Then, since the inequality in (16) is not strict, it must be true, because of WGS, that $s_{r+1,j}(\mathbf{p}_R,\mathbf{0}) = 0$ for $j > r + 1$. Additionally, by H, $s_{r+1,r+1} = 0$ and we conclude

$$s_{r+1,j}(\mathbf{p}_R,\mathbf{0}) = 0 \qquad \text{all } j \geq r + 1 \quad \text{if } k_{r+1} > k_{r+2}$$

and (17) not strict.

Now, from (18) and the fact that (17) holds with equality, we have

$$\sum_{j \in R} p_r s_{j,r+1}(\mathbf{p}_R,\mathbf{0}) = 0.$$

But $s_{r+1,r+1}(\mathbf{p}_R,\mathbf{0}) = 0$, so by WGS and the fact that $p_j > 0$, all $> r$, it must be that

$$s_{j,r+1} = 0 \qquad \text{all } j > r + 1.$$

Once again (17) must hold with s_{r+2} and k_{r+1} replaced by k_{r+2}. If the inequality is strict for this good, we again deduce (19) for "$r + 2$" and, therefore, (13) cannot hold. If not, we proceed as before to $r + 3$, and so on. If at no stage we obtain a strict inequality in the appropriate form of (17), then it must be that $s_j(\mathbf{p}_R,\mathbf{0}) = 0$ for all $j > r$. But then, since by the argument of (b) $s_j(\mathbf{p}_R,\mathbf{0}) \leq 0$, all $j \leq r$, and since $\mathbf{p}_R^* \gg \mathbf{0}$ and by assumption $(\mathbf{p}_R,\mathbf{0})$ is not an equilibrium, it follows that for some $j \leq r$, $s_j(\mathbf{p}_R,\mathbf{0}) < 0$ and so $\mathbf{p}_R^*\mathbf{s}_R(\mathbf{p}_R,\mathbf{0}) < 0$ and $\mathbf{p}_R^*\mathbf{s}_R(\mathbf{p})$ is not maximized at $(\mathbf{p}_R,\mathbf{0})$. Since $\mathbf{p}_R^*\mathbf{s}_R(\mathbf{p}_R^*,\mathbf{0}) = 0$ clearly cannot be a minimum of $\mathbf{p}_R^*\mathbf{s}_R(\mathbf{p})$, the theorem is proved.

Corollary 11. If all goods are WGS at all $\mathbf{p}$ then the set of equilibrium prices (E) is convex.

Proof. Let $\mathbf{p}^*$ and $\mathbf{p}^{**}$ be two unequal vectors in E and $\mathbf{p}(\alpha) = \alpha\mathbf{p}^* + (1 - \alpha)\mathbf{p}^{**}$: $0 \leq \alpha \leq 1$. If the corollary is false, then for some α in the given range, $\mathbf{p}(\alpha)$ is not in E. Then $\mathbf{p}(\alpha)\mathbf{s}(\mathbf{p}(\alpha)) = (\alpha\mathbf{p}^* + (1 - \alpha)\mathbf{p}^{**})\mathbf{s}(\mathbf{p}(\alpha)) = \alpha\mathbf{p}^*\mathbf{s}(\mathbf{p}(\alpha)) + (1 - \alpha)\mathbf{p}^{**}\mathbf{s}(\mathbf{p}(\alpha)) < 0$ by T.9.11, and we have a contradiction of W. Hence $\mathbf{p}(\alpha) \in E$, for all α in the range.

The results we have established for the WGS case are a good deal weaker than those that were establishable with GS, or WGS with connectedness. Yet for many purposes of economic analysis it is correct to say that the convexity of the equilibrium set is as good as uniqueness, and WAR for all comparisons in which one price belongs to E is as good as WAR for all comparisons in which one price vector is the unique equilibrium one. This will become clear later in this book. The drawback of the WGS assumption, therefore, is not the weakness of its implications for the equilibrium set, but rather the weak appeal of the assumption itself. It is only slightly less restrictive and unappealing than GS and that makes it pretty unpalatable still. There is much incentive to look for a hypothesis that is less disagreeable to common sense.

9. Diagonal Dominance

Suppose that we wished to investigate the consequences of the hypothesis that the excess demand (supply) of each good is "more sensitive" to a change in its own price than it is to a change in the prices of all other goods combined. If this idea is to be made precise, it is clear that careful attention will have to be given to the units in which goods are measured. If we imagine the demand function for a good plotted in a multi-dimensional diagram whose axes are the different prices, the slope of the resulting demand surface in any direction will depend on the units in which we have chosen to measure the various goods. It is, of course, for this reason that we use elasticities to measure the responsiveness of demand to changes in price. In formulating our hypothesis precisely, therefore, we shall wish to put it in the form: There is at $\mathbf{p}$ some way of measuring goods such that for all of them it is true that their excess demands are more sensitive to a change in their own price than they are to a change in other prices combined. We shall also impose a restriction on the sign of the term giving the change in the excess demand for a good when its own price changes.

DEFINITION 8 (DD). The economy is said to have *Diagonal Dominance* at $\mathbf{p}$ with $p_n > 0$ if

(a) $s_{ii}(\mathbf{p}) > 0$, all i,
(b) there is a vector $\mathbf{h}(\mathbf{p}) \gg \mathbf{0}$, such that

$$h_i(\mathbf{p})s_{ii}(\mathbf{p}) > \sum_{n>j\neq i} |s_{ij}(\mathbf{p})|h_j(\mathbf{p}) \qquad \text{all } i < n.$$

Part (a) of the definition means that when we come to stipulate DD for an economy, we shall be implying that the substitution terms λ_{ii} in Eq. (10) (for $j = i$), which are known to be negative, are large in absolute value relative to the income term. If that is not so, we must rely on a high responsiveness (known to be positive) in the supply of the ith good to a change in its price. We can think of examples where this is not the case, but far less readily than was the case for GS, and even less readily when DD is taken to hold locally only. By and large, assuming part (a) to hold does not appear absurd and is in conformity with much of economic theory.

Part (b) is in the spirit of our introductory remarks. Note that s_{ij} is the partial of s_i when i and j are measured in any given units; so $(h_j/h_i)s_{ij}$ will be the value of the partial when one new unit of i is now equal to h_i old units and one new unit of j is equal to h_j old units of j. Thus (b) says that there are some units in which to measure goods such that the diagonal term dominates the off-diagonal terms with $j < n$. It is reasonable to ask why we should have excluded the nth good.

First, it should be clear that the choice of n was arbitrary. If $p_s > 0$, and on excluding the sth good in the same way, but including the nth, (a) and (b) are satisfied and we should still say that the economy has DD at $\mathbf{p}$. Secondly, let h_i, $i = 1, \ldots, n$, be any set of positive numbers. Let $q_i = p_i/h_i$ and say $q_r = \max q_i$. Then, using H,

$$|h_r s_{rr}(\mathbf{p})q_r| = \left|\sum_{j \neq r} h_j s_{rj}(\mathbf{p})q_j\right| \leq q_r \sum_{j \neq r} h_j |s_{rj}(\mathbf{p})|,$$

and clearly DD is impossible if we include all goods.

Lastly, it is worth noting that DD is definitely a weaker requirement than GS for $\mathbf{p} \gg \mathbf{0}$. The latter implies DD, while DD does not imply GS. The second part of this statement is obvious. The first follows at once from H. If we set $h_j(\mathbf{p}) = p_j$, all j and $\mathbf{p}$ recall $s_{jn} > 0$, we at once verify (b) of the definition; that (a) must hold is obvious. By the same argument, DD is weaker than WGS for $\mathbf{p} \gg \mathbf{0}$ and $s_{in}(\mathbf{p}) > 0$, some i.

It is easy to establish the following results.

THEOREM 12. If for all $\mathbf{p} \in E$, the set of equilibrium prices, the economy has DD, and if N holds, then equilibrium is unique.

Proof. Let $J^+(\mathbf{P}^*)$ have elements $h_j(\mathbf{P}^*)s_{ij}(\mathbf{P}^*)$, where $\mathbf{p}^* \in E$,

($\mathbf{P} = (1/p_n)\mathbf{p}$). Suppose there exists $\mathbf{v} > \mathbf{0}$, such that $TJ(\mathbf{P}^*)T\mathbf{v} \leq \mathbf{0}$. Then, setting $w_j = v_j/h_j(\mathbf{P}^*)$, it must be that $TJ^+(\mathbf{P}^*)T\mathbf{w} \leq \mathbf{0}$. Let

$$w_r = \max_j w_j.$$

Then

$$t_{rr}^2 h_r(\mathbf{P}^*)s_{rr}(\mathbf{P}^*)w_r \leq -\sum_{j \neq r} t_{rr}h_j(\mathbf{P}^*)s_{rj}(\mathbf{P}^*)t_{jj}w_j \leq w_r \sum_{j \neq r} h_j(\mathbf{P}^*)|s_{rj}(\mathbf{P}^*)|,$$

which contradicts DD. Hence $J(\mathbf{P}^*)$ has GP, and T.9.2 establishes the result.

Corollary 12. If for all $\mathbf{p}$ the economy has DD and N holds, then equilibrium is unique.

By and large, we may rest quite satisfied with the results of this section. As we have already argued, DD is not an obviously silly restriction to impose on the system. Of course, this does not mean that all actual systems will satisfy DD. What it does mean is that it will be worthwhile, at a later stage in the book, to further investigate the properties of such economies.

10. Other Sufficient Conditions for Uniqueness

In this section we shall investigate a number of other restrictions on the excess-demand functions that are sufficient to ensure the uniqueness of an equilibrium. These conditions share the disadvantage that it is hard to give them any obvious economic motivation. However, that does not mean that they are without interest, since there is no reason to explain further the actual properties of, say, the Jacobian $J(\mathbf{P})$ of an actual economy by more or less common sense appeals to economic theory.

DEFINITION 9. A matrix A is said to be *positive definite* if for all non-zero values of the vector $\mathbf{v}$, $\mathbf{v}'A\mathbf{v} > 0$, and A is symmetric. A is said to be *positive quasi-definite* if for all non-zero values of the vector $\mathbf{v}$, $\mathbf{v}'[(A + A')/2]\mathbf{v} > 0$. ($A'$ is the transpose of A.)

THEOREM 13. If, for all $\mathbf{P}^* \in E$, $J(\mathbf{P}^*)$ is either positive definite or positive quasi-definite and if N holds, then the economy has a unique equilibrium.

Proof. We establish that $J(\mathbf{P}^*)$ has GP.

(a) Suppose that $J(\mathbf{P}^*)$ is positive definite, but does not have

GP, that is, for some T and some $\mathbf{v} > \mathbf{0}$, $TJ(\mathbf{P}^*)T\mathbf{v} \leq \mathbf{0}$. But then $(T\mathbf{v})'J(\mathbf{P}^*)T\mathbf{v} \leq 0$, which contradicts $J(\mathbf{P}^*)$ positive definite.

(b) If $J(\mathbf{P}^*)$ is positive quasi-definite, the same argument as in (a) holds since

$$\mathbf{v}'J(\mathbf{P}^*)\mathbf{v} = \mathbf{v}'\frac{J(\mathbf{P}^*) + J(\mathbf{P}^*)'}{2}\mathbf{v}.$$

But if $J(\mathbf{P}^*)$ has GP then T.9.2 establishes the theorem.

THEOREM 14. If, for all $\mathbf{P}^* \in E$, the determinant of every principal submatrix of $J(\mathbf{P}^*)$ is positive and if N holds, then the economy has a unique equilibrium.

This is a restatement of Lemma 9.2.

It should be noted that the conditions of T.9.14 are weaker than any case (except for the Hicksian with some zero equilibrium prices where no comparison is possible) we have considered so far. This is clear from the single fact that, by T.9.12, DD implies GP, which is equivalent to the condition of T.9.14, but not vice versa. The second part of this statement is obvious as a simple 2×2 example would illustrate.

The following theorem is weaker in some respects and stronger in others than T.9.14.

THEOREM 15. If $J(\mathbf{P})$ is non-singular and $J^{-1}\tilde{\mathbf{z}}(\mathbf{P})$ is continuously differentiable for all $\mathbf{P} \gg \mathbf{0}$, where $\tilde{\mathbf{z}}(\mathbf{P})$ is the vector of excess demands for the non-numeraire commodities, and if

$$\sum_i z_i(\mathbf{p})$$

approaches $+\infty$ whenever $\mathbf{p}$ approaches a limit, $\mathbf{p}^0$ with $p_i^0 = 0$, some i, then the economy has a unique, strictly positive equilibrium.

This theorem makes global rather than local assumptions about the Jacobian and, in addition, makes strong requirements with respect to the boundary, though these may be capable of relaxation. On the other hand, only the non-singularity of the Jacobian is assumed; nothing is said about the principal minors.

The proof we will give depends on dynamic arguments and is postponed to Section 12.8.

11. The Leontief Economy

We considered this economy in Section 2.11. Here we give conditions that suffice for it to have a unique equilibrium.

THEOREM 16. Let the Leontief economy satisfy A.2.10–A.2.13. Then equilibrium is unique.

Proof. Let $\pi_i(\mathbf{p})$ be the unit profit function of the ith sector, that is,

$$\pi_i(\mathbf{p}) = p_i - C_i(\mathbf{p}) \qquad i = 1, \ldots, n-1$$

where $C_i(\mathbf{p})$ is the minimum unit cost function of i (see A.2.13). If p_n^* is the equilibrium price of labor, we know (T.2.6) that $p_n^* > 0$, In addition, if $\mathbf{p}^*$ is an equilibrium, $\boldsymbol{\pi}(\mathbf{p}^*) = \mathbf{0}$ and, of course, $\pi(\mathbf{p}^* k) = k\pi(\mathbf{p}^*)$, for $k > 0$. Hence, by Euler's theorem,

$$\pi_{ii}(\mathbf{p}^*)p_i^* + \sum_{n>j\neq i} \pi_{ij}(\mathbf{p}^*)p_j^* = -\pi_{in}(\mathbf{p}^*)p_n^* \qquad i = 1, \ldots, n-1, \tag{20}$$

where $\pi_{ij}(\mathbf{p}^*) = \partial\pi_i(\mathbf{p}^*)/\partial p_j$. But we know (T.3.6) that $\pi_{in}(\mathbf{p}^*) = -a_{in}$, where a_{in} is the input of labor per unit of output of i, so the right-hand side of (20) is positive. Since $\pi_{ii}(\mathbf{p}^*) > 0$ (see T.3.6) and $\pi_{ij}(\mathbf{p}^*) \leq 0$ for $j \neq i$, (20) tells us that the matrix $H(\mathbf{p}^*) = [\pi_{ij}(\mathbf{p}^*)]$, has DD (where $H(\mathbf{p}^*)$ is $(n-1) \times (n-1)$). Hence, by proof of T.9.12, $H(\mathbf{p}^*)$ has GP. Since this must be true at every equilibrium, it follows from T.9.2 that there is only one equilibrium.

12. Economies with No Joint Production but Many Factors

The Leontief economy can be generalized by dropping the requirement that there can be only one primary factor. We retain the assumptions of constant returns to scale and no joint production and postulate that any net output requires some use of factors.

Let $\mathbf{y}$ be the vector of produced goods, $\mathbf{z}$ the vector of demands for factor inputs (taken non-negative), and $\mathbf{L}$ the vector of initial factor holdings. As before, there are no endowments of produced goods. Let $\mathbf{p}$ be the vector of prices of produced goods, $\mathbf{w}$ the vector of factor prices. Let $C(\mathbf{p},\mathbf{w})$ be the vector of minimum unit cost functions. Then, if all goods are produced, equilibrium requires that $\mathbf{p} = C(\mathbf{p},\mathbf{w})$. There are a number of questions that may be asked of this model; the "two-sector" model and factor price equalization discussed below have been much discussed in the literature.

Determination of commodity prices by factor prices. For any given factor price vector, $\mathbf{w} > \mathbf{0}$, we can regard the factors as a composite commodity; then all the assumptions of the Leontief economy are satisfied, and from T.9.16 we can find a unique vector $\mathbf{p}$ that satisfies the conditions of zero profit in each industry. Then $\mathbf{p} = \mathbf{p}(\mathbf{w})$ is a function of $\mathbf{w}$; since all the demand and cost functions are continuous, it can easily be seen that $\mathbf{p}$ is a continuous function of $\mathbf{w}$. Further, as we know, we can choose the activity levels in each industry so that supply equals demand on each produced goods market and the total value of demand for factors, at the vector $\mathbf{w}$, equals the value of initial endowment. Assume that producers supply exactly what is demanded when prices satisfy the zero-profit condition. Then we have defined an excess-supply function, $\mathbf{s}(\mathbf{p},\mathbf{w}) = \mathbf{s}[\mathbf{p}(\mathbf{w}),\mathbf{w}] = \mathbf{S}(\mathbf{w})$, say, for the factors, and this must itself satisfy W; that is, $\mathbf{w}\mathbf{S}(\mathbf{w}) = 0$, for all $\mathbf{w} > \mathbf{0}$. It then follows that $\mathbf{w}^*$ can be so chosen as to define equilibrium in the factor markets and hence, with $\mathbf{p}^* = \mathbf{p}(\mathbf{w}^*)$, a general equilibrium.

This equilibrium need not be unique, in general, but $\mathbf{p}$ is defined uniquely by $\mathbf{w}$. In fact, if we consider different economies with the same technology, but possibly different factor endowments and demand functions, we can still say that two equilibria with the same factor prices must have the same produced goods prices.

The "two-sector" model. Now consider, in particular, the uniqueness of equilibrium in the case of two primary factors. Since $\mathbf{S}$ is certainly homogeneous of degree zero in $\mathbf{w}$, we may normalize by considering $\mathbf{w} \in S_2$.

We already know that if $\mathbf{w}^*$ is an equilibrium (here assumed to exist), then $\mathbf{w}^*\mathbf{S}(\mathbf{w}) < 0$, all $\mathbf{w}$ not proportional to $\mathbf{w}^*$, is a sufficient condition for the uniqueness of the equilibrium. Here it is necessary. For example, suppose equilibrium is unique. If (0,1) is not an equilibrium, then, with the aid of W, we must have $S_1(0,1) < 0$, $S_2(0,1) = 0$, so that $\mathbf{w}^*\mathbf{S}(0,1) < 0$. Similarly, if (1,0) is not an equilibrium, $\mathbf{w}^*\mathbf{S}(1,0) < 0$. Suppose the equation $\mathbf{w}^*S(\mathbf{w}) = 0$ had a solution on the unit simplex different from $\mathbf{w}^*$, say $\mathbf{w}'$. Then $\mathbf{w}^*\mathbf{S}(\mathbf{w}') = 0$, while, by W, $\mathbf{w}'\mathbf{S}(\mathbf{w}') = 0$. Since the matrix with rows $\mathbf{w}^*,\mathbf{w}'$ is certainly non-singular, it must be that $\mathbf{S}(\mathbf{w}') = \mathbf{0}$, contrary to the assumption that $\mathbf{w}^*$ is the unique equilibrium. If $\mathbf{w}^*\mathbf{S}(\mathbf{w}) = 0$ only for $\mathbf{w} = \mathbf{w}^*$ and $\mathbf{w}^*\mathbf{S}(\mathbf{w}) < 0$ for some $\mathbf{w}$, it must be that for all $\mathbf{w} \neq \mathbf{w}^*$, $\mathbf{w}^*\mathbf{S}(\mathbf{w}) < 0$.

What we have just proved clearly holds for any two-goods economy, and we sum up this result in the following.

THEOREM 17. Let $\mathbf{p}$ be a price vector in the two-dimensional simplex, $\mathbf{z}(\mathbf{p})$ a two-dimensional excess-demand vector function. Then a necessary and sufficient condition that $\mathbf{p}^*$ is the unique equilibrium for the two-goods economy is that $\mathbf{p}^*\mathbf{z}(\mathbf{p}) > 0$ for all $\mathbf{p}$ for which $\mathbf{p} \neq \mathbf{p}^*$. (The two-goods economy is assumed to satisfy all the usual assumptions that we have used to show that at least one equilibrium exists.)

We now know that we need conditions that ensure $\mathbf{w}^*\mathbf{S}(\mathbf{w}) < 0$ for all $\mathbf{w} \neq \mathbf{w}^*$ in the simplex. Certainly it is easy to check that this will be the case if the economy is "Hicksian" in the outputs. We shall consider instead a situation that has been much discussed in the recent literature on the theory of economic growth.

Suppose there are two kinds of households; one kind labeled "1" owns all of the input labeled "1" and derives utility only from the good labeled "1," while similarly the kind labeled "2" owns all of the input with that label and derives utility only from the good labeled "2." (This can be translated to the "classical" savings assumption of growth literature.) The households in each group are Hicksian. From these assumptions we quickly verify, assuming all demands differentiable,

$$p_i \frac{\partial x_i}{\partial p_i} = -x_i \qquad i = 1, 2$$

$$p_i \frac{\partial x_i}{\partial w_i} = L_i \qquad i = 1, 2,$$

where L_i is the amount of the ith input available.

Further suppose that the production of each good requires only primary factors; neither good serves as an intermediate product. If y_i is the producers' demand for factor i, then

$$y_i(\mathbf{x},\mathbf{w}) = \sum_j a_{ji}x_j \qquad i = 1, 2,$$

where a_{ji} is the amount of factor input i per unit of output j; it depends on $\mathbf{w}$, and from T.3.6, $dp_j/dw_i = a_{ji}$, $i, j = 1, 2$.

Now consider an equilibrium $\mathbf{w}^*$. Let Z_1 $(= -S_1)$ be the excess demand for input 1, and write $Z_{12} \equiv \partial Z_1/\partial w_2$. Using these relations and the household-demand conditions and taking all derivatives at $\mathbf{w}^*$, we have

$$
\begin{aligned}
Z_{12} &= \frac{\partial y_1}{\partial x_1}\frac{\partial x_1}{\partial p_1}\frac{dp_1}{dw_2} + \frac{\partial y_1}{\partial x_2}\left(\frac{\partial x_2}{\partial p_2}\frac{dp_2}{dw_2} + \frac{\partial x_2}{\partial w_2}\right) + \frac{\partial y_1}{\partial w_2} \\
&= -a_{11}a_{12}\frac{x_1}{p_1} - a_{21}x_2\frac{a_{22}}{p} + a_{21}\frac{L_2}{p_2} + \frac{\partial y_1}{\partial w_2} \\
&= -\frac{a_{21}}{p_2}(x_2a_{22} + x_1a_{12}) + \frac{a_{21}}{p_2}L_2 + x_1a_{12}\left(\frac{a_{21}}{p_2} - \frac{a_{11}}{p_1}\right) + \frac{\partial y_1}{\partial w_2} \\
&= x_1a_{12}\left(\frac{a_{21}}{p_2} - \frac{a_{11}}{p_1}\right) + \frac{\partial y_1}{\partial w_2},
\end{aligned}
$$

since in equilibrium $L_1 = x_1a_{12} + x_2a_{22}$. Hence, $Z_{12}(\mathbf{w}^*) > 0$ if $a_{21}/p_2 > a_{11}/p_1$ since $\partial y_1/\partial w_2 \geq 0$. Since both industries are making zero profits, $p_j = a_{j1}w_1 + a_{j2}w_2$, it is easy to verify that the condition $a_{21}/p_2 > a_{11}/p_1$ is equivalent to the same condition with the subscripts "1" and "2" interchanged, so that this condition ensures $Z_{21}(\mathbf{w}) > 0$. Hence, the two inputs are gross substitutes in every equilibrium if good i uses input j ($j \neq i$) more intensively than good j does. This means that equilibrium is unique and so, by T.9.17, $\mathbf{w}^*\mathbf{S}(\mathbf{w}) < 0$, all $\mathbf{w} \neq \mathbf{w}^*$.

There are, of course, other assumptions on household behavior and the production sets that ensure uniqueness. They all, however, seem to entail the GS property (though we have not made an exhaustive check).

This example is instructive for two reasons. First of all, it shows the need to examine the economics of purely formal uniqueness conditions. Second, it makes clear how special the case of two goods is (a recurring result, e.g., T.12.1). In the present instance, the fact that $\mathbf{w}^*\mathbf{S}(\mathbf{w}) < 0$, for $\mathbf{w} \neq \mathbf{w}^*$, is necessary for uniqueness is helpful, but this property will not hold for an economy with more than two inputs.

Factor price equalization. We now consider a problem arising in the theory of international trade. In the general model with no joint production and constant returns, goods prices and factor prices satisfy the relation $\mathbf{p} = \mathbf{C}(\mathbf{p},\mathbf{w})$, as we have noted. We now assume that the number of factors, m, equals the number of goods. The question asked is this: Given $\mathbf{p}$, is there a unique $\mathbf{w}$ that solves these equations?

If (C_{ij}) is the Jacobian with element $(\partial C_i/\partial w_i)$, then if this Jacobian has GP we know that there can be only one $\mathbf{w}$ in the simplex that solves these equations. But $\partial C_i/\partial w_j$ is the intensity with which industry i uses input j (T.3.6), so for instance, if there is some ordering of inputs and sectors such that each sector uses the input with the same label more intensively than it does all other inputs combined; that is, if the Jacobian has DD, then it will also have GP and $\mathbf{w}$ will uniquely solve the above equations.

In this example the economics of our conditions are extremely unattractive. Pearce [1967] has shown that rather weaker conditions will suffice provided we are willing to extend the domain of $C(\cdot)$ to the set of all $\mathbf{w}$ that make $C(\cdot)$ non-negative. Since this includes negative factor prices the meaning of such an extension of the domain is somewhat obscure.

As our example illustrates, however, the most general uniqueness conditions discussed in this chapter are still extremely restrictive, and we must hope that acceptable weaker conditions will become available. Even so, a reformulation of the question posed at the beginning of this example does allow us to give a definite answer.

Suppose that the economy has a given endowment vector. Is it possible to have given $\mathbf{p}$, two values of $\mathbf{w}$ for which the economy is in equilibrium, and not only in the sense that unit costs are covered, but also in the sense that all markets are cleared?

Suppose there are two equilibria, $(\mathbf{p},\mathbf{w})$ and $(\mathbf{p},\mathbf{w}^*)$, with the same vector of goods prices. Let $(\mathbf{y},\mathbf{z})$ be the vector of outputs and inputs corresponding to the first equilibrium, $(\mathbf{y}^*,\mathbf{z}^*)$ to the second. Since maximum profits in either case are zero, we must have

$$\mathbf{py} - \mathbf{w}^*\mathbf{z} \leq 0 \qquad \mathbf{py}^* - \mathbf{wz}^* \leq 0. \tag{21}$$

By W, $\mathbf{py} = \mathbf{wL}$, $\mathbf{py}^* = \mathbf{w}^*\mathbf{L}$. If we add the above inequalities and make the indicated substitutions, we see that $\mathbf{wS}^* + \mathbf{w}^*\mathbf{S} \leq 0$. By definition of equilibrium, however, $\mathbf{S}^* \geq \mathbf{0}$, $\mathbf{S} \geq \mathbf{0}$, so that equality must hold. Hence, we must have $\mathbf{py} - \mathbf{w}^*\mathbf{z} = 0$ (and also $\mathbf{py}^* - \mathbf{wz}^* = 0$). If $(\mathbf{y}^i,\mathbf{z}^i)$ is the equilibrium input-output vector for the ith industry at $(\mathbf{p},\mathbf{w})$, then profit maximization implies that $\mathbf{py}^i - \mathbf{w}^*\mathbf{z}^i \leq 0$, each i; summing over i implies that $\mathbf{py} - \mathbf{w}^*\mathbf{z} \leq 0$; since we know the equality holds, it must hold for each i, since a sum of non-positive numbers is zero if and only if each one is zero. By constant returns, $\mathbf{py}^i - \mathbf{wz}^i = 0$ for each i, so $(\mathbf{w}^* - \mathbf{w})(\mathbf{z}^1 \cdots \mathbf{z}^m) = \mathbf{0}$, where $(\mathbf{z}^1 \cdots \mathbf{z}^m)$ is the matrix with columns $\mathbf{z}^i$.

Now assume that at the equilibrium $(\mathbf{p},\mathbf{w})$ all goods are produced and the input vectors of the various industries are linearly independent. Then the matrix $(\mathbf{z}^1 \cdots \mathbf{z}^m)$ is non-singular, so that $\mathbf{w}$ must equal $\mathbf{w}^*$; that is, factor prices are uniquely determined by goods prices.

13. Conclusion

Almost all economists, whether or not they are "theoretical," when asked to evaluate the fairly long-run consequences of a shift in some parameter of an economy, will attempt, certainly in the first stage, a comparison of the equilibrium before and after the change. If equilibrium is not unique this procedure may break down. In this chapter, we have explored some of the sufficient conditions for this method to have a chance. Unfortunately, necessary conditions are unlikely to be available. Nonetheless, it can be argued that the conditions we have stated are not, in general, unreasonably demanding, although the last example suggests that in some cases they may become so. Whether reasonable or not, they are the best available at this stage to help answer an important question, on which so much of current analysis depends. Probably the most appealing of the possible postulates leading to uniqueness is Diagonal Dominance. This condition, if fulfilled in fact, would give a general equilibrium system a kind of Mashallian flavor, inasmuch as the properties of the demand and supply curves in the plane of the price of the good in question and the quantity supplied or demanded are in some sense the "dominating" properties. It means that partial analysis may not make serious mistakes. When the price of a good changes and we take others as fixed, it is reasonable to suppose in many cases that, in fact, they are "almost" fixed. But then, in view of DD, the answers we obtain from the "fixed" assumption will not be very different from the correct answer. Whatever our intellectual predisposition on the matter of partial versus general equilibrium analysis may be, we all meet practical problems by a partial approach first, so these are comforting conclusions. Of course, it still remains to see how "good" the DD assumption is in fact.

Notes

The study of uniqueness by examining the Jacobian of an appropriate mapping was initiated by Samuelson [1953–54]. He thought a sufficient condition for uniqueness to be that for one permutation of the rows and columns of the Jacobian, all its leading principal minors are non-vanishing. This proposition paid insufficient attention to the domain of the mapping and Gale and Nikaidô [1965] showed it to be false by means of a counter example. They then established a sufficient condition, here called "Gale Property," which is the foundation of much of this chapter. More recently, Pearce [1967] and Pearce and Wise [unpublished] have sought to find much weaker sufficient conditions. These studies turn on theorems on covering mappings and lead to conditions that require only that over the requisite domain a certain Jacobian should not vanish. We have commented briefly on one aspect of this work in Section 9.12. The more recent work of Pearce and Wise appeared too late to be thoroughly explored here. On one matter, however, comment is appropriate.

Pearce and Wise examine the case in which $p_i s_i(\mathbf{P}) \to 0$ as $p_i \to 0$. Suppose the economy has an equilibrium $\mathbf{P}^* \gg \mathbf{0}$. We may construct a reduced economy by setting $p_i \equiv 0$ and noting that W holds for this reduced economy. (This was discussed in another context by Hahn [1965].) Let the reduced economy have an equilibrium $\mathbf{p}^{**}$, with $p_i^{**} = 0$, of course. Suppose the two economies have non-vanishing Jacobians in the neighborhoods of $\mathbf{p}^*$ and $\mathbf{p}^{**}$, respectively. Then they show that it is possible to find a $\mathbf{p} \neq \mathbf{p}^*$ that is an equilibrium, so that the mapping is not univalent. Then the economy cannot have GP, but we know that GS implies GP. Hence GS must imply $p_i s_i(\mathbf{p})$ does not go to zero as $p_i \to 0$, whence $s_i(\mathbf{p})$ must be unbounded below. This Pearce and Wise consider to be absurd.

There are two comments we should like to make on this. First, GS ensures that any equilibrium must be in the interior of the simplex and we need never be concerned with the behavior of excess supplies at, or indeed with suitable assumptions near, the boundaries. Surely they take "unbounded demand" possibilities too literally. It is true that GS forces this on us as a price goes to zero, but assuming GS over the whole simplex (including boundaries) is to be taken as an idealization (as recent measure-theoretic approaches to general equilibrium are also to be taken), which with care in application simplifies analysis without leading us astray. Second, as T.9.3. shows, only assumptions of GP or GS at equilibrium are needed.

That both weak revealed preference and GS imply uniqueness was first pointed out by Wald [1936; 1951, pp. 375–376, 385–387]. Arrow, Block, and Hurwicz [1959, p. 90] first showed that if GS holds, weak revealed preference holds as between an equilibrium price vector and any other. The weak gross substitute extensions are due to McKenzie [1960], Uzawa [1961], Morishima [1959, unpublished], and Arrow and Hurwicz [1960].

Much of the discussion of uniqueness in the literature was motivated by the theory of factor-price equalization in international trade theory. The literature since Samuelson's [1948] paper is large; the results of Section 9.12 are discussed more fully in McKenzie [1955a].

Debreu [1970] has recently reexamined the possibilities for multiple equilibria. He assumes only that excess-demand functions are differentiable functions of both prices and the distribution of endowments; the absolute value of the excess-demand vector is assumed to approach infinity as any price approaches zero, so that only strictly positive equilibria are possible. Then it is shown that there is a closed set of measure zero in the space of endowment allocations such that for all other endowment allocations there are only finitely many equilibria. This seems to be the best possible result short of the much more restrictive assumptions of the type used in this chapter.

Chapter Ten

COMPARING EQUILIBRIA

The old order changeth, yielding plac
to the new.
—A. Tennyson, *Morte d'Arthu*

1. The Problem

In analyzing the effects of a given change in the parameters of ar economy, say, taste or technology, it is often useful as a first approach to neglect the questions of adjustment to this change and to compare the equilibrium that results (if all goes well) with the equilibrium we started with. One of the questions we shall have to answer is just when this approach is in fact likely to prove useful. The method of comparing equilibria is often referred to as the method of comparative statics or comparative dynamics. The force of the terms "statics" and "dynamics" is by no means clear. For instance, for economies with all possible futures markets it is not easy to say whether we are dealing with statics, because all contracts are made at a moment of time, or with dynamics, because quantities of goods produced and stored may be changing as the future develops. We therefore think it best to avoid this terminology.

The main problem we set ourselves in this chapter is an inquiry into the power of general equilibrium models in giving unambiguous predictions of how the equilibrium of an economy will be affected by a given parameter change. As we have already argued in the previous section, this problem must be intimately related to that of the uniqueness of an equilibrium and it is pretty clear that we shall not expect to get very far without stipulating one or the other of the conditions that ensure such uniqueness. Even so, the kind of parameter changes for which predictions become possible is pretty limited.

2. Binary Changes

We start our investigation with the simplest case. Suppose there is a change in the tastes of households so that at a given $\mathbf{p} \gg \mathbf{0}$, they demand more of a certain good. Then, by W, the demand for at least one other good must be affected by the change in taste. The simplest of our cases arises when at a given price vector the demand for *two* goods only is affected by the change. We shall call such a change a "binary" change:

DEFINITION 1. A change in the parameters of an economy at $\mathbf{p}$ will be called a *binary* change, if, when $\mathbf{z}'(\mathbf{p})$ is the excess-demand vector when the parameters have changed, $\mathbf{z}(\mathbf{p}) - \mathbf{z}'(\mathbf{p})$ has only two non-zero components.

It should be noted that this definition stipulates that a change is binary at a given price. Thus a change that satisfies the requirement that it be binary at $\mathbf{p}$ need not have the same effects on $\mathbf{z}$ at some other price vector $\mathbf{p}'$. For convenience, we shall take $z_1'(\mathbf{p}) > z_1(\mathbf{p})$ and $z_2'(\mathbf{p}) < z_2(\mathbf{p})$. (The inequalities must differ, taking $p_1 > 0$, $p_2 > 0$ for the two goods because of W.)

The simplest case for this simplest of all parameter changes is the two-good economy. Here every parameter change is *ipso facto* binary. We also get a very simple result.

THEOREM 1. Let $\mathbf{p}^*$ be the unique equilibrium before and $\mathbf{p}^{**}$ the unique equilibrium after the change in parameter. Then $p_1^{**} > p_1^*$.

Proof. In T.9.17 we showed that for a two-good economy the condition $\mathbf{p}^*\mathbf{s}(\mathbf{p}) < 0$ for $\mathbf{p} \neq \mathbf{p}^*$ was necessary and sufficient for uniqueness. So in the present application,

$$\mathbf{p}^{**}\mathbf{s}'(\mathbf{p}^*) < 0$$

and, by W,

$$(\mathbf{p}^{**} - \mathbf{p}^*)\mathbf{s}'(\mathbf{p}^*) < 0.$$

By assumption $s_1'(\mathbf{p}^*) < s_1(p^*)$, and $\mathbf{p}^{**}$ and $\mathbf{p}^* \in S_2$. If the theorem is false, it must be that $p_1^{**} < p_1^*$ (since $p_1^{**} = p_1^*$ would mean $p_2^{**} = p_2^*$, which is impossible). But then $p_1^* > 0$, so that $s_1(\mathbf{p}^*) = 0$, and also $p_2^{**} > p_2^*$. Hence, $s_2'(\mathbf{p}^*) < 0 \leq s_2(\mathbf{p}^*)$ contrary to assumption. Hence $p_1^{**} > p_1^*$.

As an application, consider the "two-sector" model of 9.12. Suppose there is an exogenous increase in L_1, the amount of the factor of type 1 available. It is trivial to show that, in the notation of 9.12, this implies

$$s_1'(\mathbf{w}^*) > s_1(\mathbf{w}^*).$$

If the economy has a unique equilibrium before and after the binary change, T.10.1 tells us that $w_1^{**} < w_1^*$ (and $w_2^{**} > w_2^*$). Thus, if the factor of type 1 is "capital," the equilibrium with more capital, other things constant, must also have a lower rental of capital. It is important to understand that this prediction depends crucially on the supposition of uniqueness.

It is not hard to see that the lessons of this example can be applied to other situations, for instance to the two-country, two-good neoclassical model of international trade. Thus suppose that the country experiencing a once-over increase in the stock of capital was an exporter of the capital-intensive good. Then, assuming the world equilibrium unique, since we know that the equilibrium wage-rental ratio must go up and since this must mean that the price of the capital-intensive good must fall relatively to that of the other good, we have at once the result that the terms of trade of our country must deteriorate. These are all simple consequences of T.10.1, and it must be confessed that they will not generalize to an economy with more goods, except if the contemplated change is binary. We shall return to this question presently. First, we shall examine what can be said about binary changes in a world of many goods.

THEOREM 2. Let the parameter change be binary at $\mathbf{p}^*$, an equilibrium. Then if (a) the economy is Hicksian for all $\mathbf{p}$ and has $\mathbf{p}^* \gg \mathbf{0}$ *or* (b) all goods are GS at all $\mathbf{p}$, there is a new equilibrium price vector $\mathbf{p}^{**}$ with $p_1^{**} > p_1^*$ and $p_2^{**} < p_2^*$.

Proof. If the economy is Hicksian, then by assumption, and if GS, by Corollary 9.6, $\mathbf{p}^* \gg \mathbf{0}$. Therefore, we may choose units for the goods such that $\mathbf{p}^* = \mathbf{e}$, the unit vector. By the proof of T.9.4, T.9.9, and W, we have for either type of economy for $\mathbf{p} \neq \mathbf{p}^{**}$

$$(\mathbf{p} - \mathbf{p}^{**})\mathbf{s}'(\mathbf{p}) > 0$$

and so, in particular,

$$(\mathbf{e} - \mathbf{p}^{**})\mathbf{s}'(\mathbf{e}) > 0. \tag{1}$$

By the definition of a binary change, $s_1'(\mathbf{e}) + s_2'(\mathbf{e}) = 0$, $s_1'(\mathbf{e}) < 0$ and $s_i'(\mathbf{e}) = 0$, all $i \neq 1,2$ (since $\mathbf{p}^* \gg \mathbf{0}$). Hence from (1),

$$p_1^{**} - 1 > p_2^{**} - 1. \tag{2}$$

Then there is some $k > 0$, such that with $\hat{\mathbf{p}}^{**} = k\mathbf{p}^{**}$,

$$\hat{p}_1^{**} - 1 > 0 \quad \text{and} \quad \hat{p}_2^{**} - 1 < 0. \tag{3}$$

By H, $\hat{\mathbf{p}}^{**}$ is an equilibrium.

For the GS case we can establish a slightly stronger result by different methods.

THEOREM 3. Let the parameter change be binary at $\mathbf{p}^*$, an equilibrium. Then, if all goods are GS for all $\mathbf{p}$ and the nth good has been chosen as numeraire ($p_n = 1$ always), it must be that $p_1^{**} > p_1^*$, $p_2^{**} < p_2^*$.

Proof. By Corollary 9.6, we have $\mathbf{p}^* \gg \mathbf{0}$. Again let the units in which goods are measured be such as to give $\mathbf{p}^* = \mathbf{e}$. Let $p_k^{**} \geq p_i^{**}$, all i. Then we claim that $k = 1$. Suppose $k \neq 1$. Then by T.9.8, we have $s_k'(\mathbf{p}^*) < s_k'(\mathbf{p}^{**})$. But $s_k'(\mathbf{p}^*) = 0$ for $k \neq 1,2$ by the binary change assumption and $s_2'(\mathbf{p}^*) > 0$, by the same assumption. Hence $s_k'(\mathbf{p}^{**}) > 0$ and $\mathbf{p}^{**}$ is not an equilibrium contrary to its definition. We conclude that indeed $k = 1$. In the same way we show that if $p_h^{**} \leq p_i^{**}$; then it must be that $h = 2$. Hence the theorem is proved.

Corollary 3. Let the economy have GS for all $\mathbf{p}$. Then a binary change at $\mathbf{p}^*$, an equilibrium, will raise the equilibrium price of the good whose excess demand has increased at $\mathbf{p}^*$ in greater proportion than any other equilibrium price is raised and lower the equilibrium price of the good whose excess demand was decreased at $\mathbf{p}^*$ in greater proportion than any other equilibrium price.

Corollary 3'. Let the economy have GS at all $\mathbf{p}$. Then a binary change at $\mathbf{p}^*$ raises the prices of all goods in terms of the good whose excess demand was reduced by the binary change at $\mathbf{p}^*$.

Proof. Choose the second good as numeraire; that is, set $p_2 = 1$ everywhere. Then if, say, $p_k^{**} < p_k^*$ and $p_k^{**}/p_k^* \leq p_i^{**}/p_i^*$, all i, the familiar argument would lead to $s_k(\mathbf{p}^{**}) < 0$; if $k \neq 2$, then by the binary change assumption $s_k'(\mathbf{p}^{**}) = s_k(\mathbf{p}^{**}) < 0$ and we would thus contradict $\mathbf{p}^{**}$ as being an equilibrium. This is as it should be in view of GS: $p_2^{**} = p_2^*$, and all other prices rise relatively to that of the second good, so that the excess supply for the second good is reduced as needed, since by hypothesis $s_2'(\mathbf{p}^*) > 0$.

The application of these results to actual situations is somewhat limited simply because the supposition that the parameter change is binary is very limiting. Later we shall be able to illustrate a version of T.10.3 for more interesting situations. Here we may find an application in the analysis of the consequences for the equilibrium of an economy of a switch in government expenditure at $\mathbf{p}^*$ from one good to another or of a technical innovation in one sector of the economy that has the consequence of reducing, at $\mathbf{p}^*$, the demand for one particular input and increasing the demand for another. But no doubt all these examples are rather artificial. Before we attempt to be more adventurous, however, it will be useful to see whether the hypotheses of WGS or DD allow us to make straightforward predictions for binary changes.

We know from our discussion of the case in Chapter 9 that if one postulates WGS *and* connectedness, all the theorems established for GS continue to hold. Thus it is clear that T.10.2 and T.10.3 with its corollaries continue to be valid for this economy. Accordingly, we concentrate on the case in which connectedness is not stipulated.

THEOREM 4. Let all goods be WGS and let there be a binary change such that for all $\mathbf{p}^* \in E$, $s_2'(\mathbf{p}^*) > s_2(\mathbf{p}^*)$, $s_1'(\mathbf{p}^*) < 0$. Then there is a new set of equilibrium price vectors E' such that if $\mathbf{p}^{**} \in E'$, then for every $\mathbf{p}^* \in E$, $\mathbf{p}^{**}$ can be scaled so that $p_1^{**} > p_1^*$, $p_2^{**} \leq p_2^*$.

Proof. We note first that if $p_i^* > 0$, for either $i = 1$ or $i = 2$, then $p_i^* > 0$, for both $i = 1$ and $i = 2$. This follows from W and the postulate that the change is binary. Suppose $p_i^* = 0$ for $i = 1,2$. By T.9.11 and the assumptions that imply that $\mathbf{p}^*$ is not in E', $\mathbf{p}^{**}\mathbf{s}'(\mathbf{p}^*) < 0$. For each $i \neq 1,2$, either $s_i(\mathbf{p}^*) = 0$ or $s_i(\mathbf{p}^*) > 0$ and, therefore, $p_i^* = 0$; in the latter case, $s_i'(\mathbf{p}^*) > 0$, by the assumption of a binary change, and by T.9.10, for all $\mathbf{p}^{**} \in E'$, $p_i^{**} = 0$, so that in any case $p_i^{**}s_i'(\mathbf{p}^*) = 0$ for $i \neq 1,2$. Then we have $p_1^{**}s_1'(\mathbf{p}^*) + p_2^{**}s_2'(\mathbf{p}^*) < 0$ and so certainly $p_1^{**} > p_1^* = 0$. Since $s_2'(\mathbf{p}^*) > 0$ by assumption when $p_2^* = 0$, T.9.10 ensures that $s_2'(\mathbf{p}^{**}) > 0$, whence $p_2^{**} = 0$.

If $p_i^* > 0$ for $i = 1,2$ then we proceed as in T.10.2.

We must now note that this result is not only slightly weaker than the corresponding one for GS, but its assumptions are also stronger since we postulate the change in parameters to be of a certain type not only at a given $\mathbf{p}$, but over a whole set of $\mathbf{p}$'s. If this had not been postulated, then it might be that E and E' have price vectors in common, and so we could not have utilized the Weak Axiom in the way we in fact did. In the case of GS we found (T.10.3) that we could do without the Weak Axiom. Here this avenue is not available, for we cannot now argue that if, say, $p_k^{**} \geq p_i^{**}$, all i,

$s'_k(\mathbf{p}^{**}) > 0$ for $k \neq 1$, since it may be that the kth good belongs to the class of goods that is independent of prices, and so we could have $s'_k(\mathbf{p}) = 0$, all $\mathbf{p}$. Moreover, should $p_i^* = 0$ for $i = 1,2$, then if the change is defined in the usual way to be binary at $\mathbf{p}^*$ (not over the whole of E), evidently it is quite possible for $\mathbf{p}^{**} \in E$ and $p_i^{**} = 0$ for $i = 1,2$. Thus it would appear that the assumptions of T.10.4 are as weak as or weaker than any alternative ones we could impose in order to obtain clearcut results.

Unfortunately, the assumption that there is Diagonal Dominance, which, we argued in the last chapter, is the most attractive of the restrictions on the forms of the excess-supply functions, is not very powerful in allowing us to make definite statements when equilibria are being compared. Let us see what can be done.

Consider a binary change at $\mathbf{p}^*$ such that $s'_1(\mathbf{p}^*) - s_1(\mathbf{p}^*) = -a$ and $s'_2(\mathbf{p}^*) - s_2(\mathbf{p}^*) = b$ where $p_1^*b - p_2^*a = 0$. Then, since we shall suppose there to be DD, it follows that there will be a new unique equilibrium, which we may write as $\mathbf{p}(a)$. Now let $\{a^\nu\}$ be a sequence with $a^0 = a$, which approaches 0, and let $\mathbf{p}^\nu = \mathbf{p}(a^\nu)$. By an argument exactly similar to that used in proving Lemma 9.3, we can show that

$$\lim_{\nu\to\infty} \mathbf{p}^\nu = \mathbf{p}(\lim_{\nu\to\infty} a^\nu) = \mathbf{p}(0) = \mathbf{p}^*,$$

so that $\mathbf{p}(a)$ is continuous at $a = 0$. In fact we shall assume $\mathbf{p}(a)$ to be differentiable at $a = 0$. With this preliminary out of the way, we may now prove the following proposition.

THEOREM 5. Let $\mathbf{s}(\mathbf{p},\alpha)$ be a one-parameter family of excess-supply functions undergoing binary shifts so that $\partial s_1/\partial\alpha < 0$, all $\mathbf{p}$, and $\partial s_i/\partial\alpha = 0$, all $\mathbf{p}$ and $i \geq 3$. Suppose that $s_2(\mathbf{p},\alpha) < 0$ for all α and $\mathbf{p}$ with $p_2 = 0$ and that for all $\mathbf{p}$ the economy has GP. Then, as α increases, either good 1 is free or, if $\mathbf{p}(\alpha)$ is the equilibrium for α, $p_1(\alpha)/p_2(\alpha)$ increases.

Proof. By assumption, $p_2(\alpha) > 0$ so that we may choose the second good as numeraire and write $\mathbf{P}$ as the vector of prices in terms of a numeraire.

When α is varied, $\mathbf{P}(\alpha)$ is varied so as to ensure a new equilibrium. Hence we have

$$\frac{ds_i[\mathbf{P}(\alpha),\alpha]}{d\alpha} > 0 \quad \text{implies} \quad \frac{dP_i(\alpha)}{d\alpha} \leq 0 \tag{4}$$

and

$$\frac{ds_i[\mathbf{P}(\alpha),\alpha]}{d\alpha} < 0 \quad \text{implies} \quad \frac{dP_i(\alpha)}{d\alpha} \geq 0. \tag{5}$$

Thus, in the case of (4) we know that in the new equilibrium $P_i = 0$. So either the ith price was zero already in the previous equilibrium, or it must now become so. The inequalities of (5) have a similar explanation.

Now write $J = (\partial s_i[\mathbf{P}(\alpha),\alpha]/\partial P_j)$, $i, j \neq 2$ and $\hat{\mathbf{s}}$ for the excess-supply vector excluding the second good. Then

$$\frac{d\hat{\mathbf{s}}[\mathbf{P}(\alpha),\alpha]}{d\alpha} = J\frac{d\mathbf{P}(\alpha)}{d\alpha} + \frac{\partial\hat{\mathbf{s}}}{\partial\alpha} \tag{6}$$

Let T be the diagonal matrix with elements $+1$ or -1 such that

$$\mathbf{Q} = T\frac{d\mathbf{P}(\alpha)}{d\alpha} \geq \mathbf{0}. \tag{7}$$

If $dP_i(\alpha)/d\alpha = 0$, let t_{ii} have the opposite sign of $ds_i/d\alpha$. Thus, by (4) and (5),

$$T\frac{d\hat{\mathbf{s}}[\mathbf{P}(\alpha)\alpha]}{d\alpha} \leq \mathbf{0}, \tag{8}$$

so that if $H = TJT$ we have from (6), recalling $TT = I$,

$$H\mathbf{Q} = T\frac{d\hat{\mathbf{s}}[\mathbf{P}(\alpha),\alpha]}{d\alpha} - T\frac{\partial\hat{\mathbf{s}}}{\partial\alpha} \leq -T\frac{\partial\hat{\mathbf{s}}}{\partial\alpha},$$

but $\partial s_i/\partial\alpha = 0$ for $i \geq 3$ and $\partial s_1/\partial\alpha < 0$ by assumption. Hence $t_{11} = -1$ implies $H\mathbf{Q} < \mathbf{0}$, which contradicts GP. Thus $t_{11} = +1$ and the theorem is proved.

This result is somewhat weaker than the corresponding one for GS. There we were able to prove that whichever good may be chosen as numeraire, the equilibrium price in terms of numeraire of the good experiencing an increase in excess demand at $\mathbf{P}^*$ by the binary change must rise, while the price of the second good must fall. This cannot be shown for the DD case. Nor should this be surprising since DD allows for extremely complex relationships between goods. Thus, for instance, the excess demand for the first good caused by the binary change may be eliminated by a fall in its price in terms of numeraire, provided some other good j that is a gross complement for good 1 ($s'_{1j} > 0$) rises sufficiently in price.

A simple example in which T.10.5 might be applicable would be to trace the consequence on equilibrium wages in terms of food in a country that, in an equilibrium situation, experiences an immigration of labor that directs all its potential demand to food. If the conditions of the theorem are satisfied, then a fall in the food wage can be predicted. The rather artificial nature of this example, quite apart from the necessary assumptions, is an indication of how limited the results have been so far. It is time to see whether we can do any better.

3. More General Parameter Changes

It is not hard to see that for the GS case, certainly, we may relax the requirement that the parameter change be binary and still get some definite conclusion as to the constellation of the new equilibrium prices. Thus we easily establish the following:

THEOREM 6. Let all goods be GS at all **P**. Let there be a parameter change at $\mathbf{P}^*$, an equilibrium with the nth good as numeraire, such that $s_n'(\mathbf{P}^*) > 0$ and $s_i'(\mathbf{P}^*) \leq 0$, all $i \neq n$. Then some prices in terms of numeraire will be higher and none will be lower in the new equilibrium.

Proof. Apply the method of proof used in Corollary 3′.

Small as this extension is, it does allow us to give a more sensible formulation to the immigration example of the previous section for an economy with GS. If we chose labor as our numeraire, we can surely predict a fall in the equilibrium real wage, however that may be defined. The immigrants offer themselves on the labor market at the prevailing equilibrium prices and cause an excess supply there. At the same time, they are potential demanders of goods and so the excess demand at the prevailing prices will rise for some goods and fall for none. There seems no good reason to suppose that the immigration as such will cause a change in the existing plans of residents. The example is, as we said, more sensible, but of course, the restriction GS is correspondingly more severe than was DD.

For "small" parameter changes a somewhat more general result (than the binary ones) can be established for GS. We use the same notation as in T.10.5, but choose the nth good as numeraire. By GS, $\mathbf{P}(\alpha) \gg \mathbf{0}$, all α, and $\hat{\mathbf{s}}[\mathbf{P}(\alpha),\alpha] = \mathbf{0}$, all α. Hence equation (6) of Section 10.2 becomes

$$J\frac{d\mathbf{P}(\alpha)}{d\alpha} = -\frac{\partial\hat{\mathbf{s}}}{\partial\alpha}. \tag{9}$$

We first prove

LEMMA 1. If all goods are GS, then J has a positive root λ^* and an associated positive eigenvector $\mathbf{x}^* \gg \mathbf{0}$.

Proof. Let $\sigma > \max s_{ii}(\mathbf{P}^*)$, let I be the unit matrix, and define A by $A = \sigma I - J(\mathbf{P}^*)$. Then, by GS, A is a positive matrix, (i.e., all elements of A are positive). We know (T.A.1) that a positive matrix has a largest root α, which is positive, and an associated eigenvector $\mathbf{y} \gg \mathbf{0}$. Also (T.A.5), if $\mathbf{a}_i$ is the ith row vector in A,

$$\alpha \leq \max_i \mathbf{a}_i \mathbf{e},$$

where $\mathbf{e}$ is the unit vector. Since $\mathbf{P}^* \gg \mathbf{0}$, we may choose units of goods so that $P_i^* = 1$, all i. Then

$$\mathbf{a}_i \mathbf{e} = \sigma - \sum_{j \neq n} s_{ij}(\mathbf{P}^*) = \sigma + s_{in}(\mathbf{P}^*)$$

and so, by GS, $\alpha < \sigma$. Clearly $\lambda^* = \sigma - \alpha$ is a root of J and has the associated eigenvector $\mathbf{x}^* = \mathbf{y}$.

We now prove

THEOREM 7. Let all goods be GS and let there be a parameter change at $\mathbf{P}^*$. Then there exists a way of constructing a composite commodity and an associated price vector, such that the parameter change causes this price to move in the opposite direction to the excess supply of the composite commodity.

Proof. From (9), if $\mathbf{x}^*$ is the strictly positive eigenvector,

$$\mathbf{x}^* J \frac{d\mathbf{P}(\alpha)}{d\alpha} = -\mathbf{x}^* \frac{\partial \hat{\mathbf{s}}}{\partial \alpha}.$$

But $\mathbf{x}^* J = \lambda^* \mathbf{x}^*$. Let $\mathbf{P}^*(\alpha) = \mathbf{x}^* \mathbf{P}(\alpha)$, $\hat{\mathbf{s}}^* = \mathbf{x}^* \hat{\mathbf{s}}$. Then,

$$\lambda^* \frac{d\mathbf{P}^*(\alpha)}{d\alpha} = -\frac{\partial \hat{\mathbf{s}}^*}{d\alpha},$$

which, in view of $\lambda^* > 0$, proves the theorem.

Not much can be claimed for the usefulness of T.10.7, for it may reasonably be argued that if we know enough to calculate the eigenvectors then we certainly know enough about J to solve (9) directly. It is worth noting, however, that should the excess-supply functions be linear over a certain range, then having done our calculations once puts us in the position of making the prediction of the theorem.

Without further restricting the model that we use in comparing equilibria it does not seem possible to obtain any further results for general parameter changes. This is neither surprising nor a cause for despondency. The analysis of binary changes does in a general equilibrium context what Marshallian partial analysis achieves in a much more restricted setting; for general changes we must expect to have fairly precise quantitative information as to the relationship between goods before being able to make the kind of statement that was possible for binary changes.

4. The Constant Returns Economy

In this section we will study the L-economy of Section 2.11. Recall (T.3.6) that if $C_i(\mathbf{p})$ is the minimum unit cost function of sector i, then

$$C_{ij}(\mathbf{p}) \equiv \frac{\partial C_i}{\partial p_j} = -y'_{ij}(\mathbf{p})$$

where $-y'_{ij}(\mathbf{p})$ is the cost minimizing input of "j" per unit of good i. We give labor the subscript N.

DEFINITION 2. The economy will be called *production connected* at $\mathbf{p}$ if there is no set of goods H such that $C_{ij}(\mathbf{p}) = 0$ for all $i \in H, j \notin H$, $j < N$.

This notion of connectedness is, of course, similar to D.9.7, only here it is related to the minimum unit cost functions, that is, to the use of inputs in production. We may now prove

THEOREM 8. Let the economy be production connected at all $\mathbf{p}$ and satisfy A.2.10–A.2.14. Let a parameter change lower unit production costs for some sectors and raise it for none. Then the equilibrium price of every good in terms of labor must fall.

Note that, by T.2.6, the equilibrium price of labor is always positive, so it may be chosen as numeraire both before and after the change.

Proof. Let $R_i(\mathbf{p}) = p_i - C_i(\mathbf{p})$ and $\mathbf{R}(\mathbf{p})$ the vector with components $R_i(\mathbf{p})$. A prime denotes the value of a variable or vector after the parameter change. By assumption,

$$\mathbf{R}(\mathbf{p}^*) = \mathbf{0} \qquad \mathbf{R}'(\mathbf{p}^*) > \mathbf{0}.$$

Since $\mathbf{R}$ is homogeneous of degree one in $\mathbf{p}$, we may normalize on labor. Let $\mathbf{P}^* = \mathbf{p}^*/p_N$, $\mathbf{P}^{**} = \mathbf{p}^{**}/p_N^{**}$. Suppose that, contrary to assertion, there is a set of goods H such that

$$1 \leq k = \frac{P_h^{**}}{P_h^*} \geq \frac{P_i^{**}}{P_i^*} \qquad \text{for } h \in H,\ i < N.$$

Certainly $kP_N^* \geq P_N^{**}$, and since all sectors use labor,

$$C_h'(k\mathbf{P}^*) \geq C_h'(\mathbf{P}^{**}) \qquad h \in H,$$

and so

$$0 \leq R_h'(\mathbf{P}^*) = \frac{R_h'(k\mathbf{P}^*)}{k} \leq \frac{R_h'(\mathbf{P}^{**})}{k} \qquad h \in H.$$

If the right-hand inequality is not strict for any $h \in H$, then the sectors in H use no goods produced by the sectors not in H, in contradiction to the assumption that the economy is production connected unless H consists of all goods. In that case k cannot exceed 1, since labor, which has not risen in price, enters the production of all goods, and k cannot equal 1, for then $\mathbf{P}^* = \mathbf{P}^{**}$ cannot be an equilibrium after the change. Hence, $R_h'(\mathbf{P}^{**}) > 0$, some $h \in H$, and again $\mathbf{P}^{**}$ cannot be an equilibrium. Hence, $k < 1$.

It can be left to the reader to verify that in the absence of the connectedness assumption we prove $\mathbf{P}^* > \mathbf{P}^{**}$ with a strict inequality in those components that represent the sectors in which the productivity improvement has taken place. The advantage of the stronger assumption is that it allows us to make assertions such as: Technical progress will raise the equilibrium "real" wage of labor, however "real" wage is defined. The result is not surprising, of course, but it is worth having.

Corollary 8. In the economy of T.10.8, let the parameter change be such that the cost of production at the initial equilibrium prices, $\mathbf{P}^*$, is lowered only for good s. Then it must be that

$$\frac{P_s^{**}}{P_s^*} \leq \frac{P_i^{**}}{P_i^*} \qquad \text{all } i.$$

Proof. Suppose that the asserted inequality does not hold for "s," but for "t." Then, by the same arguments as in the proof of the theorem, we have

$$0 = R_t'(\mathbf{P}^*) = \frac{R_t'(k\mathbf{P}^*)}{k} > \frac{R_t'(\mathbf{P}^{**})}{k} = 0; \quad k = \frac{P_t^{**}}{P_t^*} < 1,$$

which is impossible.

From this we conclude that although a technical improvement in one sector only must raise the equilibrium product wage everywhere, it must raise it by the greatest proportion in the sector in which the improvement has taken place.

Let us now consider an economy in which there are a number of different non-produced inputs that enter into production. As in 9.12, we assume that there are as many non-produced inputs as there are goods. We first consider a fully integrated economy with no intermediate goods. As usual, we write $\mathbf{w}$ as the vector of input prices and consider the equilibrium

$$\mathbf{p}^* = \mathbf{C}^*(\mathbf{w}^*),$$

where $\mathbf{C}^*(\mathbf{w})$ is the vector of minimum unit-cost functions. We shall take $\mathbf{p}^* \gg \mathbf{0}$ and $\mathbf{w}^* \gg \mathbf{0}$ and consider what would be the consequence for the equilibrium prices of inputs of an autonomous change in the prices of outputs. We shall discuss the economic context of this question presently. First, we prove

THEOREM 9. Let $\mathbf{p}^* \gg \mathbf{0}$ and $\mathbf{w}^* \gg \mathbf{0}$ with $\mathbf{p}^* = \mathbf{C}^*(\mathbf{w}^*)$ in a constant returns economy using n inputs to produce n outputs in positive amounts. Let $\mathbf{p} = \mathbf{p}^* + d\mathbf{p}^*$ where $\mathbf{p} - \mathbf{p}^* \neq k\mathbf{p}^*$ for any scalar $k > 0$. Then

(a) there is at least one good in terms of which total factor income falls;

(b) there is at least one factor whose income does not fall in terms of any good.

Proof. (a) If $(C_{ij}(\mathbf{w}^*))$ is the Jacobian at $\mathbf{w}^*$ of $\mathbf{C}^*(\mathbf{w}^*)$, let $-Y = (C_{ij}(\mathbf{w}^*))$. Note (T.3.6) that $-Y_{ij}$ is the amount of factor j used in the production of one unit of good i.

For $d\mathbf{p}^*$ small enough we can find the required change, $d\mathbf{w}^*$ in factor prices that preserve equality between prices and unit production costs from

$$-Yd\mathbf{w}^* = d\mathbf{p}^*. \tag{10}$$

Let $\mathbf{x}^* \gg \mathbf{0}$ be the output column vector at $(\mathbf{p}^*,\mathbf{w}^*)$, L the column vector of available factor supplies. Then,

$$-\mathbf{x}^{*\prime} Y = \mathbf{L}'$$

where the prime denotes transposition.

Combining this last expression with (10), we have

$$-\mathbf{x}^{*\prime} Y d\mathbf{w}^* = \mathbf{L}' d\mathbf{w}^* = \mathbf{x}^{*\prime} d\mathbf{p}^*$$

so

$$\frac{\mathbf{L}' d\mathbf{w}^*}{\mathbf{L}'\mathbf{w}^*} = \frac{\mathbf{x}^{*\prime} d\mathbf{p}^*}{\mathbf{L}'\mathbf{w}^*}$$

and we note that the left-hand side of this expression measures the proportionate change in factor receipts. Let

$$h = \max_i \frac{dp_i^*}{p_i^*}.$$

Then, by the assumption of the theorem, $dp_j^*/p_j^* < h$, some j at $x_j^* > 0$, whence

$$\frac{\mathbf{x}^{*\prime} d\mathbf{p}^*}{\mathbf{L}'\mathbf{w}^*} < \frac{h\mathbf{x}^{*\prime}\mathbf{p}^*}{\mathbf{L}'\mathbf{w}^*} = h,$$

where the last equality follows from constant returns to scale, which ensures $\mathbf{x}^{*\prime}\mathbf{p}^* = \mathbf{L}'\mathbf{w}^*$. Then, if $h = dp_r^*/p_r^*$, say,

$$\frac{\mathbf{L}' d\mathbf{w}^*}{\mathbf{L}'\mathbf{w}^*} < \frac{dp_r^*}{p_r^*}$$

so that in terms of the rth good, total factor incomes fall.

(b) By the homogeneity of the cost functions and the assumption $d\mathbf{p}^* \neq k\mathbf{p}^*$, there must be an s such that

$$\frac{dw_s^*}{w_s^*} \geq \frac{dw_i^*}{w_i^*} \qquad \text{all } i$$

and

$$\frac{dw_s^*}{w_s^*} > \frac{dw_i^*}{w_i^*} \qquad \text{some } i; \tag{11}$$

for if factor prices all rose in the same proportion, so would goods prices. Taking the rth equation of (10), and recalling $-Y_{rj} \geq 0$, all r and j,

$$hp_r^* = -\sum_j Y_{rj} dw_j^* = -\sum_j (Y_{rj} w_j^*) \frac{dw_j^*}{w_j^*} \leq \frac{dw_s^*}{w_s^*} \left(-\sum_j Y_{rj} w_j^*\right) \tag{12}$$

or

$$h \leq \frac{dw_s^*}{w_s^*},$$

since by constant returns to scale $p_j^* = -\sum_j Y_{rj} w_j^*$. Hence the income of factor s in terms of good r, the good whose price has risen in the greatest proportion does not fall.

Corollary 9. If all factors are used in the production of every good then the real income of at least one factor will increase no matter how deflated.

Proof. The inequality in (12) is strict since $-Y_{rj} > 0$, all j.

These results of course in no way depend on the number of prices that are taken to be different. If, for instance, $dp_i^* = 0$, all $i \neq 1$, then the real incomes we make predictions about are incomes in terms of good 1.

If we think of a world in which prices are set by the forces of free international trade, then we may use the above results in analyzing the consequences for real factor income in a given country of a change in the world price of a given good. Alternatively, we may think of the change in the prices coming about by an imposition or removal of a tariff. In that case, for instance, our theory predicts that, tariff revenue apart, the raising of a tariff on one good must reduce the real income of factors, but that there will be at least one factor that is "not hurt" by this policy and that might gain. The question naturally arises, whether we can identify the factor that is the subject of (b) of the theorem.

THEOREM 10. Assume that there is one input for every output such that the share of that input in the revenue of the output exceeds the sum of the shares of all other inputs. If one output price increases, then the price of the corresponding input increases, in at least as great proportion.

Proof. Let the price of the first good be changed. Number inputs as stated in the theorem and note that it is assumed that

$$-Y_{ii} w_i^* > \sum_{j \neq i} (-Y_{ij}) w_j^* \qquad \text{all } i.$$

Let $s_{i1} = (dw_i^*/dp_1^*)(p_1^*/w_i^*)$ and consider r such that

$$|s_{r1}| \geq |s_{i1}| \qquad \text{all } i.$$

Then, if $r \neq 1$ we have by (10),

$$-Y_{rr} w_r^* |s_{r1}| = \left| -\sum_{j \neq r} Y_{rj} w_j^* s_{j1} \right| \leq |s_{r1}| \sum_{j \neq r} (-Y_{rj}) w_j^*,$$

which contradicts the assumption of the theorem, and so $r = 1$. Since this same assumption ensures that $-Y\hat{w}^*$ has GP (since it has DD) where $\hat{w}^*$ is the diagonal matrix with elements w_i^*, solving (10) gives $s_{r1} > 0$, and (12) establishes the theorem.

It can be argued that this result is not of very great interest since the assumptions on which it rests are very unlikely to be fulfilled in practice. If we are concerned only with a two-good, two-factor world, then the supposition that each good uses one input more intensively than the other, at least in the vicinity of an equilibrium, seems entirely plausible. But then we have replaced the unpalatable assumptions of the theorem by the equally unpalatable one that there are only two goods. It is also worth noting that the assumption of T.10.10 ensures that for every **p** there is only one **w** at which production costs are covered. (We are here assuming DD to hold globally.) This might suggest that the uniqueness of the equilibrium **w**, given **p**, and the problem of which input experiences a rise in its real wage when a given price is raised are connected problems. Assertion in some of the literature notwithstanding, this is not the case, however. Thus the reader can check that if the production functions are everywhere Cobb–Douglas with constant returns to scale, we may write the equations minimum unit cost = price as

$$\log p_i + \text{constant} = \sum \alpha_{ij} \log w_j$$

where the α_{ij}'s are the exponents of the Cobb–Douglas. Since these equations are linear, it follows that there is a unique **w** that satisfies them given **p**. On the other hand, there is no reason to suppose that the matrix (α_{ij}) has DD.

Now while it is true that the conditions of T.10.10 are only sufficient for its proposition, it is fairly clear that no very economically meaningful necessary conditions are likely. We must thus conclude that it will be only in the rather special circumstances of the theorem that, for instance, the effect of a tariff on a particular good on the real wage of a named factor can be predicted. At least T.10.9 enables us to predict that there will be one factor that will not have its real wage lowered by the tariff.

It is easy, however, to show that the output of the good whose price is changed must move in a direction not opposite to the price change. If we write $\mathbf{y}(\mathbf{p})$ as the vector of outputs of the economy at **p**, then profit maximization implies

$$\mathbf{p}^*\mathbf{y}(\mathbf{p}^*) - \mathbf{w}^*\mathbf{L} \geq \mathbf{p}^*\mathbf{y}(\mathbf{p}^{**}) - \mathbf{w}^*\mathbf{L},$$

$$\mathbf{p}^{**}\mathbf{y}(\mathbf{p}^{**}) - \mathbf{w}^{**}\mathbf{L} \geq \mathbf{p}^{**}\mathbf{y}(\mathbf{p}^*) - \mathbf{w}^{**}\mathbf{L}.$$

So combining and noting that $\Delta p_i^* = 0$, all $i \neq 1$, we have

$$\Delta p_1^*[y_1(\mathbf{p}^{**}) - y_1(\mathbf{p}^*)] \geq 0.$$

This concludes what seems possible to accomplish for this class of problem. Before we leave it, though, we must briefly see how our conclusions survive the introduction of intermediate goods. We now write the equation minimum unit cost = price as

$$\mathbf{p} = \mathbf{H}(\mathbf{p},\mathbf{w}).$$

If, as before, we write $-Y$ as the matrix of factor inputs per unit of output and $-\tilde{Y}$ as the matrix of the inputs of goods per unit of output, then (10) becomes

$$-Yd\mathbf{w}^* = (I + \tilde{Y})d\mathbf{p}^*$$

where I is the unit matrix. The net output vector, $\mathbf{x}^{*\prime}(I + \tilde{Y})$, is assumed strictly positive. If we define h as in T.10.9, $\mathbf{dp}^* < \mathbf{p}^*h$ and, therefore, $\mathbf{x}^{*\prime}(I + \tilde{Y})\mathbf{dp}^* < \mathbf{x}^{*\prime}(I + \tilde{Y})\mathbf{p}^*h$. Since certainly,

$$-\mathbf{x}^{*\prime}Y = \mathbf{L}',$$

as before, and by constant returns to scale,

$$\mathbf{L}'\mathbf{w}^* = \mathbf{x}^{*\prime}(I + \tilde{Y})\mathbf{p}^*$$

the proof of T.10.9(a) proceeds as before.

That T.10.9(b) continues to hold is clear from the modified (12),

$$h\left(p_r^* + \sum_j \tilde{Y}_{rj}p_j^*\right) \leq hp_r^* + \sum_j \tilde{Y}_{rj}dp_j^* \leq \frac{dw_s^*}{w_s^*}\left(-\sum_j Y_{rj}w_j^*\right).$$

That T.10.10 also survives the introduction of intermediate goods is now clear. Thus, to suppose the economy to be fully integrated turns out to be a harmless simplification in these problems.

We conclude this discussion of the constant returns to scale economy with a simple example.

Consider an economy of the type here considered in equilibrium with a factor endowment of $\mathbf{L}$. (We again exclude intermediate goods for simplicity of exposition.) That is, in the usual notation, $\mathbf{p}^* = \mathbf{C}(\mathbf{w}^*)$ and $-\mathbf{x}^{*\prime}Y = \mathbf{L}'$, where $\mathbf{x}^*$ is again the vector of outputs.

Suppose $\mathbf{x}^* \gg \mathbf{0}, \mathbf{L} \gg \mathbf{0}$. We are interested in predicting the new equilibrium output $\mathbf{x}^{**}$ that would result if there was a small change in the availability of input of type 1 and $\mathbf{p}^*$ were held constant. This, in the two-factor case, was first investigated by Rybczynski [1955].

Suppose $-Y$ has GP. Then we want to examine

$$-\mathbf{dx}^{*\prime} Y = (dL_1, 0, \ldots, 0).$$

By the Remark to D.9.1 (the definition of GP), the vectors $\mathbf{dx}^*$ and $\mathbf{dL}$ must have at least one component with common non-zero sign; this can only be the first, so that we conclude that $dx_1^* dL_1 > 0$.

Certainly $-Y$ will have GP if, for some numbering of the outputs and inputs, the sector i uses input i more intensively than it does all other inputs combined,

$$C_{ii}^* w_i^* > \sum_{j \neq i} C_{ij}^* w_j^*.$$

In that case, we then have the theorem that, say, an increase in the amount of input i available, all goods prices constant, will lead to a new equilibrium where more of the good using i most intensively will be produced. This result has proved useful in simple international trade theory, but it is achieved at a high cost.

5. Conclusions

The most notable conclusion of our investigations in this chapter appears to us to be that for very many interesting problems of comparing equilibria, the information provided by the foundations of the models, profit and utility maximization, are insufficient in giving us definite answers to our questions. Indeed, even if the weak axiom of revealed preference holds for the whole economy, either for comparisons involving one equilibrium or generally, we soon find that we have insufficient information when we consider parameter changes that are not binary. At one time it was thought that this paucity of definite results could be avoided, if in addition to the underlying maximizing behavior of agents, it was postulated that the equilibrium of the economy was "stable" under some adjustment process. We shall see later, however, that the necessary conditions for such stability do not provide the kind of information we require, while sufficient conditions now known involve restrictions on the excess-demand functions such as GS or DD that, as we have seen in this chapter, do not carry us a great deal further.

Now while such results as we were able to establish are useful and worth having, the main negative lesson is also useful, for it points to the dangers of partial analysis, in which it is often possible to get quite definite predictions of the consequences of a given parameter change. We now know that such results, if they are to be correct for "other things not equal" involve very special assumptions, such as DD and binary changes.

Notes

Hicks [1939] was probably the first to concern himself with the questions of this chapter in the context of a full general equilibrium model. His method, as well as that of his successors, such as Mosak [1944] and Samuelson [1947], was based on calculus and hence was concerned only with infinitesimal changes. Morishima [1959–60] was the first to exploit the Weak Axiom of Revealed Preference in binary comparisons of price situations of which one was an equilibrium. T.10.2–T.10.4, were first noted by him. T.10.8 is also closely related to a proposition of Morishima's [1964], although his analysis was in the context of a model of steady growth. Indeed, a number of results that refer to comparisons of steady states have not been treated by us since they would have required us to break off our main analysis. T.10.10 is, in the n-factor context, related to a well-known proposition of Samuelson and Stolper [1941]. The other theorems do not appear to be in the literature.

In recent years, a suggestion of Samuelson's [1947] that local comparative results might be obtainable from the sign pattern of the appropriate Jacobians has been much explored. The main references are Lancaster [1961–62, 1964, 1965], Gorman [1964], and Quirk [1968]. We have not discussed this development because it would have taken us rather far afield. As might be expected, the results so far, although interesting, have not been very encouraging. For instance, for a binary change, sign prediction is possible if and only if the matrix $(s_{ij}(\mathbf{p}))$, by permutation and multiplication by diagonal matrices with ± 1 on the diagonal, can be given the GS sign pattern or the GS sign pattern except for one column where all off-diagonal elements can be positive. The first case is, of course, GP, and using W, the second case can be shown to imply GP also (since it implies DD). On the other hand, of course, GP does not imply this sign pattern. So we seem to have the following result: Sign restrictions in the binary change case are possible from sign information on the Jacobian only if this information suffices to establish GP.

Chapter Eleven

INTRODUCTION TO STABILITY ANALYSIS

Nine in the second position means:
He allows himself to be drawn into returning.
Good fortune.

—*I Ching*

1. The Problem

The economist's interest in equilibrium situations may be justified by two kinds of arguments. An equilibrium has special claims to our attention because when we ask ourselves how to characterize a decentralized economy that is also efficient we find that it is often an economy in competitive equilibrium. This is not always so as, for instance, reflection on the case of an economy subject to increasing returns will quickly show. It is true, however, for sufficiently interesting situations and so certainly merits attention. The second argument, familiar from Marshall, is simply that there are forces at work in any actual economy that tend to drive an economy toward an equilibrium if it is not in equilibrium already. If this is correct, then for instance, the method of comparing equilibria may be a legitimate way of going about the business of predicting the consequences of given parameter changes. In any case, it is with the question of a "tendency to equilibrium" that this and two of the following chapters will be concerned. We may agree at the outset that should our investigations convince us that Marshall was mistaken, this in itself would be a conclusion of considerable importance. Not only would it have immediate negative implications for the method of comparing equilibria, but when we put on the hat of welfare economists, it would have great relevance in helping us to judge, in the manner in which welfare economists do judge, the performance of actual economic systems.

That the task we have set ourselves is a hard one seems evident. It would surely be foolish to suppose that the proper manner of proceeding would be to plunge immediately into the complex problems of agents' reactions to disequilibrium situations. Accordingly, we shall start our enquiries with a quite artificial process of adjustment, which we shall now describe and discuss.

2. A Tâtonnement

Suppose that in an economy with given tastes, endowments, and technological knowledge, agents believe that they can transact on terms given by the price vector **p** and that, of course, these terms do not depend on the amount of any given transaction. Suppose further that, given **p**, agents plan to transact in amounts such that for none of them is there an alternative set of transactions that they would prefer, but that, in fact, not all the transactions can be carried out simultaneously. This means that **p** is not an equilibrium. In practice, therefore, some agents will find their plans cannot be brought to fruition, so that when we look at them a little later, we should find that the goods they have and the production they undertake are not the goods they planned to have or the production they planned to undertake. We would then require to know just how each agent fared in carrying out his transaction plans before we could hope to carry the story further. This will be quite difficult to accomplish and it is the special feature of what we shall call a *tâtonnement*[1] that it sidesteps this difficulty by supposing that no transactions at all are carried out when the transactions planned cannot be brought to fruition simultaneously.

We may imagine, to give some flesh to the abstraction we propose to investigate, the existence of a super-auctioneer who calls a given set of prices **p** and receives transaction offers from the agents in the economy. If these do not match, he calls another set of prices, following some rule, to be discussed, but no transactions are allowed to take place. This process either comes to some end or continues indefinitely. In fact, we shall find that, like Achilles and the tortoise, the auctioneer following his rule will never be able to rectify a mistake completely, although in some proper sense, the mistake may get smaller and smaller. But that is a point that must await attention until the suitable moment has come. Here we better give a formal definition of the imaginary process.

[1] The word comes from Walras. It is not claimed that he used it in the same way as it is being used here.

DEFINITION 1. A *tâtonnement* consists of the adoption of the following rules:

(a) If $\mathbf{p}(t)$ is a price vector at time t, then this price is changed by some rule if and only if $\mathbf{p}(t)$ is not an equilibrium.
(b) Agents are permitted to transact if and only if $\mathbf{p}(t)$ is an equilibrium.

It seems pretty clear that when we have learned all we can about this kind of process, a great deal of work will remain before we shall be able to claim to have a proper understanding of the "price mechanism." It would be foolish, however, to maintain that we shall have learned nothing because the stage we have set bears too little resemblance to the actual world. For one thing, it will be agreed that a tâtonnement serves to isolate what might be called "pure price effects" from those that are due to changes in either the wealth or the composition of wealth of the agents. Since we shall certainly have to understand these price effects in any full story, it is reasonable to suppose that a study of them in isolation is a hopeful procedure.

It may also be argued that despite its abstract stance, a tatônnement is what many economists must have had in mind when they first proposed "the law of supply and demand." More than piety seems at stake in subjecting such venerable principles to the more rigorous analysis of the present time. Additionally, it may be maintained that although the process is pictured as taking place in time, this is simply a device to aid understanding, and that the calculations of the auctioneer may be taken as steps in a computer program designed, by a process of iteration, to calculate the equilibrium prices for an economy. Not too much can be made of this point because, on the one hand, the rules we shall impose on the auctioneer do, however remotely, mimic what we believe goes on in actual markets, and there is no reason why a computer program should be so restricted, and on the other, there is no reason to think the process computationally efficient.

Lastly, before turning to greater details, it may be worth noting that we could think of actual economies for which a tatônnement would not appear to be so remote a description, for instance, in a world where all goods are perishable and where the goods agents have in possession after given time intervals are independent of the transactions they have carried out. This world would not be greatly misdescribed by a process that prohibits transactions at non-equilibrium prices, simply because the change in the circumstances of agents due to transactions are quite transitory. On the other hand, we should still face a problem, endemic for perfect competition models, of how prices are changed. For, if no one can affect the terms on which he may transact, it is hard to see, without the "as if" auctioneer, how these terms ever come to be different. This is a point to which we shall return later (see Chapter 13).

3. The Auctioneer's Rules

We have already committed ourselves to one rule that we shall take the auctioneer as following: Never change any price if the given price vector is an equilibrium; never leave all prices unchanged if the given price vector is not an equilibrium. We have also supposed implicitly that the price adjustment is in continuous time. This is not an essential feature of the process and at some later stage we shall consider situations in which the adjustment is over discrete time intervals. What we shall do now, bearing in mind that we wish to attain some eventual understanding of the price mechanism, is to allow the other restrictions on the auctioneer to be what we take to be most conducive to mimicking what may be an actual process. Thus, taking F, W, C, and B of Chapter 2 to hold and writing, as usual, $z_i(\mathbf{p})$ as the excess-demand function for commodity i when the distribution of wealth between agents and its total amount can be taken as given, we stipulate the following rule for the auctioneer.

ASSUMPTION 1. Let $G_i(z_i)$ be a sign-preserving function of z_i, with $G_i(0) = 0$, and differentiable with $G_i' > 0$. Then for all i:

$$\begin{aligned} \dot{p}_i &= 0 \quad \text{if} \quad p_i \leq 0 \quad \text{and} \quad z_i(p) < 0 \\ \dot{p}_i &= G_i[z_i(\mathbf{p})] \quad \text{otherwise} \end{aligned}$$

(A dot over a symbol denotes the operation d/dt.)

The first thing to notice about this rule is that if $\mathbf{p}(0) > \mathbf{0}$, then $\mathbf{p}(t) > \mathbf{0}$ for all *finite* t (i.e., $t < +\infty$). We show this now.

Take $p_i(0) > 0$ and suppose that $p_i(t') < 0$, $t' > 0$. Then, by continuity, there is some t, where $0 < t < t'$, for which $p_i(t) = 0$. Let t'' be the time closest to t' for which the ith price is zero. Then it cannot be that $z_i(\mathbf{p}(t'')) > 0$, for the ith price is rising at t'' and would have to pass through zero again in order to become negative at t' to contradict the definition of t''. But $z_i(\mathbf{p}(t'')) \leq 0$ is also impossible for then the ith price would remain constant at zero beyond t''. Hence $p_i(t) < 0$ is not possible.

Suppose next that for some finite t' we have $\mathbf{p}(t') = \mathbf{0}$. We note that when $\dot{\mathbf{p}}(t) \neq \mathbf{0}$, it must be that for some i, $z_i(\mathbf{p}(t)) > 0$. If not, $\mathbf{z}(\mathbf{p}(t)) \leq \mathbf{0}$ and so, by D.2.1, $\mathbf{p}(t)$ is an equilibrium. It then must be true, by T.2.1, that all goods in excess supply have a zero price and no good with a positive price is in excess demand. But then $\dot{\mathbf{p}}(t) = \mathbf{0}$, contrary to assumption. Since some price is always increasing as long as prices are changing and $\mathbf{p}(0) > \mathbf{0}$, not all prices can become zero in finite time and the supposition at the beginning of the paragraph is not possible. However, the reader should note that we have not established the impossibility of $\mathbf{p}(t)$ approaching $\mathbf{0}$ as t approaches plus infinity. For reasons that will become apparent, we shall have to strengthen our requirements on the auctioneer's rules in order to exclude that possibility also. So far we have established

THEOREM 1. If A.11.1 holds, then

(a) prices change if and only if the economy is not in equilibrium;
(b) for all finite t, $\mathbf{p}(t) > \mathbf{0}$ if $\mathbf{p}(0) > \mathbf{0}$.

The "error" that causes a given price to change is a disparity between the planned transactions of agents in the market in which that price is called. It will be agreed that the last property of the rule that we are imposing seems faithful to that "law" of supply and demand to which we have already referred. Yet it has caused some disquiet on the grounds that while it is reasonable to postulate that, for instance, an actual attempt to buy more shoes at a given price than are being supplied at that price will drive up the price of shoes, it is quite another matter to say that the *plan* to buy more shoes than are planned for supply will drive up their price. It might just happen that when several markets are out of equilibrium and I have already found myself unable to buy the socks I had planned to buy, my actual pressure to have shoes supplied to me also will be less than I had planned it to be before I discovered my inability to fulfill my plans. Therefore, is it sensible to deduce from people's plans what the actual pressure on individual markets is going to be when these plans are inconsistent? There is no doubt that these objections have force in an argument designed to show that the rules we propose do not properly mimic what we think may actually take place in markets. Certainly we shall have to consider this matter at some stage. (See Chapter 13.)

It will have been noticed that A.11.1 applies the same rule of change to all prices. It must be true, then, that we are taking these as reckoned in some fictional unit of account. However, we are used to dealing with prices in terms of some numeraire, for example, money. It will be convenient to have an analysis also of a situation in which the prices called by the auctioneer are in terms of numeraire. Let us suppose that A.9.2(N) holds and consider the following modification of A.11.1 where $\mathbf{P}$ is the price vector in terms of numeraire.

ASSUMPTION 2. Let $F_i(z_i)$ have all the properties of $G_i(z_i)$ and choose the nth good as numeraire. Then for all $i \neq n$:

$$\dot{P}_i = 0 \quad \text{if} \quad P_i \leq 0 \quad \text{and} \quad z_i(\mathbf{P}) < 0$$
$$\dot{P}_i = F_i(z_i(\mathbf{P})) \quad \text{otherwise}$$

and $\dot{P}_n$ is equal to zero identically in t.

It seems unnecessary to comment further on this assumption, since what was said concerning A.11.1 applies to it also. Yet even at this stage, we may note that we shall wish to ask ourselves whether certain of the conclusions we may deduce for this process are independent of the choice of numeraire, if there are a number of goods that may be so chosen without logical objection.

Both of the auctioneer's rules suppose that when changes in prices do occur, they do so in continuous time. At some stage, it will be interesting also to consider them in discrete time. In that case, instead of $\dot{\mathbf{p}}$ or $\dot{\mathbf{P}}$ we shall write $p_i(t + \epsilon) - p_i(t)$ and $P_i(t + \epsilon) - P_i(t)$.

There are also a number of technical restrictions that we shall impose on the rules followed by the auctioneer. If we look at these rules again, we see that they are a set of simultaneous differential equations. A solution of such equations is a path depending on t and on initial conditions ($\mathbf{p}(0)$ or $\mathbf{P}(0)$). From now on we shall discuss only A.11.1; what is said about A.11.1 applies equally to A.11.2. We write a solution as $\mathbf{p}(t \mid \mathbf{p}(0))$ and note that if indeed it is a solution, it must be that $\mathbf{p}(t \mid \mathbf{p}(0))$ satisfies the rules at each t. It would be very awkward if for given initial conditions there were a number of possible different solutions; indeed, for general cases we might then find it impossible to analyze the time path of prices at all. Accordingly, we shall wish to exclude this possibility of multiple solutions. For reasons that will become apparent in the next section, we shall also wish to be able to take for granted that $\mathbf{p}(t \mid \mathbf{p}(0))$ is continuous in $\mathbf{p}(0)$, that is, in the initial conditions.

The ideal way of doing this would be to specify the class of functions $G_i(\ )$ for which we can be certain that the resulting path will have the properties we desire. Unfortunately, our insistence that prices must never become negative precludes us from using the standard sufficient restriction that the functions should satisfy a "Lipschitz condition."[1] That condition certainly will not be satisfied if the functions determining the rate of change in prices are not continuous, and our functions will not be continuous for all $\mathbf{p}$. Suppose that $\mathbf{p}$ has a zero member p_i and that $z_i(\mathbf{p}) < 0$. Then for all $\mathbf{p}'$ close to $\mathbf{p}$ with $p_i' > 0$, there is $\epsilon > 0$ such that

$$z_i(\mathbf{p}) < -\epsilon.$$

So, for some $\delta > 0$ in the same neighborhood

$$G_i(z_i(\mathbf{p}')) < -\delta.$$

But at $\mathbf{p}$, $G_i(z_i(\mathbf{p})) = 0$ so that $\mathbf{G}$ is discontinuous at $\mathbf{p}$.

Certainly, we can avoid much of this trouble if we consider only classes of excess-demand functions (such as those that satisfy GS) for which we can be certain that, if we start with a strictly positive price vector, the auctioneer will never find himself in the position of not changing a price although its excess demand is not zero. Of course, this involves a certain cost—a rather severe restriction on the excess-demand functions. Instead, we prefer to follow the rather unsatisfactory procedure of stipulating directly the consequences we desire.

ASSUMPTION 3. Let $\mathbf{p}(t \mid \mathbf{p}(0))$ be a solution of the rule in A.11.1 and $\mathbf{P}(t \mid \mathbf{P}(0))$ a solution of the rule in A.11.2. Then

(a) these solutions are uniquely determined by their initial conditions, $\mathbf{p}(0)$ or $\mathbf{P}(0)$;

(b) the solutions are continuous in $\mathbf{p}(0)$ and $\mathbf{P}(0)$, respectively.

[1] The differential equations: $\dot{\mathbf{x}} = \mathbf{f}(\mathbf{x})$, where $\mathbf{x}$ is a vector and $\mathbf{f}(\mathbf{x})$ is vector valued, are said to obey a *Lipschitz condition* if for any two values of $\mathbf{x}$, say $\mathbf{x}$ and $\mathbf{x}'$,

$$|\mathbf{f}(\mathbf{x}) - \mathbf{f}(\mathbf{x}')| \leqq K|\mathbf{x} - \mathbf{x}'|,$$

where K is a constant independent of $\mathbf{x}$.

The difficulty we have been discussing also can be overcome by modifying the auctioneer's rules. For instance, Nikaidô and Uzawa [1960] have suggested the following rule:

$$\dot{p}_i = \max[kz_i(\mathbf{p}) + p_i, 0] - p_i \qquad i = 1, \ldots, n$$

where $k > 0$ and depends on $\mathbf{p}(0)$. Certainly, $p_i = 0$ and $z_i(\mathbf{p}) < 0$ now gives $\dot{p}_i = 0$. Also, $kz_i(\mathbf{p}) + p_i \leq 0$ leads to $\dot{p}_i = -p_i$ for $p_i > 0$. It is easy to check that no discontinuity occurs at $p_i = 0$. The continuity of $\mathbf{z}(\mathbf{p})$ over the simplex and standard theorems then allows us to prove for this process what A.11.3 assumes. This is satisfactory, but the result is bought at the cost of an ad hoc postulate that is not easily made economically persuasive.

Another possibility, not noted in the literature, is the following adjustment rule:

$$\dot{p}_i = \max[p_i z_i(\mathbf{p}), z_i(\mathbf{p})] \qquad i = 1, \ldots, n.$$

Then for p_i close to zero and $z_i(\mathbf{p}) < 0$, $\dot{p}_i = p_i z_i(\mathbf{p})$ and there is no discontinuity at $p_i = 0$. Once again we may establish A.11.3 as a proposition, but as before, there is not much to recommend this particular rule.

In the analysis of the behavior of prices in the large, we shall require the solution $\mathbf{p}(t \mid \mathbf{p}(0))$ to be bounded. In a number of cases this can be proved to be the case. For others, we may wish to suppose that the adjustment rule obeys this requirement. For ease of reference, we now state this as an assumption, but we will show why it is satisfied in specific cases in the following chapter.

ASSUMPTION 4. For all admissible $\mathbf{p}(0)$, the solution $\mathbf{p}(t \mid \mathbf{p}(0))$ is bounded.

4. Some Basic Results

In this section, we shall repeat a number of mathematical results that we shall need in the next chapter to investigate the behavior over time of the prices that result from a tatônnement.

Let us start our investigation with an arbitrary $\mathbf{p}(0) > \mathbf{0}$ and stipulate A.11.1, A.11.3, and A.11.4. We have a unique solution path:

$$\mathbf{p}(t) = \mathbf{p}(t \mid \mathbf{p}(0)).$$

Since it is bounded we know from elementary analysis that there must be a convergent subsequence, $\mathbf{p}(t_\lambda) \to \mathbf{p}^*$, say. Hence the solution path has at least one limit point.

THEOREM 2. Let $\mathbf{p}(t \mid \mathbf{p}(0)) \to \mathbf{p}^*$ as $t \to +\infty$. Then $\mathbf{p}^*$ is an equilibrium of the economy.

Proof. Suppose not, so that $\mathbf{p}^*$ is not an equilibrium. This by D.2.1(E) means that for some i, $z_i(\mathbf{p}^*) > 0$. Write $G_i(z_i(\mathbf{p})) = g_i(\mathbf{p})$ and note that, by assumption, $g_i(\mathbf{p}^*) > 0$. We now show that this leads to a contradiction.

By the continuity of G_i and z_i, say,

$$\lim_{t\to\infty} g_i(\mathbf{p}(t)) = g_i(\lim_{t\to\infty} \mathbf{p}(t)) = g_i(\mathbf{p}^*) = g_i^*.$$

Since $g_i(\cdot)$ is convergent, we may choose $\epsilon > 0$ and small enough to ensure $g_i^* - \epsilon > 0$ and such that for t large enough,

$$|g_i(\mathbf{p}(t)) - g_i^*| < \epsilon$$

or

$$g_i(\mathbf{p}(t)) > g_i^* - \epsilon.$$

But $\dot{p}_i(t) = g_i(\mathbf{p}(t))$, whence

$$\dot{p}_i(t) > g_i^* - \epsilon.$$

For t large and $t' > t$, integrating the above expression from t to t' yields

$$p_i(t') > p_i(t) + (g_i^* - \epsilon)(t' - t).$$

For our choice of ϵ, then, it must be that as $t' \to +\infty$, $p_i(t') \to +\infty$, which contradicts the convergence of $\mathbf{p}(t)$ to a finite limit. Hence $g_i(\mathbf{p}^*) \leq 0$, all i, and $\mathbf{p}^*$ is an equilibrium.

We have shown that if $\mathbf{p}(t \mid \mathbf{p}(0))$ converges to $\mathbf{p}^*$, then $\mathbf{p}^*$ is an equilibrium. It will be useful to have the following definition.

DEFINITION 2. The auctioneer's rule will be called *globally stable* if for every $\mathbf{p}(0) > 0$, the solution $\mathbf{p}(t \mid \mathbf{p}(0))$ approaches an equilibrium.

If a solution $\mathbf{p}(t \mid \mathbf{p}(0))$ is convergent, say to $\mathbf{p}^*$, then of course $\mathbf{p}^*$ is the only limit point of that solution. On the other hand, since there are many different solution paths, depending on the choice of initial conditions, there may be many limit points to the paths generated by the auctioneer's rule (differential equations). All we can deduce from the information that the rule is globally stable is that every possible path will approach one of these points. However it may happen, for instance, when equilibrium for the economy is unique, that if all solutions converge, they must converge to the same limit point—the unique equilibrium. This leads to the following.

DEFINITION 3. If the rule followed by the auctioneer is globally stable and if the economy possesses a unique equilibrium, then that *equilibrium* is called *globally stable.*

If the economy possesses more than one equilibrium then no equilibrium can be globally stable.

Since the equations we are dealing with are non-linear and their number is large we shall not expect to be able to answer the question, "Are they globally stable?" by explicitly solving them, nor would that be a pleasant task to attempt if it is possible. Fortunately, we can often answer a qualitative question of this type, without actually solving the equations. To this matter we now turn.

Suppose that we can find a continuous function of $\mathbf{p}(t)$, $V[\mathbf{p}(t)]$, which has the property that it converges for every path $\mathbf{p}(t)$ can take and is constant along the path $\mathbf{p}(t \mid \mathbf{p}(0))$ if and only if $\mathbf{p}(0)$ is an equilibrium. The question is whether the existence of such a function together with the boundedness of all the paths of prices would be sufficient to allow us to deduce the global stability of the rules. We shall find that the answer is "almost" in the affirmative. We say "almost" because without one further assumption only a weaker proposition than global stability can be established. Let us see how far we can go.

Since $\mathbf{p}(t)$ is bounded, it has a converging subsequence and we may write

$$\lim_{\lambda \to \infty} \mathbf{p}(t_\lambda) = \mathbf{p}^*.$$

Consider the solution path

$$\mathbf{p}^*(t) = \mathbf{p}(t \mid \mathbf{p}^*).$$

On this path we take a limit point of $\mathbf{p}(t \mid \mathbf{p}(0))$ as our initial condition. We show that all points on this path are limit points of $\mathbf{p}(t \mid \mathbf{p}(0))$, so that the path is well named as a *limit path.*

Now, by A.11.3(a), every path is a unique function of its starting point. Let $\mathbf{p}^0$ be such a point and consider

$$\mathbf{p}(t) = \mathbf{p}(t + t_1 \mid \mathbf{p}^0)$$

so that

$$\mathbf{p}(0) = \mathbf{p}(t_1 \mid \mathbf{p}^0).$$

Since the path is uniquely defined by $\mathbf{p}^0$, $\mathbf{p}(t)$ must be the same whether we take $\mathbf{p}^0$ or $\mathbf{p}(0)$ as our initial condition, since $\mathbf{p}(t)$ is another unique path emanating from $\mathbf{p}^0$. Hence

$$\mathbf{p}(t + t_1 \mid \mathbf{p}^0) = \mathbf{p}(t \mid \mathbf{p}(t_1 \mid \mathbf{p}^0)).$$

Applying this to the limit path,

$$\begin{aligned}
\mathbf{p}^*(t) &= \mathbf{p}(t \mid \mathbf{p}^*) \\
&= \mathbf{p}\left[t \mid \lim_{\lambda \to \infty} \mathbf{p}(t_\lambda \mid \mathbf{p}(0))\right] \\
&= \lim_{\lambda \to \infty} \mathbf{p}[t \mid \mathbf{p}(t_\lambda \mid \mathbf{p}(0))] \\
&= \lim_{\lambda \to \infty} \mathbf{p}(t + t_\lambda \mid \mathbf{p}(0)),
\end{aligned}$$

so that every point of $\mathbf{p}^*(t)$ is a limit point of $\mathbf{p}(t \mid \mathbf{p}(0))$.

Now by A.11.4, the path $\mathbf{p}(t \mid \mathbf{p}(0))$ is bounded so, since $V(\cdot)$ is taken as continuous, it too is bounded. By assumption, it converges and so

$$\begin{aligned}
\lim_{t \to \infty} V[\mathbf{p}(t \mid \mathbf{p}(0))] &= \lim_{\lambda \to \infty} V[\mathbf{p}(t + t_\lambda \mid \mathbf{p}(0))] \\
&= V\left[\lim_{\lambda \to \infty} \mathbf{p}(t + t_\lambda \mid \mathbf{p}(0))\right] \\
&= V[\mathbf{p}(t \mid \mathbf{p}^*)].
\end{aligned}$$

It follows that $V[\mathbf{p}(t \mid \mathbf{p}^*)]$ is a constant; from the assumed properties of V, it follows that $\mathbf{p}^*$ is an equilibrium, and this for every limit point $\mathbf{p}^*$. Hence, if a function $V(\cdot)$ as specified can be found, every limit point of every solution path is an equilibrium, or to put it differently, every solution path converges to the set of equilibria. Let us state this formally.

DEFINITION 4. A function $V(\mathbf{p})$ that is continuous in its arguments and such that $V[\mathbf{p}(t \mid \mathbf{p}(0))]$ converges for all admissible $\mathbf{p}(0)$ and is constant if and only if $\mathbf{p}(0)$ is an equilibrium is called a *Lyapounov function.*

THEOREM 3. If the rules of A.11.1 or A.11.2, that is, the differential equations defined by it, allow the existence of a Lyapounov function and if A.11.3 and A.11.4 hold, then every solution path of prices approaches arbitrarily close to the set of equilibria of the economy.

DEFINITION 5. A set of differential equations that satisfy T.11.3 is called *quasi-globally stable.*

We see that we have finished up with quasi-global stability instead of with global stability. What that means is that so far, while we can predict that after a sufficiently long lapse of time prices will be arbitrarily close to some equilibrium, we cannot pick out any particular equilibrium for which this is true. This is better, indeed a good deal better, than nothing, yet we may choose to be more ambitious.

If there exist only two equilibrium points, say $\mathbf{p}^*$ and $\mathbf{p}^{**}$, then since any particular solution path gets arbitrarily close to this path, it must be arbitrarily close to one of these points or it must be close to one of them at one moment and close to the other at the next. Is this last, in fact, a possibility? It would appear that, unless something more is said, the path while in transit from one of these points to the other will not be close to either of them and this would lead to a contradiction of the theorem. Evidently this difficulty can be avoided if we say that $\mathbf{p}^*$ and $\mathbf{p}^{**}$ are arbitrarily close to each other; that is, any small neighborhood of one also contains the other. Then by the same token, if the equilibria of the economy do not satisfy this further restriction, that is, if on some measure of distance they are a finite distance apart, we can take it that our theorem establishes the stronger results, namely that every solution path converges on to an equilibrium. Let us make these ideas more precise.

Let $N(\mathbf{p}^*)$ be a closed neighborhood of $\mathbf{p}^*$ and $N(\mathbf{p}^{**})$ a closed neighborhood of $\mathbf{p}^{**}$ (where $\mathbf{p}^*$ and $\mathbf{p}^{**}$ are limit points of some path). We are to suppose that it is possible to find such neighborhoods with the property that no equilibrium other than $\mathbf{p}^{**}$ belongs to $N(\mathbf{p}^{**})$ and no equilibrium other than $\mathbf{p}^*$ belongs to $N(\mathbf{p}^*)$. ($\mathbf{p}^*$ and $\mathbf{p}^{**}$ are said to be *isolated.*) Then we can certainly find neighborhoods such that $N(\mathbf{p}^*)$ and $N(\mathbf{p}^{**})$ have no point in common, and we suppose that done. Now $\mathbf{p}(t)$ for t arbitrarily large must lie in $N(\mathbf{p}^*)$, for by definition, there is a sequence of points on the path such that for t large enough it has points close to $\mathbf{p}^*$. By the same argument, for t' arbitrarily large, $\mathbf{p}(t')$ must lie in $N(\mathbf{p}^{**})$. Then for some t^* such that $t < t^* < t'$, $\mathbf{p}(t^*)$ must be on the boundary of the closed neighborhood of $N(\mathbf{p}^*)$. Clearly, we may make t^* as large as we like since we may make t as large as we like. Also, the boundary of $N(\mathbf{p}^*)$ is bounded. Hence there is a sequence of point

$\mathbf{p}(t^*_\lambda)$ converging on some limit point $\mathbf{p}^{***}$, which lies on the border of $N(\mathbf{p}^*)$. This contradicts the supposition that $\mathbf{p}^*$ was an isolated limit point. Therefore, we have proved

THEOREM 4. If the set of limit points of a solution path contains more than one point, then these points cannot be isolated.

Corollary 4. If the equilibria of the economy are isolated in a given region and the conditions of T.11.3 hold, then the rule A.11.1 (or A.11.2) is globally stable.

Proof. If the set of limit points of a path $\mathbf{p}(t \mid \mathbf{p}(0))$ had more than one member, the set would not be isolated, by T.11.4. But by T.11.3, every limit point is an equilibrium, so that the set of equilibria would not be isolated, contrary to assumption.

Corollary 4′. If the conditions of T.11.3 hold and the economy has a unique equilibrium, then that equilibrium is globally stable.

Since we know quite a bit about the uniqueness of equilibrium of a competitive economy (see Chapter 9), the result we have just established should prove useful in an analysis of a tâtonnement. Of course, a good deal still depends on finding a suitable Lyapounov function in each of the cases we propose to investigate. Yet it is sometimes true that this function, and indeed the auctioneer's rule, arises quite naturally from the problem itself. A consideration of this class of cases will serve not only to illuminate the discussion up to this point, but it also holds an economic lesson that we ought to learn before we plunge into the particular details of the tatônnement process.

5. An Example: The Gradient Method

Let us consider a Hicksian economy, which we know (Section 9.6) may be treated as if it consisted of a single household. Let this household have a strictly quasi-concave utility function $U(\mathbf{x})$. We postulate a pure-exchange economy with endowment vector $\bar{\mathbf{x}} > \mathbf{0}$. In reality, if there were only one household, the economy would always be in equilibrium. As it is, the fictional household maximizes $U(\mathbf{x})$ subject to $\mathbf{p}(\mathbf{x} - \bar{\mathbf{x}}) = 0$, (rather than subject to $\mathbf{x} \leq \bar{\mathbf{x}}$), where $\mathbf{p}$ is the price vector called by the auctioneer.

We know that this economy has a unique equilibrium $\mathbf{p}^*$ and that the demand vector is a function, $\mathbf{x}(\mathbf{p})$, (rather than a correspondence) of $\mathbf{p}$. However, since $\mathbf{px}(\mathbf{p}) = \mathbf{p\bar{x}} \geq \mathbf{px}(\mathbf{p}^*)$,

$$U[\mathbf{x}(\mathbf{p})] > U[\mathbf{x}(\mathbf{p}^*)] \qquad \text{all } \mathbf{p} \neq \mathbf{p}^*.$$

In what follows, we write $V(\mathbf{p}) = U[\mathbf{x}(\mathbf{p})]$, and taking U as differentiable, we note that

$$\frac{\partial V(\mathbf{p})}{\partial p_k} \equiv V_k(\mathbf{p}) = \sum_i \left(\frac{\partial U}{\partial x_i}\right)\left(\frac{\partial x_i}{\partial p_k}\right) = -\sum_i \left(\frac{\partial U}{\partial x_i}\right)\left(\frac{\partial s_i}{\partial p_k}\right)$$

where $s_i(\mathbf{p})$ is the excess supply of goods.

For suitable λ, $\partial U/\partial x_i - \lambda p_i \leq 0$; if the strict inequality holds, $x_i(\mathbf{p}) = 0$ and indeed remains 0 for small changes in p_k, so that $\partial s_i/\partial p_k = 0$ if $\partial U/\partial s_i - \lambda p_i < 0$. Therefore,

$$V_k = -\lambda \sum_i p_i\left(\frac{\partial s_i}{\partial p_k}\right) - \sum_i \left(\frac{\partial U}{\partial x_i} - \lambda p_i\right)\left(\frac{\partial s_i}{\partial p_k}\right) = -\lambda \sum_i p_i\left(\frac{\partial s_i}{\partial p_k}\right).$$

Since

$$\sum_i p_i s_i(\mathbf{p}) \equiv 0,$$

we see, by differentiation with respect to p_k, that

$$\sum_i p_i\left(\frac{\partial s_i}{\partial p_k}\right) = -s_k(\mathbf{p}),$$

or

$$V_k(\mathbf{p}) = \lambda s_k(\mathbf{p}) \qquad \lambda > 0$$

where $s_k(\mathbf{p})$ is the excess supply of good k at $\mathbf{p}$. (If $p_k = 0$, this is to be taken as the right-hand derivative.)

Assume that the auctioneer does not know $\mathbf{p}^*$, but he does know that if $\mathbf{p}$ is not an equilibrium, $V(\mathbf{p}) > V(\mathbf{p}^*)$ and $V_k(\mathbf{p}) < 0$, some k. On the other hand, $V_k(\mathbf{p}) \geq 0$, all k, $p_k V_k(\mathbf{p}) = 0$, all k, if and only if $\mathbf{p}$ is an equilibrium. Accordingly, he argues as follows: If I follow the rule

$$\dot{p}_k = -V_k(\mathbf{p}), \text{ all } k, \text{ unless } p_k = 0,\ V_k(\mathbf{p}) > 0, \text{ when } \dot{p}_k = 0,$$

then I will ensure that $V(\mathbf{p})$ is declining as a function of time. This can mean only that $V(\mathbf{p})$ is getting nearer to its lower bound, which, wherever it is, will be at an equilibrium $\mathbf{p}$. Since, on the above rule, $V(\mathbf{p})$ acts like a Lyapounov function, the rule will indeed make the prices the auctioneer calls converge to their unique equilibrium value provided the solution path is bounded (see below).

What the auctioneer is doing in this example is following an iterative procedure for minimizing $V(\mathbf{p})$. He does this by making sure that he is always changing $\mathbf{p}$ in such a way as to be going "downhill"; in fact, he is following a gradient method for minimizing a function.

DEFINITION 6. The *gradient method* of minimizing a differentiable function $f(\mathbf{y})$ (where $\mathbf{y}$ is a vector) over a compact set is the rule: sign $\dot{y}_i = -$sign $\partial f/\partial y_i$ (if two numbers are zero they have both the same and opposite sign). If $\mathbf{y} \geq \mathbf{0}$ is a requirement of the problem, we add $y_i = 0$ if $y_i = 0$ and $\partial f/\partial y_i > 0$.

It is for the reader to state the gradient method for maximizing $f(\mathbf{y})$.

As another example, take $f(\mathbf{y})$ as a strictly concave function that we seek to maximize on a compact set; we do not preclude $y_i < 0$, some i. If we follow the gradient method, say $\dot{y}_i = w_i[f_i(\mathbf{y})]$, where w_i is sign preserving and $w_i(0) = 0, f_i(\mathbf{y}) = \partial f(\mathbf{y})/\partial y_i$, we have

$$\frac{df(\mathbf{y})}{dt} = \sum_i f_i(\mathbf{y})w_i[f_i(\mathbf{y})]$$

and this expression will be positive unless all the partial derivatives of $f(\mathbf{y})$ vanish. Since $f(\mathbf{y})$ is strictly concave, it has a unique maximum, and if we suppose this to occur at $\mathbf{y}^*$, which is not an extreme point of the set of possible $\mathbf{y}$, it is clear that we may treat $f(\mathbf{y})$ as a Lyapounov function and that the gradient method will generate a path for $\mathbf{y}$, the limit point of which is $\mathbf{y}^*$.

It should be noted now that in both the present example and the previous example, we had to make sure that a maximum or minimum existed for the function we were interested in, which we did by taking it over a compact set, and that it was extremely useful to take this maximum as unique, which we accomplished in the present example by making the function strictly concave and in the earlier example by taking $U(\mathbf{x})$ strictly quasi-concave. Granted, it is pretty clear that the gradient method in the last example will take us to a point at which all the derivatives vanish (ignoring complications with corners). Of course, this may be a minimum of $f(\mathbf{y})$ or a local maximum only. If we can take $f(\mathbf{y})$ as concave, although not strictly concave, then we can avoid difficulty—every $\mathbf{y}$ for which the derivatives vanish is a maximum of the function. Now there may be other maxima. If these are isolated, we know that nonetheless the method will drive us toward some particular maximum.

All this has important lessons for anyone interested in the behavior of a tâtonnement. If the auctioneer's rule may be treated as an intelligent method of maximizing or minimizing some relevant function, then if such a function is well behaved in the sense just discussed, we should expect the rule to exhibit global stability. Unfortunately, however, except in exceptional circumstances of which the Hicksian is one instance, the price mechanism cannot be taken to act as if someone were trying to maximize or minimize some well-behaved function of prices. It is true that we should expect "it" to recognize a situation that is not maximal in the sense that some household can be made better off without another one being made worse off, for we know that such a situation cannot be an equilibrium and we have so arranged matters that prices change when the economy is out of equilibrium. But being able to recognize that a function is not maximal at certain values of its arguments does not yet mean that we have a function of the kind for which the price mechanism is the appropriate gradient method or that this method will indeed be appropriate. We shall take up this point again in the next chapter.

6. Local Stability

We conclude this preliminary discussion of methods by noting that the requirement of global stability is extremely ambitious. For instance, when we consider a sequence of short-run equilibria in which expectations play an enormous role, we should certainly be surprised to hear that the system returns equally smoothly to an equilibrium after, say, the burning down of one factory and after half the factories have burned. Somehow we cannot help feeling that large shocks to a system will have to be treated in a qualitatively different way than small ones. This feeling may turn out to be based on misconceptions and we shall examine this again much later. Here we shall lay down rather obvious points concerning the more modest scheme of considering small deviations from equilibrium.

If we have chosen some appropriate measure of distance, say $[\sum (p_i - p_i^*)^2]^{1/2}$, where $\mathbf{p}^*$ is an equilibrium, and wish to utilize the properties of the excess-demand functions known to hold in some appropriate neighborhood of equilibrium in the examination of the path of prices two possibilities arise: If $\mathbf{p}(0)$ is in the interior of the specified neighborhood, it is true either that for all t, $\mathbf{p}(t \mid \mathbf{p}(0))$ will always remain in the neighborhood or that $\mathbf{p}(t \mid \mathbf{p}(0))$ may leave the neighborhood at some t. Evidently, in the second case we cannot stick to our resolution of examining the small neighborhood only, simply because we shall find that our quarry has left it at some moment. Thus we cannot even be certain that $\mathbf{p}$ will not, for some still larger t, re-enter our neighborhood unless we look to see what goes on outside it. In the first case, however, we can be thoroughly provincial and never consider what the world looks like outside the vicinity of the equilibrium.

DEFINITION 7. Let $\mathbf{p}^*$ be an equilibrium. We say that it is *stable in the sense of Lyapounov* if for every δ there is an ϵ such that, if $|\mathbf{p}(0) - \mathbf{p}^*| < \epsilon$, it is true also that $|\mathbf{p}(t \mid \mathbf{p}(0)) - \mathbf{p}^*| < \delta$, all $t \geq 0$.

As we have already noted, we shall expect to be able to concentrate on the behavior of a tâtonnement in some neighborhood of an equilibrium only if that equilibrium is stable in the sense of Lyapounov.

DEFINITION 8. An equilibrium is *locally asymptotically stable*, if all paths starting in a close neighborhood converge to the equilibrium and the equilibrium is stable in the sense of Lyapounov.

The idea of this definition is obvious. We impose the requirement that the equilibrium must be stable since without it we cannot rely on the "local" properties of the functions under investigation. But suppose that, while equilibrium is stable in the sense of D.11.7, the equilibrium is not locally asymptotically stable. We may conclude, evidently, that it is not globally stable either. Thus, while an analysis of local properties cannot establish global stability, it can establish a negative proposition of the kind just stated. In the next chapter we shall use this device to settle an important question.

If we make enough stability demands on a system, it can easily be seen that the system must have a unique equilibrium. Specifically, if we require global stability of the auctioneer's rule and also local asymptotic stability of every equilibrium, there can be only one such. For illustration, consider the familiar case of two commodities. As will be shown later (T.12.1), the system is always globally stable in that case; that is, the path starting from any initial set of prices always converges to some equilibrium. Then, as is well known since the days of Marshall, there will be alternating stable and unstable equilibria.

THEOREM 5. If the auctioneer's rule is globally stable and every equilibrium is locally asymptotically stable and if A.11.3 holds, then equilibrium is unique.

Proof. Since each equilibrium is locally asymptotically stable, each is surrounded by a neighborhood containing no other equilibria. The set E of equilibria is then isolated and, therefore, finite.

Suppose there is more than one equilibrium. Let C be a closed convex set containing more than one equilibrium, for example, a line segment joining two equilibria. For any $\mathbf{p}^* \in E$, let

$$C(\mathbf{p}^*) = \{\mathbf{p}^0 \in C \mid \mathbf{p}(t \mid \mathbf{p}^0) \to \mathbf{p}^*\},$$

in words, the set of points in C from which solutions converge to $\mathbf{p}^*$. Since the rule is globally stable, every point of C belongs to $C(\mathbf{p}^*)$ for some $\mathbf{p}^*$; by A.11.3(a), no point belongs to more than one such. It will be shown in Corollary B.11 that a convex set cannot be the union of two or more, but finitely many, disjoint non-null closed sets. Hence, at least one of the non-null sets $C(\mathbf{p}^*)$ is not closed; in other words, it has a limit point, $\mathbf{p}^0$, not belonging to it. Since C is closed, $\mathbf{p}^0 \in C$ and so $\mathbf{p}^0 \in C(\mathbf{p}^{**})$ for some $\mathbf{p}^{**} \neq \mathbf{p}^*$. By D.11.8, there is a neighborhood N of $\mathbf{p}^{**}$ such that $\mathbf{p}(t \mid \mathbf{p}^1) \to \mathbf{p}^{**}$ if $\mathbf{p}^1 \in N$. Since $\mathbf{p}^0 \in C(\mathbf{p}^{**})$, we can find t_1 so that $\mathbf{p}(t_1 \mid \mathbf{p}^0) \in N$. By A.11.3(b), $\mathbf{p}(t_1 \mid \mathbf{p})$ is continuous in $\mathbf{p}$; since $\mathbf{p}^0$ is a limit point of $C(\mathbf{p}^*)$, we can find $\mathbf{p}^{00} \in C(\mathbf{p}^*)$ such that $\mathbf{p}^1 = \mathbf{p}(t_1 \mid \mathbf{p}^{00}) \in N$. Then, for $t > t_1$, $\mathbf{p}(t \mid \mathbf{p}^{00}) = \mathbf{p}(t - t_1 \mid \mathbf{p}^1) \to \mathbf{p}^{**}$, a contradiction since $\mathbf{p}^{00} \in C(\mathbf{p}^*)$.

We shall use T.11.5 to establish T.9.15; the argument will be completed in Section 12.8.

7. The Auctioneer in a Constant-Returns Economy

So far we have taken it as given that F (see Chapter 2) is satisfied, which, as we know, makes it hard to consider an economy in which production is carried out under constant returns to scale. If the minimum cost functions $C_i^*(\mathbf{p})$ are well defined, however (see Chapter 3), we could consider an alternative rule for the auctioneer to follow. This time he will allow no transactions until the price of every good planned for production in positive quantity just covers its minimum unit cost. In the meantime, the auctioneer raises the price of every good for which unit cost exceeds its price unless he has been informed that there is a zero demand for the good. In all cases, he will lower the price of a good if that price exceeds its minimum unit cost. Formally:

ASSUMPTION 5. Let the economy produce everywhere under constant returns to scale. Let $x_i(\mathbf{p})$ be the demand for a produced good, i, and let there be one non-produced good only with subscript "0." Suppose that $x_i(\mathbf{p})$ is a function. Then the auctioneer follows the rule:

For all $i \neq 0$, $\dot{p}_i = 0$ if $x_i(\mathbf{p}) = 0$ and $p_i < C_i(\mathbf{p})$;
$\dot{p}_i = H_i[C_i(\mathbf{p}) - p_i]$ otherwise, where $H_i(\ )$ has the same properties as the function $G_i(\ )$ and $F_i(\ )$,
$\dot{p}_0 = 0$ identically in t.

A.11.5 is a numeraire process, and when we come to consider it, we shall have to examine whether it indeed satisfies the requirements of such a process that the good chosen as numeraire always has a positive equilibrium price. We shall also have to see whether any sensible rules can be found if there are several non-produced goods.

Notes

A well-known text for part of this chapter is E. A. Coddington and N. Levinson [1955]. The Lyapounov method is described in J. LaSalle and S. Lefschetz [1961] and in W. Hahn [1959]. The original Lyapounov paper appeared in translation in 1947.

The problems encountered by the requirement that prices must be non-negative at all times have been discussed by H. Uzawa [1958] and M. Morishima [1959]. In a series of as yet unpublished papers C. Henry of l'Ecole Polytechnique has investigated the solution of differential equations whose trajectories must lie in a closed convex set. This work appeared too late to be noticed here, but it seems clear from it that A.11.3 can be deduced as a theorem provided certain technical conditions are met by the sign preserving functions $G(\cdot)$ and $F(\cdot)$.

Chapter Twelve

STABILITY WITH RECONTRACTING

Turning and turning in the widening gyre
The falcon cannot hear the falconer.
—W. B. Yeats, *The Second Coming*

1. The Problem

Our main task in this chapter is to investigate the qualitative properties of the path of prices generated by an economy in which no contract is binding except in equilibrium, that is, a tâtonnement process (Section 11.2). In particular, we shall be interested in describing the cases for which it is true that these paths are either globally or locally stable. Since we shall show by an example that there are situations in which, for a properly constructed general equilibrium model, the tâtonnement path of prices is not stable, the "case study" approach is necessary. However, we shall consider whether it may be possible to characterize a class of cases for which the tâtonnement has either local or global stability properties.

Throughout this chapter it is rather important to remember that we are investigating as yet a laboratory situation only. Thus it would be quite wrong to conclude that the price mechanism works from a demonstration of stability, as it indeed would be wrong to conclude the reverse from demonstrations of instability. Such large conclusions, if they are to be drawn at all, must await a discussion of more acceptable models of adjustment in which the results of this chapter may well find some application.

2. The Two-Goods Economy

As is true in so much of general equilibrium analysis, there are some rather general conclusions to be drawn from a model in which there are only two goods, conclusions that cannot be established for any other case. We shall investigate this special situation because in so many parts of the literature of economic theory, for example, in the theory of international trade, it is this hypothetical economy that has engaged the most attention. The sequel will suggest that this is probably not sensible.

We prove the following, where we assume, as indeed we do elsewhere in this chapter, that A.11.3 and A.11.4 hold.

THEOREM 1. Let a two-goods economy have isolated equilibria. Then the rule A.11.1 is globally stable.

Proof. Consider $\mathbf{p}(0) \in S_2$ (the two-dimensional simplex), $E = \{\mathbf{p}^* \mid \mathbf{z}(\mathbf{p}^*) \leq \mathbf{0},\ \mathbf{p}^* \in S_2\}$. Let $\mathbf{p}(0) \notin E$ and, without loss of generality, take $z_1(\mathbf{p}(0)) > 0$. By W, $p_2(0) > 0$ and $z_2(\mathbf{p}(0)) \leq 0$. Let $\mathbf{p}^* \in E$ and consider

$$V(\mathbf{p}) = \sum_{i=1}^{2} (p_i - p_i^*)^2.$$

At $t = 0$, differentiating $V(\mathbf{p}(0))$ with respect to t and using the pricing rule gives

$$\dot{V}(\mathbf{p}(0)) = 2 \sum_i (p_i(0) - p_i^*) G_i[z_i(\mathbf{p}(0))].$$

Then, if $p_1(0) > p_1^*$, it must be that $p_2(0) < p_2^*$. By assumption, $G_1[z_1(\mathbf{p}(0))] > 0$ and $G_2[z_2(\mathbf{p}(0))] \leq 0$, so $\dot{V}(\mathbf{p}(0)) > 0$. By the pricing rule, $p_1(t) > p_1^*$, all t, since the price of the first good rises as long as $z_1(\mathbf{p}(t)) > 0$ and remains constant when $z_1(\mathbf{p}(t)) = 0$. Similarly, $p_2(t) < p_2^*(t)$, all t. Hence $\dot{V}(\mathbf{p}(t)) > 0$, all t, as long as $\mathbf{p}(t) \notin E$.

An exactly analogous argument establishes that if $p_1(0) < p_1^*$, then $\dot{V}(\mathbf{p}(t)) < 0$, all t, as long as $\mathbf{p}(t) \notin E$. Also, $\dot{V}(\mathbf{p}(t)) = 0$ if $\mathbf{p}(t) \in E$. Since $V(\mathbf{p})$ is then monotone and $\mathbf{p}(t \mid \mathbf{p}(0))$ is bounded, it must be convergent:

$$\lim_{t \to \infty} V(\mathbf{p}(t \mid \mathbf{p}(0))) = V(\lim_{t \to \infty} \mathbf{p}(t \mid \mathbf{p}(0))) = V(\mathbf{p}^{**}) = V^*.$$

By T.11.2, we know that $\mathbf{p}^{**}$ is an equilibrium. Since the equilibria are isolated, there can be only one value of $\mathbf{p}$, namely $\mathbf{p}^{**}$, for which $V(\mathbf{p}) = V^*$.

Corollary 1. A two-goods economy with a unique equilibrium is globally stable.

Proof. Directly by T.12.1 and D.11.3.

An obvious application of the above results is to the traditional question of whether in a world with two goods, freely fluctuating terms of trade would establish a world equilibrium. In the literature this question is often answered by considering the derivative of one of the excess-demand functions at an equilibrium and implicitly supposing that the adjustment mechanism is one of recontracting. Thus, for instance, if P_1 is the price of the first good in terms of the second, P_1^* a world equilibrium, then for all P_1 such that $|P_1 - P_1^*|$ is small enough we may write, assuming $P_1^* > 0$,

$$z_1(P_1) \approx z_1(P_1^*) + \left|\frac{\partial z_1}{\partial P_1}\right|_{P_1 = P_1^*} P_1 - P_1^* = \left|\frac{\partial z_1}{\partial P_1}\right|_{P_1 = P_1^*} P_1 - P_1^*$$

since $z_1(P_1^*) = 0$. Then, if $\partial z_1(\mathbf{P})/\partial P_1 < 0$ when $P_1 = P_1^*$, we may take $|P_1 - P_1^*|$ as providing a Lyapounov function provided $P_1(0)$ is in the specified neighborhood. For we can verify easily that, by application of A.11.2, this function must be monotone declining as long as it is positive. This ensures that the rule is stable in the sense of Lyapounov (i.e., we stay in the small neighborhood in which we started). Moreover, by the usual argument we can verify that the function indeed converges and show that the convergence point is P_1^*.

Recall that in Chapter 11 we distinguished two stability concepts: An adjustment rule is stable if it leads the economy to *some* equilibrium, while a particular equilibrium is stable under an adjustment process if the latter returns the economy toward that particular equilibrium. Careful scrutiny of the argument of the previous paragraph suggests that what is at stake is not the stability properties of the adjustment rule, but the question of whether a particular equilibrium is locally stable. This, of course, is a question of legitimate interest. However, it leaves the question of the behavior of the system unanswered should it turn out that the particular equilibrium is not locally stable. Let us see how we might deal with the problem of adjustment in this model in the light of what we have learned.

Suppose that P_1^* is a unique equilibrium for the world economy. Then, by Corollary 1, it is globally stable for the rule A.12.2 and so certainly locally stable. Alternatively, $(P_1 - P_1^*)z_1(\mathbf{P}) < 0$, $P_1 \neq P_1^*$, is a necessary condition for the uniqueness of an equilibrium in a two-goods economy (T.9.17). Hence, if the derivative $\partial z_1(P_1^*)/\partial P_1^* \geq 0$ at $P_1 = P_1^*$, we conclude that there must be at least one other equilibrium. From T.12.1 we then predict that the auctioneer's rule will take the economy arbitrarily close to one of the other equilibria. We note that not all equilibria can be locally stable if the economy has more than one equilibrium. From this we can say to the international trade theorist, "If you have already supposed the equilibrium to be unique, as you often do, then you need worry no more about the stability of the adjustment path. If you have not assumed uniqueness then you must be prepared to find that some equilibrium is not locally stable, but you may nonetheless be sure that your adjustment process will converge to some equilibrium."

It seems pretty clear that this more complete statement of the situation is to be much preferred to all the unpleasant elasticity formulas that keep cropping up in this subject. On the other hand, we can hardly take a two-goods world as a serious representation of what we are interested in; after all, the supposition that the adjustment mechanism is a tâtonnement is a serious enough restriction on reality already. Nor is it likely that, for instance, an analysis that allows us to consider two goods only, although there are many, by supposing the relative prices of goods in each of two groups of goods to be constant (a supposition that we know allows aggregation into groups of goods) will be closer to the mark.

3. The "Weak Axiom of Revealed Preference"

We shall start our investigation with the simplest cases. To begin with, it will prove convenient to specialize the auctioneer's rule of A.11.1 or A.11.2 by supposing that

$$G_i(z_i(\mathbf{p})) = k_i z_i(\mathbf{p}) \qquad k_i > 0. \tag{I}$$

Presently, we shall consider the more general case. It will be clear that A.11.1 specialized to (I) will give rise to solution paths that are bounded, because using (I) and W, we have

$$\frac{d(\sum p_i^2/k_i)}{dt} = 2\sum p_i z_i = 0. \tag{1}$$

THEOREM 2. Let $\mathbf{p}^*$ be an equilibrium of the economy for which $\mathbf{p}^*\mathbf{s}(\mathbf{p}) < 0$, all $\mathbf{p} \neq \mathbf{p}^*$. Then $\mathbf{p}^*$ is globally stable for both the rules A.11.1 and A.11.2 specialized to (I).

Proof. Let

$$V(\mathbf{p}) = \frac{\sum (p_i - p_i^*)^2}{k_i}$$

and let $R^*(\mathbf{p}) = \{i \mid p_i = 0;\ \ z_i(\mathbf{p}) < 0\}$ and $R(\mathbf{p})$ the complement of $R^*(\mathbf{p})$. Then, by A.11.1, (I), and W, we have

$$\frac{dV(\mathbf{p})}{dt} = 2 \sum_{i \in R(\mathbf{p})} (p_i - p_i^*) z_i(\mathbf{p}) = \sum_{i \in R(\mathbf{p})} p_i^* s_i(\mathbf{p}) \leq \mathbf{p}^*\mathbf{s}(\mathbf{p}),$$

and so $V(\mathbf{p})$ is monotonically declining along the solution path as long as $\mathbf{p} \neq \mathbf{p}^*$. Since $\mathbf{p}(t)$ is obviously bounded (quite independently of the argument under (1)), it is a Lyapounov function, and we can say that the rule is globally stable. By the assumption of the theorem, $\mathbf{p}^*$ is a unique equilibrium of the economy (see the proof of T.9.4), so that the limit point of every solution path is $\mathbf{p}^*$. So by Corollary 11.4′ the theorem is established.

Let $\mathbf{P}$ be the price vector in terms of numeraire and check that, by the assumption of the theorem, $(\mathbf{P}^* - \mathbf{P})\mathbf{s}(\mathbf{P}) < 0$ for $\mathbf{P} \neq \mathbf{P}^*$. Let $W(\mathbf{P}) = \sum (P_i - P_i^*)^2/k_i$, and by the same argument as the one just given, show that $W(\mathbf{P})$ is a Lyapounov function for A.11.2 and (I). Note that by the monotonicity of $W(\mathbf{P})$ it must be that all solution paths are bounded.

From this result we have at once,

Corollary 2. If the economy is Hicksian, or if all goods are GS, or if all goods are WGS and the economy is connected, then A.11.1 and A.11.2 specialized to (I) are globally stable and the unique equilibrium of the economy is globally stable.

Proof. By T.9.4, T.9.9, and the argument of pp. 227–228, it is true for all these cases that $\mathbf{p}^*\mathbf{s}(\mathbf{p}) < 0$ for $\mathbf{p} \neq \mathbf{p}^*$.

These results are pleasant. It is important, however, not to be misled by the monotonicity of $V(\mathbf{p})$ and $W(\mathbf{P})$ into believing that all prices are monotonically approaching the equilibrium value. The monotonicity of the Lyapounov function here is quite consistent with, say, fluctuations of individual prices of declining amplitude about their equilibrium value.

The natural question to ask next is whether we can extend T.12.2 to the case in which the auctioneer's rule does not take the special form (I). In answering this question we shall examine first the Hicksian case and then the situation in which all goods are GS. Throughout, we assume that the adjustment rule satisfies A.11.1 and A.11.2.

THEOREM 3. Let the economy be Hicksian with a total production set that is convex and differentiable. Then A.11.1 and A.11.2 are globally stable rules.

Proof. By T.9.5, we may treat the economy as if it had one household only with a strictly quasi-concave utility function $U(\mathbf{x})$, where $\mathbf{x}$ is the total consumption vector of households. Thus $\mathbf{x}(\mathbf{p})$, the consumption at $\mathbf{p}$, can be found by maximizing $U(\mathbf{x})$ subject to $\mathbf{pz}(\mathbf{p}) = 0$ (recall that all profits are distributed to households). This gives rise to first-order conditions:

$$U_i(\mathbf{x}(\mathbf{p})) \leq \lambda p_i$$

$$U_i = \frac{\partial U}{\partial x_i}$$

$$\lambda = \text{Lagrangean multiplier} \qquad \lambda > 0. \tag{2}$$

We shall now show that we may take $U(\mathbf{x}(\mathbf{p}))$ as our Lyapounov function.

We know that the strict inequality in (2) for i implies $x_i(\mathbf{p}) = 0$. Hence, using (2) we have:

$$\frac{dU(\mathbf{x}(\mathbf{p}))}{dt} = \sum_i \dot{p}_i \sum_j U_j(\mathbf{x}(\mathbf{p})) \frac{\partial x_j}{\partial p_i} \leq \sum_i \dot{p}_i \lambda \sum_j p_j \frac{\partial x_j}{\partial p_i}.$$

From $\mathbf{pz}(\mathbf{p}) \equiv 0$, we have

$$\sum_j p_j \frac{\partial x_j}{\partial p_i} = -z_i(\mathbf{p}) + \sum_j p_j \frac{\partial y_j}{\partial p_i} \tag{3}$$

where y_j is the jth component of the supply vector of producers. Since $\mathbf{py}(\mathbf{p})$ is always at a maximum, we know (Corollary 3.6) that $\partial y_j/\partial p_i = \partial y_i/\partial p_j$, and since $y_i(\mathbf{p})$ is homogeneous of degree zero in $\mathbf{p}$, the term under the summation sign on the right-hand side of (3) is zero. Hence we have

$$\frac{dU(\mathbf{x}(\mathbf{p}))}{dt} \leq \lambda \sum_i \dot{p}_i s_i(\mathbf{p}) = \lambda \sum_{i \in R(\mathbf{p})} G_i(z_i(\mathbf{p})) s_i(\mathbf{p}),$$

where $R(\mathbf{p})$ is defined as before. It is clear that the right-hand side of this expression is negative for non-equilibrium values of $\mathbf{p}$. By assumption, the solution path of prices is bounded. Since $\mathbf{x}(\mathbf{p})$ is a continuous function of $\mathbf{p}$, it too is bounded and so, therefore, is $U(\mathbf{x}(\mathbf{p}))$. Then $U(\mathbf{x}(\mathbf{p}))$ is convergent. Since the economy has a unique equilibrium (Corollary 9.5), the theorem is established.

It is left to the reader to show that the same argument may be used to show that A.11.2 gives a globally stable rule for the Hicksian economy.

The common sense of the procedure of the proof is not hard to see. The fictional household maximized utility subject to the constraint $\mathbf{pz(p)} = 0$. For an equilibrium, however, it must have maximized utility subject to $\mathbf{z} \leq \mathbf{0}$. This constraint gives choices that are wholly contained in the set of choices that are feasible for the contraint $\mathbf{pz(p)} = 0$. Hence it cannot be that the utility of the fictional household is less out of equilibrium than it is in equilibrium. By the Hicksian assumption of strict quasi-concavity of U, it must indeed be that the out-of-equilibrium utility is higher than the utility possible in an equilibrium. The auctioneer's rule then serves to reduce monotonically the difference $[U(\mathbf{x(p)}) - U(\mathbf{x(p^*)})]$. Since he raises the price of the good in excess demand and reduces the price of the goods in excess supply, it must be that all the income terms in the basic equation of demand of the fictional household are negative; in other words, the household is made "worse off" and the conclusion we reached then follows rather simply.

We next turn to the GS case, which can be handled even more easily.

THEOREM 4. Let all goods be GS. Then the rules A.11.1 and A.11.2 are globally stable.

Proof. By Corollary 9.6, we know that the unique equilibrium $\mathbf{p}^*$ is strictly positive, so we may choose units in which to measure goods that allow us to write $\mathbf{p}^* = \mathbf{e}$, the unit vector. We show that

$$V(\mathbf{p}) = \max_i (p_i - 1)$$

is a Lyapounov function. By T.9.8, the good whose price exceeds its equilibrium value in the greatest proportion must be in excess supply and the good whose price exceeds its equilibrium value in the smallest proportion must be in excess demand. By the rule A.11.1, the price of the former type of good must fall and that of the latter rise. Hence, certainly for $\mathbf{p} \neq \mathbf{e}$, $V(\mathbf{p})$ must be falling along the solution path.

$V(\mathbf{p})$ may not be differentiable everywhere, but it does not matter for our purposes since it is continuous and monotone declining. The lack of differentiability arises when

$$\max_i (p_i - 1)$$

is attained for a number of goods. We only sketch what is involved. Suppose, for instance, that $V(\mathbf{p}) = p_r - 1 = p_s - 1$ and $p_i < p_r$, all $i \neq s,r$. Then $z_r < 0$, $z_s < 0$ and the right-hand derivative $dV(\mathbf{p})^+/dt = \max(k_r z_r, k_s z_s)$. It is well defined. The left-hand derivative $dV(\mathbf{p})^-/dt = \min(k_r z_r, k_s z_s)$ and is also well defined.

Since $V(\mathbf{p})$ is evidently bounded, it is a Lyapounov function and the theorem follows.

A similar argument can be developed for the rule of A.11.2, for which we note that, by definition, the price of the numeraire good is kept equal to unity throughout.

Corollary 4. If all goods are WGS and the economy is connected, A.11.1 and A.11.2 give globally stable rules.

Proof. We know (pp. 227–228) that for this economy equilibrium is unique and strictly positive, and $\mathbf{p}^*\mathbf{s}(\mathbf{p}) < 0$ for $\mathbf{p} \neq \mathbf{p}^*$.

It is interesting to note that in the two cases we have just considered, where the process has such agreeable properties, we are able to say that the non-equilibrium situation is "superior" to the equilibrium one. In the Hicksian case this follows directly by the argument just given, and in the GS case it follows from $\mathbf{p}^*\mathbf{s}(\mathbf{p}) < 0$ (see Chapter 9). In the Hicksian case the auctioneer's rules are gradient processes for minimizing $[U(\mathbf{x}(\mathbf{p})) - U(\mathbf{x}(\mathbf{p}^*))]$. In the GS these rules are not easy to interpret as gradient processes, but they lead to the minimization of $(\mathbf{p} - \mathbf{p}^*)\mathbf{s}(\mathbf{p})$, which is a sort of measure of the gap between the welfare that households hope to attain out of equilibrium and the welfare that they can attain (of course, this is not a measure to be taken other than being suggestive).

Since, for any pair $(\mathbf{p}^*, \mathbf{p})$ where $\mathbf{p}^*$ is an equilibrium and $\mathbf{p}$ is not, $\mathbf{p}^*\mathbf{s}(\mathbf{p}) < 0$ when all goods are WGS (T.9.11), we should expect that for this case also we can establish the global stability of the rules we are investigating. This is indeed the case when (I) is stipulated as we now show, although, at first sight, the fact that in this case the equilibrium set is convex (Corollary 9.11) and so the equilibrium points are not isolated suggests that only global quasi-stability can be established.

THEOREM 5. If all goods are WGS, then the rules A.11.1 and A.11.2 of the form (I) are globally stable.

Proof. By T.9.11, $\mathbf{p}^*\mathbf{s}(\mathbf{p}) < 0$ for $\mathbf{p}^* \in E$ and $\mathbf{p} \notin E$. Hence, certainly for any $\mathbf{p}^* \in E$,

$$V(\mathbf{p}) = \frac{\sum (p_i - p_i^*)^2}{k_i}$$

is a Lyapounov function for A.11.1 (I) by the same argument as in the proof of T.12.2. In particular, $V(\mathbf{p}(t))$ converges to a unique limit V^*. Hence, if $\mathbf{p}^*(t)$ is the limit path of $\mathbf{p}(t)$, it must be that for all points on that path V takes on the value V^*; that is,

$$V(\mathbf{p}^*(t)) = V^*.$$

In the definition of $V(\mathbf{p})$ we may always choose $\mathbf{p}^*$ to be a point on $\mathbf{p}^*(t)$. We can do this because V constant identically in t means that all points on the path are equilibria. Then, evidently, it must be true that $V(\mathbf{p}^*) = 0 = V^*$. But $V(\mathbf{p}) = 0$ has a unique solution and so $\mathbf{p}^*$ must be the only point on $\mathbf{p}^*(t)$ and so $\mathbf{p}(t)$ converges on this point as t goes to plus infinity.

The question now arises whether this result depends on the special form of (I) of the auctioneer's rule. If we consider the more general form, we shall certainly have to introduce as an assumption, as we have done elsewhere, that the solution path is bounded. Having done so let us see how we fare.

Suppose first that there is some $\mathbf{p}(i)$ such that $z_i(\mathbf{p}(i)) \leq 0$. Then $z_i(\mathbf{p}) \leq 0$, all $\mathbf{p}$. Suppose not and suppose that for some $\mathbf{p}'$, $z_i(\mathbf{p}') > 0$. Then, by WGS, $z_i(\mathbf{p}'(i)) \geq z_i(\mathbf{p}') > 0$, a contradiction of the result that $z_i(\mathbf{p}'(i)) \leq 0$ since $z_i(\mathbf{p}(i)) \leq 0$ (T.9.10, Corollary 9.10). Now let N be the set of i such that $z_i(\mathbf{p}(i)) > 0$, all $\mathbf{p}(i)$. Then, by what has already been said, this set can be empty only if all $\mathbf{p} \in E$. If N is empty, $z_i(\mathbf{p}) \leq 0$, all $\mathbf{p}$ and all i, and so W confirms that all $\mathbf{p} \in E$.

Let us suppose, therefore, that N is not empty and consider

$$M(\mathbf{p}) = \max_{i \in N} \frac{G_i[z_i(\mathbf{p})]}{p_i}.$$

Let $\mathbf{p}_N$ be the price vector with components in N. It is easy to see that if $\mathbf{p}_N(0) \gg \mathbf{0}$, then $\mathbf{p}_N(t) \gg \mathbf{0}$, all t. Suppose not and let t' be the first time that some price, say the ith, $i \in N$, becomes zero. Then, certainly, since no price can have fallen in greater proportion relatively to its positive equilibrium price than i has fallen, we have, by WGS,

$$z_i[\mathbf{p}(t')] \geq 0.$$

(See T.9.8, which clearly holds in this weak form.) But, since $i \in N$, the inequality must be strict, whence by continuity, there is $t^* < t$ such that

$$z_i[\mathbf{p}(t)] > 0 \qquad t^* < t < t'.$$

For such t, the adjustment rule ensures $\dot{p}_i(t) > 0$, so that $0 = p_i(t') > p_i(t^*) \geq 0$, which is a contradiction.

Next we note that if $\mathbf{p} \in E$, $M(\mathbf{p}) = 0$. Conversely, suppose $M(\mathbf{p}) = 0$, $\mathbf{p}_N \gg \mathbf{0}$, then for all $i \in N$, $z_i(\mathbf{p}) = 0$, and for all $i \notin N$, $z_i(\mathbf{p}) \leq 0$ from our earlier discussion. Then by W, $z_i(\mathbf{p}) < 0$, $i \notin N$ must mean $p_i = 0$, whence $\mathbf{p} \in E$.

Let

$$m = \left\{ i \mid M[\mathbf{p}(t)] = G_i \frac{z_i[\mathbf{p}(t)]}{p_i(t)}, \quad i \in N \right\}.$$

Then for all $i \in m$, we have, omitting arguments from functions,

$$\frac{dz_i}{dt} = \sum z_{ij} G_j \leq \sum_{j \in N} z_{ij} G_j = \sum_{j \in N} \frac{(z_{ij} p_j) G_j}{p_j} \leq M \sum_{j \in N} z_{ij} p_j \leq 0.$$

The inequalities follow from

(a) $G_j(z_j) \leq 0$ for $j \notin N$ and $z_{ij} \geq 0, j \neq i$ by WGS;

(b) by H and WGS $|z_{ii}| p_i \geq \sum_{j \neq i} z_{ij} p_j$;

(c) $G_j \leq G_i, j \in N, i \in m$.

Now the right-hand derivative of $M(\mathbf{p}(t))$ is

$$\max_{i \in m} \frac{d}{dt} \frac{G_i(z_i)}{p_i}$$

and the left-hand derivative is

$$\min_{i \in m} \frac{d}{dt} \frac{G_i(z_i)}{p_i}.$$

Using the above inequalities, we have

$$\frac{dM[p(t)]^+}{dt} = G_i' \left[\frac{dz_i/dt}{p_i} - \frac{G_i(z_i)}{p_i^2} \right] < 0$$

if $\mathbf{p}(t) \notin E$, since by A.11.1, $G_i' > 0$. We have assumed that the solution path is bounded and so $M(\mathbf{p})$ is indeed a Lyapounov function.

In particular, if $\mathbf{p}^*(t)$ is a limit path of the solution,

$$M[\mathbf{p}^*(t)] = M^* \qquad \text{identically in } t,$$

so that every point on $\mathbf{p}^*(t)$ is an equilibrium.

By Corollary 9.11, the set of equilibria is convex when WGS holds, so that the equilibria are not isolated if there are more than one. From T.11.3 and D.11.5, therefore, quasi-global stability without global stability seems possible for this case, although we have not investigated this question. However, Arrow and Hurwicz [1962] showed that if we postulate that at least one strictly positive equilibrium exists, the adjustment process is stable. They also gave an example in which, when this extra assumption (of at least one strictly positive equilibrium) is not made, the process is quasi-globally stable, but unbounded. In their example, however, $G_i(0)$ was not finite. The question whether the process under WGS may be only quasi-globally stable, but not stable under slightly stronger conditions, is unsettled.

We sum up what we have proved or stated.

THEOREM 6. Let all goods be WGS and let $\mathbf{p}_N(0) \gg \mathbf{0}$. Then A.11.1 is globally stable provided that all solution paths are bounded. If there exists a strictly positive equilibrium, then A.11.1 is always globally stable.

While the analysis of the WGS case is rather more complex than that of GS, we see that we do almost as well with the weaker assumption as we did with the stronger. The "almost" is due to the extra fuss to ensure boundedness of the solution paths. The weakening of the assumptions is to be welcomed, but they are still pretty strong.

4. Diagonal Dominance

Let us again start with the simplest case, by supposing Diagonal Dominance and the adjustment rule to be of a special kind and the economy to be a pure-exchange economy.

Let $x_i(\mathbf{P})$ be the demand for good i at the prices (in terms of numeraire) $\mathbf{P}$. Then we write $e_{ij}(\mathbf{P}) = x_{ij}(\mathbf{P})P_j/x_i(\mathbf{P})$ as the appropriate elasticities of demand. The special form of Diagonal Dominance, which we refer to as D*D*, is this:

$$e_{ii}(\mathbf{P}) < 0 \qquad \text{all } i \neq n \text{ and } \mathbf{P};$$

$$|e_{ii}(\mathbf{P})| > \sum_{n>j\neq i} |e_{ij}(\mathbf{P})| \qquad \text{all } i \neq n \text{ and } \mathbf{P}.$$

The special adjustment form of A.11.2 is this:

$$F_i(z_i(\mathbf{P})) = P_i z_i(\mathbf{P}) \qquad \text{for } P_i > 0. \tag{II}$$

In order to be able to use this rule without complications we further stipulate:

ASSUMPTION 1. For all $\mathbf{P}$, $\mathbf{x}(\mathbf{P}) \gg \mathbf{0}$ and $z_i[\mathbf{P}(i)] > 0$, all i. ($\mathbf{P}(i)$ is $\mathbf{P}$ with the ith element replaced by zero.) Also, $z_n[\mathbf{P}(n)] > 0$.

This assumption supposes that every good is demanded in positive amount at every set of prices and that every good is in excess demand when its own price is zero. It requires also that the demand for the numeraire good is large (in excess of the fixed supply) when its price goes to zero. We do not claim that all these assumptions have a great deal to recommend them. In any event, we may now establish

THEOREM 7. If a pure-exchange economy has D*D* and it follows the tâtonnement rule (II), then, provided A.12.1 and $\mathbf{p}(0) \gg \mathbf{0}$ hold, the rule will be globally stable.

Proof. By an argument exactly analogous to that used in the proof of T.12.6 we can show that $\mathbf{P}(0) \gg \mathbf{0}$ implies that $\mathbf{P}(t) \gg \mathbf{0}$, all t, since $z_i(\mathbf{P}(i)) > 0$. Hence, certainly, the solution path is bounded from below. By A.12.1, $z_n(\mathbf{P}) > 0$ for $\sum P_i$ sufficiently large, for

$$z_n(\mathbf{P}) = z_n\left(\frac{\mathbf{P}}{\sum_{i \neq n} P_i}\right)$$

by H, so that setting $p_n = 1$, $z_n(\mathbf{P}) > 0$ when $\sum P_i = +\infty$ and so $z_n(\mathbf{P}) > 0$ for $\mathbf{P}$ sufficiently large. By W, $\sum P_i z_i(\mathbf{p}) = -z_n(\mathbf{P})$ and $(d/dt) \sum P_i = \sum P_i z_i(\mathbf{P}) < 0$ for $\sum P_i$ sufficiently large, so that the solution path is also bounded from above.

We now let

$$Z(\mathbf{P}) = \max_i |z_i(\mathbf{P})|$$

and show that it is a Lyapounov function. Let m be the set of i for which $|z_i(\mathbf{P})| = Z(\mathbf{P})$. Then, for $i \in m$, consider $\log x_i(\mathbf{P})$, which, in view of A.11.1, is well defined. Differentiating with respect to t and using (II) gives

$$\frac{d[\log x_i(\mathbf{P})]}{dt} = \sum_{j \neq n} e_{ij}(\mathbf{P}) z_j(\mathbf{P}).$$

If this expression were non-negative for non-equilibrium **P**, when $z_i > 0$, it would have to be that the following is true for $i \in m$:

$$|e_{ii}(\mathbf{P})|\,|z_i(\mathbf{P})| \leq \left| \sum_{n>j\neq i} e_{ij}(\mathbf{P})z_j(\mathbf{P}) \right|$$

$$\leq \sum_{n>j\neq i} |e_{ij}(\mathbf{P})|\,|z_j(\mathbf{P})| \leq |z_i(\mathbf{P})| \sum_{n>j\neq i} |e_{ij}(\mathbf{P})|.$$

where the last inequality follows from the definition of m. Evidently, the above inequalities contradict D*D*. Similarly, if $z_i < 0$, $d[\log x_i(\mathbf{p})]/dt$ must be positive. Hence, since we are in a pure-exchange economy, $Z(\mathbf{P})$ is declining at non-equilibrium **P**. Since we already know the solution path to be bounded, $Z(\mathbf{P})$ is indeed a Lyapounov function. Since, by T.9.12, the economy must have a unique equilibrium, the theorem is proved. (Of course, the equilibrium as well as the rule is globally stable.)

It is not hard to think of the kind of assumptions we should like to make in order to extend these results to an economy in which there is also production. We consider only one of these, the simplest.

ASSUMPTION 2. The numeraire good does not enter into the production of any good nor is it produced. Also, $\partial y_i(\mathbf{P})/\partial P_j < 0$ for all $\mathbf{P} \gg \mathbf{0}$ and $j \neq i$.

The last assumption supposes that, say, a rise in the price of good j will decrease the economy's output of good i, if that good is produced, or reduce the demand for that good (service) as input if it is not. As usual, it is easy to think of technologies that would falsify this assumption. If it is made in view of H applied to $\mathbf{y}(\mathbf{P})$, however, it follows at once from the supposition that the numeraire good does not enter production in any way, that $\partial y_i(\mathbf{P})/\partial P_i > 0$ all $\mathbf{P} \gg \mathbf{0}$ and all i.

THEOREM 8. If an economy has D*D*, follows the rule (II), and satisfies A.12.1 and A.12.2, then for all $\mathbf{P}(0) \gg \mathbf{0}$, the rule is globally stable.

Proof. Proceed as in the proof of T.12.7. For $i \in m$, we find, writing $y_{ij}(\mathbf{P}) = \partial y_i(\mathbf{P})/\partial P_j$ and using (II),

$$\frac{dy_i(\mathbf{P})}{dt} = \sum_j y_{ij}(\mathbf{P})P_j z_j(\mathbf{P}).$$

It can be left to the reader to show that this expression has the same sign as z_i for non-equilibrium **P**. As before, $Z(\mathbf{P})$ is declining for non-equilibrium **P**, and the proof proceeds as before.

The result we have just established is worth having if for no other reason that the Diagonal Dominance hypothesis, when framed in terms of elasticities, seems particularly appealing. There is also another, sadder reason. When we return to the more general form of the assumption and also to the more general form of the pricing rule, it is not at present possible to establish global stability. This, if a conjecture may be made, is likely to be due to lack of skill on our part, rather than to any global instability in fact. The kind of result that we need here is one that would allow us to deduce global stability from the postulate that the Jacobian of excess supplies has everywhere DD. No such result is available, but neither are counter-examples. In any event, we are able, at present, to prove only the following, weaker result.

THEOREM 9. Let there be units in which goods are measured such that if the economy has DD in these units, it has this property at all prices. Then A.11.2 gives a globally stable rule.

Proof. We note formally the assumption of the theorem: There is a vector $\mathbf{h} \gg \mathbf{0}$, such that for all $i \neq n$ *and* all **P**

$$|z_{ii}(\mathbf{P})|h_i > \sum_{n>j\neq i} |z_{ij}(\mathbf{P})|h_j,$$

where, of course, $z_{ii}(\mathbf{P}) < 0$, all i.

We now show that

$$H(\mathbf{P}) = \max \frac{F_i[z_i(\mathbf{P})]}{h_i}$$

is a Lyapounov function. Let m be the set of i for which $F_i[z_i(\mathbf{P})]/h_i = H(\mathbf{P})$. Then for $i \in m$,

$$\frac{dz_i(\mathbf{P})}{dt} = \sum z_{ij}(\mathbf{P})F_j[z_j(\mathbf{P})] = \frac{\sum z_{ij}(\mathbf{P})h_jF_j[z_j(\mathbf{P})]}{h_j}.$$

The right-hand side of this expression must be negative for non-equilibrium **P**. If not, then

$$|z_{ii}(\mathbf{P})|h_iH(\mathbf{P}) \leq \frac{\sum_{n>j\neq i} z_{ij}(\mathbf{P})h_jF_j[z_j(\mathbf{P})]}{h_j}$$

$$\leq H(\mathbf{P}) \sum_{n=j\neq i} |z_{ij}(\mathbf{P})|h_j,$$

which would contradict the assumption of the theorem. Hence $H(\mathbf{P})$ is declining in value at every non-equilibrium $\mathbf{P}$ and the usual argument proves the theorem.

The method of proof we have just used shows why we needed the rather special form of Diagonal Dominance. If we had taken $\mathbf{h}$ to be a function of $\mathbf{P}$, that is, $\mathbf{h} = \mathbf{h}(\mathbf{P})$, we would have required to know how $\mathbf{h}(\mathbf{P})$ behaves when $\mathbf{P}$ changes, and on this, no useful hypothesis seems available.

5. Local Stability

In all the cases we have considered so far, with the exception of WGS, we know that the equilibrium is unique, and since we have shown it to be globally stable, it must be that the equilibrium is locally stable also. The question we shall briefly pose is whether there are situations for which local, but not global, stability properties can be established. We do not propose, however, to examine local stability problems at all exhaustively.

We shall be considering the numeraire rule of A.11.2 and conducting our analysis in terms of the norm $V(\mathbf{P}) = (\mathbf{P} - \mathbf{P}^*)D(P - P^*)'$ when $\mathbf{P}$ (taken as a row vector with transposition denoted by a prime) is assumed to lie in an ϵ neighborhood of $\mathbf{P}^*$, and D is a suitably chosen diagonal matrix. Of course, what we are looking for are situations for which we can say that the norm is declining for all non-equilibrium $\mathbf{P}$, for then, on the usual argument, we shall be able to treat it as a Lyapounov function.

For a suitable choice of ϵ we may write $z_i(\mathbf{P})$ in a Taylor expansion, ignoring non-linear terms, as follows:

$$z_i(\mathbf{P}) = z_i(\mathbf{P}^*) + \sum z_{ij}(\mathbf{P}^*)(\mathbf{P}_j - \mathbf{P}_j^*)'.$$

If $\mathbf{P}^* \gg \mathbf{0}$, then we know that it must be that $\mathbf{z}(\mathbf{P}^*) = \mathbf{0}$. By A.11.2, we may then write

$$\dot{P}_i = F_i' \sum z_{ij}(\mathbf{P}^*)(P_j - P_j^*).$$

If, as usual, we write $J(\mathbf{P}^*)$ as the Jacobian of the *excess-supply* functions and f as the diagonal matrix with non-zero elements given by F_i', we have, in matrix notation,

$$\dot{\mathbf{P}}' = -fJ(\mathbf{P}^*)(\mathbf{P} - \mathbf{P}^*)'.$$

Premultiplying both sides of this expression by $(\mathbf{P} - \mathbf{P}^*)f^{-1}$,

$$(\mathbf{P} - \mathbf{P}^*)D\dot{\mathbf{P}}' = -(\mathbf{P} - \mathbf{P}^*)J(\mathbf{P}^*)(\mathbf{P} - \mathbf{P}^*)'$$

when $D = f^{-1}$. The left-hand side of this expression is equal to $[dV(\mathbf{P})/dt]/2$ and so we would like to be able to say that the right-hand side is negative for non-equilibrium $\mathbf{P}$. The reader should prove to himself that this is indeed the case for a Hicksian or GS economy. It is not necessarily true for DD because $V(\mathbf{P})$ is not a suitable form of the Lyapounov function for this case.

To proceed, it will be useful to look at the constituents of $J(\mathbf{P}^*)$. Since $s_i = \bar{x}_i + y_i - x_i$, we may write

$$J(\mathbf{P}^*) = Y(\mathbf{P}^*) - X(\mathbf{P}^*),$$

where $Y(\mathbf{P}^*)$ is the Jacobian of the production term $y(\mathbf{P}^*)$ and $X(\mathbf{P}^*)$ the Jacobian of the demand term $\mathbf{x}(\mathbf{P}^*)$ in $\mathbf{s}(\mathbf{P}^*)$. (We here assume that all these are differentiable.) From profit maximization we know that $(\mathbf{P} - \mathbf{P}^*)[(\mathbf{y}(\mathbf{P}) - \mathbf{y}(\mathbf{P}^*)] \geq 0$ (see T.3.8). By the Taylor expansion,

$$\mathbf{y}(\mathbf{P}) - \mathbf{y}(\mathbf{P}^*) = Y(\mathbf{P}^*)(\mathbf{P} - \mathbf{P}^*)'$$

and so

$$-(\mathbf{P} - \mathbf{P}^*)\,Y(\mathbf{P}^*)(\mathbf{P} - \mathbf{P}^*)' \leq 0.$$

It follows from this that if, for some cases, we can show

$$(\mathbf{P} - \mathbf{P}^*)X(\mathbf{P}^*)(\mathbf{P} - \mathbf{P}^*)' < 0$$

for non-equilibrium $\mathbf{P}$, we can then say that for these assumptions $V(\mathbf{P})$ is indeed a Lyapounov function. Thus the crucial problem is the behavior of households, not that of producers. We shall simplify matters accordingly from here on by considering only a pure-exchange economy.

We know that we may write $X(\mathbf{P}^*)$ as the sum of the matrix of substitution terms, say $[\sigma_{ij}(\mathbf{P}^*)]$, and the matrix of income terms, say $[\mu_{ij}(\mathbf{P}^*)]$. The former is known to be negative definite (see T.4.9(b)), so evidently the crux of the problem is presented by the income term matrix as no doubt we expected all along. From elementary theory, we may write the typical element of that matrix as

$$\mu_{ij}(\mathbf{P}^*) = \sum_h s_{hj}(\mathbf{P}^*)m_{hi}(\mathbf{P}^*)$$

where $s_{hj}(\mathbf{P}^*)$ is the difference between the amount of the jth good household h has at $\mathbf{P}^*$ and the amount it would like to have at $\mathbf{P}^*$, household h's excess supply of good j, and $m_{hi}(\mathbf{P}^*)$ is the household's marginal propensity to consume good i at $\mathbf{P}^*$. Since $\mathbf{P}^* \gg \mathbf{0}$, it is of course true that

$$\sum_h s_{hj}(\mathbf{P}^*) = 0.$$

This enables us to write the typical element of the income term matrix also as

$$\mu_{ij}(\mathbf{P}^*) = \sum_h s_{hj}(\mathbf{P}^*)[m_{hi}(\mathbf{P}^*) - m_i(\mathbf{P}^*)]$$

where $m_i(\mathbf{P}^*)$ is the average marginal propensity to consume good i for household as a whole. Evidently, we may interpret the foregoing expression as a covariance. If there is no reason we can think of why there should be any systematic relationship between being a net supplier or demander of good j and having a high or low marginal propensity to consume good i, then we would be inclined to say that this covariance is very close to zero. This inclination would be reinforced if the number of households was large. Of course, if this is a satisfactory description of the world, then $V(\mathbf{P})$ will indeed qualify as a Lyapounov function, provided the covariance (income terms) is sufficiently small relative to the substitution terms. Here we get additional help from the fact that the leading diagonal elements in the substitution matrix of every household must be negative (if the household consumes the good in question). Hence, as far as these terms are concerned, they are additive when we come to write down the substitution matrix for households as a whole. We cannot but think that this term at least will greatly outweigh the income term in practice. Of course, this is not enough for the task of proving stability, but it helps.

The condition that the covariance must be small ensures local stability, but it does not entail either that the economy be either Hicksian or GS or WGS or DD even in a small neighborhood of $\mathbf{P}^*$, let alone everywhere. Moreover, if the demand Jacobian is evaluated at $\mathbf{P} \neq \mathbf{P}^*$,

$$\mu_{ij}(\mathbf{P}) = \sum_h s_{hj}(\mathbf{P})[m_{hi}(\mathbf{P}) - m_i(\mathbf{P})] + s_j(\mathbf{P})m_i(\mathbf{P}).$$

The smallness of the covariance term no longer allows us to deduce desirable properties for the Jacobian. Thus, even if the covariance term is small for all **P**, this does not seem sufficient to establish a global stability result.

Indeed, local stability requires us to show that the real parts of the roots of $X(\mathbf{P}^*)$ are negative. Suppose this to be the case not only at $\mathbf{P}^*$, but at all **P**. We might conjecture, then, that provided $\mathbf{P}(t)$ is bounded and equilibrium is unique, global stability would follow. This we have not been able to prove.

It is not clear how interesting the small covariance case is, since, for instance, a stratified society may well consist of a few kinds of households only and the covariance terms may be large. Indeed, we must recognize that we have here a double-edged weapon, for it would seem clear that we ought to be able to construct at least hypothetical examples where the income terms are sufficiently large relative to the substitution terms to allow us to deduce that $V(\mathbf{P})$ is increasing for all non-equilibrium **P**. In that case we shall have not only a case of local instability, but also of course an instance of global instability should the equilibrium be unique. We shall consider such an example now.

6. An Example of Global Instability

Consider an economy with three goods, one of which, say that labelled "0," can be chosen as numeraire, and we are interested in the process described by A.11.2, (I). When examining local stability, that is, the behavior of the system in the neighborhood of an equilibrium P_1^*, P_2^*, we shall wish to ensure that the real parts of the roots of $-DJ(\mathbf{P}^*)$ are negative, if there is to be local stability. Here

$$-DJ(\mathbf{P}^*) = \begin{pmatrix} z_{11}(\mathbf{P}^*)k_1 & z_{12}(\mathbf{P}^*)k_1 \\ z_{21}(\mathbf{P}^*)k_2 & z_{22}(\mathbf{P}^*)k_2 \end{pmatrix}$$

where D is the diagonal matrix with element k_i. However, if $R(\lambda_i)$ is the real part of the ith root, we know that

$$\sum_i R(\lambda_i) = \sum z_{ii}(\mathbf{P}^*)k_i \quad \text{and} \quad \lambda_1\lambda_2 = \det(-DJ(\mathbf{P}^*)).$$

Is there anything in the underlying micro-theory of economic agents that ensures that $\sum z_{ii}(\mathbf{P}^*)k_i < 0$ and $\det(-DJ(\mathbf{P}^*)) > 0$, which is a required necessary condition for local stability?

The answer is no, as the following example due to Gale illustrates. Suppose all households are alike and that they own 12 units of the numeraire good and nothing of the other two goods. Write the budget constraint:

$$P_1x_1(\mathbf{P}) + P_2x_2(\mathbf{P}) \leq 12.$$

Let the utility function be given by

$$U(x_1,x_2) = 28x_1 + 28x_2 - 2x_1^2 - 3x_1x_2 - 2x_2^2. \tag{4}$$

The reader should check that (4) gives convex indifference curves [although they are not strictly convex for all (x_1,x_2)]. In the economy there are stocks of the two goods given by

$$\bar{x}_1 = 6 \qquad \bar{x}_2 = 1.$$

These goods are held by an agent in the economy who is always willing to trade the whole of his stock against numeraire at the going prices.

We find the unique equilibrium prices to be given by $P_1 = 1$, $P_2 = 6$. Setting $k_1 = k_2 = 1$,

$$-J(\mathbf{P}^*) = \frac{1}{56}\begin{bmatrix} 24 & -60 \\ 10 & -11 \end{bmatrix}$$

and we verify that both roots have positive real parts, so that the economy is locally unstable.

In this example, good 1 is inferior at the equilibrium prices. We easily find the marginal propensity to consume this to be $-\frac{1}{8}$. Moreover, this income effect is strong enough to outweigh the substitution effect. This means that the excess demand for this good is, at the equilibrium prices, an increasing function of its own price and the undesirable consequences follow.

Two points may be made. If there is only one good in the economy to which the Giffen paradox applies, that is sufficient to give an example of instability for some adjustment speeds. If one diagonal element of $-J(\mathbf{P}^*)$ is positive, then there is always some D such that the sum of the diagonal elements of $-DJ(\mathbf{P}^*)$, the trace, is positive, which in turn implies at least one root with positive real part. Secondly, it should be noted that examples can be constructed, as they have been by Scarf, such that all goods are normal for every household and yet some diagonal term (or terms) of $-DJ(\mathbf{P}^*)$ is positive. This is due to differences in endowments between the households that have different marginal propensities to consume the goods. Here the covariance, which we have already examined, is not small. Since this has been discussed at some length already, we shall not pursue it further.

7. The Choice of Numeraire

In describing an equilibrium of an economy, it does not matter which good with a positive exchange value we choose as numeraire. The question arises whether this is also true for the analysis of the pricing process.

Certainly, if the economy is Hicksian or if all goods are GS, the choice of numeraire cannot in any way affect the prediction of global stability. That this is so follows from the manner in which stability for these cases was established earlier. The DD postulate is not in the same boat, however, for there is nothing in either the theory of household choice or the theory of producer choice that rules out the possibility that a system may have DD for one choice of numeraire and not for another. In that case, we may find ourselves in the situation in which we can claim the auctioneer's rule to be globally stable for one choice of numeraire and possibly divergent for another. In any event, we may be unable to prove stability for the latter.

We know that if the economy has DD for some numeraire, then it must have a unique equilibrium. Here the possible lack of DD for some other numeraire, of course, cannot affect the claim of uniqueness. Thus, if there is some choice of numeraire that allows us to show that for no prices in the vicinity of the equilibrium is the equilibrium locally stable, for that choice of numeraire, we shall also have shown that the auctioneer's rules are not globally stable. Suppose there are three goods and the economy has DD when the third good is chosen as numeraire, but not when the second good is so chosen. In the first case, the Jacobian we require for local analysis is given by

$$\begin{pmatrix} z_{11}(\mathbf{P}^*) & z_{12}(\mathbf{P}^*) \\ z_{21}(\mathbf{P}^*) & z_{22}(\mathbf{P}^*) \end{pmatrix}$$

and in the second case, it is given by

$$\begin{pmatrix} z_{11}(\mathbf{Q}^*) & z_{13}(\mathbf{Q}^*) \\ z_{31}(\mathbf{Q}^*) & z_{33}(\mathbf{Q}^*) \end{pmatrix}$$

where $\mathbf{Q}^*$ is the equilibrium price vector in terms of the second good. Since we are not excluding the possibility that $z_{33}(\mathbf{Q}^*) > 0$, the second Jacobian may have a positive trace and a positive determinant, and thus both roots may have positive real parts and the second system could not then be locally stable. To clinch the case, we would need to show by example that this sort of situation can arise for some utility functions and wealth holdings of households. This indeed can be done.

Since the DD situation is the most interesting of all we have investigated, the sensitivity of the qualitative analysis of the tâtonnement to the choice of numeraire must be taken seriously. If we leave, for the moment, the abstract world we have been inhabiting, we would be inclined to argue that insofar as the tâtonnement rule simulates any aspect of reality, there would in practice be no choice of numeraire at all; prices would be quoted in terms of the medium of exchange. Therefore, the proper procedure is not to enquire whether the system has DD for any arbitrary numeraire, but to enquire whether this is the case for this particular one. This argument has some force, but it is open to at least two objections. First we must recall that the formal structure of our economy is ill-suited in its present form to accommodate what we would regard as a sensible theory of money. There is no uncertainty, and above all, we have given the economy no time sequence of transactions. This objection, then, is simply one against the importation of casual empiricism into a construction as abstract as the present one. It is an argument for postponing the discussion of the "choice of numeraire" until we have reached the stage at which we can bring empirical evidence to bear. The second objection, however, is worth noting now. It is that in a number of actual situations, whatever the power of our model to accommodate them, there is in fact a choice of numeraire. Thus, in the theory of the balance of payments, there are evidently policy choices such as whether to use a given currency (the dollar) as the currency in terms of which all others are quoted on the market for exchange or whether to use gold or some fictional unit such as bancors for this role. Thus it may well be that our laboratory procedure has uncovered a point that may yet be of practical relevance. But the answer to this awaits the stage at which it appears reasonable to draw at least tentative inference from the theory to the facts.

8. Some Other Auctioneer's Rules

We have seen that it is by no means true that, in all situations, the two rules we have examined will be successful in seeking an equilibrium for the economy. If, for a moment, we think of the auctioneer as a planner who is seeking the equilibrium by trial and error and forget all about simulating market procedures, it is reasonable to enquire whether there is some other rule that would lead to an equilibrium whatever the fine properties of the excess-demand functions might be.

We shall not attempt to answer this question in its full generality, since it is a little too farfetched to merit detailed attention. We shall discuss one interesting example, however.

Let $\mathbf{P}$ be the price vector in terms of numeraire. Suppose the planner can observe not only excess-demand vector $\tilde{\mathbf{z}}(\mathbf{P})$ for the non-numeraire goods, but also their Jacobian $-J(\mathbf{P})$. If this Jacobian is non-singular, the planner can calculate what the equilibrium price vector, call it $\mathbf{Q}$, of the economy would be if the excess-demand functions were linear with the coefficients $J(\mathbf{P})$; that is, he solves

$$\tilde{\mathbf{z}}(\mathbf{P}) - J(\mathbf{P})(\mathbf{Q} - \mathbf{P}) = \mathbf{0} \quad \text{or} \quad (\mathbf{Q} - \mathbf{P}) = J(\mathbf{P})^{-1}\tilde{\mathbf{z}}(\mathbf{P}),$$

which is Newton's method for solving non-linear equations.

Of course, in general, the excess-demand functions are not linear. However, the planner follows the rule of raising the price of good i if $Q_i > P_i$ and lowering it when $Q_i < P_i$. At each stage of the process he must recalculate $\mathbf{Q}$, which depends on $\mathbf{P}$. He may justify this procedure simply by the argument that he is always moving prices in the direction of the only approximation to equilibrium that he is able to calculate.

Evidently, this manner of adjusting prices will be possible in this simple way only if for all $\mathbf{P}$ generated, $J(\mathbf{P})$ is non-singular. There are other difficulties as well. Certainly, there is no guarantee that $\mathbf{Q}$ will always have non-negative components. It may be argued that this does not matter so long as $\mathbf{P} \gg \mathbf{0}$, since although the planner realizes that $\mathbf{Q}$ with negative components cannot be an equilibrium price vector, $Q_i - P_i$ still indicates the direction in which P_i should be changed. Yet if P_i itself is zero, we certainly cannot let the planner reduce it any further.

Suppose that

$$\sum_j z_j(\mathbf{P}) \to +\infty \quad \text{as} \quad P_i \to 0, \quad \text{any } i,$$

and take $\mathbf{P}(0) \gg \mathbf{0}$. The planner follows the rule

$$\dot{\mathbf{P}} = \mathbf{Q} - \mathbf{P} = J(\mathbf{P})^{-1}\tilde{\mathbf{z}}(\mathbf{P})$$

whence

$$\frac{d}{dt}[\tilde{\mathbf{z}}'(\mathbf{P})\tilde{\mathbf{z}}(\mathbf{P})] = -2[\tilde{\mathbf{z}}'(\mathbf{P})\tilde{\mathbf{z}}(\mathbf{P})] \leq 0$$

with equality if and only if $\mathbf{P}$ is an equilibrium. Then, since $\tilde{\mathbf{z}}'(\mathbf{P})\tilde{\mathbf{z}}(\mathbf{P})$ is never increasing, it follows from our assumption that no P_i can approach zero during this process.

This argument shows also that $[\tilde{\mathbf{z}}'(\mathbf{P})\tilde{\mathbf{z}}(\mathbf{P})]$ is a Lyapounov function. Therefore, the planner's procedure, under the given assumptions, will lead to an equilibrium, provided that

(a) A.11.3 is satisfied;
(b) the solution path is bounded.

For (a), a Lipschitz condition is sufficient (see Section 11.3 and footnote). Since $\tilde{\mathbf{z}}'(\mathbf{P})\tilde{\mathbf{z}}(\mathbf{P})$ is non-increasing, the path remains in a compact set away from the boundaries. Hence, if we assume, as we did in the hypothesis of T.11.15, that $J^{-1}\tilde{\mathbf{z}}(\mathbf{P})$ is continuously differentiable, it follows that, in the relevant region, the derivatives are uniformly bounded and, therefore, the Lipschitz condition must certainly hold. To see (b), note that we have already shown that our assumptions assure that $\mathbf{P}(t)$ is bounded below. To ensure that it is bounded above and, in any case, to assure that the numeraire process can lead to an equilibrium, we made the numeraire assumption A.11.2. This implies that as $|\mathbf{P}(t)| \rightarrow +\infty$ the excess demand for the numeraire good goes to plus infinity. Then, by W and $\|\mathbf{P}\|$ large enough, $[\tilde{\mathbf{z}}'(\mathbf{P})\tilde{\mathbf{z}}(\mathbf{P})]$ must be increasing if $\|\mathbf{P}\|$ increases further, and this we know to be impossible.

We have shown, therefore, that under fairly restrictive conditions, which, however, do not by themselves imply any of the stability conditions so far discussed, there exists a price adjustment process that ensures stability. It is important to note that this is not a process that mimicks the invisible hand—for instance, the price of a good may be raised even though it is in excess supply.

The most restrictive of the conditions is that that requires $J(\mathbf{P})$ to be non-singular for all $\mathbf{P}$. To clarify this, we show that the assumption implies that there is a unique equilibrium with $\mathbf{P} \gg \mathbf{0}$. (This is the promised proof of T.9.15.)

Certainly, if $J(\mathbf{P}^*)$ is non-singular at some equilibrium $\mathbf{P}^* \gg \mathbf{0}$, then by a classical result in analysis there cannot be another equilibrium in a small neighborhood of $\mathbf{P}^*$; that is, if there are many equilibria, they must be isolated. Moreover, for a small enough neighborhood and $\mathbf{J(P)}$ uniformly bounded, the planner's rule gives

$$\dot{\mathbf{P}} = J(\mathbf{P})^{-1}\tilde{\mathbf{z}}(\mathbf{P}) \approx -\mathbf{J}(\mathbf{P})^{-1}\mathbf{J}(\mathbf{P}^*)(\mathbf{P} - \mathbf{P}^*).$$

For $|\mathbf{P} - \mathbf{P}^*|$ small enough, $\mathbf{J}(\mathbf{P})^{-1}\mathbf{J}(\mathbf{P}^*)$ must have a dominant diagonal, so it is easy to see that $\mathbf{P}(t)$ converges to $\mathbf{P}^*$; that is, every equilibrium $\mathbf{P}^*$ is locally asymptotically stable.

We already know that the adjustment process is globally stable as well, so by T.11.5, we see that there can be only one equilibrium $\mathbf{P}^* \gg \mathbf{0}$.

There is yet another procedure we might take the auctioneer as following, a procedure that also fails to mimic the market, but deserves attention if for no other reason than that Walras found it worthy of attention. As a matter of fact, it is useful to consider it also as an example of a process taking place in discrete rather than continuous time.

We now take the auctioneer as concentrating on one market at a time. By this we mean, in the first place, that if the system is not in equilibrium at t, then in the time interval, $(t, t + 1)$, only one price is changed. Secondly, if it is the ith price that is changed, then the auctioneer changes it to the value that, given all the other prices, will ensure that the ith market is in equilibrium. Of course, we must assume that one such value of the price exists, and we shall find it safe to assume also that there is only one such value. Formally, if this process started at $t = 0$, then the price vector at m will be

$$p(m) = \{p_1(1), p_2(2) \cdots p_m(m), \quad p_{m+1}(0) \cdots p_n(0)\},$$

where we have supposed that the markets are numbered in the order in which they attract the attention of the auctioneer and that if one of these is in equilibrium, then prices do not change at all for one period.

It is fairly clear that this sequential price adjustment method will not converge to an equilibrium for all possible forms of the excess-demand functions. But it is not hard to show that making some of the now very familiar assumptions, such as GS, will be sufficient to ensure stability. Thus stipulate GS. Consider the jth market at time t. Let $M(\mathbf{p}) = \max(p_i - 1)$, $m(\mathbf{p}) = \min(p_i - 1)$, where, as usual in such a case, we take the unit vector $\mathbf{e}$ as the unique equilibrium of the economy. Suppose that in order to bring the jth market into equilibrium the auctioneer has to choose $p_j(t + 1)$

such that $(p_j(t + 1) - 1) \geq M[\mathbf{p}(t)]$. Then, by T.9.8, since the jth price would exceed its equilibrium value in the greatest proportion, it must be that $z_j[\mathbf{p}(t + 1)] < 0$, contradicting the manner in which the auctioneer has been supposed to determine the th price. By the same argument, it is not possible to have $(p_j(t + 1) - 1) \leq m[\mathbf{p}(t)]$. Hence, certainly the price solution must be bounded since no price can ever exceed its equilibrium by more than $M[\mathbf{p}(0)]$ or fall short of it by more than $m[\mathbf{p}(0)]$. Also $M(\mathbf{p}) - m(\mathbf{p})$ is a Lyapounov function and so stability follows.

It can be readily seen also that similar results can be established with a strictly positive equilibrium for the case of DD when this property holds at all prices for some particular choice of units in which to measure goods. Letting $M'(\mathbf{p}) = \max(p_j - 1)/h_j$ and similarly modifying the definition of $m(\mathbf{p})$, we can argue in exactly the same way as we did in the case of GS. If, say, it were true that the auctioneer has to choose p_j such that $(p_j(t + 1) - 1)/h_j \geq M'(\mathbf{p}(t))$, then it must be true that we can find a sequence of prices $\mathbf{p}^\nu$ starting at $\mathbf{e}$ such that, at all ν,

$$\epsilon \geq \frac{|p_j^\nu - p_j^{\nu-1}|}{h_j} \geq \frac{|p_i^\nu - p_i^{\nu-1}|}{h_i} \qquad \text{all } i,$$

where this sequence converges to $\mathbf{p}(t + 1)$. Then, at each step of this sequence, it follows from DD that, if ϵ is sufficiently small,

$$z_j(\mathbf{p}^\nu) - z_j(\mathbf{p}^{\nu-1}) < 0,$$

and since $z_j(\mathbf{p}^0) = 0$, we again have a contradiction of the supposed manner in which the auctioneer determines prices. A similar argument holds, of course, to ensure that $[p_j(t + 1) - 1]/h_j > m'(\mathbf{p})$.

The proof that the rule now under consideration will also be stable if the economy is Hicksian is left to the reader. The rule does not seem to permit a proof of stability for any cases that might be regarded as less restrictive than those we considered for the "normal" rules. Indeed, this successive tâtonnement procedure has rather little to recommend it. Not only does it not imitate the market, but it is doubtful whether it imitates an efficient computational program for finding an equilibrium. It is, in fact, what is known as a Gauss–Seidel method of solving a set of simultaneous equations, a method that is not particularly attractive as a computational means.

To conclude this section on alternative rules, let us return to the market-imitative A.11.1 and A.12.2, but for discrete time. In particular, consider the rule

$$p_i(t+1) = \max\{0, p_i(t) + kz_i(\mathbf{p}(t))\} \qquad k > 0, \tag{5}$$

which is reminiscent of the mapping whose fixed point was discussed in Chapter 2. Evidently, (5) ensures that prices are always non-negative. We shall not investigate this process for all of our cases, since we are mainly interested in one particular lesson, which we can learn by taking the GS situation only.

As usual, the units we choose to measure goods allow us to write the unique equilibrium as $\mathbf{e}$. We consider $V(\mathbf{p}) = (\mathbf{p} - \mathbf{e})(\mathbf{p} - \mathbf{e})'$ to see whether it will make a suitable Lyapounov function. We take $\mathbf{p}(0) \gg \mathbf{0}$ and note that because of GS we may take $\mathbf{p}(t) \gg \mathbf{0}$, all t, because the good with the lowest price at t must be in excess demand. Now what we wish to show, of course, is that for all $\mathbf{p}(t) \neq \mathbf{e}$,

$$V[\mathbf{p}(t+1)] - V[\mathbf{p}(t)] < 0.$$

This evidently enables us to kill two birds with one stone: The solution path of price will be bounded and V will indeed be a Lyapounov function. But $V(\mathbf{p}(t)) = \sum p_i^2(t) - 2\sum p_i(t) + n$, where n is the number of goods. By (5) and W, we have

$$\sum [p_i(t+1)]^2 = \sum p_i^2(t) + k^2 \sum z_i^2[\mathbf{p}(t)],$$

so that

$$V[\mathbf{p}(t+1)] = \sum p_i^2(t) + k^2 \sum z_i^2(\mathbf{p}(t)) - 2\sum p_i(t+1) + n$$

and

$$V[\mathbf{p}(t+1)] - V[\mathbf{p}(t)] = k^2 \sum z_i^2(\mathbf{p}(t)) - 2\sum [p_i(t+1) - p_i(t)].$$

By (5),

$$\sum [\, p_i(t+1) \;- p_i(t)] = k \sum z_i(\mathbf{p}(t))$$

and so finally,

$$V[\mathbf{p}(t+1)] - V[\mathbf{p}(t)] = k^2 \sum z_i^2[\mathbf{p}(t)] - k\mathbf{ez}[\mathbf{p}(t)].$$

We know, however, that since all goods are GS, it must be that $\mathbf{ez}[\mathbf{p}(t)] > 0$ for all $\mathbf{p}(t) \neq \mathbf{e}$ by T.9.9. Consider the ratio

$$r[\mathbf{p}(t)] = \frac{\mathbf{ez}[\mathbf{p}(t)]}{\mathbf{ez}^2[\mathbf{p}(t)]} \qquad \mathbf{p}(t) \neq \mathbf{e},$$

where the denominator vector $\mathbf{z}^2$ has components z_i^2. Clearly $r[\mathbf{p}(t)] > 0$ and, therefore, must be bounded away from zero for all non-equilibrium $\mathbf{p}^*$.

Let $R = \{\mathbf{p} \mid |\mathbf{z}(\mathbf{p})| \geq \epsilon, \quad \epsilon > 0\}$. Then, from what has been said, we may choose k^* such that $k^* < (r(\mathbf{p}))$ for $\mathbf{p} \in R$. Inserting k^* in (5) shows that $V[\mathbf{p}(t)]$ will be monotonically declining for all $\mathbf{p}(t) \in R$. Hence, for T large enough, $|\mathbf{z}[\mathbf{p}(t)]| < \epsilon$, all $t > T$. Thus there is a choice of k^* such that prices converge to any given small neighborhood of the equilibrium.

The lesson we seem to have learned is that in the finite time adjustment rule stability depends on the fine properties of the adjustment rule itself even when so convenient a hypothesis as GS is made. This is in marked contrast to what we found to be true in the continuous time case. It is not hard to see that this conclusion does not really depend on the manner in which we choose to try to prove the stability of the process. If we take the set of all $\mathbf{p}$, such that $|\mathbf{p} - \mathbf{e}| = \epsilon$, then for that set there will be some $\mathbf{p}'$ that maximizes $r(\mathbf{p})$. If we then choose $k > r(\mathbf{p})$, it will be true that $V(\mathbf{p})$ is increasing at every point of that set of prices. Then, if $|\mathbf{p}(0) - \mathbf{e}| > \epsilon$, it is clear that the adjustment process could never return us to the equilibrium. This is a sad lesson. So far we have been content to let the auctioneer imitate the market in the sense of raising prices in response to excess demand, and so on, but of course, any proper imitation would also have to take account of the lag structures we find in the world. Given the great variety of these structures and given the lesson just learned, it is fairly clear that we shall not be able to predict, in general, stability of any such process from a knowledge only of the kinds of excess-demand functions with which we are dealing. Such knowledge will still be relevant and helpful; it just will not be sufficient.

There is a notable exception to this conclusion, however, namely the case of the Hicksian economy. In such an economy any rule that raises the prices of goods in excess demand and lowers those of goods in excess supply must, whatever the lag structure, serve to lower the utility of the fictional household whose behavior we may take as generating the actual excess demands we observe. Therefore, we may take this household's utility function as our Lyapounov function. Of course, the Hicksian case is exceptional. But the argument showing that, for that case, stability is assured for a wide variety of lag structures in the adjustment mechanism suggests that it may well be the artificial restriction we have imposed on the problem, namely that there shall be no transactions out of equilibrium, that is at least partly responsible for our predicament. Is it not reasonable to suppose that when exchange is permitted at all **p**, it will take place only if it is to the advantage of the transactors and, therefore, that in such a world we may hope to use the utility indicators of households as our Lyapounov function as we use that of the fictional household in the Hicksian case? These matters will be discussed in Chapter 13 and we reserve judgment until then.

9. Short-Period Equilibrium

So far our analysis can well apply to an abstract economy with all possible futures markets. Of course, this makes it even more remote from reality. It is worthwhile to enquire whether some of our results will survive a change in model that is designed to allow for the possibility that the only way of undertaking intertemporal transactions may be by means of storage of one or more goods. This probably errs on the side of pessimism as to the existence of futures markets.

We shall consider a pure-exchange economy because it is simpler and because if such an economy permits a stable adjustment process, then under the usual assumption on the production set, a more realistic construction will also have this property. We suppose that time is divided into the present, a finite time interval, and the future, also a finite time interval. The only good that may be transferred from the present to the future is the good with the index n. The price vector ruling in the present is written as **p**. Households are assumed also to form expectations as to the prices that will rule in the future. We assume that they do not subdivide the future into smaller time periods and write **q** as the price vector expected to rule over the entire future. At this stage, we do not distinguish between the expectations of the various households and take it that they are all the same. We are concerned only with the excess-demand vector of the present, which, as usual, we write as **z**, but it will now depend not only on **p**, but also on **q**: **z(p,q)** is the excess-demand vector at **p** and **q**. It is homogeneous of degree zero in these arguments and W holds: **pz(p,q)** = 0. We also take it to be differentiable where required. In Chapter 2 we discussed an economy of which the present one is a special instance. We showed that if we can take $\mathbf{q}$ to be a continuous function of $\mathbf{p}$, there would then exist a $\mathbf{p}^*$ such that the economy is in equilibrium in the present. We do not enquire how it will fare in the future. We shall refer to this economy as the short-period economy (SP).

The auctioneer operates in the present on the basis of the excess demands observable to him in the present. This may cause a conceptual difficulty. Is it possible to say that the auctioneer's rule is stable, when that notion seems to imply time going to infinity and we are confining ourselves to a finite time interval? The answer is that we have used time as an expository device so far; what is really at stake is that the number of steps—price changes undertaken by the auctioneer—goes to infinity, and that is clearly possible in a finite time interval. While in a formal way we can avoid being silly, it is true that in practice price adjustments do take time and that if the tâtonnement is to be taken seriously as in some sense connected with reality, then it must face the objection that even if the process is stable it is only asymptotically that equilibrium is attained. We shall take the formal way out of the difficulty and continue to use time differentials, although these must be taken to refer to steps.

Let us consider the simple adjustment process (II) and take all goods to be GS. Here "all goods" includes future goods. We take $\mathbf{p}(0) \gg \mathbf{0}$, and the usual argument will show that $\mathbf{p}(t) \gg \mathbf{0}$ all t so that (II) does not run into difficulties. We also postulate the following simple expectation formation mechanisms:

$$q_j = q_j(p_j) \qquad q_j > 0 \text{ when } p_j > 0. \tag{E}$$

Thus we make the price expected to rule for the jth good in the future dependent only on the price called for that good by the auctioneer in the present. Here the word "rule" should be interpreted as the expected equilibrium price of the future, that is, the price at which households expect to be able to transact then. The assumption evidently has no very great appeal, but it will serve in allowing us to learn some of the most important economic lessons that arise in these constructions. We shall also be making use of the Hicksian elasticity of expectations ϵ_j, which, of course, is given by

$$\epsilon_j = \frac{d \log q_j}{d \log p_j}.$$

To be able to utilize this concept we take all the expectation formation functions to be differentiable.

Let

$$V(\mathbf{p},\mathbf{q}) = \max_i z_i(\mathbf{p},\mathbf{q}),$$

a function that is positive for all non-equilibrium $\mathbf{p}$. We write $z_{in+j} = \partial z_i/\partial q_j$ and take it for granted that all the partials are evaluated at $(\mathbf{p},\mathbf{q})$. Also m is the set of i for which $z_i(\mathbf{p},\mathbf{q}) = V(\mathbf{p},\mathbf{q})$, and N is the set of i for which $z_i(\mathbf{p},\mathbf{q}) < 0$. Then we have, for any i,

$$\dot{z}_i = \sum_j z_{ij}p_j z_j + \sum_j z_{i,n+j}q'_j p_j z_j \qquad \text{where } q'_j = \frac{dq_j}{dp_j}.$$

Then for $i \in m$, it must be that

$$\dot{z}_i < \sum_{j \notin N} z_{ij}p_j z_j + \sum_{j \notin N} z_{i,n+j}q_j\epsilon_j z_j \leq V(\mathbf{p},\mathbf{q})\left(\sum_{j \notin N} z_{ij}p_j + \sum_{j \notin N} z_{i,n+j}q_j\epsilon_j\right),$$

where the strict inequality follows from the fact that out of equilibrium, N cannot be empty in view of W and GS. Then, using H, it is surely true[1] that for all $i \in m$, $\dot{z}_i < 0$, provided that

$$\epsilon_j \leq 1 \qquad \text{all } j \text{ and all } (\mathbf{p},\mathbf{q}) \gg \mathbf{0}.$$

Thus, certainly V is declining for all non-equilibrium prices if that condition holds. We know that the path of $\mathbf{p}$ is bounded, so since $\mathbf{q}$ is a continuous function of $\mathbf{p}$, it must be that $\mathbf{q}$ is also bounded and, hence, certainly $V(\mathbf{p},\mathbf{q})$ is a Lyapounov function.

Since we may write $\mathbf{q} = \mathbf{q}(\mathbf{p})$, we may also write $\mathbf{z}[\mathbf{p},\mathbf{q}(\mathbf{p})] = \mathbf{Z}(\mathbf{p})$, say. But $\mathbf{Z}$ will have H in $\mathbf{p}$ if all $\epsilon_j = 1$ and it will have DD if some $\epsilon_j < 1$ and no $\epsilon_j > 1$. The reader should check this by differentiating $\mathbf{z}$ and using the known property H for $\mathbf{z}(\mathbf{p},\mathbf{q})$ in $(\mathbf{p},\mathbf{q})$. Hence, for these cases, the economy has a unique equilibrium since our theorems on GS apply to $\mathbf{Z}(\mathbf{p})$ if it has H and our theorems on DD apply to $\mathbf{Z}(\mathbf{p})$ if it does not. We have therefore proved

THEOREM 9. Let an SP economy have the expectation formation E with $\epsilon_j(\mathbf{p},\mathbf{q}) \leq 1$, all $(\mathbf{p},\mathbf{q})$. Then the economy has a unique short-period equilibrium if all goods are GS. For $\mathbf{p}(0) \gg \mathbf{0}$, and the auctioneer's rule (II), $\mathbf{p}^*$ is globally stable.

[1] By H,

$$z_{ii}p_i + \sum_{j \neq i} z_{ij}p_j + \sum z_{i,n+j}q_j = 0.$$

All the terms under the summation signs are positive by GS. Hence, since N is not empty and $\epsilon_j \leqq 1$,

$$\sum_{j \notin N} z_{ij}p_j + \sum_{j \notin N} z_{i,n+j}q_j\epsilon_j < 0.$$

But $V(\mathbf{p},\mathbf{q}) > 0$.

It is quite easy to show that an exactly similar theorem can be established for the case of DD, provided this property holds for units in which goods are measured that are independent of $(\mathbf{p},\mathbf{q})$ and provided we may take it that $\mathbf{p}(t) \gg \mathbf{0}$, all t. This is just a simple exercise in the method just described and we shall not spell it out beyond noting that the appropriate V is then max z_i/h_i where h_i has the usual meaning. It is also interesting to note that these results can still be shown to hold by exactly the same method of proof if we replace (II) by

$$\frac{d \log p_i}{dt} = G_i[z_i(\mathbf{p},\mathbf{q})]. \tag{II$'$}$$

In that case the appropriate form of V is max G_i. Insofar as we take the auctioneer as imitating the market, it would seem that (II′) has a good deal to recommend it. Curiously enough, it does not seem possible to extend all these results to the Hicksian case. The utility function of the fictional household with which we have worked in this case in the past will not do now as a Lyapounov function. The reason is simply that while the auctioneer's rule, as usual, serves to make the fictional household worse off, the consequential adjustment in expected price may make it better off. Thus, if the household plans an excess demand for a good in the present and an excess supply of the good in the future, the rise in present price will make it worse off, but the consequential rise in expected price will make it better off. There may be a way of showing stability for the Hicksian case also, but we have not been able to find it.

Now it is not at all hard to think of alternative expectation formation hypotheses and no doubt a good many "theorems" could be generated. It does not seem appropriate to attempt a fuller catalog of possibilities here, especially since it seems likely that we already have sufficient to draw the qualitative moral that is likely to apply to all cases. This moral is that, contrary to what was proposed in *Value and Capital*,[1] we cannot draw any stability conclusions from knowledge of the expectation formation hypothesis alone. To do so we require information also on the form of the excess-demand

[1] "Technically, then, the case where elasticities of expectation are equal to unity marks the dividing line between stability and instability." Hicks [1939, p. 255]. Hicks, of course, was concerned with stability in a different sense than used here.

functions *and* on the rule followed by the auctioneer. In particular, $\epsilon_j \leq 1$, all j, is neither a necessary nor a sufficient condition for stability. That it is not sufficient follows from the fact that we can easily construct an example for $\mathbf{Z}(\mathbf{p})$ with ϵ_j's obeying the restriction imposed, but nonetheless it is a case of instability. That it is not necessary follows from our manner of proof of T.12.9. If we had information on the upper bounds of the partial coefficients of the excess-demand function, then stability might be established for logically possible cases with $\epsilon_j > 1$, some j. This is quite an important point to understand since there is often talk in economics of *destabilizing expectations* when all that is meant is that the elasticity of expectation may somewhere exceed unity. After all, it is common sense to enquire how expected prices enter into present excess demands before assenting to the adjective "destabilizing." Indeed, the SP economy is very rich in qualitative possibilities and it seems rather doubtful that any either very simple or very general stability propositions can be proved.

Although we have determined not to examine a catalog of expectation hypotheses, there is one to which we must briefly pay some attention because it is often used. We imagine the typical household to have a memory of all the prices that have been called by the auctioneer and to formulate its expectations as to the prices that will rule in the future by taking an exponentially weighted average of past observed prices. In such an artificial setting, this assumption probably does not command much credence, but since matters are otherwise in other settings, it is not without interest to consider it here. Accordingly, we postulate

$$\dot{q}_j(t) = \mu_j(p_j(t) - q_j(t)) \qquad \mu_j \geq 0. \tag{E$'$}$$

We refer to expectations formed according to (E′) as *adaptive*. On integrating this expression we find that the expected price is an exponentially weighted average of past prices. Note that $\mu_j = \infty$ implies $q_j = p_j$, all t, a case often referred to as "stationary expectations." We may interpret all this to mean that the price expected to rule in the future is the same as that expected to be called "next" by the auctioneer, so that if the actual price differs from the one expected in the future, it also differs from the one expected to be called next. It is here that the artificiality of the construct is most apparent since, as a matter of plain common sense, no household can have any interest in predicting what price will be called next by the auctioneer. In any event, we note that equilibrium requires $\mathbf{q} = \mathbf{p}$. Moreover, if we start in the vicinity of an equilibrium, then since μ_j cannot exceed infinity, $\mathbf{q}$ can at most change in the same proportions as $\mathbf{p}$, so that in the appropriate sense, the elasticity of the previous discussion can never exceed unity. This is the important point to remember when we show that in the GS case stability is assured to rule (I) whatever the precise value of μ_j may be. Adaptive expectations are conservative in the sense of Hicks, and in view of the foregoing, the result should cause no surprise nor tempt us into unnecessarily and unjustifiably startling claims that expectations do not matter for stability.

The proof of stability is very simple. We choose $V(\mathbf{p},\mathbf{q})$ as follows:

$$V(\mathbf{p},\mathbf{q}) = \max\left\{\frac{z_1}{p_1}, \ldots, \frac{z_n}{p_n}, \quad \frac{\mu_1(p_1 - q_1)}{q_1} \ldots \frac{\mu_n(p_n - p_n)}{q_n}\right\}.$$

We first show that $V(\mathbf{p},\mathbf{q}) = 0$ implies $\mathbf{z}(\mathbf{p},\mathbf{q}) = 0$, $\mathbf{p} = \mathbf{q}$. If not, it follows from W that

$$\begin{aligned} \mathbf{z}(\mathbf{p},\mathbf{q}) &= \mathbf{0} \\ p_i - q_i &\leq 0 \quad \text{all } i \\ p_i - q_i &< 0 \quad \text{some } i. \end{aligned} \tag{6}$$

If we write $\mathbf{Z}(\mathbf{p}) = \mathbf{z}(\mathbf{p},\mathbf{p})$ and use the mapping 2.(4) we see that the economy has an equilibrium $(\mathbf{p}^*,\mathbf{q}^*)$ with $\mathbf{p}^* = \mathbf{q}^*$. By GS, $\mathbf{p}^* \gg \mathbf{0}$. Choose units such that $\mathbf{p}^* = \mathbf{e} = \mathbf{q}^*$. Then, if for some current price p_r,

$$\begin{aligned} p_r &\leq p_i \quad \text{all } i, \\ p_r &\leq q_i \quad \text{all } i, \end{aligned}$$

it follows from T.9.8 that $z_r(\mathbf{p},\mathbf{q}) > 0$ unless $(\mathbf{p},\mathbf{q})$ is proportional to $(\mathbf{e},\mathbf{e})$. This contradicts the hypothesis, but since $(\mathbf{p},\mathbf{q})$ is not proportional to $(\mathbf{e},\mathbf{e})$, there must be an expected price q_s with

$$\begin{aligned} q_s &\leq p_i \quad \text{all } i, \\ q_s &\leq q_i \quad \text{all } i. \end{aligned}$$

But $q_i \geq p_i$, all i, by assumption, so $q_s = p_s$ and by the same argument as before $z_s(\mathbf{p},\mathbf{q}) > 0$. Hence (6) is impossible.

Now consider (I) with $k_i = 1$, all i. It is left to the reader to verify that $\mathbf{q}(0) \gg \mathbf{0}$, GS, and (E′) ensure $\mathbf{q}(t) \gg \mathbf{0}$, all t. We treat $V(\mathbf{p},\mathbf{q})$ as differentiable and note that by the same argument as in the proof of T.12.6, we can easily modify the analysis when it is not differentiable.

Let

$$\frac{z_j}{p_j} = v_j \qquad \frac{\mu_j(p_j - q_j)}{q_j} = w_j;$$

suppose that

$$V(\mathbf{p},\mathbf{q}) = v_r \neq 0.$$

By W, $v_r > 0$. Also

$$\begin{aligned} \dot{V}(\mathbf{p},\mathbf{q}) &= \dot{v}_r \\ &= \frac{1}{p_r}\left[\sum z_{rj} p_j v_j + \sum z_{rn+j} q_j w_j\right] - v_r^2 \\ &\leq \frac{v_r}{p_r}\left[\sum z_{rj} p_j + \sum z_{rn+j} q_j\right] - v_r^2 \\ &< 0 \end{aligned} \tag{7}$$

where the first inequality follows from GS and the definition of v_r and the second inequality from H.

Next suppose that

$$V(\mathbf{p},\mathbf{q}) = w_s \neq 0,$$

so

$$\dot{V}(\mathbf{p},\mathbf{q}) = \dot{w}_s = \frac{\mu_s}{q_s}(p_s v_s - q_s w_s) - w_s^2$$

Certainly $w_s > 0$; if not, since $\mathbf{z}(\mathbf{p},\mathbf{q}) \neq \mathbf{0}$, W implies that $z_i > 0$, some i, contradicting $V(\mathbf{p},\mathbf{q}) = w_s$. If $v_s \leq 0$, then certainly $\dot{V}(\mathbf{p},\mathbf{q}) < 0$. So suppose $v_s < 0$. Then $v_s(p_s - q_s) \geq (p_s v_s - q_s w_s)$, since $w_s \geq v_s$, so

$$\dot{V}(\mathbf{p},\mathbf{q}) \leq v_s w_s - w_s^2 < 0. \tag{8}$$

Thus $V(\mathbf{p},\mathbf{q})$ is declining for non-equilibrium $(\mathbf{p},\mathbf{q})$. Since it is easy to verify that the solution path of prices is bounded, we have proved

THEOREM 10. Let the SP economy have GS and the expectation rule (E′). Then there is a unique equilibrium with $\mathbf{p} = \mathbf{q}$. Moreover, the auctioneer's rule (I) with all $k_i = 1$ and $\mathbf{p}(0)$, $\mathbf{q}(0) \gg \mathbf{0}$ makes this equilibrium globally stable.

As we noted earlier, the theorem has nothing to say concerning the size of μ_j. As we also argued earlier, this should not be surprising.

10. The Constant-Returns Economy

We now consider an economy in which production is everywhere carried out under constant returns to scale and in which there is only one non-produced input. In particular, we shall take the economy to be connected and postulate A.2.10–A.2.13. The pricing rule is that given in A.11.5.

By our assumptions, it must be true that for all i and $\mathbf{p} > \mathbf{0}$, the minimum unit cost of producing i, $(C_i(\mathbf{p}))$, is strictly positive. It is clear, therefore, that all solution paths generated by the pricing rule, starting with non-negative prices, will be bounded from below. We also know (T.9.16) that the economy has a unique equilibrium, $\mathbf{p}^* \gg 0$. Let $k(\mathbf{p}) = p_r/p_r^* \geq p_i/p_i^*$, all i. Then, by the homogeneity of the minimum unit cost function and the definition of an equilibrium,

$$p_r = k(\mathbf{p})p_r^* = C_r(k(\mathbf{p})\mathbf{p}^*).$$

To pass from $k(\mathbf{p})\mathbf{p}^*$ to $\mathbf{p}$, at least one price, namely that of the non-produced input, must be lowered, so certainly

$$C_r(\mathbf{p}) < C_r(k(\mathbf{p})\mathbf{p}^*) = p_r.$$

Thus, by A.11.5, $\dot{p}_r < 0$, unless $\mathbf{p} = \mathbf{p}^*$, (i.e., $k(\mathbf{p}) = 1$). It follows from all this that the solution path of prices is bounded also from above. Moreover, it is immediate that

$$V(\mathbf{p}) = \max\left|\frac{p_i}{p_i^*} - 1\right|$$

will now serve as a Lyapounov function that is declining for all non-equilibrium $\mathbf{p}$. We have proved, therefore,

THEOREM 11. The equilibrium of a connected constant-returns economy satisfying A.2.10 to A.2.13 is globally stable for the rule of A.11.5.

This rather pleasing result is, unfortunately, very heavily dependent on the supposition that there is only one non-produced input, and therefore, it is not likely to find ready application in a more realistic setting. If it were not for this limitation, we would be tempted to argue that we have here the beginnings, admittedly only rudimentary ones, of a mark-up theory of price formation.

If there are a number of non-produced inputs, then we know (Section 2.11) that we cannot determine equilibrium prices independently of demand considerations and, therefore, we cannot expect a pure cost-determined theory of price adjustment to prove adequate. To see some of the difficulties that arise we now consider an economy in which there are as many non-produced inputs as there are outputs and in which no intermediate goods are used in production. It is the economy discussed in Section 10.4, and we employ the same notation.

Since demand factors are now relevant to price formation and since we cannot employ supply functions under constant returns to scale, we must somehow sidestep the difficulty this creates. We propose to do this as follows. We know that if $\mathbf{w}$ is the vector of input prices, we may solve for $\mathbf{p}$, the vector of output prices at which unit costs will be covered in all lines of production, from $\mathbf{p} = \mathbf{h}(\mathbf{w})$. If the production sets are strictly convex, then $\mathbf{w}$ determines the vector $\mathbf{p}$ uniquely. We now suppose that the auctioneer calls the prices of inputs, $\mathbf{w}$, and simultaneously solves $\mathbf{h}(\mathbf{w}) = \mathbf{p}$ and calls the resulting prices of outputs. Since minimum unit costs are exactly covered at all times in all lines of production, producers stand ready to supply whatever is demanded of the produced goods. We shall take it that for all $(\mathbf{w}, \mathbf{h}(\mathbf{w}))$, every produced good is demanded in positive quantity by households. The consequence of these assumptions is that we can never observe anything but a zero excess demand for produced goods. On the other hand, it may not be feasible to produce all the goods in the quantities in which they are demanded. This would be the case if, at the prices called and the consequential supply plans to meet household demands, some input were to be in excess demand. Now the natural thing to assume is that the auctioneer acts in the markets for inputs as we imagined him earlier in this chapter acting in all markets: He raises the price of the input in excess demand and lowers it for that in excess supply. Thus the auctioneer's activity is responsive to demand considerations only insofar as they appear in the market for inputs. Let $\mathbf{z}_I$ be the excess-demand vector for inputs. Then we may put what has just been said formally.

ASSUMPTION 3. (a) For all $t \geq 0$, $\mathbf{p}(t) = \mathbf{h}(\mathbf{w}(t))$.

(b) For any $i \in I$, $\dot{w}_i = G_i(z_i)$, unless $w_i = 0$ and $z_i < 0$ when $\dot{w}_i = 0$.

(c) The household (net) demand vector $\mathbf{x}(\mathbf{p},\mathbf{w}) - \bar{\mathbf{x}}$ is strictly positive for all $(\mathbf{p},\mathbf{w})$.

Since we may write $\mathbf{z}_I = \mathbf{z}_I(\mathbf{p},\mathbf{w}) = \mathbf{z}_I(\mathbf{h}(\mathbf{w}),\mathbf{w}) = \mathbf{Z}_I(\mathbf{w})$, say, and since $\mathbf{w}\mathbf{Z}_I = 0$, all $\mathbf{w}$, we may think of the market for inputs as constituting a "reduced" general equilibrium system.[1] Stability conclusions can be drawn by making assumptions about the reduced excess demands, $\mathbf{Z}_I$, so that we may appeal to our earlier results, in which these properties were taken to hold for the non-reduced system. The difficulty is simply that these postulates are now only indirectly related to what might be the appropriate preferences of households and the production sets of producers. Thus, for instance, if Z_{ij} is the partial coefficient of Z_i with respect to its jth argument,

$$Z_{ij} = \sum_k \frac{\partial z_i}{\partial p_k}\frac{\partial p_k}{\partial w_j} + \frac{\partial z_i}{\partial w_j}.$$

We certainly may take $\partial p_k/\partial w_j > 0$, all k, and it is easy to argue for $\partial z_i/\partial w_j > 0$, $i \neq 0$. It is much harder to postulate anything sensible concerning the $(\partial z_i/\partial p_k)$'s.

If we suppose that from the point of view of households all goods are GS, then a rise, say, in the price of the produced good k will reduce the demand for that good and increase the demand for other goods. By our assumptions, the supply of good k will be lower and that of others higher. This does not give us enough information to determine the final effect on the demand for any particular input; to do that we need to know some of the finer properties of the household demand functions and of the production sets. This should come as no surprise since we found this to be the case when we investigated the two-sector neoclassical model, which is similar to the present one in all respects except that it was restricted to the case of two inputs and outputs. Thus, while we may make such formal statements as, "If $\mathbf{Z}_I$ has GS, then the unique equilibrium of the economy will be globally stable for the rule of A.12.3," and while such results are not without use, it must be admitted that they are not of very great interest.

It is of some importance to understand why these difficulties are a peculiar feature of the present case. When constant returns are not stipulated, we need only quite general restrictions on the production sets and household preferences to enable us to say that the rise in the price of a produced good will raise the demand for a given input, or

[1] This discussion partly recapitulates what was said in 9.12.

at least will not lower it. Such a rise cannot lead to the reduction in the planned supply of the good if production sets are convex and it leaves the planned supplies of all other goods unchanged. Accordingly, we should be justified in saying that the demand for no input is reduced. On the other hand, the rise in the price of the produced good will not increase the supply of any input either if the latter is not subject to household choice or, if it is, if we may take it that leisure is not an inferior good. Thus, while some restrictions on the production sets and household preferences are required, if we want to be able to say that a rise in the price of good k does not reduce the excess demand for any input, these are far less "fine" than needed in the constant-returns case. This is due to the necessity of circumventing the absence of a supply "function" in this case by stipulating that whatever is demanded is also supplied provided minimum unit costs are covered.

There is one case, however, for which we can be quite definite in our conclusions; this arises when it is true that all households satisfy the requirement that the economy be Hicksian, if all inputs are household services and households own no stocks of any good. If we write $\mathbf{L}$ as the supply vector of household services (taken to have non-negative components) and $\mathbf{x}$ as the vector of household demand for produced goods, we may write the budget constraint of the fictional household that we always examine in the Hicksian case as

$$B = \mathbf{h}(\mathbf{w})\mathbf{x} - \mathbf{w}\mathbf{L} = 0.$$

Write $h_{ij}(\mathbf{w}) = \partial h_i/\partial w_j$ and differentiate the budget constraint with respect to w_j to find, when $\mathbf{x}$ and $\mathbf{L}$ are *held constant* (denoted by an asterisk),

$$\frac{\partial B^*}{\partial w_j} = \sum_i h_{ij}(\mathbf{w})x_i - L_j$$

$h_{ij}(\mathbf{w})$ is the amount of input j employed per unit of output of good i and so

$$\frac{\partial B^*}{\partial w_j} = Z_j(\mathbf{w})$$

since by assumption whatever is demanded of a produced good is also supplied (if unit costs are covered). Then, using the auctioneer's rule A.12.3, we have

$$\frac{dB^*}{dt} = \sum \frac{\partial B^*}{\partial w_j}\dot{w}_j = \sum Z_j(\mathbf{w})G_j(Z_j(\mathbf{w})),$$

an expression that must always be positive out of equilibrium. However, $dB^*/dt > 0$ must mean that the fictional household is made worse off by each successive calling of prices of inputs. Provided the rule gives rise to a bounded sequence, $\mathbf{w}(t)$ (as it will, for instance, if $G_i(Z_i) = Z_i$), we may use the utility function of the fictional household as a Lyapounov function, as usual. We have therefore proved

THEOREM 12. Let the constant-returns economy have as many non-produced inputs as it has produced outputs, there being no joint production. Let households own no stocks of any good and suppose that A.12.3 holds. Then, if the economy is Hicksian, the auctioneer's rule will be globally stable if the price path is bounded.

We see that the Hicksian hypothesis is sufficiently powerful to allow us to deduce definite stability results without any further fine specification of the production sets and of household preferences; it seems to be the only such case.

11. The Correspondence Principle

In Section 1.6 we briefly mentioned the contention, due to Samuelson, that the postulate that the economy was stable would carry with it implications that would be helpful in the task of comparing equilibria. We are now in a better position to assess this claim.

At first sight it would appear to be wholly justified, since it is true that we have been able to prove stability for just those cases for which we also found it possible to reach certain conclusions as to the effects of parameter changes on the economy's equilibrium. It is on such grounds that an "intimate connection between stability and comparative statics" has been proposed. Yet the conclusion is too hasty and the impression delusory, for we are asked to compare equilibria, not given the information that the economy has GS or is Hicksian, etc., but given the information that the equilibrium is locally or globally stable. The following example will make clear that this latter information is not enough. Consider an economy with four goods. Write the excess-demand function for good 1 as $z_1(\mathbf{p},\alpha)$, where α is a shift parameter such that $z_{1\alpha} = \partial z_1/\partial\alpha > 0$. We assume that α enters into the excess-demand function of only the first and fourth goods and that the latter is the chosen numeraire.

If $\mathbf{P}^*$ is an equilibrium, we may be interested in the sign of $dP_1^*/d\alpha$, which we go about determining from

$$J(\mathbf{P}^*)\left\{\frac{dP_i^*}{d\alpha}\right\} = \{z_{1\alpha},0,0\}$$

in our usual notation. If all goods are, say, GS, then we know that it must be that $dP_1^*/d\alpha > 0$. It will be true also that for the usual auctioneer's rule, $\mathbf{P}^*$ will be locally stable. But suppose that we are given only the latter information. We conclude from the requirements of local stability that all the real parts of the roots of $J(\mathbf{P}^*)$ are positive. This is consistent with the determinant formed from $J(\mathbf{P}^*)$ by deleting the first row and column having the same or the opposite sign of the determinant of $J(\mathbf{P}^*)$ itself. Hence, from the given information, we cannot deduce how the equilibrium price of the first good will be changed as a result of a change in α. The necessary conditions for local stability are too weak for the comparison task. This is even more striking, of course, when the number of goods is large and when global stability is at stake.

Thus what the "correspondence principle" amounts to is this: Most of the restrictions on the form of the excess-demand functions that are at present known to be sufficient to ensure global stability are also sufficient to allow certain exercises in comparing equilibria. It should be added that these same conditions also turn up in the discussion of the uniqueness of a competitive equilibrium. All these restrictions share the characteristic that they are not necessary for the task for which they were invented; they are only sufficient and this explains why the correspondence principle "isn't."

12. Conclusions

Although we set ourselves the task of investigating "the price mechanism" in a highly simplified setting, it will probably be agreed that the task is not simple, and that it has not been definitively completed. There is a distressingly anecdotal air about our investigation; case succeeds case, but it was not found possible to lay down any general principles.

Some of the difficulties we have encountered may be due to the abstraction of a tâtonnement; this will be discussed in the next chapter. Even if it had been possible to show that in a perfectly competitive economy a tâtonnement is always stable, it is not clear that such a result could have been given much weight in forming a judgment of the performance of the price mechanism in actual economics. The fiction of an auctioneer is quite serious, since without it we would have to face the paradoxical problem that a perfect competitor changes prices that he is supposed to take as given. In addition, the processes investigated in this chapter assume that, disequilibrium notwithstanding, there is only a single price for each good at any moment. It is also postulated that at each moment, the plans of agents are their equilibrium plans. Lastly, of course, there is no trade out of equilibrium. All of these postulates are damaging to the tâtonnement exercise. It may be that some of the theorems and some of the insights gained will have application when a more satisfactory theory of the price mechanism has been developed. At the moment the main justification for the chapter is that there are results to report on the tâtonnement while there are no results to report on what most economists would agree to be more realistic constructions.

Notes

Walras [1874, 1877] first formulated the idea of a tâtonnement although in his more formal account of it he seemed to conceive of it as the Gauss–Seidel process discussed in Section 12.8.

The modern concern with a rigorous analysis of the problem in a general equilibrium context started with Hicks [1939], but the proper dynamic formulation came from Samuelson [1941–42; see also 1947]. A number of important local stability results were soon thereafter proved. Global stability analysis was inaugurated by Arrow and Hurwicz [1958] and notably contributed to by Uzawa [1961].

The gross-substitute case (after the concept was first formulated by Mosak [1944]) was analyzed by Metzler [1945], Hahn [1958], and Negishi [1958] in the local context, and by Arrow and Hurwicz [1958] and Arrow, Block, and Hurwicz [1959] in the global context. The weak gross-substitute case has been studied by McKenzie [1960a] and Arrow and Hurwicz [1960]. Diagonal Dominance was fully explored by McKenzie [1960b] for local results and by Arrow, Block, and Hurwicz [1959] for global ones. A number of other cases have been investigated for local stability, notably by Morishima [1952], but we have not discussed them in this chapter.

The first example to show the possibility of global instability was that of Scarf [1960]. The simpler case presented in Section 12.6 is due to Gale [1963].

Uzawa [1959–60] formulated the discrete time process and proved the main results.

Enthoven and Arrow [1956] and Arrow and Nerlove [1958] studied local stability when expected prices entered the excess-demand functions; global stability with adaptive expectations was studied by Arrow and Hurwicz [1962].

Chapter Thirteen

TRADING OUT OF EQUILIBRIUM: A PURE-EXCHANGE ECONOMY

Pleasure or businesse, so, our soules admit
For their first mover and are whirled by it.

—John Donne, *Good Friday, 1613, Riding Westward.*

1. The Problem

In the preceding chapter we concerned ourselves with the investigation of an extremely artificial formulation of the "price mechanism." In particular, we insisted that no trade take place out of equilibrium. This restriction, strictly interpreted, is not only obviously unrealistic, but also seems to carry the logical implication that trade never takes place. If the auctioneer's rule is not stable, trading is not permitted *a fortiori*, while if it is, trading will be permitted only "in the limit" (i.e., as t approaches infinity), for it is only in the limit that equilibrium and "called" prices coincide. Although there are obvious ways of interpreting the process less strictly, it would be highly desirable nonetheless to be able to do without the recontract assumption.

Accordingly, in this chapter we shall remove the restriction of no trade for non-equilibrium situations. In two important respects, however, the analysis will continue to be both abstract and unrealistic: We shall continue to suppose that there is an auctioneer who calls prices and we shall assume that no productive activities are carried on in the economy. It is not uninstructive to consider why, as it were, we continue to tie our hands behind our backs.

The role of the auctioneer is twofold; at any moment of time he establishes unique and public terms on which goods may be traded, and he adjusts these terms in the light of market observations by some particular rule. If we did not stipulate the existence of such an auctioneer, we would have to describe how it comes about that at any moment of time two goods exchange on the same terms wherever such exchange takes place and how these terms come to change under market pressure.

It is clear that the stipulation of a single rate of exchange between any two goods at any one moment of time could itself be viewed as the outcome of some adjustment with some information process to make participants aware of disparities in the terms of exchange. Alternatively, we could decide to allow a variety of exchange rates between any two goods at every moment of time for which the economy was out of equilibrium and consider a sequence of outcomes that might result from a large number of bilateral bargains between a variety of individuals. In either case, our task would be a good deal more difficult. Although we shall return to this problem later, the idealization of postulating an auctioneer is not an obviously illegitimate shortcut through these problems, and the question, "How do prices come to change in the absence of an auctioneer?" is much more difficult to deal with. If we decide that the terms of exchange facing any unit of decision shall be independent of the course of action that unit might wish to pursue, it is decidedly odd to imagine any one decision unit changing prices under "market pressure." Thus, for instance, in a production economy, if every firm faces a horizontal demand curve (or thinks that it faces such a curve), it is not easy to visualize any firm changing the price at which its product is sold. What is happening now is that, having decided on one idealization (perfect competition), we run into what must be taken to be logical difficulties unless we import a further idealization: the auctioneer. It would be a vulgar mistake to suppose that this can be taken as evidence that the analysis has nothing to teach us about the world. The question really turns on the "mistakes" we can see ourselves making by adopting the perfectly competitive view. We cannot form any adequate judgment of these "mistakes" until we have discovered where the idealization is taking us, and so we now adopt it.

The simplification that there is no production is of great importance for the results to be established in this chapter and for an understanding of these results. We shall show that in the pure-exchange economy with trade permitted at all times, relatively modest assumptions will allow us to deduce that the economy converges to an equilibrium. If, as in the theory of the trade cycle, we also wish to maintain that in many situations the process of decentralized decisions is not convergent, it is likely that we shall have to look for the causes on the "production side." This in itself is valuable information. If we can also learn why the arguments to be developed in this chapter would fail in an economy with production, we may also be well on the way to understanding why such an economy may get into "difficulties."

2. The Relation to Stability with Recontract

Let there be H households, each endowed with a collection of goods represented by the vector $\bar{\mathbf{x}}_h$. Write $\bar{X}$ as the matrix with columns $\bar{\mathbf{x}}_h$. Then since we are proposing to treat $\bar{X}$ as variable (by exchange), we write the excess-demand function as:

$$z_i = z_i(\mathbf{p},\bar{X}) \qquad i = i, \ldots, n.$$

In general, we can expect the equilibrium prices to depend on $\bar{X}$.

Suppose we continue to postulate a price adjustment mechanism given by

$$\dot{p}_i = z_i(\mathbf{p},\bar{X}) \qquad i = i, \ldots, n.$$

In addition, there will be some process of exchange. This process must satisfy two conditions if it is to be feasible:

$$\mathbf{p}\dot{\bar{\mathbf{x}}}_h(t) = 0 \qquad \text{all } h,\ t \geq 0 \tag{1}$$

$$\sum_h \dot{\bar{\mathbf{x}}}_h(t) = \mathbf{0} \qquad \text{all } t \geq 0. \tag{2}$$

The first of these establishes that no household can change its wealth by exchange; the value of what it buys must clearly be equal to the value of what it sells. The second confirms that we are in a pure-exchange economy without production. Let

$$\dot{\bar{X}} = G[\bar{X},\mathbf{p}]$$

be a process of exchange that satisfies (1) and (2) (we shall discuss an example in a subsequent section).

Given the mechanism of exchange and of price change, let us calculate $\dot{z}_i$. Let

$$w_h(t) = \mathbf{p}\bar{\mathbf{x}}_h(t).$$

Then, by elementary demand theory,

$$\frac{\partial z_i}{\partial \bar{x}_{hj}} = \frac{\partial x_{hi}}{\partial w_h} p_j - \delta_{ij}$$

where, as usual, x_{hi} is the utility-maximizing choice of good i of h at $\mathbf{p}$, $\bar{\mathbf{x}}_h$, and $\delta_{ij} = 1$ if $i = j$, 0 if $i \neq j$. Then

$$\sum_h \sum_j \frac{\partial z_i}{\partial \bar{x}_{hj}} \dot{\bar{x}}_{hj} = \sum_h \frac{\partial x_{hi}}{\partial w_h} \sum_j p_j \dot{\bar{x}}_{hj} - \sum_j \delta_{ij} \sum_h \dot{\bar{x}}_{hj} = 0$$

by (1) and (2). So it follows that along any path of the economy,

$$\begin{aligned} \dot{z}_i &= \sum_j z_{ij}(\mathbf{p}, \bar{X}) \dot{p}_j + \sum_h \sum_j \left(\frac{\partial z_i}{\partial \bar{x}_{hj}}\right) \dot{\bar{x}}_{hj} \\ &= \sum_j z_{ij}(\mathbf{p}, \bar{X}) \dot{p}_j \end{aligned}$$

where

$$z_{ij} = \frac{\partial z_i}{\partial p_i}.$$

Before we allowed exchange to take place, we were able to show (Chapter 12), that the pricing process was stable if all goods were gross substitutes, or if there was a dominant diagonal (with constant units of measurement), or if all households were "alike." The striking point is this: If we are willing to postulate any of these properties here and suppose these to hold for all $\bar{X}$, then the pricing process is again stable. Therefore, it turns out that for the cases known, the assumption of recontract was not required for the desired result.

The reader can verify this for himself by the arguments of Chapter 12. Here we take the gross-substitute case as an illustration. Let

$$V(\mathbf{p}, \bar{X}) = \max_j \frac{z_i(\mathbf{p}, \bar{X})}{p_i}.$$

(We can divide by p_i because it can easily be shown that $\mathbf{p}(t) \gg \mathbf{0}$, all t, if $\mathbf{p}(0) \gg \mathbf{0}$.) With the usual qualification (see proof of T.12.4), $V(\mathbf{p}, \bar{X})$ is differentiable, and using the above results, we find

$$\dot{V}(\mathbf{p}, \bar{X}) = \frac{1}{p_r} \sum_j z_{rj} p_j \frac{z_j}{p_j} - \frac{z_r^2}{p_r^2}$$

where

$$\frac{z_r(\mathbf{p}, \bar{X})}{p_r} = \max_i \frac{z_i(\mathbf{p}, \bar{X})}{p_i}.$$

By gross substitutability and the definition of V,

$$z_{rr} p_r \frac{z_r}{p_r} + \sum_{j \neq r} z_{rj} p_j \frac{z_j}{p_j} \leq \frac{z_r}{p_r} \sum_j z_{rj} p_j = 0$$

and so $\dot{V} < 0$ if $V \neq 0$. We may use the usual argument to show that $\mathbf{z}(t) \rightarrow 0$. Furthermore, if $\mathbf{z}(\mathbf{p}, \bar{X}) = \mathbf{0}$, then $\dot{\mathbf{p}} = \mathbf{0}$, and we already know that $\dot{\mathbf{z}} = \mathbf{0}$, so that any exchange that continues to take place must leave equilibrium prices unchanged.

From all this we expect that as long as we continue to use the same pricing rule, allowing exchange even out of equilibrium not only cannot deprive us of any existing stability results, but also may well give us stronger results. This, as we shall now see, is indeed the case.

The reader should note, however, that the results just given show convergence to some equilibrium, which of course depends on $\bar{X}$ and $\mathbf{p}(0)$, and not to any arbitrarily preassigned equilibrium. This means the process is stable, although no given equilibrium need be stable.

3. Conditions for Trade

Let $B_h(\mathbf{p})$ represent the collection of goods a household could acquire at $\mathbf{p}$ without violating its budget constraint, that is, $B_h(\mathbf{p}) = \{\mathbf{x} \mid \mathbf{p}\mathbf{x}_h \leq \mathbf{p}\bar{\mathbf{x}}_h\}$, and let X be the matrix with columns $\mathbf{x}_h$. Write $\mathbf{e}$ for the H-dimensional column vector with all elements equal to unity. We propose to work with the following assumption.

ASSUMPTION 1. Exchange will take place at $\mathbf{p} \gg \mathbf{0}$, if and only if there is an X, with $\mathbf{x}_h \in B_h(\mathbf{p})$, all h, and $X\mathbf{e} = \bar{X}\mathbf{e}$, such that $U_h(\mathbf{x}_h) \geq U_h(\bar{\mathbf{x}}_h)$, all h, and $U_h(\mathbf{x}_h) > U_h(\bar{\mathbf{x}}_h)$, some h.

What this amounts to is an assertion that trade will take place if and only if it is feasible for the households at $\mathbf{p}$, feasible for the economy, and leads to a Pareto-superior allocation. (We are supposing that there is no consumption so that the total endowment of goods in the economy is the same before and after trade; this assumption can be ignored at the cost of some complications.) At first sight, the assertion sounds extremely reasonable, but further thought quickly shows that, in fact, the proposed conditions are quite restrictive. Thus we note that it is quite possible that an individual who experiences a loss in utility from a given exchange may be prepared nonetheless to undertake it if he expects that the next $\mathbf{p}$ called by the auctioneer will put him in an advantageous position to make large gains as a consequence of the exchanges he has currently made. In other words, it is possible for households to engage in speculative transactions that, while they imply a utility loss when they are made, are anticipated to yield a net gain eventually. Hence, if we are prepared to accept the proposed assumption, we would be wise to think of households as having stationary expectations. We shall return to this point later. Even so, we are not yet out of the woods. If two individuals who can gain from exchange are actually to do so, it must be possible for them to find each other. Given enough time and a random search of households for profitable exchanges, we could attempt to demonstrate that the probability of the two households finding each other goes to one as time of search goes to infinity. However, since this procedure is no less unrealistic than the supposition that it is part of the auctioneer's job to freely disseminate offers to buy and sell, we prefer to make the latter assumption. Once again, however, we are giving the auctioneer an uncomfortably large role. At the moment, our concern is limited to dispelling the notion that A.13.1 is innocuous.

One immediate consequence of A.13.1 is that no exchange will take place if $\bar{X}$ is Pareto efficient. On the other hand, it is clear that $\bar{X}$'s being Pareto efficient does not imply that **P** is an equilibrium for the economy in the sense that all excess demands are zero. Less obvious, perhaps, is the fact that A.13.1 might not permit trade to take place even though $\bar{X}$ is not Pareto efficient. Let us examine this.

It will be convenient to suppose that all utility functions are differentiable where required, and we write $U_{hi}(\bar{\mathbf{x}}_h) = \bar{U}_{hi}$ as the partial differential coefficient of U_h at $\bar{\mathbf{x}}_h$ with respect to its ith argument. We take it, at least for the moment, that these marginal utilities are everywhere positive and define

$$R_{hi} = \frac{\bar{U}_{hi}}{\bar{U}_{hn}} \qquad \mu_{hi} = \frac{R_{hi}}{P_i} - 1, \qquad i = 1, \ldots, n - 1,$$

where **P** is the price vector in terms of good n. We also adopt the convention that two quantities, v and w, are of "the same sign" if they are both positive, or negative, or zero.

Now, if no trade is possible at $\bar{X} > 0$, it follows from A.13.1 that for all i, μ_{hi} must have the same sign for all h. If not, since, say, the marginal rate of substitution between goods i and n would exceed their relative prices for some household, but not for some other household, it is clear that the first household, could gain by exchanging i for n while the other household would not lose by this, provided the exchange is made at the ruling prices. The condition that for all i, μ_{hi} must be of the same sign for all h, is not enough to exclude the possibility of exchange in accordance with A.13.1 between goods other than i and n. To ensure that, we must suppose that for all possible pairs i and j, $\mu_{hi} - \mu_{hj}$ is of the same sign for all h. Suppose, to take an example, that this difference is positive for h and zero for k. Then

$$\frac{R_{hj}}{P_j}\frac{R_{hi}P_j}{R_{hj}P_i - 1} > 0 \qquad \frac{R_{kj}}{P_j}\frac{R_{ki}P_j}{R_{kj}P_i - 1} = 0$$

so that, evidently, h would gain by exchanging some of good i for good j at the terms P_j/P_i, while household k would be indifferent to such an exchange. On the other hand, if for all possible pairs i and j, $\mu_{hi} - \mu_{hj}$ is of the same sign for all h, then it must be that the marginal rate of substitution between any pair of goods bears the same relation (equal, greater than, less than) to the terms by which they can be exchanged, for all households, and thus exchange is not possible in accordance with A.13.1. We have established, therefore,

THEOREM 1. A necessary condition for no exchange to be possible in accordance with A.13.1 at $\bar{X} > 0$ and $\mathbf{p} \gg \mathbf{0}$ is:

(a) For all i, μ_{hi} must be of the same sign for all h.
(b) For all possible pairs i and j, $\mu_{hi} - \mu_{hj}$ must have the same sign, all h.

Clearly, conditions (a) and (b) are not equivalent to the requirement that for all i, R_{hi} must be of the same magnitude for all h, and so even though $\bar{X}$ is not Pareto efficient, no trade is possible at $\mathbf{P} \gg \mathbf{0}$.

4. Prices When No Trade Occurs

Consider the pricing rule

$$\begin{aligned} \dot{p}_i &= z_i, \qquad i = 1, \ldots, n-1; \\ \dot{p}_n &= 0 \end{aligned} \tag{I}$$

where, as usual, z_i is the excess demand for good i and depends, of course, on $\mathbf{p}$ and $\bar{X}$. We wish to investigate the behavior of the solution path of this rule on the assumption that $\bar{X}$ is constant for all t, that is, that no exchange takes place even though it is permitted.

Since we are permitting exchange, this assumption is equivalent to the assertion that conditions (a) and (b) of T.13.1 hold for $\bar{X}$ and $\mathbf{p}(t)$, all t.

Let us write $\mathbf{z}_h(\mathbf{p},\bar{\mathbf{x}}_h)$ as the excess-demand vector of household h; its components are $x_{hi}(\mathbf{p},\bar{\mathbf{x}}_h) - \bar{x}_{hi}$. Then, if $\mathbf{z}_h \neq \mathbf{0}$, it must be, assuming preferences strictly convex, that

$$U_h(\bar{\mathbf{x}}_h + \mathbf{z}_h) > U_h(\bar{\mathbf{x}}_h), \tag{3}$$

and for any λ_j, $0 < \lambda \leq 1$,

$$U_h[\lambda(\bar{\mathbf{x}}_h + \mathbf{z}_h) + (1 - \lambda)\bar{\mathbf{x}}_h] = U_h(\lambda\mathbf{z}_h + \bar{\mathbf{x}}_h) > U_h(\bar{\mathbf{x}}_h).$$

Also for λ small,

$$0 < U_h(\lambda\mathbf{z}_h + \bar{\mathbf{x}}_h) - U_h(\bar{\mathbf{x}}_h) \approx \sum_i \bar{U}_{hi}\lambda z_{hi}. \tag{4}$$

If $\mathbf{P}$ is the price vector in terms of good n (nth component $= 1$), $\mathbf{P}\mathbf{z}_h = 0$, by the budget constraint for h. Subtracting $\lambda\mathbf{P}\mathbf{z}_h$ from the right-hand side of (4) after dividing this by $\bar{U}_{hn}$, we find

$$\lambda \sum_i \alpha_{hi} > 0 \tag{5}$$

where $\alpha_{hi} = P_i\mu_{hi}$, $\alpha_{hn} = 0$, and some $\alpha_{hi} \neq 0$.

Now suppose $\bar{\mathbf{x}}_h \gg \mathbf{0}$, all h, and $\mathbf{p} \gg \mathbf{0}$, and consider household k. If this household were to satisfy the demand $\lambda\mathbf{z}_h$ of household h, the transaction would be feasible for λ small enough (since $\bar{\mathbf{x}}_k \gg \mathbf{0}$). Moreover, $\mathbf{p}\bar{\mathbf{x}}_k - \mathbf{p}\lambda\mathbf{z}_h = \mathbf{p}\bar{\mathbf{x}}_k$. Its utility change, then, is given by

$$U_k(\bar{\mathbf{x}} + \lambda(-\mathbf{z}_h)) - U_k(\bar{\mathbf{x}}_k).$$

This expression must be negative since we have postulated that no exchange is possible. Then, certainly, for λ small enough, it must be that

$$-\lambda \sum_i \bar{U}_{ki} z_{hi} < 0,$$

and so proceeding as before,

$$\lambda \sum_i \alpha_{ki} z_{hi} > 0.$$

Evidently, (6) must be true for all $k \neq h$, so letting

$$\alpha_i = \sum_k \alpha_{ki},$$

summing (6) over $k \neq h$, and adding (5) gives

$$\lambda \sum_i \alpha_i z_{hi} > 0. \tag{7}$$

But (7) must hold for all h with $\mathbf{z}_h \neq \mathbf{0}$, so summing over h, we finally have

$$\sum_i \alpha_i z_i > 0 \qquad \text{if } \mathbf{z}_h \neq \mathbf{0}, \text{ some } h. \tag{8}$$

We may now prove

THEOREM 2. Let $\bar{X}$ be strictly positive and $\mathbf{p} \gg \mathbf{0}$. Then, if all utility functions are strictly quasi-concave and have positive partial differential coefficients at $\mathbf{x}_h$ and no exchange is possible at $\mathbf{p}$, $\mathbf{z}(\mathbf{p},\bar{X}) = \mathbf{0}$ implies that $\bar{X}$ is Pareto efficient.

Proof. If not, then some $\mathbf{z}_h \neq \mathbf{0}$ and so for some h and i, $\alpha_{hi} \neq 0$, and from T.13.1(a), $\alpha_{hi} \neq 0$ and of the same sign, all h. But then, in view of $\mathbf{z} = \mathbf{0}$, we contradict (8). Hence $\mathbf{z}_h = \mathbf{0}$, all h.

We proceed to introduce

ASSUMPTION 2. Let $\mathbf{p}(i)$ be the price vector with zero in the ith place. Then, for all feasible $\bar{X}$ and all $\mathbf{p}(i)$, $z_i[\mathbf{p}(i),\bar{X}] > 0$, all i.

The purpose of this assumption is to keep all prices positive and to ensure that the path of prices is bounded (see below). We now prove

THEOREM 3. If A.13.2 and the assumptions of T.13.1 hold, if no exchange takes place anywhere on the path, and if $\mathbf{p}(0) \gg \mathbf{0}$, then the adjustment rule is globally stable.

Proof. Certainly, if $\mathbf{p}$ is not an equilibrium, $(\mathbf{z}(\mathbf{p},\bar{X}) \neq \mathbf{0})$, it must be that some $z_h \neq 0$, and so some $\alpha_i(\mathbf{p},\bar{X}) \neq 0$. Let

$$V(\mathbf{p},\bar{X}) = \sum_i \alpha_i^2 = \sum_i \sum_h (R_{hi} - P_i)^2.$$

Certainly, $V(\mathbf{p},\bar{X}) > 0$ for all non-equilibrium $\mathbf{P}$. Differentiating V with respect to t gives, using (I),

$$\dot{V} = -2 \sum_i \alpha_i z_i$$

and so, in view of (8), $\dot{V} < 0$ for non-equilibrium $\mathbf{P}$. V may be taken as a Lyapounov function, since we know (12.(1)) that A.13.2

ensures that the solution paths of (I) are bounded. If $\mathbf{p}^*$ is a limit point of $\mathbf{p}(t)$, since for t large enough $\mathbf{p}(t)$ must be arbitrarily close to $\mathbf{p}^*$, then by the usual argument (see the proof of T.11.3), $\mathbf{p}^*$ is an equilibrium, and since by assumption $\mathbf{p}^* \gg \mathbf{0}$, it must be that $\mathbf{z}(\mathbf{p}^*,\bar{X}) = \mathbf{0}$. By T.13.2, $\bar{X}$ is Pareto efficient. From this it follows that $\mathbf{p}(t)$ can have only one limit point, since $\alpha_i(\mathbf{p},\bar{X}) = 0$, all i, can have only one solution. This is enough to establish the global stability of (I).

We have shown, therefore, that the supposition implies that $\bar{X}$ is Pareto efficient and that the latter property of the distribution matrix implies, in turn, that (I) is globally stable. This result plays an important role in the analysis that follows.

5. The Exchange Process

We shall now consider the story in which not only prices are changing in accordance with rule (I), but exchange also is taking place whenever it is possible in accordance with A.13.1.

It is not easy to state a sensible rule for the rate at which exchange is taking place between households at any one moment of time. There may be a considerable variety of exchanges possible at any $\mathbf{p}$ and $\bar{X}$, and it is not clear what simple rule of choice is appropriate. We propose to ignore this difficulty at the moment and postulate the existence of a continuous function, T, that obeys the requirements of A.13.1 and such that

$$\dot{\bar{X}} = \mathbf{T}(\mathbf{p},\bar{X}). \qquad \text{(II)}$$

Later we shall give an example of such a function. We shall suppose also that $\mathbf{z}(\cdot)$ and $\mathbf{T}(\cdot)$ satisfy a Lipschitz condition so that (I) and (II) combined give rise to solutions $\bar{X}(t)$ and $\mathbf{p}(t)$, which are uniquely defined by the initial conditions $\bar{X}(0)$ and $\mathbf{p}(0)$ and are continuous in these. Lastly, we shall suppose that for all t, $\mathbf{p}(t) \gg \mathbf{0}$ and $\bar{X}(t)$ are positive. Of course, this implies certain restrictions on the utility functions of households.

Consider the function $W(\mathbf{p},\bar{X})$ defined by

$$W(\mathbf{p},\bar{X}) = \sum_h U_h(\bar{\mathbf{x}}_h).$$

By A.13.1, it must be true that as long as exchange is going on, $\dot{W} > 0$, and that in any case, W cannot decline. Therefore, we may take W as a Lyapounov function, which, since $\mathbf{p}(t)$ and $\bar{X}(t)$ are bounded, approaches a limiting value W^* as t approaches infinity. In particular,

$$\lim_{t \to \infty} \sum U_h(\bar{\mathbf{x}}_h(t)) = \sum U_h^*,$$

since every U_h is non-decreasing (i.e., monotone), and therefore, must approach a unique limit. Then let $\bar{X}^*$ be any limit distribution of $\bar{X}(t)$, $\mathbf{p}^*$ any limit point of $\mathbf{p}(t)$ and consider the limit paths $\bar{X}^*(t)$ and $\mathbf{p}^*(t)$, generated by taking $\bar{X}^*$ and $\mathbf{p}^*$ as initial conditions. Then, certainly,

$$U_h^* = U_h(\bar{\mathbf{x}}_h^*) = U_h(\bar{\mathbf{x}}_h^*(t)) \qquad \text{all } h,$$

and so by A.13.1 and strict convexity of preferences it must be that $\bar{\mathbf{x}}_h^* = \bar{\mathbf{x}}_h^*(t)$, all h and t; that is, $\bar{X}^* = \bar{X}^*(t)$, all t. Then, on the limit path $\mathbf{p}^*(t)$, we may take $\bar{X}(t)$ constant at $\bar{X}^*$, all t, and so by T.13.3, $\mathbf{p}^*(t)$ converges to $\mathbf{p}^*$ such that $\mathbf{z}(\mathbf{p}^*,\bar{X}^*) = \mathbf{0}$. By T.13.2, it follows then that $\bar{X}^*$ is Pareto optimal. Thus we have proved

THEOREM 4. Let $\bar{X}(t)$ and $\mathbf{p}(t)$ be strictly positive for all t. Let all utility functions be strictly quasi-concave and have partial differential coefficients positive everywhere. Then the process (I) and (II) is globally stable and the limit is a competitive equilibrium of the economy; that is, $\mathbf{z}(\mathbf{p},\bar{X}) = \mathbf{0}$ (and Pareto efficient).

It is important to recall that showing that a process is globally stable is not the same thing as asserting that a particular equilibrium of the economy is globally stable. In particular, in the present case, while we can assert that the economy will approach some equilibrium, we cannot say which, until it has approached it. Evidently, the exact nature of the exchanges undertaken along any path determines which of the infinite number of Pareto-efficient allocations the economy will approach. The outcome here is not independent of the path. It was the desire to avoid this, in part at least, that led to the development of the recontract analysis. In that respect, therefore, recontract results are often stronger than our present one, since they may enable us to declare one particular equilibrium globally (or locally) stable.

Let us now return to the question of exchange processes that satisfy A.13.1. It is not hard to construct one that, while not necessarily sensible, is of the type (II) that we have used.

Let $S[U_1(\mathbf{x}_1) \cdots U_H(\mathbf{x}_H)]$ be a strictly quasi-concave social welfare function. Imagine it maximized for any $\mathbf{p}$ and $\bar{X}$, subject to the constraints that for all h,

$$\mathbf{p}\mathbf{x}_h = \mathbf{p}\bar{\mathbf{x}}_h \qquad U_h(\mathbf{x}_h) \geq U_h(\bar{\mathbf{x}}_h)$$

and

$$\sum_h \mathbf{x}_h = \sum_h \bar{\mathbf{x}}_h.$$

Elementary theory of such maximization assures us that, since the individual utility functions are strictly quasi-concave, a unique solution, which we write as the matrix $\bar{X}(\mathbf{p},\bar{X})$, can be found. If we imagine the household utility functions to be such that the marginal utility of any good to any household becomes infinitely great as the quantity of that good goes to zero, we may take it that $\bar{X}(\mathbf{p},\bar{X})$ is a positive matrix. We also take $\bar{X}(0)$ to be positive. We may now let $\mathbf{T}$ in (II) be given by

$$\dot{\bar{X}} = [\bar{X}(\mathbf{p},\bar{X}) - \bar{X}].$$

Certainly, $\bar{X}(\mathbf{p},\bar{X})$ will be continuous in its arguments and the reader should verify that by our assumptions, $\bar{\mathbf{x}}_h(t) > \mathbf{0}$, all t and h, if $\bar{X}(0)$ is positive.

We cannot claim that this process has much to recommend it on the grounds of realism; it is simply given to show that it is possible to find processes such as (II). A more sensible procedure is the following, which we merely sketch. Given $\bar{X}(t)$ and $\mathbf{p}$, we can define a small neighborhood of $\bar{X}(t)$ and note all the distribution matrices in this small neighborhood that can be reached in accordance with A.13.1. We could argue that the probability of any one of these matrices being reached is the same as that of reaching any other one. Thus the status of the economy at $t + \epsilon$ is given by $\mathbf{p}(t + \epsilon)$ and any one of the admissible matrices. We do not know which of these possible states actually will materialize, but for each such state, we can calculate again a class of neighborhood matrices and the rate at which prices are changing. Thus we are involved in a branching process. Along every branch the utilities of households are non-diminishing, and as long as exchange is taking place, they are increasing. We can be sure, then, that each branch terminates in some distribution matrix since the attainable utilities are bounded above. For each of these "terminal" matrices we can use T.13.2 and T.13.3 to show that the associated price process is now convergent and that each terminal matrix is Pareto efficient. There are calculable probabilities of the system converging on any one of these equilibria. Thus, while this is not a rigorous demonstration, it is not likely that the conclusions of T.13.4 are vitally dependent on the existence of deterministic exchange processes such as (II).

While it seems pretty safe to assert that our result is not very sensitive to a change in the assumptions concerning the process of exchange, it is not clear, unfortunately, that it is equally robust with respect to some of the other assumptions. Let us remove the requirement that $\bar{X}(t)$ be positive for all t (but retain all other postulates). In other words, now we permit situations in which it may happen that at some point in the exchange process, individuals hold zero quantities of some good or goods. Since the demonstration that the exchange process will lead $\bar{X}(t)$ to approach a distribution, $\bar{X}^*$, is not dependent on the hypothesis that $\bar{X}(t)$ are positive for all t, we can continue to use this result. However, $\bar{X}^*$ may have some zero components. This has the unpleasant consequence that the inequality (8) of Section 13.4 can no longer be established. In the notation of that section, consider the following possibility:

$$\lambda \sum \alpha_{hi} z_{hi} > 0 \qquad \lambda \sum \alpha_{ki} z_{hi} < 0.$$

If h received $\lambda \mathbf{z}_h$ from exchange with k, while the latter received $-\lambda \mathbf{z}_h$, both would be better off, and we might conclude, therefore, that exchange is possible at $\bar{X}^*$. This would be too hasty. We must be sure that exchange is feasible. In particular, for some $\lambda > 0$, it must be that $\bar{\mathbf{x}}_k - \lambda \mathbf{z}_h$ has no negative components. We could be certain of this when $\bar{\mathbf{x}}_k \gg \mathbf{0}$. Now clearly we cannot, and so we cannot establish inequality (8) and the theorems dependent on it. This in turn means that we have lost the crucial information that allowed us to declare the price path that results with the limiting distribution $\bar{X}^*$ to be stable.

Since the assumption that every household always owns positive stocks of every good is not a very happy one, we cannot really claim very much for our results. On the other hand, it is clear that any of the assumptions leading to the stability of the recontract process investigated in the last chapter will now serve to show that the process that allows exchange in accordance with A.13.1 is also stable. Since to permit exchange during the process is more realistic than not doing so, we can claim to have improved to that extent on the analysis, at least for a pure-exchange economy.

The assumption that $\mathbf{p}(t) \gg \mathbf{0}$, all t, we can relax without serious difficulties. In the first place, we note that it is no longer true that $\mathbf{z}_h \neq 0$ implies that $U_h(\bar{\mathbf{x}}_h + \mathbf{z}_h) > U_h(\bar{\mathbf{x}}_h)$, since it may happen that the only non-zero component of $\mathbf{z}_h$ is negative and its price is equal to zero, whence by free disposal, the household's utility cannot be changed by disposing. On the other hand, (8) must still hold for all $\mathbf{z}_h \neq \mathbf{0}$, $z_{hi} > 0$, some i. (We are again taking $\bar{X}^*$ to be positive, of course.) Now consider the proof of T.13.2. From the fact that $\mathbf{p}^*$ is a limit point of $\mathbf{p}(t)$ we deduce that $\mathbf{z}(\mathbf{p}^*,\bar{X}^*) \leq \mathbf{0}$. By the argument just given, it must be true that $\mathbf{z}_h(\mathbf{p}^*,\mathbf{x}_h^*) \leq \mathbf{0}$, all h, and so certainly $\bar{X}$ is Pareto efficient. It must be true, then, that for all $p_i^* > 0$, $\alpha_i(\mathbf{p}^*,\bar{X}^*) \leq 0$. But clearly there can be only one $\mathbf{p}^*$ satisfying these conditions. Thus T.13.2 and consequently T.13.4 are not at all dependent on the assumption that prices are strictly positive throughout, although the methods of proof originally employed are. (We still require an equilibrium in which the exchange value of the numeraire is positive.)

The assumption that the partial differential coefficients of the utility functions are everywhere positive is closely related to the one that insists that all households at all times have positive quantities of all goods. Should it be possible for the marginal utility of some good to be zero when none of that good is held, we will be back in the troubled waters that we have already traversed. If the assumption $\bar{X}(t)$ positive for all t can be maintained, however, the reader can check that all of our analysis will continue to hold, provided only that we may take it that the marginal utility of numeraire is nowhere zero.

We can sum up the state of affairs at this stage as follows. At no point will the exchange process fail to converge to an equilibrium if conditions are such that every recontract process is stable. On the other hand, to show the exchange process to be always stable (whatever the form of the excess-demand functions might be) has required, so far, the assumption that every good is held in positive quantity by every household and a restriction to the case of the pure-exchange economy.

6. A Monetary Economy

The results of the last section depend entirely on the assumptions that ensure that at every stage of the process, the utilities of households are non-decreasing and those of some households are increasing, as long as equilibrium has not been attained. In fact, the exchange economy may behave like a gradient process in the vector of household utilities. The economy we have been considering, although it is one in which the auctioneer regulates the terms at which goods shall exchange, is essentially one of barter; all acts of exchange are completed between two households exchanging one good for another. In the world in which we live, however, most acts of exchange are exchanges of goods for money and money for goods, and one feature of this arrangement is that it cannot sensibly be argued that every such act of exchange increases the utility of at least one of the participants and diminishes that of no participant. A real household, if constrained to the mediation of money, may be willing to exchange something of one good for money on the supposition that the money so acquired will be used in exchange for some other good. Should the second leg of this transaction fail to materialize, then it may well be that had the household anticipated this it would never have embarked on the first leg; in other words, the first transaction by itself leads to a fall in utility. Some rather perplexing problems now come up.

Of course, our model is in no shape to give a satisfactory formal account of the role of money. In particular, it would be hard to "explain" the holding of money or why it mediates in most acts of exchange. For the moment, we sidestep these portentous issues by making assumptions that, while hard to justify in the context of a simple pure-exchange economy, are not altogether off the mark in a more satisfactory and complicated world (see Chapter 14).

The first thing to notice is that if some commodity called money indeed must mediate in exchange, this in itself does not yet damage our conclusions of the previous section if we can take it that sales and purchases are simultaneous. In this case, there is no "first leg" and "second leg" of a transaction and we could continue to postulate that every transaction is of a kind that does not decrease the utility of the transactors. If this is the case, however, we certainly would be hard put to explain why any household should hold any money at all (here, of course, we are abstracting from price uncertainty). On the other hand, if we postulate that a purchase at any moment of time cannot be financed from the sales of that moment then every transaction of a household is speculative in the sense that the utility change from any one transaction is contingent on the completion of all other transactions. Now we encounter difficulties of exactly the sort we would have encountered in our earlier analysis had we not stipulated that every household believed firmly that the present terms on which goods exchange would continue indefinitely. Of course, this picture could be somewhat modified if we made the further concession to reality of permitting lending and borrowing, but we shall not do so here.

Let us write m for the good that must mediate in exchange and suppose that in other respects it is like other goods, in the sense that it yields its holder direct utility that does not depend on its exchange value. In other words, at the end of the transaction process, households plan to have a certain amount of m, which they determine in the same manner in which they determine the quantities of other goods they plan to have (see below). Of course, this is bad monetary theory, but our object here is not to examine a theory for which the pure-exchange model is in any event peculiarly ill suited, but rather to concentrate on the single problem to which the necessity of mediation gives rise in the analysis of such an exchange process. (We shall assume that over the relevant range, the marginal utility of m is positive for all h.)

The amount of each good, including money, that the household plans to have when its transactions have been completed is found by maximizing $U_h(\mathbf{x}_h,\mathbf{m}_h)$ subject to

$$\mathbf{P}\mathbf{z}_h + m_h - \bar{m}_h = 0.$$

($\mathbf{P}$ is now the price vector in terms of m.) The resulting excess demands we call *target* excess demands, and the resulting utility is the *target* utility. By assumption, however, if the superscript "+" to a vector denotes that subvector whose components are non-negative, at any moment t the household is further constrained by

$$\mathbf{P}\mathbf{z}_h^+(t) \leq \bar{m}_h(t) \tag{9}$$

(where we take the dimension of $\mathbf{P}$ from the context). If the constraint is binding at t, then the household must plan a sequence of transactions in order to attain its target utility.

Every household will be taken to believe that its transactions will succeed. If we take the interval between transactions to be very small, we may suppose that the household does not care by what sequence it attains its target. Accordingly, we shall stipulate a rule of thumb that the household will be taken to follow. We write

$a_{hi}(t)$ as the household's excess demand at moment t for good i and $\mathbf{a}_h(t)$ as the vector with these components. The latter is such to be consistent with both the budget and the financial constraint (9).

ASSUMPTION 3. For $z_{hi}(t) > 0$,

$$a_{hi}(t) = k_h(t)z_{hi}(t) \qquad k_h(t) = \min\left(1, \frac{\bar{m}_h(t)}{\mathbf{P}\mathbf{z}_h^+(t)}\right).$$

For $z_{hi}(t) \leq 0$,

$$a_{hi}(t) = z_{hi}(t).$$

This rule is arbitrary, of course. It supposes that when financial constraints are binding, target purchases all are reduced in the same proportion. Also, it assumes that the household is prepared to spend all its money at t. Evidently, a number of alternative hypotheses are available. The important point to emphasize is that the vector $\mathbf{a}_h(t)$, which we shall call the *active* excess-demand vector of household h, represents the actual transactions the household is willing to undertake at t.

In formulating the price adjustment rule we may take advantage of the extra realism the present construction affords. Instead of supposing that prices are moved by target excess demands, we now ensure that active excess demands are responsible. This is some improvement since target excess demands are private to individuals while active excess demands are public.

ASSUMPTION 4. $\dot{p}_i = 0$ for $i = m$ and for $p_i = 0$, $a_i \leq 0$; $\dot{p}_i = a_i$ otherwise, where $a_i = \sum_h a_{hi}$.

Since we are taking money as the numeraire we take A.13.2 to hold for z_m. Since $\sum P_i a_i \leq \sum P_i z_i = -z_m$, we use an argument like that employed in the proof of T.12.7 to show that prices will be bounded.

We now turn to the process of exchange. Our concept of active excess demands allows us to think of a proper market for a good i, one that brings together agents willing to exchange i for money and vice-versa. We suppose that if there are willing sellers and willing buyers, the two groups will transact. Should prices remain constant for some time, we would expect a positive (negative) aggregate excess demand in market i to be possible only if no agent has a negative (positive) active excess demand for the good. It is at this point that we propose to start the story.

Let $a_{hi}(t)$ be the active excess demand for i by h at t and define $a_i(t)$ similarly. Then

ASSUMPTION 5. For any h and i,

$$a_{hi}(0) \neq 0 \quad \text{implies} \quad a_{hi}(0)a_i(0) > 0.$$

Note that A.13.5 implies that $a_i(0) = 0$ if and only if $a_{hi}(0) = 0$, all h.

We would like the conditions of A.13.5 to hold for all $t \geq 0$. Let

$$x^a_{hi}(t) = a_{hi}(t) + \bar{x}_{hi}(t),$$

so that $x^a_{hi}(t)$ is the stock of the ith good h would actively wish to have at t. Also let

$$H(i,t) = \{h \mid a_i(t)\dot{x}^a_{hi}(t) < 0, \quad a_{hi}(t) = 0\}$$

and note that from A.13.3, if $\bar{m}_h(t) > 0$, then $a_{hi}(t) = 0$, only if $z_{hi}(t) = 0$. Finally let a superscript "+" denote a non-negative variable and a superscript "−" denote a negative variable. We now introduce

ASSUMPTION 6. (a) For i such that $a_i(t) \neq 0$,

$$\dot{\bar{x}}_{hi}(t) = \dot{x}^a_{hi}(t) \qquad \text{if } h \in H(i,t),$$

$$\dot{\bar{x}}_{hi}(t) = -\frac{a_{hi}(t)}{a_i(t)} \sum_{h \in H(i,t)} \dot{x}^a_{hi}(t) \qquad \text{if } h \notin H(i,t).$$

(b) For i such that $a_i(t) = 0$,

$$\dot{\bar{x}}_{hi}(t) = \min[1, v_i(t)]\dot{x}^a_{hi}(t) \qquad \text{if } \dot{x}^a_{hi}(t) \geq 0$$

$$\dot{\bar{x}}_{hi}(t) = \min[1, v_i^{-1}(t)]\dot{x}^a_{hi}(t) \qquad \text{if } \dot{x}^a_{hi}(t) < 0$$

where

$$v_i(t) = -\frac{\sum_h \dot{x}^{a-}_{hi}(t)}{\sum_h \dot{x}^{a+}_{hi}(t)}.$$

This assumption is pretty cumbersome, but it has a simple interpretation.

(a) The first part says that a household with zero excess demand can transact at the desired level if its excess demand is changing in a direction opposite to the prevailing aggregate active excess demand.

The second part states that there is a "rationing" of available "new" sales and purchases among unsatisfied buyers and sellers.

(b) Suppose $a_i(t) = 0$ does imply $a_{hi}(t) = 0$, all h. Certainly this is true at $t = 0$, by A.13.5. New transactions in this market depend on the excess demand of one h becoming positive and of some other h negative. The assumptions ensure that not more can be bought than is being newly supplied and no more can be sold than is being newly demanded. Moreover, there is once again a rationing process when not all new demands or supplies can be met.

We can easily verify that A.13.6 ensures

$$\sum_h \dot{\bar{x}}_{hi}(t) = 0 \qquad \text{all } i.$$

Moreover, in conjunction with A.13.5 we now have, provided that for all h and all $t \geq 0$, $\bar{m}_h(t) > 0$,

$$a_{hi}(t)a_i(t) > 0 \qquad \text{if } a_{hi}(t) \neq 0, \text{ all } h, i \text{ and } t \geq 0. \tag{10}$$

Suppose that at T, two active excess demands, say $a_{hi}(T)$ and $a_{ki}(T)$, become of opposite sign for the first time. One of them, at least, must be zero at T, supposing $a_{ki}(T) = 0$. Then $k \in H(i,T)$ and $\dot{a}_{ki}(T) = 0$, making it impossible that at T the two excess demands are becoming oppositely signed.

The reason the story seems a little strained is that we have chosen to work in continuous time. If we imagined an interval between each price change that is long enough to allow all transactions to be completed, it would not be fanciful to suppose that there are no willing sellers or buyers left in the same market at the end of the interval.

There is one objection to A.13.6(a). To ensure continuity in the transactions, we must suppose that there are very many agents. Otherwise, the sum

$$\sum_{h \in H(i,t)} \dot{x}_{hi}(t)$$

may change discontinuously when a new agent enters the set $H(i,t)$. It is not clear how serious a problem this is for the analysis (Lipschitz conditions are in danger of being violated), but the reader must suppose that there are sufficiently many agents.

The above continuity difficulty can be avoided at the cost of economic realism. For instance, we can assume that for $a_i \neq 0$ the ratio a_{hi}/a_i is kept constant by transactions. Thus, for example, assume $a_i(0) \neq 0$, all i, and

$$\dot{\bar{x}}_{hi}(t) = \dot{x}^a_{hi}(t) - \frac{a_{hi}(t)}{a_i(t)} \sum_i \dot{x}^a_{hi}(t).$$

Summing these equations over h and using the definition of $x^a_{hi}(t)$ gives

$$\frac{\dot{a}_{hi}(t)}{a_{hi}(t)} = \frac{\dot{a}_i(t)}{a_i(t)}.$$

We can easily check

$$\sum_h \dot{\bar{x}}_{hi}(t) = 0.$$

Clearly, the preceding process preserves what we want—$a_i(t)a_{hi}(t) \geq 0$, all h, i, or t—and no continuity problems arise. But it has less to recommend it on economic grounds. In what follows we shall use A.13.6 with the premise of "sufficiently many agents," but the reader can readily check that all our conclusions will hold also for the above process.

Now we may easily establish the following preliminary results:

LEMMA 1. Let $H(t) = \{h \mid \bar{m}_h(t) = 0\}$. Then, if $H(t) = \varnothing$, all $t \geq 0$, $\dot{U}_h(t) \leq 0$, all h.

Proof. From the budget constraint,

$$\dot{\mathbf{P}}(t)\mathbf{z}_h(t) + \mathbf{P}(t)\dot{\mathbf{x}}_h(t) + \dot{m}_h(t) - [\mathbf{P}(t)\dot{\bar{\mathbf{x}}}_h(t) + \dot{\bar{m}}_h(t)] = 0 \quad (11)$$

Since $H(t) = \varnothing$, all $t \geq 0$, it follows from A.13.3 that

$$z_{hi}(t)a_{hi}(t) \geq 0 \qquad \text{all } i.$$

From (10), then,

$$z_{hi}(t)a_i(t) \geq 0 \qquad \text{all } i,$$

and so by A.13.4, the first term in (11) is non-negative. The last term in (11) is zero since a household cannot change its wealth by exchange. Hence

$$\mathbf{P}(t)\dot{\mathbf{x}}_h(t) + \dot{m}_h(t) \leq 0. \quad (12)$$

But from target utility maximization,

$$\dot{U}_h(t) = \sum_i U_{hi}(t)\dot{x}_{hi}(t) + \dot{m}_h(t)\lambda_h(t)$$
$$= \lambda_h(t)[P(t)\dot{x}_h(t) + \dot{m}_h(t)].$$
$$\left(\lambda_h(t) = \frac{\partial U_h(t)}{\partial m_h(t)} > 0.\right)$$

Using (12), then, proves the lemma.

Corollary to Lemma 1. If $H(t) = \varnothing$, all $t \geq 0$, and $a_i(t) \neq 0$, some i, then $\dot{U}_h(t) \leq 0$, all h, and $\dot{U}_h(t) < 0$, some h.

Proof. Evidently the first term in (11) must be strictly positive for some h and so (12) is strictly negative for some h.

These results suggest that we may be able to make the target utilities serve the same role in the analysis of the present process as did the actual utilities in the previous section. In the latter case the actual utilities were never declining, while here, as long as $H(t)$ is always empty, the target utilities are never increasing. Unfortunately there are no simple means by which we can ensure that $H(t) = \varnothing$, all t, and for the moment, we shall simply postulate that this is the case.

THEOREM 5. If $H(t) = \varnothing$, all $t > 0$, then the economy has a globally stable adjustment process under assumptions A.13.3–A.13.6.

Proof. (a) By definition, $U_h[\mathbf{x}_h(t),m_h(t)] \geq [U_h(\bar{\mathbf{x}}_h)(t), \bar{m}_h(t)]$. Moreover, we may take $U_h[\mathbf{x}_h(t),m_h(t)]$ as bounded from below.

(b) Let

$$V(t) = \sum_h U_h[\mathbf{x}_h(t),m_h(t)].$$

Then, by the Corollary to Lemma 1, $\dot{V}(t) < 0$ when $a_i(t) \neq 0$. On the other hand, $a_i(t) = 0$, all i, must mean $a_{hi}(t) = 0$, all h and i, and since $H(t) = \varnothing$, $z_{hi}(t) = z_i(t) = 0$, all i and h. Then

$$m(t) = \sum_h m_h(t) = \bar{m} = \sum_h \bar{m}_h(t).$$

Hence $\dot{V}(t) = 0$ if and only if the economy is in equilibrium, and so $V(t)$ is a Lyapounov function, in view of (9).

(c) We now have, in view of Lemma 1 (which makes $\dot{U}_h(t) > 0$ impossible),

$$\lim_{t\to\infty} U_h(t) = U_h[(\mathbf{x}_h(\mathbf{P}^*,\bar{\mathbf{x}}_h^*,\bar{m}_h^*),\quad m_h(\mathbf{P}^*,\bar{\mathbf{x}}_h^*,m_h^*)] = U_h^* \quad (13)$$

where $\mathbf{P}^*$, $\bar{\mathbf{x}}_h^*$, and $\bar{m}_h^*$ are limit points of the path of prices and of endowments. Let $\mathbf{x}_h^* = \mathbf{x}_h(\mathbf{P}^*,\bar{\mathbf{x}}_h^*,\bar{m}_h^*)$, $m_h^* = m_h(\mathbf{P}^*,\bar{\mathbf{x}}_h^*,\bar{m}_h^*)$. It must be that $\sum \mathbf{x}_h^* = \sum \bar{\mathbf{x}}_h$, $\sum m_h^* = \bar{m}$. If not, some $a_i^* \neq 0$ and $\dot{U}_h^*(\mathbf{x}_h^*,m_h^*) < 0$, some h, a contradiction of the definition of U^*. Then suppose that $\mathbf{x}_h^{**} = \mathbf{x}_h(\mathbf{P}^{**},\bar{\mathbf{x}}_h^{**},\bar{m}_h^{**})$ and

$$m_h^{**} = m_h(\mathbf{P}^{**},\bar{\mathbf{x}}_h^{**},\bar{m}_h^{**})$$

comprise another possible set of limiting target demands. Then

$$U_h(\mathbf{x}_h^*, m_h^*) = U_h(\mathbf{x}_h^{**}, m_h^{**}) = U_h^* \qquad \text{all } h,$$

and so, by the strict quasi-concavity of U_h,

$$\mathbf{P}^*(\mathbf{x}_h^* - \mathbf{x}_h^{**}) + m_h^* - m_h^{**} < 0 \qquad \text{all } h.$$

Summing over h leads to a contradiction of $\sum \mathbf{x}_h^* = \sum \bar{\mathbf{x}}_h = \sum \mathbf{x}_h^{**}$, $\sum m_h^* = \bar{m} = \sum m_h^{**}$. Hence there is only one limiting set of target demands. But $\mathbf{x}_h^* = \bar{\mathbf{x}}_h^*$, for if not, $a_i^* \neq 0$. Hence there is also a unique set of limit endowments: $\bar{\mathbf{x}}_h^*, \bar{m}_h^*$. Evidently, then, $\mathbf{P}^*$ is also the limit point of the price sequence, and the process is globally stable.

It is clear that this result is heavily dependent on the supposition that at all moments of time, households are in a position to purchase if they so desire. To use Keynesian language, we have assumed that at least a part of every positive demand for a good can be translated, at all times, into "effective" demand. When this is not true, and there is nothing to ensure that it should be true, then we certainly break the thread that links the analysis of the process to the behavior of utilities over time and it is clear that additional assumptions must be introduced in order to ensure that the process is stable. Evidently, if a household's positive target excess demand for some good cannot be translated into a positive active excess demand because of the financial restraint, it is quite possible that the active excess demand for this good in the economy as a whole is negative. In that case, the arguments of Lemma 1 no longer apply.

It is clear that there are other assumptions that could be invoked to allow the exchange process to converge even if we cannot ensure that households have positive stocks of money at every stage of the process. We have pursued this matter far enough to learn the main lessons, however. In a pure-exchange economy the necessity of mediation of some good in exchange introduces a speculative element that, in itself, will not prevent convergence to an equilibrium provided no household is prevented from an act of exchange by lack of the medium of exchange. When this is not the case—and a good deal of modern analysis suggests that this is the more interesting hypothesis—convergence must be in doubt and, in any case, requires further study. We shall return to this question in our examination of the Keynesian economy.

Lastly, the reader is reminded that the "monetary theory" of this section is extremely rudimentary.

7. Conclusions

The economy investigated in this chapter is still only a distant relative of the economy we know. Nevertheless we may claim to have learned something. In particular, since A.13.1 is not unreasonable in its context and since T.13.4 is rather general in content, we must conclude that failure of the market mechanism to establish an equilibrium—if such failures are in fact observable—must be due to the elements of the actual economy that the economy of Section 13.4 neglects. This information is worth having.

The most conspicuous neglects in the analysis up to Section 13.5 are speculative exchanges, mediation, and production. Of these, we have investigated only one. The conclusions that the necessity of mediation itself introduces a "speculative" element into the process of exchange and that general convergence results à la T.13.4 seem available only when rather strong special assumptions are made are perhaps of interest. Speculation of the traditional kind, that is, purchases with a view to resale and vice versa, are best treated in a model that includes consumption and production. We should not be surprised if we find, when we briefly turn to this matter in Chapter 14, that stability may become problematical. In particular, the absence of production in our analysis so far is significant. If we recall the "stock-flow" problems associated with the existence of durable purchases we may conjecture that we shall find it much harder to ensure a "well-behaved" market mechanism in a production economy.

Notes

The first study of a process without recontract was reported by Negishi [1961]. He allowed endowments of households to vary out of equilibrium in a continuous way and stipulated GS. The process of Section 13.1 was first studied by Uzawa [1962] and, in a somewhat different form, by Hahn [1962]. The assumption that the signs of private and aggregate excess demands for each good were always the same was first investigated by Hahn and Negishi [1962] and further extended to include adaptive expectations by Negishi [1964]. The discussion on the modification of the analysis when a medium of exchange is present owes its point of departure to Clower [1965].

Chapter Fourteen

THE KEYNESIAN MODEL

Things fall apart, the center does not hold.
—W. B. Yeats, *The Second Coming*

1. Introduction

Keynes was concerned with what we have called temporary equilibrium (Sections 2.10 and 6.3). However, our previous analysis requires some modification before it can be applied to the Keynesian case. This is so for two reasons. In Section 6.3 we supposed that at the moment an equilibrium was to be shown to exist, economic agents had no commitments left from the past, and secondly, the economy discussed was not explicitly a monetary one. One of the questions we shall study in this chapter is whether the appropriate, required modifications may lead us to modify the proposition that a temporary equilibrium always exists. This is a matter of interest because Keynes has often been interpreted as claiming that, in fact, a temporary equilibrium (as we have defined it) may not exist.

There is another, less formal possible interpretation of the General Theory. In this view, Keynes was more concerned with demonstrating a "failure" of the price mechanism than arguing that there exist no prices that make equilibrium possible. Considering the amount of attention he gave to matters such as expectations and speculation, this is a very plausible interpretation. The out-of-equilibrium behavior of an economy in which transactions take place at all prices we know to be hard to analyze. We shall do no more than consider a number of rather general problems raised by such an undertaking.

This chapter as a whole, of course, is not concerned with either a full exposition of Keynes or a detailed analysis of all the problems raised. We are solely concerned with relating certain features of this model to what has gone before in this book.

2. Some Preliminaries

We cannot here attempt a detailed and full analysis of a monetary economy. However, there are certain features that it is useful to discuss before we proceed.

Money. So far in this book, except in Chapter 8 and briefly in Chapter 13, the existence of markets has been taken for granted. Once economic agents know market prices they take it that they can transact to any extent on these terms. The process of exchange is entirely anonymous—no bargain need be struck between any two agents. It is pretty clear that this would be entirely unrealistic in an economy with no medium of exchange. Consider three individuals, A, B, and C, where A has quantities of goods X and Y and derives no utility from good Z, B has quantities of goods Y and Z and derives no utility from good X, and C has quantities of Z and X and derives no utility from Y. It is perfectly clear that there are no terms on which any two of the agents could beneficially trade with each other, although there may be available, at some terms of exchange, triangular trades that are Pareto superior to the present allocation. To make sure that the equilibrium of this economy is Pareto efficient we would have to assume that all possible triangular trades have been explored by the three households. It is easy to construct examples in which chains of arbitrarily many links would have to be taken as explored by each agent before the resulting equilibrium could be shown to be Pareto efficient.

Such explorations have two features: They are costly, and since they may involve a household in an exchange that, as such, is not "beneficial," but is undertaken for the expectation of another that is, they may involve speculation. Of course, one of the advantages of a monetary economy is that it makes it possible to have anonymous markets such that every agent need make, at most, two separate transactions if he desires to exchange a given "non-money" good for another. We have seen (Chapter 13) that this does not entirely remove the speculative element from transactions, but it greatly economizes in the number of such transactions. In particular, only one transaction is needed in the exchange of money for any good.

While a monetary economy greatly economizes in the number of transactions it does not make them costless; we still have wholesalers, retailers, and brokers, whose function it is to reduce the costs of transactions such as the search for information, but who themselves do not perform costlessly. Moreover, most transactions take time and perhaps some effort, such as traveling.

From these considerations alone it is possible to construct an explanation of why an economic agent should hold part of his wealth in a medium of exchange with zero rate of return even when there are other assets yielding a positive rate of return. Of course, insofar as money is held (and here money is supposed to be intrinsically worthless), it is held for future transactions. This would not occur if there were in existence all the futures markets discussed in Section 2.9. The cost of organizing all these markets is one reason we do not have them and, thus, one reason we use money. Costs also are responsible for the fact that sales and purchases do not always coincide in time. Thus, for instance, if a household sells services to a firm, the latter will have an incentive to economize in the frequency of payment, that is, in the number of transactions. On the other hand, should the household buy only after it has actually sold (been paid), it would be involved in storage costs.

It will be noted that so far we have not made the point that the future is uncertain and that in the absence of the requisite number of contingent futures markets, well-known propositions in the theory of choice under uncertainty can be invoked to explain why agents should include money in their portfolio of assets. In this view, the rate of return foregone in holding money is a kind of insurance premium against the possibility that, in fact, the rate of return on other assets may turn out to be negative. Of course, if the "best guess" is that the return on other assets will be negative, no further explanation for the holding of money is required. We shall not pursue the uncertainty problem here.

We can formalize some of the above arguments in the spirit of Section 6.3, but it should be emphasized that only the most primitive monetary ideas are treated here.

Let the subscript "m" stand for money that we now regard as the non-interest-paying debt of some agency outside our formal system, say the government. Household h, as in Section 6.3, has an anticipated volume of receipts given by $\bar{x}_{hb}$. (For the moment we ignore past debts.) Receipts are measured in unit of account, but not necessarily in terms of money. In addition, the household has a stock of money, $\bar{x}_{hm}$. The anticipated receipts of period 2 do not include the money stock transferred from period 1 to period 2. The two budget constraints read:

$$\mathbf{p}^1\mathbf{x}_h^1 + p_b(x_{hb} - \bar{x}_{hb}) + p_m(x_{hm} - \bar{x}_{hm}) \leq \mathbf{p}^1\bar{\mathbf{x}}^1 + \sum_f d_{hf}(\mathbf{p}\mathbf{y}_f) + \sum_f (d_{hf} - d_{hf})K_f, \quad (1)$$

$$\mathbf{p}_h^2\mathbf{x}_h^2 \leq x_{hb} + p_{hm}^2 x_{hm}. \quad (2)$$

In addition to these budget constraints, the household is constrained by transaction costs, which depend on the money stocks it holds, prices, and the transactions it proposes to carry out. Recall the time constraint on the amount of labor services supplied that was introduced in Section 3.1. We shall now write

$$J(\mathbf{x}_h^2,\mathbf{p}_h^2,p_{hm}^2 x_{hm}) \leq T. \quad (3)$$

The left-hand side indicates the necessity of supplying some labor time for transactions in period 2. The amount required declines with the money stock and increases with the value of transactions. We take $J(\ )$ to be continuous in its arguments.

Evidently, (3) is a pretty crude device to capture some of the problems discussed in this section, but for our purposes it will serve. Now, if $\mathbf{x}_h = (\mathbf{x}_h^1,x_{hb},x_{hm})$, the first-period derived utility function, D.6.18, is given by

$$U_h(\mathbf{x}_h) = \max U_h^{12}(\mathbf{x}_h^1,\mathbf{x}_h^2) \qquad \text{s.t. (2) and (3).}$$

Note that the "true" utility function, $U_h^{12}(\ )$, depends only on consumption of goods and leisure, but that the derived function depends on the money stock chosen for transfer to period (2). It is likely that more sophisticated versions of the demand for money also would allow the construction of a derived utility function of which the money stock is an argument.

In Section 6.3 we showed that our consumption assumptions allowed us to deduce that $U_h(\mathbf{x}_h)$ was semi-strictly quasi-concave, where $\mathbf{x}_h$ did not include money. Here we may assume

ASSUMPTION 1. $J(\mathbf{x}_h^2,\mathbf{p}_h^2,p_{hm}^2 x_{hm})$ is, for given $\mathbf{p}_h^2$, $p_{hm}^2 x_{hm}$, a convex function of $\mathbf{x}_h^2$.

This assumption can be justified by arguing that there are increasing time costs of transactions with a given stock of money. (Strictly speaking, a transaction takes place only when $x_{hi}^2 \neq \bar{x}_{hi}^2$. We have not thought it worthwhile to introduce the extra elaboration required.) If A.14.1 holds, the proof of p.144 can be used to establish that $U_h(\mathbf{x}_h)$ is semi-strictly quasi-concave when $\mathbf{x}_h = (\mathbf{x}_h^1, x_{hb}, x_{hm})$. We need note only that $\mathbf{x}_h^2$, as there defined, satisfies the constraint (3).

Lastly, it is easy to see that if $J(\ )$ becomes large enough as $p_{hm}^2 x_{hm}$ becomes small for $\mathbf{x}_h^2$, $\mathbf{p}_h^2$ given, the household will always transfer some money from period 1 to period 2.

The Past. In Section 6.3 all households started period 1 with no commitments from the past. This plainly is not realistic since we are not considering period 1 to be the beginning of the world. Indeed, in the present context, history may have peculiar significance.

To examine the matter further we need a rather more elaborate structure than that of Section 6.3.

Let there be three time intervals: 0, 1, and 2. If the agent is viewed as acting in period 0, then 1 is an interval of the future and 2 is the remaining future. If the agent is acting in period 1, then 0 is the past and 2 is the future. We give a variable the superscript "$0F$" to denote the expectation that was formed in 0 of the values to be taken on by that variable from period 1 on, that is, in periods 1 and 2. We give a superscript "ij," $j \neq F$, to denote the expectation formed in i of the values of the variable in j. A single superscript "i" denotes that we are dealing with the actual variable value in i.

In this notation, for instance, $\mathbf{p}_h^{0F}\bar{\mathbf{x}}_h^{0F}$ is what the agent h believes in period 0 will be the present value of his endowment in period 1, that is,

$$\mathbf{p}_h^{0F}\bar{\mathbf{x}}_h^{0F} = \mathbf{p}_h^{01}\bar{\mathbf{x}}_h^{01} + p_b^{01}(\mathbf{p}_h^{02}\bar{\mathbf{x}}_h^{02}).$$

Similarly, $\mathbf{p}_f^{0F}\mathbf{y}_f^{0F}$ is the present value of the profits in period 1 of firm f on the expectations formed in period 0.

Let us now view period 1 as the present. We assume that the bonds issued by firm f in period 0 are repaid in period 1, but that, as before, the firm issues a quantity of new bonds, $\mathbf{p}_f^{12}\mathbf{y}_f^{12}$, equal to the profits it expects in 1 to make in 2. (The reader should note that $\mathbf{y}_f^{12}$ now has quite a different meaning from that given it in Section 6.3). We write $\bar{x}_{hb}^1$ as the actual value of receipts in period 1 plus the present value of receipts expected then for period 2. By the assumptions of Section 6.3,

$$\bar{x}_{hb}^1 = \mathbf{p}^1\bar{\mathbf{x}}_h^1 + p_b^1(\mathbf{p}_h^{12}\bar{\mathbf{x}}_h^{12}) + \sum_f d_{hf}^1[\mathbf{p}^1\mathbf{y}_f^1 + p_b^1(\mathbf{p}_f^{12}\mathbf{y}_f^{12}) - \mathbf{p}_f^{0F}\mathbf{y}_f^{0F}]$$
$$+ p_b^1 \sum_f d_{hf}^1[\max_h(\mathbf{p}_h^{12}\mathbf{y}_f^{12}) - \mathbf{p}_f^{12}\mathbf{y}_f^{12}] \quad (4)$$

The first two terms are straightforward; they give the receipts from current endowment sale and the present expected value from future endowment sale. The first square bracket, for any f, gives the net payment of f to shareholders after repayment of the bonds issued in 0. The second square bracket gives the profit expected by the most optimistic household in period 2 after repayment of the bonds issued in period 1. As before $d^1_{hf} = 0$ if h is not the most optimistic household.

If we write K^1_f as the capital value of firm f in period 1, then it is given by the first square bracket plus p^1_b times the second square bracket for f. That is,

$$K^1_f = \mathbf{p}^1\mathbf{y}^1_f + p^1_b \max_h [(\mathbf{p}^{12}_h\mathbf{y}^{12}_f) - \mathbf{p}^{0F}_f\mathbf{y}^{0F}_f]. \tag{5}$$

This should be compared with D.6.15 and D.6.16. Since the economy now has a history, the firm has past commitments, that must be taken into account in the valuation placed on it in period 1. It is plain that we now cannot assume $K^1_f \geq 0$. If $K^1_f < 0$, then the household with a share d^0_{hf} in the firm is responsible for $d^0_h K^1_f$ of the net debt and cannot escape this obligation:

ASSUMPTION 2. $K^1_f < 0$ implies $d^1_{hf} = d^0_{hf}$.

Now we may write (4) also as

$$\bar{x}^1_{hb} = \mathbf{p}^1\bar{\mathbf{x}}^1_h + p^1_b(\mathbf{p}^{12}_h\bar{\mathbf{x}}^{12}_h) + \sum_f d^1_{hf}K^1_f. \tag{4'}$$

To (4′) we add the net repayment of bonds to the household, $(x^0_{hb} - \bar{x}^{0F}_{hb})$, and the money stocks transferred to period one, $\mathbf{p}^1_m.x^0_{hm}$. But

$$\bar{x}^{0F}_{hb} = \mathbf{p}^{0F}_f\bar{\mathbf{x}}^{0F}_h + \sum_f d^{01}_{hf}K^{01}_f + \sum_f (d^0_{hf} - d^{01}_{hf})K^{01}_f. \tag{6}$$

Here K^{01}_f is the capital value of firm f in period 1 as expected in period 0. Also, d^{01}_{hf} are the planned holdings of h for period 1 of the shares of firm f. Note that

$$\begin{aligned} K^{01}_f &= [\max_h (\mathbf{p}^{0F}_h\mathbf{y}^{0F}_f) - \mathbf{p}^{0F}_f\mathbf{y}^{0F}_f] \\ &= \max_h[\mathbf{p}^{01}_h\mathbf{y}^{01}_f + p^{01}_b(\mathbf{p}^{02}_h\mathbf{y}^{02}_f) - \mathbf{p}^{0F}_f y^{0F}_f] \end{aligned}$$

so that, by the assumptions of Section 6.3, $K^{01}_f \geq 0$.

The resources at the disposal of the household at the beginning of period 1 are

$$\bar{x}^1_{hb} + (x^0_{hb} - \bar{x}^{0F}_{hb}) + p^1_m x^0_{hm}$$

or, using (4) and (6),

$$[\mathbf{p}^1\bar{\mathbf{x}}^1_h + p^1_b(\mathbf{p}^{12}_h\mathbf{x}^{12}_h) - \mathbf{p}^{0F}_f\bar{\mathbf{x}}^{0F}_h] + \left[\sum_f (d^1_{hf}K^1_f - d^{01}_{hf}K^{01}_f)\right] - \sum_f (d^0_{hf} - d^{01}_{hf})K^{01}_f + x^0_{hb} + p^1_m x^0_{hm}. \quad (7)$$

We refer to (7) as the wealth of h at the beginning of period 1 and write it as w^1_h. If $d^1_{hf} = d^{01}_{hf} = d^0_{hf}$, as we could take to be the case if all expectations are fulfilled and no one buys "short" in period 0, and if indeed all expectations are correct, then $w^1_h = \mathbf{x}^0_{hb} + \mathbf{p}^0_m\mathbf{x}^0_{hm}$, which is exactly (except for the monetary component) what we deduced to be the form of the wealth transferred to the "future" in Section 6.3.

Since households and firms have different expectations in period 0, it cannot be that all expectations are fulfilled in period 1. Thus, in general:

(a) The value of the endowment of a household in 1 will differ from what was expected at 0 (the first square bracket in (7)). If it is less, then the first term in (7) is negative.

(b) K^1_f may be negative (and differ from K^{01}_f) because the value of the firm's production plan in 1 is less than it was expected to be in 0. This may be so for three related reasons: First-period prices may be different than they had been expected to be; the price expected in period 1 to rule in period 2 may be different than period 2 prices were expected to be in period 0; the production plan of the firm in period 1 may differ from what was expected in period 0.

(c) The actual share, d^1_{hf}, in firm f may differ from its planned value for all the reasons already given.

Now several situations that did not arise in our previous work are possible. As before, let $\mathbf{p} = (\mathbf{p}^1, p^1_b)$.

(a) Suppose $\mathbf{p}$ such that $\mathbf{p}^1\mathbf{y}^1_f + p^1_b\mathbf{p}^{12}_f\mathbf{y}^{12}_f - \mathbf{p}^{0F}_f\mathbf{y}^{0F}_f < 0$. Then the firm f cannot repay the debt of the previous period. We could say that the firm is bankrupt. Since there may be shareholders more optimistic than the firm, however, we might wish to assume that they will repay the short-fall on the firm's debt as long as they are not involved in loss. From this reasoning (b) follows.

(b) The firm is bankrupt when at some **p**, $K_f^1 < 0$. As long as the present value of profits of the firm is positive, however, it evidently pays to continue operating.

(c) If at **p**, K_f^1 is sufficiently negative to cause $w_h^1 < 0$, the bankruptcy point of household h has been passed. We must suppose that, in fact, the household hands over to its creditors all its assets, including the present value of its wages and its share in the firm. The creditors may value the future profits of the firm, the debtor's share of which they claim, quite differently than the debtor did, so they (the creditors) might experience a discontinuous change in wealth.

(d) To be even remotely realistic, we must add that the management of the firm and thus its production plans may change at any stage in (a), (b), or (c). In (a) the shareholders may install new management, in (b) the creditors may demand a change, and in (c) the creditors own a fraction of the firm. Any such change in the identity of the management, since it will be accompanied by a change in the expectations, will generally lead to a discontinuous change of production plans.

Clearly, the actual bankruptcy procedure is at least partly a matter of law, but it seems plain that the history of the economy may make it impossible to guarantee the continuity properties of the various functions and correspondences and this is bad for existence proofs. It is to this, one of our main concerns in this chapter, that we now turn.

3. The Existence of Keynesian Temporary Equilibrium

There are two, rather distinct questions that we must investigate. The first, straightforward question is whether it can be argued that Keynes discovered features of an economy that lead to the failure of one or the other of our assumptions of Section 6.3 and thus make it impossible to establish the existence of a temporary equilibrium. (It should be emphasized that for our purposes temporary equilibrium implies the clearing of all markets including that for labor. The next section looks at a different kind of equilibrium.) The second question is whether such an equilibrium, even if it can be shown to exist, is "sensible."

By "sensible," of course, we can mean all sorts of things. Certainly, though, we should not be much interested in an equilibrium with a zero real wage. This is not the only desideratum, however. Keynes was concerned with a monetary economy, and in any case we have agreed that all of our constructions presuppose the absence of barter. It is rather essential, then, that once money has been introduced explicitly as the means of effecting exchanges, we should not finish up with an equilibrium in which money has zero exchange value, that is, one in which $p_m^1 = 0$, in the notation of the previous section. In other words, we must show the existence of an equilibrium restrained further by the requirement that $p_m^1 > 0$.

Our procedure will be to assume first that if an equilibrium exists it will satisfy $p_m^1 > 0$. This allows us to take money as the numeraire. Later we shall re-examine this matter.

From what we have learned already we know that we must be able to establish the appropriate continuity properties of the behavioral function or correspondences and of those constructed from them in order to demonstrate that an equilibrium exists. The possibility that at some point in the price space the entire resources of one agent become the property of other agents, in the present context, is associated in general with a discontinuity, so the existence proof is endangered.

Suppose that household c is the sole creditor of firm f from period 0 and that household h owns all the shares of firm f. Then household c includes among the resources available to it in period 1 $\mathbf{p}_f^{0F}\mathbf{y}_f^{0F}$, the repayment of its loan to firm f, made in period 0. If at $\mathbf{p}$, however, household h has $w_h^1 = 0$, then it cannot borrow and transfers all its resources to c. As far as h is concerned they are just equal in value to its debt of $\mathbf{p}_f^{0F}\mathbf{y}_f^{0F}$. But household h expected to receive $\mathbf{p}_h^{12}\mathbf{y}_f^{12}$ in period 2, while household c expects $\mathbf{p}_c^{12}\mathbf{y}_f^{12}$ and the two amounts may differ. Also, of course, the future "earning power" of h from its own resources was $\mathbf{p}_h^{12}\bar{\mathbf{x}}_h^2$, while household c values them at $\mathbf{p}_c^{12}\bar{\mathbf{x}}_h^2$. Hence, at the bankruptcy point, c may experience a discontinuous change in wealth.

To this must be added the equally important difficulty caused by a change in management resulting from the bankruptcy of the firm.

In addition to all this another problem arises. It will be recalled that the strategy of our existence proofs was to establish the existence of a compensated equilibrium and then to show that it was, in fact, a competitive equilibrium. For this last step we needed to ensure that in the compensated equilibrium every household disposed of a value of resources that exceeded the value of its minimum consumption vector. It is plain that this last step may not be possible now, even if the existence of a compensated equilibrium could be demonstrated. In a compensated equilibrium, if a household is bankrupt it disposes of no resources, and we cannot use our assumption of resource relatedness to reach the desired conclusion. The fact that some household has an "effective" demand for the resources of the bankrupt household does not help the latter to any "disposable" resources.

In his Chapter 19, "Changes in Money-Wages," Keynes really addressed himself to the problems of this section, although he was not concerned with a formal existence analysis. He argued that lower money wages might not reduce unemployment. He adduced various well-known reasons, including one not yet mentioned here, namely the possibility that expected prices may not be continuous functions of current price. This is not unimportant if we consider, for instance, the likelihood that the bankruptcy of firms and households is information separate from current price information, which may influence agents' views of the future. But Keynes also wrote, "Indeed if the fall in wages and prices goes far, the embarrassment of those entrepreneurs who are heavily indebted may soon reach the point of insolvency—with severely adverse effects on Investment," (p. 264).

This leads us to another point of some importance: The problem of bankruptcy is not unrelated to the good or goods in terms of which debts are contracted. Keynes realistically took it that they were contracted in terms of money. We have hitherto taken them as contracted in abstract unit of account. Consider again the creditor household c. If it has a contract to receive money, then it will receive $p_m^1(\mathbf{p}_f^{0F}\mathbf{y}_f^{0F})p_m^{01}$, and this is the amount of money the debtor household also is contracted to deliver. Evidently then, the set of $\mathbf{p}$ at which $w_h^1 = 0$ when debt is fixed in unit of account will not coincide, in general, with the set of $\mathbf{p}$ at which $w_h^1 = 0$ when debt is present in terms of money. The terms in which contracts are made matter. In particular, if money is the good in terms of which contracts are made, then the prices of goods in terms of money are of special significance. This is not the case if we consider an economy without a past and without a future. Keynes wrote that "the importance of money essentially flows from it being a link between the present and the future," to which we may add that it is important also because it is a link between the past and the present. If a serious monetary theory comes to be written, the fact that contracts are indeed made in terms of money will be of considerable importance.

We now have a great deal of evidence that establishing the existence of a temporary equilibrium for the economy we are now considering may not be smooth sailing. Of course, general "non-existence" theorems are not to be sought. Therefore it may be helpful to sketch an example.

To avoid aggregation problems, let us suppose that the economy is capable of producing a single good. For the purpose of this example only, we write y^t as the output of the good at time t (not to be confused with the vector $\mathbf{y}^t$). The good may be consumed or used in subsequent production. Let S_t be the amount of the good available at the end of period t for production at $t + 1$ and let L_t be the amount of the single kind of labor service used in production at t. Then the production function is

$$y^t = S_{t-1}^{\beta} L_t^{\alpha} \qquad \alpha > 0, \beta > 0, \alpha + \beta < 1. \tag{8}$$

Note that there are diminishing returns to scale and that only stocks set aside in the previous period are available for production. It will be convenient to take units such that

$$S_0 = 1.$$

Let p be the actual price of the good in period 1 (i.e., we omit the superscript), p_f^2 the price expected by the firm for period 2. Similarly w is the current wage and w_f^2 the wage expected by the firm for period 2. All prices are measured in terms of money. Then, assuming that the present value of profits are maximized, routine calculations give

$$\pi_f = p(\alpha r)^a(1 - \alpha) + p_b(p_f^2)^{1/b} b(1 - \alpha)(\alpha r_f^2)^u \left(\frac{q}{\beta}\right)^{-\beta/b(1-\alpha)} \tag{9}$$

where π_f is the present value of profits as seen by the firm and

$$r = \frac{p}{w}, \quad r_f^2 = \frac{p_f^2}{w_f^2}, \quad q = \frac{p}{p_b},$$

$$a = \frac{\alpha}{1 - \alpha}, \quad b = \frac{1 - (\alpha + \beta)}{1 - \alpha}, \quad u = \frac{a}{b}.$$

Also

$$y^1 = (\alpha r)^a. \tag{10}$$

Next let us consider households. We shall assume that they have identical utility functions, although they may have different expectations. For reasons we will not examine, a household will always deliver one unit of labor in each period. (This assumption makes the example easier, but is in no way essential.) The maximum amount of leisure it can have in each period is also one unit. Part of the leisure, however, may have to be used in transactions (see (3)). To make this precise, let c_h^t be the amount of the good bought by h in period t and let m_h^{t-1} be the amount of money transferred from period $(t-1)$ to period t. Then, if λ_h^t is the leisure consumed by h in period t, we postulate

$$\lambda_h^t = \min\left(1, \frac{m_h^{t-1}}{p^t c_h^t}\right). \tag{11}$$

The idea behind (11) is sufficiently obvious, as is the amount of simplification involved. It is worth noting that $1 - \lambda_h^t$, the amount of leisure used for transaction purposes, is indeed a convex function of the transactions to be made in the range in which $\lambda_h^t \leq 1$.

The utility function we shall use is

$$(\nu \log c_h^1 + \mu \log \lambda_h^1) + \delta(\nu \log c_h^2 + \mu \log \lambda_h^2)$$

where $\delta > 0$ and $\nu > \mu > 0$. The constraint on the household, besides (11), is:

$$pc_h^1 + p_b p_h^2 c_h^2 + (1 - p_b) m_h^1 = w_h^1, \tag{12}$$

where w_h^1 is the total present wealth, including "human wealth," of h.

Proceeding in the usual way we find

$$m_h^1 = g \frac{pc_h^1}{1 - p_b} \quad g = \frac{\delta\mu}{\nu - \mu}, \qquad \text{for } p_b < \frac{\nu - \mu}{\nu} \tag{13}$$

$$pc_h^1 = \bar{c} w_h^1 \qquad \bar{c} = \frac{1}{1 + \delta + g}. \tag{14}$$

If there are H households, the labor supply in period 1 is equal to H. The demand for labor is $(\alpha r)^a/\alpha$ and so, neglecting the case $w = 0$, a condition of equilibrium is

$$H = \frac{(\alpha r)^a}{\alpha}, \tag{15}$$

and this uniquely determines r^*.

Next we want

$$\sum_h m_h^1 = \bar{m}, \tag{16}$$

where $\bar{m}$ is the total stock of money in the economy. Also let

$$I = S_1;$$

then we require

$$I + \sum_h c_h^1 = y^1 = (\alpha r^*)^a. \tag{17}$$

Since the debt of a firm is really the debt of the households that own its shares, we find, on the assumption that $w_h^1 > 0$, all h,

$$\sum w_h^1 \equiv w^1 = \sum_h m_h^0 + p + \sum_h w_h^1 + p_b \sum_h w_h^2 + py_f^1 - wL_f^1 + p_b[\max(p_h^2 y_f^2 - w_h^2 L_f^2)] \tag{18}$$

(where it should be recalled that $S_0 = 1$ so that $pS_0 = p$). Also,

$$I = \left[\frac{q}{\beta p_f^2}(\alpha r_f^2)^{-a}\right]^{-\frac{1}{b}} - 1 \tag{19}$$

and

$$y_f^2 = (\alpha r_f^2)^a (I + 1)^{\beta/(1-\alpha)}. \tag{20}$$

From (19), we may write

$$I = I(q).$$

Also, if

$$\hat{w} = \frac{1}{p}\sum_h w_h^1,$$

then from (18), (19), and (20),

$$\hat{w} = \hat{w}(p,q).$$

If $\hat{w}_p = \partial\hat{w}/\partial p'$ and so on, we find $\hat{w}_p < 0$, $\hat{w}_q < 0$, and in similar notation, $I_q < 0$.

We may now write (16) and (17) as

$$\left.\begin{aligned} g\bar{c}\hat{w}(p,q) + (q^{-1} - p^{-1})\bar{m} &= 0, \quad (16') \\ I(q) + \bar{c}\hat{w}(p,q) - (\alpha r^*)^a &= 0, \quad (17') \end{aligned}\right\} p_b < \frac{(\nu - \mu)}{\nu}.$$

When $p_b \geq (\nu - \mu)/\nu$, then (13) is not appropriate, since in that case $\lambda_h^2 = 1$. Also, it has been supposed that m_h^0 has a value that allows the solution $\lambda_h^1 < 1$. For the purpose of this example we suppose that the economy finds an equilibrium in the range for which $\lambda_h^1 < 1$ and $\lambda_h^2 < 1$. In Figure 14-1, OA has slope $\nu/(\nu - \mu)$ so that every point above OA satisfies $p_b < (\nu - \mu)/\nu$, since $q/p = 1/p_b$.

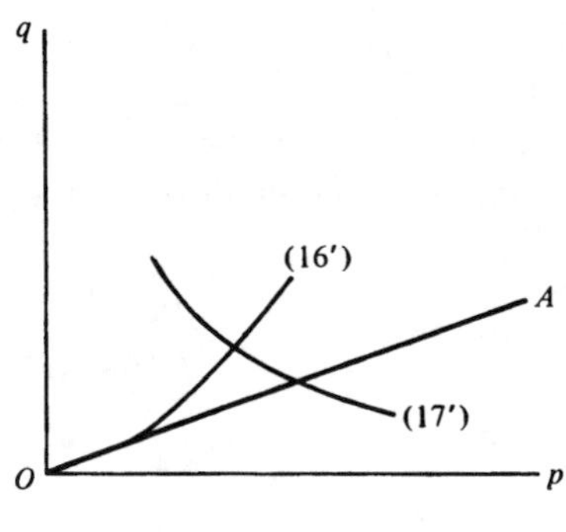

Figure 14-1

We have also plotted equations (16′) and (17′), and the signs of their slopes can be checked from what has gone before. The intersection of the two curves gives the unique equilibrium of the economy. It should be noted that as p varies, so does w_0 (the money wage) in the same proportion, since r is fixed at r^*.

However, we have supposed in deriving these curves that $w_h^1 > 0$ throughout. Now suppose that there are only two households: the creditor household and the debtor household, so-called according to their respective commitments in period 0. In Figure 14-2 the curve B is the bankruptcy locus of the debtor. If (p,q) lies on this curve, then the debtor hands his assets (in the sense of the previous section) to the creditor. If the creditor has a less sanguine expectation of future profits than did the debtor, there will be a discontinuous fall in the creditor's wealth. Hence, in order that the demand for output should equal its supply, at any p, p_b will have to be higher than it would have been otherwise. For the same reason, and because the creditor must now demand all the money there is, at any p, p_b will have to be higher than it would have been otherwise if the demand for money is to equal what is available.

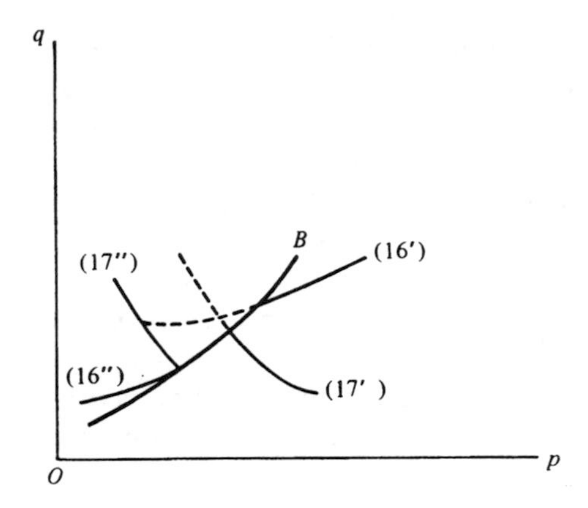

Figure 14-2

At all points to the left of B and on B, the debtor is bankrupt. The dashed part of (16′) and (17′) are the continuations of Figure 14-1 if bankruptcy had not occurred. The discontinuity caused by bankruptcy means that no equilibrium exists. It should be noted that the construction takes full account of cash balance effects. Indeed, if it did not, (17′) would be an equation in q only. Note also that when the debtor is bankrupt, equilibrium in the money market implies an excess demand for goods, while if he is not bankrupt, it implies an excess supply of goods, where these are "full employment" excess demands.

As usual, it is not possible to prove for the general case that no equilibrium exists. The example is sufficient, however, to show that if we take the Keynesian construction seriously, that is, as of a world with a past as well as a future and in which contracts are made in terms of money, no equilibrium may exist.

Let us now turn to the second problem we have set ourselves: If an equilibrium exists, is it one in which money has a positive exchange value?

Before answering this question it is worthwhile drawing attention to a paradox that may arise from an ill-formulated monetary theory. By this we may mean a theory in which the demand for money is simply derived by putting "real cash balances" into the utility function, not as a proxy for something else, but to account for convenience and the like. If nothing else is said, and if the usual continuity properties are taken to hold, then we can argue as follows:

Consider the case in which the price of money is made identically equal to zero. Ignoring the supply and demand for money altogether, we have an economy in which there is one less good. Of course, Walras' law and the other usual assumptions hold. The economy has an equilibrium. Yet there must be an equilibrium also for the "full" economy with money, since at a zero price no one will wish to hold money and it will be in excess supply. Thus a "monetary economy" so loosely specified always has an equilibrium in which money plays no part. This result, of course, is due entirely to the fact that a proper function for money has not been formulated, so that when money is worthless, transactions can be carried out as before.

To avoid such nonsense it is best to regard the model as defined, or viable, only for the case $p^1_m > 0$. This becomes an additional constraint. We may assume more sensibly that the demand for money will always be positive—say, by the kind of argument used in the example.

Since we are now concerned specifically with the problems arising from requiring $p^1_m > 0$, it is best to return to the construction of Section 6.3, that is, to a world without a past and, therefore, one in which bankruptcy difficulties cannot occur. We shall consider the case of fixed expected prices only.

Let

$$\bar{k}\bar{\mathbf{x}}_m = \bar{k}\{\bar{x}_{1m}, \ldots, \bar{x}_{Hm}\} \qquad \bar{k} \text{ a scalar}$$

be the initial endowment vector of household money balances. Set $p^1_m \equiv 1$ and consider $\mathbf{p} = (\mathbf{p}^1, p_b, k)$, where k is a scalar by which we propose to multiply $\bar{\mathbf{x}}_m$, $k \geq 0$. Then, if $\mathbf{p}$ is a temporary price equilibrium, so is $h\mathbf{p}$, $h > 0$, if we make the following assumption: The utility of every household is unchanged if the quantity of money it can hold and all money prices are changed in the same proportion. This is a sufficiently well-known postulate that does not require elaboration; it is in accordance with what we said concerning the derived utility function in Section 14.2 (Money). It should be noted that changing p_b to hp_b is equivalent to multiplying the present prices of all future goods by h. Also, the amount of money each household transfers to period 2 from period 1 is multiplied by h. Certainly, therefore, we may normalize $\mathbf{p}$ to lie in the unit simplex.

Now the method of proof of the existence of a temporary equilibrium, with rather obvious modifications, can proceed as before with $\mathbf{p}$ given its present definition and $\mathbf{x}_h = (\mathbf{x}_h^1, x_{hb}, x_{hm}^1)$. As before, for any Pareto-efficient utility allocation we can find a set of $\mathbf{p}$ that support it and penalize households who "overspend" at $\mathbf{p}$, in the same way as before. It does not seem worthwhile going through this again step by step.

We know that there exists $\mathbf{p}^0$, a competitive equilibrium. Since $p_m \equiv 1$, we know that there will be some demand for money and so $k^0 = 0$ is impossible. Hence $k^0 > 0$. Set $p_m^0 = k^0$ and we have found the actual equilibrium price of money. Therefore, if the assumptions made here and in Section 6.3 hold, an equilibrium always exists for a monetary economy. It is worth noting that $k^0 > 0$ implies $p_b^0 < 1$, so that the equilibrium is reached at a positive "interest rate."

4. Target and Active Excess Demands

In the previous chapter, where we assumed that money was required for every act of exchange, we found it necessary to distinguish between target and active excess demands. The distinction is quite similar to the Keynesian distinction between desired purchase and effective demand. Strictly speaking, this distinction arises also in a barter economy: A household may have to acquire some one good before it can exchange it for the desired one. Still, it is best to stick to the economy we know, that is, a monetary one.

We wish to extend the analysis of Chapter 13 to include a production vector. Also, we shall be concerned with temporary equilibrium.

As before, we shall write

$$\mathbf{y}^1 = \sum_f \mathbf{y}_f^1$$

as the current production vector that would maximize profits—call it the target production vector. Also, $\bar{x}_{h0}^1$ is the stock of leisure (there is only one kind) available to h in period 1 and x_{h0}^1 is its demand for leisure. Write

$$\bar{x}_0^1 = \sum_h \bar{x}_{h0}^1$$

$$x_0^1 = \sum_h x_{h0}^1 \qquad y_0^1 = \sum_f y_{f0}^1.$$

We shall take firms as sufficiently integrated so as to be able to ignore intermediate goods. This is not a good assumption, but it is quite harmless to the main point of this section. It means that we take y_0^1 as the only non-positive component of $\mathbf{y}_f^1$. It is also supposed that firms can always "finance" their demands. Then, if $\mathbf{y}^{1a}$ is the actual production vector we have

ASSUMPTION 3. $\mathbf{y}^{1a} \neq \mathbf{y}^1$ if and only if $y_0^1 + (\bar{x}_0^1 - x_0^1) < 0$.

That is, actual and target production fail to coincide only if firms cannot get all the labor they want. Let $z_0 = x_0^1 - \bar{x}_0^1 - y_0^1$, the target excess demand for labor.

The money available to households consists of the following: the stock transferred from the previous period, the receipts from all actual sales, including that of bonds (since firms do not buy bonds, households as a whole have no net receipts from bonds), and receipts of profits from the firms. These consist of current profits only, since firms finance the payment currently of the present value of future profits out of the sale of bonds (see Section 6.3). Thus households as a group can augment their inherited money stock only by sales of labor and receipts of profits.

Let $\mathbf{x}^{1a}$ be the vector of active demands by households taken together and $\bar{\mathbf{x}}^1$ the stock of goods they hold, where both vectors exclude money and labor. Write $\mathbf{z}^{1a} = (\mathbf{x}^{1a} - \bar{\mathbf{x}}^1)$. Corresponding to these definitions let $\mathbf{z}^1$ be the target value of $\mathbf{z}$, that is, when it is derived without the constraint, no purchase without money. Then we postulate

ASSUMPTION 4. $\mathbf{z}^{1a+} \neq \mathbf{z}^{1+}$ implies $\mathbf{y}^{1a} = \mathbf{y}^1$, where the superscript "+" denotes a vector with non-negative components.

What this means is that if households fail to achieve their targets, they have not sold their target amount of labor to firms. Then, by A.14.3, firms cannot have failed to buy the target quantity of labor. The assumption thus excludes the possibility of households selling their target quantity of labor, but failing to achieve their target borrowing. Once again the main point of the discussion is not vitally affected by this.

From what has already been said, the available monetary resources of the households are

$$\mathbf{p}^1\mathbf{y}^1 + \bar{x}_m - p_0^1 y_0^1.$$

So, if $\mathbf{z}^{1a+} \neq \mathbf{z}^{1+}$, we have

$$\sum_{i \neq 0} p_i^1 z_i^{1a+} + p_b z_b^{1a+} + x_m^{1a} - \bar{x}_m^0 = \sum_{i \neq 0} p_i^1 y_i^1.$$

Or, if $\hat{z}_i^1 = z_i^{1a+} - y_i^1$,

$$\sum_{i \neq 0} p_i^1 \hat{z}_i^1 + p_b z_b^{1a+} + x_m^{1a} - \bar{x}_m^0 = 0, \tag{21}$$

which is Walras' law for active excess demands. It is different from the usual (target) form; in particular, the excess supply of labor makes no appearance. Hence, as far as active excess demands are concerned, active attempts to sell more labor are not mirrored in active attempts to buy more than is being offered for sale.

It is important not to misunderstand (21). It is *not* being proposed that sometimes the usual (target) Walras' law holds and sometimes it does not. It *always* holds. What is being argued is that for certain purposes of analysis it is not the most appropriate accounting identity. Thus if, as we have implicitly been doing, we think of a two-stage analysis in which households first sell to firms and then buy, (21) easily emerges. It is a much too tidy affair, of course, as can be seen from the assumptions. But it makes again the important point that in a monetary economy intentions to buy become relevant signals only when coupled with both the willingness and ability to pay in money. Lastly, the reader familiar with the Keynesian literature will recognize (21) as the accounting identity used there. In particular, note that $\hat{z}_i^1$ depends on what has been sold, that is, on income as well as on prices.

A certain difficulty with (21) must now be noted. In deriving this relation we supposed that households actually receive what are in fact the target profits of period 1, $\mathbf{p}^1\mathbf{y}^1$. If targets cannot be met, actual profits may differ from target profits. There are two ways in which actual profits and target profits may differ: Active demand for goods may be less than actual supply; target production may differ from actual production for the reasons already given. To overcome this complication we suppose that firms actually pay households the target profits for period 1 out of their cash balances, so that a discrepancy between target and actual profits is reflected in the firms' second-period assets and so in the valuation of households of their next period's profit. This way we can keep the accounting straight although an obvious simplification of reality is involved.

In view of what has just been said we can easily check that the appropriate accounting identity when $z_0 \geq 0$ is the usual Walras' law. Households receive target profits and target receipts from the sale of labor. The discrepancy between $\mathbf{y}^1$ and $\mathbf{y}^{1a}$ is reflected in the expected future receipts from firms, that is, in the stock of bonds.

Now consider the possibility, much discussed in recent years (e.g., by Phillips), that changes in money wages obey the law

$$\dot{p}_0 = F(z_0 + B) \qquad B > 0,$$

where F is a sign-possessing function, $F(0) = 0$. Then it is possible that at some set of prices $-z_0 = B$, $\hat{z}^1 = 0$, $z_b^{1a+} = 0$, $z_m^{1a} = 0$. This suggests $\dot{p}_i = 0$, all i, and we call the situation a *quasi-equilibrium*. Clower has argued that there is good reason to suppose that this corresponds to Keynes' unemployment equilibrium. Of course, it is not an equilibrium in any of the senses used in this book; it is consistent with target excess supply in one market and it is not Pareto efficient.

It is not at all clear that, for arbitrary B, such an equilibrium need exist. Sometimes, however, the Keynesian wage mechanism is interpreted as

$$\dot{p}_0 = F[\max(0,z_0)]$$

so that money wages can rise, but not fall. A *quasi-equilibrium* is now any set of prices at which active excess demands are zero, but $z_0 < 0$. In certain circumstances we can show that either a quasi-equilibrium in this sense or a proper temporary equilibrium exists. To do so we cannot use a procedure that depends on the fixed point being Pareto efficient. If we are willing to deal with functions rather than correspondences, however, we can use the method of Chapter 2, provided the required continuity properties hold. We replace z_0 by $\max(0,z_0) = \hat{z}_0$ and use (21). We must suppose that there are no discontinuities at the point at which households cease to be able to meet their targets.

5. Some Concluding Remarks

So far we have been concerned with the modification of our earlier discussion of temporary equilibrium to make it possible to include some of the features of an economy stressed by Keynes. It is arguable, however, that Keynes was as much concerned with the actual behavior of an economy out of equilibrium as he was with the description of an equilibrium or quasi-equilibrium. Indeed the idea of a quasi-equilibrium is rather closely connected with the postulated behavior of the economy (in particular, of course, the labor market) out of equilibrium.

We shall discuss briefly the Keynesian view of the economy when it is not in quasi-equilibrium. Consider the following quotations from the *General Theory*:

> . . . if labor were to respond to conditions of gradually diminishing employment by offering its services at a gradually diminishing money wage, this would not, as a rule, have the effect of reducing real wages and might even have the effect of increasing them. . . . The chief result of this policy would be to cause a great instability of prices, so violent perhaps as to make business calculations futile. . . . To suppose that a flexible wage policy is a right and proper adjunct of a system which on the whole is one of *laissez faire*, is the opposite of the truth. (p. 269)

> For if competition between unemployed workers always led to a very great reduction in the money wage there would be violent instability in the price level. Moreover there might be no position of stable equilibrium except in conditions consistent with full employment. (p. 253)

> In particular it is an outstanding characteristic of the economic system in which we live that, whilst it is subject to severe fluctuations in respect of output and employment, it is not violently unstable. (p. 249)

Keynes in fact takes the evidence of the third statement to imply that the contingencies considered in the first and second do not occur; that is, wages do not fall, in particular they do not fall very much in response to a target excess supply of labor. On the other hand, the end of statement 2 seems to entail the possibility that if wages fell rapidly enough, full equilibrium could possibly be established. In view of statement 1, however, we must take this as not likely.

It is plain that it will not be easy to make any simple connection between the adjustment process so far discussed and the kind of forces Keynes thought to be important. This is partly due to the fact that he was quite imprecise in these matters, but largely because a precise formulation would be extremely complex. For instance, part of an argument designed to show the possible inefficacy of falling money wages is to say that they may induce the expectation of falling money prices. Just how large such an expectation must be, in absolute magnitude, to give the predicted "violent instability" in any moderately realistic model would be fairly hard to calculate. Moreover, since the whole process, unlike a tâtonnement, takes place in real time, the consequences of disequilibrium transactions at one moment in the behavior of the economy in a subsequent moment would be very difficult to trace. In addition, the actual path may be strewn with bankruptcies.

We cannot attempt to pursue these difficult matters here. It is certainly sufficiently clear that models constructed to discuss Keynes' view, that is, models that pay no attention to expectations, cannot illuminate or enable us to criticize this view. Suppose we return to the simple model of Section 14.3. Let z_g be the active excess demand for output and z_0 the target excess demand for labor. Suppose that for some B, there are prices such that $-z_0 = B$, $z_g = 0$, that is, that a quasi-equilibrium exists.

If we calculate $\partial z_g/\partial p$ and $\partial z_g/\partial w$ on the assumption of fixed expectations, we find the first term negative and the second term positive. Since $\partial z_0/\partial w < 0$, $\partial z_0/\partial p > 0$, the process $\dot{p} = z_g$, $\dot{w} = F(z_0 + B)$ will be stable since it is a gross-substitute case.

Now suppose that all agents have the same expectations and that expected prices are the same as current prices. (Keynes would never have denied that lower money wages, say, are good for employment if they and prices are lower relative to their future expected value.) We find

$$p\frac{\partial z_g}{\partial p} = \bar{c}p_b y = \left[a\alpha + \frac{\beta}{1-\alpha}\frac{a}{b}\right] - \bar{c}\frac{\bar{m}}{p} - sy^1 a\alpha + (I+1)\frac{a}{b},$$

where

$$s = 1 - \bar{c} \qquad w\frac{\partial z_g}{\partial w} = -\bar{c}\frac{\bar{m}}{p} - p\frac{\partial z_g}{\partial p}.$$

Simple though the construction is, it can now accommodate some of the more important Keynesian points. Certainly, in the vicinity of quasi-equilibrium we may have $\partial z_g/\partial p > 0$. For instance, since expected prices are also lower, lower prices will reduce investment and expected future incomes. This reduction in demand may more than offset the reduction in current output, even allowing for the rise in real cash balances. Moreover, if this is the case, $\partial z_g/\partial w < 0$ and the reader can easily find the quasi-equilibrium totally unstable.

Then, whether the economy may move to a full equilibrium depends, of course, on whether it exists and on the global properties of z_g.

Certainly we may interpret what Keynes says in quotation 2 in this light. (We have taken p_b as fixed and relied on the cash balance effect to do the work Keynes ascribes to changing interest rates. A full analysis would have to do without this simplification.) It is even possible to imagine a case in which $\partial z_g/\partial p < 0$ and $\partial z_g/\partial w > 0$, in which case the economy would exhibit oscillatory behavior, which may or may not be damped. The faster wages change in this case, the less likely is it that oscillations will be damped.

From all this, as well as from our existence discussions, we conclude that the Keynesian revolution cannot be understood if proper account is not taken of the powerful influence exerted by the future and past on the present and by the large modifications that must be introduced into both value theory and stability analysis, if the requisite futures markets are missing. Clearly, it is not possible, on the basis of this single example, to judge whether Keynes was right or wrong in his view that a price mechanism confined mainly to current markets for current goods is likely to go astray. He was certainly right in arguing that the theoretical evidence to be adduced from constructions in which these problems did not arise is not relevant. Indeed it could be argued that much of the literature devoted to explaining Keynes has really not concerned itself with this central point. This chapter can be taken as no more than a beginning of taking seriously the Keynes of the chapters on expectations and the functions of money.

Notes

The literature on this subject is vast, and this chapter has been influenced by many writers. The problems of proving the existence of an equilibrium in a monetary economy were first discussed by Hahn [1965] and later by Glustoff [1968]. The distinction between target and active excess demands is that of Clower [1965], and it has been extensively discussed by Leijonhufvud [1968].

Appendix A

POSITIVE MATRICES

This appendix proves the theorems on positive matrices that are used in this book. It is not an exhaustive treatment.

Notation. Let A be $n \times n$, with elements a_{ij}. If $a_{ij} > 0$, all i,j, write $A \gg 0$. If $a_{ij} \geq 0$, all i,j, and $a_{ij} > 0$, some i,j, write $A > 0$ If $a_{ij} \geq 0$, all i,j, write $A \geq 0$. As usual, S_n is the unit simplex in n space. Also, let

$$\Lambda = \{\lambda \mid \mathbf{x}A \geq \lambda\mathbf{x} \quad \text{for some } \mathbf{x} \in S_n, \lambda \geq 0\}.$$

Remark 1. For any matrix A, Λ is compact, that is, closed and bounded. For any $\lambda \in \Lambda$, let $\mathbf{x}$ be the vector for which $\mathbf{x}A \geq \lambda\mathbf{x}$, $\mathbf{x} \in S_n$, and let x_i be the largest component of $\mathbf{x}$. Then certainly $x_i \geq 1/n$. Furthermore, since S_n is compact, the range of $\mathbf{x}A$ as $\mathbf{x}$ ranges over S_n is bounded so that, for some M, $(\mathbf{x}A)_i \leq M$ for all $\mathbf{x} \in S_n$ and all i. Then

$$\lambda \leq n\lambda x_i \leq n(\mathbf{x}A)_i \leq nM,$$

so that Λ is bounded. Now let $\lambda^\nu \in \Lambda$, all ν, $\lambda^\nu \to \lambda^0$, and by definition, choose $\mathbf{x}^\nu \in S_n$ such that

$$\mathbf{x}^\nu A \geq \lambda^\nu \mathbf{x}^\nu.$$

Since S_n is compact, the sequence $\{\mathbf{x}^\nu\}$ has a limit point, say $\mathbf{x}^0$, in S_n. Then $\mathbf{x}^0 A \geq \lambda^0 \mathbf{x}^0$ so that $\lambda^0 \in \Lambda$, and Λ is closed as well as bounded. Note also that for $A > 0$, Λ is non-null (put $\lambda = 0$). Let

$$\lambda_0 = \max_{\lambda \in \Lambda} \lambda;$$

the maximum is attained for compact and non-null Λ. From the definition of λ_0, it is clearly real and is non-negative if $A > 0$.

THEOREM 1 (Perron). Let $A \gg 0$. Then

(a) there exists $\mathbf{x}^0 \gg \mathbf{0}$ such that $\mathbf{x}^0 A = \lambda_0 \mathbf{x}^0$,
(b) λ_0 exceeds the moduli of all other characteristic roots $\mathbf{x}$ of A.

(It is clear that $\lambda_0 > 0$.)

Proof. (a) There is some $\mathbf{x}^0 > \mathbf{0}$ such that $\mathbf{x}^0 A \geq \lambda_0 \mathbf{x}^0$. Let $\mathbf{y} = \mathbf{x}^0 A$. Then $\mathbf{y} \gg \mathbf{0}$ (since $A \gg 0$ and $\mathbf{x}^0 > \mathbf{0}$). Then, unless $\mathbf{x}^0 A = \lambda_0 \mathbf{x}^0$ (in which case $\mathbf{x}^0 \gg \mathbf{0}$), we have $\mathbf{y} > \lambda_0 \mathbf{x}^0$ or $\mathbf{y} - \lambda_0 \mathbf{x}^0 > \mathbf{0}$, so that $(\mathbf{y} - \lambda_0 \mathbf{x}^0) A \gg \mathbf{0}$ or $\mathbf{y}\mathbf{A} \gg \lambda_0 \mathbf{y}$. In that case, however, for some $\epsilon > 0$,

$$\mathbf{y} A \geq (\lambda_0 + \epsilon)\mathbf{y}.$$

Since $\mathbf{y} \gg \mathbf{0}$, $\mathbf{y}\mathbf{e} > 0$ (where it will be recalled that $\mathbf{e}$ is the vector all of whose components are 1). If $\mathbf{z} = \mathbf{y}/(\mathbf{y}\mathbf{e})$, then $\mathbf{z} \in S_n$, and

$$\mathbf{z} A \geq (\lambda_0 + \epsilon)\mathbf{z},$$

a contradiction of the definition of λ_0. This proves (a).

(b) Let $\lambda \neq \lambda_0$ be a characteristic root of A, and $\mathbf{z}$ the corresponding characteristic vector, $\mathbf{z}A = \lambda \mathbf{z}$. Let $\mathbf{z}^+$ be the vector in which all elements of z are replaced by their moduli; since $\mathbf{z} \neq \mathbf{0}$, $\mathbf{z}^+ > \mathbf{0}$. Since the modulus of a sum does not exceed the sum of the moduli and $A \geq 0$, $\mathbf{z}^+\mathbf{A} \geq |\lambda|\mathbf{z}^+$. From the construction of λ_0, $|\lambda| \leq \lambda_0$. Suppose $|\lambda| = \lambda_0$. Let $\delta > 0$ and small enough so that $A - \delta I \gg 0$. Evidently, $\lambda_0 - \delta$ is the largest positive characteristic root of $A - \delta I$ and bounds in absolute value all other roots of this matrix. But since $|\lambda| = \lambda_0$ and $\lambda \neq \lambda_0$, the imaginary part of λ is non-zero. An easy calculation shows that $|\lambda - \delta| > \lambda_0 - \delta$, a contradiction. Hence $\lambda_0 > |\lambda|$.

THEOREM 2. Let $A > 0$. Then

(a) there exists $\mathbf{x}^0 > \mathbf{0}$ such that $\mathbf{x}^0 A = \lambda_0 \mathbf{x}^0$,
(b) if λ is a characteristic root of A, then $|\lambda| \leq \lambda_0$.

Proof. Let U be the matrix all of whose elements are 1. Then for all $\delta > 0$, $A + \delta U \gg 0$. Thus, T.A.1 holds for this matrix for all $\delta > 0$. By an immediate limiting argument on δ, T.A.2 is established.

DEFINITION 1. A matrix, A, is said to be *decomposable* if there exists a permutation that, when applied simultaneously to the rows and columns, puts A in the form:

$$\begin{pmatrix} A_1 & A_2 \\ 0 & A_4 \end{pmatrix}.$$

If A is not decomposable, it is said to be *indecomposable*.

THEOREM 3. Let $A > 0$ and indecomposable. Then there exists $\mathbf{x}^0 \gg \mathbf{0}$ such that $\mathbf{x}^0 A = \lambda_0 A$, where λ_0 is the root described in T.A.2.

Proof. Suppose $\mathbf{x}^0$, as described in T.A.2, has zero components. Let $\mathbf{x}^0 = (\mathbf{x}^{01},\mathbf{x}^{02})$, where $\mathbf{x}^{01} \gg \mathbf{0}$ and $\mathbf{x}^{02} = \mathbf{0}$. Partition A conformably, and consider the equation

$$(\mathbf{x}^{01},\mathbf{x}^{02})\begin{pmatrix} A_1 & A_2 \\ A_3 & A_4 \end{pmatrix} = \lambda_0(\mathbf{x}^{01},\mathbf{x}^{02}).$$

Then $\mathbf{x}^{01}A_2 + \mathbf{x}^{02}A_4 = \lambda_0\mathbf{x}^{02}$ or, since $\mathbf{x}^{02} = \mathbf{0}$, $\mathbf{x}^{01}A_2 = 0$. Since $A_2 \geq 0$ and $\mathbf{x}^{01} \gg \mathbf{0}$, this is possible only if $A_2 = 0$. Then A is decomposable, contrary to hypothesis.

THEOREM 4. Let $A > 0$ and indecomposable, and $s > \lambda_0$. Then $sI - A$ is non-singular and $B = (sI - A)^{-1} \gg 0$.

Proof. (a) Suppose $sI - A$ singular. Then there exists $\mathbf{x} \neq \mathbf{0}$ so that $\mathbf{x}A = s\mathbf{x}$. Then $s > \lambda_0$ would be a characteristic root of A, contrary to T.A.2.

(b) From T.A.3 and hypothesis, $\mathbf{y}^0 \equiv \mathbf{x}^0(sI - A) = (s - \lambda_0)\mathbf{x}^0 \gg \mathbf{0}$. Now consider $\mathbf{x}(sI - A) = \mathbf{y}$, with $\mathbf{y} > \mathbf{0}$. The assertion $B \gg 0$ is equivalent to the statement $\mathbf{x} \gg \mathbf{0}$ for each such y. First it is shown that $\mathbf{x} > \mathbf{0}$.

Let

$$\theta = \min_i \frac{x_i}{x_i^0} \qquad \mathbf{z} = \mathbf{x} - \theta\mathbf{x}^0.$$

Then $\mathbf{z} \geq \mathbf{0}$, $z_r = 0$ for some r.

$$\mathbf{z}(sI - A) = \mathbf{y} - \theta\mathbf{y}^0 > -\theta\mathbf{y}^0,$$

or

$$s\mathbf{z} > \mathbf{z}A - \theta\mathbf{y}^0 \geq -\theta\mathbf{y}^0$$

since $\mathbf{z} \geq \mathbf{0}$ and $A > 0$. For the rth component this inequality becomes

$$0 = sz_r \geq -\theta y_r^0,$$

and since $y_r^0 > 0$, $\theta \geq 0$. By definition of θ, $\mathbf{x} \geq \mathbf{0}$, but since $\mathbf{x} \neq \mathbf{0}$ (otherwise $\mathbf{y} = \mathbf{0}$), $\mathbf{x} > \mathbf{0}$.

(c) We show that, in fact, $\mathbf{x} \gg \mathbf{0}$. Suppose not. Let $\mathbf{x} = (\mathbf{x}^1,\mathbf{x}^2)$, where $\mathbf{x}^1 \gg \mathbf{0}$ and $\mathbf{x}^2 = \mathbf{0}$. Partition $(sI - A)$ conformably, and consider

$$(\mathbf{x}^1,\mathbf{x}^2)\begin{pmatrix} sI - A_1 & -A_2 \\ -A_3 & sI - A_4 \end{pmatrix} > 0.$$

Then $\mathbf{0} \leq \mathbf{x}^1(-A_2) + \mathbf{x}^2(sI - A_4) = -\mathbf{x}^1 A_2$, and since $\mathbf{x}^1 \gg \mathbf{0}$ and $A_2 \geq 0$, this is possible only if $A_2 = 0$, which contradicts the hypothesis of indecomposability. Hence $\mathbf{x} \gg \mathbf{0}$.

Remark 2. If $A > 0$, but decomposable, and we know that for some $\mathbf{u} \gg \mathbf{0}$, $\mathbf{u}(sI - A) \gg \mathbf{0}$, then we may proceed as in (a) and (b) of the preceding proof to show that $(sI - A)^{-1} > 0$.

THEOREM 5. Let $A > 0$ and indecomposable,

$$r_i = \sum_j a_{ij}.$$

Then

$$\min_i r_i \leq \lambda_0 \leq \max_i r_i.$$

Proof. (a) Let $B > 0$ be a matrix of the same order as A, such that $A - B \geq 0$. Let μ be a characteristic root of B, and $\mathbf{y}$ the associated right characteristic vector. We show that $|\mu| \leq \lambda_0$. We have $B\mathbf{y} = \mu\mathbf{y}$ and $\mathbf{x}^0 A = \lambda_0 \mathbf{x}^0$. Let $\mathbf{y}^+$ have components $|y_i|$. Then $|\mu|\mathbf{y}^+ \leq B\mathbf{y}^+ \leq A\mathbf{y}^+$, and hence

$$|\mu|\mathbf{x}^0\mathbf{y}^+ \leq \mathbf{x}^0 A\mathbf{y}^+ = \lambda_0\mathbf{x}^0\mathbf{y}^+.$$

But $\mathbf{x}^0 \gg \mathbf{0}$, $\mathbf{y}^+ > \mathbf{0}$, so that $\mathbf{x}^0\mathbf{y}^+ > 0$ and $|\mu| \leq \lambda_0$.

(b) Let B be derived from A by multiplying every element in the jth row of A by

$$\frac{(\min r_i)}{r_j} \quad \text{for each } j.$$

Then every row sum of B is

$$\min_i r_i,$$

$B > 0$ and indecomposable. Let μ_0 be the dominant root of B as defined by T.A.2 and T.A.3 and $\mathbf{y}$ the associated right characteristic vector. By T.A.3, $\mathbf{y} \gg \mathbf{0}$. From (a), $\lambda_0\mathbf{y} \geq \mu_0\mathbf{y} = B\mathbf{y}$. Let

$$y_r = \min_i y_i.$$

Then

$$\lambda_0 y_r \geq \sum_j b_{rj} y_j \geq \left(\sum_j b_{rj}\right) y_r = (\min_i r_i) y_r,$$

which, since $y_r > 0$, establishes

$$\min_i r_i \leq \lambda_0.$$

It is left to the reader to establish the second part of the inequality.

Remark 3. By considering A', T.A.5 establishes also that

$$\min_j c_j \leq \lambda_0 \leq \max_j c_j,$$

where

$$c_j = \sum_j a_{ij}.$$

Appendix B

CONVEX AND RELATED SETS

1. Basic Definitions

Most of the concepts to be introduced in this section need little elaboration.

DEFINITION 1. A *linear space*, L, is a set of vectors such that

(a) if $\mathbf{x} \in L$, then $t\mathbf{x} \in L$ for any real t;
(b) if $\mathbf{x}^1 \in L$ and $\mathbf{x}^2 \in L$, then $\mathbf{x}^1 + \mathbf{x}^2 \in L$.

Sets are partially ordered by set inclusion. Hence, for any given family of sets, we can speak of a *minimal* member of the family, meaning a set in the family such that no other member is a subset of it. Similarly, a *maximal* member of the family is one that is not included in any other member.

Any set, S, may be included in a linear space modified by having the origin displaced to another point, that is, a set of the form $L + \{\mathbf{a}\}$, for some $\mathbf{a}$. Then for any $\mathbf{x} \in S$, $\mathbf{x} = \mathbf{x}' + \mathbf{a}$, for some $\mathbf{x}' \in L$, or equivalently, $\mathbf{x} - \mathbf{a} \in L$. Take any fixed $\mathbf{x}^0 \in S$, so that $\mathbf{x}^0 - \mathbf{a} \in L$. Since L is a linear space, $\mathbf{a} - \mathbf{x}^0 = (-1)(\mathbf{x}^0 - \mathbf{a}) \in L$, and so does $\mathbf{x} - \mathbf{x}^0 = (\mathbf{x} - \mathbf{a}) + (\mathbf{a} - \mathbf{x}^0)$. Hence, if $S \subset L + \{\mathbf{a}\}$ for some $\mathbf{a}$, $S \subset L + \{\mathbf{x}^0\}$ for any fixed $\mathbf{x}^0 \in S$. Then let $S \subset L + \{\mathbf{a}\}$ and also $S \subset L' + \{\mathbf{a}'\}$, where L and L' are linear spaces. Choose any $\mathbf{x}^0 \in S$; then $S \subset L + \{\mathbf{x}^0\}$, $S \subset L' + \{\mathbf{x}^0\}$, or $\mathbf{x} - \mathbf{x}^0$ belongs to both L and L', and therefore, to their intersection. Thus, if L'' is the intersection of all linear spaces L such that $S \subset L + \{\mathbf{a}\}$ for some $\mathbf{a}$, it is also true that $S \subset L'' + \{\mathbf{x}^0\}$. Since the intersection of any family of linear spaces is again a linear space, L'' must be the minimal linear space with the property $S \subset L + \{\mathbf{a}\}$ for some $\{\mathbf{a}\}$.

DEFINITION 2. The *linear space of* S, $L(S)$, is the minimal linear space with the property $S \subset L + \{\mathbf{a}\}$ for some $\mathbf{a}$. By the *dimension* of S, dim S, is meant the dimension of $L(S)$.

In what follows, a *relative neighborhood* of a point $\mathbf{x}^0 \in S$ is defined to be the intersection of a neighborhood of $\mathbf{x}^0$ with $L(S) + \{\mathbf{x}^0\}$. Then $\mathbf{x}^0$ is a *relative interior point* of S if it possesses a relative neighborhood entirely contained in S; $\mathbf{x}^0$ is a *relative boundary point* of S if every relative neighborhood of $\mathbf{x}^0$ contains points of both S and $\tilde{S}$ (the complement of S).

DEFINITION 3. For any finite set T, $\mathbf{x}'$ is said to be a *convex combination* of T if there exists a real-valued function, $\alpha(\mathbf{x})$, defined on T, such that

$$\alpha(\mathbf{x}) \geq 0 \qquad \text{all } \mathbf{x} \in T,$$

$$\sum_{\mathbf{x} \in T} \alpha(\mathbf{x}) = 1,$$

$$\mathbf{x}' = \sum_{\mathbf{x} \in T} \alpha(\mathbf{x})\mathbf{x}.$$

We will also say that T *spans* $\mathbf{x}'$ under the same circumstances. The point $\mathbf{x}'$ will be said to be a *proper convex combination* of T if, in addition to the above, $\alpha(\mathbf{x}) > 0$, all $\mathbf{x} \in T$. A *line segment* $[\mathbf{x}^1,\mathbf{x}^2]$ is the set of convex combinations of the set containing just the two elements $\mathbf{x}^1$ and $\mathbf{x}^2$.

DEFINITION 4. For any set S and any two points, $\mathbf{x}^1$ and $\mathbf{x}^2$, $\mathbf{x}^1$ is *visible* in S from $\mathbf{x}^2$ if $[\mathbf{x}^1,\mathbf{x}^2] \subset S$.

DEFINITION 5. S is *star shaped* (with *center* $\mathbf{x}^0$) if every point of S is visible from $\mathbf{x}^0$.

DEFINITION 6. S is *strictly star shaped* (with *center* $\mathbf{x}^0$) if there is a relative neighborhood N of $\mathbf{x}^0$ such that every point of S is visible from every point of N.

DEFINITION 7. S is *convex* if every point of S is visible from any other.

LEMMA 1. If S is convex, then it is strictly star shaped for some center.

Proof. Take any $\mathbf{x}^0 \in S$. Then, if $r = \dim S$, it follows from D.B.2 that there exist r elements of S, $\mathbf{x}^i$ $(i = 1, \ldots, r)$ such that the vectors $\mathbf{x}^i - \mathbf{x}^0$ are linearly independent. Let $\bar{\mathbf{x}}$ be any proper convex combination of the points $\mathbf{x}^i$ $(i = 0, \ldots, r)$. Now any point in S can be written uniquely as

$$\mathbf{x} = \mathbf{x}^0 + \sum_{i=1}^{r} \lambda_i(\mathbf{x}^i - \mathbf{x}^0) = \sum_{i=0}^{r} \lambda_i \mathbf{x}^i \qquad \text{with} \sum_{i=0}^{r} \lambda_i = 1.$$

If we write

$$\bar{\mathbf{x}} = \sum_{i=0}^{r} \bar{\lambda}_i \mathbf{x}^i \qquad \text{where } \bar{\lambda}_i > 0, \ \sum_{i=0}^{r} \bar{\lambda}_i = 1$$

we see that for any $\mathbf{x}$ in a sufficiently small relative neighborhood of $\bar{\mathbf{x}}$, the corresponding λ_i's must be non-negative, so that $\mathbf{x}$ is a convex combination of the points $\mathbf{x}^i$ $(i = 0, \ldots, r)$ and, therefore, belongs to S. Since S is convex, every point of S is visible from every point in this neighborhood.

2. Gauge Functions

For any set, S, and a given point, $\mathbf{x}^0$, we can define a function over $L(S)$ that in effect indicates how far along a line segment starting at $\mathbf{x}^0$ the set S extends.

DEFINITION 8. The *gauge function* $p(\mathbf{x} \mid \mathbf{x}^0, S)$ for a given set S and point $\mathbf{x}^0$ in the relative interior of S is defined for all $\mathbf{x} \in L(S)$ as

$$p(\mathbf{x} \mid \mathbf{x}^0, S) = \inf\left\{p \mid p > 0, \quad \mathbf{x}^0 + \frac{\mathbf{x}}{p} \in S\right\}.$$

Since $\mathbf{x}^0$ is a relative interior point, there will always exist some $p > 0$ for which $\mathbf{x}^0 + (\mathbf{x}/p) \in S$ for any $\mathbf{x} \in L(S)$, so that the gauge function is always defined.

Where the context makes the designation of $\mathbf{x}^0$ and S clear or unnecessary, the gauge function will be referred to simply as $p(\mathbf{x})$. To state some properties of gauge functions, we define two properties of real-valued functions.

DEFINITION 9. The function $f(\mathbf{x})$ defined over a linear space is said to be *positive homogeneous* if $f(t\mathbf{x}) = tf(\mathbf{x})$ for all $\mathbf{x}$ and all $t > 0$.

DEFINITION 10. The function $f(\mathbf{x})$ defined over a linear space is said to be *subadditive* if for every $\mathbf{x}^1$ and $\mathbf{x}^2$, $f(\mathbf{x}^1 + \mathbf{x}^2) \leq f(\mathbf{x}^1) + f(\mathbf{x}^2)$.

THEOREM 1. The following properties hold for gauge functions:

(a) $p(\mathbf{0}) = \mathbf{0}$;
(b) $p(\mathbf{x})$ is positive homogeneous;
(c) if S is bounded, then $p(\mathbf{x} \mid \mathbf{x}^0, S) > 0$ for all $\mathbf{x} \neq \mathbf{0}$;
(d) if $p(\mathbf{x} \mid \mathbf{x}^0, S) > p$, then $\mathbf{x}^0 + (\mathbf{x}/p) \notin S$;
(e) if S is star shaped with center $\mathbf{x}^0$ and $p(\mathbf{x} \mid \mathbf{x}^0, S) < p$, then $\mathbf{x}^0 + (\mathbf{x}/p) \in S$;
(f) if $p(\mathbf{x} - \mathbf{x}^0 \mid \mathbf{x}^0, S) > 1$, then $\mathbf{x} \notin S$;
(g) if S is star shaped with center $\mathbf{x}^0$ and $\mathbf{p}(\mathbf{x} - \mathbf{x}^0 \mid \mathbf{x}^0, S) < 1$, then $\mathbf{x} \in S$;
(h) if S is closed and star shaped with center $\mathbf{x}^0$, then $\mathbf{x} \in S$ if and only if $p(\mathbf{x} - \mathbf{x}^0 \mid \mathbf{x}^0, S) \leq 1$;
(i) $p(\mathbf{x})$ is bounded on every bounded subset of the linear space on which it is defined;
(j) if S is convex, then $p(\mathbf{x} \mid \mathbf{x}^0, S)$ is subadditive.

Proof. Parts (a)–(d) follow immediately from the definitions. Suppose the hypothesis of (e) holds. Then, by D.B.8, there exists $p' < p$ such that $\mathbf{x}^0 + (\mathbf{x}/p') \in S$. But

$$\mathbf{x}^0 + \frac{\mathbf{x}}{p} = \frac{p'}{p}\left(\mathbf{x}^0 + \left(\frac{\mathbf{x}}{p'}\right)\right) + \left(1 - \frac{p'}{p}\right)\mathbf{x}^0.$$

Since $\mathbf{x}^0 + (\mathbf{x}/p')$ is visible from $\mathbf{x}^0$ by hypothesis, and $p' < p$ by construction, $\mathbf{x}^0 + (\mathbf{x}/p) \in S$, as claimed. Parts (f) and (g) follow from (d) and (e), respectively, if $\mathbf{x}$ is replaced by $\mathbf{x} - \mathbf{x}^0$ and p set equal to 1. In view of (f) and (g) it is sufficient to show that $p(\mathbf{x} - \mathbf{x}^0) = 1$ implies that $\mathbf{x} \in S$ to prove (h). For such $\mathbf{x}$, $\mathbf{x}^0 + (\mathbf{x} - \mathbf{x}^0)/p \in S$ for all $p > 1$, by (e); for closed S, then $\mathbf{x} = \mathbf{x}^0 + (\mathbf{x} - \mathbf{x}^0)/1 \in S$.

If (i) did not hold, then there would be a bounded sequence $\{\mathbf{x}^\nu\}$ for which $p(\mathbf{x}^\nu) \to \infty$. Then we could certainly choose a sequence $\{p^\nu\}$ such that $p^\nu < p(\mathbf{x}^\nu)$, $p^\nu \to \infty$. By (d), $\mathbf{x}^0 + (\mathbf{x}^\nu/p^\nu) \notin S$. But this sequence approaches $\mathbf{x}^0$, in contradiction to D.B.8, which requires that $\mathbf{x}^0$ be a relative interior point of S.

Finally, to prove (j), we can choose $p_i > p(\mathbf{x}^i)$, $i = 1,2$, so that $\mathbf{x}^0 + (\mathbf{x}^i/p_i) \in S$ by (e). Since S is convex, the point

$$\mathbf{x}^0 + \frac{\mathbf{x}^1 + \mathbf{x}^2}{p_1 + p_2} = \frac{p_1}{p_1 + p_2}\left(\mathbf{x}^0 + \frac{\mathbf{x}^1}{p_1}\right) + \frac{p_2}{p_1 + p_2}\left(\mathbf{x}^0 + \frac{\mathbf{x}^2}{p_2}\right)$$

also belongs to S. By definition, $p(\mathbf{x}^1 + \mathbf{x}^2) \leq p_1 + p_2$, but p_i

can be chosen arbitrarily close to $p(\mathbf{x}^i)$, so it must be that $p(\mathbf{x}^1 + \mathbf{x}^2) \leq p(\mathbf{x}^1) + p(\mathbf{x}^2)$.

In Section 6.4, it turned out to be useful to show that a strictly star-shaped set is equivalent in certain essential ways to a compact convex set; more exactly, it is a continuous image of such a set. This follows easily from the continuity of the gauge function for such sets.

THEOREM 2. If S is strictly star shaped with center $\mathbf{x}^0$, then the gauge function for the point $\mathbf{x}^0$ and S is continuous.

Proof. Let $\{\mathbf{x}^\nu\}$ be a sequence such that $\mathbf{x}^\nu \to \mathbf{x}$. By T.B.1(i), then, the sequence $\{p(\mathbf{x}^\nu)\}$ is bounded. Let p^* be any limit point; we seek to prove that $p^* = p(\mathbf{x})$.

For notational convenience let $\mathbf{x}^0 = \mathbf{0}$; there is clearly no loss of generality.

Let $\{\epsilon_\nu\}$ be a sequence of positive real numbers converging to 0, $p_\nu = p(\mathbf{x}^\nu) + \epsilon_\nu$. By T.B.1(e), $\mathbf{x}^\nu/p_\nu \in S$, all ν. By the hypothesis that S is strictly star shaped, it is possible to choose $\epsilon > 0$ such that every element of S is visible from every $\mathbf{x}$ for which $|\mathbf{x}| \leq \epsilon$. In particular, therefore, $\mathbf{x}^\nu/p_\nu$ is visible from $\epsilon(\mathbf{x} - \mathbf{x}^\nu)/|\mathbf{x} - \mathbf{x}^\nu|$, all ν. Let

$$\begin{aligned}\mathbf{x}'^\nu &= \frac{\mathbf{x}}{p_\nu + (|\mathbf{x} - \mathbf{x}^\nu|/\epsilon)} \\ &= \frac{\epsilon p_\nu}{\epsilon p_\nu + |\mathbf{x} - \mathbf{x}^\nu|}\frac{\mathbf{x}^\nu}{p_\nu} + \frac{|\mathbf{x} - \mathbf{x}^\nu|}{\epsilon p_\nu + |\mathbf{x} - \mathbf{x}^\nu|}\frac{\epsilon(\mathbf{x} - \mathbf{x}^\nu)}{|\mathbf{x} - \mathbf{x}^\nu|};\end{aligned}$$

then $\mathbf{x}'^\nu$ must lie in S; by the definition of a gauge function, then,

$$p(\mathbf{x}) \leq p_\nu + (|\mathbf{x} - \mathbf{x}^\nu|/\epsilon).$$

By letting ν approach infinity, we see that $p(\mathbf{x}) \leq p^*$. The argument is illustrated in Figure B-1a.

It remains to show that $p(\mathbf{x}) \geq p^*$; this part of the proof is illustrated in Figure B-1b. Note that $p(\mathbf{x}) = |\mathbf{x}|p(\mathbf{x}/|\mathbf{x}|)$ if $\mathbf{x} \neq 0$ by T.B.1(b). Since $p(\mathbf{x}/|\mathbf{x}|)$ is bounded, by T.B.1(i), it easily follows that

$$\lim_{\mathbf{x}\to\mathbf{0}} p(\mathbf{x}) = 0 = p(\mathbf{0}),$$

by T.B.1(a). Furthermore, if $\mathbf{x} \neq \mathbf{0}$, then it follows also that it suffices to prove continuity for all $\mathbf{x}$ such that $|\mathbf{x}| = 1$. Let $\mathbf{x}^1\mathbf{x}^2$ denote the usual *inner product* of $\mathbf{x}^1$ and $\mathbf{x}^2$, that is,

$$\mathbf{x}^1\mathbf{x}^2 = \sum_i x_i^1 x_i^2.$$

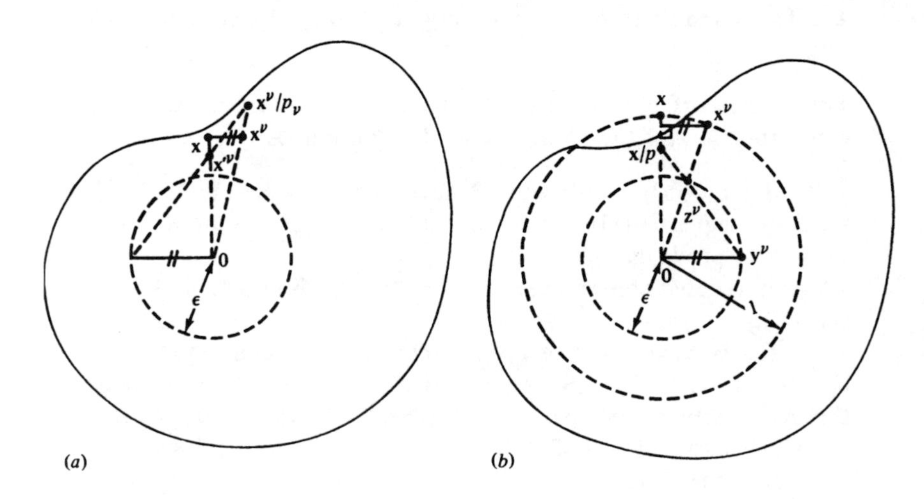

LEGEND: // Two lines so marked are parallel

⌟ Right angle

Figure B-1

By a well-known inequality,

$$(\mathbf{x}^\nu\mathbf{x})^2 \leq |\mathbf{x}^\nu|^2|\mathbf{x}|^2 = 1.$$

Then we can define $D_\nu = \sqrt{1 - (\mathbf{x}^\nu\mathbf{x})^2}$; clearly $D_\nu \to 0$. Also,

$$\begin{aligned}|\mathbf{x}^\nu - (\mathbf{x}^\nu\mathbf{x})\mathbf{x}|^2 &= |\mathbf{x}^\nu|^2 - 2(\mathbf{x}^\nu\mathbf{x})^2 + (\mathbf{x}^\nu\mathbf{x})^2|\mathbf{x}|^2 \\ &= 1 - (\mathbf{x}^\nu\mathbf{x})^2 = D_\nu^2,\end{aligned}$$

or $|\mathbf{x}^\nu - (\mathbf{x}^\nu\mathbf{x})\mathbf{x}| = D_\nu$. For all ν for which $D_\nu > 0$, let

$$\mathbf{y}^\nu = \frac{\epsilon}{D_\nu}[\mathbf{x}^\nu - (\mathbf{x}^\nu\mathbf{x})\mathbf{x}].$$

Then $|\mathbf{y}^\nu| = \epsilon$ for all ν for which $D_\nu > 0$; choose $\mathbf{y}^\nu$ arbitrarily subject to the condition $|\mathbf{y}^\nu| = \epsilon$ for all ν for which $D_\nu = 0$.

Choose $p > p(\mathbf{x})$, so that $\mathbf{x}/p \in S$, by T.B.1(e). Then $\mathbf{x}/p$ is visible from $\mathbf{y}^\nu$, all ν. By construction,

$$\mathbf{x}^\nu = (\mathbf{x}^\nu\mathbf{x})p\,\frac{\mathbf{x}}{p} + \frac{D_\nu}{\epsilon}\,\mathbf{y}^\nu.$$

Since $D_\nu/\epsilon \geq 0$ while $(\mathbf{x}^\nu\mathbf{x})p \to p > 0$, it follows that for ν large,

$$\mathbf{z}^\nu = \frac{\mathbf{x}^\nu}{(\mathbf{x}^\nu\mathbf{x})p + (D_\nu/\epsilon)}$$

is a convex combination of $\mathbf{x}/p$ and $\mathbf{y}^\nu$ and therefore belongs to S, by hypothesis. Therefore, $p(\mathbf{x}^\nu) \leq (\mathbf{x}^\nu\mathbf{x})p + (D_\nu/\epsilon)$. Let ν approach infinity; then $p^* \leq p$. Since p was any number exceeding $p(\mathbf{x})$, $p^* \leq p(\mathbf{x})$, as was to be proved.

Corollary 2. If S is convex, then for some $\mathbf{x}^0$, the gauge function, $p(\mathbf{x} \mid \mathbf{x}^0, S)$ is continuous.

Proof. T.B.2, Lemma B.1.

THEOREM 3. For any compact, strictly star shaped set S, there is a compact convex set C and a continuous function $\mathbf{T}(\mathbf{x})$ that maps C into S and whose unique inverse maps S into C.

Proof. Take C to be the unit sphere, $\{\mathbf{x} \mid |\mathbf{x}| \leq 1\}$. Let $\mathbf{x}^0$ be a center of the strictly star shaped set S as defined in D.B.6. Let the mapping be defined by

$$\mathbf{T}(\mathbf{x}) = \begin{cases} \mathbf{x}^0 + \dfrac{\mathbf{x}|\mathbf{x}|}{p(\mathbf{x})} & \text{if } \mathbf{x} \neq \mathbf{0}, \\ \mathbf{x}^0 & \text{if } \mathbf{x} = \mathbf{0}. \end{cases}$$

Here $p(\mathbf{x})$ is the gauge function for S from $\mathbf{x}^0$. Note that $\mathbf{T}(\mathbf{x})$ is well defined since $p(\mathbf{x}) > 0$ for $\mathbf{x} \neq \mathbf{0}$ by T.B.1(c). From T.B.2, $\mathbf{T}(\mathbf{x})$ is clearly continuous for $\mathbf{x} \neq 0$. Also, for $\mathbf{x} \neq 0$, it follows from the positive homogeneity of $p(\mathbf{x})$ that

$$\mathbf{T}(\mathbf{x}) = \mathbf{x}^0 + \frac{\mathbf{x}}{p(\mathbf{x}/|\mathbf{x}|)}.$$

Let B be the boundary of the unit sphere; since p is continuous and positive there, $p(\mathbf{x})$ is bounded away from 0 for $\mathbf{x} \in B$. If $\mathbf{x} \neq \mathbf{0}$, $\mathbf{x}/|\mathbf{x}| \in B$, so that $p(\mathbf{x}/|\mathbf{x}|)$ is bounded away from 0 for $\mathbf{x} \neq 0$. Hence, as $\mathbf{x}$ approaches $\mathbf{0}$, $\mathbf{x}/p(\mathbf{x}/|\mathbf{x}|)$ approaches 0, so that $\mathbf{T}(\mathbf{x})$ approaches $\mathbf{x}^0$ and is continuous.

Again using the positive homogeneity of the gauge function,

$$p[\mathbf{T}(\mathbf{x}) - \mathbf{x}^0] = p\left(\frac{\mathbf{x}|\mathbf{x}|}{p(\mathbf{x})}\right) = \frac{|\mathbf{x}|}{p(\mathbf{x})}p(\mathbf{x}) = |\mathbf{x}|.$$

From T.B.1(h), $\mathbf{T}(\mathbf{x}) \in S$ if and only if $|\mathbf{x}| \leq 1$, so that S is indeed the image of C under the mapping $\mathbf{T}(\mathbf{x})$. It is easy to see that $\mathbf{T}(\mathbf{x})$ has a unique inverse.

3. Support and Separation Theorems

Consider a convex set C and the linear space $L(C)$. A hyperplane in $L(C)$ defines two half-spaces, the sets of points not above and not below the hyperplane. A *separating hyperplane* for two disjoint sets, C_1 and C_2, is one such that C_1 is contained in one and C_2 in the other of the half-spaces.

In establishing the existence of separating hyperplanes, we shall make use of the gauge function and of the Hahn–Banach theorem for finite-dimensional spaces.

DEFINITION 11. The function $f(\mathbf{x})$ defined over a linear space is said to be *linear* if $f(t\mathbf{x}) = tf(\mathbf{x})$ for all real t and $f(\mathbf{x}^1 + \mathbf{x}^2) = f(\mathbf{x}^1) + f(\mathbf{x}^2)$ for all $\mathbf{x}^1$ and $\mathbf{x}^2$.

THEOREM 4. Let $p(\mathbf{x})$ be a positive homogeneous, subadditive function defined on a linear space L and $f(\mathbf{x})$ a linear function defined on a linear space L' contained in L. If $f(\mathbf{x}) \leq p(\mathbf{x})$ for all $\mathbf{x} \in L'$, then there exists a linear function $F(\mathbf{x})$ defined on L such that

(a) $F(\mathbf{x}) = f(\mathbf{x})$ for all $\mathbf{x} \in L'$,
(b) $F(\mathbf{x}) \leq p(\mathbf{x})$ for all $x \in L$.

Proof. It suffices to establish the theorem for the case in which the dimension of L is one greater than that of L', for then the general case follows by straightforward induction.

In that case, let $\mathbf{u}^0$ be any element of L not in L'. Then obviously any $\mathbf{x} \in L$ can be written $\mathbf{x} = \mathbf{x}' + t\mathbf{u}^0$, where $\mathbf{x}' \in L'$, and this in only one way.

Now take any $\mathbf{x}^i \in L'$ $(i = 1,2)$. By hypothesis and the definitions,

$$\begin{aligned} f(\mathbf{x}^1) + f(\mathbf{x}^2) &= f(\mathbf{x}^1 + \mathbf{x}^2) \leq p(\mathbf{x}^1 + \mathbf{x}^2) \\ &= p[(\mathbf{x}^1 - \mathbf{u}^0) + (\mathbf{x}^2 + \mathbf{u}^0)] \\ &\leq p(\mathbf{x}^1 - \mathbf{u}^0) + p(\mathbf{x}^2 + \mathbf{u}^0), \end{aligned}$$

the last by the subadditivity of $p(\mathbf{x})$. Equivalently,

$$f(\mathbf{x}^1) - p(\mathbf{x}^1 - \mathbf{u}^0) \leq -f(\mathbf{x}^2) + p(\mathbf{x}^2 + \mathbf{u}^0) \qquad \text{all } \mathbf{x}^1, \mathbf{x}^2 \in L'.$$

Since the left-hand side depends only on $\mathbf{x}^1$ and the right-hand side on $\mathbf{x}^2$ and these two variables are independent, there must be a scalar α such that

$$f(\mathbf{x}^1) - p(\mathbf{x}^1 - \mathbf{u}^0) \leq \alpha \leq -f(\mathbf{x}^2) + p(\mathbf{x}^2 + \mathbf{u}^0), \quad \text{all } \mathbf{x}^1, \mathbf{x}^2 \in L'. \tag{1}$$

Then we define $F(\mathbf{x}) = f(\mathbf{x}') + \alpha t$ when $\mathbf{x} = \mathbf{x}' + t\mathbf{u}^0$, $\mathbf{x}' \in L'$. Clearly, $F(\mathbf{x})$ is a linear function, and it coincides with $f(\mathbf{x})$ for $\mathbf{x} \in L'$, that is, when $t = 0$. It remains to show that $F(\mathbf{x}' + t\mathbf{u}^0) \leq p(\mathbf{x}' + t\mathbf{u}^0)$ for $\mathbf{x} \in L'$, $t \neq 0$. First assume $t > 0$. Then use the second inequality in (1) with $\mathbf{x}^2 = \mathbf{x}'/t$.

$$\begin{aligned} F(\mathbf{x}' + t\mathbf{u}^0) &= f(\mathbf{x}') + \alpha t \leq f(\mathbf{x}') - tf\left(\frac{\mathbf{x}'}{t}\right) + tp\left(\frac{\mathbf{x}'}{t} + \mathbf{u}^0\right) \\ &= f(\mathbf{x}') - f(\mathbf{x}') + p(\mathbf{x}' + t\mathbf{u}^0) = p(\mathbf{x}' + t\mathbf{u}^0), \end{aligned}$$

where use has been made of the properties $tf(\mathbf{x}') = f(t\mathbf{x}')$, all t, $tp(\mathbf{x}) = p(t\mathbf{x})$ for $t > 0$.

For the case $t < 0$, use the first inequality in (1), and let $\mathbf{x}^1 = -\mathbf{x}'/t$; positive homogeneity of $p(\mathbf{x})$ implies $-tp(\mathbf{x}) = p(-t\mathbf{x})$.

$$\begin{aligned} F(\mathbf{x}' + t\mathbf{u}^0) &= f(\mathbf{x}') + \alpha t \leq f(\mathbf{x}') + tf\left(\frac{-\mathbf{x}'}{t}\right) - tp\left(\frac{-\mathbf{x}'}{t} - u^0\right) \\ &= p(\mathbf{x}' + t\mathbf{u}^0), \end{aligned}$$

as was to be proved.

THEOREM 5 (First Separation Theorem). Let C be a convex set, $\mathbf{x}^1$ belong to $L(C)$, but not to C. Then there exists a point $\mathbf{x}^0$ in the relative interior of C and a linear function, $F(\mathbf{x})$, defined on $L(C)$, such that for all $\mathbf{x} \in C$, $F(\mathbf{x} - \mathbf{x}^0) \leq F(\mathbf{x}^1 - \mathbf{x}^0)$, with $F(\mathbf{x})$ not identically 0. If C is closed, then there is a constant $c < F(\mathbf{x}^1 - \mathbf{x}^0)$ such that $F(\mathbf{x} - \mathbf{x}^0) \leq c$ for all $\mathbf{x} \in C$.

Proof. Choose $\mathbf{x}^0$ in the relative interior of C, and let $p(\mathbf{x}) = p(\mathbf{x} \mid \mathbf{x}^0, C)$ be the gauge function. Let L' be the one-dimensional space consisting of all points $\mathbf{x} = t(\mathbf{x}^1 - \mathbf{x}^0)$ for all t. On L', define $f(\mathbf{x}) = tp(\mathbf{x}^1 - \mathbf{x}^0)$; it is certainly a linear function. For $t > 0$, $f(\mathbf{x}) = p[t(\mathbf{x}^1 - \mathbf{x}^0)] = p(\mathbf{x})$, by the homogeneity of p; for $t \leq 0$, $f(\mathbf{x}) \leq 0 \leq p(\mathbf{x})$, so that $f(\mathbf{x}) \leq p(\mathbf{x})$, all $\mathbf{x} \in L'$. By T.B.4, there exists a linear function $F(\mathbf{x})$ on $L(C)$ such that $f(\mathbf{x}) = F(\mathbf{x})$ for $\mathbf{x} \in L'$, $F(\mathbf{x}) \leq p(\mathbf{x})$ for all $\mathbf{x} \in L(C)$. From T.B.1(f), $p(\mathbf{x} - \mathbf{x}^0) \leq 1$

for $\mathbf{x} \in C$. Let $c = 1$; then $F(\mathbf{x} - \mathbf{x}^0) \leq p(\mathbf{x} - \mathbf{x}^0) \leq c$ for all $\mathbf{x} \in C$. Since $\mathbf{x}^1 \notin C$, it follows from T.B.1(g) that $p(\mathbf{x}^1 - \mathbf{x}^0) \geq 1 = c$, while if C is closed, we must have $p(\mathbf{x}^1 - \mathbf{x}^0) > c$ by T.B.1(h). Finally, by construction, $F(\mathbf{x}^1 - \mathbf{x}^0) = f(\mathbf{x}^1 - \mathbf{x}^0) = p(\mathbf{x}^1 - \mathbf{x}^0)$.

Corollary 5. Let C be a convex set of the full dimensionality of the space, $\mathbf{x}^1 \notin C$. Then there exists a row vector $\mathbf{y} \neq 0$ such that $\mathbf{yx} \geq \mathbf{yx}^1$ for all $\mathbf{x} \in C$. If C is closed, there is a constant $c > \mathbf{yx}^1$ such that $\mathbf{yx} \geq c$ for all $\mathbf{x} \in C$.

Proof. Let $F(\mathbf{x})$ have the properties specified in T.B.5. Then $F(\mathbf{x})$ is a linear function over the entire space. Let $\mathbf{e}^i$ be the ith unit vector (with 1 in the ith place and 0 elsewhere); then any vector $\mathbf{x}$ can be written as

$$\mathbf{x} = \sum_i x_i \mathbf{e}^i.$$

Then

$$-F(\mathbf{x}) = -F\left(\sum_i x_i \mathbf{e}^i\right) = -\sum_i x_i F(\mathbf{e}^i) = \sum_i y_i x_i = \mathbf{yx},$$

where $\mathbf{y}$ is the row vector with components $y_i = -F(\mathbf{e}^i)$. Since $F(\mathbf{x})$ is not identically zero, $\mathbf{y} \neq 0$. Then by T.B.5, $\mathbf{y}(\mathbf{x} - \mathbf{x}^0) \geq \mathbf{y}(\mathbf{x}^1 - \mathbf{x}^0)$, all $\mathbf{x} \in C$, or, equivalently, $\mathbf{yx} \geq \mathbf{yx}^1$.

THEOREM 6 (Second Separation Theorem). Let C_1 be a convex set of the full dimensionality of the space, C_2 a convex set disjoint from C_1. Then there exists $\mathbf{y} \neq \mathbf{0}$ and scalar c such that $\mathbf{yx} \geq c$, all $\mathbf{x} \in C_1$, $\mathbf{yx} \leq c$, all $\mathbf{x} \in C_2$.

Proof. Let $C = C_1 - C_2$. If $\mathbf{x}^1$ is an interior point of C_1 (one exists by hypothesis) and $\mathbf{x}^2$ any element of C_2, then $\mathbf{x}^1 + \mathbf{u} \in C_1$ for all $\mathbf{u}$ sufficiently small in absolute value, so that, by definition, $\mathbf{x}^1 + \mathbf{u} - \mathbf{x}^2 = (\mathbf{x}^1 - \mathbf{x}^2) + \mathbf{u} \in C_1 - C_2$ for all such $\mathbf{u}$. By definition, $\mathbf{x}^1 - \mathbf{x}^2$ is an interior point of $C_1 - C_2$, which must therefore have the full dimensionality of the space. Also, since C_1 and C_2 are disjoint, it is impossible that $\mathbf{x}^1 - \mathbf{x}^2 = 0$ for any $\mathbf{x}^1 \in C_1$, $\mathbf{x}^2 \in C_2$; hence, $\mathbf{0} \notin C_1 - C_2$. Then Corollary 5 implies that for some $\mathbf{y} \neq \mathbf{0}$, $\mathbf{yx} \geq 0$ for all $\mathbf{x} \in C_1 - C_2$, or by definition, $\mathbf{yx}^1 \geq \mathbf{yx}^2$ for all $\mathbf{x}^1 \in C_1$, $\mathbf{x}^2 \in C_2$. Since the two variables are independent, there must be a constant c such that

$$\mathbf{yx}^1 \geq c \geq \mathbf{yx}^2 \qquad \text{for all } \mathbf{x}^1 \in C_1,\ \mathbf{x}^2 \in C_2.$$

4. Convex Hulls and Vector Sums

DEFINITION 12. The *convex hull* of a set S, con S, is the minimal convex set that includes S.

That every set possesses a convex hull can easily be seen. First, note that the intersection of the members of any family of sets containing S must itself contain S. Now consider the intersection of any family of convex sets. If $\mathbf{x}^1$ and $\mathbf{x}^2$ are any two members of the intersection, they belong to all members of the family. Since each is convex, each contains the line segment $[\mathbf{x}^1,\mathbf{x}^2]$, which by the preceding remark, must also be contained in the intersection. Thus, the intersection of a family of convex sets is also convex. From these remarks, it follows that the intersection of all convex sets containing S is a convex set containing S; by construction, this intersection is included in any convex set containing S and is therefore the minimal set of this type. We note an obvious characterization of convex hulls.

THEOREM 7. (a) If S is finite, con S is the set of all convex combinations of S.

(b) For any S, con $S = \{\mathbf{x} \mid T$ spans $\mathbf{x}$ for some finite subset T of S with at most $n + 1$ elements$\}$, where n is the dimensionality of the space.

Proof. It is obvious that if $T \subset S$, then con $T \subset$ con S, and we shall use this fact repeatedly. First, we note that if T is a finite subset of a convex set C and T spans $\mathbf{x}$, then $\mathbf{x} \in C$. We prove this by induction on the number of elements of T. If T contains two elements, this statement is just the definition of convexity. Suppose true when T has m members, and let T with $m + 1$ members span $\mathbf{x}$. Then there is a real-valued function $\alpha(\mathbf{x}')$ defined on T, with

$$\mathbf{x} = \sum_{\mathbf{x}' \in T} \alpha(\mathbf{x}')\mathbf{x}' \qquad \sum_{\mathbf{x}' \in T} \alpha(\mathbf{x}') = 1,$$

$$\alpha(\mathbf{x}') \geq 0, \qquad \text{all } \mathbf{x}' \in T.$$

Choose $\mathbf{x}^0 \in T$ so that $\alpha(\mathbf{x}^0) < 1$, and let $T' = T \sim \{\mathbf{x}^0\}$; T' has m members. Let $\beta(\mathbf{x}') = \alpha(\mathbf{x}')/[1 - \alpha(\mathbf{x}^0)]$ for $\mathbf{x}' \in T'$. Then

$$\mathbf{x} = [1 - \alpha(\mathbf{x}^0)]\mathbf{x}^1 + \alpha(\mathbf{x}^0)\mathbf{x}^0,$$

where

$$\mathbf{x}^1 = \sum_{\mathbf{x}' \in T'} \beta(\mathbf{x}')\mathbf{x}'.$$

Since $\mathbf{x}^1$ is spanned by T', $\mathbf{x}^1 \in C$ by the induction hypothesis; $\mathbf{x}^0 \in C$ by hypothesis; hence $\mathbf{x} \in C$ by the definition of convexity.

If C is convex and T a finite subset of C, then every convex combination of T belongs to C. (2)

(a) In (2) if we replace T by S and C by any convex set containing S, then we can see that every convex combination of S belongs to every convex set containing S. But the set of convex combinations of S is easily seen to be itself convex. Hence the set of convex combinations of S must be the convex hull of S by D.B.12, since it is a convex set containing S and contained in every convex set containing S.

(b) For general S, con $T \subset$ con S, for T a finite subset of S. Let $S^* = \{\mathbf{x} \mid T \text{ spans } \mathbf{x} \text{ for some finite subset } T \text{ of } S\}$. Then clearly $S^* \subset$ con S. By considering the one-element subsets of S, in particular, it is obvious that $S \subset S^*$ and therefore con $S \subset$ con S^*. Hence it is necessary only to show that S^* is convex. If $\mathbf{x}$ is spanned by T, it is certainly spanned by any finite set containing T; we need only extend the definition of $\alpha(\mathbf{x})$ by letting $\alpha(\mathbf{x}) = 0$ for $\mathbf{x} \notin T$. Then, if $\mathbf{x}^1$ and $\mathbf{x}^2 \in S^*$, they are spanned by finite subsets T_1 and T_2, respectively. Then both are spanned by the finite subset $T_1 \cup T_2$, and hence any convex combination of them is spanned by $T_1 \cup T_2$ and therefore belongs to S^*.

It remains to show that if $\mathbf{x} \in S^*$, $\mathbf{x}$ is spanned by a finite subset of S with no more than $n + 1$ elements. For any $\mathbf{x} \in S^*$, let T be the spanning set with the least number of members. If

$$\mathbf{x} = \sum_{\mathbf{x} \in T} \alpha(\mathbf{x}')\mathbf{x}',$$

where

$$\alpha(\mathbf{x}') \geq 0 \qquad \sum_{\mathbf{x}' \in T} \alpha(\mathbf{x}') = 1,$$

then it must be that $\alpha(\mathbf{x}') > 0$ for all $\mathbf{x}' \in T$; otherwise such an $\mathbf{x}'$ could be deleted and the remainder of the set would still span $\mathbf{x}$, whereas we have chosen T to have the least possible number of members. Suppose, then, $\alpha(\mathbf{x}') > 0$, all $\mathbf{x}' \in T$, and T has more than $n + 1$ members. Associate with each member of T the corresponding $(n + 1)$-dimensional vector obtained by adding 1 as the $(n + 1)$st component. Write such a vector as $(\mathbf{x}',1)$, where $\mathbf{x}' \in T$. Since there are more than $n + 1$ of them, they are linearly dependent. We can find a real function $c(\mathbf{x}')$ defined for $\mathbf{x}' \in T$ such that

$$\sum_{\mathbf{x}' \in T} c(\mathbf{x}')(\mathbf{x}',1) = 0 \qquad c(\mathbf{x}') \neq 0 \text{ for some } \mathbf{x}' \in T.$$

Then

$$\sum_{\mathbf{x}' \in T} c(\mathbf{x}')\mathbf{x}' = 0 \qquad \sum_{\mathbf{x}' \in T} c(\mathbf{x}') = 0.$$

Let $\beta(\mathbf{x}') = \alpha(\mathbf{x}') + tc(\mathbf{x}')$; then

$$\sum_{\mathbf{x}' \in T} \beta(\mathbf{x}') = 1 \qquad \sum_{\mathbf{x}' \in T} \beta(\mathbf{x}')\mathbf{x}' = \mathbf{x}.$$

Since $-c(\mathbf{x}')$ satisfies the same conditions as $c(\mathbf{x}')$, we can assume without loss of generality that $c(\mathbf{x}') < 0$ for some $\mathbf{x}' \in T$. Then $\beta(\mathbf{x}') > 0$ for all $\mathbf{x}' \in T$ when $t = 0$, $\beta(\mathbf{x}') < 0$ for some $\mathbf{x}'$ for t sufficiently large. There is, then, a largest $t = \bar{t}$ for which $\beta(\mathbf{x}') \geq 0$, all $\mathbf{x}' \in T$. For this value, $\beta(\mathbf{x}') = 0$ for some $\mathbf{x}'$, so that $\mathbf{x}$ is spanned by a smaller set, contrary to hypothesis. Hence T contains, at most, $n + 1$ elements.

The operation of taking a convex hull commutes with that of forming a vector sum.

Lemma 2. For any sets S_i $(i = 1, \ldots, m)$,

$$\text{con} \sum_{i=1}^{m} S_i = \sum_{i=1}^{m} \text{con } S_i.$$

Proof. It suffices to consider the case $m = 2$; the general case follows by an obvious induction.

First, let $\mathbf{x} \in \text{con}(S_1 + S_2)$. Then $\mathbf{x}$ can be written

$$\mathbf{x} = \sum_i \alpha_i \mathbf{x}^i,$$

where $\mathbf{x}^i \in S_1 + S_2$. Then $\mathbf{x}^i = \mathbf{x}^{i1} + \mathbf{x}^{i2}$, where $\mathbf{x}^{i1} \in S_1$, $\mathbf{x}^{i2} \in S_2$. Hence,

$$\mathbf{x} = \sum_i \alpha_i \mathbf{x}^{i1} + \sum_i \alpha_i \mathbf{x}^{i2},$$

and is therefore the sum of a vector in con S_1 and of one in con S_2.

Now let $\mathbf{x} \in \text{con } S_1 + \text{con } S_2$. Then $\mathbf{x} = \mathbf{x}^1 + \mathbf{x}^2$, where

$$\mathbf{x}^1 = \sum_i \alpha_i \mathbf{x}^{1i} \qquad \mathbf{x}^2 = \sum_j \beta_j \mathbf{x}^{2j},$$

where $\mathbf{x}^{1i} \in S_1$, all i, $\mathbf{x}^{2j} \in S_2$, all j.

Then it is easily calculated that

$$\mathbf{x} = \sum_i \sum_j \alpha_i \beta_j (\mathbf{x}^{1i} + \mathbf{x}^{2j}),$$

and since $\mathbf{x}^{1i} + \mathbf{x}^{2j} \in S_1 + S_2$ for every pair i and j, $\mathbf{x} \in \text{con}(S_1 + S_2)$.

Another elementary consequence of the definitions is the following.

LEMMA 3. The convex hull of a compact set is compact.

Proof. If S is bounded, then $|\mathbf{x}| \leq M$ for all $\mathbf{x} \in S$, for some suitably chosen M. Then, if $\mathbf{x} \in \text{con } S$, we can find a finite subset T of S and a real non-negative function $\alpha(\mathbf{x}')$ defined on T such that

$$\sum_{\mathbf{x}' \in T} \alpha(\mathbf{x}') = 1 \qquad \mathbf{x} = \sum_{\mathbf{x}' \in T} \alpha(\mathbf{x}')\mathbf{x}'.$$

By the triangle inequality,

$$|\mathbf{x}| \leq \sum_{\mathbf{x}' \in T} \alpha(\mathbf{x}')|\mathbf{x}'| \leq \sum_{\mathbf{x}' \in T} \alpha(\mathbf{x}')M = M,$$

so that con S is bounded.

Now let $\{\mathbf{x}^\nu\}$ be a sequence in con S, with $\mathbf{x}^\nu \to \mathbf{x}$. We seek to show that $\mathbf{x} \in \text{con } S$. For each ν we can find a set $T^\nu \subset S$ with not more than $n + 1$ elements and a non-negative function $\alpha^\nu(\mathbf{x}')$ defined on T^ν such that

$$\sum_{\mathbf{x}' \in T} \alpha^\nu(\mathbf{x}') = 1 \qquad \sum_{\mathbf{x}' \in T} \alpha^\nu(\mathbf{x}')\mathbf{x}' = \mathbf{x}^\nu.$$

Without loss of generality we can suppose that T^ν contains $n + 1$ elements, each ν; we need only add elements for which we define $\alpha^\nu(\mathbf{x}') = 0$. For each ν enumerate the elements of T^ν in some arbitrary order; call them $\mathbf{x}'^{i\nu}$ $(i = 1, \ldots, n + 1)$. Let $\alpha_i^\nu = \alpha^\nu(\mathbf{x}'^{i\nu})$. Then

$$\sum_{i=1}^{n+1} \alpha_i^\nu = 1 \qquad \sum_{i=1}^{n+1} \alpha_i^\nu \mathbf{x}'^{i\nu} = \mathbf{x}^\nu.$$

The numbers α_i^ν can be considered components of a vector $\boldsymbol{\alpha}^\nu$, which belongs to the unit simplex S_n. Then the vectors $\mathbf{x}'^{i\nu}$, $\boldsymbol{\alpha}^\nu$ taken together belong to the Cartesian product

$$\left(\mathop{\times}_{i=1}^{n+1} S\right) \times S_n;$$

as the Cartesian product of compact sets, it is itself compact. Hence, by choice of a suitable subsequence, we can find vectors $\boldsymbol{\alpha} \in S_n$, $\mathbf{x}'^i \in S$ (each i) such that $\boldsymbol{\alpha}^\nu \to \boldsymbol{\alpha}$, $\mathbf{x}'^{i\nu} \to \mathbf{x}'^i$ along the subsequence. Then

$$\mathbf{x} = \sum_{i=1}^{n+1} \alpha_i \mathbf{x}'^i,$$

so that $\mathbf{x} \in \text{con } S$.

We now come to the main point of this section for our purposes, a theorem due to L. Shapley and J. H. Folkman (unpublished but reported by Starr [1969, pp. 35–37]) of the extent to which vector sums of bounded sets are approximately convex. We first need the concept of the "facial dimension" of a point in a convex set, that is, the dimension of the face on which it lies (note that convex hulls typically have flat sections on their boundary); this theory is due to Karlin and Shapley [1953, pp. 6–7].

Definition 13. The vector $\mathbf{y}$ is a *facial direction* at $\mathbf{x}$ in C if $\mathbf{x} + t\mathbf{y} \in C$ for all $|t|$ sufficiently small. The set of all facial directions at $\mathbf{x}$ in C is called the *facial space* at $\mathbf{x}$ in C.

If C is convex, the facial space, after displacement of the origin to $\mathbf{x}$, is the hyperplane of highest dimension such that $\mathbf{x}$ lies in the relative interior of the intersection of C with that hyperplane. In Figure B-2, $\mathbf{y}$ is a facial direction at $\mathbf{x}$ in C, and L is the facial space there. At $\mathbf{x}^1$ or $\mathbf{x}^2$, the only facial direction is $\mathbf{0}$.

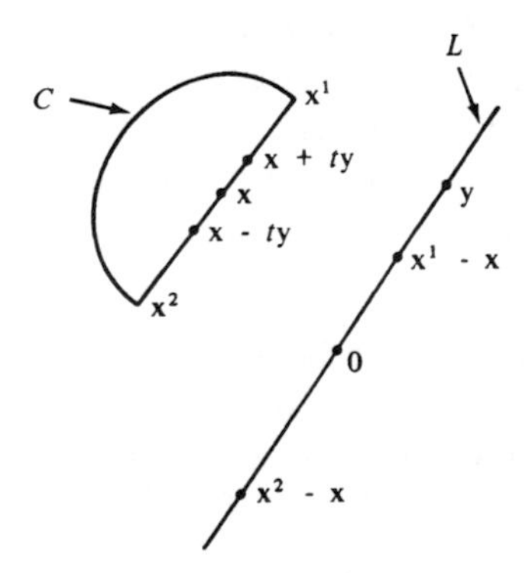

Figure B-2

From this definition, it is obvious that if $\mathbf{y}$ is a facial direction, then so is $t\mathbf{y}$ for any scalar t. Now suppose C is convex and $\mathbf{y}^1$ and $\mathbf{y}^2$ are both facial directions at some point $\mathbf{x}$ in C. By definition, $\mathbf{x} + t_i\mathbf{y}^i \in C$ for $|t_i|$ small ($i = 1,2$). Since C is convex,

$$\mathbf{x} + \frac{t_1}{2}\mathbf{y}^1 + \frac{t_2}{2}\mathbf{y}^2 \in C$$

for $|t_1|$, $|t_2|$ sufficiently small, so that $\mathbf{x} + t(\mathbf{y}^1 + \mathbf{y}^2) \in C$ for $|t|$ sufficiently small, and therefore, $\mathbf{y}^1 + \mathbf{y}^2$ is a facial direction also.

LEMMA 4. If C is convex and $\mathbf{x} \in C$, then the facial space at $\mathbf{x}$ in C is a linear space.

DEFINITION 14. The *facial dimension* of $\mathbf{x}$ in C, $d(\mathbf{x} \mid C)$, is the dimension of the facial space at $\mathbf{x}$ in C.

In Figure B-2, the facial dimension of $\mathbf{x}$ in C is 1, while that of $\mathbf{x}^1$ is 0.

Suppose $\mathbf{x}$ and $\mathbf{x}^1$ both belong to a convex set C and also suppose that the movement from $\mathbf{x}$ to $\mathbf{x}^1$ lies on a face; that is, $\mathbf{x}^1 - \mathbf{x}$ is a facial direction at $\mathbf{x}$ in C. Then any facial direction at $\mathbf{x}^1$ must also be a facial direction at $\mathbf{x}$; the converse will not hold if $\mathbf{x}^1$ is at the edge of the face, as can be seen from Figure B-2.

LEMMA 5. If $\mathbf{x}$ and $\mathbf{x}^1$ belong to the convex set C and $\mathbf{x}^1 - \mathbf{x}$ is a facial direction at $\mathbf{x}$ in C, then every facial direction at $\mathbf{x}^1$ is also a facial direction at $\mathbf{x}$.

Proof. Since $\mathbf{x}^1 - \mathbf{x}$ is a facial direction at $\mathbf{x}$, $\mathbf{x}^0 = \mathbf{x} + t(\mathbf{x}^1 - \mathbf{x}) \in C$ for some $t < 0$, so that $\mathbf{x} = (1 - \alpha)\mathbf{x}^0 + \alpha\mathbf{x}^1$, where $\alpha = -t/(1 - t)$, and therefore, $0 < \alpha < 1$. Let $\mathbf{y}$ be a facial direction at $\mathbf{x}^1$; then $\mathbf{x}^1 + t\mathbf{y} \in C$ for $|t|$ sufficiently small. Then $\mathbf{x} + \alpha t\mathbf{y} = (1 - \alpha)\mathbf{x}^0 + \alpha(\mathbf{x}^1 + t\mathbf{y}) \in C$ for all $|t|$ sufficiently small and therefore for all $|\alpha t|$ sufficiently small. Hence, by definition, $\mathbf{y}$ is a facial direction at $\mathbf{x}$.

LEMMA 6. If $\mathbf{x}$ and $\mathbf{x}^1$ both belong to a convex set C and if $\mathbf{x}^1 - \mathbf{x}$ is a facial direction at $\mathbf{x}$ in C, then $d(\mathbf{x}^1 \mid C) \leq d(\mathbf{x} \mid C)$. The equality holds if and only if $\mathbf{x}^1 - \mathbf{x}$ is also a facial direction at $\mathbf{x}^1$ in C.

Proof. The weak inequality follows from Lemma B.5. If $\mathbf{x}^1 - \mathbf{x}$ is also a facial direction at $\mathbf{x}^1$, then so is $\mathbf{x} - \mathbf{x}^1 = (-1)(\mathbf{x}^1 - \mathbf{x})$.

Hence, interchanging $\mathbf{x}$ and $\mathbf{x}^1$, the weak inequality holds also in the reverse direction, so equality holds. If $\mathbf{x}^1 - \mathbf{x}$ is not a facial direction at $\mathbf{x}^1$, then, by Lemma B.5, the set of facial directions at $\mathbf{x}^1$ is a proper subset of that at $\mathbf{x}$; but since both are linear spaces, by Lemma B.4, the facial space at $\mathbf{x}^1$ must have a lower dimension than that at $\mathbf{x}$.

We now consider faces formed when the convex hull of a set is taken. A point in the convex hull of a set is spanned by a finite subset of the convex hull. We show that the difference between the point and any element of the spanning set is a facial direction in the convex hull. In Figure B-3, $\mathbf{x}^1 - \mathbf{x}$ and $\mathbf{x}^2 - \mathbf{x}$ are facial directions at $\mathbf{x}$ in the convex hull of the illustrated set.

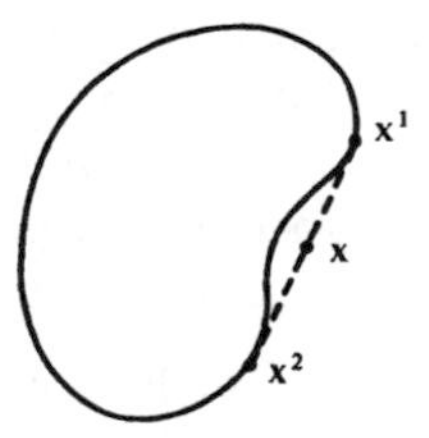

Figure B-3

LEMMA 7. If $\mathbf{x} \in$ con S, then there is a finite subset T of S such that T spans $\mathbf{x}$ and $\mathbf{x}' - \mathbf{x}$ is a facial direction at $\mathbf{x}$ in con S for all $\mathbf{x}' \in T$.

Proof. By T.B.7(b), there is a finite subset T of S and a function $\alpha(\mathbf{x}')$ defined on T such that

$$\sum_{\mathbf{x}' \in T} \alpha(\mathbf{x}') = 1,$$

$$\alpha(\mathbf{x}') \geq 0 \qquad \text{all } \mathbf{x}' \in T,$$

$$\mathbf{x} = \sum_{\mathbf{x}' \in T} \alpha(\mathbf{x}')\mathbf{x}'.$$

If we delete all elements of T for which $\alpha(\mathbf{x}') = 0$, obviously the same relations hold. Hence we can assume $\alpha(\mathbf{x}') > 0$ for all $\mathbf{x}' \in T$. Choose any fixed $\mathbf{x}'' \in T$, and let

$$\mathbf{x}^1 = (1 - t)\mathbf{x} + t\mathbf{x}'' = t\mathbf{x}'' + (1 - t) \sum_{\mathbf{x}' \in T} \alpha(\mathbf{x}')\mathbf{x}'.$$

Let $\beta(\mathbf{x}') = (1 - t)\alpha(\mathbf{x}')$ when $\mathbf{x}' \neq \mathbf{x}''$, $\beta(\mathbf{x}'') = (1 - t)\alpha(\mathbf{x}'') + t$. Then

$$\mathbf{x}^1 = \sum_{\mathbf{x}' \in T} \beta(\mathbf{x}')\mathbf{x}',$$

$$\sum_{\mathbf{x}' \in T} \beta(\mathbf{x}') = t + (1 - t) \sum_{\mathbf{x}' \in T} \alpha(\mathbf{x}') = t + (1 - t).$$

Finally, since $\alpha(\mathbf{x}') > 0$, all $\mathbf{x}' \in T$, we can ensure $\beta(\mathbf{x}') \geq 0$, all $\mathbf{x}' \in T$, by making $|t|$ sufficiently small. Hence $\mathbf{x}^1 \in \text{con}\, T \subset \text{con}\, S$ for such t. If we write $\mathbf{x}^1 = \mathbf{x} + t(\mathbf{x}'' - \mathbf{x})$, we see, by D.B.13, that $\mathbf{x}'' - \mathbf{x}$ is a facial direction at $\mathbf{x}$ in con S, and this for any $\mathbf{x}'' \in T$.

We now state the first theorem that shows that, in one sense, the vector sum of a large number of sets is approximately convex. Consider any point in the convex hull of the vector sum. By Lemma B.2, the point can be written as a vector sum of points in the convex hulls of the individual sets. This representation is, in general, not unique; it will be shown that the points can be chosen so that all but a fixed number (equal to the dimensionality of the space) are actually in the individual sets and not merely in their convex hulls.

THEOREM 8. Let F be a finite family of compact sets,

$$\mathbf{x} \in \text{con} \sum_{S \in F} S.$$

Then F can be divided into two subfamilies, F_1 and F_2, where F_1 has at most n members (where n is the dimensionality of the space) such that

$$\mathbf{x} \in \text{con} \sum_{S \in F_1} S + \sum_{S \in F_2} S.$$

Before proceeding to the general proof, we shall illustrate the theorem and the method of proof in a very simple case. Let the space be the set of real numbers, therefore of dimension 1, and let the family F consist of m sets, each of which consists of the numbers 0 and 1. Call the sets $S_1, \ldots, S_m$. Then

$$\sum_{S \in F} S = \sum_{i=1}^{m} S_i$$

consists of the integers $0, \ldots, m$,

$$\text{con} \sum_{i=1}^{m} S_i$$

is the closed interval $\langle 0,m \rangle$, and con S_i is the interval $\langle 0,1 \rangle$. For each i, x_i has facial dimension 1 in con S_i if $0 < x_i < 1$ and facial dimension 0 if $x_i = 0$ or 1. If x is any real number between 0 and m, it can be written in many ways as

$$x = \sum_{i=1}^{m} x_i,$$

where $0 \leq x_i \leq 1$, but among these ways there is at least one for which x_i is either 0 or 1 except, at most, for one value of i. Specifically, if $x = r$, an integer, then we can let $x_i = 1$ $(i = 1, \ldots, r)$, $x_i = 0$ $(i = r + 1, \ldots, m)$, while if x is not an integer and r is the largest integer less than x, let $x_i = 1$ $(i = 1, \ldots, r)$, $x_i = 0$ $(i = r + 1, \ldots, m - 1)$, $x_m = x - r$. Although in this case the result is obvious, we çan also prove it by a method that generalizes. Among the many solutions to the equations and inequalities

$$\sum_{i=1}^{m} x_i = x \qquad 0 \leq x_i \leq 1,$$

choose the one that minimizes the sum of the facial dimensions of x_i in con S_i. If this solution has more than one x_i satisfying $0 < x_i < 1$, suppose this holds for $i = 1,2$. Let $x_i(t) = x_1 + t$, $x_2(t) = x_2 - t$, $x_i(t) = x_i$ $(i > 2)$. Increase t from 0 until either $x_1(t)$ reaches 1 or $x_2(t)$ reaches 0; that is, let $t = \min(1 - x_1, x_2)$. Note that

$$\sum_{i=1}^{m} x_i(t) = x \qquad 0 \leq x_i(t) \leq 1.$$

Further, the facial dimension of $x_i(t)$ in con S_i remains unchanged for each i except for the one that reaches 1 or 0, respectively, for which the facial dimension drops from 1 to 0, in contradiction to the choice of the x_i's. Hence the solution in question can have, at most, one x_i that is neither 0 nor 1.

Proof. By Lemma B.2,

$$\mathbf{x} = \sum_{S \in F} \mathbf{x}(S),$$

where $\mathbf{x}(S) \in \text{con } S$. Among all choices of $\mathbf{x}(S)$ satisfying these conditions, choose the one that minimizes

$$\sum_{S \in F} d[\mathbf{x}(S) \mid \text{con } S];$$

since the function to be minimized takes on only non-negative integer values, it must have a minimum. By Lemma B.7, we must have, for each S, a point $\mathbf{x}'(S)$ such that $\mathbf{x}'(S) \in S$ and $\mathbf{x}'(S) - \mathbf{x}(S)$ is a facial direction at $\mathbf{x}(S)$ in con S. Let $F_1 = \{S \mid \mathbf{x}'(S) \neq \mathbf{x}(S)\}$, $F_2 = \{S \mid \mathbf{x}'(S) = \mathbf{x}(S)\}$. For $S \in F_2$, $\mathbf{x}(S) \in S$; hence

$$\begin{aligned}\mathbf{x} &= \sum_{S \in F_1} \mathbf{x}(S) + \sum_{S \in F_2} \mathbf{x}(S) \in \sum_{S \in F_1} \text{con } S + \sum_{S \in F_2} S \\ &= \text{con} \sum_{S \in F_1} S + \sum_{S \in F_2} S,\end{aligned}$$

by Lemma B.2.

It remains to show that F_1 has, at most, n members. Suppose it had more. Then the vectors $\mathbf{x}'(S) - \mathbf{x}(S)$, $S \in F_1$, would be linearly dependent; that is, there would exist real numbers $c(S)$, not all 0, such that

$$\sum_{S \in F_1} c(S)[\mathbf{x}'(S) - \mathbf{x}(S)] = 0.$$

For each S in F_1, let

$$\mathbf{x}(t \mid S) = \mathbf{x}(S) + c(S)[\mathbf{x}'(S) - \mathbf{x}(S)]t.$$

By construction,

$$\sum_{S \in F_1} \mathbf{x}(t \mid S) = \sum_{S \in F_1} \mathbf{x}(S),$$

so that

$$\mathbf{x} = \sum_{S \in F_1} \mathbf{x}(t \mid S) + \sum_{S \in F_2} \mathbf{x}(S).$$

Hence, if $\mathbf{x}(t \mid S) \in \text{con } S$, all $S \in F_1$, it follows from the choice of $\mathbf{x}(S)$ as minimizing

$$\sum_{S \in F} d[\mathbf{x}(S) \mid \text{con } S]$$

that

$$\sum_{S \in F_1} d[\mathbf{x}(t \mid S) \mid \text{con } S] + \sum_{S \in F_2} d[\mathbf{x}(S) \mid \text{con } S] \geq \sum_{S \in F} d[\mathbf{x}(S) \mid \text{con } S],$$

or

$$\sum_{S \in F_1} d[\mathbf{x}(t \mid S) \mid \text{con } S] \geq \sum_{S \in F_1} d[\mathbf{x}(S) \mid \text{con } S] \tag{3}$$

if $\mathbf{x}(t \mid S) \in \text{con } S$ for all $S \in F_1$. Let $A = \{t \mid t \geq 0, \ \mathbf{x}(t \mid S) \in \text{con } S$ for all $S \in F_1\}$. Obviously, A is a closed interval containing 0. Furthermore, since $\mathbf{x}'(S) - \mathbf{x}(S)$ is a facial direction at $\mathbf{x}(S)$ in con S for each S, $\mathbf{x}(t \mid S) \in \text{con } S$ for $|tc(S)|$ sufficiently small and, therefore, for all $|t|$ sufficiently small, so that A contains a positive value of t. Suppose A were unbounded. Since $\mathbf{x}'(S) - \mathbf{x}(S) \neq 0$ for $S \in F_1$, it follows that the range of $\mathbf{x}(t \mid S)$ as t varies over A is unbounded also if $c(S) \neq 0$, which must be true for at least one $S \in F_1$. For $t \in A$, $\mathbf{x}(t \mid S) \in \text{con } S$; since S is compact by hypothesis, so is con S, by Lemma B.3, a contradiction. Hence (3) can be written

$$\sum_{S \in F_1} d[\mathbf{x}(t \mid S) \mid \text{con } S] \geq \sum_{S \in F_1} d[\mathbf{x}(S) \mid \text{con } S] \qquad \text{for } t \in A, \quad (4)$$

and A is a closed bounded non-degenerate interval with lower bound 0.

Since $\mathbf{x}'(S) - \mathbf{x}(S)$ is a facial direction at $\mathbf{x}(S)$ in con S, so is $c(S)[\mathbf{x}'(S) - \mathbf{x}(S)]t$; by Lemma B.6,

$$d[\mathbf{x}(t \mid S) \mid \text{con } S] \leq d[\mathbf{x}(S) \mid \text{con } S]$$

for all $S \in F_1$. From (4),

$$d[\mathbf{x}(t \mid S) \mid \text{con } S] = d[x(S) \mid \text{con } S] \qquad \text{for all } S \in F_1 \text{ if } t \in A.$$

Again from Lemma B.6, it must be that $\mathbf{x}(t \mid S) - \mathbf{x}(S)$ is a facial direction at $\mathbf{x}(t \mid S)$. Then, by definition,

$$\mathbf{x}(t \mid S) + u[\mathbf{x}(t \mid S) - \mathbf{x}(S)] \in \text{con } S$$

for $|u|$ sufficiently small if $t \in A$. In particular, take $u > 0$. Since $\mathbf{x}(t \mid S) + u[\mathbf{x}(t \mid S) - \mathbf{x}(S)] = \mathbf{x}(S) + c(S)[\mathbf{x}'(S) - \mathbf{x}(S)](1 + u)t$, it follows that if $t \in A$, so does $(1 + u)t$ for some $u > 0$. Thus there is no largest positive element of A, in contradiction to its being a closed bounded non-degenerate interval. It has been shown, therefore, that the elements of F_1 cannot be linearly dependent and therefore there are no more than n of them.

We now proceed to state the fundamental result of Shapley and Folkman, which gives a bound on the degree to which the vector sum of a large number of uniformly bounded sets can differ from its convex hull. We define the *radius* of any compact set as that of the smallest sphere that includes it.

DEFINITION 15. The radius of a compact set is defined by

$$\text{rad}(S) = \min_{\mathbf{x}} \max_{\mathbf{y} \in S} |\mathbf{x} - \mathbf{y}|.$$

THEOREM 9 (Shapley–Folkman). Let F be a family (not necessarily finite) of compact sets S such that, for some number L, $\text{rad}(S) \leq L$ for all $S \in F$. Then

for any finite subfamily $F' \subset F$ and any $\mathbf{x} \in \text{con} \sum_{S \in F'} S$, there is a $\mathbf{y} \in \sum_{S \in F'} S$ such that $|\mathbf{x} - \mathbf{y}| \leq L\sqrt{n}$,

where n is the dimensionality of the space.

Proof. We will establish:

For any finite family F of compact sets and any $\mathbf{x} \in \text{con} \sum_{S \in F} S$, there exists $\mathbf{y} \in \sum_{S \in F} S$ such that $|\mathbf{x} - \mathbf{y}|^2 \leq \sum_{S \in F} [\text{rad}(S)]^2$. (5)

Suppose (5) has been established. Let F' be any finite subfamily of F satisfying the hypotheses of the theorem. Let m be the number of members of F'. If $m \leq n$, then from (5),

$$|\mathbf{x} - \mathbf{y}|^2 \leq \sum_{S \in F'} [\text{rad}(S)]^2 \leq \sum_{S \in F'} L^2 = mL^2 \leq nL^2.$$

Suppose then $m > n$. By T.B.8, $\mathbf{x} = \mathbf{x}^1 + \mathbf{x}^2$, where

$$\mathbf{x}^1 \in \text{con} \sum_{S \in F_1'} S \qquad \mathbf{x}^2 \in \sum_{S \in F_2'} S,$$

F_1' and F_2' constitute a partition of F' into two disjoint subfamilies and F_1' has, at most, n elements. Then

$$\mathbf{x} - \mathbf{x}^2 \in \text{con} \sum_{S \in F_1'} S;$$

since F_1' has, at most, n elements, it follows from what has already been established that there exists

$$\mathbf{y}^1 \in \sum_{S \in F_1'} S$$

such that $|\mathbf{x} - \mathbf{x}^2 - \mathbf{y}^1| \leq L\sqrt{n}$. But if $\mathbf{y} = \mathbf{y}^1 + \mathbf{x}^2$, then

$$\mathbf{y} \in \sum_{S \in F'} S,$$

and the theorem is established.

It remains to prove (5); we proceed by induction on m, the number of members of F. First, suppose $m = 1$. Then

$$\mathbf{x} = \sum_{\mathbf{y} \in T} \alpha(\mathbf{y})\mathbf{y},$$

for some finite $T \subset S$ and some function $\alpha(\mathbf{y})$ with $\alpha(\mathbf{y}) \geq 0$, all $\mathbf{y}$, and

$$\sum_{\mathbf{y} \in T} \alpha(\mathbf{y}) = 1.$$

Let $\mathbf{x}^*$ minimize

$$\max_{\mathbf{y} \in S} |\mathbf{x} - \mathbf{y}|,$$

so that

$$\text{rad}(S) = \max_{\mathbf{y} \in S} |\mathbf{x}^* - \mathbf{y}|.$$

$$\mathbf{0} = \mathbf{x} - \mathbf{x} = \mathbf{x} - \sum_{\mathbf{y} \in T} \alpha(\mathbf{y})\mathbf{y} = \sum_{\mathbf{y} \in T} \alpha(\mathbf{y})(\mathbf{x} - \mathbf{y}).$$

Take the inner product of both sides with $\mathbf{x} - \mathbf{x}^*$.

$$0 = \sum_{\mathbf{y} \in T} \alpha(\mathbf{y})(\mathbf{x} - \mathbf{x}^*)(\mathbf{x} - \mathbf{y}).$$

It is clearly impossible that $(\mathbf{x} - \mathbf{x}^*)(\mathbf{x} - \mathbf{y}) > 0$ for all $\mathbf{y}$ in T. Therefore, $(\mathbf{x} - \mathbf{x}^*)(\mathbf{x} - \mathbf{y}) \leq 0$ for some $\mathbf{y} \in S$. But

$$\begin{aligned}[\text{rad}(S)]^2 &\geq |\mathbf{x}^* - \mathbf{y}|^2 = |(\mathbf{x} - \mathbf{x}^*) - (\mathbf{x} - \mathbf{y})|^2 \\ &= |\mathbf{x} - \mathbf{y}|^2 + |\mathbf{x} - \mathbf{x}^*|^2 - 2(\mathbf{x} - \mathbf{x}^*)(\mathbf{x} - \mathbf{y}) \geq |\mathbf{x} - \mathbf{y}|^2,\end{aligned}$$

as was to be proved.

Now suppose that (5) holds for m; we seek to prove it when F has $m + 1$ members. Let S' be any set in the family F, and let F' be the family of remaining members of which there are m. Then, if

$$\mathbf{x} \in \text{con} \sum_{S \in F} S = \text{con} \sum_{S \in F} S + \text{con}\, S'$$

(by Lemma B.2), we can write $\mathbf{x} = \mathbf{x}^1 + \mathbf{x}^2$, where

$$\mathbf{x}^1 \in \text{con} \sum_{S \in F'} S \qquad \mathbf{x}^2 \in \text{con}\, S'.$$

By the induction hypothesis, we can find

$$\mathbf{y}^1 \in \sum_{S \in F'} S$$

such that

$$|\mathbf{x}^1 - \mathbf{y}^1|^2 \leq \sum_{S \in F'} [\text{rad}(S)]^2.$$

Now choose $\mathbf{z}^0$ to minimize $|\mathbf{x} - \mathbf{y}^1 - \mathbf{z}|$ for $\mathbf{z} \in \text{con } S'$. Since S' is compact, so is con S', by Lemma B.3, so the minimum exists. Since $\mathbf{x}^2 \in \text{con } S'$, we have, in particular,

$$|\mathbf{x} - \mathbf{y}^1 - \mathbf{z}^0|^2 \leq |\mathbf{x} - \mathbf{y}^1 - \mathbf{x}^2|^2 = |\mathbf{x}^1 - \mathbf{y}^1|^2 \leq \sum_{S \in F'} [\text{rad}(S)]^2. \tag{6}$$

For any $\mathbf{z} \in \text{con } S'$, $t\mathbf{z} + (1 - t)\mathbf{z}^0 \in \text{con } S'$ for $0 < t \leq 1$. Then,

$$\begin{aligned} |\mathbf{x} - \mathbf{y}^1 - \mathbf{z}^0|^2 &\leq |\mathbf{x} - \mathbf{y}^1 - [t\mathbf{z} + (1 - t)\mathbf{z}^0]|^2 \\ &= |\mathbf{x} - \mathbf{y}^1 - \mathbf{z}^0 - t(\mathbf{z} - \mathbf{z}^0)|^2 \\ &= |\mathbf{x} - \mathbf{y}^1 - \mathbf{z}^0|^2 - 2t(\mathbf{x} - \mathbf{y}^1 - \mathbf{z}^0)(\mathbf{z} - \mathbf{z}^0) \\ &\qquad + t^2|\mathbf{z} - \mathbf{z}^0|^2. \end{aligned}$$

Add $2t(\mathbf{x} - \mathbf{y}^1 - \mathbf{z}^0)(\mathbf{z} - \mathbf{z}^0) - |\mathbf{x} - \mathbf{y}^1 - \mathbf{z}^0|^2$ to both sides, divide by $2t$ (with $t > 0$), and then let t approach 0.

$$(\mathbf{x} - \mathbf{y}^1 - \mathbf{z}^0)(\mathbf{z} - \mathbf{z}^0) \leq 0 \qquad \text{for all } \mathbf{z} \in \text{con } S'. \tag{7}$$

According to Lemma B.7, we can find a finite subset T of S' that spans $\mathbf{z}^0$, since $\mathbf{z}^0 \in \text{con } S'$. Since $\mathbf{z}^0 \in \text{con } T$, it follows by (5) for $m = 1$ that we can choose $\mathbf{y}^2 \in T \subset S'$ such that

$$|\mathbf{y}^2 - \mathbf{z}^0|^2 \leq [\text{rad}(T)]^2 \leq [\text{rad}(S')]^2. \tag{8}$$

Since it is also true, by Lemma B.7, that $\mathbf{y}^2 - \mathbf{z}^0$ is a facial direction at $\mathbf{z}^0$ in con S', $\mathbf{z}^0 + t(\mathbf{y}^2 - \mathbf{z}^0) \in \text{con } S'$ for $|t|$ sufficiently small. If we substitute for $\mathbf{z}$ in (7), we see that

$$t(\mathbf{x} - \mathbf{y}^1 - \mathbf{z}^0)(\mathbf{y}^2 - \mathbf{z}^0) \leq 0$$

for all $|t|$ sufficiently small. Since t can be of either sign, we must have

$$(\mathbf{x} - \mathbf{y}^1 - \mathbf{z}^0)(\mathbf{y}^2 - \mathbf{z}^0) = 0. \tag{9}$$

Let $\mathbf{y} = \mathbf{y}^1 + \mathbf{y}^2$; then

$$\mathbf{y} \in \sum_{S \in F} S.$$

From (6), (8), and (9),

$$\begin{aligned} |\mathbf{x} - \mathbf{y}|^2 &= |\mathbf{x} - \mathbf{y}^1 - \mathbf{y}^2|^2 = |(\mathbf{x} - \mathbf{y}^1 - \mathbf{z}^0) - (\mathbf{y}^2 - \mathbf{z}^0)|^2 \\ &= |\mathbf{x} - \mathbf{y}^1 - \mathbf{z}^0|^2 - 2(\mathbf{x} - \mathbf{y}^1 - \mathbf{z}^0)(\mathbf{y}^2 - \mathbf{z}^0) + |\mathbf{y}^2 - \mathbf{z}^0|^2 \\ &\leq \sum_{S \in F} [\text{rad}(S)]^2. \end{aligned}$$

Important as this theorem is, it can be usefully strengthened. For example, consider the case in which all the sets in the family F are themselves convex. Then the vector sum is convex and coincides with its convex hull, so that the upper bound given above is too weak. Starr [1969, p. 37] extended the Shapley–Folkman theorem by measuring the non-convexity of the sets in F. For each point in the convex hull of a set S, we can find all the finite subsets of S that span it and choose among them the one having the smallest radius (which will be zero if the point belongs to S). The minimum radius of spanning set, in general, will vary as x varies over con S; the maximum attained is a measure of the non-convexity of the set, since it will certainly be zero if every point of the convex hull belongs to S itself.

DEFINITION 16. The *inner radius* of S is defined by

$$r(S) = \sup_{\mathbf{x} \in \operatorname{con} S} \inf_{\substack{T \text{ spans } \mathbf{x} \\ T \subset S}} \operatorname{rad}(T).$$

THEOREM 10 (Starr). Let F be a family (not necessarily finite) of compact sets S such that, for some number L, $r(S) \leq L$ for all $S \in F$. Then for every finite subfamily F' and any

$$\mathbf{x} \in \operatorname{con} \sum_{S \in F'} S,$$

there is a

$$\mathbf{y} \in \sum_{S \in F'} S$$

such that $|\mathbf{x} - \mathbf{y}| \leq L\sqrt{n}$, where n is the dimensionality of the space.

Proof. If

$$\mathbf{x} \in \operatorname{con} \sum_{S \in F'} S,$$

then

$$\mathbf{x} = \sum_{S \in F'} \mathbf{x}(S),$$

where $\mathbf{x}(S) \in \operatorname{con} S$. By D.B.16, we can find $T(S) \subset S$, where $T(S)$ spans $\mathbf{x}(S)$ and $\operatorname{rad}[T(S)] \leq r(S) + \epsilon$, for any given $\epsilon > 0$. Then $\mathbf{x}(S) \in \operatorname{con} T(S)$, and

$$\mathbf{x} \in \sum_{S \in F'} \operatorname{con} T(S) = \operatorname{con} \sum_{S \in F'} T(S).$$

Consider the family of all finite subsets T of any S in F for which $\text{rad}(T) \leq L + \epsilon$. The family of sets $T(S)$ for $S \in F'$ is certainly a finite subfamily of this family, and we can use T.B.9. Then there is a point,

$$\mathbf{y} \in \sum_{S \in F'} T(S),$$

such that $|\mathbf{x} - \mathbf{y}| \leq (L + \epsilon)\sqrt{n}$. Note that

$$\mathbf{y} \in \sum_{S \in F'} S.$$

The chosen $\mathbf{y}$ may vary with ϵ, but since it lies in a compact set, by choosing a suitable sequence of ϵ's approaching 0, we can approach a point,

$$\mathbf{y} \in \sum_{S \in F} S,$$

such that $|\mathbf{x} - \mathbf{y}| \leq L\sqrt{n}$.

5. The Connectedness of Convex Sets

We shall prove here that a closed convex set cannot be expressed as the union of two or more (but finitely many) closed sets; this result was used in the proof of T.11.5. To accord with the formulations of textbooks in analysis, we will state definitions and results slightly more generally than actually employed. Some of these definitions have found other uses in mathematical economics.

DEFINITION 17. The set C is *closed* in the set S if any limit point of C that is in S is also in C.

Note that if C is closed in the usual sense, that is, in its natural space, then C is closed in S for any S. We actually need only this case.

DEFINITION 18. If C is a non-null proper subset of S and both C and $S \sim C$ are closed in S, then C is a *component* of S.

Intuitively, C is isolated from the rest of S, for no sequence of points in $S \sim C$ can approach a point in C, and no sequence of points of C can approach a point in $S \sim C$. Of course, if C is a component, so is $S \sim C$.

Definition 19. S is *connected* if it has no components.

Lemma 8. S is connected if and only if it is not the union of two or more, but finitely many disjoint non-null sets each closed in S.

Proof. Suppose S is not connected. Then it has a component C; by D.B.18, S is the union of C and $S \sim C$, both non-null and closed in S. Conversely, suppose S is the union of $C_1, \ldots, C_m$, mutually disjoint and each non-null and closed in S, with $m > 1$. Then $S \sim C_1$ is the union of $C_2, \ldots, C_m$ and, therefore, is non-null and closed in S, since the union of finitely many closed sets is closed. Then C_1 is a component of S, which therefore is not connected.

Another rendering of the intuitive concept of connectedness, appropriate to vector spaces, is that any two points in the set can be joined by a continuous path or arc lying entirely in the set.

Definition 20. S is *arcwise connected* if, for every $\mathbf{x}^0, \mathbf{x}^1 \in S$, there is a continuous vector-valued function, $\mathbf{x}(t)$, defined for $0 \leq t \leq 1$, such that $\mathbf{x}(0) = \mathbf{x}^0$, $\mathbf{x}(1) = \mathbf{x}^1$, and $\mathbf{x}(t) \in S$, all t, $0 \leq t \leq 1$.

Theorem 11. Every arcwise connected set is connected.

Proof. Suppose S arcwise connected, but not connected. Let C be any component. Choose $\mathbf{x}^0 \in C$, $\mathbf{x}^1 \in S \sim C$, and let $\mathbf{x}(t)$ be the arc joining them, as defined in D.B.20. Let

$$C' = \{t \mid \mathbf{x}(t) \in C'\} \qquad C'' = \{t \mid x(\mathbf{t}) \in S \sim C\}.$$

Since C and $S \sim C$ are closed in S and $\mathbf{x}(t)$ is continuous, C' and C'' are disjoint closed sets whose union is the unit interval. By construction, $0 \in C'$, $1 \in C''$; hence neither is null. Since C'' is closed and bounded from below, it must have a minimum element, $\underline{t}$, which must be positive since $0 \in C'$. Then $t \in C'$ for all $t < \underline{t}$, by definition of a minimum; but this statement implies that $\underline{t}$ is a limit point of C', a contradiction to either the disjointness of C' and C'' or the closedness of C'.

Corollary 11. No convex set is the union of two or more, but finitely many disjoint non-null closed sets.

Proof. Every pair of points in a convex set is joined in the set by the line segment defined by them; hence every convex set is arcwise connected and, therefore, connected so that Lemma B.8 applies.

Appendix C

FIXED-POINT THEOREMS AND RELATED COMBINATORIAL ALGORITHMS

1. Preliminary Remarks

A basic role in the proofs of the existence theorems in competitive equilibrium has been played by fixed-point theorems. In each case, there is some kind of continuous mapping of a set into itself, and the aim is to demonstrate that at least one point of the set remains invariant under the mapping. For our purposes, it suffices to confine attention to domains that are subsets of finite-dimensional vector spaces.

The nature of the domain over which the mapping is defined is crucial to the validity of a fixed-point theorem. Thus, if we consider the set defined by the circumference of a circle, a 45° rotation is a continuous transformation that has no fixed point; on the other hand, if we consider the entire circle, interior and circumference, such a rotation leaves the center invariant. Though more general theorems are known, it will suffice to assume the domain to be a convex set, a condition that eliminates the first counter-example.

It is obviously necessary also to restrict attention to sets that are closed and bounded. Thus, map the open interval, $(0,1)$, into itself by moving each point halfway to the upper boundary, that is, mapping x into $(x + 1)/2$. This mapping has no fixed point in the open interval; on the other hand, if it is closed by adding the end-points, then 1 is a fixed point. Boundedness is also essential: The mapping x into $x + 1$ maps the entire real line into itself, but has no fixed point.

We thus restrict ourselves to mappings of compact convex sets into themselves. The basic theory can be worked out for a special case, in which the domain is a simplex, and then easily extended to the general case of a compact convex set.

DEFINITION 1. A *simplex* is the convex hull of a finite set of linearly independent vectors.

A particular simplex has been used repeatedly in Chapters 2–5:

DEFINITION 2. The *fundamental simplex* in n space is the set of n vectors,

$$S_n = \left\{ \mathbf{x} \mid \mathbf{x} \geq \mathbf{0}, \ \sum_{i=1}^{n} x_i = 1 \right\}.$$

It is easy to verify that S_n is the convex hull of the unit n vectors, $\mathbf{e}^i$ ($i = 1, \ldots, n$), where $\mathbf{e}^i$ is a vector with 1 in the ith place and 0 elsewhere.

The basic fixed-point theorem for the fundamental simplex is

THEOREM 1 (Brouwer's Fixed-Point Theorem). If $\mathbf{f}(\mathbf{x})$ is a continuous mapping of the fundamental simplex, S_n, into itself, then there exists $\mathbf{x}^* \in S_n$ such that $\mathbf{f}(\mathbf{x}^*) = \mathbf{x}^*$.

Proofs of this theorem can be found in many books on topology. It is possible to give proofs that do not depend on other topological theorems; for excellent self-contained presentations see Tompkins [1964] or Burger [1963, Appendix]. In the following sections, however, we present a new theory, due to Scarf [1967; a, b, c], of a general combinatorial algorithm that yields not only a proof of Brouwer's theorem, but a method of computing the fixed point, at least to any desired degree of approximation. The algorithm actually does a great deal more; it proves the more general Kakutani fixed-point theorem (see Section B.4), which, as we have seen, is essential to proving the existence of equilibrium in the general model of Chapters 3–5, and it enables us to calculate the core in market and more general games. This appendix is based on the exposition in Hansen and Scarf [1969]; see also Kuhn [1968], who has related Scarf's theory to earlier proofs of fixed-point theorems.

First, since the following account is fairly difficult, we shall discuss the method somewhat intuitively before working it precisely. We shall need some well-known results from the theorem on linear programming so we recapitulate.

Let Y be an m-element set of n-dimensional vectors, where $m > n$ and Y is taken to include the n vectors $\mathbf{e}^i$. If $\mathbf{b} \geq \mathbf{0}$ is any given vector, we are interested in the fundamental solution of

$$\sum_{\mathbf{y} \in Y} \mathbf{y} w(\mathbf{y}) = \mathbf{b} \qquad w(\mathbf{y}) \geq 0. \tag{1}$$

(a) In Y there is at least one subset, B, (a basis) of n linearly independent vectors such that (1) holds with $w(\mathbf{y}) = 0$ for $\mathbf{y} \in Y \sim B$. To see this, let $B = I$, the unit matrix.

(b) Suppose $\mathbf{y}' \in Y \sim B$ for some basis B. We ask whether there is another basis, B', that includes $\mathbf{y}'$ and all but one element of B such that (1) can be satisfied with $w(\mathbf{y}) = 0$, all $\mathbf{y} \in Y \sim B'$. Note that $B \sim \{\mathbf{y}''\} = B' \sim \{\mathbf{y}'\}$, where $\mathbf{y}''$ is the element in $B \sim B'$.

DEFINITION 3. B' is said to be the *insertion* of $\mathbf{y}'$ in B if B and B' are both feasible bases for (1) and $B' \sim B = \{\mathbf{y}'\}$.

By the definition of B there are numbers $r(\mathbf{y})$ so that

$$\mathbf{y}' = \sum_{\mathbf{y} \in B} \mathbf{y} r(\mathbf{y}). \tag{2}$$

Let $\theta \geq 0$ be a scalar and write (1) as

$$\sum_{\mathbf{y} \in B} \mathbf{y} w(\mathbf{y}) - \theta \mathbf{y}' + \theta \mathbf{y}' = \mathbf{b}. \tag{1'}$$

Substitute from (2) into (1′):

$$\sum_{\mathbf{y} \in B} \mathbf{y}[w(\mathbf{y}) - \theta r(\mathbf{y})] + \theta \mathbf{y}' = \mathbf{b}. \tag{1''}$$

Let $w(\mathbf{y},\theta) = w(\mathbf{y}) - \theta r(\mathbf{y})$ for $\mathbf{y} \in B$, $= \theta$ for $\mathbf{y} = \mathbf{y}'$, and $= 0$ otherwise.

Suppose $r(\mathbf{y}) \leq 0$, all $\mathbf{y} \in B$. Then (1) would be satisfied for θ arbitrarily large with $w(\mathbf{y}) = w(\mathbf{y},\theta)$. We exclude this possibility by supposing that the *set of solutions of* (1) *is bounded* so that $r(\mathbf{y}) > 0$ some $y \in B$. Let

$$\theta^* = \min_{\substack{\mathbf{y} \in B \\ r(\mathbf{y}) > 0}} \frac{w(\mathbf{y})}{r(\mathbf{y})} = \frac{w(\mathbf{y}'')}{r(\mathbf{y}'')}.$$

If this minimum is unique with $w(\mathbf{y}) > 0$, then setting $\theta = \theta^*$ in (1″) gives us a new solution of (1):

$$\sum_{\mathbf{y} \in B} \mathbf{y} w'(\mathbf{y}) = \mathbf{b} \qquad w'(\mathbf{y}) = w(\mathbf{y}) - \theta^* r(\mathbf{y})$$
$$\mathbf{y} \in B,\ w(\mathbf{y}') = \theta^*$$

If the minimum is not unique and/or $w(\mathbf{y}) = 0$, there is said to be *degeneracy*.

(c) We deal with degeneracy in the following way (see Dantzig [1951, pp. 365–367]; Charnes [1952]). Let us say that the vector

$\mathbf{w}^1$ is *lexicographically greater* than the vector $\mathbf{w}^2$ if $w_j^1 > w_j^2$ when $j = \min\{i \mid w_i^1 \neq w_i^2\}$. We write this as $\mathbf{w}^1 >_L \mathbf{w}^2$.

Now let $\mathbf{w}(\mathbf{y})$ be $(n + 1)$-dimensional with the coordinates indexed $(0, \ldots, n)$, and consider the equation and inequalities:

$$\sum_{\mathbf{y} \in B} \mathbf{y}\mathbf{w}(\mathbf{y}) = (\mathbf{b}, I), \qquad \mathbf{w}(\mathbf{y}) >_L \mathbf{0} \text{ all } \mathbf{y} \in B, \tag{3}$$

where B is a basis. If (3) can be satisfied, we say that B is a feasible basis and note that the solution of (3) contains as the coordinate labeled "0" the solution to problem (1).

Now suppose that $\mathbf{y}' \in Y \sim B$ and that there is a new feasible basis B' where $B \sim \{\mathbf{y}''\} = B' \sim \{\mathbf{y}'\}$. Then there is a vector $\mathbf{v}$ such that

$$\sum_{\mathbf{y} \in B} \mathbf{y}\mathbf{w}(\mathbf{y}) - \mathbf{y}'\mathbf{v} + \mathbf{y}'\mathbf{v} = \sum_{\mathbf{y} \in B} \mathbf{y}[\mathbf{w}(\mathbf{y}) - \mathbf{v}r(\mathbf{y})] + \mathbf{y}\mathbf{v} = (\mathbf{b}, I) \tag{3'}$$

and

$$\mathbf{v} = \frac{\mathbf{w}(\mathbf{y}'')}{r(\mathbf{y}'')}.$$

Certainly $\mathbf{v} >_L \mathbf{0}$. So we need show only that $\mathbf{y}''$ is the only element removed from B, that is, that

$$\min_{\substack{\mathbf{y} \in B \\ r(\mathbf{y}) > 0}} \frac{\mathbf{w}(\mathbf{y})}{r(\mathbf{y})}$$

is unique.

If not, then $\mathbf{w}(\mathbf{y}'') = [r(\mathbf{y}'')]/[r(\mathbf{y}^1)]\mathbf{w}(\mathbf{y}^1)$, for $\mathbf{y}^1 \neq \mathbf{y}''$. Let W be the $n \times n$ matrix, the rows of which are the n-dimensional vectors ${}^0\mathbf{w}(\mathbf{y})$ formed from $\mathbf{w}(\mathbf{y})$ by deleting the first element. Let $[\mathbf{y}]_B$ be the matrix formed for $\mathbf{y} \in B$. Then, by (3), $[\mathbf{y}]_B W = I$. Postmultiply both sides of the equation by the vector $\mathbf{k}$ and note $W\mathbf{k} = \mathbf{0}$ implies $\mathbf{k} = \mathbf{0}$, so W is non-singular. Then it is impossible for two rows, ${}^0\mathbf{w}(\mathbf{y}'')$, ${}^0\mathbf{w}(\mathbf{y}^1)$ of W to be proportional and so the minimum must be unique.

The Scarf algorithm requires us to consider another set, which for the moment we write as Z, and, also for the moment, take to have as its elements n-dimensional vectors $\mathbf{z}$. In Z we are interested in certain subsets with the property that all of its elements are "close" to each other. Such a set will be called a *primitive set* of Z. We shall consider a one-to-one mapping from subsets of Z to subsets of Y.

Suppose there is $D \subset Z$ such that the mapping takes D into a basis B in Y, where B is feasible for problem (1). Suppose also that D can be chosen so that all but one of its elements are the same as that of a primitive set in Z. We could try to bring the two sets into "agreement" (have them contain the same elements) by either removing the non-agreeing element from the primitive set and finding another one to replace it, or inserting the element of the primitive set that is not in D into D and, accordingly, removing one element from D. The latter operation, given the mapping, involves finding a new feasible basis for problem (1); the first operation involves finding a new primitive set from a given primitive set. If it is the case that there is always a unique way of performing these operations (as we already know to be the case with changes in feasible base) and if the steps never cycle, we can show that the attempt to bring D into agreement with a primitive set of Z will eventually be accomplished.

To see why this algorithm can lead to a fixed-point theorem, let $\mathbf{b} = \mathbf{e}'$ in (1), where $\mathbf{e}'$ is the n-dimensional row vector with one in every place. Let Z be a finite subset of the n-dimensional simplex and $\mathbf{f}(\mathbf{z})$ a single-valued continuous map of the simplex into itself. Let $\mathbf{y}(\mathbf{z})$ be the mapping from Z to Y referred to above and write

$$\mathbf{y}(\mathbf{z}) = \mathbf{f}(\mathbf{z}) - \mathbf{z} + \mathbf{e}'.$$

Suppose that when the algorithm terminates we have

$$\sum_{\mathbf{z} \in P} \mathbf{y}(\mathbf{z}) w(\mathbf{z}) = \sum_{\mathbf{z} \in P} [\mathbf{f}(\mathbf{z}) - \mathbf{z} + \mathbf{e}'] w(\mathbf{z}) = \mathbf{e}', \tag{4}$$

where P is the primitive set in Z with which the algorithm terminates.

Since $\mathbf{e}\mathbf{f}(\mathbf{z}) = \mathbf{e}\mathbf{z} = 1$, we have $\mathbf{e}[\mathbf{f}(\mathbf{z}) - \mathbf{z} + \mathbf{e}'] = n$ whence premultiplying (4) by $\mathbf{e}$ gives

$$n \sum_{\mathbf{z} \in P} w(\mathbf{z}) = n$$

or

$$\sum_{\mathbf{z} \in P} w(\mathbf{z}) = 1. \tag{5}$$

Now suppose that the elements of P are so "close" that we may take them as identical. Here we are thinking of a limiting operation that of course will require Z to be suitably dense (see Lemmas C.1 and C.2). Then, in view of (5), (4) becomes $\mathbf{f}(\mathbf{z}) - \mathbf{z} = 0$, which is the Brouwer fixed point.

While these remarks may serve to motivate the discussion that follows, there are a good many complications that we have neglected and that account for some of the special procedures we adapt.

(a) We can define a primitive set of Z as follows. Let P be an n-element subset of Z. Let $\hat{\mathbf{z}}$ be the vector formed by making each of its components equal to the smallest corresponding component of any vector in P. Consider the set $\mathbf{z} \in Z$ such that $\mathbf{z} \geq \hat{\mathbf{z}}$. Then we can say that P is primitive if the set just defined has an empty interior. If so, there are no elements of Z that can be expressed as convex mixtures of elements in P and so there are no elements of Z that lie "between" the elements of P in that case.

However, difficulties similar to those discussed under the heading of degeneracy in linear programming arise if there are elements in P with zero coordinates and if there is more than one vector in P that has a given smallest coordinate. The algorithm requires us to remove one element from P and uniquely replace it by another in order to form a new primitive set.

(b) It will be recalled that Y contains the n vectors $\mathbf{e}^i$ and that we concern ourselves with mapping points from another set into Y. It will be convenient to replace Z by the set $X \cup J$ where X is a set of n-dimensional vectors and J the set of integers $1, \ldots, n$. In our mapping we shall associate with any $j \in J$ the vector $\mathbf{e}^j$ in Y.

To form a primitive set in $X \cup J$ to allow us to pass from one such set to another, we must induce an order on the elements of $X \cup J$. To avoid degeneracy we wish to avoid "ties." This we can accomplish by a cyclic permutation of the series $1, \ldots, n$. The formal theory follows in the next section, but we shall consider an illustration here.

Let the vectors in X be three-dimensional and $J = 1, 2, 3$. Consider a cyclic permutation of the indexes, 2, 3, 1, which we might call a "2-ordering" since 2 is now the leading term. Then in this ordering $1 > 3$, since 1 comes after 3. Also, of course, $1 > 2$.

Now consider a 2-ordering of the coordinates of elements in X. That is, the coordinate labeled "2" is the first entry of each vector, the coordinate labeled 3 is the second, and that labeled 1 is the third. Consider in the ordering two elements $\mathbf{x}, \mathbf{x}'$ in X, $\mathbf{x} \neq \mathbf{x}'$. Certainly they must differ in at least one coordinate. Find the 2-smallest such coordinate, that is, the first coordinate in the 2-ordering in which they differ. Suppose it has the label "3." Then we shall say $\mathbf{x} >_2 \mathbf{x}'$ if $x_3 > x_3'$ and $\mathbf{x} <_2 \mathbf{x}'$ if $x_3 < x_3'$.

To compare an element of J with an element of X requires a convention and we chose the following. In a 2-order, we regard $2 <_2 \mathbf{x}$, all $\mathbf{x} \in X$, and all other integers, that is, 1 or 3, are 2-greater than every element of X.

It is plain that in this illustration the choice of a 2-order was arbitrary—we could have taken instead a 3-order or, indeed, a 1-order.

We note that for unequal vectors in X either $\mathbf{x} >_2 \mathbf{x}'$ or $\mathbf{x}' >_2 \mathbf{x}$ so that they are strictly ordered. Moreover, there is a complete 2-order of all elements in $X \cup J$, and since it is strict, there is a unique 2-minimum element.

With these conventions, let Q be an n-element subset of $X \cup J$. Let $\bar{\mathbf{x}}^i(Q)$ be the i-minimum element in Q. Then we say that Q is primitive if there is no $\mathbf{x}$ in $X \cup J$ such that $\mathbf{x} >_i \bar{\mathbf{x}}^i(Q)$, all i. If there is such an $\mathbf{x}$ we say that it dominates Q. In our example i takes on the values 1, 2, 3.

To illustrate, let X be the set of three vectors: $\mathbf{x}^1 = (3,7,6)$, $\mathbf{x}^2 = (3,5,1)$, $\mathbf{x}^3 = (5,4,1)$. Also let $\mathbf{x}^4 = 1$, $\mathbf{x}^5 = 2$, $\mathbf{x}^6 = 3$. Suppose Q has the elements $\mathbf{x}^1$, $\mathbf{x}^2$, and $\mathbf{x}^4$. Then $\bar{\mathbf{x}}^1(Q) = \mathbf{x}^4$, $\bar{\mathbf{x}}^2(Q) = \mathbf{x}^2$, $\bar{\mathbf{x}}^3(Q) = \mathbf{x}^2$. Then certainly $\mathbf{x}^1 >_i \bar{\mathbf{x}}^i(Q)$, all i, and the set cannot be primitive.

Next let Q have the elements $\mathbf{x}^1$, $\mathbf{x}^4$, and $\mathbf{x}^6$. Then $\bar{\mathbf{x}}^1(Q) = \mathbf{x}^4$, $\bar{\mathbf{x}}^2(Q) = \mathbf{x}^1$, $\bar{\mathbf{x}}^3(Q) = \mathbf{x}^6$. It is plain that no element of Q dominates Q. Also, we have $\mathbf{x}^5 <_2 \bar{\mathbf{x}}^2(Q)$, $\mathbf{x}^2 <_2 \bar{\mathbf{x}}^2(Q)$, and $\mathbf{x}^3 <_2 \mathbf{x}^2(Q)$, so no element outside Q dominates Q. Hence $(\mathbf{x}^1,\mathbf{x}^4,\mathbf{x}^6)$ is a primitive set.

Notice that when we were considering the set $(\mathbf{x}^1,\mathbf{x}^2,\mathbf{x}^4)$, we had $\mathbf{x} = \bar{\mathbf{x}}^i(Q)$ for more than one i and found that the set was not primitive. Indeed, it is easy to show (see (17)) that if Q is primitive, $\mathbf{x} = \bar{\mathbf{x}}^i(Q)$ for exactly one i. Also note that a primitive set cannot consist of elements of J only, since by definition, $\mathbf{x} >_i i$, if $\mathbf{x} \in X$.

Suppose we start with the primitive set Q: $(\mathbf{x}^1,\mathbf{x}^4,\mathbf{x}^6)$ and are told to remove $\mathbf{x}^4$ from it. The problem is to find a replacement for this element so that a new primitive set Q' will be formed. Call this element $\mathbf{x}''$—we still have to find it, but first assume that indeed a new primitive set Q' can be formed. We proceed by steps.

(a) $\mathbf{x}^4$ is 1-minimum in Q. We show that $\mathbf{x}''$ cannot be 1-minimum in Q'. This is easy, for the sets $Q \sim \{\mathbf{x}^4\}$ and $Q' \sim \{\mathbf{x}''\}$ are the same. Hence, if $\mathbf{x}''$ is 1-minimum in Q', we have

$$\bar{\mathbf{x}}^2(Q') = \mathbf{x}^1 \qquad \bar{\mathbf{x}}^3(Q') = \mathbf{x}^6.$$

But also $\mathbf{x}'' \neq \mathbf{x}^4$ so either $\mathbf{x}'' >_1 \mathbf{x}^4$ or $\mathbf{x}'' <_1 \mathbf{x}^4$. In the first case, since $\mathbf{x}'' >_2 \mathbf{x}^1$ and $\mathbf{x}'' >_3 \mathbf{x}^6$, $\mathbf{x}''$ would dominate Q, contradicting that it is primitive. In the second case $\mathbf{x}^4 >_2 \mathbf{x}^1$, $\mathbf{x}^4 >_3 \mathbf{x}^6$, and $\mathbf{x}^4 >_1 \mathbf{x}'' = \mathbf{x}^1(Q')$, contradicting that Q' is primitive. Hence $\mathbf{x}'' \neq \bar{\mathbf{x}}^1(Q')$.

(b) Then $\bar{\mathbf{x}}^1(Q') = \mathbf{x}^1$ or $\mathbf{x}^6$. But $\mathbf{x}^6 >_i \mathbf{x}$, all $\mathbf{x} \in X$, $i \neq 3$, and so $\bar{\mathbf{x}}^1(Q') = \mathbf{x}^1$. (This shows that if we had removed $\mathbf{x}^1$ from Q no new primitive set could have been found. For $\mathbf{x}^1$ is 2-minimum and neither $\mathbf{x}^4$ nor $\mathbf{x}^6$ could be 2-minimum in Q'. That is, we cannot proceed with the algorithm if, after the removal of an element from Q, we are left with only elements in J. Not only is $\mathbf{x}^1$ the 1-minimum element in Q', but clearly it is also the 1-minimum element in $Q \sim \{\mathbf{x}^4\} = (\mathbf{x}^1,\mathbf{x}^6)$.)

(c) Since we have shown that $\mathbf{x}^1$ is 1-minimum in Q' and we know that $\mathbf{x}^6$ is 3-minimum in Q', it must be that $\mathbf{x}''$ is 2-minimum in Q'. To find $\mathbf{x}''$ consider the set R of elements of $X \cup J$ that are 1-greater than $\mathbf{x}^1$ and 3-greater than $\mathbf{x}^6$. Certainly this set has at least one member since $\mathbf{x}^5$ satisfies the criteria. Also, of course, $\mathbf{x}''$ must be a member of this set, being the 2-minimum element of Q' and not i-minimum for $i \neq 2$. Find the 2-maximum element of the set we have defined and call it $\mathbf{x}^{**}$. Then $\mathbf{x}^{**} >_1 \mathbf{x}^1$, $\mathbf{x}^{**} >_3 \mathbf{x}^6$. If $\mathbf{x}^{**} >_2 \mathbf{x}''$, then $\mathbf{x}^{**}$ would dominate $Q' = (\mathbf{x}^1,\mathbf{x}^6,\mathbf{x}^4)$, so $\mathbf{x}^{**} = \mathbf{x}''$.

Since $\mathbf{x}^2 <_1 \mathbf{x}^1$ in our example, $\mathbf{x}^2$ is not a candidate for $\mathbf{x}''$. But $\mathbf{x}^3 >_1 \mathbf{x}^1$ and $\mathbf{x}^3 >_3 \mathbf{x}^6$, so $\mathbf{x}^3$ as well as $\mathbf{x}^5$ is a candidate. But $\mathbf{x}^5 <_2 \mathbf{x}$, all $\mathbf{x}$ in X, so $\mathbf{x}^5 <_2 \mathbf{x}^3$, $\mathbf{x}^3 = \mathbf{x}''$, or $Q' = (\mathbf{x}^1,\mathbf{x}^6,\mathbf{x}^3)$. It is easily checked directly that Q' is indeed primitive. But we can also argue as follows. Suppose there is an $\mathbf{x}$ that dominates Q'. Then certainly $\mathbf{x}$ must be 1-greater than $\mathbf{x}^1$ and 3-greater than $\mathbf{x}^6$ and thus $\mathbf{x} \in R$. But also of course $\mathbf{x} >_2 \mathbf{x}''$, and this contradicts the definition of $\mathbf{x}''$ as the 2-maximum element of R.

Hopefully these samples will make it easier to understand the formal presentation that follows.

2. Primitive Sets and Replacements

Several new concepts will be introduced as part of Scarf's proof; the more traditional proofs of fixed-point theorems also require the introduction of concepts peculiar to them, though different from Scarf's.

Let X be a set of non-negative vectors and J the set of integers

$1, \ldots, n$. The set $X \cup J$, is then a well-defined, though somewhat strange, set composed of n vectors and integers. We are interested in sets Q that are n-element subsets of $X \cup J$. The idea is that the integer elements of Q, that is, the set $J \cap Q$, designate certain dimensions that are treated in a special manner. Then, since Q has n elements, there are exactly as many members of $J \sim Q$ as there are of $X \cap Q$, and they will be put into one-to-one correspondence in appropriate ways.

We want to rank elements of X according to their ith coordinate, but analogous to our treatment of the degeneracy in Section C.1, we shall supplement the rules so as to avoid ties; that is, if the ith coordinates are equal, they will rank one element above another according to the relative values of some other coordinates. Also, we want to rank elements of X relative to those of J; we agree that i itself is "smaller in the ith coordinate" than any element of X, but that an integer $j \neq i$ is "larger in the ith coordinate" than any element of X.

Although there are several ways of introducing the desired ranking, it will be most convenient, both theoretically and computationally, to order the integers according to a cyclic permutation with the integer i placed first; then we order the elements of X according to the lowest-ranking tie-breaking component, where the components are ordered according to this cyclic permutation. Specifically, we introduce an i-ordering on J,

$$j <_i j' \quad \text{if} \quad i \leq j < j' \quad \text{or} \quad i \leq j,\ j' < i \quad \text{or} \quad j < j' < i. \tag{6}$$

This amounts to putting the integers $i, \ldots, n$ before the integers $1, \ldots, i-1$ and then ordering them. The relation "$j <_i j'$" will be read, "j is i-smaller than j'."

We now order the elements of X according to the ith coordinate if possible; if not, because of a tie, we order them according to the first unequal coordinate in the i-ordering of coordinates.

For two elements, $\mathbf{x},\mathbf{x}'$ in X, let $I(\mathbf{x},\mathbf{x}')$ be the set of coordinates i for which $x_i \neq x_i'$, and let j be the i-minimum element of $I(\mathbf{x},\mathbf{x}')$. Then we define

$$\mathbf{x} <_i \mathbf{x}' \quad \text{to mean that} \quad x_j < x_j'. \tag{7}$$

Note that if $x_i \neq x_i'$, then i itself is the i-minimum element of $I(\mathbf{x},\mathbf{x}')$ and $\mathbf{x} <_i \mathbf{x}'$ or $\mathbf{x}' <_i \mathbf{x}$ according as $x_i < x_i'$ or $x_i' < x_i$.

We complete the definition of the i-ordering to permit comparisons of elements of J with elements of X.

$$i <_i \mathbf{x} \qquad \text{for all } \mathbf{x} \text{ in } X; \tag{8}$$

$$\mathbf{x} <_i j \qquad \text{for all } \mathbf{x} \text{ in } X \text{ and all } j \neq i, j \in J. \tag{9}$$

It can easily be verified that the i-ordering is an ordering, that is, transitive and connected, and indeed a strict ordering, so that for $\mathbf{x} \neq \mathbf{x}'$ one and only one of the relations $\mathbf{x} <_i \mathbf{x}'$ and $\mathbf{x}' <_i \mathbf{x}$ holds. It follows that for any subset of $X \cup J$ there is a unique i-minimum. Specifically, for any n-element subset, Q, of $X \cup J$, let

$$\bar{\mathbf{x}}^i(Q) \text{ be the } i\text{-minimum element of } Q. \tag{10}$$

We note some elementary consequences of these definitions. From (8) and (9), if $i \in J \cap Q$, then $\bar{\mathbf{x}}^i(Q) = i$. If $i \notin J \cap Q$, so that $i \in J \sim Q$, then $J \cap Q$ has at most $n - 1$ members, so that Q contains at least one member of X. Hence, from (9), it is impossible that $\bar{\mathbf{x}}^i(Q) = j$ for $j \in J, j \neq i$.

$$\begin{aligned} &\text{If } i \in J \cap Q, \text{ then } \bar{\mathbf{x}}^i(Q) = i; \\ &\text{if } i \in J \sim Q, \text{ then } \bar{\mathbf{x}}^i(Q) \in X \cap Q. \end{aligned} \tag{11}$$

If $\bar{x}^i_i(Q) > x_i$ for some $\mathbf{x}$ in $X \cap Q$, it certainly could not be true that $\bar{\mathbf{x}}^i(Q)$ is the i-minimum element.

$$\text{If } i \in J \sim Q, \text{ then } \bar{x}^i_i(Q) = \min_{\mathbf{x} \in Y \cap Q} x_i. \tag{12}$$

We will associate with Q a cone contained in the non-negative orthant. Define a vector $\boldsymbol{\xi}(Q)$ by the coordinate relations:

$$\xi_i(Q) = \begin{cases} 0 & \text{if } i \in J \cap Q \\ \bar{x}^i_i(Q) & \text{if } i \in J \sim Q \end{cases} \tag{13}$$

Then define a convex cone,

$$T(Q) = \{\mathbf{x} \mid \mathbf{x} \geq \boldsymbol{\xi}(Q)\}. \tag{14}$$

The above definitions amount to saying that we choose $m \leq n$ elements of X and a corresponding number of coordinate directions; then $T(Q)$ is the smallest cone similar to the non-negative orthant containing these points and unrestricted in all other coordinate directions.

Now define,

DEFINITION 4. An element $\mathbf{x}$ in X *dominates* an n-element subset, Q, of $X \cup J$, $\mathbf{x}$ dom Q, if and only if $\mathbf{x} >_i \bar{\mathbf{x}}^i(Q)$, all i. Q is said to be *primitive* if it is undominated by any element of X.

If $T(Q)$ had an element of X in its interior, then it would certainly be dominated.

$$\text{If } Q \text{ is primitive, then the interior of } T(Q) \text{ is disjoint from } X. \tag{15}$$

The converse is not quite true, because of the possibility of ties in any one coordinate that are broken by looking at another coordinate.

We first note some elementary properties of primitive sets. Suppose Q contained no elements of X, that is, $Q \subset J$. Since Q and J both have n elements, $Q = J$. Then $\bar{\mathbf{x}}^i(Q) = i$, all i; but, by (8), $\mathbf{x}$ dom Q for any $\mathbf{x} \in X$.

$$\text{If } Q \text{ is primitive, } X \cap Q \text{ is non-null.} \tag{16}$$

Suppose $\mathbf{x} \in Q$, $\mathbf{x} \neq \bar{\mathbf{x}}^i(Q)$. By (10), then, $\mathbf{x} >_i \bar{\mathbf{x}}^i(Q)$. Hence, if Q is primitive, for all $\mathbf{x} \in Q$, $\mathbf{x} = \bar{\mathbf{x}}^i(Q)$ for some i, for otherwise $\mathbf{x}$ dom Q. Since both J and Q have n elements, it is impossible that $\mathbf{x} = \bar{\mathbf{x}}^i(Q)$ for more than one i, since then there would be some $\mathbf{x}' \neq \bar{\mathbf{x}}^i(Q)$, all i.

$$\text{If } Q \text{ is primitive, then for all } \mathbf{x} \in Q,\ \mathbf{x} = \bar{\mathbf{x}}^i(Q) \text{ for exactly one } i. \tag{17}$$

If $\mathbf{x} \in X \cap Q$, $\xi_i(Q) > x_i$, then $\xi_i(Q) > 0$; from (13), $i \in J \sim Q$, and then there is a contradiction from (13) and (12). Therefore,

$$x_i \geq \xi_i(Q) \qquad \text{for } \mathbf{x} \in X \cap Q, \text{ all } i.$$

It follows from (16) that

$$T(Q) \cap X \text{ is non-null.} \tag{18}$$

A primitive set is, in some suggestive ways, analogous to a basis in linear programming; the set $J \cap Q$ is analogous to the set of slack vectors. A key step in linear programming is the pivotal transformation by which one element is removed from a basis and replaced by another. In general, this replacement is unique. The following definition introduces an analogous step.

DEFINITION 5. Q' is said to be *a replacement of* $\mathbf{x}'$ *in* Q if Q and Q' are primitive sets and $Q \sim Q' = \{\mathbf{x}'\}$.

In other words, $\mathbf{x}'$ is removed from the primitive set Q and replaced by another element of $X \cup J$, say $\mathbf{x}''$, in such a way that the new set, Q', is also primitive.

THEOREM 2. If Q is primitive and $\mathbf{x}' \in Q$, then there is no replacement of $\mathbf{x}'$ in Q if $Q \sim \{\mathbf{x}'\} \subset J$ and exactly one replacement otherwise.

Proof. We suppose that such a replacement exists and find necessary conditions. Let $\mathbf{x}''$ be the sole element of $Q' \sim Q$, that is, the new element in Q'. From (17), we can assume, without loss of generality, that

$$\mathbf{x}' = \bar{\mathbf{x}}^1(Q).$$

First, suppose that $\mathbf{x}'' = \bar{\mathbf{x}}^1(Q')$; we show that this is impossible. From (17), we would have, for $i > 1$, $\bar{\mathbf{x}}^i(Q) \in Q \sim \{\mathbf{x}\}$, $\bar{\mathbf{x}}^i(Q') \in Q' \sim \{\mathbf{x}''\}$. Since $\bar{\mathbf{x}}^i(Q)$ is i-minimum in Q, it is certainly i-minimum in the subset, $Q \sim \{\mathbf{x}'\}$, and similarly, $\bar{\mathbf{x}}^i(Q')$ is i-minimum in $Q' \sim \{\mathbf{x}''\}$, which, however, is the same set.

$$\bar{\mathbf{x}}^i(Q) = \bar{\mathbf{x}}^i(Q') \qquad \text{for } i > 1.$$

From (10) and (17), $\mathbf{x}' >_i \bar{\mathbf{x}}^i(Q) = \bar{\mathbf{x}}^i(Q')$ for $i > 1$, and similarly $\mathbf{x}'' >_i \bar{\mathbf{x}}^i(Q)$ for $i > 1$. Since $\mathbf{x}' \neq \mathbf{x}''$, either $\mathbf{x}' >_1 \mathbf{x}''$ or $\mathbf{x}'' >_1 \mathbf{x}'$. Since $\mathbf{x}' = \bar{\mathbf{x}}^1(Q)$, $\mathbf{x}'' = \bar{\mathbf{x}}^1(Q')$, we have in the first case that $\mathbf{x}'$ dom Q' and in the second that $\mathbf{x}''$ dom Q, both of which contradict the assumed primitivity of Q and Q'. Thus the supposition $\mathbf{x}'' = \bar{\mathbf{x}}^1(Q')$ leads to a contradiction.

Then, $\bar{\mathbf{x}}^1(Q')$ must belong to $Q' \sim \{\mathbf{x}''\} = Q \sim \{\mathbf{x}'\}$. Let

$$\mathbf{x}^* = \bar{\mathbf{x}}^1(Q'). \tag{19}$$

Since $\mathbf{x}^* \in Q$, $\mathbf{x}^* = \bar{\mathbf{x}}^i(Q)$, some i, but $\mathbf{x}^* \neq \mathbf{x}' = \bar{\mathbf{x}}^1(Q)$, so that $i > 1$. Without loss of generality, we may suppose

$$\mathbf{x}^* = \bar{\mathbf{x}}^2(Q). \tag{20}$$

If $\mathbf{x}^* \in J$, then we have to have, by (11), $\mathbf{x}^* = 1$, from (19), and $\mathbf{x}^* = 2$, from (20), a contradiction.

$$\mathbf{x}^* \in X \cap [Q \sim \{\mathbf{x}'\}]. \tag{21}$$

This statement already shows that it is necessary for the existence of a replacement of $\mathbf{x}'$ in Q that $X \cap [Q \sim \{\mathbf{x}'\}]$ be non-null. Hence, if $Q \sim \{\mathbf{x}'\} \subset J$, then there is no such replacement, so the first part of T.C.2 is confirmed.

From (10), $\mathbf{x}^*$ is 1-minimum in Q'; from (21),

$$\mathbf{x}^* \text{ is 1-minimum in } X \cap [Q' \sim \{\mathbf{x}''\}] = X \cap [Q \sim \{\mathbf{x}'\}], \qquad (22)$$

so that $\mathbf{x}^*$ is uniquely defined and by a constructive procedure.

From (19) and (17), $\mathbf{x}^*$ is not 2-minimum in Q'. From (20), $\mathbf{x}^*$ is 2-minimum in Q and therefore in $Q \sim \{\mathbf{x}'\} = Q' \sim \{\mathbf{x}''\}$; hence

$$\mathbf{x}'' = \bar{\mathbf{x}}^2(Q'). \qquad (23)$$

Now $Q \sim [\{\mathbf{x}'\} \cup \{\mathbf{x}^*\}] = Q' \sim [\{\mathbf{x}''\} \cup \{\mathbf{x}^*\}]$. For $i > 2$, $\bar{\mathbf{x}}^i(Q)$ is i-minimum in the first of these sets and $\bar{\mathbf{x}}^i(Q')$ in the second.

$$\bar{\mathbf{x}}^i(Q) = \bar{\mathbf{x}}^i(Q') \qquad \text{for } i > 2. \qquad (24)$$

We seek a characterization of $\mathbf{x}''$. Define the set

$$R = \{\mathbf{x} \mid \mathbf{x} \in X \cup J, \mathbf{x} >_1 \mathbf{x}^*, \mathbf{x} >_i \bar{\mathbf{x}}^i(Q) \qquad \text{for } i > 2\}. \qquad (25)$$

First, note that R is necessarily non-null, for $2 \in R$; from (9), $2 >_i \mathbf{x}$ for all $\mathbf{x} \in X$ if $i \neq 2$, while from (6), $2 >_i i$ for all $i \in J$, $i \neq 2$. Also, we note that, from (23) and (17), $\mathbf{x}'' \in R$. Let $\mathbf{x}^{**}$ be the 2-maximum element of R. From (19) and (24), it follows from the definition of R that,

$$\mathbf{x}^{**} >_i \bar{\mathbf{x}}^i(Q') \qquad \text{for } i \neq 2.$$

If $\mathbf{x}^{**} >_2 \mathbf{x}''$, then, from (23), $\mathbf{x}^{**}$ dom Q', contrary to assumption. Therefore, $\mathbf{x}^{**} = \mathbf{x}''$, by definition of a 2-maximum element.

$$\mathbf{x}'' \text{ is the 2-maximum element of } R. \qquad (26)$$

From (22), $\mathbf{x}^*$ is uniquely defined, and therefore, so is $\mathbf{x}''$, by (25) and (26). Thus, there is, at most, one replacement of $\mathbf{x}'$ in Q. It remains to show that these conditions are sufficient for a replacement. Since Q', defined as $[Q \sim \{\mathbf{x}'\}] \cup \{\mathbf{x}''\}$, has n elements, it suffices to show that it is primitive. First, we will show that $\bar{\mathbf{x}}^i(Q')$ are indeed as given in (19), (23), and (24). If $1 \in Q$, then $\mathbf{x}' = 1$, so that, in any case, $1 \notin Q \sim \{\mathbf{x}'\}$. It then follows from (22) and (9) that $\mathbf{x}^*$ is 1-minimum in $Q \sim \{\mathbf{x}'\} = Q' \sim \{\mathbf{x}''\}$. From (25) and (26), $\mathbf{x}'' >_1 \mathbf{x}^*$, so that (19) is confirmed. Similarly, for $i > 2$, $\bar{\mathbf{x}}^i(Q)$ is i-minimum in Q and therefore in $Q \sim \{\mathbf{x}'\} = Q' \sim \{\mathbf{x}''\}$, while $\mathbf{x}'' >_i \bar{\mathbf{x}}^i(Q)$, so that (24) holds.

From (25), $\mathbf{x}^*$ does not belong to R. Suppose that $\mathbf{x}'' >_2 \mathbf{x}^*$. Since $\mathbf{x}^* = \bar{\mathbf{x}}^2(Q)$, from (20), we have, from (25), $\mathbf{x}'' >_i \bar{\mathbf{x}}^i(Q)$ for $i > 1$. Since $\mathbf{x}^* >_1 \bar{\mathbf{x}}^1(Q)$, from (20), and $\mathbf{x}'' >_1 \mathbf{x}^*$, by definition of R, we have, by transitivity, that $\mathbf{x}'' >_1 \bar{\mathbf{x}}^1(Q)$, so that $\mathbf{x}''$ dom Q, contrary to hypothesis. Hence, $\mathbf{x}^* >_2 \mathbf{x}''$. Again from (20), $\mathbf{x}^*$ is 2-minimum in Q and therefore in $Q \sim \{\mathbf{x}'\} = Q' \sim \{\mathbf{x}''\}$, so that (23) must hold.

It is now easy to show that Q' is primitive. If $\mathbf{x}$ dom Q', it follows from (19), (24), and (25) that $\mathbf{x} \in R$, while also $\mathbf{x} >_2 \bar{\mathbf{x}}^2(Q')$, a contradiction to (26). This completes the proof of the theorem.

Corollary 2. If Q' is the replacement of $\mathbf{x}'$ in Q and $\mathbf{x}''$ is the sole element of $Q' \sim Q$, then Q is the replacement of $\mathbf{x}''$ in Q.

This follows immediately from the uniqueness of the replacement and its definition.

Remark. It has been shown that the unique replacement of $\mathbf{x}'$ in Q can be achieved in a finite number of steps, by (22), (25), and (26). The determination of $\mathbf{x}^*$ in (22) involves a search among, at most, $n - 1$ alternatives, and n usually will be taken in application to be a fixed number (for example, the number of commodities). However, the set X will be taken to be very large; indeed, in the determination of a fixed point, the larger the set X, the better the approximation. It would appear on the face of it that the determination of the set R requires searching through the entire $X \cup J$, which is not very appealing. In general, this is true, but it is possible to reduce the calculation to a minor exercise if X happens to be the set of elements of S_n with rational coordinates and a fixed denominator, that is,

$$X_N = \left\{\mathbf{x} \mid x_i = \frac{a_i}{N}, \quad a_i \text{ non-negative integers}, \sum_i x_i = 1\right\}.$$

For details, see Hansen and Scarf [1969, Section IV] and Kuhn [1968, pp. 1240–1242].

3. Scarf's Theorem

THEOREM 3. Let X be a set of n vectors, $\mathbf{y}(\mathbf{x})$ a function mapping X into a set Y of n vectors, I the set of unit vectors and J the set of integers $1, \ldots, n$. If $\mathbf{b} \geq \mathbf{0}$ and if the set of inequalities,

$$\sum_{\mathbf{y} \in Y \cup I} \mathbf{y} w(\mathbf{y}) = \mathbf{b} \qquad w(\mathbf{y}) \geq 0,$$

has a bounded set of solutions, then there exists a feasible basis B for the system of inequalities and a primitive set Q for the set $X \cup J$ such that B is the image of Q under the mapping $\mathbf{y}(\mathbf{x})$, where it is understood that $\mathbf{y}(j) = \mathbf{e}^j$ for $j \in J$.

Proof. The ingenious combinatorial argument parallels one introduced by Lemke and Howson [1964] for finding the equilibrium points of a two-person non-zero sum game with finitely many strategies for each player; for excellent expositions and greatly widened range of applications, see Lemke [1968] and Dantzig and Cottle [1968].

For the purposes of this proof, an n-element subset C of $X \cup J$ will be termed a feasible basis if its image under the mapping $\mathbf{y}(\mathbf{x})$, denoted by $\mathbf{y}(C)$, is a feasible basis. A feasible basis C is said to *agree* with a primitive set Q if $Q = C$. We seek to show that there exists a pair (C,Q) such that C agrees with Q. A feasible basis C is said to *almost agree* with a primitive set Q if $C \sim Q = \{1\}$; that is, $n - 1$ elements of $B = \mathbf{y}(C)$ correspond to elements of Q, but B also contains the first unit vector.

This method of proof is to begin with a pair (C_0, Q_0) that almost agrees and then continue with a series of transformations that take an almost agreeing pair into either an almost agreeing pair or an agreeing pair. It will be shown that the sequence can never repeat; since there are only finitely many possible pairs, the process must eventually terminate in an agreeing pair, which not only demonstrates the theorem, but exhibits a finite algorithm for arriving at a basis that is both feasible and primitive.

If C almost agrees with Q, $Q \sim C$ must contain exactly one element; define

$$\mathbf{x}(C,Q) \text{ is the sole element of } Q \sim C. \tag{27}$$

If C is a feasible basis, then $\mathbf{y}(C)$ is a feasible basis in its appropriate set $Y \cup I$. Since both sets have n elements, the mapping $\mathbf{y}(\mathbf{x})$ has a unique inverse for $\mathbf{x} \in C$. If $\mathbf{x}' \notin C$, we define C' to be the *insertion* of $\mathbf{x}'$ in C essentially if C' is the inverse of the insertion of $\mathbf{y}(\mathbf{x}')$ in $\mathbf{y}(C)$. In more detail, if $\mathbf{y}''$ is the eliminated element in this insertion, then $\mathbf{y}'' = \mathbf{y}(\mathbf{x}'')$ for some unique $\mathbf{x}''$, and we define C' as $[C \sim \{\mathbf{x}''\}] \cup \{\mathbf{x}'\}$. It can happen that $\mathbf{y}(\mathbf{x}')$ is in fact already an element of $\mathbf{y}(C)$; that is, $\mathbf{y}(\mathbf{x}') = \mathbf{y}(\mathbf{x}'')$ for some $\mathbf{x}'' \in C$. There cannot be more than one such $\mathbf{x}''$, since the elements of $\mathbf{y}(C)$ are distinct. The insertion of $\mathbf{y}(\mathbf{x}')$ in $\mathbf{y}(C)$ has no meaning in this case, or more precisely, the "insertion" simply leaves the basis unchanged, but we can still define C' in exactly the same way, and C' is different from C.

If C almost agrees with Q, we say that the pair (C',Q') is *adjacent* to (C,Q) if either of the following is possible.

(a) $C = C', Q'$ is the replacement of $\mathbf{x}(C,Q)$ in Q;
(b) $Q = Q', C'$ is the insertion of $\mathbf{x}(C,Q)$ in C.

From linear programming theory, the transformation (b) is always possible. We show that the transformation (a) is possible if and only if $C \neq J$. First, suppose $C = J$. Then $C \cap Q$ must consist of the integers $2, \ldots, n$. Since C and Q do not agree, $\mathbf{x}(C,Q)$ must be an element of X. Thus, $Q \sim \{\mathbf{x}(C,Q)\} \subset J$, and by T.C.2, no replacement is possible.

Now suppose $C \neq J$. Then C contains an element, $\mathbf{x}$, of X. Since $C \sim Q = \{1\}$, $\mathbf{x} \in Q$. But $\mathbf{x} \neq \mathbf{x}(C,Q)$, from (27), so that $Q \sim \{\mathbf{x}(C,Q)\}$ contains an element of X, and a replacement is possible. We have shown that if $C \neq J$, both transformations (a) and (b) are possible, while if $C = J$, only (b) is possible.

$$(C,Q) \text{ has one adjacent pair if } C = J, \text{ two adjacent pairs otherwise.} \tag{28}$$

If (C',Q') is adjacent to (C,Q) and C' almost agrees with Q', then it follows from Corollary 2 that (C,Q) is adjacent to (C',Q').

We also observe that if $C = J$, there is only one possible Q that almost agrees with C. As already seen, Q must contain $2, \ldots, n$. Then $\bar{\mathbf{x}}^i(Q) = i$, $i > 1$, while $\bar{\mathbf{x}}^1(Q) \in X$. Let $\mathbf{x}^*$ be the 1-maximum element of X. Then $\mathbf{x}^* >_i i$ $(i > 1)$; if also $\mathbf{x}^* >_1 \bar{\mathbf{x}}^1(Q)$, then $\mathbf{x}^*$ dominates Q, and Q would not be primitive. Hence, if $C = J$ and C almost agrees with Q, then Q consists of $\mathbf{x}^*$ and the integers $2, \ldots, n$; call this set Q_0.

We now generate a sequence of pairs, (C_ν,Q_ν), as follows. Let $C_0 = J$ and Q_0 be as just specified. Then there is precisely one pair adjacent to (C_0,Q_0); call it (C_1,Q_1). In general, if $C_\nu \neq J$, there are two pairs adjacent to (C_ν,Q_ν); let $(C_{\nu+1},Q_{\nu+1})$ be adjacent to (C_ν,Q_ν) and distinct from $(C_{\nu-1},Q_{\nu-1})$. By induction, it is immediately verified that if C_ν almost agrees with Q_ν, then $(C_{\nu-1},Q_{\nu-1})$ is adjacent to (C_ν,Q_ν), so that $(C_{\nu+1},Q_{\nu+1})$ is uniquely specified.

Note also that, from the definition of adjacency, if C almost agrees with Q and (C',Q') is adjacent to (C,Q), then C' either agrees or almost agrees with Q'.

Now we demonstrate that the sequence never repeats; that is, it is impossible that $(C_\mu,Q_\mu) = (C_{\nu+1},Q_{\nu+1})$ for $\mu \leq \nu$. Otherwise, pick the smallest such ν. Since two adjacent pairs are never equal, it is impossible that $\mu = \nu$, and by the construction, it is impossible that $\mu = \nu - 1$. Hence $\mu < \nu - 1$.

Suppose $\mu = 0$. Then (C_ν,Q_ν) would be adjacent to (C_0,Q_0) as would (C_1,Q_1). But there is only one pair adjacent to (C_0,Q_0); hence $(C_1,Q_1) = (C_\nu,Q_\nu)$. Since $\nu > 1$, as just seen, this contradicts the choice of ν as the smallest value for which $(C_\mu,Q_\mu) = (C_{\nu+1},Q_{\nu+1})$, for some $\mu \leq \nu$.

Suppose $\mu > 0$. Then $(C_{\mu-1},Q_{\mu-1})$, $(C_{\mu+1},Q_{\mu+1})$, and (C_ν,Q_ν) would all be adjacent to (C_μ,Q_μ). In view of (28) two would have to be equal; but such equality contradicts the choice of ν.

Therefore, all the elements of the sequence (C_ν,Q_ν) are distinct. The sequence can be continued as long as C_ν almost agrees with Q_ν; on the other hand, there are only finitely many possible bases and, *a fortiori*, only finitely many pairs (C,Q) that almost agree. Hence, since all elements of the sequence either agree or almost agree, and the sequence terminates in the first case, it follows that in finitely many steps the algorithm reaches an agreeing pair.

4. Brouwer's and Kakutani's Fixed-Point Theorems

Scarf's theorem yields a remarkably rapid proof of Brouwer's fixed-point theorem, T.C.1. For any given integer, N, we consider the set X to be the set X_N defined in the Remark to T.C.2 and then make a suitable choice of $\mathbf{y}(\mathbf{x})$. The theorem follows by a limiting argument.

LEMMA 1. Let Q_N be any primitive set for $X_N \cup J$, and let $\mathbf{x}_N$ be any element of $X_N \cap Q_N$. By choosing an appropriate subsequence, we can find a proper subset, J^*, of J, and a point, $\mathbf{x}^*$, such that $J \cap Q_N = J^*$ and $\mathbf{x}_N \to \mathbf{x}^*$ along the subsequence, and $x_i^* = 0$ for all $i \in J^*$. The subsequence and the limit point $\mathbf{x}^*$ are independent of the manner of choosing $\mathbf{x}_N$ from $X_N \cap Q_N$.

Proof. Recall the definition of $T(Q_N)$ in (14). Since $X_N \subset S_n$, it follows from (18) that $T(Q_N) \cap S_n$ is non-null; let $\mathbf{x}$ be an element.

Then $\mathbf{ex} = 1$ and, from (14),

$$\mathbf{e}\xi(Q_N) \leq 1. \tag{29}$$

Let U be the subset of the non-negative orthant consisting of all points on or below the fundamental simplex, that is,

$$U = \{\mathbf{x} \mid \mathbf{x} \geq \mathbf{0}, \quad \mathbf{ex} \leq 1\}.$$

The set $T(Q_N)$ is geometrically similar to the non-negative orthant, and therefore the set $U \cap T(Q_N)$ is similar to the set U, with all dimensions reduced in the proportion $1 : 1 - \mathbf{e}\xi(Q_N)$. Consider, in particular, the radius of the largest neighborhood contained in $T(Q_N) \cap S_n$, where the neighborhood is taken relative to S_n; this radius is proportional to $1 - \mathbf{e}\xi(Q_N)$. For N large, the set X_N can be made as dense as desired in S_n, so that the radius of the largest neighborhood relative to S_n that is disjoint from X_N approaches 0 as N approaches infinity. Since, by (15), the interior of $T(Q_N)$ is disjoint from X_N, the same is true of any neighborhood contained in $T(Q_N) \cap S_n$. From all this, it follows that

$$\lim_{N \to \infty} \mathbf{e}\xi(Q_N) = 1. \tag{30}$$

For each N, $J \cap Q_N$ is a proper subset of J; since there are only finitely many such sets, there must be at least one set, J^*, such that $J \cap Q_N = J^*$ for infinitely many N. From now on, consider only such N. The sequence $\xi(Q_N)$ is bounded; hence we can choose another subsequence such that

$$\xi(Q_N) \to \mathbf{x}^*. \tag{31}$$

From the definition of $\xi(Q)$ in (13), $\xi_i(Q_N) = 0$ for $i \in J^*$, so that certainly $x_i^* = 0$ for $i \in J^*$, as claimed. Finally, since $\mathbf{x}_N \in X_N \cap Q_N$, we have both $\mathbf{x}_N \in S_n$ and $\mathbf{x}_N \in T(Q_N)$, so that

$$\mathbf{ex}_N = 1 \qquad \mathbf{x}_N \geq \xi(Q_N).$$

Then it follows from (29)–(31) that $\mathbf{x}_N \to \mathbf{x}^*$ along the subsequence.

We now state a lemma that exhibits, in general, the manner of going to a limit in the application of Scarf's theorem; this lemma is used not only to prove Brouwer's and Kakutani's fixed-point theorems, but also to prove a large variety of other results (for example, see Section C.5).

LEMMA 2. If $\mathbf{y}(\mathbf{x})$ is a bounded mapping from S_n to n space, $\mathbf{b} \geq \mathbf{0}$, and the sets of solutions to the inequalities

$$\sum_{\mathbf{x} \in X \cup J} \mathbf{y}(\mathbf{x}) w(\mathbf{x}) = \mathbf{b} \qquad w(\mathbf{x}) \geq 0$$

for all finite subsets X of S_n are bounded uniformly, then there exists a proper subset, J^*, of J, $\mathbf{u}^* \geq \mathbf{0}$, $v_j^* \geq 0$ $(j = 1, \ldots, m)$, where m is the number of elements in $J \sim J^*$, $\mathbf{x}^*$ in S_n, and $\mathbf{y}^j$ $(j = 1, \ldots, m)$, where, for each j, $\mathbf{y}^j$ is a limit point of $\mathbf{y}(\mathbf{x})$ as $\mathbf{x}$ approaches $\mathbf{x}^*$, such that

(a) $\mathbf{u}^* + \sum_{j=1}^{m} v_j^* \mathbf{y}^j = \mathbf{b}$,

(b) $u_i^* = 0$ for $i \in J \sim J^*$,
$x_i^* = 0$ for $i \in J^*$.

Proof. By T.C.3, for each N, there exists Q_N, which is both a primitive set and a feasible basis for the inequalities

$$\sum_{\mathbf{x} \in X_N \cup J} \mathbf{y}(\mathbf{x}) w(\mathbf{x}) = \mathbf{b} \qquad w(\mathbf{x}) \geq 0.$$

Then, by definition of a feasible basis, we can find $w_N(\mathbf{x}) \geq 0$, $\mathbf{x} \in Q_N$, such that

$$\sum_{\mathbf{x} \in Q_N} \mathbf{y}(\mathbf{x}) w_N(\mathbf{x}) = \mathbf{b}. \tag{32}$$

Choose the subsequence of Lemma C.1 and the corresponding J^*. Let $u_i^N = w_N(i)$ for $i \in J^*$, $u_i^N = 0$ for $i \in J \sim J^*$. Since $\mathbf{y}(i) = \mathbf{e}^i$,

$$\sum_{\mathbf{x} \in J^*} \mathbf{y}(\mathbf{x}) w(\mathbf{x}) = \sum_{i \in J^*} u_i^N \mathbf{e}^i = \sum_{i=1}^{n} u_i^N \mathbf{e}^i = \mathbf{u}^N,$$

where $\mathbf{u}^N$ is the vector with components u_i^N. Enumerate the m elements of $Q_N \sim J^*$ arbitrarily as $\mathbf{x}^{1N}, \ldots, \mathbf{x}^{mN}$, and let $w_N(\mathbf{x}^{jN}) = v_j^N$. Then (32) can be written

$$\mathbf{u}^N + \sum_{j=1}^{m} v_j^N \mathbf{y}(\mathbf{x}^{jN}) = \mathbf{b},$$

where $\mathbf{u}^N \geq 0$, $v_j^N \geq 0$, $u_i^N = 0$ for $i \in J \sim J^*$. From Lemma C.1 there exists $\mathbf{x}^*$ such that $\mathbf{x}^{jN} \to \mathbf{x}^*$ for all j on a suitable subsequence, and $\mathbf{x}_i^* = 0$ for $i \in J^*$. From the boundedness hypothesis of the lemma, the sequences $\mathbf{u}^N$, v_j^N, and $\mathbf{y}(\mathbf{x}^{jN})$ are all bounded; hence, by choosing a further subsequence, we can ensure that

$$\mathbf{u}^N \to \mathbf{u}^* \qquad v_j^N \to v_j^* \qquad \mathbf{y}(\mathbf{x}^{jN}) \to \mathbf{y}^j,$$

so that (a) and (b) hold; that $u_i^* = 0$ for $i \in J \sim J^*$ follows from the fact that $u_i^N = 0$ for those i for all N.

Proof of T.C.1. We now apply Lemma C.2 with an appropriate choice of $\mathbf{y}(\mathbf{x})$ and $\mathbf{b}$. Brouwer's theorem assumes that $\mathbf{f}(\mathbf{x})$ is a continuous mapping of S_n into itself. Hence $\mathbf{ef}(\mathbf{x}) = 1 = \mathbf{ex}$, for all $\mathbf{x} \in S_n$.

Define now

$$\mathbf{y}(\mathbf{x}) = \mathbf{f}(\mathbf{x}) - \mathbf{x} + \mathbf{e}', \quad \mathbf{b} = \mathbf{e}', \qquad \text{for } \mathbf{x} \in S_n, \tag{33}$$

where $\mathbf{e}'$ is the column vector all of whose components are 1. First, we verify that the boundedness hypotheses are verified. Obviously, $\mathbf{y}(\mathbf{x})$ is a bounded function. Let X be any finite subset of S_n, and consider the equations and inequalities

$$\sum_{\mathbf{x} \in X \cup J} \mathbf{y}(\mathbf{x}) w(\mathbf{x}) = \mathbf{e}' \qquad w(\mathbf{x}) \geq 0.$$

Since $\mathbf{y}(i) = \mathbf{e}^i$ for $i \in J$, by letting $u_i = w(i)$ and $\mathbf{u}$ be the vector with components u_i, we can write this system as

$$\mathbf{u} + \sum_{\mathbf{x} \in X} \mathbf{y}(\mathbf{x}) w(\mathbf{x}) = \mathbf{e}' \qquad \mathbf{u} \geq \mathbf{0},\ w(\mathbf{x}) \geq 0, \text{ all } \mathbf{x} \in X. \tag{34}$$

From (33), it is obvious that $\mathbf{ey}(\mathbf{x}) = \mathbf{ef}(\mathbf{x}) - \mathbf{ex} + \mathbf{ee}' = \mathbf{ee}' = n$, all $\mathbf{x} \in X$. Also, $\mathbf{eu} \geq 0$, $\mathbf{eu} = 0$ if and only if $\mathbf{u} = \mathbf{0}$. If we multiply through in (34) on the left by $\mathbf{e}$,

$$\mathbf{eu} + n \sum_{\mathbf{x} \in X} w(\mathbf{x}) = n,$$

so that

$$\begin{aligned} &\sum_{\mathbf{x} \in X} w(\mathbf{x}) \leq 1 && w(\mathbf{x}) \geq 0, \text{ all } \mathbf{x} \in X; \\ &\sum_{\mathbf{x} \in X} w(\mathbf{x}) = 1 && \text{if and only if } \mathbf{u} = \mathbf{0}, \end{aligned} \tag{35}$$

and the solutions for $w(\mathbf{x})$ ($\mathbf{x} \in X$) are, in particular, bounded; from (34), the same must hold for $\mathbf{u}$.

We can therefore apply Lemma C.2 so that

$$\mathbf{u}^* + \sum_{j=1}^{m} v_j^* \mathbf{y}^j = \mathbf{e}', \tag{36}$$

where also Lemma C.2(b) holds, and from (35),

$$\sum_{j=1}^{m} v_j^* \leq 1 \quad \text{and equality implies that} \quad \mathbf{u}^* = 0. \tag{37}$$

Here, $\mathbf{y}^j$ is a limit point of $\mathbf{y}(\mathbf{x})$ as $\mathbf{x}$ approaches $\mathbf{x}^*$. From (33) then

$$\mathbf{y}^j + \mathbf{x}^* - \mathbf{e}' \text{ is a limit point of } \mathbf{f}(\mathbf{x}) \text{ as } \mathbf{x} \text{ approaches } \mathbf{x}^*. \tag{38}$$

Since $\mathbf{f}(\mathbf{x})$ is assumed continuous,

$$\mathbf{y}^j + \mathbf{x}^* - \mathbf{e}' = \mathbf{f}(\mathbf{x}^*) \qquad \text{all } j. \tag{39}$$

Now let $\mathbf{d}$ be the row vector, with $d_i = 0$ for $i \in J^*$, $d_i = 1$ for $i \in J \sim J^*$. From Lemma C.2(b), $\mathbf{du}^* = 0$. Also, $d_i \neq e_i$ only for $i \in J^*$ and therefore only if $x_i^* = 0$, by Lemma C.2(b); hence $\mathbf{dx}^* = \mathbf{ex}^* = 1$. Finally, $\mathbf{d} \leq \mathbf{e}$, so that $\mathbf{df}(\mathbf{x}) \leq \mathbf{ef}(\mathbf{x}) = 1$. From (38) or (39),

$$\mathbf{d}(\mathbf{y}^j + \mathbf{x}^* - \mathbf{e}') \leq 1 \qquad \text{each } j.$$

Since $\mathbf{dx}^* = 1$, this statement can be written $\mathbf{dy}^j \leq \mathbf{de}'$. If we premultiply (36) by $\mathbf{d}$, then we find

$$(\mathbf{de}') \sum_{j=1}^{m} v_j^* \geq \mathbf{de}'.$$

In conjunction with (37), we see that

$$\sum_{j=1}^{m} v_j^* = 1 \qquad \mathbf{u}^* = 0.$$

If we substitute into (36), then we have

$$\mathbf{y}^* = \mathbf{e}' \quad \text{where} \quad \mathbf{y}^* = \sum_{j=1}^{m} v_j^* \mathbf{y}^j \quad \text{and}$$

$$\sum_{j=1}^{m} v_j^* = 1, v_j^* \geq 0, \text{all } j. \tag{40}$$

If we multiply (39) by v_j^* and then sum over j, we have

$$\mathbf{y}^* + \mathbf{x}^* - \mathbf{e}' = \mathbf{f}(\mathbf{x}^*),$$

which, in view of (40) establishes Brouwer's theorem.

We now state and prove Kakutani's generalization of Brouwer's theorem. We first repeat the definition already given in Chapter 4.

DEFINITION 6. A *correspondence* is a mapping of points into sets. A correspondence, $\Phi(\mathbf{x})$, is said to be *upper semi-continuous* if for any sequences $\{\mathbf{x}^\nu\}$, $\{\mathbf{y}^\nu\}$, the conditions $\mathbf{x}^\nu \to \mathbf{x}$, $\mathbf{y}^\nu \to \mathbf{y}$, $\mathbf{y}^\nu \in \Phi(\mathbf{x}^\nu)$, all ν, imply that $\mathbf{y} \in \Phi(\mathbf{x})$.

THEOREM 4 (Kakutani's Fixed-Point Theorem). Let C be a compact convex set and $\Phi(\mathbf{x})$ an upper semi-continuous correspondence defined on C such that $\Phi(\mathbf{x}) \subset C$, $\Phi(\mathbf{x})$ convex, for each $\mathbf{x} \in C$. Then there exists $\mathbf{x}^* \in C$ such that $\mathbf{x}^* \in \Phi(\mathbf{x}^*)$.

Note that if $\Phi(\mathbf{x})$ consists of a single point for each $\mathbf{x}$, this reduces to Brouwer's theorem for a general compact convex domain.

Proof. The above proof of Brouwer's theorem suffices, with slight modifications, to establish Kakutani's theorem for the case in which C is the fundamental simplex, S_n. Then the general case can be handled simply.

For each $\mathbf{x} \in S_n$, choose $\mathbf{f}(\mathbf{x})$ to be an arbitrary element of $\Phi(\mathbf{x})$. Then define $\mathbf{y}(\mathbf{x})$ as before. The entire argument through (38) makes no use of the continuity of $\mathbf{f}(\mathbf{x})$ and so remains valid; also, (40) still holds. Since $\mathbf{f}(\mathbf{x}) \in \Phi(\mathbf{x})$, which is upper semi-continuous, it follows from (38) and D.C.6 that

$$\mathbf{y}^j + \mathbf{x}^* - \mathbf{e}' \in \Phi(\mathbf{x}^*), \qquad \text{each } j.$$

Since, from (40),

$$v_j^* \geq 0, \qquad \text{each } j,$$

and

$$\sum_{j=1}^{m} v_j^* = 1$$

and since $\Phi(\mathbf{x}^*)$ is convex by hypothesis,

$$\sum_{j=1}^{m} v_j^*(\mathbf{y}^j + \mathbf{x}^* - \mathbf{e}') \in \Phi(\mathbf{x}^*),$$

which can be written,

$$\mathbf{y}^* + \mathbf{x}^* - \mathbf{e}' \in \Phi(\mathbf{x}^*).$$

From (40), this establishes Kakutani's theorem.

To extend this to the case in which the domain is a general compact convex set, first note that there is really no loss of generality in assuming that C is a subset of a fundamental simplex. Suppose that the dimensionality of C is $n - 1$; this is the dimensionality of the smallest linear space containing C. Choose a coordinate system in this space of $n - 1$ dimensions; this can be taken to be a linear transformation of the original variables. By shifting origin, we can assume that C is contained in the non-negative orthant. Since C is bounded, $\mathbf{ex}$ is bounded on C; by another simple transformation we can assume that $\mathbf{ex} \leq 1$. Finally, we map C linearly into a subset of S_n by adding an nth coordinate, $1 - \mathbf{ex}$. Thus, C is linearly equivalent to a compact convex subset of S_n and has the same dimensionality. Since all transformations are linear, the hypotheses of Kakutani's theorem remain valid.

Now choose $\mathbf{x}^0$ to be any point of C that is internal relative to the linear space defined by the equation, $\mathbf{ex} = 1$, and let $p(\mathbf{x})$ be the gauge function of C relative to this space (see D.B.8, T.B.1(h)). Then $p(\mathbf{x})$ is continuous, and $p(\mathbf{x} - \mathbf{x}^0) \leq 1$ if and only if $\mathbf{x} \in C$, for $\mathbf{x}$ in this space and in particular for $\mathbf{x} \in S_n$. Let $q(\mathbf{x}) = \max[p(\mathbf{x} - \mathbf{x}^0), 1]$ so that $\mathbf{x} \in C$ if and only if $q(\mathbf{x}) = 1$. Define a mapping,

$$T(\mathbf{x}) = \mathbf{x}^0 + \frac{\mathbf{x} - \mathbf{x}^0}{q(\mathbf{x})};$$

this maps an element of C into itself and an element $\mathbf{x}$ of $S_n \sim C$ into that element of C that is closest to $\mathbf{x}$ on the line segment joining $\mathbf{x}^0$ to $\mathbf{x}$. Since $q(\mathbf{x})$ is bounded away from 0, $\mathbf{T}(\mathbf{x})$ is continuous. Finally, define the correspondence

$$\Phi_1(\mathbf{x}) = \Phi[\mathbf{T}(\mathbf{x})] \qquad \text{for all } \mathbf{x} \in S_n.$$

For $\mathbf{x}$ in C, this is simply the original correspondence. Φ_1 is upper semi-continuous, since Φ is upper semi-continuous and $\mathbf{T}(\mathbf{x})$ is continuous; $\Phi_1(\mathbf{x}) = \Phi[\mathbf{T}(\mathbf{x})]$, where $\mathbf{T}(\mathbf{x}) \in C$ for all $\mathbf{x} \in S_n$, so that for each such $\mathbf{x}$, $\Phi_1(\mathbf{x})$ is convex and $\Phi_1(\mathbf{x}) \subset C \subset S_n$. Hence $\Phi_1(\mathbf{x})$ satisfies all the hypotheses of Kakutani's theorem for the fundamental simplex, and there is a point, $\mathbf{x}^* \in S_n$, such that $\mathbf{x}^* \in \Phi_1(\mathbf{x}^*)$. Since, by construction, $\Phi_1(\mathbf{x}) \subset C$ for all $\mathbf{x} \in S_n$, $\mathbf{x}^* \in C$; then $\mathbf{T}(\mathbf{x}^*) = \mathbf{x}^*$ and $\Phi_1(\mathbf{x}^*) = \Phi(\mathbf{x}^*)$, so that Kakutani's theorem holds for the set C.

Remark. From the computational view, the extension of Kakutani's theorem to a general compact convex set creates only one possible difficulty, namely, the mapping, $T(\mathbf{x})$ of the simplex onto the set. Although the definition is very simple in principle, computation might turn out to be very difficult if the set C is not defined in some simple way.

5. A Direct Computation of Equilibrium in a Simple Model

We conclude this appendix by presenting Scarf's [1967c] algorithm for computing equilibrium in a simple model involving both production and exchange. Although, in principle, all equilibrium computations can be done by using the general reduction to a fixed-point problem, as in Chapter 5, it is frequently preferable from the viewpoint of computational simplicity to use Scarf's theorem directly with a new interpretation of $\mathbf{y}(\mathbf{x})$.

In the present section, the symbols have economic interpretations and therefore the notation of the text will be used. The underlying variable is the price vector, $\mathbf{p}$, which ranges over S_n. Household demand, $\mathbf{x}(\mathbf{p})$, is assumed single valued, continuous, and nonnegative, over S_n. The social production possibility set is taken to be a closed convex cone, Y, which satisfies the conditions of Chapter 4, in particular, A.4.4, so that production without inputs and reversibility are both ruled out. Then T.4.2 holds, so that the set of feasible production vectors,

$$\hat{Y} = Y \cap \{\mathbf{y} \mid \mathbf{y} + \bar{\mathbf{x}} \geq \mathbf{0}\},$$

is compact, where $\bar{\mathbf{x}}$ is the vector of initial endowments. Since profits at equilibrium are 0 for Y, a cone, we can assume

$$\mathbf{p}\mathbf{x}(\mathbf{p}) = \mathbf{p}\bar{\mathbf{x}} \qquad \text{for all } \mathbf{p}; \tag{41}$$

more precisely, we define $\mathbf{x}(\mathbf{p})$ to be household demand from an income generated solely by sale of household possessions. To avoid difficult cases, we assume that $\bar{\mathbf{x}} \gg \mathbf{0}$, so that $\mathbf{p}\bar{\mathbf{x}} > 0$, all $\mathbf{p} \in S_n$.

Equilibrium, allowing for inequalities, can be defined by the relations

$$\mathbf{u}^* + \mathbf{x}(\mathbf{p}^*) = \mathbf{y}^* + \bar{\mathbf{x}}, \qquad \mathbf{u}^* \geq \mathbf{0}, \qquad \mathbf{p}^*\mathbf{u}^* = \mathbf{0}, \qquad \mathbf{y}^* \in Y,$$
$$\mathbf{p}^*\mathbf{y}^* = 0, \qquad \mathbf{p}^*\mathbf{y} \leq 0, \qquad \text{all } \mathbf{y} \in Y. \tag{42}$$

If we define

$$Y^- = \{\mathbf{p} \mid \mathbf{p}\mathbf{y} \leq 0 \quad \text{for all } \mathbf{y} \in Y\} \tag{43}$$

the last condition can be written $\mathbf{p}^* \in Y^-$. (Y^- is frequently referred to as the *polar cone* to Y.)

Now we use again Lemma C.2. With the present notation, we replace $\mathbf{y}(\mathbf{x})$ by $\mathbf{q}(\mathbf{p})$. To define this, note that if $\mathbf{p} \notin Y^-$, then $\mathbf{p}\mathbf{y} > 0$ for some $\mathbf{y} \in Y$; since Y is a cone, we have, for all $\lambda > 0$,

$\lambda\mathbf{y} \in Y$ and $\mathbf{p}(\lambda\mathbf{y}) > 0$. Therefore, for two arbitrary numbers, $0 < M < \overline{M}$, we can require $M \leq |\mathbf{y}| \leq \overline{M}$. Then choose $\mathbf{q}(\mathbf{p})$ so that

$$\mathbf{q}(\mathbf{p}) = -\mathbf{y}, \tag{44}$$

where $\mathbf{py} > 0$, $\mathbf{y} \in Y$, $M \leq |\mathbf{y}| \leq \overline{M}$, for $\mathbf{p} \notin Y^-$, and

$$\mathbf{q}(\mathbf{p}) = \mathbf{x}(\mathbf{p}) \qquad \text{for } p \in Y^-. \tag{45}$$

Let P be any finite subset of S_n. We first establish that the solutions of the inequalities,

$$\mathbf{u} + \sum_{\mathbf{p} \in P} \mathbf{q}(\mathbf{p})w(\mathbf{p}) = \bar{\mathbf{x}} \qquad \mathbf{u} \geq \mathbf{0},\ w(\mathbf{p}) \geq 0,$$

are bounded uniformly in the choice of P. From (44) and (45), these can be written,

$$\mathbf{u} + \sum_{\mathbf{p} \in P \cap Y^-} \mathbf{x}(\mathbf{p})\mathbf{w}(\mathbf{p}) = \sum_{\mathbf{p} \in P \sim Y^-} [-\mathbf{q}(\mathbf{p})]w(\mathbf{p}) + \bar{\mathbf{x}}. \tag{46}$$

Since $-\mathbf{q}(\mathbf{p}) \in Y$ for $\mathbf{p} \in P \sim Y^-$, $w(\mathbf{p}) \geq 0$, all $\mathbf{p}$, and Y is a convex cone,

$$\sum_{\mathbf{p} \in P \sim Y} [-\mathbf{q}(\mathbf{p})]w(\mathbf{p}) = \mathbf{y} \in Y. \tag{47}$$

Since the left-hand side of (46) is certainly non-negative, $\mathbf{y} \in \hat{Y}$ and therefore is bounded. Then, since $|-\mathbf{q}(\mathbf{p})| \geq M$ for $\mathbf{p} \in P \sim Y^-$, it follows from (47) that $w(\mathbf{p})$ is uniformly bounded for such $\mathbf{p}$. Also, from (41), $\mathbf{x}(\mathbf{p}) \neq 0$ for any $\mathbf{p} \in S_n$, so that $|\mathbf{x}(\mathbf{p})|$ is bounded away from 0 on S_n, since it is a continuous function. Since the right-hand side of (46) is bounded, the left-hand side must be; thus, both $\mathbf{u}$ and

$$\sum_{\mathbf{p} \in P \cap Y} \mathbf{x}(\mathbf{p})w(\mathbf{p})$$

are bounded. But since $|\mathbf{x}(\mathbf{p})|$ is bounded uniformly from below, it must be that $w(\mathbf{p})$ is bounded from above for $\mathbf{p} \in P \cap Y^-$.

From the definitions (44) and (45), the function $\mathbf{q}(\mathbf{p})$ is certainly bounded. Hence Lemma C.2 is applicable.

$$\mathbf{u}^* + \sum_{j=1}^{m} v_j^* \mathbf{q}^j = \bar{\mathbf{x}} \qquad \mathbf{u}^* \geq \mathbf{0},\ v_j^* \geq 0; \tag{48}$$

for some set J^*, $u_i^* = 0$ for $i \in J \sim J^*$, $p_i^* = 0$ for $i \in J^*$, so that

$$\mathbf{p}^*\mathbf{u}^* = 0, \tag{49}$$

and, for each $j = 1, \ldots, m$, $\mathbf{q}^j$ is a limit point of $\mathbf{q}(\mathbf{p})$ as $\mathbf{p}$ approaches $\mathbf{p}^*$. Then let

$$\mathbf{q}^j = \lim_{\nu \to \infty} \mathbf{q}(\mathbf{p}^{j\nu}) \qquad \text{where } \lim_{\nu \to \infty} \mathbf{p}^{j\nu} = \mathbf{p}^*.$$

We can classify the indices j into two sets according as the sequence $\{\mathbf{p}^{j\nu}\}$ does or does not have infinitely many members in Y^-. Let the indices in the second set be numbered $1, \ldots, r$, and in the first, $r + 1, \ldots, m$: It still has to be shown that $r < m$, that is, that for some j, $\mathbf{p}^{j\nu} \in Y^-$ for infinitely many ν. For $j > r$, then, $\mathbf{q}(\mathbf{p}^{j\nu}) = \mathbf{x}(\mathbf{p}^{j\nu})$ for infinitely many ν, and $\mathbf{p}^*$ is the limit of a sequence in Y^-; since $\mathbf{x}(\mathbf{p})$ is continuous and Y^- is closed,

$$\mathbf{q}^j = \mathbf{x}(\mathbf{p}^*) \quad \text{for } j > r; \qquad \mathbf{p}^* \in Y^- \quad \text{if } r < m. \tag{50}$$

For $j \leq r$, $-\mathbf{q}(\mathbf{p}^{j\nu}) \in Y$ and $\mathbf{p}^{j\nu}[-\mathbf{q}(\mathbf{p}^{j\nu})] > 0$, all ν. Since Y is closed,

$$-\mathbf{q}^j \in Y, \ -\mathbf{p}^*\mathbf{q}^j \geq 0 \qquad \text{for } j \leq r. \tag{51}$$

From (50) and (51), (48) can be rewritten

$$\mathbf{u}^* + v^*\mathbf{x}(\mathbf{p}^*) = \mathbf{y}^* + \bar{\mathbf{x}}, \tag{52}$$

where

$$v^* = \sum_{j=r+1}^{m} v_j^*$$

and

$$\mathbf{y}^* = \sum_{j=1}^{r} v_j^*(-\mathbf{q}^j).$$

Since Y is a convex cone, it follows from (51) that

$$\mathbf{y}^* \in Y \qquad \mathbf{p}^*\mathbf{y}^* \geq 0.$$

Premultiply both sides of (52) by $\mathbf{p}^*$ and use (49) and (41):

$$(v^* - 1)\mathbf{p}^*\bar{\mathbf{x}} = \mathbf{p}^*\mathbf{y}^*.$$

Then $v^* \geq 1$, $v^* = 1$ if $\mathbf{p}^*\mathbf{y}^* = 0$. But $v^* > 0$ certainly implies that $r < m$; from (50) and the definition of Y^-,

$$\mathbf{p}^*\mathbf{y} \leq 0 \qquad \text{all } \mathbf{y} \in Y,$$

and certainly $\mathbf{p}^*\mathbf{y}^* = 0$ and therefore $v^* = 1$, so that (42) is satisfied.[1]

[1] Attention should be drawn to another algorithm for finding a competitive equilibrium, due to Cottle [1966]; it is applicable to economies in which a slightly stronger version of the Gale property holds, specifically, where all the principal minors of the Jacobian of excess supplies are positive and bounded away from zero and infinity.

BIBLIOGRAPHY

American Mathematical Society [1968]. *The Mathematics of the Decision Sciences.* Providence, Rhode Island: The American Mathematical Society, 2 vols.

Arrow, K. J. [1951]. "An extension of the basic theorems of classical welfare economics," in J. Neyman (ed.), *Proceedings of the Second Berkeley Symposium on Mathematical Statistics and Probability.* Berkeley: University of California Press, pp. 507–532.

Arrow, K. J. [1953]. "Le rôle des valeurs boursières pour la répartition la meilleure des risques," *Econometrie.* Paris: Centre National de la recherche scientifique, pp. 41–48.

Arrow, K. J. [1963]. "Uncertainty and the welfare economics of medical care," *American Economic Review,* **53**, 941–973. Reprinted in Arrow [1970, pp. 177–219].

Arrow, K. J. [1963–1964]. "The role of securities in the optimal allocation of risk-bearing," *Review of Economic Studies,* **31**, 91–96. English translation of Arrow [1953]. Reprinted in Arrow [1970, 121–133].

Arrow, K. J. [1965]. *Aspects of the Theory of Risk-Bearing.* Helsinki: Academic Bookstore. Reprinted in Arrow [1970, 44–120, 134–143].

Arrow, K. J. [1968]. "Economic equilibrium," in *International Encyclopedia of the Social Sciences.* Macmillan and the Free Press, **4**, 376–386.

Arrow, K. J. [1970]. *Essays in the Theory of Risk-Bearing.* Chicago: Markham; London: North-Holland.

Arrow, K. J. [1971]. "The firm in general equilibrium theory," in R. Marris and A. Wood (eds.), *The Corporate Economy: Growth, Competition, and Innovative Potential.* London: Macmillan; Cambridge, Mass.: Harvard University Press, pp. 68–110.

Arrow, K. J., H. D. Block, and L. Hurwicz [1959]. "On the stability of the competitive equilibrium II," *Econometrica,* **27**, 82–109.

Arrow, K. J., and G. Debreu [1954]. "Existence of equilibrium for a competitive economy," *Econometrica,* **22**, 265–290.

Arrow, K. J. and L. Hurwicz [1958]. "On the stability of the competitive equilibrium I," *Econometrica,* **26**, 522–552.

Arrow, K. J., and L. Hurwicz [1960]. "Competitive stability under weak gross substitutability: the 'Euclidean distance' approach," *International Economic Review*, **1**, 38–49.

Arrow, K. J., and L. Hurwicz [1962]. "Competitive equilibrium under weak gross substitutability: non-linear price adjustment and adaptive expectation," *International Economic Review*, **3**, 233–255.

Arrow, K. J., and M. Nerlove [1958]. "A note on expectations and stability," *Econometrica*, **26**, 297–305.

Aumann, R. J. [1964]. "Markets with a continuum of traders," *Econometrica*, **32**, 39–50.

Aumann, R. J. [1966]. "Existence of competitive equilibria in markets with a continuum of traders," *Econometrica*, **34**, 1–17.

Bator, F. M. [1961]. "Convexity, efficiency, and markets," *Journal of Political Economy*, **69**, 480–483.

Becker, G. [1965]. "A theory of the allocation of time," *Economic Journal*, **75**, 495–517.

Bernoulli, D. [1738]. "Specimen theoriae novae de mensura sortis," *Commentarii Academiae Scientiarum Imperiales Petropolitanae*, **5**, 175–192.

Bernoulli, D. [1954]. "Exposition of a new theory of the measurement of risk," *Econometrica*, **12**, 23–36. English translation by L. Sommer of Bernoulli [1738].

Bohm, P. [1963]. *External Economies in Production.* Stockholm: Almqvist & Wiksell. Stockholm Economic Studies, Pamphlet Series 3.

Bowen, R. [1968]. "A new proof of a theorem in utility theory," *International Economic Review*, **9**, 374.

Burger, E. [1963]. *Introduction to the Theory of Games.* Englewood Cliffs, N.J.: Prentice-Hall.

Bushaw, D. W., and R. W. Clower [1957]. *Introduction to Mathematical Economics.* Homewood, Ill.: Irwin.

Cassel, G. [1924]. *The Theory of Social Economy.* New York: Harcourt, Brace.

Chamberlin, E. H. [1948]. "Proportionality, divisibility, and economies of scale," *Quarterly Journal of Economics*, **62**, 229–262.

Chamberlin, E. H. [1949]. "Proportionality, divisibility, and economies of scale: reply," *Quarterly Journal of Economics*, **63**, 137–143.

Chamberlin, E. H. [1956]. *The Theory of Monopolistic Competition*, 7th Edition. Cambridge, Mass.: Harvard University Press.

Charnes, A. [1952]. "Optimality and degeneracy in linear programming," *Econometrica*, **17**, 160–170.

Chipman, J. S. [1970]. "External economies of scale and competitive equilibria," *Quarterly Journal of Economics*, **84**, 347–385.

Clower, R. W. [1965]. "The Keynesian counterrevolution: a theoretical appraisal," in F. H. Hahn and F. P. R. Brechling (eds.), *The Theory of Interest Rates.* London: Macmillan; New York: St. Martin's Press.

Coddington, E. A., and N. Levinson [1955]. *Theory of Ordinary Differential Equations.* New York: McGraw-Hill.
Cottle, R. W. [1966]. "Nonlinear programs with positively bounded Jacobians," *SIAM Journal of Applied Mathematics*, **14**, 147–158.
Cottle, R. W., and G. B. Dantzig [1968]. "Complementary pivot theory of mathematical programming," in *American Mathematical Society* [1968, I: 115–136].
Cournot, A. A. [1838]. *Recherches sur les principes mathématiques de la théorie des richesses.* Paris: Librairie des sciences politiques et sociales, M. Rivière & cie. Translated by Nathaniel T. Bacon [1897]. *Researches into the Mathematical Principles of the Theory of Wealth.* New York: Macmillan.
Dantzig, G. B. [1951]. "Application of the simplex method to a transportation problem," in Koopmans [1951a], Chapter XXIII, pp. 359–373.
Dantzig, G. B., A. Orden, and P. Wolfe [1955]. "The generalized simplex method for minimizing a linear form under inequality restraints," *Pacific Journal of Mathematics*, **5**, 183–195.
Debreu, G. [1951]. "The coefficient of resource utilization," *Econometrica*, **19**, 273–292.
Debreu, G. [1954]. "Representation of a preference ordering by a numerical function," in R. M. Thrall, C. H. Coombs, and R. L. Davis (eds.), *Decision Processes.* New York: Wiley; London: Chapman & Hall, Chapter XI, pp. 159–166.
Debreu, G. [1959]. *Theory of Value.* New York: Wiley.
Debreu, G. [1962]. "New concepts and techniques for equilibrium analysis," *International Economic Review*, **3**, 257–273.
Debreu, G. [1964]. "Continuity properties of Paretian utility," *International Economic Review*, **5**, 285–293.
Debreu, G. [1970]. "Economies with a finite set of equilibria," *Econometrica*, **38**, 387–392.
Debreu, G., and H. Scarf [1963]. "A limit theorem on the core of an economy," *International Economic Review*, **4**, 235–246.
Edgeworth, F. Y. [1881]. *Mathematical Psychics.* London: C. Kegan Paul.
Eilenberg, S. [1941]. "Ordered topological spaces," *American Journal of Mathematics*, **63**, 37–45.
Enthoven, A. C., and K. J. Arrow [1956]. "A theorem on expectations and the stability of equilibrium," *Econometrica*, **24**, 288–293.
Farrell, M. J. [1959]. "The convexity assumption in the theory of competitive markets," *Journal of Political Economy*, **67**, 377–391.
de Finetti, B. [1937]. "La prévision: ses lois logiques, ses sources subjectives," *Annales de l'Institut Henri Poincaré*, **7**, 1–68. English translation by H. E. Kyburg in Kyburg and Smokler [1964, 95–158].
Gale, D. [1957]. "General equilibrium for linear models." Unpublished.
Gale, D., and H. Nikaidô [1965]. "The Jacobian matrix and global univalence of mappings," *Mathematische Annalen*, **159**, 81–93.

Georgescu-Roegen, N. [1951]. "Some properties of a generalized Leontief model," in Koopmans [1951a, Chapter X, 165–173]. Reprinted in enlarged form in N. Georgescu-Roegen [1966]. *Analytical Economics.* Cambridge, Mass.: Harvard University Press, Chapter 9, pp. 316–337.

Gillies, D. B. [1953]. "Some theorems on *n*-person games." Ph.D. thesis, Princeton University.

Glustoff, E. [1968]. "On the existence of a Keynesian equilibrium," *Review of Economic Studies*, **35**, 327–334.

Gorman, W. M. [1953]. "Community preference fields," *Econometrica*, **21**, 63–80.

Gorman, W. M. [1964]. "More scope for qualitative economics," *Review of Economic Studies*, **31**, 65–68.

Hahn, F. H. [1949]. "Proportionality, divisibility, and economies of scale: comment," *Quarterly Journal of Economics*, **63**, 131–137.

Hahn, F. H. [1958]. "Gross substitutes and the dynamic stability of general equilibrium," *Econometrica*, **26**, 169–170.

Hahn, F. H. [1962]. "On the stability of pure exchange equilibrium," *International Economic Review*, **3**, 206–213.

Hahn, F. H. [1965]. "On some problems in proving the existence of equilibrium in a monetary economy," in F. H. Hahn and F. P. R. Brechling (eds.), *The Theory of Interest Rates.* London: Macmillan; New York: St. Martin's Press.

Hahn, F. H., and T. Negishi [1962]. "A theorem on non-tâtonnement stability," *Econometrica*, **30**, 463–469.

Hahn, W. [1959]. *Theorie und Anwendung der direkten Methoden von Lyapunov.* Berlin: Springer.

Hansen, T., and H. Scarf [1969]. "On the applications of a recent combinatorial algorithm." Cowles Foundation Discussion Paper, No. 272.

Hawkins, D., and H. Simon [1949]. "Note: some conditions of macroeconomic stability," *Econometrica*, **17**, 245–248.

Hicks, J. R. [1939]. *Value and Capital.* Oxford: Clarendon Press.

Hicks, J. R. [1965]. *Capital and Growth.* Oxford: Clarendon Press.

Hildenbrand, W. [1970]. "On economies with many agents," *Journal of Economic Theory*, **2**, 161–188.

Hotelling, H. [1932]. "Edgeworth's taxation paradox and the nature of demand and supply functions," *Journal of Political Economy*, **40**, 571–616.

Isnard, A. N. [1781]. *Traité des richesses.* London.

Jenkin, F. [1870]. "The graphic representation of the laws of supply and demand, and other essays on political economy," in Sir Alexander Grant (ed.), *Recess Studies*, pp. 76–106. Edinburgh. Reprinted in 1931. No. 9 in series of Reprints of Scarce Tracts in Economic and Political Science. London: London School of Economics.

Kakutani, S. [1941]. "A generalization of Brouwer's fixed-point theorem," *Duke Mathematical Journal*, **8**, 451–459.

Kaldor, N. [1935]. "Market imperfection and excess capacity," *Economica N.S.*, **2**, 33–50.

Karlin, S. [1959]. *Mathematical Methods and Theory in Games, Programming, and Economics.* Reading, Mass.: Addison-Wesley, 2 vols.

Karlin, S., and L. S. Shapley [1953]. "Geometry of moment spaces," *Memoirs of the American Mathematical Society*, **12**.

Keynes, J. M. [1936]. *The General Theory of Employment Interest and Money.* New York: Harcourt, Brace.

Knight, F. H. [1935]. "The Ricardian theory of production and distribution," *Canadian Journal of Economic and Political Science*, **1**, 3–25, 171–196. Reprinted in Frank H. Knight [1956]. *On the History and Method of Economics.* Chicago: University of Chicago Press, pp. 37–88.

Koopmans, T. C. (ed.) [1951a]. *Activity Analysis of Allocation and Production.* New York: Wiley.

Koopmans, T. C. [1951b]. "Analysis of production as an efficient combination of activities," in Koopmans [1951a], Chapter III, pp. 33–97.

Kuhn, H. W. [1968]. "Simplicial approximation of fixed points," *Proceedings of the National Academy of Sciences*, **61**, 1238–1242.

Kyburg, H. E., Jr., and H. E. Smokler (eds.) [1964]. *Studies in Subjective Probability.* New York: Wiley.

Lancaster, K. [1961–62]. "The scope of qualitative economics," *Review of Economic Studies*, **29**, 99–123.

Lancaster, K. [1964]. "Partitionable systems and qualitative economics," *Review of Economic Studies*, **31**, 69–72.

Lancaster, K. [1965]. "The theory of qualitative linear systems," *Econometrica*, **33**, 395–408.

La Salle, J., and S. Lefschetz [1961]. *Stability by Lyapounov's Direct Method with Applications.* New York: Academic Press.

Leijonhufvud, A. [1968]. *On Keynesian Economics and the Economics of Keynes: A Study of Monetary Theory.* New York: Oxford University Press.

Lemke, C. [1968]. "On complementary pivot theory," in *American Mathematical Society* [1968, I: 95–114].

Lemke, C., and J. T. Howson, Jr. [1964]. "Equilibrium points of bimatrix games," *Journal of the Society for Industrial and Applied Mathematics*, **12**, 412–423.

Leontief, W. W. [1936]. "Composite commodities and the problem of index numbers," *Econometrica*, **4**, 39–59.

Leontief, W. W. [1941]. *The Structure of the American Economy, 1919–1939*, First Edition. New York: Oxford University Press.

Lyapounov, A. [1947]. *Problème général de la stabilité du mouvement, Annals of Mathematics Study 17.* Princeton, N.J.: Princeton University Press.

Marris, R. [1964]. *The Economic Theory of "Managerial" Capitalism.* New York: Free Press.

McKenzie, L. [1954]. "On equilibrium in Graham's model of world trade and other competitive systems," *Econometrica*, **22**, 147–161.

McKenzie, L. [1955a]. "Equality of factor prices in world trade," *Econometrica*, **23**, 239–257.

McKenzie, L. [1955b]. "Competitive equilibrium with dependent consumer preferences," in National Bureau of Standards and Department of the Air Force, *The Second Symposium on Linear Programming*. Washington, D.C.

McKenzie, L. [1956–57]. "Demand theory without a utility index," *Review of Economic Studies*, **24**, 185–189.

McKenzie, L. [1959]. "On the existence of general equilibrium for a competitive market," *Econometrica*, **27**, 54–71.

McKenzie, L. [1960a]. "Stability of equilibrium and the value of positive excess demand," *Econometrica*, **28**, 606–617.

McKenzie, L. [1960b]. "Matrices with dominant diagonal and economic theory," in K. J. Arrow, S. Karlin, and P. Suppes (eds.), *Mathematical Methods in the Social Sciences, 1959*. Stanford, Calif.: Stanford University Press, Chapter 4, pp. 47–62.

McKenzie, L. [1961]. "On the existence of general equilibrium: some corrections," *Econometrica*, **29**, 247–248.

Menger, K. [1954]. "The laws of return; a study in metaeconomics," in O. Morgenstern (ed.), *Economic Activity Analysis*. New York: Wiley, pp. 419–481.

Metzler, L. [1945]. "The stability of multiple markets: the Hicks conditions," *Econometrica*, **13**, 277–292.

Morishima, M. [1952]. "On the law of change of price-system in an economy which contains complementary commodities," *Osaka Economic Papers*, **1**, 101–113.

Morishima, M. [1959]. "Gross substitutability, homogeneity, and the Walras' Law." Unpublished manuscript.

Morishima, M. [1959–60]. "On the three Hicksian laws of comparative statics," *Review of Economic Studies*, **27**, 195–201.

Morishima, M. [1964]. *Equilibrium, Stability, and Growth*. Oxford: Clarendon Press.

Mosak, Jacob L. [1944]. *General Equilibrium Theory in International Trade*. Bloomington, Indiana: Principia Press.

Nash, J. F., Jr. [1950]. "Equilibrium in *N*-person games," *Proceedings of the National Academy of Sciences*, **36**, 48–49.

Nataf, A. [1953]. "Possibilité d'agrégation dans le cadre de la théorie des choix," *Metroeconomica*, **5**, 22–30.

Negishi, T. [1958]. "A note on the stability of an economy where all goods are gross substitutes," *Econometrica*, **26**, 445–447.

Negishi, T. [1960]. "Welfare economics and existence of an equilibrium for a competitive economy," *Metroeconomica*, **12**, 92–97.

Negishi, T. [1960–61]. "Monopolistic competition and general equilibrium," *Review of Economic Studies*, **28**, 196–201.

Negishi, T. [1961]. "On the formation of prices," *International Economic Review*, **2**, 122–126.

Negishi, T. [1964]. "Stability of exchange and adaptive expectations," *International Economic Review*, **5**, 104–111.

Neisser, H. [1932]. "Lohnhöhe und Beschäftigungsgrad im Marktgleichgewicht," *Weltwirtschaftliches Archiv*, **36**, 415–455.

von Neumann, J. [1937]. "Über ein ökonomisches Gleichungssystem und eine Verallgemeinerung des Brouwerschen Fixpunktsatzes," *Ergebnisse eines Mathematischen Kolloquiums*, **8**, 73–83.

von Neumann, J. [1945]. "A model of general economic equilibrium," *Review of Economic Studies*, **13**, 1–9. English translation of von Neumann [1937].

von Neumann, J., and O. Morgenstern [1944]. *Theory of Games and Economic Behavior*. Princeton, N.J.: Princeton University Press.

von Neumann, J., and O. Morgenstern [1947]. *Theory of Games and Economic Behavior*, Second Edition. Princeton, N.J.: Princeton University Press.

Nikaidô, H. [1956]. "On the classical multilateral exchange problem," *Metroeconomica*, **8**, 135–145.

Nikaidô, H., and H. Uzawa [1960]. "Stability and non-negativity in a Walrasian tâtonnement process," *International Economic Review*, **1**, 50–59.

Nishino, H. [1970]. "Kokan-keisai no Core to sono Kyokugenteiri" (The cores of exchange economies and the limit theorems), in M. Suzuki (ed.), *Kyoso-shakai no Game no Riron* (*Theory of Games in Competitive Society*). Tokyo: Keiso-shobo, pp. 131–168.

Pareto, V. [1909]. *Manuel d'économie politique*. Paris: Girard & Briere.

Pearce, I. F. [1967]. "More about factor price equalization," *International Economic Review*, **8**, 255–270.

Pearce, I. F., and J. Wise [forthcoming]. "On the uniqueness of competitive equilibrium."

Quirk, J. P. [1968]. "Comparative statics under Walras' law: the case of strong dependence," *Review of Economic Studies*, **35**, 11–21.

Rader, J. T. [1963]. "The existence of a utility function to represent preferences," *Review of Economic Studies*, **30**, 229–232.

Radner, R. [1968]. "Competitive equilibrium under uncertainty," *Econometrica*, **36**, 31–58.

Ramsey, F. P. [1926]. "Truth and Probability," in F. P. Ramsey [1931]. *The Foundations of Mathematics and Other Logical Essays*. London: K. Paul, Trench, Trubner and Co., pp. 156–198. Reprinted in Kyburg and Smokler [1964, 63–92].

Robinson, J. [1933]. *The Economics of Imperfect Competition*. London: Macmillan.

Rothenberg, J. [1960]. "Non-convexity, aggregation, and Pareto optimality," *Journal of Political Economy*, **68**, 435–468.

Rybczynski, T. M. [1955]. "Factor endowment and relative commodity prices," *Economica N.S.*, **22**, 336–341.

Saito, M. [1961]. "Professor Debreu on 'Theory of Value'; a review article," *International Economic Review*, **2**, 231–237.

Samuelson, P. A. [1941, 1942]. "The stability of equilibrium," *Econometrica*, **9**, 97–120; **10**, 1–25. Reprinted in Samuelson [1966, I: 539–562, 565–589].

Samuelson, P. A. [1947]. *Foundations of Economic Analysis.* Cambridge, Mass.: Harvard University Press.

Samuelson, P. A. [1948]. "International trade and the equalisation of factor prices," *Economic Journal*, **58**, 163–184. Reprinted in Samuelson [1966, II: 847–868].

Samuelson, P. A. [1951]. "Abstract of a theorem concerning substitutability in open Leontief Models," in Koopmans [1951a, Chapter VII, 142–146]. Reprinted in Samuelson [1966, I: 515–519].

Samuelson, P. A. [1953–54]. "Prices of factors and goods in general equilibrium," *Review of Economic Studies*, **21**, 1–20. Reprinted in Samuelson [1966, II: 888–908].

Samuelson, P. A. [1957]. "Wages and interest: a modern dissection of Marxian economic models," *American Economic Review*, **47**, 884–912. Reprinted in Samuelson [1966, I: 341–369].

Samuelson, P. A. [1959]. "A modern treatment of the Ricardian economy," *Quarterly Journal of Economics*, **73**, 1–35, 217–231. Reprinted in Samuelson [1966, I: 373–421].

Samuelson, P. A. [1966]. *The Collected Scientific Papers of Paul A. Samuelson.* Cambridge, Mass.: M.I.T. Press, 2 vols.

Samuelson, P. A., and W. F. Stolper [1941–42]. "Protection and real wages," *Review of Economic Studies*, **9**, 58–73. Reprinted in Samuelson [1966, II: 831–846].

Savage, L. J. [1954]. *The Foundations of Statistics.* New York: Wiley.

Scarf, H. [1962]. "An analysis of markets with a large number of participants," *Recent Advances in Game Theory.* Princeton, N.J.: Princeton University Press.

Scarf, H. [1967a]. "The core of an *N*-person game," *Econometrica*, **35**, 50–69.

Scarf, H. [1967b]. "On the approximation of fixed points of a continuous mapping," *SIAM Journal on Applied Mathematics*, **15**, 1328–1343.

Scarf, H. [1967c]. "On the computation of equilibrium prices," in W. Fellner et al., *Ten Economic Studies in the Tradition of Irving Fisher.* New York: Wiley, Chapter 8.

Schelling, T. C. [1960]. *The Strategy of Conflict.* Cambridge, Mass.: Harvard University Press.

Schlesinger, K. [1933–34]. "Über die Produktionsgleichungen der ökonomische Wertlehre," *Ergebnisse eines mathematischen Kolloquiums*, **6**, 10–11.

Scitovsky, T. [1944–45]. "Some consequences of the habit of judging quality by price," *Review of Economic Studies*, **12**, 100–105.

Shubik, M. [1959]. "Edgeworth market games," in A. W. Tucker and R. D. Luce (eds.), *Contributions to the Theory of Games*, IV. Princeton: Princeton University Press.

Slutzky, E. [1915]. "Sulla teoria del bilancio del consumatore," *Giornale degli Economisti*, **51**, 19–23.

von Stackelberg, H. [1933]. "Zwei Kritische bemerkungen zur preistheorie Gustav Cassels," *Zeitschrift für Nationalökonomie*, **4**, 456–472.

Starr, R. [1969]. "Quasi-equilibria in markets with nonconvex preferences," *Econometrica*, **37**, 25–38.

Theocharis, R. [1961]. *Early Developments in Mathematical Economics.* London: Macmillan.

Tompkins, C. B. [1964]. "Sperner's lemma and some extensions," in E. F. Beckenbach (ed.), *Applied Combinatorial Mathematics.* New York: Wiley, Chapter 15.

Triffin, R. [1940]. *Monopolistic Competition and General Equilibrium Theory.* Cambridge, Mass.: Harvard University Press.

Uzawa, H. [1958]. "Gradient method for concave programming, II: global stability in the strictly concave case," in K. J. Arrow, L. Hurwicz, and H. Uzawa, *Studies in Linear and Non-Linear Programming.* Stanford, Calif.: Stanford University Press, Chapter 7, pp. 127–132.

Uzawa, H. [1959–60]. "Walras' tâtonnement in the theory of exchange," *Review of Economic Studies*, **27**, 182–194.

Uzawa, H. [1961]. "The stability of dynamic processes," *Econometrica*, **29**, 617–631.

Uzawa, H. [1962]. "On the stability of Edgeworth's barter process," *International Economic Review*, **3**, 218–232.

Veblen, T. [1899]. *The Theory of the Leisure Class.* New York: Macmillan.

Wald, A. [1933–34]. "Über die eindeutige positive Lösbarkeit der neuen Produktions-gleichungen," *Ergebnisse eines mathematischen Kolloquiums*, **6**, 12–20.

Wald, A. [1934–35]. "Über die Produktionsgleichungen der ökonomische Wertlehre," *Ergebnisse eines mathematischen Kolloquiums*, **7**, 1–6.

Wald, A. [1936]. "Über einige Gleichungssysteme der mathematischen Ökonomie," *Zeitschrift für Nationalökonomie*, **7**, 637–670.

Wald, A. [1951]. "On some systems of equations of mathematical economics," *Econometrica*, **19**, 368–403. English translation of Wald [1936].

Walras, L. [1874, 1877]. *Eléments d'économie politique pure.* Lausanne: L. Corbaz. English translation of the definitive edition by William Jaffé [1954]. *Elements of Pure Economics.* London: Allen and Unwin.

Whitin, T. M., and M. H. Peston [1954]. "Random variations, risk, and returns to scale," *Quarterly Journal of Economics*, **68**, 603–612.

Williamson, O. E. [1964]. *The Economics of Discretionary Behavior: Managerial Objectives in a Theory of the Firm.* Englewood Cliffs, N.J.: Prentice-Hall.

Wold, H. [1943–44]. "A synthesis of pure demand analysis," I–III, *Skandinavisk Aktuarietidskrift*, **26**, 85–118, 220–263; **27**, 69–120.

Zeuthen, F. [1932]. "Das Prinzip der Knappheit, technische Kombination und ökonomische Quälitat," *Zeitschrift für Nationalökonomie*, **4**, 1–24.

INDEXES

Author Index

Subject Index

LaVergne, TN USA
09 December 2010
208145LV00002B/16/A